Lecture Notes in Computer Science   9115

Commenced Publication in 1973
Founding and Former Series Editors:
Gerhard Goos, Juris Hartmanis, and Jan van Leeuwen

More information about this series at http://www.springer.com/series/7407

Raymond Devillers · Antti Valmari (Eds.)

Application and Theory
of Petri Nets
and Concurrency

36th International Conference, PETRI NETS 2015
Brussels, Belgium, June 21–26, 2015
Proceedings

 Springer

Editors
Raymond Devillers
Université Libre de Bruxelles
Brussels
Belgium

Antti Valmari
Tampere University of Technology
Tampere
Finland

ISSN 0302-9743   ISSN 1611-3349   (electronic)
Lecture Notes in Computer Science
ISBN 978-3-319-19487-5   ISBN 978-3-319-19488-2   (eBook)
DOI 10.1007/978-3-319-19488-2

Library of Congress Control Number: 2015939435

LNCS Sublibrary: SL1 – Theoretical Computer Science and General Issues

Springer Cham Heidelberg New York Dordrecht London

Printed on acid-free paper

Springer International Publishing AG Switzerland is part of Springer Science+Business Media
(www.springer.com)

Preface

This volume constitutes the proceedings of the 36th International Conference on Application and Theory of Petri Nets and Concurrency (Petri Nets 2015). This series of conferences serves as an annual meeting place to discuss progress in the field of Petri nets and related models of concurrency. These conferences provide a forum for researchers to present and discuss both applications and theoretical developments in this area. Novel tools and substantial enhancements to existing tools can also be presented. This year, the satellite program of the conference comprised four workshops, two Petri net courses, two advanced tutorials, and a model checking contest.

Petri Nets 2015 was co-located with the Application of Concurrency to System Design Conference (ACSD 2015). Both were organized by the Département d'Informatique (Science Faculty) of the Université Libre de Bruxelles (ULB) and took place in Brussels, Belgium, June 21–26, 2015. We would like to express our deepest thanks to the Organizing Committee chaired by Gilles Geeraerts for the time and effort invested in the local organization of the conference.

This year, 30 regular papers and four tool papers were submitted to Petri Nets 2015. The authors of the submitted papers represented 21 different countries. We thank all the authors. Each paper was reviewed by at least three reviewers. The Program Committee (PC) meeting took place electronically, using the EasyChair conference system for the paper selection process. The PC selected 12 regular papers and two tool papers for presentation. After the conference, some authors were invited to submit an extended version of their contribution for consideration in a special issue of the *Fundamenta Informaticae* journal.

We thank the PC members and other reviewers for their careful and timely evaluation of the submissions before the meeting, and the fruitful discussions during the electronic meeting. The Springer LNCS team and the EasyChair system provided excellent support in the preparation of this volume.

We are also grateful to the invited speakers for their contribution:

Robert Lorenz (Modeling Quantitative Aspects of Concurrent Systems using Weighted Petri Net Transducers)

Marlon Dumas (Process Mining Reloaded: Event Structures as a Unified Representation of Process Models and Event Logs)

Marta Kwiatkowska (On Quantitative Modelling and Verification of DNA Walker Circuits Using Stochastic Petri nets)

June 2015   Raymond Devillers
                                                                                          Antti Valmari

Organization

Steering Committee

W. van der Aalst,
  The Netherlands
G. Ciardo, USA
J. Desel, Germany
S. Donatelli, Italy
S. Haddad, France
K. Hiraishi, Japan
J. Kleijn, The Netherlands
F. Kordon, France
M. Koutny, UK (Chair)

L.M. Kristensen, Norway
C. Lin, China
W. Penczek, Poland
L. Pomello, Italy
W. Reisig, Germany
G. Rozenberg, The Netherlands
M. Silva, Spain
A. Valmari, Finland
A. Yakovlev, UK

Program Committee

Kamel Barkaoui	Conservatoire National des Arts et Métiers, France
Marco Beccuti	Università degli Studi di Torino, Italy
Robin Bergenthum	FernUniversität in Hagen, Germany
Luca Bernardinello	Università di Milano-Bicocca, Italy
Hanifa Boucheneb	Polytechnique Montréal, Canada
Didier Buchs	University of Geneva, Switzerland
Josep Carmona	Universitat Politècnica de Catalunya, Spain
Piotr Chrzastowski-Wachtel	Warsaw University, Poland
Gianfranco Ciardo	Iowa State University, USA
David de Frutos Escrig	Complutense University of Madrid, Spain
Raymond Devillers (Co-chair)	Université Libre de Bruxelles, Belgium
João M. Fernandes	Universidade do Minho, Portugal
Henri Hansen	Tampere University of Technology, Finland
Monika Heiner	Brandenburg University of Technology, Germany
Joost-Pieter Katoen	Aachen University, Germany
Ekkart Kindler	Technical University of Denmark, Denmark
Hanna Klaudel	Université d' Evry-Val d' Essonne, France
Lars Michael Kristensen	Bergen University College of Applied Sciences, Norway
Ranko Lazic	University of Warwick, UK
Irina Lomazova	Higher School of Economics, Moscow, Russia
Hiroshi Matsuno	Yamaguchi University, Japan
Daniel Moldt	Universität Hamburg, Germany
Madhavan Mukund	Chennai Mathematical Institute, India

Artem Polyvyanyy	Queensland University of Technology, Australia
Riadh Robbana	Carthage University, Tunisia
Stefan Schwoon	ENS Cachan and Inria, France
Carla Seatzu	Università di Cagliari, Italy
Natalia Sidorova	Technische Universiteit Eindhoven, The Netherlands
Yann Thierry-Mieg	Laboratoire d'Informatique de Paris 6, France
Antti Valmari (Co-chair)	Tampere University of Technology, Finland
Michael Westergaard	Technische Universiteit Eindhoven, The Netherlands
Mengchu Zhou	New Jersey Institute of Technology, USA

Organizing Committee

Romain Brenguier	Axel Haddad	Guillermo A. Pérez
Ami Kumar Dhar	Ismaël Jecker	Jean-François Raskin
Emmanual Filiot	Stéphane Le Roux	Ocan Sankur
Gilles Geeraerts (Chair)	Benjamin Monmege	

Workshops and Tutorials Chairs

Jörg Desel	FernUniversität in Hagen, Germany
Jetty Kleijn	Universiteit Leiden, The Netherlands

Tools Exhibition Chair

Thomas Brihaye	University of Mons, Belgium

Publicity Chair

Thierry Massart	ULB, Belgium

Additional Reviewers

Amparore, Elvio Gilberto	Kılınç, Görkem	Ribeiro, Óscar R.
Bashkin, Vladimir	Langar, Mahjoub	Rohr, Christian
Cabac, Lawrence	Ma, Ziyue	Rosa-Velardo, Fernando
Chaouiya, Claudine	Macià, Hermenegilda	Schwarick, Martin
Colange, Maximilien	Mosteller, David	Sfaxi, Lilia
Costa, Aniko	Munoz-Gama, Jorge	Slaats, Tijs
Gabarro, Joaquim	Nakamura, Morikazu	Valero, Valentin
Gomes, Luis	Noll, Thomas	Wagner, Thomas
Göller, Stefan	Pinna, G. Michele	Wu, Hao
Haustermann, Michael	Racordon, Dimitri	Yamaguchi, Shingo
Herajy, Mostafa	Rataj, Artur	

Contents

On Quantitative Modelling and Verification of DNA Walker Circuits
Using Stochastic Petri Nets 1
   Benoît Barbot and Marta Kwiatkowska

Process Mining Reloaded: Event Structures as a Unified Representation
of Process Models and Event Logs 33
   Marlon Dumas and Luciano García-Bañuelos

Modeling Quantitative Aspects of Concurrent Systems Using Weighted
Petri Net Transducers 49
   Robert Lorenz

On Interval Process Semantics of Petri Nets with Inhibitor Arcs 77
   Mohammed Alqarni and Ryszard Janicki

An SRN-Based Resiliency Quantification Approach 98
   Dario Bruneo, Francesco Longo, Marco Scarpa, Antonio Puliafito,
   Rahul Ghosh, and Kishor S. Trivedi

Non-atomic Transition Firing in Contextual Nets 117
   Thomas Chatain, Stefan Haar, Maciej Koutny, and Stefan Schwoon

Discrete Parameters in Petri Nets 137
   Nicolas David, Claude Jard, Didier Lime, and Olivier H. Roux

Negotiation Programs 157
   Javier Esparza and Jörg Desel

Nested-Unit Petri Nets: A Structural Means to Increase Efficiency
and Scalability of Verification on Elementary Nets 179
   Hubert Garavel

Charlie – An Extensible Petri Net Analysis Tool (Tool Paper) 200
   Monika Heiner, Martin Schwarick, and Jan-Thierry Wegener

Petri Nets with Structured Data 212
   Eric Badouel, Loïc Hélouët, and Christophe Morvan

On the Reversibility of Live Equal-Conflict Petri Nets 234
   Thomas Hujsa, Jean-Marc Delosme, and Alix Munier-Kordon

SNAKES: A Flexible High-Level Petri Nets Library (Tool Paper) 254
   Franck Pommereau

Characterizing Stable Inequalities of Petri Nets   266
    Marvin Triebel and Jan Sürmeli

Process Discovery Using Localized Events   287
    Wil M.P. van der Aalst, Anna Kalenkova, Vladimir Rubin,
    and Eric Verbeek

New Search Strategies for the Petri Net CEGAR Approach   309
    Ákos Hajdu, András Vörös, and Tamás Bartha

Workflow Management Principles for Interactions Between Petri
Net-Based Agents   329
    Thomas Wagner and Daniel Moldt

Author Index   351

On Quantitative Modelling and Verification of DNA Walker Circuits Using Stochastic Petri Nets

Benoît Barbot$^{(\boxtimes)}$ and Marta Kwiatkowska$^{(\boxtimes)}$

Department of Computer Science, University of Oxford,
Wolfson Building, Parks Road, Oxford OX1 3QD, UK
{benoit.barbot,marta.kwiatkowska}@cs.ox.ac.uk

Abstract. Molecular programming is an emerging field concerned with building synthetic biomolecular computing devices at the nanoscale, for example from DNA or RNA molecules. Many promising applications have been proposed, ranging from diagnostic biosensors and nanorobots to synthetic biology, but prohibitive complexity and imprecision of experimental observations makes reliability of molecular programs difficult to achieve. This paper advocates the development of design automation methodologies for molecular programming, highlighting the role of quantitative verification in this context. We focus on DNA 'walker' circuits, in which molecules can be programmed to traverse tracks placed on a DNA origami tile, taking appropriate decisions at junctions and reporting the outcome when reaching the end of the track. The behaviour of molecular walkers is inherently probabilistic and thus probabilistic model checking methods are needed for their analysis. We demonstrate how DNA walkers can be modelled using stochastic Petri nets, and apply statistical model checking using the tool Cosmos to analyse the reliability and performance characteristics of the designs. The results are compared and contrasted with those obtained for the PRISM model checker. The paper ends by summarising future research challenges in the field.

1 Introduction

Molecular programming is an emerging field concerned with building synthetic biomolecular computing devices at the nanoscale, for example from DNA or RNA molecules. Several nanotechnologies have been developed, of which *DNA strand displacement (DSD)* [55,56] is particularly popular, since it uses only DNA molecules, is enzyme-free, and easy to synthesize chemically. DSD has ben used to implement logic circuits [41,44], diagnostic biosensors [29] and controllers programmed in DNA [11]. Further, DNA self-assembly technologies such as origami folding [43] have enabled novel designs, including *DNA walker systems* that can traverse tracks 'printed' on origami tiles and deliver cargo [51,54].

Molecular computing devices built from DNA are *autonomous* – they can interact with the biochemical environment, process information, make decisions and act on them – and *programmable*, that is, they can be systematically

© Springer International Publishing Switzerland 2015
R. Devillers and A. Valmari (Eds.): PETRI NETS 2015, LNCS 9115, pp. 1–32, 2015.
DOI: 10.1007/978-3-319-19488-2_1

configured to perform specific computational or mechanical tasks. The computational power of such systems has been shown to be equivalent to Turing computability [45]. The future potential of these developments is tremendous, particularly for smart therapeutics, point-of-care diagnostics and synthetic biology. For example, *biosensing* involves a decision process that aims to detect various input biomarkers in an environment, such as strands of messenger RNA within a cell, and take action based on the detected input.

Since such systems can perform information processing within living cells, their use is envisaged in healthcare applications, where safety is paramount. As argued in [32], this paper advocates the development of design automation methodologies for molecular programming. There are similarities to existing work in design automation for silicon circuits and hardware verification, but we must consider inherent *stochasticity* of the underlying molecular interactions, the need to state requirements in *quantitative* form, and the importance to consider *control* of molecular systems. Therefore, *probabilistic modelling* and *automated, quantitative verification* and *synthesis* techniques are needed [31,33,34].

In this paper, we focus on DNA walker circuits introduced in [8,50,51]. The behaviour of molecular walkers is inherently probabilistic and we have studied their performance and reliability in [14–16]. In [38], we have developed techniques to automatically synthesise rates so that a given quantitative requirement is guaranteed to be satisfied. The models of DNA walkers were developed in PRISM's modelling language, a notation based on reactive modules [34]. DNA walkers, however, perform spatially localised computation by following programmable tracks. Therefore, graphical notations such as Petri nets are particularly well suited to their modelling and analysis. We demonstrate how DNA walker circuits can be modelled using stochastic Petri nets, matching the layout of the original circuit designs, and analyse the reliability and performance characteristics of the designs. In view of state-space explosion observed in the original study [15,16], we focus on evaluating the potential of statistical model checking using the tool Cosmos. We develop a family of models, some designed by biochemist and some artificial schemes aimed to exhibit design challenges, and a range of quantitative requirements. The results are compared and contrasted with those obtained for the PRISM model checker using state-of-the-art numerical techniques (uniformisation and fast adaptive uniformisation [14,21]) and PRISM's statistical model checking implementation known as approximate model checking [34]. We conclude that statistical model checking significantly benefits from parallelisation and enables efficient analysis of much larger models at no great loss of accuracy compared to numerical methods. The paper ends by summarising future research challenges in the field.

2   Background on Molecular Walkers

DNA computing has so far mainly focused on designing logic circuits that perform computation *in vitro*, by transforming DNA strands using strand displacement systems as e.g. demonstrated experimentally in [41,44]. However, this approach has limitations, in that the strands are cascaded through a series of logic gates in solution, which may lead to unintended interference [36] and consequently incorrect outcomes. An alternative approach is to design localised computation by 'printing' circuits on origami tiles as proposed in [9,41]. In this paper we focus on DNA walker systems [8,50,51], and particularly the programmable walkers of [48].

A DNA walker system consists of a *track* of strands, called *anchorages*, that are tethered to a DNA origami tile and traversed by a *walker* strand [48]. Origami tiles [43] are long circular single-stranded DNA scaffolds that can be folded into the tile shape with complementary short DNA strands that hybridize with the scaffold. The tracks can fork at junctions, and the walkers can be programmed to take a left or the right branch by selectively unblocking the anchorages that the walker can follow. Fig. 1 shows an example of a double-junction circuit that we will study later, where the two directions at the first junction are respectively labelled X and $\neg X$.

The stepping process is shown in Fig. 2. The walker, which carries a quencher (Q), is initially bound (hybridized) to the initial anchorage. The target anchorages at the end of the tracks have fluorophores (F) attached to them. After some initial preparation, the walker is able to autonomously step from one anchorage to another, eventually reaching the target anchorages and quenching the fluorophores. The programming of the tracks is achieved as follows. Initially, the anchorages are hybridized to the tile, and are either *unblocked*, meaning that the walker can bind to them, or *blocking*, that is, initially bound to a blocking strand that will prevent the walker from binding to them. Sections of the track can be reprogrammed by selectively unblocking them through the addition of strands that are complementary to the blocking strand; see Fig. 2 (Pane 2), where $\neg X$ is unblocked but X remains blocked.

After the walker is placed at the initial anchorage, a nicking enzyme is added to the solution. It binds to the walker-anchorage complex, melting the top of the anchorage away, which frees the top of the walker. This enables the walker strand to bind to the next anchorage through a displacement reaction (Panes 3 and 4 of Fig. 2). The process repeats, and the walker thus continues along the unblocked section of the track, through junctions, towards the final anchorage, where it reports the outcome by quenching the fluorophore.

Formally, the system can be viewed as a planar graph, composed from undirected tracks (consecutive anchorages) and gates (track junction points) that connect at most three tracks. [48] experimentally demonstrated that a walker can be directed to any leaf in a complete two-level binary tree by selectively unblocking the anchorages. In [15,16], we have studied the expressive power of DNA walker circuits implemented by this technology and showed that the circuits can compute any Boolean function through reduction to 3-CNF. Compared to DNA strand displacement systems in solution, an advantage of this technology is its spatial locality, but we have found that the undirected nature of the tracks imposes limitations on the use of parallelism. Other walker technologies that work with directed tracks have been demonstrated, so this limitation does not apply to all walker systems.

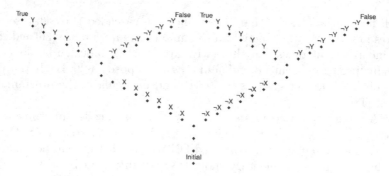

Fig. 1. A double-junction DNA walker circuit ([16])

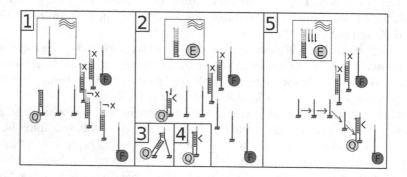

Fig. 2. The stepping action of the walker ([16])

Computing Boolean functions using nanotechnologies such as the DNA walker systems has application in biosensing, for example to detect the presence of certain molecules. However, experiments have shown that the computation is quite unreliable, in the sense that walkers may release from a track, jump over two anchorages, or a blockade can fail to block an anchorage, delaying or diverting the walker to a different anchorage, thus returning wrong result. To study the reliability and performance of such systems, in [15,16] we also developed a stochastic model of DNA walker systems based on [8,48,50]. Note that, since we are considering localised computation, standard mass action kinetics which applies to well-mixed solution cannot be used, and we instead derive a model from experimental observations.

The model can be configured to a specific circuit layout, where we can vary the topology of the circuit, the number of anchorages in each section, and their physical spacing. We also model the different modes of anchorages, such as *blocked, unblocked, empty* or *bound* to the walker. The stepping process of Fig. 2 has been abstracted into a single walker step transition, taking the walker from one anchorage to the next. The rate of the stepping transition is dependent on the distance between anchorages, and was derived using rate constants estimated in [50]. Maximum interaction distance was observed to be $d_M = 24$ nm. Taking into account the average distance between anchorages in the experiment of 6.2 nm, we have defined the walker stepping rate k to be a function of the distance d_a and the base rate k_s given by:

$$k = \begin{cases} k_s = 0.009\text{s}^{-1} & \text{when } d \leq 1.5d_a \\ k_s/50 & \text{when } 1.5d_a < d \leq 2.5d_a \\ k_s/100 & \text{when } 2.5d_a < d \leq d_M \\ 0 & \text{otherwise} \end{cases} \tag{1}$$

This determines a sphere of reach of up to d_M around the walker-anchorage complex, within which the walker may step onto an uncut anchorage. We note that this abstraction of the stepping rate makes certain simplifying assumptions, such as we do not consider walker moving between intact anchorages or stepping backwards; these aspects have been experimentally observed and the model can be refined further in future.

One aspect that we do consider, however, and which also has been observed experimentally, is the failure of the blocking mechanism. We can allow the anchorages to spontaneously unblock and assume that the unblocking is uniform. If this happens, the walker may step onto such an unblocked anchorage and follow an incorrect track. The failure rate of 30% was estimated based on [48]. We have not modelled the failure of other mechanisms, such as missing anchorages or the failure of the reporting mechanisms, but these could again be added to the model.

In [15,16], we have constructed a family of models for a variety of circuits, fitting the rates from the single-junction circuit experiments [48], and then evaluating the quality of the model on the double-junction circuits. We found good alignment of model predictions with the experimental data, in particular also observing the effect of *leakage* transitions, that is, when the walker unintentionally transfers to the neighbouring track because of its proximity. In addition, we have considered a range of circuit designs and analysed their performance and reliability using the probabilistic model checker PRISM [34].

3   Stochastic Models and Analysis Techniques

As discussed in the previous section, stochasticity is an important aspect that we need to consider when designing molecular circuits, particularly localised computation such as DNA walkers placed on origami tiles. In this section we introduce the background notation and briefly overview existing stochastic models and analysis methods applicable to molecular systems.

3.1   Continuous-Time Markov Chains (CTMC)

The evolution of molecular systems is naturally modelled as a stochastic process tracking the probability of molecular populations over time. This process, under the assumption of constant volume and temperature, is a (homogeneous) *continuous-time Markov chain (CTMC)*.

Formally, a CTMC $\mathcal{C}$ is a tuple $(S, s_0, \mathbf{R})$, where S is a set of states, $s_0 \in [0,1]^S$ is the initial distribution over states, and $\mathbf{R}$ is the rate transition matrix with $\forall s, s' \in S$, $\mathbf{R}(s, s') \geq 0$, $\mathbf{R}(s, s) = 0$.

Each CTMC can be unfolded into execution paths from the start state as follows. The residence time in state s is exponentially distributed with exit rate $\lambda_s = \sum_{s' \in S} \mathbf{R}(s, s')$. Once the residence time expires, the probability to move to state s' from s is $\frac{\mathbf{R}(s,s')}{\lambda_s}$. We refer to the discrete-time Markov chain encoding the discrete transition probabilities for each state as the *embedded DTMC*.

Alternatively, for a CTMC the probability over time (*transient probability distribution*) is given by the Chemical Master Equation (CME) [23] $\frac{d}{dt}\pi_t = \pi_t \cdot \mathbf{Q}$, where $\mathbf{Q}$ is the infinitesimal generator matrix, defined as $\mathbf{Q}(s, s') = \mathbf{R}(s, s')$ if $s \neq s'$, and $1 - \sum_{s'' \neq s} \mathbf{R}(s, s'')$ otherwise, and $\pi_0 = s_0$.

A CTMC can be extended with a reward structure (ρ, ι), where ρ and ι are respectively a vector and matrix of non-negative reals. $\rho(s)$ is a state reward, and defines the rate at which the reward is acquired when $\mathcal{C}$ remains in state s for t time units. The function $\iota(s, s')$, $s, s' \in S$, defines the transition reward acquired each time the transition (s, s') occurs.

All Markov processes with countable state spaces and continuous distributions of time may be described as CTMCs, since the exponential distribution is the only continuous distribution with the Markov property. We usually work with finite state CTMCs, though some of the analysis techniques generalise to countable CTMCs.

In the context of verification CTMCs are enriched with *atomic propositions* that label states. Formally, a *labelled* CTMC is a tuple $(AP, L, S, s_0, \mathbf{R})$ such that $(S, s_0, \mathbf{R})$ is a CTMC, AP is a set of atomic propositions and $L : S \to 2^{AP}$ is a labelling function that assigns atomic propositions to the states. When considering molecular systems, the set of atomic propositions usually includes inequalities over the number of each molecule type, for example, "there are at least 5 molecules x" (written $x \geq 5$).

3.2   Quantitative Verification for CTMCs

To specify quantitative properties of CTMCs, a number of formalisms can be used. These are divided into two families, linear time and branching time. Linear time formalisms specify accepting paths, and contain a single outer probabilistic operator. They include:

- temporal logics LTL (linear-time temporal logic) [40] and BLTL (bounded linear-time temporal logic) [28];
- deterministic timed automata specifications [6,19], where timed paths are accepted only if they are in the language of the automaton;
- deterministic linear hybrid automata specifications [5], an extension of timed automata with clocks evolving at different speed;

– temporal logic MTL (metric temporal logic) [10]which is an extension of BLTL with real-time constraints on the until operator.

Branching-time formalisms, on the other hand, contain nested probabilistic operators, and include:

– temporal logics PCTL [24] and PCTL* (probabilistic computation tree logic) [1], based on CTL/CTL* with the probabilistic operator added (for untimed properties);
– temporal logic CSL (continuous stochastic logic) [2], an extension of PCTL where temporal operators are equipped with real-time constraints and with an additional operator to specify steady state distribution.

These formalism can be extends with rewards. In this paper we will work with linear-time properties that we introduce using random variables. The key properties of interest are $\mathbb{P}_{=?}[X_\phi]$, the probability of the path formula ϕ being satisfied from a given state over time (X_ϕ is a random variable defined over paths from s equal to 1 if the path satisfies ϕ and 0 otherwise); and $\mathbb{E}_{=?}[X_{(\rho,\iota)}]$, the expected cumulative reward in a given state over time ($X_{(\rho,\iota)}$ is a random variable defined over paths annotated with rewards (ρ,ι) that computes the total reward cumulated up to t). Path formulas ϕ include the temporal operators 'until' and 'future', both unbounded and time-bounded variants; for example, $(x \geq 1)\mathbb{U}(x = 0)$ denotes a path along which molecules x eventually degrade, and $\mathbb{F}^{<100}(x \geq 1) \wedge (y = 0)$ a path which reaches a state where there is at least one x molecule and no y molecules within 100 time units.

A number of techniques are available to analyse CTMCs. Since precise solution of the CME is in general intractable, the prevailing method is stochastic simulation, e.g. using the Gillespie algorithm [23], which generates forward trajectories from the initial state or distribution. Quantitative verification aims to compute the probability or expectations of certain events specified using the above temporal logic or automata formalisms. For CSL formulas, the computation of probability over time reduces to transient analysis on a modified model. Given an automaton representation of the property (which can be derived from LTL formulas or provided directly, e.g. as a timed automaton), it is necessary first to build the product of the automaton and the model, and then compute transient probability distributions on the product. Quantitative verification of expected reward properties is similar.

Transient analysis usually proceeds through numerical methods or simulation-based analysis known as statistical model checking, which we describe next.

3.3   Numerical Verification Methods for CTMCs

Numerical methods require that the state space and rate matrix of the CTMC be constructed. Typically, the numerical computation of transient distribution proceeds through discretisation of the CTMC, resulting in approximate probability values. These methods are more efficient on branching-time formalisms, in particular for CSL, where they take advantage of the strict alternation of probabilistic and temporal operators. On linear-time properties one first has to build an automaton from the specification, and then build the product of the automaton and the CTMC, which increases the state space. Two methods have been developed for transient analysis, *uniformisation* and its variant *fast adaptive uniformisation* that neglects states with insignificant probability mass, thus improving performance of the computation.

Uniformisation. Uniformisation (see e.g. [35] translates the problem of computing transient distribution of a CTMC to the computation of transient distribution of its discretisation, called the *uniformised DTMC*, and can be summarised as follows.

- For any CTMCs where there exists a bound on the maximal exit rate, the uniformised DTMC can be computed over the same state space, where each step in the DTMC corresponds to one exponentially distributed delay in the CTMC with rate equal to the maximal exit rate.
- Transient probability of the CTMC at time t can be computed as an infinite summation of i jumps in the uniformised DTMC weighted by Poisson probabilities.
- The Poisson weights of the infinite summation are derived using the Fox & Glynn algorithm [22], which also determines the upper bound on the number of summation terms needed to meet a given error bound.

Uniformisation involves operations on the stochastic matrix of the uniformised DTMC, and thus can suffer from state-space explosion.

Fast Adaptive Uniformisation (FAU). Fast adaptive uniformisation (FAU) [18,39] can reduce the size of the explored state space by neglecting states with insignificant probability mass. It is an approximate method for computing the transient distribution of a CTMC and can be summarised as follows:

- Transient probability distributions are computed forward from the initial state in the embedded DTMC. States with low probability of occurrence (below a threshold δ) are discarded. Therefore, FAU only explores a subset of the state space.
- The maximal exit rate of the CTMC is approximated and computed on the fly on the set of states that have not been discarded. The upper bound on the infinite summation is also computed on the fly.

The FAU method can greatly improve the time and memory consumption of the transient probability computation when the state space is large and exit rates of states span several orders of magnitude. It has also been extended to the computation of rewards [14].

Numerical model checking for CTMCs against CSL probability and reward formulas has been implemented in PRISM [34] using uniformisation (symbolic, hybrid, sparse and explicit engine) and FAU (explicit engine).

3.4 Statistical Model Checking

Instead of constructing the rate matrix of the CTMC, an alternative when dealing with large state spaces is to use statistical methods. The *statistical model checking* approach relies on Monte Carlo simulation algorithm to estimate the probability of interest. These methods are better suited to linear-time properties due to the difficulty of dealing with nested probabilistic operators. In [53] an algorithm for nested probabilistic operators is provided, but the simulation time greatly increases with the depth of the nesting. More precisely, statistical methods are applied as follows: for a path formula ϕ, a Bernoulli random variable X is defined which takes 1 as value on a path that satisfies ϕ and 0 otherwise. The probability estimate is thus obtained as the ratio of the number of paths satisfying ϕ to the total number of paths, where the Monte Carlo algorithm simulates a large number, say N, of paths. The random variable Z is defined as the mean of N independent copies of X:

$$Z = \frac{1}{N} \sum_{i=1}^{N} X_i$$

An advantage of statistical model checking is that it can be parallelised very easily: it suffices to run several simulators of the system on different processors and take the mean result of paths from all simulators. Particular attention needs to be paid to the random number generator to ensure that all generated paths are independent, but otherwise the overhead of parallelisation is low. Statistical model checking can be naturally extended to computing expected rewards, that is, the expected value of a random variable whose values depend on rewards cumulated over simulated paths.

Confidence Intervals. When one computes a probability estimate for some random variable X, and the exact value cannot be computed, it is important to know how far this estimate is from the actual value. Statistical methods cannot guarantee that the numerical value we obtain is at a given distance to the actual value. This is because using a fixed number of samples the simulation may avoid certain parts of the system with non-zero probability, thus biasing the estimation. Nevertheless, probabilistic guarantees on the obtained result can be given in the form of confidence interval, namely, confidence in the fact that the actual value is close enough to the realisation, defined as follows.

Let $(X_i)_1^N$ be independent random variables following a common distribution including a parameter θ. Let $0 < \gamma < 1$ be a confidence level. Then a *confidence interval* for θ with level at least γ is given by two random variables $l(X_1, \ldots, X_N)$ and $u(X_1, \ldots, X_N)$ such that for all θ:

$$\mathbb{P}\left[l(X_1, \ldots, X_N) \leq \theta \leq u(X_1, \ldots, X_N)\right] \geq \gamma$$

Classical statistical inequality can be used to derive confidence intervals from a set of realisations of a random variable. As a general rule, these inequalities link together the confidence *level*, the *number* of samples and the *width* of the confidence interval, such that the user specifies two of them and the third is derived from the inequality.

The simplest approach is Gaussian analysis, which uses central limit theorem to approximate the distribution of the mean value of the observations of the random variable. When a random variable follows normal distribution, confidence interval can be computed using Gaussian error function.

A variant of this approach is to approximate the distribution of the random variable to a normal distribution and use the cumulative distribution function of the student-t distribution to compute confidence intervals. This confidence interval is more conservative than the one of the normal distribution when the number of samples is small, but as the number of samples increases they converge to each other.

When more conservative results are required and bounds on the value taken by the random variable are known, then Chernoff-Hoeffding inequality can be used to produce confidence intervals.

Sequential Estimation. Using additional hypotheses, the required number of samples can be computed on the fly; the simulation is then stopped as soon as the number of samples is sufficient. These methods are called *sequential estimation*.

Given a confidence level and a confidence interval width, the Chow and Robbin algorithm [12] requires the same hypothesis as Gaussian analysis and that the width of the confidence interval tends to zero. The algorithm provides the optimal stopping rules for the simulation and returns a confidence interval with expected width and variance.

When one is not interested in the actual expected value of a random variable but rather in deciding whether this value is above or below a threshold, then hypothesis testing can be used. Given a confidence level, a threshold and an open interval around this threshold called indifference region, the Sequential Probability Ratio Test (SPRT) [46,53] returns whether the value is above or below the threshold. If the true expected value is in the indifference region the test result has no probabilistic guarantee. Otherwise, the test result is correct with a probability equal to the confidence level. Two different confidence levels may be used for values above and below the threshold to make the test asymmetric (type I and type II errors).

Rare Events. One of the main limitations of statistical model checking is the rare event problem. When the probability that we want to compute is very small (usually smaller than 10^{-6}, statistical model checking becomes inefficient. Recently, several methods have addressed this limitation using *importance sampling* [7,26,42] or *splitting* [27], summarised below.

– Importance sampling relies on biasing the model such that the satisfaction of the formula is no longer a rare event. During simulation an the overall bias is estimated to produce an accurate estimation of the rare event. The difficulty lies in the choice of bias.

– Splitting relies on defining a sequence of successive embeddedings of subsets of the state space. The smallest subset only contains states satisfying the property of interest, while the largest contains all states. During simulation, each time a path reaches the next subset it is split into several copies. The probability that one path reaches the smaller subset is higher than the initial probability. Appropriately choosing the subsets is crucial to obtain precise results.

Statistical model checking for CTMCs has been implemented in a number of tools, to mention PRISM and Cosmos. In particular, PRISM [34] implements the confidence interval and SPRT methods for time-bounded CSL properties (also known as approximate probabilistic model checking), whereas Cosmos [3, 4] provides a range of statistical model checking methods, including importance sampling, for a more expressive specification language.

3.5   Stochastic Petri Nets

CTMC models of molecular systems are complex, and high-level modelling languages facilitate their construction. Such languages include stochastic extensions of process algebras (cf PEPA [13]), reactive modules (cf PRISM [34]) or Petri nets (cf Cosmos [3,4]). We focus here on *stochastic Petri nets (SPNs)*, a graph of places connected by transitions, where the time for a transition to fire is distributed according to exponential distributions. SPNs are naturally interpreted as CTMCs whose state space is the set of reachable marking. They have been widely studied, for example in [17].

Formally, an SPN is a tuple $\mathcal{N} = (P, T, W^-, W^+, m_0, \Lambda)$, where P is a finite set of places, T is a finite set of transitions, $W^- : P \times T \to \mathbb{N}$ is the pre incidence matrix, $W^+ : P \times T \to \mathbb{N}$ is the post incidence matrix, $m_0 \in \mathbb{N}^P$ is the initial marking, and $\Lambda : \mathbb{N}^P \times T \to \mathbb{R}$ is the rate function which associates a rate to each marking and transition.

SPNs can be endowed with CTMC semantics, which for $\mathcal{N} = (P, T, W^-, W^+, m_0, \Lambda)$ is given as the CTMC $\mathcal{C} = (S, s_0, \mathbf{R})$ defined by:

– $S = Reach(\mathcal{N}, m_0)$, the set of reachable markings
– $s_0(m_0) = 1$, $\forall s \in S \backslash \{m_0\}, s_0(s) = 0$
– $\mathbf{R}(m, m') = \sum_{t \in T, \ s.t. \ m \xrightarrow{t} m'} \Lambda(m, t)$.

A common extension of SPNs are *generalized stochastic Petri nets (GSPN)*, which additionally use immediate transitions with Dirac distributions. Weights are added to resolve concurrent firing of immediate transitions. As immediate transitions are memoryless, the semantics of a GSPN is still Markovian as long as there is no cycle of immediate transitions [20]. Such cycles can be detected by an analysis of the structure of the net. Adding such immediate transitions is convenient for modelling stochastic systems and may reduce the size of the set of reachable markings [30].

GSPNs are supported by a number of tools, including Cosmos and Marcie [25].

4   Modelling DNA Walkers

In [15,16], DNA walkers were modelled in the native language of PRISM, which represents each walker circuit as a synchronised parallel composition of reactive modules, each specified using guarded commands whose updates are annotated with rates. Since DNA walker circuits are planar, GSPNs are well suited to their modelling, with the layout of the GSPN closely corresponding to the layout of the original circuit: the state of each anchorage is modelled using an independent place, while the steps of the walker are modelled with transitions that are exponentially distributed.

The blocking mechanism used to steer the movement of the walker may fail with some probability; this failure occurs before the walker is released and thus before any walker movement. In PRISM, this is modelled with transitions with very high rates (a billion times larger than walker movement rates), which makes the computation intractable when uniformisation is used. In GSPN this blocking mechanism is modelled using instantaneous transitions.

More precisely, each DNA walker circuit comprises several tracks (sequences of anchorages) and transitions correspond to walker taking a step from one anchorage to another nearby. The states of each anchorage are modelled as follows:

- Each anchorage is modelled with a single place, to preserve the layout of the original circuit placement. The relative placement of each place corresponds to that of the corresponding anchorage on the origami.
- Intact anchorages are modelled with places containing one token.
- Anchorages where the top has melted away are modelled by empty places.
- The anchorage to which the walker is attached is modelled by a place with two tokens.
- Blocked anchorages are modelled like anchorages where the top has melted away, with empty places.

Fig. 3 illustrates a transition encoding a displacement reaction between two anchorages a and b. Place a encodes the anchorage to which to walker is currently bound. Place b encodes an intact, unblocked anchorage. The transition consumes two tokens in the place corresponding to a and one token in the place corresponding to b, and produces two tokens in the place corresponding to b. Indeed, after the transition is fired the place corresponding to a is left empty, which models the anchorage where the top has melted away.

The walker may move between two anchorages that are sufficiently close. Each such movement is modelled with independent transitions. The rate of each transition depends on the distance between the two anchorages as specified on page 5.

Blocked anchorages do not initially contain tokens. In order to model the possibility of failure of the blocking mechanism, a place with initially one token and two immediate concurrent transitions are added to each blocked anchorage. Fig. 4 illustrates this. With failure probability $f = 0.3$, a token is added to the place for anchorage a. In this case the anchorage is no longer blocked.

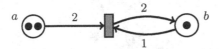

Fig. 3. Transition modelling movement of the walker from anchorage a to anchorage b

Fig. 4. Two transition model of the failure of the blocking mechanism of anchorage a

Our modelling approach ensures modularity of the design and that the layout of the Petri net closely resembles that of the original walker system. Different circuits can be composed together easily by merging together initial and final anchorages and by adding transitions between places encoding nearby transitions. Additional behaviours of the circuit, such as a missing anchorage, may be added easily by adding or removing tokens. An alternative modelling approach would have been to use colour to model the position of the walker, similarly to works in [37], but this would not preserve the layout of the original walker.

The walker models that we study are complex and have large number of transitions, but can nevertheless be viewed on screen and zoomed in. As an example, Fig. 5 shows one of the smallest models. In the following, for the sake of clarity we will hide most of the transitions when displaying a Petri net.

The state space of the walker systems increases exponentially with the number of anchorages. Table 1 shows the number of places and transitions, together with the size of the state space for models of DNA walkers that we studied. For the larger models it was not possible to build the state space due to memory limits.

The size of the state space makes the analysis of these models difficult. Qualitative analysis is still possible using symbolic representation of the state space for the smaller examples. For quantitative analysis, numerical computation of transient probability via uniformisation requires the storage of a vector of probabilities (one floating point number per state). Currently, the maximal amount of memory in a computer is in the order of 100 GByte using single precision, namely, at most $100 \cdot 1024 \cdot 1024 \cdot 1024/4 \approx 27 \cdot 10^9$ states. This neglects the amount of memory required to store the transition matrix, let alone the time to compute with such a large vector. Unfortunately, the state space of some of the models of DNA walkers that we consider exceeds this limit. This problem can be partially alleviated using FAU. However, when the state space is too large to be constructed the only viable alternative is to use statistical model checking for the analysis.

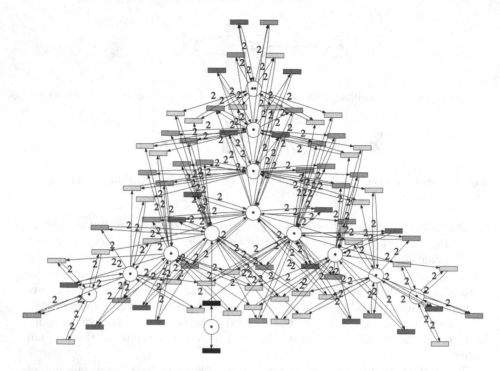

Fig. 5. A single junction circuit. The walker is initially in the upper anchorage. The anchorage on the left of the junction is blocked. Gray-scale used for the transitions indicate the tree possible rates $(k_s, k_s/50, k_s/100)$. Black transitions correspond to immediate transitions.

5   Experiments and Results

In this paper, we model a variety of DNA walker circuits using stochastic Petri nets and analyse their reliability and performance. We focus on the application of statistical model checking, which we compare to numerical solution methods implemented in PRISM. We first briefly describe the tools used, followed by an overview of the results and analysis of the advantages of each method and the corresponding trade offs that can serve as guidelines when selecting software tools for quantitative modelling and verification of similar systems.

5.1   Tools

We use three modelling and analysis tools to perform computational experiments, namely Marcie [25], PRISM [34] and Cosmos [3,4]. We also use Graphviz for the visualisation of Petri nets.

Marcie supports qualitative and quantitative analysis of generalised stochastic Petri nets. The tool has been developed for the study of chemical reaction networks and thus facilitates the modelling of such systems. It employs Interval Decision Diagrams (IDD) to symbolically represent the state space of the

Table 1. Size of the state space of DNA walker models studied

Model	Places	Transitions	States	Model	Places	Transitions	States
control	8	34	172	ringLL	27	260	27,950,678
controlMissing1	7	22	50	ringRL	27	260	27,950,678
controlMissing2	6	13	13	ringLR	27	260	28,209,796
controlMissing7	7	27	82	ringRR	27	260	28,209,796
track12Block1	13	82	3,795	ringLLLarge	33	312	1,885,372,776
track12Block2	14	84	5,459	ringRLLarge	33	312	1,885,372,776
track12BlockBoth	14	84	5,248	ringLRLarge	33	312	1,860,879,029
track28LL	34	250	432,884,827	ringRRLarge	33	312	1,860,879,029
track28LR	34	250	435,340,831	redundantChoiceL	43	490	-
track28RL	34	250	435,340,831	redundantChoiceR	43	490	-
track28RR	34	250	432,884,827				

Petri net. The implementation of IDD is mostly parallel, taking advantage of multicore architectures. The tool has recently been extended with a simulation engine for model checking of PLTL (propositional linear-time temporal logic) formulas. Marcie can deal with unbounded until properties as long as the user guarantees termination. We use Marcie to compute the size of the state space in our experiments.

PRISM is a probabilistic model checker that supports a variety of probabilistic models and probabilistic temporal logics, including CTMCs and temporal logic CSL. A CTMC model is provided in the PRISM modelling language as a synchronised parallel composition of reactive modules, but model imports, e.g. via SBML, are also supported. Verification of CSL properties can proceed via numerical methods (uniformisation or fast adaptive uniformisation) or statistical model checking (confidence interval and SPRT), known as approximate probabilistic model checking. We use PRISM to perform quantitative verification using numerical methods and approximate model checking.

Cosmos is a statistical model checker for generalised stochastic Petri nets with general distributions. It takes Hybrid Automata Stochastic Logic (HASL), based on linear hybrid automata, as a specification language. Efficient simulation is obtained using code generation that generates lightweight optimised C++ code. The generated code implements a simulator for the product of the model with the automaton underlying the specification. We use Cosmos for the evaluation of the models using statistical model checking.

5.2   The Setting

We perform experiments with Cosmos and PRISM on several circuit designs that have either been experimentally studied by biochemists or present design challenges. To ensure that the model given to each tool encodes the same system, the following workflow is used:

1. Each circuit defines a set of anchorages; for each anchorage, the position is specified as well as whether it is an initial or final anchorage. Additionally, the correct final anchorage is specified.

2. From this description of the circuit a GSPN is built.
3. The GSPN is exported in the GrML (Graph Markup Language) file format for Cosmos; the ANDL (Abstract Net Description Language) for Marcie; and the DOT language for Graphviz and the PRISM language. All these exports are simple except for PRISM, for which the GSPN is transformed into a single module, where each place is transformed into one variable and each transition into one guarded command. The property that the GSPN is 2-safe is used to bound variables.
4. From the GSPN and the initial description of the circuit, properties are provided as logical formulas for PRISM and as automata for Cosmos.

On each model we define atomic propositions of the form $Ax = y$, with Ax indicating an anchorage name, x either a place name or a PRISM variable, and y an integer. Labels and reward structures on states are also added to express certain properties, as described below.

For each model we perform the following initial analysis. The first four formulas are simple bounded reachability properties that can be expressed in many logics, for example BLTL or CSL with rewards. For the two remaining ones, we give the specification. We compute after 200 min the following properties:

1. The probability of reaching a deadlock state, where we assume an atomic proposition `deadlock` labelling deadlock states:

$$\text{Deadlock} := \mathbb{P}_{=?} \, \mathbb{F}^{\leq 12000} \, \texttt{deadlock}$$

2. The probability of reaching a final anchorage, define using a state label (`final`):

$$\text{Finish} := \mathbb{P}_{=?} \, \mathbb{F}^{\leq 12000} \, \texttt{final}$$

3. The average time spent in an anchorage that was supposed to be blocked but the failure mechanism failed; this is defined using reward structure `block` that increases linearly with the time spent in a blocked anchorage:

$$\text{Blockade} := \mathbb{R}\{\texttt{block}\}_{=?} \, C^{<=12000}$$

4. The expected number of steps of the walker, defined using reward structure `steps` that is increased by one for each firing of a transition:

$$\text{Steps} := \mathbb{R}\{\texttt{steps}\}_{=?} \, \mathbb{C}^{<=12000}$$

5. The reliability of the walker computation, written as an algebraic expression over (quantitative) CSL or BLTL formulas:

$$\text{Reliability} := \frac{\mathbb{P}_{=?} \, \mathbb{F}^{\leq 12000} \, \texttt{finalCorrect}}{\mathbb{P}_{=?} \, \mathbb{F}^{\leq 12000} \, \texttt{final}}$$

6. The probability that a path reaches the correct final anchorage while visiting a blocked anchorage, defined in BLTL using state label `blockAnchorage`:

$$\text{uB} := \mathbb{P}_{=?} \, ((\mathbb{F}^{\leq 12000} \, \texttt{blockAnchorage}) \wedge (\mathbb{F}^{\leq 12000} \, \texttt{finalCorrect}))$$

The first five properties were already studied in [15] for some of the models.

The tool Cosmos takes deterministic Linear Hybrid Automata (LHA) as a specification formalism. Compared to timed automata, in LHA clocks are replaced by piecewise linear variables. Cosmos implements the synchronisation of a GSPN with an LHA. The main features of a property automaton are illustrated in Fig. 6. The locations of the automaton are labelled with invariants, which are atomic propositions of the GSPN. Locations are labelled with the rate of each variable; for clarity only rates different from 0 are labelled in the figure except for variable t, whose rate is always equal to 1. Accepting locations of the automaton are labelled with a name (in Fig. 6 names are **sl,fc,fnc**). The transitions of the automaton are of two types: *synchronized* transitions are labelled with a set of GSPN transition names, or the symbol A for any transition, and are synchronised with the firing of the GSPN transition. They can be labelled with a time guard; *autonomous* transitions, indicated with symbol #, are not synchronised and occur as soon as the time guard is satisfied. More detail on the synchronisation of GSPN and LHA can be found in [3].

In addition to the property automata, Cosmos relies on several HASL expressions that specify which value to estimate from the automaton. For our properties the expressions are as follows:

- The probability of reaching a deadlock state is expressed as follows:

$$\mathbb{P}_{=?}\,\mathbf{dl}$$

  and is interpreted as the probability for an accepting trajectory of the GSPN to end in location **dl**;
- The probability of reaching a final anchorage is expressed as follows:

$$\mathbb{P}_{=?}\,\mathbf{fc} \vee \mathbf{fnc}$$

- The average time spent in an anchorage that was supposed to be blocked, but the failure mechanism failed, is expressed as follows:

$$\mathbb{E}_{=?}\,bt$$

  and is interpreted as the average value of variable bt in accepting states;
- The reliability property is expressed as:

$$\frac{\mathbb{P}_{=?}\,\mathbf{fc}}{\mathbb{P}_{=?}\,\mathbf{fc} \vee \mathbf{fnc}}$$

- The probability that a path reaches the correct final anchorage while visiting a blocked anchorage is defined as:

$$\frac{\mathbb{P}_{=?}\,(ub = 1) \wedge \mathbf{fc}}{\mathbb{P}_{=?}\,\mathbf{fc}}$$

The sixth property is expressed with a slightly more involved automaton, which is not reported here for reasons of space. In this automaton a variable s is added to count the number of steps of the walker; it is increased by 1 on each synchronised transition except the one that loops over the initial state. The HASL expression is $\mathbb{E}_{=?}\ s$. More details and formal specification of HASL expressions can be found in [3].

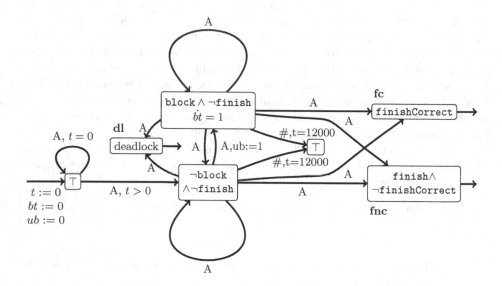

Fig. 6. LHA for the first four of the properties. This LHA contains two variables: t is a clock which is never reset, and bt is a piecewise linear variable with respect to time whose derivative is equal to 0 everywhere except in states where **block** holds. Symbol A indicates that the automaton reads any action of the model.

In the remainder of this section we describe the models and report on the results of verifying the above properties using statistical model checking methods. In Section 6 we compare and contrast the outcomes produced by the different tools and methods on each model, as well as the time and memory requirements.

5.3   Control Model

We begin by analysing the experimental designs of DNA walker models introduced in [47,52], which were modelled and analysed in [15,16]. These circuits comprise several anchorages in a straight line, where some anchorages have been removed. Fig. 7 depicts the control model where, for clarity, the transitions of the Petri net have been omitted except for the self-loops on final anchorages. The positioning of places corresponding to each anchorage is consistent with the positioning of the anchorage on the circuit layout. The initial position of the walker is in the upper left corner and is encoded with two tokens. The final position is in the lower right corner. There are three variants of this model. In the first, the anchorage 4 is omitted. In the second, anchorages 4 and 5 are omitted. In the third anchorage, 7 is omitted.

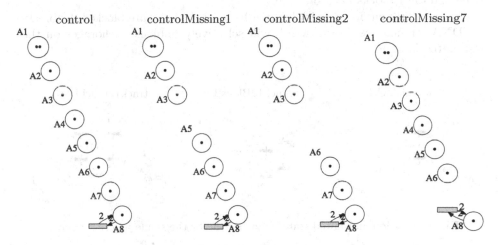

Fig. 7. Simplified Petri nets of control models

The results for this control model are reported in Table 2. We compute the average number of steps (Steps), the probability of deadlock (Deadlock) and the probability to reach the final anchorage in 200 minutes (Finish).

Table 2. Experimental results for the control model

Model	Steps	Deadlock	Finish
control	6.8756	0.0033	0.9618
controlMissing1	5.5141	0.0002	0.8528
controlMissing2	3.8529	0.0194	0.5909
controlMissing7	5.1453	0.0305	0.1755

We observe that the number of steps is directly proportional to the number of anchorages, and the probability to reach the final anchorage within the time bound greatly decreases when an anchorage is missing. From these two observations, we can deduce that the predominant path in these models is the one that successively visits each anchorage, which is consistent with wetlab experiments [47] (Fig. 2).

5.4   Single Junction Circuit

The second set of models is a single junction circuit based on the experimental setup described in [49]. Blocked anchorages are used to steer the walker in a specific direction. Fig. 8 shows three model variants. In the first, one anchorage is blocked. The second model employs two blocked anchorages on the same branch, while the third blocks both branches.

For each branch, in the initial state all the anchorages are blocked. Unblocking DNA strands are added, which will selectively unblock anchorages on the designated branch.

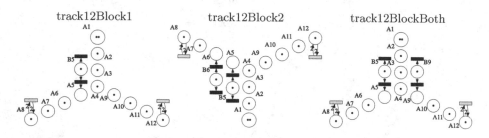

Fig. 8. Position and initial state of anchorage for the single junction circuit

Table 3 presents the results of our analysis for single junction models. We observe that the probability of deadlock (Deadlock) is very small, and with high probability the walker reaches a final anchorage within the time bound (Finish).

We observe that the model with two blockades is more reliable than that with only one: 0.84 instead of 0.77. In [16] (Fig. 11), an extensive study of the impact of blockade length on the reliability is presented.

For the third model, one of the final anchorages is chosen arbitrarily as the correct one.

Table 3. Experimental results for the single junction circuit

Model	uB	Blockade	Steps	Deadlock	Finish	Reliability
track12Block1	0.1796	46.8615	7.0494	0.0009	0.9715	0.7746
track12Block2	0.2083	315.508	6.9504	0.0016	0.9592	0.8452
track12BlockBoth	0.4794	104.292	6.551	0.0007	0.9227	0.4999

These results are consistent with those experimentally observed. In [49] (Fig. 2), for a single blockade the dependability of 0.76 is reported and for a double blockade the dependability of 0.87 is reported. When the two branches are blocked, no bias is observed between the two branches.

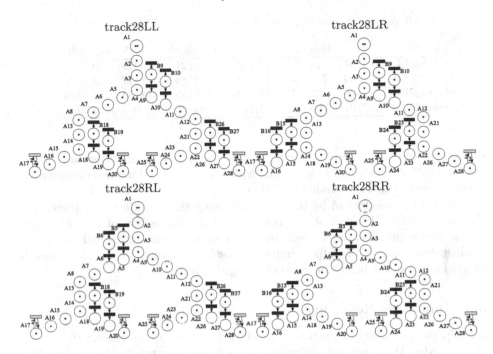

Fig. 9. Position and initial state of anchorage for the two level junction circuit

5.5 Two-Level Junction Circuit

These models are an extension of the junction circuit with two levels, which were also studied in the wetlab in [49] (Fig. 3).

Table 4 shows numerical results. We observe that the reliability varies for the four different configurations. We note that that final anchorages reached on the outside of the model show greater reliability: 0.766 versus 0.7326. The other properties also show that the circuit with final anchorages on the inside are more likely to deadlock, that the walker performs more steps, spends more time in blocked anchorages, and that the probability for the walker to bind to a blocked anchorage before reaching the final location is higher. As expected by the symmetry, the two circuits with final anchorages on the outside (respectively on the inside) have very similar results and the difference can be explained by the statistical error due to simulation. Fig. 10 shows the evolution of the probability of the presence of the walker on each final anchorage. This can be explained by the proximity of the two innermost tracks, which allows the walker to jump from one track to the other.

The plot of Fig. 10 corresponds to the wetlab experiments of [49] (Fig. 3) with similar qualitative results; the numerical value differs probably due to a

Table 4. Experimental results for the two-level binary tree

Model	uB	Blockade	Steps	Deadlock	Finish	Reliability
track28LL	0.3707	711.003	11.7339	0.0121	0.8959	0.7658
track28LR	0.3809	740.849	11.7688	0.0183	0.8847	0.7326
track28RL	0.3806	741.85	11.7684	0.0182	0.8853	0.7326
track28RR	0.3701	708.867	11.7363	0.012	0.8964	0.766

different setting. The results in Fig. 10 have been computed statistically using Cosmos with $200,000$ simulations. The width of confidence intervals around each point of each graph is bounded by 0.006.

Even if this model can be built by composing three single junction circuits, the overall reliability cannot be computed as a composition of the reliability of the single junction, which will be equal for the four configurations. Thus, quantitative analysis of walker circuit cannot be performed at the level of each individual gate but has to be done at the global level.

5.6   Improving Reliability

In [16], the reliability of junction circuits is improved by increasing the length of blockades. We propose a different design based on a two-level junction with redundant choice and time constraints.

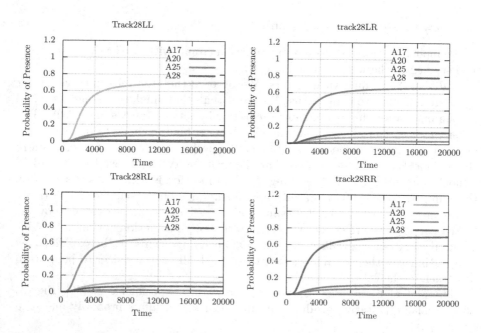

Fig. 10. Evolution over time of the probability of the presence of the walker on each final anchorage (Track28)

Table 5. Experimental results for the two-level choice

Model	uB	Blockade	Steps	Deadlock	Finish	Reliability
redundantChoice10	0.7296	1869.53	17.0304	0.2178	0.5554	0.7219
redundantChoice01	0.7298	1871.98	17.0307	0.2171	0.5559	0.7215

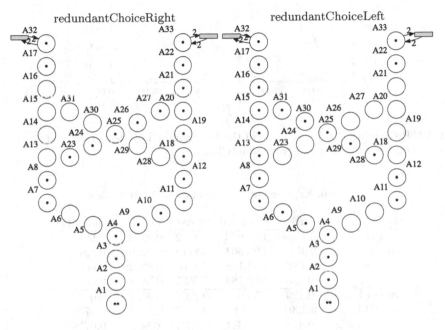

Fig. 11. Position and initial state of anchorage

Results in Table 5 demonstrate that the reliability after 200 minutes does not increase compared to the single junction circuit, and in fact is even worse than the single junction circuit with two blockades. However, since paths which end in the incorrect final anchorage had to follow a longer path, in a short amount of time the reliability is much higher. In Figure 12 we plot the probability to reach each final anchorage over time T, as well as the reliability. At time $T = 1200s$ the reliability reaches 0.935, at the cost of fewer paths reaching the final anchorage. This demonstrates that timing constraints can play an important role in DNA computation designs, and can be used to produce small circuits with comparable reliability compared to those obtained by increasing blockade length.

5.7 Exclusive Disjunction

This model implements the exclusive disjunction logical function (XOR) as a two-level junction circuit, where final anchoraged have been merged together

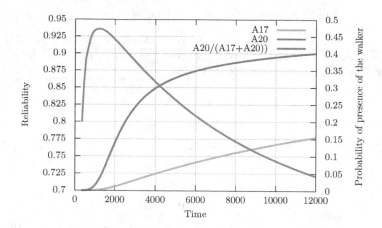

Fig. 12. Probability density function of the time required by the correct and incorrect path to reach final anchorages (redundantChoice)

Table 6. Experimental results for the XOR models

Model	uB	Blockade	Steps	Finish	Reliability
ringLL	0.4509	607.693	7.8712	0.9273	0.6981
ringRL	0.4511	606.561	7.8714	0.9269	0.6975
ringLR	0.4527	664.121	7.651	0.8982	0.6661
ringRR	0.453	664.188	7.6565	0.8978	0.6665
ringLLLarge	0.429	584.601	9.7267	0.8622	0.6737
ringRLLarge	0.4291	585.6	9.7287	0.8624	0.6745
ringLRLarge	0.428	581.341	9.7391	0.865	0.6719
ringRRLarge	0.4283	579.661	9.7379	0.8651	0.6717

forming a ring with the initial state in the middle (see Fig. 13). It illustrates the limits of increasing the length of tracks to improve the reliability. Fig. 13 shows two designs of the XOR function with different track length. The reliability does not always increase, as reported in table 6. First, note that the design is not symmetrical for the small ring, which explains the different results. The reliability increases (from 0.666 to 0.672) in two cases (LR) and (RR), but decreases (from 0.698 to 0.674) for (LL) and (RL). This model as been studied in [15] (Fig. 6) with various track lengths; for conciseness we report here only two different designs.

6   Comparison of Model Checkers

In this section we compare the performance in time and memory of tools Cosmos and PRISM. All experiments have been conducted on a computer with "Core

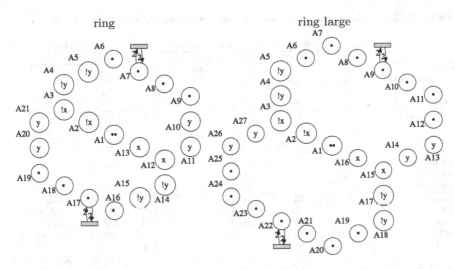

Fig. 13. Position and initial state of anchorage for XOR for a small and large design

i7-2600" CPU with 4 cores and 8GB of RAM. The maximal execution time for each experiment is set to 20 hours.

When using PRISM we apply three different methods:

- PRISM Num: Numerical model checking using PRISM's hybrid engine, uniformisation and the default numerical solver for linear equation systems (Jacobi) with threshold $\varepsilon = 10^{-6}$.
- PRISM FAU: Numerical model checking using fast adaptive uniformisation (explicit engine) with $\delta = 10^{-10}$ and $\varepsilon = 10^{-8}$.
- PRISM Sim: Simulation-based approximate model checking that involves simulating $2,000,000$ paths with confidence level of 0.99.

For Cosmos we also use $2,000,000$ paths and 0.99 confidence level. This value allows us to obtain tight confidence intervals for the results we are interested in. Cosmos simulation times are reported with 1 thread (Cosmos 1T) and 8 threads (Cosmos 8T)[1] to show how statistical methods benefit from parallelisation.

Table 7 reports time and memory[2] requirement of the different methods. Memory is omitted for statistical methods, as it is negligible compared to numerical methods since there is no need to construct the matrix. All times are reported in seconds.

---

[1] Experiments are performed on a machine with 4 cores and 2 threads per core. Experimentally, using 8 threads for the simulation is faster by around 30% than using 4 of them, whereas the speed up between 1 and 4 threads is around 370%.

[2] The memory consumption for PRISM with the FAU method is measured with the Unix 'time' utility, which includes a large constant overhead due to the Java virtual machine GC. By comparison, the uniformisation method precisely reports the memory consumption.

Table 7. Time and memory measurements for statistical and numerical methods

	Cosmos 8T	Cosmos 1T	Prism Sim	Prism Num		Prism FAU	
	Time	Time	Time	Time	Memory(KB)	Time	Memory(MB)
control	2.4	11.1	29.4	0.04	40.2	1	127.18
controlMissing1	1.5	6.8	18.9	0.01	7.8	0.9	98.82
controlMissing2	0.8	3.6	11.2	0	7.3	0.09	81.58
controlMissing7	1.9	8.6	22.6	0.02	26	0.92	113.76
track12Block1	4.7	22.4	68	>20H	388.3	3.95	245.11
track12Block2	4.7	22.2	76.4	-	530.8	4.84	296.03
track12BlockBoth	4.4	20.8	71.9	-	509.4	4.76	279.55
track28LL	10.6	51.5	395.5		>8GB	879.35	1,042.62
track28LR	11.1	53.3	393.8	-		927.59	1,061.37
track28RL	11.2	54.4	382	-		929.39	1,076.57
track28RR	10.6	52.2	393.3	-		870.48	1,047.32
ringLL	10.9	53.7	360	>20H	700MB	748.83	1,139.35
ringRL	11.1	55	339.1	-	700MB	755.69	1,131.96
ringLR	11	54.9	348.3	-	700MB	754.01	1,164.21
ringRR	10.9	53.4	346.3	-	700MB	757.72	1,154.43
ringLLLarge	12.7	62.7	423.7		>8GB	1,864.83	2,206.84
ringRLLarge	12.9	63.7	471.7	-		1,802.69	2,201.96
ringLRLarge	13	64.1	442	-		1,994.9	2,206.27
ringRRLarge	12.7	62.2	555.2	-		2,056.98	2,211.3
redundantChoice10	27.1	131.8	1,258.2		>8GB		>8GB
redundantChoice01	26.6	128.9	1,239.8	-			

We observe that uniformisation takes a very long time except for the smallest model. This is due to a large summation bound computed by the Fox & Glynn algorithm. This is due to the following two factors:

- the time bound of properties (12000 time units) is very large;
- the PRISM language does not support instantaneous transitions, and thus instantaneous transitions are encoded using stochastic transitions with a large rate (1000000).

The FAU method, on the other hand, is the fastest on small models. Compared to standard uniformisation, which uses a very large time horizon in the uniformised DTMC, FAU performs a small number of iterations. This is due to the algorithm neglecting states that did not fire transitions that encode the failure of blockade after some time. As these states have transitions with large rates, neglecting them allows FAU to use smaller uniformisation constants, resulting in fewer iterations.

For the two-level junction circuits the statistical methods are faster, while uniformisation fails due to excessive time or memory requirements. Comparing the two statistical model checking tools, Cosmos achieved better runtimes. The parallel version of Cosmos, in particular, shows that statistical methods can take advantage of parallel architecture. The difference of runtime between the two statistical tools can be explained by two main factors.

- For small models, Cosmos is twice as fast as PRISM, which can be explained by the programming language of each tool. PRISM's simulator is written in Java, while that of Cosmos consists of C++ code generated from the model

and compiled into a native executable. The choice of the language can be
explained by the history of the two tools. PRISM was designed to perform
numerical model checking, whereas Cosmos was designed from the start as
a statistical model checker.
- Cosmos exploits the structure of Petri nets to generate code, which results in
  fast simulation performance. In Petri nets, all the possible events of a system
  are the firings of the transitions. In the PRISM language, events are firings
  of guarded transitions with possible synchronisations between component.
  To avoid checking whether each event is enabled, Cosmos analyses the Petri
  net structure to compute how transitions affect each other. This is used to
  produce a simulator that checks only a subset of the transitions after each
  firing of transitions and explains the difference of runtime of about a tenth
  on the larger models.
  The analysis of the dependencies between transitions is easier to perform
  on Petri nets, as they can be expressed as graph properties. There is no
  theoretical limitation to adapt the same ideas in the PRISM simulator by
  building a dependency graph between commands, based on the content of
  their guard and updates.

Table 8 present comparison of the quality of results for statistical model
checking and FAU. Two properties are used for the comparison: the expected
number of steps before reaching a final anchorage (Steps) and the probability to
reach the correct final anchorage (FinishCorrect). As numerical methods are not
available due to time or memory constraints, only the statistical model checking
methods can be compared with each other.

The results obtained by Cosmos and the approximate model checking procedure of PRISM are indistinguishable. Thanks to the large number of paths, the
confidence intervals of the two tools converge to a very similar value.

For each property, we report the expected value for each method, as well as
a measure of the error. For the statistical methods the error is measured with
the width of the absolute confidence interval, which is reported. For the FAU
method, the total probability lost is reported.

The two error bounds are of rather different nature, and thus only their
order of magnitude can be compared. There are three distinct behaviours in the
results:

- For the control and the single junction models, the FAU method is more
  precise by two orders of magnitude. The returned values for this model are
  almost indistinguishable, and the result returned by FAU is inside the confidence interval of the statistical methods.
- For the two-level junction models and exclusive disjunction, confidence interval width and lost probability have the same order of magnitude. Most of
  the time the value computed with FAU is smaller than the left bound of the
  confidence interval.
- For the remaining models, statistical methods are more precise, with significantly smaller confidence intervals width than probability lost, 0.0018

Table 8. Comparison of the quality of result return by statistical and numerical methods

| | Steps | | | | Finish Correct | | | |
| | Statistical | | FAU | | Statistical | | FAU | |
Model	Value	Width	Value	Lost P	Value	Width	Value	Lost P
control	6.876	1.62E-3	6.876	1.94E-7	0.962	6.98E-4	0.9618	1.88E-7
controlMissing1	5.514	3.53E-3	5.514	3.17E-8	0.853	1.29E-3	0.8528	3.17E-8
controlMissing2	3.853	5.20E-3	3.855	1.79E-8	0.591	1.79E-3	0.5918	1.79E-8
controlMissing7	5.145	1.56E-3	5.145	3.18E-8	0.175	1.39E-3	0.1751	2.58E-8
track12Block1	7.049	3.39E-3	7.049	2.19E-5	0.753	1.57E-3	0.7526	1.55E-5
track12Block2	6.95	2.97E-3	6.95	1.96E-5	0.811	1.43E-3	0.811	1.80E-5
track12BlockBoth	6.551	3.67E-3	6.552	2.17E-5	0.461	1.82E-3	0.4613	1.54E-5
track28LL	11.734	5.00E-3	11.707	9.49E-3	0.686	1.69E-3	0.6843	9.42E-3
track28LR	11.769	5.20E-3	11.74	1.00E-2	0.648	1.74E-3	0.6465	9.96E-3
track28RL	11.768	5.20E-3	11.74	1.00E-2	0.649	1.74E-3	0.6465	9.96E-3
track28RR	11.736	5.00E-3	11.707	9.49E-3	0.687	1.69E-3	0.6843	9.42E-3
ringLL	7.871	9.94E-3	7.869	9.40E-3	0.647	1.74E-3	0.643	7.87E-4
ringRL	7.871	9.94E-3	7.869	9.40E-3	0.647	1.74E-3	0.643	7.87E-4
ringLR	7.651	1.06E-2	7.65	1.08E-2	0.598	1.78E-3	0.5948	8.80E-4
ringRR	7.656	1.06E-2	7.65	1.08E-2	0.598	1.78E-3	0.5948	8.80E-4
ringLLLarge	9.727	1.40E-2	9.708	3.10E-2	0.581	1.80E-3	0.5725	4.81E-3
ringRLLarge	9.729	1.40E-2	9.708	3.10E-2	0.582	1.80E-3	0.5725	4.81E-3
ringLRLarge	9.739	1.40E-2	9.723	3.16E-2	0.581	1.80E-3	0.5716	4.89E-3
ringRRLarge	9.738	1.40E-2	9.723	3.16E-2	0.581	1.80E-3	0.5716	4.89E-3
redundantChoiceL	17.03	1.30E-2	15.709	0.205	0.401	1.79E-3	0.3374	0.205
redundantChoiceR	17.031	1.30E-2	15.709	0.205	0.401	1.79E-3	0.3374	0.205

against 0.2. The value computed by FAU is significantly smaller than the left bound of the confidence interval, which is due to FAU neglecting small probability values during the computation.

7   Conclusion

We have analysed a range of DNA walker circuits against quantitative properties using the Cosmos tool, and established its usefulness as part of design automation technologies for molecular programming. Petri net models closely reflect the spatial designs of walker systems devised by experimentalists. The efficiency and accuracy of the analysis, as well its alignment with experimental observations, has been demonstrated, improving over the numerical techniques implemented in PRISM for very large models.

However, there are significant challenges ahead for this field. These include programming languages and abstractions tailored to molecular programming and nanorobotics, which need to account for not just molecular kinetics, but also thermodynamics of molecular systems; scalability of the verification, for example via modular designs and compositional analysis; and synthesis techniques, including controller synthesis and circuit synthesis from quantitative specifications. Finally, integration of the verification and synthesis tools with molecular programming toolkits such as CADNANO is desirable.

Acknowledgments. This paper has been supported by ERC Advanced Grant VERIWARE.

References

1. Baier, C.: On algorithmic verification methods for probabilistic systems. Habilitation thesis, Fakultät für Mathematik & Informatik, Universität Mannheim (1998)
2. Baier, C., Katoen, J.-P., Hermanns, H.: Approximate symbolic model checking of continuous-time markov chains (extended abstract). In: Baeten, J.C.M., Mauw, S. (eds.) CONCUR 1999. LNCS, vol. 1664, p. 146. Springer, Heidelberg (1999)
3. Ballarini, P., Barbot, B., Duflot, M., Haddad, S., Pekergin, N.: HASL: A new approach for performance evaluation and model checking from concepts to experimentation. Performance Evaluation, 2015. To appear
4. Ballarini, P., Djafri, H., Duflot, M., Haddad, S., Pekergin, N.: Cosmos: a statistical model checker for the hybrid automata stochastic logic. In: 2011 Eighth International Conference on Quantitative Evaluation of Systems (QEST), pp. 143–144. IEEE (2011)
5. Ballarini, P., Djafri, H., Duflot, M., Haddad, S., Pekergin, N.: HASL: an expressive language for statistical verification of stochastic models. In: Samson Lasaulce, P.H., Fiems, D., Vandendorpe, L. (eds.) Proceedings of the 5th International Conference on Performance Evaluation Methodologies and Tools (VALUETOOLS'11), pp. 306–315. ICST, Cachan (2011)
6. Barbot, B., Chen, T., Han, T., Katoen, J.-P., Mereacre, A.: Efficient CTMC model checking of linear real-time objectives. In: Abdulla, P.A., Leino, K.R.M. (eds.) TACAS 2011. LNCS, vol. 6605, pp. 128–142. Springer, Heidelberg (2011)
7. Barbot, B., Haddad, S., Picaronny, C.: Coupling and importance sampling for statistical model checking. In: Flanagan, C., König, B. (eds.) TACAS 2012. LNCS, vol. 7214, pp. 331–346. Springer, Heidelberg (2012)
8. Bath, J., Green, S.J., Turberfield, A.J.: A free-running DNA motor powered by a nicking enzyme. Angewandte Chemie 44, 4358–61 (2005)
9. Chandran, H., Gopalkrishnan, N., Phillips, A., Reif, J.: Localized hybridization circuits. DNA Computing and Molecular Programming 6937, 64–83 (2011)
10. Chen, T., Diciolla, M., Kwiatkowska, M., Mereacre, A.: Time-bounded verification of CTMCs against real-time specifications. In: Fahrenberg, U., Tripakis, S. (eds.) FORMATS 2011. LNCS, vol. 6919, pp. 26–42. Springer, Heidelberg (2011)
11. Chen, Y.-J., Dalchau, N., Srinivas, N., Phillips, A., Cardelli, L., Soloveichik, D., Seelig, G.: Programmable chemical controllers made from DNA. Nature Nanotechnology 8(10), 755–762 (2013)
12. Chow, Y.S., Robbins, H.: On the asymptotic theory of fixed-width sequential confidence intervals for the mean. The Annals of Mathematical Statistics, 457–462 (1965)
13. Ciocchetta, F., Hillston, J.: Bio-PEPA: A framework for the modelling and analysis of biological systems. Theoretical Computer Science 410(33–34), 3065–3084 (2009)
14. Dannenberg, F., Hahn, E.M., Kwiatkowska, M.: Computing cumulative rewards using fast adaptive uniformisation. In: Gupta, A., Henzinger, T.A. (eds.) CMSB 2013. LNCS, vol. 8130, pp. 33–49. Springer, Heidelberg (2013)
15. Dannenberg, F., Kwiatkowska, M., Thachuk, C., Turberfield, A.J.: DNA walker circuits: computational potential, design, and verification. In: Soloveichik, D., Yurke, B. (eds.) DNA 2013. LNCS, vol. 8141, pp. 31–45. Springer, Heidelberg (2013)

16. Dannenberg, F., Kwiatkowska, M., Thachuk, C., Turberfield, A.: Dna walker circuits: Computational potential, design, and verification. Natural Computing (2014)
17. Diaz, M.: Petri Nets: Fundamental models, verification and applications. Wiley (2010)
18. Didier, F., Henzinger, T.A., Mateescu, M., Wolf, V.: SABRE: A tool for stochastic analysis of biochemical reaction networks. In: Seventh International Conference on the Quantitative Evaluation of Systems QEST 2010, Williamsburg, Virginia, USA, September 15–18, pp. 193–194 (2010)
19. Donatelli, S., Haddad, S., Sproston, J.: CSL TA: an expressive logic for continuous-time markov chains. In: Fourth International Conference on the Quantitative Evaluation of Systems, QEST 2007, pp. 31–40. IEEE (2007)
20. Eisentraut, C., Hermanns, H., Katoen, J.-P., Zhang, L.: A semantics for every GSPN. In: Colom, J.-M., Desel, J. (eds.) PETRI NETS 2013. LNCS, vol. 7927, pp. 90–109. Springer, Heidelberg (2013)
21. Dannenberg, E.M.H.F., Kwiatkowska, M.: Computing cumulative rewards using fast adaptive uniformisation. ACM Transactions on Modeling and Computer Simulation, Special Issue in Computational Methods in Systems Biology (2014)
22. Fox, B.L., Glynn, P.W.: Computing poisson probabilities. Commun. ACM **31**(4), 440–445 (1988)
23. Gillespie, D.: Exact stochastic simulation of coupled chemical reactions. The Journal of Physical Chemistry **93555**, 2340–2361 (1977)
24. Hansson, H., Jonsson, B.: A logic for reasoning about time and reliability. Formal Aspects of Computing **6**(5), 512–535 (1994)
25. Heiner, M., Rohr, C., Schwarick, M.: MARCIE – model checking and reachability analysis done efficiently. In: Colom, J.-M., Desel, J. (eds.) PETRI NETS 2013. LNCS, vol. 7927, pp. 389–399. Springer, Heidelberg (2013)
26. Jegourel, C., Legay, A., Sedwards, S.: Cross-entropy optimisation of importance sampling parameters for statistical model checking. In: Madhusudan, P., Seshia, S.A. (eds.) CAV 2012. LNCS, vol. 7358, pp. 327–342. Springer, Heidelberg (2012)
27. Jegourel, C., Legay, A., Sedwards, S.: Importance splitting for statistical model checking rare properties. In: Sharygina, N., Veith, H. (eds.) CAV 2013. LNCS, vol. 8044, pp. 576–591. Springer, Heidelberg (2013)
28. Jha, S.K., Clarke, E.M., Langmead, C.J., Legay, A., Platzer, A., Zuliani, P.: A bayesian approach to model checking biological systems. In: Degano, P., Gorrieri, R. (eds.) CMSB 2009. LNCS, vol. 5688, pp. 218–234. Springer, Heidelberg (2009)
29. Jung, C., Ellington, A.D.: Diagnostic applications of nucleic acid circuits. Accounts of Chemical Research (2014, to appear)
30. Kartson, D., Balbo, G., Donatelli, S., Franceschinis, G., Conte, G.: Modelling with generalized stochastic Petri nets. Wiley (1994)
31. Kwiatkowska, M.: Quantitative verification: models, techniques and tools. In: Proc. 6th Joint Meeting of the European Software Engineering Conference and the ACM SIGSOFT Symposium on the Foundations of Software Engineering (ESEC/FSE), pp. 449–458. ACM Press (September 2007)
32. Kwiatkowska, M.: Challenges in automated verification and synthesis for molecular programming. In: Abadi, M., Gardner, P., Gordon, A.D., Mardare, R. (eds.) Essays for the Luca Cardelli Fest, Volume MSR-TR-2014-104 of Technical Report, pp. 155–170. Microsoft Research (2014)
33. Kwiatkowska, M., Norman, G., Parker, D.: Stochastic model checking. In: Bernardo, M., Hillston, J. (eds.) SFM 2007. LNCS, vol. 4486, pp. 220–270. Springer, Heidelberg (2007)

34. Kwiatkowska, M., Norman, G., Parker, D.: PRISM 4.0: verification of probabilistic real-time systems. In: Gopalakrishnan, G., Qadeer, S. (eds.) CAV 2011. LNCS, vol. 6806, pp. 585–591. Springer, Heidelberg (2011)
35. Kwiatkowska, M., Norman, G., Parker, D.: Stochastic model checking. In: Bernardo, M., Hillston, J. (eds.) SFM 2007. LNCS, vol. 4486, pp. 220–270. Springer, Heidelberg (2007)
36. Lakin, M., Parker, D., Cardelli, L., Kwiatkowska, M., Phillips, A.: Design and analysis of DNA strand displacement devices using probabilistic model checking. Journal of the Royal Society Interface 9, 1470–1485 (2012)
37. Liu, F., Heiner, M.: Colored petri nets to model and simulate biological systems. In: Proceedings of the Workshops of the 31st International Conference on Application and Theory of Petri Nets and Other Models of Concurrency (PETRI NETS 2010) and of the 10th International Conference on Application of Concurrency to System Design (ACSD 2010), Braga, Portugal (June 2010) pages 71–85, 2010
38. Češka, M., Dannenberg, F., Kwiatkowska, M., Paoletti, N.: Precise parameter synthesis for stochastic biochemical systems. In: Mendes, P., Dada, J.O., Smallbone, K. (eds.) CMSB 2014. LNCS, vol. 8859, pp. 86–98. Springer, Heidelberg (2014)
39. Mateescu, M.-E.-C.: Propagation Models for Biochemical Reaction Networks. PhD thesis (2011)
40. Pnueli, A.: The temporal logic of programs. In: 18th Annual Symposium on Foundations of Computer Science, pp. 46–57. IEEE (1977)
41. Qian, L., Winfree, E.: Scaling up digital circuit computation with DNA strand displacement cascades. Science 332, 1196–1201 (2011)
42. Reijsbergen, D., de Boer, P.-T., Scheinhardt, W., Haverkort, B.: Automated rare event simulation for stochastic petri nets. In: Joshi, K., Siegle, M., Stoelinga, M., D'Argenio, P.R. (eds.) QEST 2013. LNCS, vol. 8054, pp. 372–388. Springer, Heidelberg (2013)
43. Rothemund, P.: Folding DNA to create nanoscale shapes and patterns. Nature 440, 297–302 (2006)
44. Seelig, G., Soloveichik, D., Zhang, D., Winfree, E.: Enzyme-free nucleic acid logic circuits. Science 314, 1585–1588 (2006)
45. Soloveichik, D., Seelig, G., Winfree, E.: DNA as a universal substrate for chemical kinetics. Proceedings of the National Academy of Science 107(12), 5393–5398 (2010)
46. Wald, A.: Sequential tests of statistical hypotheses. The Annals of Mathematical Statistics 16(2), 117–186 (1945)
47. Wickham, S.F., Endo, M., Katsuda, Y., Hidaka, K., Bath, J., Sugiyama, H., Turberfield, A.J.: Direct observation of stepwise movement of a synthetic molecular transporter. Nature Nanotechnology 6(3), 166–169 (2011)
48. Wickham, S.F.J., Bath, J., Katsuda, Y., Endo, M., Hidaka, K., Sugiyama, H., Turberfield, A.J.: A DNA-based molecular motor that can navigate a network of tracks. Nature Nanotechnology 7, 169–173 (2012)
49. Wickham, S.F.J., Bath, J., Katsuda, Y., Endo, M., Hidaka, K., Sugiyama, H., Turberfield, A.J.: A dna-based molecular motor that can navigate a network of tracks. Nat Nano 7(3), 169–173 (2012)
50. Wickham, S.F.J., Endo, M., Katsuda, Y., Hidaka, K., Bath, J., Sugiyama, H., Turberfield, A.J.: Direct observation of stepwise movement of a synthetic molecular transporter. Nature Nanotechnology 6, 166–169 (2011)
51. Yin, P., Yan, H., Daniell, X.G., Turberfield, A.J., Reif, J.H.: A unidirectional DNA walker that moves autonomously along a track. Angewandte Chemie International Edition 43, 4906–4911 (2004)

52. Yin, P., Yan, H., Daniell, X.G., Turberfield, A.J., Reif, J.H.: A unidirectional dna walker that moves autonomously along a track. Angewandte Chemie International Edition **43**(37), 4906–4911 (2004)
53. Younes, H., Simmons, R.: Statistical probabilistic model checking with a focus on time-bounded properties. Information and Computation **204**(9), 1368–1409 (2006)
54. Yurke, B., Turberfield, A., Mills, A., Simmel, F., Neumann, J.: A DNA-fuelled molecular machine made of DNA. Nature **406**(6796), 605–8 (2000)
55. Zhang, D., Seelig, G.: Dynamic DNA nanotechnology using strand displacement reactions. Nature Chemistry **3**, 103–113 (2011)
56. Zhang, D.Y., Turberfield, A.J., Yurke, B., Winfree, E.: Engineering entropy-driven reactions and networks catalyzed by DNA. Science **318**(5853), 1121 (2007)

Process Mining Reloaded: Event Structures as a Unified Representation of Process Models and Event Logs

Marlon Dumas[✉] and Luciano García-Bañuelos

University of Tartu, Tartu, Estonia
marlon.dumas@ut.ee

Abstract. Process mining is a family of methods to analyze event logs produced during the execution of business processes in order to extract insights regarding their performance and conformance with respect to normative or expected behavior. The landscape of process mining methods and use cases has expanded considerably in the past decade. However, the field has evolved in a rather ad hoc manner without a unifying foundational theory that would allow algorithms and theoretical results developed for one process mining problem to be reused when addressing other related problems. In this paper we advocate a foundational approach to process mining based on a well-known model of concurrency, namely event structures. We outline how event structures can serve as a unified representation of behavior captured in process models and behavior captured in event logs. We then sketch how process mining operations, specifically automated process discovery, conformance checking and deviance mining, can be recast as operations on event structures.

1 Introduction

Process mining [1,2] is a family of methods concerned with the analysis of event records produced during the execution of business processes. Process mining methods allow analysts to understand how a given process is executed on a day-to-day basis and to detect and analyze deviations with respect to performance objectives or normative pathways. Process mining has gained significant practical adoption in recent years, as evidenced by a growing number of case studies and commercial tools. An overview of methods, tools and case studies in this field is maintained by the IEEE Task Force on Process Mining.[1]

The main input of a process mining method is a *business process event log*, that is, a collection of event records relevant to a given business process. An event log is generally structured as a set of traces. Each *trace* consists of the sequence of events produced by one execution of the process (a.k.a. a *case*). An event in a trace denotes the start, end, abortion or other relevant state change of the process or an activity therein.

---

[1] http://www.win.tue.nl/ieeetfpm

© Springer International Publishing Switzerland 2015
R. Devillers and A. Valmari (Eds.): PETRI NETS 2015, LNCS 9115, pp. 33–48, 2015.
DOI: 10.1007/978-3-319-19488-2_2

Most typically, event logs used in the context of process mining consist of events that signal the start or the end of each activity of the process. As a minimum, an event record contains an identifier of the case of the process to which the event refers, a timestamp and an *event class*, that is, a reference to an activity in the process under observation. Each event in a trace may additionally carry a payload consisting of attributes such as the resource(s) involved in the execution of an activity or other data recorded alongside the event – for example if an event represents the creation of a loan application, possible attributes include the name of the applicant and the amount of the requested loan.

A simplified example of a log of a loan application process is sketched in Table 1. In this table, CID stands for "Customer Identifier" and constitutes the primary key that should be used to group the records in the log into traces.

Table 1. Extract of a loan application log

CID	Event Type	Timestamp	...
13219	Enter Loan Application	2007-11-09 11:20:10	...
13219	Retrieve Applicant Data	2007-11-09 11:22:15	...
13220	Enter Loan Application	2007-11-09 11:22:40	...
13219	Compute Installments	2007-11-09 11:22:45	...
13219	Notify Eligibility	2007-11-09 11:23:00	...
13219	Approve Simple Application	2007-11-09 11:24:30	...
13220	Compute Installments	2007-11-09 11:24:35	...
...	...	...	...

The output of process mining can be manifold, ranging from a model of the process, to a summarized view of the most frequent paths of the process or a description of the deviations of the process with respect to normative or expected behavior.

Process mining has been an active field of research for over a decade [1,2]. During this time, a number of process mining operations have been extensively studied. One widely studied operation is *automated process discovery*. This operation takes as input a log L and produces a process model M that is "likely" to have generated the traces in log L. For example, given the log in Table 1, the output of an automated process discovery method could be the process model shown in Figure 1, which uses the standard Business Process Model and Notation (BPMN) [3].

Another widely researched operation is conformance checking, which given a model and a log, produces an enumeration of their differences, that is, a description of the behavior observed in the log but not in the model, as well as behavior allowed by the model but not observed in the log. Related to the latter is *model repair*, where instead of simply enumerating the differences between a model M and a log L, the goal is to produce a process model M' that is "similar" to M and can parse every trace in the log.

Until now, process mining methods have been developed on a case-by-case basis using disparate approaches and representations. Attempts have been made

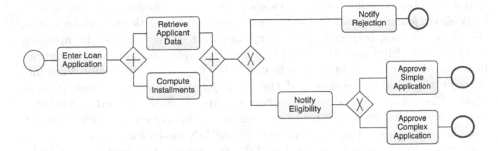

Fig. 1. Process model corresponding to the log extract in Table 1

at identifying a small number of primitive operations from which other operations can be defined [2] – but each of these primitives has been formally defined and developed independently, without an underpinning foundational theory.

In this paper we advocate a foundational approach to process mining based on a well-known model of concurrency, namely event structures [4]. We show that event structures can be used to represent both models and logs in a unified manner and that this unified representation can serve to define process mining operations that have until now been approached using different formalisms.

2 Overview of Process Mining Operations

Following a well-accepted classification in the broader field of data mining, process mining methods can be broadly classified into offline methods and online methods. Offline process mining methods aim at providing insights about the process as it is or as it has been observed in the logs. Online process mining methods on the other hand aim at providing insights about currently running cases of a process, like for example predicting the completion time of an ongoing case, or predicting whether an ongoing case will lead to a positive or a negative outcome [5]. For the sake of scoping the discussion, we hereby focus on offline process mining methods. Online process mining methods come with strong non-functional requirements, particularly with respect to performance and scalability, that deserve a separate treatment.

From the literature on process mining, one can distill the following broad classes of offline process mining operations: (i) automated process discovery and model enhancement; (ii) conformance checking and model repair; and (iii) deviance mining. Other classes of process mining operations include concept drift analysis [6] and variant identification [7], but we shall herein concentrate on the former three classes of operations for the sake of illustration.

Automated process discovery is a family of methods that given a log L generate a model M that "approximates" log L. A range of algorithms for automated process discovery have been proposed over the past decade, based on various representations of behavior. For example, the α-algorithm [8] starts by inferring a matrix of behavioral relations between pairs of event classes in the log, specifically *direct follows*, *causality*, *conflict* and *concurrency* relations. Given a matrix capturing all such relations, the algorithm constructs a Petri net by applying a set of rules. Similarly, the heuristics miner [9] relies on behavioral relations between all pairs of event classes found in the log, but additionally takes into account the relative frequency of the *direct follows* relation between pairs of tasks. These data are used to construct a graph of events (called a Heuristics net), where edges are added based on a number of heuristics. The Heuristics net can then be converted into a Petri net or a BPMN model for example. Van der Werf et al. [10] propose a process model discovery method where behavioral relations observed in the logs are translated to an Integer Linear Programming (ILP) problem, while Carmona et al. [11] approach the problem of automated process discovery using theory of regions. Finally, the InductiveMiner [12] discovers a tree where each internal node represents a block-structured control-flow construct (e.g. block-structured parallelism or block-structured choice). Such trees can then be trivially transformed into a block-structured Petri net for example.

Automated process discovery methods can be evaluated along four dimensions: fitness, precision, generalization and complexity [1,13]. Fitness measures to what extent the traces in a log can be parsed by a model. Precision measures the additional behavior allowed by a discovered model not found in the log. A model with low precision is one that parses a proportionally large number of traces that are not in the log. Generalization captures how well the discovered model generalizes the behavior found in the log. For example, if a model discovered using 90% of traces in the log can parse all or most of the remaining 10% of traces in the log, it is said the model generalizes well the log. Finally, process model complexity is intended as a proxy for understandability. It can be measured in terms of size (number of nodes and/or edges) or using a number of structural complexity metrics such as cyclomatic complexity or density that have been empirically shown to be correlated with understandability and error-proneness [14].

Related to automated process discovery is a family of methods known as *process model enhancement* [15], which given a model M and a log L (such that L is likely to have been produced by M) generate an annotated process model M'. A sub-family of model enhancement methods produce annotations referring to performance measures such as waiting times and processing times for each activity and branching probabilities for each branch of a decision point. Another family of model enhancement methods produce annotations related to resources: who performs which activity and who hands-over work to whom? In any case, from an algorithmic perspective, process model enhancement generally does not bring additional challenges with respect to automated process discovery.

Conformance checking is concerned with describing how and where actual process executions (recorded in an event log) deviate with respect to a given process model. This problem has been approached using replay techniques [15] and trace alignment techniques [16]. Replay takes as input one trace at a time and determines what maximal prefix of the trace (if any) can be parsed by the model.

When it is found that a prefix can no longer be parsed by the model, error-recovery techniques are used to correct the parsing error and to continue parsing as much as possible the remaining input trace. Alignment-based techniques on the other hand seek to find for each trace in the log, the closest corresponding trace(s) produced by the model and to determine where exactly in these traces the model and the log diverge.

Closely related to the problem of conformance checking is that of *model repair* [17], where instead of simply enumerating the differences between a model M and a log L, the goal is to generate a process model M' that is similar to M and can parse all the traces in the log. Model repair can be seen as a generative counter-part of conformance checking.

Deviance mining [18] is a family of process mining methods that aim at detecting and explaining differences between executions of a business process that lead to a positive outcome vs. those that lead to a negative outcome – with respect to a given labeling of cases into positive vs. negative ones. For example, one specific deviance mining problem is that of explaining the differences between executions of a process that fulfill a given service-level objective vs. those that do not.

Existing approaches to deviance mining can be classified into two categories [18]: *model delta analysis* [19,20] and *sequence classification*. The idea of model delta analysis is to apply automated process discovery methods to the traces of positive cases and to the traces of negative cases separately. The discovered process models are then visually compared in order to identify distinguishing patterns. This approach however does not scale up to large and complex logs. Sequence classification methods [20–22] construct a classifier (e.g. a decision tree) that can determine with sufficient accuracy whether a given trace belongs to the positive or the negative class. The crux of these methods is how sequences are encoded as feature vectors for classifier learning. Several sequence mining techniques have been explored for feature extraction in this setting. These techniques generally extract patterns of the form activity A occurs before activity B, which are frequent in (e.g.) positive cases but not in negative ones or vice-versa. An evaluation of these techniques on real-life logs has shown however that their explanatory power is rather limited [18], meaning that dozens or hundreds of rules are required to explain the differences between positive and negative cases.

Observations The above overview illustrates that various process mining problems have been approached from different angles and using disparate representations and approaches. Automated process discovery for example has been approached using representations based on binary relations between event classes as well as tree-based representations of (block-structured) process models. Meanwhile, conformance checking has been approached using replay (parsing) as well as trace alignment – techniques that are in essence disconnected from those used for automated process discovery. On the other hand, deviance mining has been approached using sequence mining techniques, which reason in terms of sequences and patterns on sequences. Again, these techniques are disconnected from the previous ones. As a further case in point, the problem of concept drift analysis [6] – where the goal is to detect and explain how the behavior of a given process has evolved over time – has been approached using sequence patterns as well as abstractions of sets of traces based on polyhedra [23].

Underpinning these observations is the fact that the representations used to reason about the behavior captured in process models are different from those used to reason about the behavior captured in event logs. When reasoning on process models, representations based on behavioral relations or Petri nets tend to be favored. When reasoning from the perspective of logs, representations based on sequences are often preferred. Below we advocate for a unified representation of process models and event logs that provides a unified perspective into existing process mining problems and methods.

3   Event Structures as a Foundation for Process Mining

We contend that event structures [4] – a well-known model of concurrency – can serve as a common representation of process models and event logs for the purpose of defining and implementing process mining operations. Below we provide a brief overview of event structures and their relation with process models and event logs. We then sketch how conformance checking and deviance mining can be recast as problems of comparison of event structures, and we briefly discuss how automated process discovery could be tackled under this framework.

3.1   Event Structures

A Prime Event Structure (PES) [4] is a graph of events, where an event e represents the occurrence of an action (e.g. a task) in the modeled system (e.g. a business process). If a task occurs multiple times in a run, each occurrence is represented by a different event. The order of occurrence of events is defined via binary relations: i) *Causality* ($e < e'$) indicates that event e is a prerequisite for e'; ii) *Conflict* ($e \# e'$) implies that e and e' cannot occur in the same run; iii) *Concurrency* ($e \parallel e'$) indicates that no order can be established between e and e'.

Definition 1 (Labeled Prime Event Structure [4]). *A Labeled Prime Event Structure over the set of event labels $\mathcal{L}$ is the tuple $\mathcal{E} = \langle E, \leq, \#, \lambda \rangle$ where*
- *E is a set of events (e.g. tasks occurrences),*
- *$\leq \subseteq E \times E$ is a partial order, referred to as causality,*
- *$\# \subseteq E \times E$ is an irreflexive, symmetric conflict relation,*
- *$\lambda : E \to \mathcal{L}$ is a labeling function.*

We use $<$ to denote the irreflexive causality relation. The concurrency relation of $\mathcal{E}$ is defined as $\parallel = E^2 \setminus (< \cup <^{-1} \cup \#)$. Moreover, the conflict relation satisfies the principle of conflict heredity, i.e. $e \# e' \wedge e' \leq e'' \Rightarrow e \# e''$ for $e, e', e'' \in E$.

For illustration, Fig. 2 presents side-by-side a BPMN process model and a corresponding PES $\mathcal{E}^1$. Nodes are labelled by an event identifier followed by the

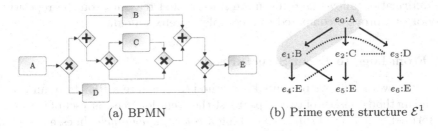

(a) BPMN   (b) Prime event structure $\mathcal{E}^1$

Fig. 2. Sample BPMN process model and corresponding PES

label of the represented task, e.g. "e_2:C" tells us that event e_2 represents an occurrence of task "C". The causality relation is depicted by solid arcs whereas the conflict relation is depicted by dotted edges. For the sake of simplicity, transitive causal and hereditary conflict relations are not depicted. Every pair of events that are neither directly nor transitively connected are in a concurrency relation. Note that three different events refer to the task with label "E". This duplication is required to distinguish the different states where task "E" occurs.

A state on an event structure (hereby called a *configuration*) is characterized by the set of events that have occurred so far. For instance, set $\{e_0$:A$, e_1$:B$\}$ – highlighted in Fig. 2(b) – is the configuration where tasks "A" and "B" have occurred. In this configuration, event $\{e_3$:D$\}$ can no longer occur because it is in conflict with $\{e_1$:B$\}$. On the other hand, events $\{e_2$:C$\}$ and $\{e_4$:E$\}$ can occur, but the occurrence of one precludes that of the other. Formally:

Definition 2 (Configuration). *Let $\mathcal{E} = \langle E, \leq, \#, \lambda \rangle$ be a prime event structure. A configuration of $\mathcal{E}$ is the set of events $C \subseteq E$ such that*
- *C is causally closed, i.e. $\forall e' \in E, e \in C : e' \leq e \Rightarrow e' \in C$, and*
- *C is conflict-free, i.e. $\forall e, e' \in C \Rightarrow \neg(e \# e')$.*

The local configuration *of an event $e \in E$ is the set $\lfloor e \rfloor = \{e' \mid e' \leq e\}$. Similarly, the (set of) strict causes of an event $e \in E$ is defined as $\lfloor e) = \lfloor e \rfloor \setminus \{e\}$.*

We denote by $Conf(\mathcal{E})$ the set of all possible configurations of $\mathcal{E}$ and by $MaxConf(\mathcal{E})$ the subset of maximal configurations with respect to set inclusion. In the running example, $MaxConf(\mathcal{E}^1) = \{\{e_0, e_1, e_2, e_5\}, \{e_0, e_1, e_4\}, \{e_0, e_3, e_6\}\}$.

Prime event structures can be extracted from Petri nets using well-known unfolding techniques. In the case of acyclic nets, a full unfolding can be computed and a PES can be trivially derived therefrom. In the case of bounded Petri nets with cycles, it is possible to calculate a finite *prefix unfolding* that captures all the behavior in the original net. A PES can then be derived from such prefix unfolding. Several prefix unfoldings have been defined in the literature, such as the *complete prefix unfolding* [24]. In [25] we defined a type of unfolding that additionally captures all the causes of every event – including events inside a cycle – thus allowing us to pinpoint which events are repeated and which are not.

This information allows us to do more fine-grained reasoning on the repetitive behavior of a process compared to a complete prefix unfolding.

3.2   From Logs to Event Structures

In previous work [26], we presented a method to generate a PES from an event log. The method consists of two steps. First the event log, seen as a set of traces, is transformed into a set of runs by invoking a *concurrency oracle*. In essence, each trace is turned into a run by relaxing the total order induced by the trace into a partial order such that two events are not causally related if the concurrency oracle has determined that they occur concurrently. The concurrency oracle is left open. Existing concurrency oracles such as those proposed in the α process mining algorithm [8] or in [27] can be used for this purpose.

Second, the set of runs are merged into an event structure in a lossless manner, meaning that the set of maximal configurations of the resulting event structure is exactly equal to the set of runs. In this way and modulo the accuracy of the concurrency oracle, we ensure that the resulting event structure is a lossless representation of the input log.

For example, consider the log given in Figure 3(a). This event log consists of 10 traces, including 3 instances of distinct trace t_1 (as specified in column "N"), 2 instances of t_2, so on and so forth. Using the concurrency oracle of the α algorithm we conclude that event classes B and C are in a concurrency relation, thus we construct the set of runs in Figure 3(b). In this latter figure, the notation e:A indicates that event e represents an occurrence of event class A in the original log. By merging together events with the same label and the same history (i.e. same prefix), we obtain the PES in Figure 3(c). In this figure, the notation $\{e_1, e_2 \ldots e_i\}$:A indicates that events $\{e_1, e_2 \ldots e_i\}$ represent occurrences of event class A in different runs.

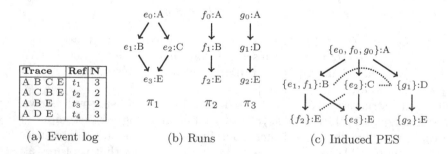

Trace	Ref	N
A B C E	t_1	3
A C B E	t_2	2
A B E	t_3	2
A D E	t_4	3

(a) Event log   (b) Runs   (c) Induced PES

Fig. 3. Example of construction of a PES from a set of traces

3.3   Comparison of Event Structures

In previous work [25], we presented a technique for comparing pairs of event structures. This technique operates by performing a *Partially Synchronized Product* (PSP) of the event structures, which is in essence a synchronized simulation starting from the empty configurations. At each step, the events that can occur given the current configuration in each of the two event structures (i.e. the *enabled* events) are compared. If they match, the simulation adds those events to the current configurations and continues. If on the other hand an enabled event in the current configuration of one event structure does not match with an enabled event in the current configuration in the other event structure, a mismatch is declared and this mismatch will be reflected in a *difference statement* that tells us that there is a pair of matching configurations where an event can occur or a behavioral relation holds in one event structure, but not in the other. Having diagnosed the difference, the unmatched event is "hidden" and the simulation jumps to the next matching configurations.

Figure 5 presents an excerpt of the PSP for $\mathcal{E}^1$ and $\mathcal{E}^2$, shown in Figure 2 and Figure 4 respectively. Note that $MaxConf(\mathcal{E}^2) = \{\{f_0, f_1, f_2, f_4\}, \{f_0, f_3, f_5\}\}$. Clearly, all maximal configurations of $\mathcal{E}^2$ can be matched to configurations of $\mathcal{E}^1$. The right-hand leaf node in the PSP illustrates the matching of configuration $\{e_0, e_1, e_2, e_5\}$ from $\mathcal{E}^1$ and $\{f_0, f_1, f_2, f_4\}$ from $\mathcal{E}^2$. There, the set m records the fact that all the events in both configuration have been matched, lh records that none of the events from $\mathcal{E}^1$ (the one to the left of the "product") has been hidden, and rh records that no event from $\mathcal{E}^2$ has been hidden. Similarly, the leaf node at the left-hand side corresponds to the best matching of configurations $\{e_0, e_1, e_4\}$ and $\{f_0, f_1, f_2, f_4\}$, respectively from $\mathcal{E}^1$ and $\mathcal{E}^2$. The cloud at the top indicates that some states precedes to the matching of a pair of events sharing the label "B". The label on the edge from the cloud to the node just below records such matching. The configuration $\{e_0, e_1\}$ enables the occurrence of e_4:E but that occurrence precludes the occurrence of e_2:C. This gives rise to a behavioral mismatch, that is resolved by hiding f_2:C. The red arrow in the PSP captures this hiding: the event f_2:C from $\mathcal{E}^2$ (right-hand side model in the product) is hidden. Note that in the target box, m remains the same, i.e. no additional matching, whereas rh records now the hiding of f_2:C. By aggregating the information in the states and edges associated to the moves "rhide C" and "match C" on the PSP, it is possible to diagnose that "Task 'C' in model 1 can be skipped, whereas the same task is always executed in model 2".

Further details on the event structures comparison method are given in [25]. A tool implementing this method, namely BP-Diff, is described in [28]. BPDiff takes as input two process models captured in standard BPMN notation and outputs a number of statements describing their behavioral differences. Each difference is verbalized in natural language and can also be visually represented on top of the process model. The tool performs the comparison at the level of event structures. Prior to the comparison step, BP-Diff converts the input BPMN process model into a Petri net and unfolds the latter into an event structure.

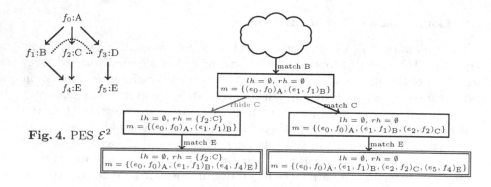

Fig. 4. PES $\mathcal{E}^2$

Fig. 5. Fragment of PSP of the PESs in Figs. 2(b) and 3

3.4   Folding of Event Structures

The PES derived from a given Petri net is generally not a space-efficient representation of behavior as it may contain significant amount of duplication (several events referring to the same task). A more compact representation can be obtained by using asymmetric event structures [29], which replace the symmetric conflict relation of PES with an asymmetric one. AES lend themselves to applying folding techniques. The idea of such folding techniques is to identify sets of events in the AES that can be merged into a single event while preserving behavior. This folding of events can be performed when two events with the same label are future-equivalent, meaning they have the same possible continuations. Under such conditions, such events can be merged into a single one thanks to the asymmetric conflict relation. The resulting folded AES is more compact and thus more convenient for the purpose of comparing pairs of process models, insofar as their comparison produces less statements of differences. In [25] we discuss how to derive a canonically folded AES from a PES, which can be used to provide a more compact diagnosis of the differences between two given PES.

We foresee that similar folding techniques can be used more widely to simplify an event structure produced from a given event log, such that the simplified event structure can be used to synthesize a process model. By allowing events to be folded even in situations where some behavior is lost or added, we can strike different tradeoffs between the four quality dimensions of discovered process models mentioned in Section 2 (precision, recall, generalization and complexity). A similar idea has been applied in [30] in order to simplify process models generated by existing automated process discovery methods.

To illustrate how folding can be used to simplify event structures at the expense of precision, consider the event structure $\mathcal{E}$ in Figure 6(a). A Petri net synthesized from this net is shown in Figure 6(b). We note that events e_3:D and e_4:D refer to the same task D. Furthermore, the set of possible futures of e_3:D is included in that of e_4:D – the latter having an additional possible future consisting of an occurrence of F. If we define a rule that folds two events under such conditions, we would fold e_5:E and e_6:E into $\{e_5, e_6\}$:E (with an empty future) and then we would fold e_3:D and e_4:D into $\{e_3, e_4\}$:D – with $\{e_5, e_6\}$:E and e_7:F as its futures. The resulting event structure then leads to the simpler net in Figure 6(c), which has more behavior (i.e. generalizes) the net in Figure 6(b).

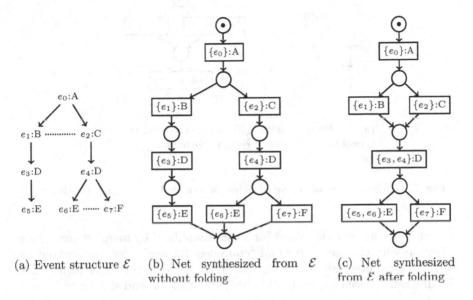

(a) Event structure $\mathcal{E}$ (b) Net synthesized from $\mathcal{E}$ without folding   (c) Net synthesized from $\mathcal{E}$ after folding

Fig. 6. Nets synthesized from an unfolded and a folded event structure with added behavior

We also foresee that a similar approach can serve to identify opportunities to introduce cycles when synthesizing a Petri net from an event structure. Consider for example the event structure in Figure 7(a). Event m_1:B and m_4:B share a common future consisting of an occurrence of D – with m_1:B having a an additional future consisting of occurrences of C, B and D. Under these conditions, one could generalize the behavior by allowing $m1 : B$ and $m3 : B$ to be folded, so that the net in 7 can be synthesized thereon.

3.5   Process Mining Operations and Event Structures

To recap, we have observed that:

- Event structures can be losslessly derived both business process models via unfoldings of Petri nets
- Event structured can be losslessly derived from event logs via concurrency oracles and merging of runs.
- Event structures allow fine-grained comparison of behavior, which can be materialized as difference statements in natural language or graphical form.

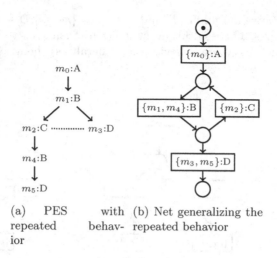

(a)   PES   with (b) Net generalizing the
repeated   behav- repeated behavior
ior

Fig. 7. Generalization of repeated behavior as a cycle during net synthesis

- Event structures can be folded (and thus simplified) by merging occurrences of events with the same label and "equivalent futures" – with or without loss of behavioral precision depending on the choice of future equivalence. This folding can be used to trade-off behavioral precision and simplicity.

These operations on event structures can be used to recast the previously reviewed process mining problems as follows:

- Deviance mining can be achieved by computing an event structure from each of the sub-logs induced by the labeling function (e.g. the log of "positive" cases and the log of "negative" cases) and comparing the two logs. In other words, this is a log-to-log comparison problem. In [26] we have empirically shown that the difference diagnostics produced in this way is more compact (less and simpler statements) than deviance diagnostics obtained using sequence classification techniques.
- Conformance checking an event log against a process model can be achieved by computing an event structure from the model, another from the log and comparing the resulting event structures to enumerate their differences. In other words, conformance checking is a model-to-log comparison problem.
- Automated process discovery of a process model from an event log can be achieved by: (i) computing an event structure from a log; (ii) transforming the resulting event structure via folding rules that achieve a trade-off between simplicity and behavioral accuracy (measured by means of fitness and precision); and (iii) utilizing the information in the resulting event structure in order to supplement a model synthesis algorithm.

Similarly although not covered in this paper, business process drift analysis can also be recast as a log-to-log comparison problem: comparing the log before and after a hypothesized change point. Meanwhile, model repair can be approached as a problem of repairing an event structure, by adding and deleting a minimal amount of relations and events in such a way that the new event structure is an accurate (or more accurate) representation of the runs in the log than the original model.

The above relations between operations on event structures and process mining operations are summarized in Figure 8.

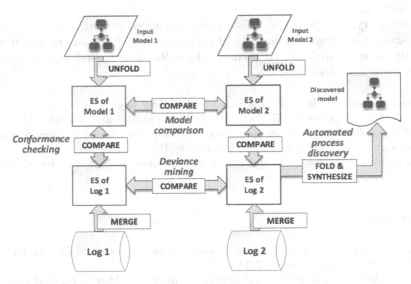

Fig. 8. Process mining operations recast as operations on Event Structures (ES)

4   Outlook

We have outlined a vision for a principled approach to process mining based on event structures as a unified representation of process models and event logs. The realization of this vision however requires a number of challenges to be addressed.

A key challenge is handling repeated behavior. Complete prefix unfoldings allow us to fully capture the behavior of a cyclic (bounded) process model. In turn, the information in this prefix unfolding can be directly encoded in an event structure. However, comparing event structures obtained from process models with those obtained from event logs is challenging because in the event structure derived from a log repeated behavior is not explicitly captured: It exists by virtue of a sub-event structure appearing multiple times in the event structure. Similarly, synthesizing a process model from the event structure derived from a log requires being able to detect and isolate repeated behavior.

Regarding automated process discovery, defining the right folding rules to simplify the event structure produced from the log is a crucial step. These folding rules will have to trade off simplicity versus accuracy – a tradeoff that existing process mining algorithms try to strike as well. In this respect, event structures merely provide us a way of studying such tradeoffs from a new perspective. Also, the use of event structures for process model synthesis would require new techniques to be developed or existing ones to be heavily adapted, e.g. adapting existing synthesis techniques based on merging of runs [31].

Finally, scalability might become a challenge, not so much in the log-to-log comparison case [26], but rather when cycle detection and folding operations come into play.

In summary, the proposed vision offers numerous opportunities to revisit long-standing challenges in the field of process mining from an angle that will hopefully allow algorithms and theoretical results to be reused across different problems and use cases.

Acknowledgments. The vision presented in this paper owes a lot to our discussions with Abel Armas-Cervantes, Nick van Beest, Dirk Fahland and Marcello La Rosa. Some of the definitions and examples used in this paper are taken from our joint previous work. This research is partly supported by the Estonian Research Council via the Institutional Grants scheme and ERDF via the Estonian Centre of Excellence in Computer Science.

References

1. van der Aalst, W.: Process Mining: Discovery, Conformance and Enhancement of Business Processes. Springer (2011)
2. van der Aalst, W., et al.: Process mining manifesto. In: Daniel, F., Barkaoui, K., Dustdar, S. (eds.) BPM 2011 Workshops, Part I. LNBIP, vol. 99, pp. 169–194. Springer, Heidelberg (2012)
3. Object Management Group: Business Process Model and Notation (BPMN) Version 2.0. Technical report, Object Management Group Final Adopted Specification (2011). http://www.omg.org/spec/BPMN/2.0/
4. Nielsen, M., Plotkin, G.D., Winskel, G.: Petri Nets, Event Structures and Domains, Part I. Theoretical Computer Science **13**, 85–108 (1981)
5. Maggi, F.M., Di Francescomarino, C., Dumas, M., Ghidini, C.: Predictive monitoring of business processes. In: Jarke, M., Mylopoulos, J., Quix, C., Rolland, C., Manolopoulos, Y., Mouratidis, H., Horkoff, J. (eds.) CAiSE 2014. LNCS, vol. 8484, pp. 457–472. Springer, Heidelberg (2014)
6. Bose, R.J.C., van der Aalst, W.M., Zliobaite, I., Pechenizkiy, M.: Dealing with concept drifts in process mining. IEEE Transactions on Neural Networks and Learning Systems **25**(1), 154–171 (2014)
7. Folino, F., Greco, G., Guzzo, A., Pontieri, L.: Mining usage scenarios in business processes: Outlier-aware discovery and run-time prediction. Data Knowl. Eng. **70**(12), 1005–1029 (2011)
8. van der Aalst, W.M.P., Weijters, T., Maruster, L.: Workflow mining: discovering process models from event logs. IEEE TKDE **16**(9), 1128–1142 (2004)
9. Weijters, A.J.M.M., Ribeiro, J.T.S.: Flexible heuristics miner (FHM). In: CIDM, pp. 310–317. IEEE (2011)

10. van der Werf, J.M.E.M., van Dongen, B.F., Hurkens, C.A.J., Serebrenik, A.: Process discovery using integer linear programming. Fundam. Inform. **94**(3–4), 387–412 (2009)
11. Carmona, J., Cortadella, J., Kishinevsky, M.: New region-based algorithms for deriving bounded petri nets. IEEE Trans. Computers **59**(3), 371–384 (2010)
12. Leemans, S.J.J., Fahland, D., van der Aalst, W.M.P.: Discovering block-structured process models from event logs - a constructive approach. In: Colom, J.-M., Desel, J. (eds.) PETRI NETS 2013. LNCS, vol. 7927, pp. 311–329. Springer, Heidelberg (2013)
13. Weerdt, J.D., Backer, M.D., Vanthienen, J., Baesens, B.: A multi-dimensional quality assessment of state-of-the-art process discovery algorithms using real-life event logs. Inf. Syst. **37**(7), 654–676 (2012)
14. Reijers, H., Mendling, J.: A study into the factors that influence the understandability of business process models. IEEE T. Syst. Man Cy. A **41**(3), 449–462 (2011)
15. Rozinat, A.: Process Mining Conformance and Extension. PhD thesis, Technische Universiteit Eindhoven (2010)
16. Adriansyah, A., van Dongen, B., van der Aalst, W.: Conformance checking using cost-based fitness analysis. In: EDOC, pp. 55–64. IEEE (2011)
17. Fahland, D., van der Aalst, W.P.: Model repair - aligning process models to reality. Inf. Syst. **47**, 220–243 (2015)
18. Nguyen, H., Dumas, M., La Rosa, M., Maggi, F.M., Suriadi, S.: Mining business process deviance: a quest for accuracy. In: Meersman, R., Panetto, H., Dillon, T., Missikoff, M., Liu, L., Pastor, O., Cuzzocrea, A., Sellis, T. (eds.) OTM 2014. LNCS, vol. 8841, pp. 436–445. Springer, Heidelberg (2014)
19. Suriadi, S., Wynn, M.T., Ouyang, C., ter Hofstede, A.H.M., van Dijk, N.J.: Understanding process behaviours in a large insurance company in australia: a case study. In: Salinesi, C., Norrie, M.C., Pastor, Ó. (eds.) CAiSE 2013. LNCS, vol. 7908, pp. 449–464. Springer, Heidelberg (2013)
20. Lakshmanan, G.T., Rozsnyai, S., Wang, F.: Investigating clinical care pathways correlated with outcomes. In: Daniel, F., Wang, J., Weber, B. (eds.) BPM 2013. LNCS, vol. 8094, pp. 323–338. Springer, Heidelberg (2013)
21. Bose, R.P.J.C., van der Aalst, W.M.P.: Abstractions in process mining: a taxonomy of patterns. In: Dayal, U., Eder, J., Koehler, J., Reijers, H.A. (eds.) BPM 2009. LNCS, vol. 5701, pp. 159–175. Springer, Heidelberg (2009)
22. Lo, D., Cheng, H., Han, J., Khoo, S.C., Sun, C.: Classification of software behaviors for failure detection: a discriminative pattern mining approach. In: KDD, pp. 557–566. ACM (2009)
23. Carmona, J., Gavaldà, R.: Online techniques for dealing with concept drift in process mining. In: Hollmén, J., Klawonn, F., Tucker, A. (eds.) IDA 2012. LNCS, vol. 7619, pp. 90–102. Springer, Heidelberg (2012)
24. Esparza, J., Römer, S., Vogler, W.: An improvement of mcmillan's unfolding algorithm. Formal Methods in System Design **20**(3), 285–310 (2002)
25. Armas-Cervantes, A., Baldan, P., Dumas, M., García-Bañuelos, L.: Behavioral comparison of process models based on canonically reduced event structures. In: Sadiq, S., Soffer, P., Völzer, H. (eds.) BPM 2014. LNCS, vol. 8659, pp. 267–282. Springer, Heidelberg (2014)
26. van Beest, N., Dumas, M., García-Bañuelos, L., La Rosa, M.: Log delta analysis: Interpretable differencing of business process event logs. Eprint no. 83018. Queensland University of Technology (2015)
27. Cook, J.E., Wolf, A.L.: Event-based detection of concurrency. In: FSE, pp. 35–45. ACM (1998)

28. Armas-Cervantes, A., Baldan, P., Dumas, M., García-Bañuelos, L.: Bp-diff: a tool for behavioral comparison of business process models. In: Limonad, L., Weber, B. (eds.) Proceedings of the BPM Demo Sessions 2014 Co-located with the 12th International Conference on Business Process Management (BPM 2014). CEUR Workshop Proceedings, vol. 1295, pp. 1–6. CEUR-WS.org (2014)
29. Baldan, P., Corradini, A., Montanari, U.: Contextual Petri Nets, Asymmetric Event Structures, and Processes. Information and Computation **171**, 1–49 (2001)
30. Fahland, D., van der Aalst, W.M.P.: Simplifying discovered process models in a controlled manner. Inf. Syst. **38**(4), 585–605 (2013)
31. van Dongen, B.F., Desel, J., van der Aalst, W.M.P.: Aggregating causal runs into workflow nets. T. Petri Nets and Other Models of Concurrency **6**, 334–363 (2012)

Modeling Quantitative Aspects of Concurrent Systems Using Weighted Petri Net Transducers

Robert Lorenz[✉]

Department of Computer Science, University of Augsburg, Augsburg, Germany
robert.lorenz@informatik.uni-augsburg.de

Abstract. In this paper we present a basic framework for weighted Petri net transducers (PNTs) for the weighted translation of partial languages (consisting of partial words) as a natural generalisation of weighted finite state transducers (FSTs). Weights may represent cost, time consumption, reward, reliability or probability of a transition execution, i.e. PNTs may serve as a general model to consider such quantitative aspects of process calculi represented by arbitrary partial words.

Concerning weights, we use the algebraic structure of concurrent semirings which is based on bisemirings and induces a natural order on its elements. Using the operations of this algebra, the weight of general partial words can be defined in a natural way and turns out to be compositional.

As desirable, complex PNTs can be composed from simple PNTs through composition operations like union, product, closure, parallel product and also language composition, lifting standard composition operations on FSTs. Composed PNTs yield a compositional computation of weights, except for the case of language composition.

For the quick construction of PNTs and evaluation of PNT-algorithms we developed the tool PNT$_\varepsilon^{\text{ooL}}$. PNT$_\varepsilon^{\text{ooL}}$ is a python library based on the framework SNAKES allowing for the modular construction of PNTs through composition operations, the visualization of PNTs, and the simulation of constructed PNTs. We present basic simulation algorithms and use PNTool to show illustrating examples.

Keywords: Petri net · Petri net transducer · Weighted transducer · Labelled partial order · Weighted labelled partial order · Partial language · Semiring · Bisemiring · Concurrent semiring · Cleanness

1 Introduction

In [25] we presented a basic framework for weighted Petri Net Transducers (PNTs). A PNT is essentially a *place/transition net (PT-net)* having transitions equipped with input symbols, output symbols and weights. An labelled partial order (LPO)[1] over the set of input symbols (input-LPO) is translated

---

[1] Also called *partial words* [14] or *pomsets* [29].

© Springer International Publishing Switzerland 2015
R. Devillers and A. Valmari (Eds.): PETRI NETS 2015, LNCS 9115, pp. 49–76, 2015.
DOI: 10.1007/978-3-319-19488-2_3

into an LPO over the set of output symbols (output-LPO) via weighted LPO-runs (partially ordered runs) of the net, where weights are coming from an algebraic bisemiring structure. These weights may represent cost, time consumption, reward, reliability or probability of a transition execution. The underlying bisemiring structure provides binary operations of addition, sequential multiplication and parallel multiplication of weights. The sequential multiplication is used for determining the weight of transitions occurring sequentially and the parallel multiplication for determining the weight of transitions occurring in parallel. Each translation of an input-LPO into an output-LPO is assigned a weight which is obtained by the sum of the weights of the LPO-runs of the net relating the input-LPO to the output-LPO. Thus, PNTs define (in a natural way) a weighted translation between partial languages, consisting of general LPOs, over different alphabets and may serve as a general model to consider quantitative aspects of process calculi represented by such LPOs.

We use a special bisemiring structure called *concurrent semirings* [16][2] to represent weights. Concurrent semirings are a bisemiring structure with some additional laws interrelating its operations. They where already used by Gischer [13], who showed that the set of all extension closed sets of LPOs can be equipped with algebraic operations yielding a concurrent semiring. In particular, concurrent semirings have an idempotent addition inducing a natural order on the set of weights. This feature allows to define the weight of a general LPO in a natural way as the supremum of all weights of its sequential parallel extensions (w.r.t. this order). As a fundamental result we showed in [25] that concurrent semirings are the least restrictive idempotent bisemiring structure such that LPOs with less dependencies have bigger weights. Moreover, this weight definition is compositional, i.e. the weight of (sequential or parallel) composed LPOs equals the corresponding bisemiring composition of the weights of its components.

In practical applications, it is important to be able to create complex transducers through composition of simple ones. To this end in [25] we introduced *cleanness* of PNTs and composition operations of union, product, closure, parallel product and language composition on clean PNTs. Cleanness ensures that runs always terminate properly and is shown to be preserved by the above operations. Moreover, we showed that the presented composition operations are compatible with suitable notions of equivalent PNTs.

The presented framework mainly aims at an application in the field of semantic dialogue modelling as described in [40]. In [22,23] we applied PNTs to small case studies in this area, in particular we proposed the translation between utterances (represented by words) and meanings (represented by general LPOs) using PNTs. Other application areas of PNTs are, for example, the specification of man-machine-dialogues or the coordination of intelligent machines (for more details see the related work section).

---

[2] In [16] concurrent semirings are applied in a trace model of programme semantics. Another axiomatic approach to partial order semantics using algebraic structures extending semirings by an additional operation of concurrent composition is [5] using the notion of trioids.

In order to be able to apply PNTs to practical relevant problems, it is necessary to develop efficient algorithms for the composition of PNTs, the analysis and optimization of PNTs, the computation of weights of weighted LPOs and the translation of partial words. As a basis for the implementation and evaluation of such algorithms, we are developing the tool PNT_ε^{ooL}. PNT_ε^{ooL} is a python library whose basic functionalities were developed in the bachelor thesis [32] and presented in [18,24]. Actually, it supports the modular construction of PNTs through composition operations, an export of PNTs in all standard picture formats, in TikZ-format and in an XML-format based on the standard PNML format. All figures in this paper showing PNTs were generated with PNT_ε^{ooL}.

In [31] algorithms for the computation of weights of weighted LPOs and for the translation of partial words were developed. At present we are integrating these algorithms in PNT_ε^{ooL} in an optimized form.

The paper gives an overview of our research on PNTS. It summarizes and integrates the main results and developments from [18,24,25] extended by several examples and remarks and by central algorithms from [31]. It is organised as follows: In section 2 we recall basic definitions, including LPOs, Petri nets and concurrent semirings. In section 3 we introduce weighted LPOs and present fundamental relationships between the weight of LPOs and the algebraic weight structure of concurrent semirings. Then (section 4) we give syntax, semantics, equivalence and composition operations of PNTs. In section 5 we propose algorithms for the computation of LPO weights and the translation of partial word by PNTs and in section 6 we give a brief description of PNT_ε^{ooL}. Finally, we summarize related word in section 7 and give an detailed outlook on future work in section 8.

2   Basic Definitions and Notations

In this section we recall basic definitions and mathematical notations.

2.1   Mathematical Preliminaries

By N_0 we denote the set of *non-negative integers*, by N the set of *positive integers*. Given a finite set X, the symbol $|X|$ denotes the *cardinality* of X.

The set of all *multisets* over a set X is the set N_0^X of all functions $m : X \to N_0$. Addition $+$ on multisets is defined by $(m + m')(x) = m(x) + m'(x)$. The relation $\leq$ between multisets is defined through $m \leq m' \iff \exists m''(m+m'' = m')$. We write $x \in m$ if $m(x) > 0$. A set $A \subseteq X$ is identified with the multiset m_A satisfying $m_A(x) = 1 \iff x \in A \land m_A(x) = 0 \iff x \notin A$. A multiset m satisfying $m(a) > 0$ for exactly one element a we call *singleton multiset* and denote it by $m(a)a$.

Given a binary relation $R \subseteq X \times Y$ and a binary relation $S \subseteq Y \times Z$ for sets X, Y, Z, their composition is defined by $R \circ S = \{(x, z) \mid \exists y \in Y((x,y) \in R \land (y,z) \in S)\} \subseteq X \times Z$. For $X' \subseteq X$ and $Y' \subseteq Y$ the restriction of R onto $X' \times Y'$ is denoted by $R|_{X' \times Y'}$. For a binary relation $R \subseteq X \times X$ over a set X, we denote $R^1 = R$ and $R^n = R \circ R^{n-1}$ for $n \geq 2$. The symbol R^+ denotes the *transitive closure* $\bigcup_{n \in \mathbb{N}} R^n$ of R.

Let A be a finite set of symbols. A *(linear) word* over A is a finite sequence of symbols from A. For a word w its length $|w|$ is defined as the number of its symbols. The symbol ε denotes the *empty word* satisfying $|\varepsilon| = 0$. The empty word is the neutral element w.r.t. concatenation of words: $w\varepsilon = \varepsilon w = w$. By A^* we denote the set of all words over A, including the empty word. A *language over A* is a (possibly infinite) subset of A^*.

A *step over A* is a multiset over A. A *step sequence* or *step-wise linear word* over A is an element of $(\mathbb{N}_0^A)^*$ and a *step language over A* is a (possibly infinite) subset of $(\mathbb{N}_0^A)^*$.

A *directed graph* is a pair $G = (V, \rightarrow)$, where V is a finite *set of nodes* and $\rightarrow \subseteq V \times V$ is a binary relation over V, called the *set of edges*. The *preset* of a node $v \in V$ is the set $^\bullet v = \{u \mid u \rightarrow v\}$. The *postset* of a node $v \in V$ is the set $v^\bullet = \{u \mid v \rightarrow u\}$. A *path* is a sequence of (not necessarily distinct) nodes $v_1 \ldots v_n$ $(n > 1)$ such that $v_i \rightarrow v_{i+1}$ for $i = 1, \ldots, n - 1$. A path $v_1 \ldots v_n$ is a *cycle*, if $v_1 = v_n$. A directed graph is called *acyclic*, if it has no cycles. An acyclic directed graph $G' = (V, \rightarrow')$ is an *extension* of an acyclic directed graph $G = (V, \rightarrow)$ if $\rightarrow \subseteq \rightarrow'$. In this case we write $G' \leq G$. An acyclic directed graph $(V', \rightarrow)$ is a *prefix* of an acyclic directed graph $(V, \rightarrow)$ if $V' \subseteq V$ and $(v' \in V') \wedge (v \rightarrow v') \Rightarrow (v \in V')$.

An *irreflexive partial order* over a set V is a binary relation $< \subseteq V \times V$ which satisfies $\forall v \in V(v \not< v)$ (irreflexivity) and $< = <^+$ (transitivity). We identify a finite irreflexive partial order $<$ over V with the directed graph $(V, <)$. Two nodes $v, v' \in V$ of an irreflexive partial order $po = (V, <)$ are called *independent* if $v \not< v'$ and $v' \not< v$. By $co_< \subseteq V \times V$ we denote the set of all pairs of independent nodes of V. The set of minimal nodes of an irreflexive partial order is $\min(po) = \{v \mid {^\bullet v} = \emptyset\}$ and the set of maximal nodes $\max(po) = \{v \mid v^\bullet = \emptyset\}$. We denote by $po|_W = (W, < |_{W \times W})$ the restriction of po to a subset $W \subset V$.

A *reflexive partial order* over V is a binary relation $\leq \subseteq V \times V$ which satisfies $\forall v \in V(v \leq v)$ (reflexivity) and $\forall v \in V(v \leq w \wedge w \leq v \implies v = w)$ (antisymmetry) and which is transitive.

A *semiring* is a quintuple $\mathscr{S} = (S, \oplus, \otimes, \overline{0}, \overline{1})$, where $(S, \oplus, \overline{0})$ is a commutative monoid, $(S, \otimes, \overline{1})$ is a monoid, $\otimes$ (the *S-multiplication*) distributes over $\oplus$ (the *S-addition*) from both sides of $\otimes$ and the zero $\overline{0}$ is absorbing w.r.t. $\otimes$ ($\overline{0} \otimes x = x \otimes \overline{0} = \overline{0}$). If $\otimes$ is commutative, then the semiring is called *commutative*.

2.2   Labelled Partial Orders

We use irreflexive partial orders labelled by action names to represent single non-sequential runs of concurrent systems. The nodes of such a labelled partial order represent events and its arrows an "earlier than"-relation between them in the sense that one event can be observed earlier than another event. If there are no arrows between two events, then these events are independent and are called *concurrent*. Concurrent events can be observed in arbitrary sequential order and simultaneously.

Formally, a *labelled partial order (LPO) over a set X* is a 3-tuple $(V, <, l)$, where $(V, <)$ is an irreflexive partial order and $l : V \to X$ is a labelling function on V. In particular, LPOs are directed graphs, thus all notions introduced w.r.t. directed graphs may also be used for LPOs. LPOs over X are also called *partial words over X*.

In most cases, we only consider LPOs up to isomorphism, i.e. only the labelling of events is of interest, but not the event names. Formally, two LPOs $(V, <, l)$ and $(V', <', l')$ are *isomorphic*, if there is a bijective renaming function $I : V \to V'$ satisfying $l(v) = l'(I(v))$ and $v < w \Leftrightarrow I(v) <' I(w)$. If an LPO *lpo* is of the form $(\{v\}, \emptyset, l)$, then it is called a *singleton LPO* and denoted by $lpo = l(v)$. A set of pairwise non-isomorphic LPOs we call a *partial language*. If L is a partial language, then an LPO *lpo* $\in L$ is called *minimal (in L)*, if there is no extension of *lpo* in L. In figures, in general we do not show the names of the nodes of an LPO, but only their labels and we often omit transitive arrows of LPOs for a clearer presentation.

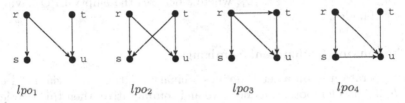

Fig. 1. An N-form (lpo_1) together with its minimal sequential parallel extensions (lpo_2, lpo_3, lpo_4).

A *step-wise linear LPO* is an LPO $(V, <, l)$ where the relation $co_<$ is transitive. The maximal sets of independent events of such an LPO are called *steps*. The steps of a step-wise linear LPO are linearly ordered. Thus, step-wise linear LPOs can be identified with step sequences. A *step-linearisation* of an LPO *lpo* is a step-wise linear LPO which is an extension of *lpo*.

The set of *sequential parallel* LPOs (*sp-LPOs*) is the smallest set of LPOs containing all singleton LPOs (over a set X) and being closed under the sequential and parallel product of LPOs. The *sequential product* of two LPOs $lpo_1 = (V_1, <_1, l_1)$ and $lpo_2 = (V_2, <_2, l_2)$ is defined by $lpo_1 ; lpo_2 = (V_1 \cup V_2, <_1 \cup <_2 \cup (V_1 \times V_2), l_1 \cup l_2)$, where V_1 and V_2 are assumed to be disjoint. Their *parallel product* is defined by $lpo_1 \parallel lpo_2 = (V_1 \cup V_2, <_1 \cup <_2, l_1 \cup l_2)$, where again V_1 and V_2 are assumed to be disjoint.

Each sp-LPO (over X) is defined by an *sp-term (over X)*. Such terms are defined as follows:

- Each $x \in X$ is an sp-term.
- If s, t are sp-terms, then also $s ; t$ and $s \parallel t$ are sp-terms.

For an LPO *lpo* we denote by $SP(lpo)$ the set of all sequential parallel extensions of *lpo* and by $SP_{min}(lpo)$ the set of all minimal sequential parallel extensions of *lpo* in $SP(lpo)$.

Given an LPO $lpo = (V, <, l)$, an *N-form* of lpo is a sub-LPO consisting of four nodes $u, v, x, y \in V$ satisfying $u < x$, $u < y$, $v < y$ and $u\ co_< v$, $v\ co_< x$, $x\ co_< y$. An LPO is *N-free*, if it does not contain an N-form. There is the following important relationship between sp-LPOs and N-free LPOs:

Theorem 1. *An LPO is N-free if and only if it is sequential parallel.*

A proof can be found in [13]. This proof is constructive: Given an N-free LPO, it shows a method to construct an sp-term defining the LPO. We will describe and use this method later on.

Figure 1 shows four LPOs: LPO lpo_1 consists of an N-form and the LPOs $lpo_2 = (r \parallel t);(s \parallel u)$, $lpo_3 = r;(s \parallel (t;u))$ and $lpo_4 = ((r;s) \parallel t);u$ are its minimal sequential parallel extensions.

The sequential and parallel product of LPOs is extended to sets of LPOs A, B in the obvious way: $A \parallel B = \{a \parallel b \mid a \in A, b \in B\}$ and $A;B = \{a;b \mid a \in A, b \in B\}$. Moreover, we define the closure of a set of LPOs A by $A^* = \{a_1; \ldots; a_n \mid n \in \mathbb{N}, a_i \in A\} \cup \{\varepsilon\}$, where ε denotes the empty LPO having an empty set of nodes.

2.3   Continuous Concurrent Semirings

A binary operation $\oplus$ on a set S defines a binary relation on S via $a \leq_\oplus b :\Leftrightarrow a \oplus b = b$. If $\oplus$ is idempotent, associative and commutative, then this relation is reflexive, transitive and antisymmetric, hence a reflexive partial order. Moreover, if S is equipped with the partial order $\leq_\oplus$, then $\forall a, b \in S : a \oplus b = \sup\{a, b\}$, where the supremum is taken w.r.t. $\leq_\oplus$.

If $(S, \oplus, \overline{0})$ is a monoid, and if $T \subseteq S$ is an arbitrary subset, then $\bigoplus T := \bigoplus_{t \in T} t := \sup(T)$, where the supremum of the empty set is understood to be the neutral element of the monoid. A semiring $(S, \oplus, \otimes, \overline{0}, \overline{1})$ is called *idempotent*, if $\oplus$ is idempotent. An idempotent semiring is called *continuous* [7], if, for any subset $T \subseteq S$, the supremum is well-defined in S (that means the semiring is *complete*), and $\otimes$ distributes over the supremum from both sides: $\forall s \in S : s \otimes \bigoplus T = \bigoplus_{t \in T} s \otimes t$ and $(\bigoplus T) \otimes s = \bigoplus_{t \in T} t \otimes s$.

A *bisemiring* is a six-tuple $\mathscr{S} = (S, \oplus, \otimes, \boxtimes, \overline{0}, \overline{1})$, where $(S, \oplus, \otimes, \overline{0}, \overline{1})$ is a semiring and $(S, \oplus, \boxtimes, \overline{0}, \overline{1})$ is a commutative semiring.[3] The binary operation $\boxtimes$ on the set S is called *S-parallel multiplication*. If $\otimes$ distributes over $\boxtimes$ from both sides, the bisemiring is called *distributive*, if $\oplus$ is idempotent, the bisemiring is called *idempotent*, and if both semirings $(S, \oplus, \otimes, \overline{0}, \overline{1})$ and $(S, \oplus, \boxtimes, \overline{0}, \overline{1})$ are continuous, the bisemiring is called *continuous*.

According to [16], a *concurrent semiring* is an idempotent bisemiring $(S, \oplus, \otimes, \boxtimes, \overline{0}, \overline{1})$ satisfying

$$\forall a, b, c, d \in S : \quad (a \boxtimes b) \otimes (c \boxtimes d) \leq_\oplus (a \otimes c) \boxtimes (b \otimes d). \qquad \textbf{(CS)}$$

---

[3] In particular, both multiplications share the same unit. A similar algebraic structure without requiring commutativity of the second semiring is defined in [6], where it is called *Q-Algebra* and coined for application in quality management. In [20] a slightly different notion of bisemirings is used where parallel multiplication may miss a unit.

Concurrent semirings will be used to define the weight of a run of a Petri net transducer. $\otimes$ will be used to model the composition of weights of a sequence of runs and $\boxtimes$ models the composition of weights of concurrent runs. Therefore, $\boxtimes$ is required to be commutative. The unit $\overline{1}$ can be thought of as the weight of the empty run (the analogue of the empty word). It is shared by $\otimes$ and $\boxtimes$, since the sequential or concurrent execution of a run r and the empty run does not change r. Using $\otimes$ and $\boxtimes$, the weight of a sequential parallel run can be defined then in the standard way (for details see the next section).

As explained above, idempotence of $\oplus$ induces a natural order on the set of weights. We will define the weight of a general run in a natural way as the supremum of all weights of its sequential parallel extensions w.r.t. this order. Condition (**CS**) will ensure that runs with fewer dependencies have bigger weights.

Example 1. If $\mathscr{S} = (S, \oplus, \otimes, \overline{0}, \overline{1})$ is an idempotent semiring such that $\leq_{\oplus}$ is a total order and $\overline{1}$ is maximal w.r.t. to that order, then we have $\mathscr{S} = (S, \max, \otimes, \overline{0}, \overline{1})$, and $(S, \max, \otimes, \min, \overline{0}, \overline{1})$ is a concurrent semiring extending $\mathscr{S}$.

If $\mathscr{S} = (S, \oplus, \otimes, \overline{0}, \overline{1})$ is an idempotent and commutative semiring, then the *doubled semiring* $(S, \oplus, \otimes, \otimes, \overline{0}, \overline{1})$ is a concurrent semiring extending $\mathscr{S}$.

Example 2. Based on the well-known *Viterbi semiring* $([0,1], \max, \cdot, 0, 1)$ representing probabilities of actions, the structure $\mathscr{V} := ([0,1], \max, \cdot, \min, 0, 1)$ yields a continuous concurrent semiring.

The structure $\mathscr{T} := ([0, \infty], \min, +, \max, \infty, 0)$ is a continuous concurrent semiring. It is based on the well-known *tropical semiring* $([0, \infty], \min, +, \infty, 0)$ representing execution times of actions.

Note that $\mathscr{V}$ and $\mathscr{T}$ are isomorphic, e.g. an isomorphism is given by $t - -\log(v)$. Both concurrent semirings extend a semiring as in the first construction of example 1.

An example of a concurrent semiring, which is not of the above kind, is $\mathscr{A} := (\{-\infty\} \cup [0, \infty[, \max, +, \boxtimes, -\infty, 0)$, where $a \boxtimes b := a + b + \min(a, b)$. It is based on the *arctic semiring* or *max-plus-algebra*.

2.4 Petri Nets

A *net* is a 3-tuple $N = (P, T, F)$, where P is a finite set of *places*, T is a finite set of *transitions* disjoint from P and $F \subseteq (P \times T) \cup (T \times P)$ is the *flow relation*. A *marking* of a net assigns to each place $p \in P$ a number $m(p) \in \mathbb{N}_0$, i.e. a marking is a multiset over P. A *marked net* is a net $N = (P, T, F)$ together with an *initial marking* m_0.

A *place/transition Petri net* (*PT-net*) is a 4-tuple $N = (P, T, F, W)$, where (P, T, F) is a net and $W : (P \times T) \cup (T \times P) \to \mathbb{N}_0$ is a *flow weight function* satisfying $W(x, y) > 0 \Leftrightarrow (x, y) \in F$. For (transition) steps τ over T we introduce the two multisets of places $^{\bullet}\tau(p) = \sum_{t \in T} \tau(t) W(p, t)$ and $\tau^{\bullet}(p) = \sum_{t \in T} \tau(t) W(t, p)$. A transition step τ *can occur* in m, if $m \geq {}^{\bullet}\tau$. If a transition step τ occurs in m, then the resulting marking m' is defined by $m' = m - {}^{\bullet}\tau + \tau^{\bullet}$. We write $m \xrightarrow{\tau} m'$ to denote that τ can occur in m and that its occurrence leads to m'. A *step execution in m* of a PT-net is a finite sequence of multisets of transitions $\sigma = \tau_1 \ldots \tau_n$ such that there are markings $m_1, \ldots, m_n$ satisfying $m \xrightarrow{\tau_1} m_1 \xrightarrow{\tau_2} \ldots \xrightarrow{\tau_n} m_n$. The markings which can be reached from the initial marking m_0 via step executions are called *reachable*.

We use LPOs over T to represent single non-sequential runs of PT-nets, i.e. the events of an LPO represent transition occurrences. An LPO $lpo = (V, <, l)$ over T is an *LPO-run* of a marked PT-net $N = (P, T, F, W, m_0)$ if each step-linearisation of lpo is a step execution of N in m_0. If an LPO-run $lpo = (V, <, l)$ occurs in a marking m, the resulting marking m' is defined by $m' = m - \Sigma_{v \in V} {}^\bullet l(v) + \Sigma_{v \in V} l(v)^\bullet$. We write $m \xrightarrow{lpo} m'$ to denote the occurrence of an LPO-run lpo. An LPO-run lpo of N is said to be *minimal*, if there exists no other LPO-run lpo' of N such that lpo is an extension of lpo'.

3   Weighted LPOs

For the representation of runs of weighted Petri net transducers (PNTs), we consider weighted LPOs (WLPOs) which are LPOs with additional node weights [25]. We assume that the set of possible weights is equipped with the algebraic structure of a *concurrent semiring*. Then the total weight of a WLPO is computed from the node weights using binary operations of this algebraic structure. As a central property we showed in [25], that the use of a concurrent semiring ensures that total weights of runs can be computed in a compositional way and that runs with fewer dependencies have bigger weights (w.r.t. the order induced by the idempotent addition operation).

A *weighted LPO* (WLPO) over an alphabet $\mathscr{A}$ and a bisemiring $\mathscr{S} = (S, \oplus, \otimes, \boxtimes, \overline{0}, \overline{1})$ is a quadruple $(V, <, l, \nu)$ such that $(V, <, l)$ is an LPO over $\mathscr{A}$ and $\nu : V \to S$ is an additional *weight function*. We use all notions introduced for LPOs also for WLPOs. Figure 2 shows examples of WLPOs, where labels $l(v) = t$ and weights s are annotated to a node v in the form t/s.

The total weight of sp-WLPOs can be defined through applying $\otimes$ to the sequential product and $\boxtimes$ to the parallel product of sub-WLPOs.

Definition 1 (Weight of sp-WLPOs [25]). *We define the weight $\omega(wlpo)$ of an sp-WLPO $wlpo = (V, <, l, \nu)$ over a bisemiring inductively as follows:*

- *If $V = \{v\}$, then $\omega(wlpo) = \nu(v)$.*
- *If $wlpo = wlpo_1 ; wlpo_2$, then $\omega(wlpo) = \omega(wlpo_1) \otimes \omega(wlpo_2)$.*
- *If $wlpo = wlpo_1 \parallel wlpo_2$, then $\omega(wlpo) = \omega(wlpo_1) \boxtimes \omega(wlpo_2)$.*

This is the standard technique to define weights of sp-LPOs [20] with weights coming from a bisemiring. In particular, the given weight of sp-WLPOs is well-defined, since the set of sp-WLPOs as well as the sub-structure $(S, \otimes, \boxtimes)$ of a bisemiring $(S, \oplus, \otimes, \boxtimes, \overline{0}, \overline{1})$ form an sp-algebra admitting an sp-algebra homomorphism from the set of sp-WLPOs into the bisemiring.

In [25] we proposed the following weight definition for a general WLPO based on the weigths of its sequential parallel extensions.

Definition 2 (Sequential-Parallel Weight of WLPOs [25]). *Let* $wlpo = (V, <, l, \omega)$ *be a WLPO. Then its* sp-weight *is defined by*

$$\omega_{sp}(wlpo) = \bigoplus_{wlpo' \in SP(wlpo)} \omega(wlpo').$$

As the considered bisemiring of weights is idempotent, the sp-weight of a WLPO-run equals the maximal weight of its sequential parallel extensions.

As a fundamental result we showed in [25] that condition (**CS**) of concurrent semirings is the minimal requirement on idempotent bisemirings such that less restrictive weighted LPOs yield bigger weights.

Theorem 2 ([25]). *Let* $\mathscr{A}$ *be an alphabet and* $\mathscr{S} = (S, \oplus, \otimes, \boxtimes, \bar{0}, \bar{1})$ *be an idempotent bisemiring. Then the following assertions are equivalent:*

(A) *If* u_1, u_2 *are sp-WLPOs over* $\mathscr{A}$ *and* $\mathscr{S}$ *and if* u_1 *is an extension of* u_2, *then* $\omega(u_1) \leq_\oplus \omega(u_2)$.
(B) $\mathscr{S}$ *is a concurrent semiring.*

Obviously, one gets a similar result, if inequation **CS** is reversed.

Corollary 1. *Let* $\mathscr{A}$ *be an alphabet and* $\mathscr{S} = (S, \oplus, \otimes, \boxtimes, \bar{0}, \bar{1})$ *be an idempotent bisemiring. Then the following assertions are equivalent:*

(A) *If* u_1, u_2 *are sp-WLPOs over* $\mathscr{A}$ *and* $\mathscr{S}$ *and if* u_1 *is an extension of* u_2, *then* $\omega(u_1) \geq_\oplus \omega(u_2)$.
(B) $\mathscr{S}$ *satisfies*

$$\forall a, b, c, d \in S : \quad (a \boxtimes b) \otimes (c \boxtimes d) \geq_\oplus (a \otimes c) \boxtimes (b \otimes d). \tag{CS'}$$

Moreover, the use of concurrent semirings ensures that the sp-weight of WLPOs can be computed in a modular way using bisemiring-operations [25].

Theorem 3 ([25]). *Let* $\mathscr{A}$ *be an alphabet and* $\mathscr{S} = (S, \oplus, \otimes, \boxtimes, \bar{0}, \bar{1})$ *be a concurrent semiring. Then the following assertions hold for weighted LPOs* $wlpo_1, wlpo_2$ *over* $\mathscr{A}$ *and* $\mathscr{S}$:

(C) $\omega_{sp}(wlpo_1 ; wlpo_2) = \omega_{sp}(wlpo_1) \otimes \omega_{sp}(wlpo_2)$.
(D) $\omega_{sp}(wlpo_1 \| wlpo_2) = \omega_{sp}(wlpo_1) \boxtimes \omega_{sp}(wlpo_2)$.

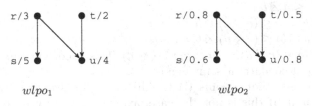

Fig. 2. WLPOs over the concurrent semirings $\mathscr{T}$ ($wlpo_1$) and $\mathscr{V}$ ($wlpo_2$).

Example 3. Consider the concurrent semiring $\mathcal{T}$ defined in subsection 2.3. It can be used to compute the minimal execution time of a run given by an arbitrary WLPO *wlpo* of a concurrent system.

The WLPO $wlpo_1$ shown in figure 2 is a WLPO over $\mathcal{T}$. The weights of its minimal sp-extensions (see figure 1) are:

- $\omega((r \parallel t);(s \parallel u)) = \max(3,2) + \max(5,4) = 8,$
- $\omega(((r;s) \parallel t);u) = \max(3+5,2) + 4 = 12,$
- $\omega(r;(s \parallel (t;u))) = 3 + \max(5,2+4) = 9.$

Thus, the minimal execution time is $\min(8,12,9) = 8$. Note, however, that there is a more efficient method to compute the minimal execution time of a general LPO computing the maximal weigth of a line of the LPO.

Example 4. Consider the concurrent semiring $\mathcal{V}$ defined in subsection 2.3. The decision for min as parallel multiplication can be interpreted as follows: If $wlpo = wlpo_1 \parallel wlpo_2$, then $wlpo_1$ and $wlpo_2$ are both necessary but independent parts of the run *wlpo* of a concurrent system and the probability of *wlpo* cannot be better than the probability of one of its parts. In [39] we give a justification for that choice of min in the context of semantic dialogue modelling.

The WLPO $wlpo_2$ shown in figure 2 is a WLPO over $\mathcal{V}$. The weights of its minimal sp-extensions (see figure 1) are:

- $\omega((r \parallel t);(s \parallel u)) = \min(0.8,0.5) \cdot \min(0.6,0.8) = 0.3,$
- $\omega(((r;s) \parallel t);u) = \min(0.8 \cdot 0.6, 0.5) \cdot 0.8 = 0.384,$
- $\omega(r;(s \parallel (t;u))) = 0.8 \cdot \min(0.6, 0.8 \cdot 0.5) = 0.32.$

Thus, the weight (probability) of $wlpo_2$ is $\max(0.3, 0.384, 0.32) = 0.384$.

Remark 1. Concurrent semirings are probably not the most abstract algebraic structure yielding the previous results.

There may be abstractions of the underlying structure of idempotent bisemirings in two directions:

- It is possible to define natural partial orders on non-idempotent semirings via $a < b :\Leftrightarrow \exists c : a \oplus c = b$ [7].
- It is possible to consider structures having no shared unit for $\otimes$ and $\boxtimes$. In this context, in [16] the following axioms are used to define so called *concurrent semigroups*:
    - (i) $a \otimes b \leq a \boxtimes b.$
    - (ii) $(a \boxtimes b) \otimes c \leq (a \otimes c) \boxtimes b.$
    - (iii) $c \otimes (a \boxtimes b) \leq (c \otimes a) \boxtimes b.$
    - (iv) $(a \boxtimes b) \otimes (c \boxtimes d) \leq (a \otimes c) \boxtimes (b \otimes d)$ (this condition equals condition (**CS**) of concurrent semirings).

    It is easy to see that axioms (i) to (iii) follow from axiom (iv), if $\otimes$ and $\boxtimes$ share a unit. If this is not the case, axioms (i) to (iv) are irreducible as proven in [16]. The axioms (i) to (iv) seem to be suitable to derive similar results as for concurrent semirings.

We decided to use concurrent semirings because they appear in a natural way in the context of sets of extension closed sp-LPOs as shown by Gischer [13]. However, the mentioned more abstract algebraic structures may make accessible additional practical problems using PNTs. This is a topic of further research.

4   Petri Net Transducers

A PNT is a Petri net which, for every transition occurrence, may read a symbol x from an input alphabet Σ and may print a symbol y from an output alphabet Δ. Additionally, a weight s from a bisemiring is assigned to each transition. If no input symbol should be read or no output symbol should be printed, we use the empty word symbol ε as annotation. We use the basic Petri net class of PT-nets to define PNTs. In graphics an input symbol x, an output symbol y and a weight s of a transition t are annotated to t in the form $x{:}y/s$, and annotations of the form $\varepsilon{:}\varepsilon/\overline{1}$ are not shown.

Definition 3 (Petri Net Transducer [25]). *A Petri net transducer (PNT) over a bisemiring $\mathscr{S} = (S, \oplus, \otimes, \boxtimes, \overline{0}, \overline{1})$ is a tuple $N = (P, T, F, W, p_I, p_F, \Sigma, \sigma, \Delta, \delta, \omega)$, where*

- *(P, T, F, W) is a marked PT-net (called the underlying PT-net),*
- *$p_I \in P$ is the source place satisfying $^\bullet p_I = \emptyset$,*
- *$p_F \in P$ is the sink place satisfying $p_F^\bullet = \emptyset$,*
- *Σ is a set of input symbols,*
- *$\sigma : T \to \Sigma \cup \{\varepsilon\}$ is the input mapping,*
- *Δ is a set of output symbols,*
- *$\delta : T \to \Delta \cup \{\varepsilon\}$ is the output mapping.*
- *$\omega : T \to S$ is the weight function.*

We call the marking $m_0 = p_I$ the initial marking and $m_F = p_F$ the final marking. A PNT is called clean, *if the final marking is the only reachable marking m with $m(p_F) > 0$.*

A WLPO $wlpo = (V, <, l, \nu)$ over T is a weighted LPO-run of N, if the underlying LPO $lpo = (V, <, l)$ is an LPO-run of N with $m_0 \xrightarrow{lpo} m_F$ and if $\nu(v) = \omega(l(v))$ for each $v \in V$. We denote by $WLPO(N)$ the set of all weighted LPO-runs of N.

The cleanness property is similar to cleanness of Boxes [4] or soundness of workflow nets [35] and ensures that PNT semantics are closed under (sequential) product and closure. The final marking can be reached only from a finite set of reachable markings [15].

Considering non-sequential semantics of Petri nets, a PNT can be used to translate a partial language into another partial language, where so called input words are related to so called output words. Input and output words are defined as LPOs $lpo_\varepsilon = (V, <, l_\varepsilon)$ with a labelling function $l_\varepsilon : V \to \mathscr{A} \cup \{\varepsilon\}$ for some input or output alphabet $\mathscr{A}$. Such LPOs we call ε-LPOs. For each such ε-LPO we construct the *corresponding ε-free LPO lpo* $= (W, < |_{W \times W}, l_\varepsilon|_W)$ by deleting ε-labelled nodes together with their adjacent edges via $W = V \setminus l_\varepsilon^{-1}(\varepsilon)$. Since partial orders are transitive, this does not change the order between the remaining nodes.

Definition 4 (Input and Output Labels of Runs [25]). *Let $N = (P, T, F, W, p_I, p_F, \Sigma, \sigma, \Delta, \delta, \omega)$ be a PNT and let $wlpo = (V, <, l, \nu) \in WLPO(N)$.*

The input *of wlpo is the ε-free LPO $wlpo_\Sigma$ corresponding to the ε-LPO $(V, <, \sigma \circ l)$.*

The output *of wlpo is the ε-free LPO $wlpo_\Delta$ corresponding to the ε-LPO $(V, <, \delta \circ l)$.*

For LPOs u over Σ and v over Δ, we denote by $WLPO(N, u)$ the subset of all WLPOs wlpo from $WLPO(N)$ with input $wlpo_\Sigma = u$, and by $WLPO(N, u, v)$ the subset of all WLPOs from $WLPO(N, u)$ with output $wlpo_\Delta = v$.

The input language $L_I(N)$ *of N is the set of all inputs of weighted LPO-runs. Its elements are also called* input words. *The* output language $L_O(N)$ *of N is the set of all outputs of weighted LPO-runs. Its elements are also called* output words.

The language $L(N)$ *of N is the set of all pairs of LPOs (u, v) over $\Sigma \times \Delta$ with $WLPO(N, u, v) \neq \emptyset$.*

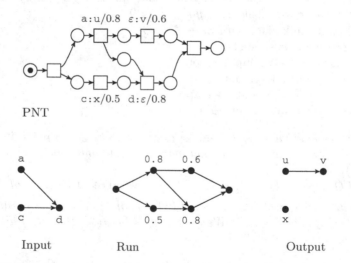

Fig. 3. A PNT together with an LPO-run and associated input and output.

The input and output language of a PNT N are extension closed, since $WLPO(N)$ is extension closed. The *output weight* of a PNT assigned to all pairs of LPOs u over Σ and v over Δ is based on weights of its WLPO-runs.

Definition 5 (Output Weight of PNTs [25]). *Let $N = (P, T, F, W, p_I, p_F, \Sigma, \sigma, \Delta, \delta, \omega)$ be a PNT over a concurrent semiring $\mathscr{S} = (S, \oplus, \otimes, \boxtimes, \overline{0}, \overline{1})$, u be* *an LPO over Σ and v be an LPO over Δ. The output weight $N(u,v)$ is defined by*

$$N(u,v) = \bigoplus_{wlpo \in WLPO(N,u,v)} \omega_{sp}(wlpo),$$

when this sum is well-defined in S (note that the sum may be infinite). We set $N(u,v) = \overline{0}$ if $WLPO(N,u,v) = \emptyset$.

The output weight equals the supremum of all weights of corresponding runs, since $\oplus$ is idempotent. If the concurrent semiring is continuous, the supremum always exists in S [7]. From the considerations in the previous section we immediately deduce that it is enough to consider minimal weighted sp-runs in the defining sum of the output weight using condition (**CS**) of concurrent semirings.

Corollary 2 ([25]). *Let $N = (P,T,F,W,p_I,p_F,\Sigma,\sigma,\Delta,\delta,\omega)$ be a PNT over a concurrent semiring $\mathscr{S} = (S,\oplus,\otimes,\boxtimes,\overline{0},\overline{1})$, u be an LPO over Σ and v be an LPO over Δ. Then*

$$N(u,v) = \bigoplus_{wlpo \in WLPO_{min}(N,u,v),\, wlpo' \in SP_{min}(wlpo)} \omega(wlpo'),$$

when this sum is well-defined in S, where $WLPO_{min}(\cdot)$ is the subset of all minimal WLPOs in $WLPO(\cdot)$.

Figure 3 shows an example of a PNT together with an LPO-run and associated input and output. The figure illustrates the translation of partial words in the presence of ε-inputs and -outputs. According to example 4 the output weight of the shown input-output-pair equals 0.384.

In practical applications, it is important to be able to create complex transducers through composition of simple ones. For this purpose we introduced in [25] composition operations of union, product, closure and parallel product for clean PNTs. Cleanness ensures that runs always terminate properly and is preserved by the above operations.

For each operation, there are a functional definition defining the output weight of the composed PNT based on the output weights its components and bisemiring-operations and an effective (and more or less straightforward) construction of the composed PNT. In the following, we recall the functional definitions and illustrate the constructions (explicitly given in [25]) in figure 4, where for a compact presentation input symbols, output symbols and weights of transitions are omitted if possible.

The *sum (or union)* $N_1 \oplus N_2$ of two PNTs N_1 and N_2 over $\mathscr{S}$ with the same input alphabet Σ and output alphabet Δ is defined as a PNT over $\mathscr{S}$ in such a way that for each pair of LPOs u over Σ and v over Δ:

$$(N_1 \oplus N_2)(u,v) = N_1(u,v) \oplus N_2(u,v).$$

The *product (concatenation)* $N_1 \otimes N_2$ of two PNTs N_1 and N_2 over $\mathscr{S}$ with the same input alphabet Σ and output alphabet Δ is defined as a PNT over $\mathscr{S}$

in such a way that for each pair of LPOs u over Σ and v over Δ:

$$(N_1 \otimes N_2)(u,v) = \bigoplus_{u=u_1\,;\,u_2,\,v=v_1\,;\,v_2} N_1(u_1,v_1) \otimes N_2(u_2,v_2).$$

The product of $n > 0$ instances of a PNT N we denote by N^n. By convention $N^0 = \mathcal{I}$, where $\mathcal{I}$ is the PNT satisfying $\mathcal{I}(u,v) = \overline{1}$ if u and v are both the empty LPO $(\emptyset, \emptyset, \emptyset)$ and $\mathcal{I}(u,v) = \overline{0}$ otherwise.

The *closure* N^* of a PNT N over $\mathcal{S}$ with input alphabet Σ and output alphabet Δ is defined as a PNT over $\mathcal{S}$ in such a way that for each pair of LPOs u over Σ and v over Δ:

$$N^*(u,v) = \bigoplus_{n=0}^{\infty} N^n(u,v).$$

The *parallel product* $N_1 \boxtimes N_2$ of two PNTs N_1 and N_2 over $\mathcal{S}$ with the same input alphabet Σ and output alphabet Δ is defined as a PNT over $\mathcal{S}$ in such a way that for each pair of LPOs u over Σ and v over Δ:

$$(N_1 \boxtimes N_2)(u,v) = \bigoplus_{u=u_1\|u_2,\,v=v_1\|v_2} N_1(u_1,v_1) \boxtimes N_2(u_2,v_2).$$

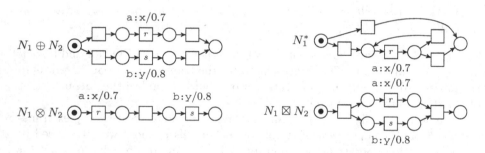

Fig. 4. Illustration of the union, (sequential) product, closure and parallel product of PNTs $N_1 = N(a,x,.7)$ and $N_2 = N(b,y,.8)$ over $\mathcal{V}$.

Moreover, we proposed the following construction of the central transducer composition operation of language composition [25]:

Let N_1 be a PNT over $\mathcal{S}$ with input alphabet Σ_1 and output alphabet Δ_1 and a N_2 be a PNT over $\mathcal{S}$ with input alphabet $\Sigma_2 = \Delta_1$ and output alphabet Δ_2. The composed PNT $N_1[\otimes]N_2$ is constructed as the parallel product of N_1 and N_2, where each transition t_1 from N_1 is merged with each transition t_2 from N_2 satisfying $\delta(t_1) = \sigma(t_2)$ to a transition t with input symbol $\sigma(t) = \sigma(t_1)$ and output symbol $\delta(t) = \delta(t_2)$, weight $\omega(t) = \omega(t_1) \otimes \omega(t_2)$ and connections $^\bullet t = {}^\bullet t_1 + {}^\bullet t_2$ and $t^\bullet = t_1^\bullet + t_2^\bullet$. Moreover, all transitions of N_1 having empty output symbol, as well as all transitions of N_2 having empty input symbol are kept with unchanged input symbols, output symbols, weights and connections. All other transitions of N_1 and N_2 are omitted. Figure 5 illustrates the construction.

We proved in [25] that this construction perserves cleaness and yields the following properties concerning compositionality w.r.t. weights:

Theorem 4 ([25]). *The PNT $N_1[\otimes]N_2$ satisfies the following properties:*

(i) If $\mathscr{S}$ is the doubled semiring, then

$$(N_1[\otimes]N_2)(u,w) = \bigoplus_v N_1(u,v) \otimes N_2(v,w),$$

where the sum runs over all LPOs over $\Sigma_2 = \Delta_1$ representing outputs of weighted LPO-runs of N_1 and inputs of weighted LPO-runs of N_2.

(ii) If $(N_1[\otimes]N_2)(u,w) = \bigoplus_v N_1(u,v)$ op $N_2(v,w)$, where the sum runs over all LPOs v over $\Sigma_2 = \Delta_1$ representing outputs of weighted LPO-runs of N_1 and inputs of weighted LPO-runs of N_2 and op is a semiring operation, then op $= \otimes$ and $\mathscr{S}$ is the doubled semiring.

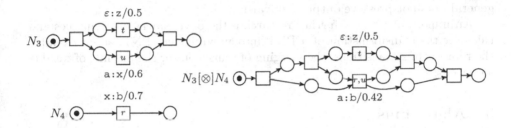

Fig. 5. Language composition for $N_3 = N(x,b,.6) \boxtimes N(\varepsilon,z,.5)$ and $N_4 = N(a,x,.7)$ over $\mathscr{V}$.

Concerning PNT semantics, only the input output behaviour is relevant. Since transitions also may have empty input and/or empty output, there are always (infinitely) many PNTs having the same semantics. For practical application, such PNTs are equivalent.

Definition 6. *Equivalent PNTs [25]] Let N_1, N_2 be two PNTs.*

(a) N_1 and N_2 are called structure equivalent, *if $L(N_1) = L(N_2)$.*

(b) If N_1 and N_2 are structure equivalent, then they are called output equivalent, *if $N_1(u,v) = N_2(u,v)$ for all $(u,v) \in L(N_1) = L(N_2)$.*

Two structure equivalent PNTs perform the same translation between input and output words, but the weights of these translations may be different. Two output equivalent PNTs perform the same weighted translation between input and output words, but the distribution of weights within WLPO-runs may be different.

Example 5. Consider a fixed concurrent semiring serving as the set of weights. We denote by $N(a,b,w)$ the clean PNT consisting of no other places than the source and sink place and exactly one transition with input symbol a, output symbol b and weight w connecting the source with the sink place.

The following PNTs are structure equivalent: $N_1 = N(a,b,w)$, $N_2 = N(a,\epsilon,u) \otimes N(\epsilon,b,v)$ and $N_3 = N(a,\epsilon,x) \boxtimes N(\epsilon,b,y)$. They are output equivalent if $w = u \otimes v = x \boxtimes y$. Moreover, the following PNTs are output equivalent: $N_2 = N(a,\epsilon,u) \otimes N(\epsilon,b,v)$, $N_5 = N(a,\epsilon,v) \otimes N(\epsilon,b,u)$ and $N_6 = N(a,\epsilon,u \otimes v) \otimes N(\epsilon,b,\overline{1})$.

An important application of equivalence in practise is the transformation of a PNT into an equivalent and simpler PNT allowing for more efficient algorithms. A central technique to do this is to replace parts of a complex composed PNT by equivalent parts. This technique requires that equivalence is consistent with composition operations.

To this end, we showed in [25], that the composition operations of union, sequential product, closure and parallel product preserve output equivalence of PNTs and that language composition perserves structure equivalence, but in general does not preserve output equivalence.

An important topic of further research is the deveopment of techniques and rules for the transformstion of a PNT into an equivalent PNT, as for example the removal of ε-transitions, the merging of transitions or the pushing of weights along paths.

5   Algorithms

In order to be able to apply PNTs to practical relevant problems, it is necessary to develop efficient algorithms for the composition of PNTs, the analysis and optimization of PNTs, the computation of weights of weighted LPOs and the translation of partial words. In [18,24] we presented the tool PNT$_\varepsilon^{\circ\circ L}$, which supports the modular construction of PNTs through composition operations and an export of PNTs in all standard picture formats, in TikZ-format and in an XML-format based on the standard PNML format (see the following section).

In this section we briefly present algorithms for the computation of the weight of general WLPOs, of the input and output language and of the output weight of input-output-pairs of PNTs. Basic versions of these algorithms were developed in the master thesis [31]. At present we are integrating these algorithms in PNT$_\varepsilon^{\circ\circ L}$.

5.1   Computing the weight of WLPOs

For the computation of the weight of some WLPO we can distinguish between WLPOs which are sequential parallel and WLPOs which are not sequential parallel.

In the first case of sp-WLPOs, according to definition 1, the weight can be computed directly from the sp-term defining the underlying LPO using the binary operations of the concurrent semiring of weights. That means, given a WLPO $wlpo$ we need to do the following:

1. Decide, whether $wlpo$ is sequential parallel (or, equivalently, N-free).

2. Compute the sp-term defining the LPO underlying $wlpo$, if the answer to the first step is yes.

From the proof of theorem 1 in [13] we can deduce a method, given an N-free LPO, to construct the sp-term defining the LPO in a top down way. The proof shows that if this method fails at some point, then the LPO must contain an N-form. Thus, we can use this method for both steps.

The method is as follows, where we denote the sp-term defining an sp-LPO $lpo = (V, <, l)$ by $sp(lpo)$:

(I) If $V = \{v\}$, then $sp(lpo) = l(v)$.

(II) If the undirected graph underlying lpo is not connected, then it can be decomposed into its connected components $lpo_1, \ldots, lpo_n$ and we get
$sp(lpo) = sp(lpo_1) \| \cdots \| sp(lpo_n)$.
Proceed with step (I) applied to $lpo_1, \ldots, lpo_n$.

(III) If $\min(lpo) = \{v\}$ then $sp(lpo) = l(v); sp(lpo|_W)$ with $W = V \setminus \{v\}$.
Proceed with step (I) applied to $lpo|_W$.

(IV) Denote $D = \{v \mid \forall v' \in \min(lpo)(v' < v)\}$. If lpo is N-free, then $D \neq \emptyset$ and $lpo = lpo|_{V \setminus D}; lpo|_D$, i.e. $sp(lpo) = sp(lpo|_{V \setminus D}); sp(lpo|_D)$.
Proceed with step (I) applied to $lpo|_{V \setminus D}$ and $lpo|_D$.

If the construction of step (IV) fails ($D = \emptyset$ or $lpo \neq lpo|_{V \setminus D}; lpo|_D$), then an N-form can be found in linear time.

It is easy to see by symmetrie, that the above construction can be completed by the following criteria for the N-freeness of an LPO:

(III)' If $\max(lpo) = \{v\}$ then $sp(lpo) = sp(lpo|_W); l(v)$ with $W = V \setminus \{v\}$.

(IV)' Denote $E = \{v \mid \forall v' \in \max(lpo)(v < v')\}$. If lpo is N-free, then $E \neq \emptyset$ and $lpo = lpo|_E; lpo|_{V \setminus E}$.

Using these facts, it is possible to adapt the described method also for the computation of the weight of WLPOs which are not N-free. In this case, according to definition 2, it is necessary to compute the maximum of the weights of all minimal sequential parallel extensions. That means we need to compute the sp-terms defining all minimal sequential parallel extensions. This can be done by extending each N-form, which is found in step (IV), in a minimal way. There are three possibilities of minimal extensions of N-forms, all shown in figure 1. We get the following algorithm for the computation of all sp-terms defining minimal sequential parallel extensions of a general LPO:

(I) If $V = \{v\}$, then $sp(lpo) = l(v)$.

(II) If the undirected graph underlying lpo is not connected, then it can be decomposed into its connected components $lpo_1, \ldots, lpo_n$ and we get
$sp(lpo) = sp(lpo_1) \| \cdots \| sp(lpo_n)$.
Proceed with step (I) applied to $lpo_1, \ldots, lpo_n$.

(III) (a) If $\min(lpo) = \{v\}$ then $sp(lpo) = l(v); sp(lpo|_W)$ with $W = V \setminus \{v\}$.
Proceed with step (I) applied to $lpo|_W$.

(b) If $\max(lpo) = \{v\}$ then $sp(lpo) = sp(lpo|_W); l(v)$ with $W = V \setminus \{v\}$.
   Proceed with step (I) applied to $lpo|_W$.

(IV) Denote $D = \{v \mid \forall v' \in \min(lpo)(v' < v)\}$ and $E = \{v \mid \forall v' \in \max(lpo)(v < v')\}$.

(a) If $D = \emptyset$ or $lpo \neq lpo|_{V \setminus D}; lpo|_D$, and $E = \emptyset$ or $lpo \neq lpo|_E; lpo|_{V \setminus E}$:
   Find an N-form and *proceed with step (III) for each minimal extension of lpo w.r.t. this N-form.*

(b) If $lpo = lpo|_{V \setminus D}; lpo|_D$: $sp(lpo) = sp(lpo|_{V \setminus D}); sp(lpo|_D)$.
   Proceed with step (I) applied to $lpo|_{V \setminus D}$ and $lpo|_D$.

(c) If $lpo \neq lpo|_E; lpo|_{V \setminus E}$: $sp(lpo) = sp(lpo|_E); sp(lpo|_{V \setminus E})$.
   Proceed with step (I) applied to $lpo|_{V \setminus E}$ and $lpo|_E$.

This is a recursive procedure splitting into three paths for each found N-form. That means, its running time is exponential in the number of N-forms contained in the considered LPO. Moreover, a minimal extension of an LPO w.r.t. an N-form may produce additional N-forms. As an example, see LPO lpo_1 from figure 6: If the N-form defined by $\{a, b, c, d\}$ is extended by the edge $b < d$, then the new N-form defined by $\{b, x, c, d\}$ is produced.

On the other side, if a PNT is composed using operation for union, sequential product, closure and/or parallel product, then the above algorithms needs to be applied only to LPO-runs of its PNT-components, since the computation of weights is compositional.

Furthermore, there a several possibilities to optimize the step (IV) concerning the definition of D and E and the choice of the next N-form. For example, we can use the following constructions in order to find possibilities for a sequential composition in a more effective way::

If $D \neq \emptyset$ and $lpo \neq lpo|_{V \setminus D}; lpo|_D$, then there is an N-form with nodes in D and in $V \setminus D$. If we delete all nodes from D belonging to an N-form which is not completely contained in D, we may get a non-empty subset $D' \subset D$ satisfying $lpo = lpo|_{V \setminus D'}; lpo|_{D'}$. As an example, see LPO lpo_2 from figure 6: If we delete the node d belonging to the N-form defined by $\{a, b, c, d\}$ from the set $D = \{d, x, y\}$, we get the set $D' = \{x, y\}$ satisfying $lpo_2 = lpo_2|_{V \setminus D'}; lpo_2|_{D'}$. An analoguous construction holds for E.

If $D = \emptyset$ or $lpo \neq lpo|_{V \setminus D}; lpo|_D$, in general many N-forms can be found. If we minimally extend one of these N-forms, also some other N-forms may be minimally extended because of transitivity. In step (IV)(a) we should choose such an N-form, whose extension also extends a maximal number of other N-forms. As an example, see LPO lpo_3 from figure 6: The N-form defined by $\{a, b, c, d\}$ causes many other N-forms due to transitivity, as for example $\{a, x, c, d\}$, $\{a, b, c, y\}$ or $\{a, b, x, y\}$ (and so on). If we extend the N-form $\{a, x, c, d\}$ by the edge $x < d$, then also the other mentioned N-forms are extended. In this example, the extension $x < d$ of the N-form $\{a, x, c, d\}$ extends a maximal number of other N-forms. A similar argumentation holds for the extension $c < b$ of the N-form $\{a, b, c, d\}$ and the extension $a < v$ of the N-form $\{a, b, v, d\}$. Again, an analoguous construction holds for E.

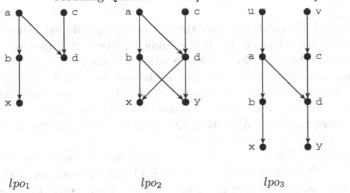

lpo_1 lpo_2 lpo_3

Fig. 6. Example-LPOs illustrating the computation of minimal series parallel extensions.

An exact and formal definition of such optimizations and their implementation, as well as experimental results are topics of further research. Moreover, it is necessary to have a closer look at the language composition of PNTs. On the one side, the weight of LPO-runs is not compositional w.r.t. to language composition, but on the other side, the structure of LPO-runs of a composed PNT can be determined from LPO-runs of its components. This may be used to construct sp-extensions of LPO-runs of a composed PNT from sp-extensions of LPO-runs of its components.

5.2   Computing the output weight of input-output-pairs

In order to compute the language of a PNT (the set of input-output-pairs), it is necessary to compute all of its LPO-runs. The most effective algorithm doing this for PT-nets is the token flow unfolding algorithm [3].

For PT-nets (underlying a PNT) having a finite set of LPO-runs, the token flow unfolding is finite and contains all LPO-runs of the net.

If a PT-net has infinitely many LPO-runs, then there are two possibilities. The first possibility is, that the PT-net is bounded. In this case the set of reachable markings is finite and it is possible to compute the so called complete finite prefix of the token flow unfolding. This prefix contains for each reachable marking at least one LPO-run leading to this marking. Since it is possible to compute all these markings, we may restrict the finite prefix to those LPO-runs leading to the final marking and we may use the algorithm to test, whether the PT-net is clean.

Note that the behavior of a bounded PNT may contain cycles (leading from a reachable marking back to the same marking). If all cycles produce empty input (empty output), then the input language (output language) is finite, otherwise infinite. It is possible during the computation of the finite prefix, to save additionally all sub-LPOs of LPO-runs which form a cycle. This information makes it possible later on to decide, whether a given input (output) belongs to the input language (output language) of the PNT.

The second possibility is, that the PT-net is unbounded. Then there is at least one unbounded place. If an unbounded place contributes to a reachable marking, from which the final marking can be reached, then the PT-net is not clean. If an unbounded place does not contribute to a reachable marking, from which the final marking can be reached, then it belongs to a useless part of the PNT. Therefore we do not want to consider PNTs having unbounded places.[4] The token flow unfolding algorithm can easily be extended in such a way that unbounded places are recognized.

In concrete applications it may not be of interest to compute the whole behavior of a PNT, but to test, whether a PNT has a given input and/or output. Consider the case of a given input. Then it is possible to restrict the computation of the token flow unfolding to such LPO-runs having the given input. Cycles not having empty input should not be cut (as it is the case for the computation of the finite prefix), but unfolded as many times as needed to get or to exceed the given input. When constructing such a restricted unfolding, special care need transitions having empty input. In particular, cycles with empty input must be cut after their first occurrence and stored for the weight computation. Analoguous considerations hold for the case of a given output and the case of a given input-output-pair.

Finally, if an input-output-pair belongs to the behavior of a PNT, its weight is computet as the supremum of the weights of all LPO-runs producing the input-output-pair. Note that the set of all such LPO-runs may be infinite if there are cycles with empty input and empty output - in this case the weight computation needs special care and depends on the used concurrent semiring.

6   Tool Support

For the modular construction of concrete PNTs in case studies and practical applications and as a basis for the implementation and evaluation of algorithms for analysis, simulation and optimisation of PNTs we are developing the tool PNT_ε^{ooL}. Its basic functionality was developed in the bachelor thesis [32] and presented in [18,24].

PNT_ε^{ooL} is a python [36] library and implemented within the framework SNAKES supporting the rapid prototyping of new Petri net formalisms and providing many basic Petri net components and functionality [27,28]. PNT_ε^{ooL} is mainly targeted at researchers in the area of PNTs. By the use of SNAKES it is relatively easy to implement and evaluate extensions, variations and new algorithms, as for example: Composition operations, algebraic weight structures, simulation algorithms and optimisation algorithms.

Constructed PNTs can be exported in an XML-format which is based on the standard PNML format developed for basic Petri net variants [33]. Moreover, PNTs can be visualised and pictures can be exported in all standard formats.

---

[4] Note that this implies that the sequential language of a PNT is regular. In order to deal with more general languages it would be necessary to use more general net classes combined with the concept of cleanness, as for example inhibitor nets.

The support of graphical output serves both as a possibility to check the implementation and as a handy utility in the process of writing scientific papers. PNT$_\varepsilon^{ool}$'s functionality supports fast construction of concrete example PNTs for case studies. PNML export can be used to analyse constructed example PNTs with other Petri net tools.

In the context of our research activities, PNT$_\varepsilon^{ool}$ serves as a scientific prototype for the development of an open library openPNT of efficient algorithms for the construction, composition, simulation and optimisation of PNTs which can be used in real world examples.

PNT$_\varepsilon^{ool}$ can be downloaded from our website [17] as a ZIP-archive. Assumed you have a working installation of Python, SNAKES, Graphviz, and dot2tex you only need to copy the py-files into the plugins sub-directory of your SNAKES installation.

6.1 Functionality

In this subsection we show how PNT$_\varepsilon^{ool}$ is used to construct and compose PNTs. We list the source code of the examples.

To use PNT$_\varepsilon^{ool}$ one has to create a text file and put the following code into it. These lines load the SNAKES library and the transducer-plugin.

```
1   import snakes.plugins
2   snakes.plugins.load(['transducer'], 'snakes.nets', 'pnts')
3   from pnts import *
```

Using the class method N from the class PetriNet a PNT consisting of a source place with one token, a sink place, and a single transition in between can be created (line 4). The parameters of this single transition are provided as named parameters to N.

In lines 5 and 6 graphical output of the PNTs is generated. The format of the output is controlled by the extension of the file-name given to the method draw as first argument. The orientation of the generated graphs is controlled by the parameter leftright of the method draw. This parameter is only effective if TikZ-output is to be created. For more available export formats one may consult the documentation of the Graphviz [12] package which is utilised by SNAKES for the export.

A PNT can be saved in PNML-format using the function savePNML – a wrapper of SNAKES methods – taking a file-name as second argument (line 7). For loading we provide loadPNML.

```
4   n = PetriNet.N('N1', weight = .5, input_symbol = eps,
        output_symbol = 'b')
5   n.draw("N.tikz", leftright = True)
6   n.draw("N.png")
7   savePNML(n, "N.pnml")
```

It is also possible to construct the same PNT (and also more complex PNTs) by adding all components (places with markings, transitions, edges with weights) separately:

```
8    n = PetriNet('N1')
9    n.add_place(Place('p_I', 1), is_source = True)
10   n.add_place(Place('p_F'), is_sink = True)
11   n.add_transition( Transition('t_1', input_symbol=eps,
         output_symbol='b'),weight=0.5)
12   n.add_input('p_I', 't_1')
13   n.add_output('p_F', 't_1')
```

Finally, PNTs can be composed by several compsition operations. An example for the use the operation of parallel composition is shown in line 14.

```
14   n1 = n | n
```

The other available operators are: * for concatenation, + for union, ~ for closure, and > for language composition.

There are many possibilities to influence the graphical output, like renaming of transitions, using subscripts in transition names, adjustment of label positions, and more. Moreover, it is possible to change the marking of a PNT be firing transitions. For details we refer to [18].

6.2   Architecture

PNT$_\varepsilon^{\circ\circ L}$ is implemented as a bunch of plugins on top of SNAKES and thus as a Python library. Actually SNAKES implements so-called coloured Petri nets [19] where Python objects and expressions are used for the annotations. However PNT$_\varepsilon^{\circ\circ L}$ does not use most of these features.

A plugin for SNAKES is a separate Python library which specialises already defined classes or adds new classes to SNAKES. Plugins can be loaded and are stacked onto each other. This way a class hierarchy is established. A function extend has to be implemented and some rules have to be followed for which the interested reader should refer to the SNAKES homepage. A plugin can depend on other plugins and can even mention conflicting plugins.

In the following we briefly describe each of the plugins that comprise PNT$_\varepsilon^{\circ\circ L}$. The first and fourth plugin can be used independently from the other plugins while the remaining three build upon each other.

The d2t-Plugin. This plugin extends the features of the gv-plugin which is delivered with SNAKES. By the use of that plugin a representation of Petri nets in the dot-language from Graphviz [12] can be produced which is then processed by Graphviz to compute a layout and eventually produce a graphical output. Our d2t-plugin adds several features to the graphical output routine, like the possibilties to use subscripts in object names, to rename objects for the graphical output, and to use the export format TikZ.

The pt-Plugin. As already said, SNAKES implements coloured Petri nets. Since the underlying net of a PNT is actually a place/transition Petri net we decided to write a plugin which restricts the nets of SNAKES by only allowing those constructs which are needed for them.

The terminal-Plugin. By using the pt-plugin and adding a few features to the class PetriNet, this plugin implements Petri nets that have a single source place and single sink place. Although SNAKES delivers the label-plugin to add properties to any node of a net we decided to implement our own mechanism because we only need a fraction of its functionality.

With these properties it is possible to define several composition operations. While SNAKES delivers the ops-plugin which implements composition operations according to [4] we implemented our own mechanism because the definitions of the operations defer.

Additionally, we provide a notation to create a *singleton* net consisting of a source and a sink place and a transition in between. This feature is implemented as the class method N of the class PetriNet.

The bisemiring-Plugin. We implemented the class Bisemiring and the association of weights to transitions in a separate plugin. Bisemiring objects hold definitions of the set of weights, neutral elements and functions for binary addition, sequential multiplication and parallel multiplication of a bisemiring.

A PNT contains an object of class Bisemiring which is the Viterbi-bisemiring as default. Every transition has a weight which can be checked against the bisemiring of the net.

The transducer-Plugin. The last plugin builds on top of the terminal- and bisemiring-plugin and equips transitions with input- and output-symbols which can be arbitrary Python objects. An additional class implements the ε-symbol. The N-method is extended to support weights and input- and output-symbols for the single transition. This plugin implements the additional composition operation of language composition. Also the graphical output of transitions is changed using the functionality of d2t-plugin. The generated TikZ-code uses definitions from a separate sty-file to provide adaptable graphics.

7 Related Work

There are several less general models using weigths with underlying algebraic structure.

Weighted finite automata are classical non-deterministic finite automata in which transitions carry weights [8]. These weights may represent cost, time consumption or probability of a transition execution. The behaviour of such automata is defined by a function associating with each word the weight of its execution. For a uniform definition of the behaviour, the set of weights is equipped with the underlying algebraic structure of a semiring. The multiplication operation of the semiring is used for determining the weight of a path, and the weight of a word is obtained by the sum of the weights of its underlying paths. If each transition additionally is equipped with an output symbol, the resulting automaton is called a transducer. Such transducers are used for the translation between languages over different alphabets for example in natural language processing. For weighted finite automata and transducers (also called finite state transducers or FSTs) there are efficient implementations of composition and optimisation operations in standard libraries [26,41].

There are generalisations of weighted finite automata to weighted automata over discrete structures other than finite words, some of them introducing concurrency into the model through considering LPOs not consisting of a total order on their symbols but of a partial order.

In [11] an overview is given on weighted finite automata (and transducers) processing tree structures. They are used to recognise weighted context-free languages with weights coming from semirings and do not consider concurrency.

In [10] weighted asynchronous cellular automata accepting weighted traces, a special restricted kind of LPOs, are described. Here also only semirings are used to describe weights, i.e. no difference is made between the combination of weights of transitions occurring in sequential order and occurring in parallel.

In [20] weighted branching automata accepting weighted sp-LPOs are introduced. Here, weights come from bisemirings where the algebraic structure of semirings is extended by a third operation of parallel multiplication (which in this case needs no unit) used for the combination of weights of concurrent transition occurrences.

For all these automata models there are widely developed theories concerning equivalent representations as rational expressions or logic formulae, useful composition operations and closure properties [8].

Another extended automata model are Q-Automata [6] whose computations are step sequences. Q-Automata are coined for application in quality management with weights modelling costs and coming from a bisemiring, whose parallel multiplication may not be commutative.

PNTs, as introduced in this paper, are a natural generalisation of all these automata based weighted transducer models working on finite words, traces or sp-LPOs. If a semiring can be extended to a concurrent semiring, then each FST over this semiring is output equivalent to a PNT [25]. However, since not each semiring can be extended to a concurrent semiring, not each FST can be represented by an equivalent PNT. In [25] we examine several conditions of semirings, which allow an extension to concurrent semirings.

There are already several publications introducing PNTs and applying them in different application areas [34,37,38]. However, these are mainly case studies lacking a common basic formal definition and without any theoretical development. Moreover, these publications only make use of sequential semantics of PNTs and do not consider weights.

Another Petri net model with transitions having assigned weights are stochastic Petri nets (SPNs). SPNs introduce a temporal specification of probabilistic nature and are applied to the performance analysis of timed systems. The weights have no underlying algebraic structure and are used to compute firing probabilities of untimed transitions.

8   Further Work

Up to now, we have developed a basic theoretical framework of PNTs and basic tool support providing the computation of weights of PNT-runs, the computation of PNT-languages and several composition operations on PNTs. Moreover, we applied PNTs in some case studies in the field of semantic dialogue modelling.

In order to apply PNTs to practical relevant problems, there are important further research steps in several directions. First, the presented theoretical framework needs to be completed:

- There are several additional composition operations of FSTs (for example inversion or reversal) which need to be examined also w.r.t. PNTs.
- In order to get more efficient algorithms, optimisation techniques must be developed as in the case of FSTs (for example elimination of ε-transitions or pushing and merging of weights alongs paths).
- For analysis purpose, we need to examine which classical Petri net properties (as for example boundedness) are consistent with composition operations.

The presented simulation algorithms need to be improved as described in section 5. Moreover, for practical application in the field of semantic dialogue modelling and speech recognition the algorithms developed so far need to be improved and extended:

- We need on-the-fly simulation algorithms computing the N best runs of a PNT (similar to N-best-paths algorithms for FSTs in the field of natural language processing).
- It is necessary to develop semi-automatic procedures to construct PNTs for the translation between the syntactic and semantic level from experimental audio data (generated in Wizard-of-Oz experiments), for example using Petri net synthesis methods [21].
- Possibily, algorithms can be fine tuned concerning the concurrent Viterbi semiring (used in this application field).

As described, we use PNT$^{\circ\circ L}$ for the quick construction of PNTs for the use in case studies and as a scientific prototype for the development of an open library openPNT of efficient algorithms for the construction, composition, simulation and optimisation of PNTs which can be used in real world examples (similar to the open library openFST [1] for FST-algorithms).

Finally, the framework can be extended w.r.t. several aspects:

- It is possible to consider other Petri net classes, either with the aim to increase the expressiveness of the model (for example using inhibitor nets), or with the aim to restrict expressiveness in order to get more effective algorithms and improved analysis and compositionality properties (for exapmle using free choice nets).
- On the other side, more usefull examples of concurrent semirings can be collected and described. Moreover, the algebraic structure of concurrent semirings used as the weight model can be generalized in order to broaden the field of possible applications.
- Concepts which are more general than cleanness can be considered for ensuring compositionality (for example adapting generlized versions of soundness).

References

1. Allauzen, C., Riley, M.D., Schalkwyk, J., Skut, W., Mohri, M.: OpenFst: a general and efficient weighted finite-state transducer library. In: Holub, J., Žd'árek, J. (eds.) CIAA 2007. LNCS, vol. 4783, pp. 11–23. Springer, Heidelberg (2007)
2. Aéma, P., Balbo, G. (eds.): Application and Theory of Petri Nets 1997. Lecture Notes in Computer Science, vol. 1248. Springer, Heidelberg (1997)
3. Bergenthum, R., Mauser, S., Lorenz, R., Juhás, G.: Unfolding Semantics of Petri Nets Based on Token Flows. Fundam. Inform. **94**, 331–360 (2009)
4. Best, E., Devillers, R.R., Hall, J.G.: The Box Calculus: a New Causal Algebra with Multi-label Communication. In: Rozenberg [30], pp. 21–69
5. Boudol, G., Castellani, I.: On the semantics of concurrency: partial orders and transition systems. In: Ehrig, H., Kowalski, R.A., Levi, G., Montanari, U. (eds.) TAPSOFT '87. LNCS, vol. 249. Springer, Heidelberg (1987)
6. Chothia, T., Klejin, J.: Q-Automata: Modelling the Resource Usage of Concurrent Components. Electronic Notes in Theoretical Computer Science **175**(175), 153–167 (2007)
7. Droste, M., Kuich, W.: Semirings and Formal Power Series. In: Droste et al. [8], ch. 1, pp. 3–28 (2009)
8. Droste, M., Kuich, W., Vogler, H. (eds.): Handbook of Weighted Automata. Monographs in Theoretical Computer Science. Springer (2009)
9. Esposito, A., Esposito, A.M., Vinciarelli, A., Hoffmann, R., Müller, V.C. (eds.): Cognitive Behavioural Systems. LNCS, vol. 7403. Springer, Heidelberg (2012)
10. Fichtner, I., Kuske, D., Meinecke, I.: Traces, series-parallel posets, and Ppictures: a weighted study. In: Droste et al. [8], ch. 10, pp. 405–452 (2009)
11. Fülöp, Z., Vogler, H.: Weighted tree automata and tree transducers. In: Droste et al. [8], ch. 9, pp. 313–404 (2009)
12. Gansner, E.R., North, S.C.: An open graph visualization system and its applications to software engineering. SOFTWARE - PRACTICE AND EXPERIENCE **30**(11), 1203–1233 (2000)
13. Gischer, J.L.: The Equational Theory of Pomsets. Theoretical Computer Science **61**, 199–224 (1988)
14. Grabowski, J.: On Partial Languages. Fundamenta Informaticae **4**(2), 428–498 (1981)
15. Hack, M.: Petri net languages. Technical Report Memo 124, computation structures group, massachusetts institute of technology (1975)

16. Hoare, T., Möller, B., Struth, G., Wehrman, I.: Concurrent Kleene Algebra and its Foundations. The Journal of Logic and Algebraic Programming **80**, 266–296 (2011)
17. Huber, M.: PNTool-Homepage (2014). www.informatik.uni-augsburg.de/lehrstuehle/inf/mitarbeiter/huber/software/
18. Huber, M., Lorenz, R.: Constructing Petri Net Transducers with PNTool. In: Moldt, D., Rölke, H. (eds) Proceedings of the International Workshop on Petri Nets and Software Engineering, Co-located with 35th International Conference on Application and Theory of Petri Nets and Concurrency (PetriNets 2014) and 14th International Conference on Application of Concurrency to System Design (ACSD 2014), Tunis, Tunisia, June 23–24, 2014, vol. 1160 of CEUR Workshop Proceedings, pp. 339–341. CEUR-WS.org (2014)
19. Jensen, K.: Coloured Petri Nets - Basic Concepts, Analysis Methods and Practical Use, vol. 1 of EATCS Monographs in Theoretical Computer Science. Springer (1992)
20. Kuske, D., Meinecke, I.: Branching Automata with Costs - A Way of Reflecting Parallelism in Costs. Theoretical Computer Science **328**, 53–75 (2004)
21. Lorenz, R., Desel, J., Juhás, G.: Models from Scenarios. T Petri Nets and Other Models of Concurrency **7**, 314–371 (2013)
22. Lorenz, R., Huber, M.: Petri Net Transducers in Semantic Dialogue Modelling. In: Proceedings of "Elektronische Sprachsignalverarbeitung (ESSV)", vol. 64 of Studientexte zur Sprachkommunikation, pp. 286–297 (2012)
23. Lorenz, R., Huber, M.: Realizing the Translation of utterances into meanings by petri net transducers. In: Proceedings of "Elektronische Sprachsignalverarbeitung (ESSV)", vol. 65 of Studientexte zur Sprachkommunikation (2013)
24. Lorenz, R., Huber, M., Straßner, D.: Constructing petri net transducers with PNTool. In: Proceedings of "Elektronische Sprachsignalverarbeitung (ESSV)", vol. 71 of Studientexte zur Sprachkommunikation (2014)
25. Lorenz, R., Huber, M., Wirsching, G.: On weighted petri net transducers. In: Ciardo, G., Kindler, E. (eds.) PETRI NETS 2014. LNCS, vol. 8489, pp. 233–252. Springer, Heidelberg (2014)
26. Mohri, M.: Weighted Automata Algorithms. In: Droste et al. [8], ch. 6, pp. 213–254 (2009)
27. Pommereau, F.: Quickly Prototyping Petri Nets Tools with SNAKES. In: Simu-Tools, p. 17. ICST (2008)
28. Pommereau, F.: The SNAKES toolkit (2013). https://www.ibisc.univ-evry.fr/fpommereau/SNAKES
29. Pratt, V.: Modelling Concurrency with Partial Orders. Int. Journal of Parallel Programming **15**, 33–71 (1986)
30. Rozenberg, G. (ed.): APN 1992. LNCS, vol. 609. Springer, Heidelberg (1992)
31. Schlosser, C.: Entwurf und Implementierung von Algorithmen zur gewichteten Übersetzung partieller Wörter mit Petrinetz-Transduktoren. Master thesis, Augsburg University (2014)
32. Strassner, D.: Prototypische Implementierung von Petrinetz-Transduktoren mit SNAKES. Bachelor thesis, Augsburg University (2013)
33. P. team. PNML.org: The Petri Net Markup Language home, p. 8 (2011). http://www.pnml.org
34. van Biljon, W.R.: Extending Petri nets for specifying man-machine dialogues. Int. J. Man-Mach. Stud. **28**(4), 437–455 (1988)
35. van der Aalst, W.M.P.: Verification of Workflow Nets. In: Aéma and Balbo [2], pp. 407–426

36. van Rossum, G., Drake, F.L.: The Python Language Reference Manual. Python-Labs, Virginia (2001)
37. Wang, F.-Y., Mittmann, M., Saridis, G.N.: Coordination specification for CIRSSE robotic platform system using Petri net transducers. Journal of Intelligent and Robotic Systems **9**, 209–233 (1994)
38. Wang, F.-Y., Saridis, G.N.: A model for coordination of intelligent machines using Petri nets. In: Proceedings of the IEEE International Symposium on Intelligent Control, pp. 28–33. IEEE Comput. Soc. Press (1989)
39. Wirsching, G., Huber, M., Kölbl, C.: Zur logik von bestenlisten in der dialogmodellierung. In: Proceedings of "Elektronische Sprachsignalverarbeitung (ESSV)", vol. 61 of Studientexte zur Sprachkommunikation, pp. 309–316 (2011)
40. Wirsching, G., Huber, M., Kölbl, C., Lorenz, R., Römer, R.: Semantic dialogue modeling. In: Esposito et al. [9], pp. 104–113
41. Wolff, M.: Akustische Mustererkennung. Habilitation (2009)

On Interval Process Semantics of Petri Nets with Inhibitor Arcs

Mohammed Alqarni$^{(\boxtimes)}$ and Ryszard Janicki

Department of Computing and Software, McMaster University,
Hamilton, ON L8S 4K1, Canada
{alqarnma,janicki}@mcmaster.ca

Abstract. Interval order semantics of Petri nets with inhibitor arc is
discussed. Both the operational semantics and process, i.e. concurrent
history, semantics are defined and their mutual relationship is discussed.
It is shown that if operational semantics is restricted to stratified orders
(i.e. step sequences) the proposed model is equivalent to models based
on step processes and comtraces.

1 Introduction

Standard operational semantics of majority of concurrency models is defined in
terms of either firing sequences or firing step sequences, while standard concurrent history semantics is usually defined in terms of partial orders, stratified
order structures (or structures equivalent to them as net processes).

Nevertheless, it is commonly assumed (first argued by N. Wiener in 1914
[26] and analysed in details in [13]) that any system run (execution) that can
be observed by a single observer *must* be an interval order of event occurrences.
This means that the most precise observational semantics is defined in terms of
interval orders. Moreover, representing observations as interval orders allows to
capture behaviours that neither of the standard semantics can really describe.
However generating interval orders directly is problematic for most models of
concurrency, as the only feasible *sequence representation* of interval order is by
using Fishburn Theorem [6] and appropriate sequences of *beginnings* and *endings*
of events involved. It was shown by Janicki and Koutny [15] that concurrent
histories involving interval orders can be represented by *interval order structures*
(proposed in [12,19]), but how these interval order structures could be derived
for particular concurrent systems was not clear.

While validity of operational semantics is usually obvious, the validity of
concurrent history/behaviour semantics is often not. It relies on the validity
of the definition of a concurrent history/behaviour, which is often not trivial
and may involve complex reasoning (cf. [3,10,11,22]). On the other hand, the
process semantics (in the sense of [4,18,22,24]), does not usually require much

---

Mohammed Alqarni—Supported by the Ministry of Higher Education in Saudi
Arabia through The Saudi Arabian Cultural Bureau in Canada.
Ryszard Janicki—Partially supported by NSERC grant of Canada.

R. Devillers and A. Valmari (Eds.): PETRI NETS 2015, LNCS 9115, pp. 77–97, 2015.
DOI: 10.1007/978-3-319-19488-2_4

validation as intuitively it is just a set of system unfoldings, so it is as natural as any operational semantics (c.f. [17, 22, 25]). Hence it can be used as a benchmark for validity of other types of history/behaviour semantics, they just have to be equivalent to the process semantics (c.f. [4, 17, 18]).

In this paper we present an *interval* process semantic for Petri Nets with Inhibitor Arcs. Various process semantics for Petri Nets with Inhibitor Arcs that started from various assumptions have been proposed in the past, the most representative and prolific are probably [4, 14, 16, 17, 20, 25, 27], but *they all assume that the operational semantics is defined in terms of sequences* [20, 25, 27] *or step sequences* [4, 14, 16, 17]. None of these models is able to deal with observations (system runs) that are neither step sequences nor semantically equivalent to any step sequence.

The paper is organized as follows: We start by providing standard mathematical definitions for different orders and their structures, then we overview Petri nets with inhibitor arcs and its operational semantics, and then introduce interval representation of Petri nets with inhibitor arcs as well as the interval order operational semantics. After that we review process semantics of Petri nets with inhibitor arcs and generalize the concept of *net process* to represent the set of *equivalent* executions modeled by interval orders. Finally we will show that our interval processes correspond to appropriate *interval order structures*, and they can define interval operational, interval process, and interval 'true concurrency' semantics of Petri nets with inhibitor arcs.

We will also show that our model covers-and is consistent with-the models where sequences or step sequences were used to represent system runs. The paper extends the ideas used for step sequences in [14, 17] to interval orders. Figure 3 shows our running example and illustrates the intuition of our approach.

2   Partial, Total, Stratified and Interval Orders

We will start the formal part of our paper with a short introduction to partial orders (c.f. [7]), as they are the principal tool to describe executions and operational semantics of concurrent systems.

Definition 1. *A relation $< \subseteq X \times X$ is a (strict) **partial order** if it is irreflexive and transitive, i.e. for all $a, c, b \in X$, $a \not< a$ and $a < b < c \implies a < c$. We also define:*
$$a \frown_< b \overset{df}{\iff} \neg(a < b) \land \neg(b < a) \land a \neq b, \text{ and}$$
$$a <^\frown b \overset{df}{\iff} a < b \lor a \frown_< b.$$
Note that $a \frown_< b$ means a and b are incomparable (w.r.t. $<$) elements of X. □

Let $<$ be a partial order on a set X. Then:

1. $<$ is **total** if $\frown_< = \emptyset$. In other words, for all $a, b \in X$, $a < b \lor b < a \lor a = b$;
2. $<$ is **stratified** if $a \frown_< b \frown_< c \implies a \frown_< c \lor a = c$, i.e., the relation $\frown_< \cup id_X$ is an equivalence relation on X;
3. $<$ is **interval** if for all $a, b, c, d \in X$, $a < c \land b < d \implies a < d \lor b < c$. In other words, $<$ is interval if all its four element restrictions are different from $<_4$ in Figure 1.

It is clear from these definitions that every total order is stratified and every stratified order is interval. Partial orders are usually represented as *Hasse diagrams*[1]. Figure 1 illustrates the above definitions. Every finite total order is uniquely represented by a sequence. For example the order $<_1$ of Figure 1 is represented by a sequence $abcd$. Similarly, every stratified order is uniquely represented by a step sequence. For example the order $<_2$ of Figure 1 is represented by a step sequence $\{a\}\{b,c\}\{d\}$. The opposite is also true, every sequence uniquely defines a total order if it is enumerated elements, and every step sequence uniquely defines a stratified order if it is enumerated elements.

Each sequence of events represents a total order of *enumerated events* in a natural way. For precise definitions see for example [14], here we will be using the following notation.

Notation 1   1. *For each set of events Σ, let $\widehat{\Sigma} = \{a^i \mid a \in \Sigma, i \geq 1\}$ denote the set of* enumerated *events generated by Σ.*
2. *For each sequence $x \in \Sigma^*$ and each step sequence $z \in (2^\Sigma)^*$, let $\hat{x} \in \widehat{\Sigma}^*$ and $\hat{z} \in (2^{\widehat{\Sigma}})^*$ denote their* enumerated *representations.*
   For example, if $x = abbaa$ then $\hat{x} = a^1 b^1 b^2 a^2 a^3$, and if $z = \{a,b\}\{a,b,c\}\{a\}$ then $\hat{z} = \{a^1, b^1\}\{a^2, b^2, c^1\}\{a^3\}$.
3. *For every sequence $x \in \Sigma^*$, $\lhd_x$ is the* total order *defined by the enumerated sequence $\hat{x}$. For example:* $\lhd_{abbaa} = a^1 \to b^1 \to b^2 \to a^2 \to a^3$.
4. *For every step sequence $z \in (2^\Sigma)^*$, $\lhd_z$ is the* stratified order *defined by the enumerated step sequence $\hat{z}$.*
   For example: $\lhd_{\{a,b\}\{a,b,c\}\{a\}} = \{a^1, b^1\} \to \{a^2, b^2, c^1\} \to \{a^3\}$.   □

The two orders on the far right of Figure 1 illustrate points (3) and (4) of the notation presented above.

For the interval orders, the name and intuition follows from Fishburn's Theorem:

Theorem 1 (Fishburn [6]). *A partial order $<$ on X is* **interval** *iff there exists a total order $\lhd$ on some T and two mappings $B, E : X \to T$ such that for all $x, y \in X$,*

1. $B(x) \lhd E(x)$,
2. $x < y \iff E(x) \lhd B(y)$.   □

Usually $B(x)$ is interpreted as the beginning and $E(x)$ as the end of an *interval* x. The intuition of Fishburn's theorem is also illustrated in Figure 1 with $<_3$ and $\lhd_3$. For all $x, y \in \{a, b, c, d\}$, we have $B(x) \lhd_3 E(x)$ and $x <_3 y \iff E(x) \lhd_3 B(y)$. For better readability we will skip parentheses in $B(x)$ and $E(x)$ in the future. Note that the interval order $<_3$ is (*not* uniquely) represented by a sequence that represents $\lhd_3$, i.e. $BaEaBbBcEbBdEcEd$. Fishburn's Theorem will be essential in interval semantics of inhibitor nets.

---

[1] A Hasse diagram of a partial order $<$ is the smallest relation R such that the transitive closure of R, i.e. R^+, is equal to $<$ (c.f. [7]).

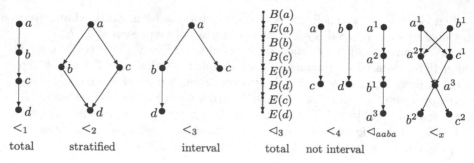

Fig. 1. Various types of partial orders (represented as Hasse diagrams), the total order defined by the sequence $aaba$, and the stratified order defined by the step sequence $x = \{a,b\}\{a,c\}\{a\}\{b,c\}$

We will say that a total order $\lhd$ on X *extends* a partial order $<$ on X, if for all $x, y \in X$ $x < y \Rightarrow x \lhd y$, and for every partial $<$, total($<$) denotes the set of all *total extensions* of $<$.

3   Stratified and Interval Order Structures

When the system runs are represented by stratified or interval orders, or when we want to express not only "earlier than" but also "no later than" relationship, partial orders alone are not enough, we need to use pairs or relations called order structures (c.f. [10,11,17]).

Definition 2 (Stratified Order Structures [8,12]). *A **stratified order structure** is a relational structure $S = (X, \prec, \sqsubset)$ such that for all $a, b, c \in X$;*

S1. $a \not\sqsubset a$ *S3.* $a \sqsubset b \sqsubset c \wedge a \neq c \Rightarrow a \sqsubset c$

S2. $a \prec b \Rightarrow a \sqsubset b$ *S4.* $a \sqsubset b \prec c \wedge a \prec b \sqsubset c \Rightarrow a \prec c$ □

We will say that a *stratified order* $<$ on X *extends* the structure S, if $\prec \subseteq <$ and $\sqsubset \subseteq <^{\frown}$. The set of all such extensions of S will be denoted by $strat(S)$. If $<$ is a stratified order on X, then the triple $(X, <, <^{\frown})$ is a stratified order structure. The axioms $S1$–$S4$ can be seen as an abstraction and generalization of the relationship between $<$ and $<^{\frown}$ when $<$ is a stratified order (c.f. [13,15]).

The formalism provided by interval order structures is more general than those provided by partial orders and stratified order structures. Interval order structures models concurrent behaviour that neither partial orders nor stratified order structures can model.

Definition 3 (Interval Order Structures [12,19]). *An **interval order structure** is a relational structure $S = (X, \prec, \sqsubset)$ such that for all $a, b, c, d \in X$:*

I1. $a \not\sqsubset a$

I2. $a \prec b \Rightarrow a \sqsubset b$

I3. $a \prec b \prec c \Rightarrow a \prec c$

I4. $a \prec b \sqsubset c \wedge a \sqsubset b \prec c \Rightarrow a \sqsubset c$

I5. $a \prec b \sqsubset c \prec d \Rightarrow a \prec d$

I6. $a \sqsubset b \prec c \sqsubset d \Rightarrow a \sqsubset d \vee a = d$ □

Note that *every stratified order structure is also an interval order structure.*

We will say that an *interval order* $<$ on X *extends* the structure S, if $\prec \subseteq <$ and $\sqsubset \subseteq <^\frown$. The set of all such extensions of S will be denoted by *interv(S)*. If $<$ is an interval order on X, then the triple $(X, <, <^\frown)$ is an interval order structure. The axioms $I1$–$I4$ can be seen as an abstraction and generalization of the relationship between $<$ and $<^\frown$ when $<$ is an interval order (c.f. [13, 15]).

In both order structures the relations $\prec$ and $\sqsubset$ are called *causality* and *weak causality* respectively, and in both models $\prec$ is an abstraction of "earlier than" relation while $\sqsubset$ is an abstraction of "no later than" relation. In both models $\prec$ is always a partial order, while $\sqsubset$ does not have to be. The fundamental difference is that for Stratified Order Structures the system runs/executions are assumed to be modeled by at most stratified orders, while for Interval Order Structures the system runs/executions are assumed to be modeled by general interval orders.

For interval order structures we have the following equivalent of Fishburn Theorem (Theorem 1).

Theorem 2 (Abraham, Ben-David, Magidor [1]).
A triple $S = (X, \prec, \sqsubset)$ is an interval order structure if and only if there exists a partial order $<$ on some Y and two mappings $B, E : X \rightarrow Y$ such that $B(X) \cap E(X) = \emptyset$ and for each $x, y \in X$:

1. $Bx < Ex$,
2. $x \prec y \iff Ex < By$,
3. $x \sqsubset y \iff Bx < Ey$ □

The partial order $<$ from Theorem 2 is not unique and does not need to be interval. For more on the theory of order structures and their applications, the reader is referenced to [10, 11, 15].

4   Elementary Nets with Inhibitor Arcs

Inhibitor arcs allow a transition to check for an *absence* of a token. They have been introduced in [2] to solve a synchronization problem not expressible in classical Petri nets. In principle they allow 'test for zero', an operator the standard Petri nets do not have (c.f. [21, 23]). *Activator arcs* (also called 'read', or 'contextual' arcs [3, 20]), formally introduced in [14, 20], are conceptually orthogonal to the inhibitor arcs, they allow a transition to check for a *presence* of a token.

Elementary nets with inhibitor arcs [14] are very simple. They are just classical *elementary nets* of [22, 24] extended with inhibitor arcs. Nevertheless they can easily express complex behaviours involving 'not later than' cases or non-transitive simultaneity. The net N in Figure 2 is an example of ENI.

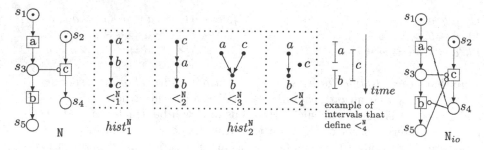

Fig. 2. Inhibitor nets N and N_{io} and all their behaviours involving one occurrence of a, b and c. The net N generates $<_1^N, <_2^N, <_3^N, <_4^N$, and two concurrent histories, while N_{io} generates only an interval order $<_4^N$. Partial orders are represented by Hasse diagrams. All orders except $<_4^N$ are stratified.

Definition 4 ([2,14]). *An **Elementary Net with Inhibitor Arcs** (ENI) is a tuple $N = (P, T, F, C_{init}, I)$ such that*

1. *P and T are finite and disjoint sets of places and transitions represented, respectively, as circles and rectangles;*
2. *$F \subseteq (P \times T) \cup (T \times P)$ is the flow relation of N - represented as directed arcs between places and transitions;*
3. *$C_{init} \subseteq P$ is the initial marking of N (generally, any $C \subseteq P$ is a marking); and*
4. *$I \subseteq P \times T$ is a set of inhibitor arcs - represented as arcs with small circles as arrowheads.* □

For every $x \in P \cup T$ we define its input ${}^\bullet x = \{y \mid (y, x) \in F\}$ and its output $x^\bullet = \{y \mid (x, y) \in F\}$. We assume that for every $t \in T$, ${}^\bullet t \neq \emptyset \neq t^\bullet$ and ${}^\bullet t \cap t^\bullet = \emptyset$. Moreover, for each $t \in T$, the set ${}^\circ t = \{p \mid (p, t) \in I\}$ is the set of places that are connected with transition t by inhibitor arcs. We also define, in a standard way, for any subset U of T: ${}^\bullet U = \bigcup_{t \in U} {}^\bullet t$, $U^\bullet = \bigcup_{t \in U} t^\bullet$ and ${}^\circ U = \bigcup_{t \in U} {}^\circ t$.

The **operational semantics** of ENI is defined through the "token game" which simulates the occurrence of transitions and the changes of tokens in places. ENI differs from ordinary elementary Petri nets only by introducing a requirement that a transition cannot be enabled if there is a token in a place to which it is connected by an inhibitor arc. A transition t is enabled at a configuration C if ${}^\bullet t \subseteq C$ and $(t^\bullet \cup {}^\circ t) \cap C = \emptyset$. An enabled transition t can fire leading to a new configuration $C' = (C \setminus {}^\bullet t) \cup t^\bullet$. We denote this by $C[t\rangle C'$. We will also write $C[t_1 \ldots t_n\rangle C'$ if $C[t_1\rangle C_1 \ldots C_{n-1}[t_n\rangle C'$ for some configurations $C_1, \ldots, C_{n-1}$.

There are two standard operational semantics for ENI, one in terms of **firing sequences** and another in terms of **firing step sequences** (c.f. [5]).

A **firing sequence** of an ENI is any sequence of transitions $t_1, \ldots, t_n$ for which there are markings $C_1, \ldots, C_n$ satisfying:

$$C_{init}[t_1\rangle C_1[t_2\rangle C_2 \ldots [t_n\rangle C_n.$$

The definition above can be generalized to sequences of sets of transitions occurring simultaneously. Let $U \subseteq T$ be a non-empty set such that for all distinct $t_1, t_2 \in U$:

$$(t_1^\bullet \cup {}^\bullet t_1) \cap (t_2^\bullet \cup {}^\bullet t_2) = \emptyset.$$

Then U is enabled at a marking C if ${}^\bullet U \subseteq C$ and $(U^\bullet \cup {}^\circ U) \cap C = \emptyset$. We also denote this by $C[U\rangle C'$ where, $C' = (C \setminus {}^\bullet U) \cup U^\bullet$.

A *firing step sequence* is a sequence of sets (or steps) $U_1, \ldots, U_n$ for which there are markings $C_1, \ldots, C_n$ satisfying:

$$C_{init}[U_1\rangle C_1[U_2\rangle C_2 \ldots [U_n\rangle C_n.$$

For the ENI system N in Figure 2, there are two firing sequences and three step sequences that involve an occurrence of a, b and c. The firing sequences are namely abc and cab and they correspond to the total orders $<_1^N$ and $<_2^N$ respectively. The step firing sequences are $\{a\}\{b\}\{c\}$, $\{c\}\{a\}\{b\}$ and $\{a, c\}\{b\}$, and they correspond to the total orders $<_1^N$ and $<_2^N$ and the stratified order $<_3^N$, respectively.

Firing sequence semantics is sometimes called 'a-posteriori' while firing step sequence semantics is sometimes called 'a-priori' (see [5, 14]). It is often assumed that if the events (transitions) are interpreted as representations of activities whose completion takes some time, then 'a-priori' model is frequently preferable, however if the events (transitions) are instantaneous, i.e. their occurrence takes zero time, then simultaneous executions must be excluded [10, 14], so only firing sequence approach remains.

Assume that when a non-instantaneous transition t begins its firing, the tokens that it consumes disappear for consumption by other transitions but continue to inhibit other transitions, if connected to an inhibitor arc. Such interpretation allows possible executions where transitions overlap, so they can be interpreted as interval orders.

Considering Figure 2, note that intuitively the *interval* order $<_4^N$ can also be considered as a possible run/execution that involves occurrences of a, b and c, for both N and N_{io}. Intuitively, if the events a, b and c are not instantaneous, one can imagine a situation where b follows a but c overlaps with both a and b. This means that for the net N and N_{io} of Figure 2, one can, intuitively, hold on to a token taken from s_2 until a token taken from s_1 is placed in s_5. We will provide a tool that allow us to generate the interval order $<_4^N$ as well. However $<_4^N$ can be described by neither a standard firing sequence nor a firing step sequence.

Finally we would like to point out that for the net N_{io} from Figure 2 the set of all firing sequences that start from the marking $\{s_1, s_2\}$ and end at the marking $\{s_4, s_5\}$ is empty and the set of all firing step sequences that start from the marking $\{s_1, s_2\}$ and end at the marking $\{s_4, s_5\}$ is also empty, and the only observation/system run that starts from the marking $\{s_1, s_2\}$ and ends at the marking $\{s_4, s_5\}$ is the interval order $<_4^N$.

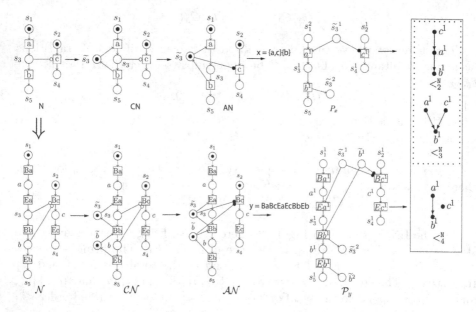

Fig. 3. An example of an inhibitor net, its interval representation, processes and concurrent histories they generate. The process P_x generates a concurrent history $\{<_2^N, <_3^N\}$ while the process $\mathcal{P}_y$ generates $\{<_2^N, <_3^N, <_4^N\}$.

5   Interval Elementary Net with Inhibitor Arcs

This section contains the first part of our contribution.

Since every interval order of events can be represented by some total order (i.e. an appropriate sequence) of event beginnings and ends (Theorem 1 by Fishburn), if we figure out how a given inhibitor net can generate appropriate sequences of event beginnings and ends, we might be able to describe all interval orders the net generates.

The basic idea of defining the set of firing interval sequences i.e. sequences of beginnings and ends (will be formally defined shortly) for a given inhibitor net N is briefly presented in Figure 3 by the vertical transformation of the net N into the net $\mathcal{N}$.

In the approach used in this paper, we assume that the events (transitions) in the ENI systems are not instantaneous. On the contrary, they are interpreted as representations of activities whose completion takes some time. However, their beginnings and ends are instantaneous.

If inhibitor arcs are not involved (i.e. the case of elementary nets), to represent transitions by their beginnings and ends, we might just replace each transition $\boxed{t}$ by the net $\boxed{Bt} \rightarrow (t) \rightarrow \boxed{Et}$ as proposed for example by Zuberek in [28] for Timed Petri nets. However, the inhibitor arcs cause some problems. In Figure 3, while the inhibitor arc (s_3, Bc) in the net $\mathcal{N}$ is obvious, the inhibitor arc (b, Bc) is not. We need it to prevent sequences as $BbBcEcEb$, which defines a stratified order corresponding to the step sequence $\{a\}\{b,c\}$, from being a firing sequence of $\mathcal{N}$ since it is not a firing step sequence of N.

We *assume* that the net $\mathcal{N}$ fully describes the behaviour of the net N and later provide some justification of this claim.

Below we provide a formal transformation of inhibitor nets into their interval representations.

Definition 5 (Transforming ENI into its interval representation).
Let $N = (P, T, F, I, C_{init})$ *be an ENI system. We define* $\mathcal{N} = (\mathcal{P}, \mathcal{T}, \mathcal{F}, \mathcal{I}, C_{init})$, *its* **interval representation** *as follows:*

1. $\mathcal{P} = P \cup T$
2. $\mathcal{T} = \{Bt \mid t \in T\} \cup \{Et \mid t \in T\}$
3. $\forall\, p \in P.\, t \in T.\;\; (p, t) \in F \iff (p, Bt) \in \mathcal{F}$
4. $\forall\, p \in P.\, t \in T.\;\; (t, p) \in F \iff (Et, p) \in \mathcal{F}$
5. $\forall\, t \in T.\;\; (Bt, t), (t, Et) \in \mathcal{F}$
6. $\forall\, p \in P.\, t \in T.\;\; (p, t) \in I \iff (p, Bt) \in \mathcal{I} \wedge (\forall r \in p^{\bullet}.\, (r, Bt) \in \mathcal{I})$. □

The nets N and $\mathcal{N}$ in Figure 3 illustrate the above definition. Note that for example each of the following sequences $BaBcEaBbEbEc$, $BaBcEaBbEcEb$, $BcBaEaBbEbEc$, and $BcBaEaBbEcEb$ are *firing sequences* of $\mathcal{N}$, and each of them represents the *interval order* $<^N_4$ from Figure 2 via Fishburn Theorem (Theorem 1). *This means that event b follows event a and event c overlaps both events a and b in the original net* N.

Directly from the above definition we have the following convenient result.

Fact 1   *Let* $N = (P, T, F, I, C_{init})$ *be an ENI system and* $\mathcal{N} = (\mathcal{P}, \mathcal{T}, \mathcal{F}, \mathcal{I}, C_{init})$ *its interval representation. Then for each* $t \in T$ *we have:* ${}^{\bullet}Bt = {}^{\bullet}t$, $Bt^{\bullet} = \{t\}$, ${}^{\bullet}Et = \{t\}$, $Et^{\bullet} = t^{\bullet}$, ${}^{\circ}Bt = {}^{\circ}t \cup ({}^{\circ}t)^{\bullet}$, *and* ${}^{\circ}Et = \emptyset$. □

Since $\mathcal{N}$ is just another inhibitor net, we may use the standard definition of a firing sequence from Section 4, but with the following caveat: not every sequence from $\mathcal{T}^*$ can be interpreted as an interval order, for example $BaBcBb$ represents no interval order.

Let $\mathcal{D} \subseteq \mathcal{T}$ and let $s \in \mathcal{T}^*$. We define the projection of s onto $\mathcal{D}$ standardly as: $\;\pi_{\mathcal{D}}(\epsilon) \stackrel{df}{=} \epsilon,\;\; \pi_{\mathcal{D}}(s\alpha) \stackrel{df}{=} \begin{cases} \pi_{\mathcal{D}}(s)\alpha & \text{if } \alpha \in \mathcal{D}, \\ \pi_{\mathcal{D}}(s) & \text{if } \alpha \notin \mathcal{D}. \end{cases}$

For example $\pi_{\{Ba, Ea\}}(BbBaEbBaEaEc) = BaBaEa$ and $\pi_{\{Ba, Ea, Bc, Ec\}}(BbBaEbBaEaEc) = BaBaEaEc$. We say that a string $x \in \mathcal{T}^*$ is an **interval sequence** iff

$$\forall Bt, Et \in \mathcal{T}^*.\, \pi_{\{Bt, Et\}}(x) \in (BtEt)^*.$$

We use $\mathsf{InSeq}(\mathcal{T}^*)$ to denote the set of all interval sequences of $\mathcal{T}^*$.

Definition 6. *Let* $\mathcal{N} = (\mathcal{P}, \mathcal{T}, \mathcal{F}, \mathcal{I}, C_{init})$ *be an interval representation of ENI. A sequence* $x = \alpha_1 \ldots \alpha_n \in \mathcal{T}^*$ *is an* **interval firing sequence** *of* $\mathcal{N}$ *if there are markings* $C_1, \ldots, C_n$ *satisfying:*

$$C_{init}[t_1\rangle\rangle C_1 [t_2\rangle\rangle C_2 \ldots [t_n\rangle\rangle C_n.$$ □

To improve readability, we use $[\![\alpha\rangle\!\rangle$ to denote firing transition α in some configuration of the net $\mathcal{N}$.

For example, for $\mathcal{N}$ from Figure 3, we have $\{s_1, s_2\}[\![BcBaEaBbEcEb\rangle\!\rangle\{s_4, s_5\}$.

The following result validates the above definition.

Proposition 1. *If x is an interval firing sequence of $\mathcal{N}$, then $x \in \mathsf{InSeq}(\mathcal{T}^*)$.*

Proof. We have to show that for each $a \in T$, $\pi_{\{Ba, Ea\}}(x) \in (BaEa)^*$.

Let $x = y\,Ba\,z$ and $C_{init}[\![y\,Ba\rangle\!\rangle C'$. Since $Ba^\bullet = \{a\}$, $a \in C'$. We also have: for any $C_a \subseteq P \cup T$, if $a \in C_a$, then Ba is not enabled in C_a, and the only way to remove a from C_a is to fire Ea (as $^\bullet Ea = \{a\}$). Hence we must have $x = y\,Ba\,w\,Ea\,v$, where $\pi_{\{Ba, Ea\}}(w) = \varepsilon$. $\qquad\square$

Since all transitions of interval representation of ENI are instantaneous, simultaneous executions of any kind are disallowed [2], so the only operational semantics for interval representations, is the firing sequences semantics.

The net $\mathcal{N}$ from Figure 3 has ten interval firing sequences that involve all elements of $\mathcal{T} = \{Ba, Ea, Bb, Eb, Bc, Ec\}$, namely $BaEaBbEbBcEc$ - which represents a total order $<_1^{\mathsf{N}}$ from Figure 2; $BcEcBaEaBbEb$ - which represents a total order $<_2^{\mathsf{N}}$; $BaBcEcEaBbEb$, $BaBcEaEcBbEb$, $BcBaEcEaBbEb$, $BcBaEaEcBbEb$ - all four represent a stratified order $<_3^{\mathsf{N}}$ of Figure 2; and $BaBcEaBbEbEc$, $BaBcEaBbEcEb$, $BcBaEaBbEbEc$, $BcBaEaBbEcEb$ - all four represent an interval order $<_4^{\mathsf{N}}$ of Figure 2. It is important to stress that if observations are not allowed to be recorded as interval firing sequences, then $<_4^{\mathsf{N}}$ can be generated neither by firing sequence nor by firing step-sequence. This order is an interval order, but it is not stratified, so step-sequences do not work.

The following proposition shows soundness and completeness of the interval representation from Definition 5 with respect to firing step sequence operational semantics[3]. It shows that firing a step A in the net N is properly simulated by firing an appropriate sequence from $\mathcal{T}^*$ in the net $\mathcal{N}$. Moreover, while the net $\mathcal{N}$ defines behaviours that cannot be defined by N (as $<_4^{\mathsf{N}}$ for the net from Figure 2), it does not generate any new behaviour that can be described by firing step sequences of N.

For every $A = \{t_1, ..., t_k\} \subseteq T$, let $A^{BE} \subseteq \mathcal{T}^*$ be defined as follows. $A^{BE} = \{Bt_{i_1}...Bt_{i_k}Et_{j_1}...Et_{j_k} \mid i_1, ..., i_k$ and $j_1, ..., j_k$ are permutations of $1, 2, ..., k\}$.

For example
$$\{a, b\}^{BE} = \{BaBbEaEb, BaBbEbEa, BbBaEaEb, BbBaEbEa\}.$$

---

[2] Defining interval firing step sequences is mathematically possible but it does not make much sense as Bt and Et are interpreted as event beginning and end, i.e. they are *instantaneous*, so their simultaneous occurrence is not observable (cf. [10]).

[3] A separate analysis of firing sequence semantics is not needed as each sequence $a_1 ... a_n$ is uniquely represented by a step sequence $\{a_1\}...\{a_n\}$.

Proposition 2. *For every two configurations $C, C' \subseteq P \subseteq \mathcal{P}$ and every $A \subseteq T$,*

$$C \, [A\rangle \, C' \iff \forall x \in A^{BE}. \, C \, [\![x\rangle\!\rangle \, C'.$$

Proof. ($\Rightarrow$)   Let $A = \{t_1, ..., t_k\}$. This means, if $i \neq j$ then $(t_i^\bullet \cup {}^\bullet t_i) \cap (t_j^\bullet \cup {}^\bullet t_j) = \emptyset$, ${}^\bullet A \subseteq C$, $(A^\bullet \cap {}^\circ A) \cap C = \emptyset$, and $C' = (C \setminus {}^\bullet A) \cup A^\bullet$. Let $y = Bt_{i_1}...Bt_{i_k}$ and $z = Et_{j_1}...Et_{j_k}$, where $i_1, ..., i_k$ and $j_1, ..., j_k$ are permutations of $1, 2, ..., k$. Since ${}^\bullet t_i = {}^\bullet Bt_i$ and ${}^\circ t_i = {}^\circ Bt_i$, we have $C \, [\![y\rangle\!\rangle \, C_B$, where $C_B = (C \setminus ({}^\bullet Bt_{i_1} \cup ... {}^\bullet Bt_{i_k})) \cup (Bt_{i_1}^\bullet \cup ... Bt_{i_k}^\bullet) = (C \setminus {}^\bullet A) \cup (Bt_{i_1}^\bullet \cup ... Bt_{i_k}^\bullet)$. But $Bt_i^\bullet = \{t_i\}$, so $C_B = (C \setminus {}^\bullet A) \cup A$. However, ${}^\bullet Et_i = \{t_i\}$, so $C_B \, [\![z\rangle\!\rangle \, C_E$, where $C_E = (C_B \setminus ({}^\bullet Et_{j_1} \cup ... \cup {}^\bullet Et_{j_k})) \cup (Et_{j_1}^\bullet \cup ... Et_{j_k}^\bullet)$. Since ${}^\bullet Et_i = \{t_i\}$ and $Et_i^\bullet = t_i^\bullet$, $C_E = (C_B \setminus A) \cup A^\bullet = (((C \setminus {}^\bullet A) \cup A) \setminus A) \cup A^\bullet = (C \setminus {}^\bullet A) \cup A^\bullet = C'$.

Hence $C \, [A\rangle \, C' \implies \forall x \in A^{BE}. \, C \, [\![x\rangle\!\rangle \, C'$.

($\Leftarrow$)   Let $A = \{t_1, ..., t_k\}$ and $C \, [\![yz\rangle\!\rangle \, C'$. Hence there are configurations $C_B^0, C_B^1, ..., C_B^k, C_E^0, C_E^1, ..., C_E^k$ in N^{BE} such that $C = C_B^0$, $C_B^k = C_E^0$, $C_E^k = C'$, and $C_B^0 \, \{[Bt_{i_1}\rangle\!\rangle \, C_B^1 \, [Bt_{i_2}\rangle\!\rangle \, C_B^2 ... C_B^{k-1} \, [\![Bt_{i_k}\rangle\!\rangle \, C_B^k \, [\![Et_{j_1}\rangle\!\rangle \, C_E^1 \, [\![Et_{j_2}\rangle\!\rangle \, C_E^2 ... C_E^{k-1} \, [\![Et_{j_k}\rangle\!\rangle \, C_E^k$. We have $C_B^{l+1} = (C_B^l \setminus {}^\bullet Bt_{i_l}) \cup Bt_{i_l}^\bullet$, and $C_E^{l+1} = (C_E^l \setminus {}^\bullet Et_{j_l}) \cup Et_{j_l}^\bullet$, for $l = 0, ..., k - 1$. Because ${}^\bullet Bt_i = {}^\bullet t_i$, and $Bt_i^\bullet = \{t_i\}$, then $C_E^0 = C_B^k = (C_B^0 \setminus {}^\bullet A) \cup A = (C \setminus {}^\bullet A) \cup A$. However, ${}^\bullet Et_i = \{t_i\}$ and $Et_i^\bullet = t_i^\bullet$, so $C_E^k = (C_E^0 \setminus A) \cup A^\bullet$. Thus, $C' = C_E^k = (C_E^0 \setminus A) \cup A^\bullet = (((C \setminus {}^\bullet A) \cup A) \setminus A) \cup A^\bullet = (C \setminus {}^\bullet A) \cup A^\bullet$. But this means $C \, [A\rangle \, C'$. $\square$

We will end this section with an analysis of the example from Figure 4. The nets N_{io}, CN_{io} and AN_{io} are clearly equivalent and none of them can generate a sequence or step sequence that leads from the marking $\{s_1, s_2\}$ to the marking $\{s_4, s_5\}$.

When our approach is used, the nets N_{io}, CN_{io} and AN_{io} are assumed to be equivalently represented by their interval representations $\mathcal{N}_{io}$, $\mathcal{CN}_{io}$ and $\mathcal{AN}_{io}$. For the latter nets, a firing sequence $z = BaBcEaBbEcEb$ leads from the marking $\{s_1, s_2\}$ to the marking $\{s_4, s_5\}$. Moreover the sequence z is an interval sequence, and by Theorem 1, the total order $\lhd_z$ uniquely represents the interval order $<_4^N$, as intuitively expected (skip the net $\mathcal{P}_z$ at this moment).

6   Process Semantics for Elementary Nets with Inhibitor Arcs

This section comprises the main results of [14, 16, 17] as our approach presented in the next section is partially based on them.

One of the essential parts of concurrent processing is that many different system runs/executions are equivalent, but this aspect is difficult to capture when only operational semantics is considered. Abstractions of these equivalent executions are often called *concurrent histories* or *non-sequential execution histories*, and dependent on the assumptions about systems and system runs, are usually modeled by partial orders [9, 22], stratified order structures or interval order structures [12, 14, 17].

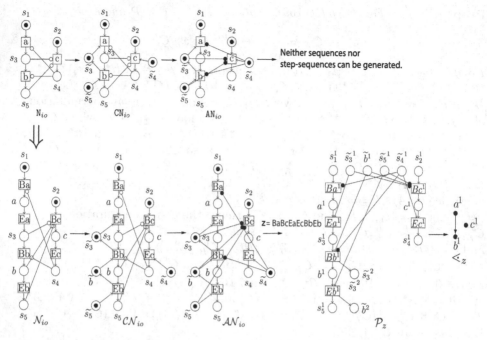

Fig. 4. An example of an inhibitor net that generates *only* interval orders. Our method results in the process $\mathcal{P}_z$ and the interval order $<_z$, which is isomorphic to $<^N_4$ of Figure 2, while all techniques based on either firing sequences or firing step sequences (c.f. [4,14,16,17,20,25,27]) produce empty set.

For the net N from Figure 2, the runs $<^N_2, <^N_3$, and $<^N_4$ are equivalent as in all cases we have event c no later than event a, so N has two concurrent histories involving all three events a, b, c. In $<^N_1$, a and b occur before c, so $<^N_1$ belongs to a different concurrent history[4] (see [10,11] for details).

In the case of Petri nets, with or without inhibitor arcs, *occurrence nets* are usually used to capture non-sequential execution histories. For nets without inhibitor arcs, an occurrence net generated by a firing sequence or a step sequence x, is just a net unfolding caused by the execution of x (c.f. [9,17,24]).

However, it was shown in [14,17] that for nets *with* inhibitor arcs, plain unfolding does not work, since the absence of a token, unlike the presence of a token, cannot be tested. Hence we have to replace inhibitor arcs by appropriate activator arcs. The idea is that an *inhibitor arc* which tests whether a place is empty, can be simulated by an *activator arc* which tests whether its *complement place* is not empty. To do such simulation, each inhibitor place must have its complements, if it does not we can always add it, as it *does not change the*

---

[4] A concurrent history is a set of runs that agree on causality invariants as "always earlier than" or "always not later than" (see [10,11] for formal arguments).

net behaviour (c.f. [9,14,17,22]). This construction is illustrated in Figure 3, the upper part for a firing step sequence and the lower part for a firing sequence.

Definition 7 ([9]). *Places $p, q \in P$ are **complementary** (p is a complement of q and vice versa) if $p \neq q$, $^\bullet p = q^\bullet$ and $p^\bullet = {}^\bullet q$, and $|C_{init} \cap \{p, q\}| = 1$.*   □

If p and q are complementary we will write $p = \widetilde{q}, q = \widetilde{p}$, and clearly $p = \widetilde{\widetilde{p}}, q = \widetilde{\widetilde{q}}$.

We may now assume that *every inhibitor place has its complement*, i.e. $(p, t) \in I \implies \widetilde{p} \in P$. We will call the nets with this property *complement closed*. This idea is illustrated in Figure 3 where the nets N and $\mathcal{N}$ are not complement closed, so they are extended to CN and $\mathcal{CN}$. Clearly the behaviours of N and CN, and of $\mathcal{N}$ and $\mathcal{CN}$ are identical (see [17]) for details.

We will now provide formal definitions of processes for elementary nets with inhibitor arcs $N = (P, T, F, I, C_{init})$, first generated by a firing sequence $y = t_1 \ldots t_n, t_i \in T$ and next generated by a step sequence $x = U_1 \ldots U_n, U_i \subseteq T$.

We define the processes generated by $y = t_1 \ldots t_n$ as $P_y = N_n$, where N_n is the last *activator occurrence net* in the sequence $N_0, \ldots, N_n$. Each net $N_k = (B_k, E_k, R_k, A_k), 0 \leq k \leq n$, is a net with *activator arcs* that model an unfolding of the net N by the sequence $t_1 \ldots t_k$. The first three components of N_k correspond to places P, transitions T, and flow relation F of the underlying net N, while $A_k \subseteq B_k \times E_k$ is the set of activator arcs derived from inhibitors arcs I.

The elements of $B_k \cup E_k$ are of the form r^i, where $r \in P \cup T$ and $i \geq 1$. We will denote $l(r^i) = r$. Moreover, for every $r \in P \cup T$ and $k \leq n$, Δr is the number of nodes of N_{k-1} labelled by r (i.e. the number of $\alpha \in B_k \cup E_k$ such that $l(\alpha) = r$.)

Algorithm 1 (Constructing P_y, for $y = t_1 \ldots t_n$, [14,17])

- *Step 0.* $N_0 = (\{(p^1) \mid p \in C_{init}\}, \emptyset, \emptyset, \emptyset)$
- *Step k.* Given N_{k-1}, we define N_k in the following way:
  - $B_k = B_{k-1} \cup \{p^{1+\Delta p} \mid p \in t_k^\bullet\}$
  - $E_k = E_{k-1} \cup \{t_k^{1+\Delta t_k}\}$
  - $R_k = R_{k-1} \cup \{(p^{\Delta p}, t_k^{1+\Delta t_k}) \mid p \in {}^\bullet t_k\} \cup \{(t_k^{1+\Delta t_k}, p^{1+\Delta p}) \mid p \in t_k^\bullet\}$
  - $A_k = A_{k-1} \cup \{(\widetilde{p}^{\Delta \widetilde{p}}, t_k^{1+\Delta t_k}) \mid p \in {}^\circ t_k\}$ □

The above algorithm is illustrated in Figure 3. When it is applied to the net $\mathcal{N}$ (actually to $\mathcal{CN}$) with the (standard) *firing sequence* $y = BaBcEaEcBbEb$ it results in the process P_y. When applied to the net N (actually CN) with the firing sequence $x = cab$, it results in the process P_x. Intuitively, P_y is a standard unfolding of $\mathcal{AN}$ according to $BaBcEaEcBbEb$, while P_x is a standard unfolding of AN according to cab. The net $\mathcal{N}$ is a standard elementary net with inhibitor arcs, and the only additional assumption is that the transitions are instantaneous, so Algorithm 1 can be applied.

An extension of Algorithm 1 to the case of firing step sequence $x = U_1 \ldots U_n$ (first proposed in [14]) is rather straightforward.

Algorithm 2 (Constructing P_x for $x = U_1 \ldots U_n$, [14,17])

- *Step 0.* $N_0 = (\{(p^1) \mid p \in C_{init}\}, \emptyset, \emptyset, \emptyset)$
- *Step k. Given N_{k-1}, we define N_k in the following way:*
  - $B_k = B_{k-1} \cup \{p^{1+\Delta p} \mid p \in U_k^{\bullet}\}$
  - $E_k = E_{k-1} \cup \{t^{1+\Delta t} \mid t \in U_k\}$
  - $R_k = R_{k-1} \cup \{(p^{\Delta p}, t^{1+\Delta t}) \mid t \in U_k \wedge p \in {}^{\bullet}t\} \cup$
    $\{(t^{1+\Delta t}, p^{1+\Delta p}) \mid t \in U_k \wedge p \in t^{\bullet}\}$
  - $A_k = A_{k-1} \cup \{(\widetilde{p}^{\Delta \widetilde{p}}, t^{1+\Delta t}) \mid t \in U_k \wedge p \in {}^{\circ}t\}$ ☐

The upper part of Figure 3 illustrates Algorithm 2. When it is applied to the net N (actually CN) with the *step sequence* $x = \{a, c\}\{b\}$, it results in the process P_x. Note that the step sequence $\{c\}\{a\}\{b\}$ also generates the same process P_x.

The occurrence nets generated by both algorithms can be viewed as partial unfoldings of the original net such that each event in the process represents a transition occurrence of the original net while each condition corresponds to the presence of a token in a place in the original net. If the original net does not have any inhibitor arcs, the generated occurrence nets are the same as these for standard elementary nets (c.f. [14,22]).

We will now show how processes, i.e. occurrence nets, can be interpreted as *concurrent histories*. When a process P_y is generated from a firing sequence $y = t_1 \ldots t_n$ using Algorithm 1, P_y can be interpreted as some partial order $<_y$. The partial order $<_y$ is obtained by first transforming P_y into a *directed acyclic graph* $<_y^{init}$ using the rules described in the upper part of Figure 5 and then constructing a transitive closure of $<_y^{init}$ (i.e. $<_y = (<_y^{init})^+$, see [17] and Definition 8 in the next section for details).

When a process P_x is generated from a firing step sequence $x = A_1 \ldots A_n$ using Algorithm 2, the process P_x can be interpreted as some stratified order structure $S^x = (E_n, \prec_x, \sqsubset_x)$ (where E_n is from the last step of Algorithm 2). The stratified order structure S^x is obtained by first transforming P_x into a tuple $(E_n, \prec_x^{init}, \sqsubset_x^{init})$ using the rules described also in the upper part of Figure 5 and then constructing ◊-closure (i.e. a transitive closure for stratified relational structures [14]) of $(E_n, \prec_x^{init}, \sqsubset_x^{init})$. Due to the lack of space we will not discuss this construction in detail, the reader is referenced to [11,14,17,18].

Both constructions are illustrated in Figure 5. Note that $P_{cab} = P_{\{c\}\{a\}\{b\}}$, but $<_{cab}$ is a partial order, while $S^{\{c\}\{a\}\{b\}}$ is a stratified order structure.

The partial order $<_y$ defines a concurrent behaviour comprising all total extensions of $<_y$ (this includes the total order defined by the sequence y). For the case from Figure 5, $<_{cab}$ is a total order, equal to $<_2^N$ of Figure 2 so its only total extension is $<_2^N$. Note that concurrent history $hist_2^N$, when restricted to total orders, is equal to $\{<_2^N\}$.

The stratified order structure $S^x = (E_n, \prec_x, \sqsubset_x)$ defines a concurrent behaviour comprising all stratified order extensions of S^x. For the case from Figure 5, $S^{\{a,c\}\{b\}} = S^{\{c\}\{a\}\{b\}}$ and after identifying a^1 with a, b^1 with b, and c^1 with c, $strat(S^{\{a,c\}\{b\}}) = \{<_2^N, <_3^N\}$, where $<_2^N$ and $<_3^N$ are these from Figure 2. If we restrict the concurrent history $hist_2^N$ to stratified orders only, it is equal to $\{<_2^N, <_3^N\}$.

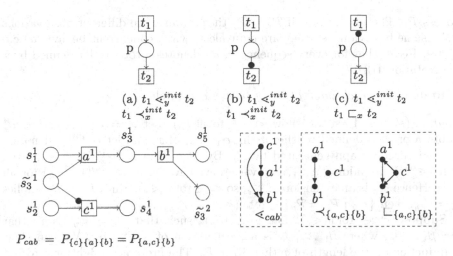

$$P_{cab} = P_{\{c\}\{a\}\{b\}} = P_{\{a,c\}\{b\}}$$

Fig. 5. An example of deriving a partial order and a stratified order structure from an activator occurrence net

However, neither approach from this section can generate the interval order $<_4^N$ nor any abstract structure that comprises it.

7   Interval Processes and Interval Order Structures

This section contains the second part of our contribution.

We will now introduce interval processes and show how they represent interval runs/executions as well as how they relate to interval order structures.

Let $N = (P, T, F, I, C_{init})$ be an ENI system, $\mathcal{N} = (\mathcal{P}, \mathcal{T}, \mathcal{F}, \mathcal{I}, C_{init})$ be its interval representation and let $x = \alpha_1 \ldots \alpha_n$ be an interval firing sequence of $\mathcal{N}$. Since $\mathcal{N}$ is just another inhibitor nets, we can use Algorithm 1 (with $\mathcal{CN}$) and produce a process (an occurrence net) $\mathcal{P}_x$ generated by $x = \alpha_1 \ldots \alpha_n$. Assume that $\mathcal{P}_x = \mathcal{N}_n = (\mathcal{B}_n, \mathcal{E}_n, \mathcal{R}_n, \mathcal{A}_n)$, where $\mathcal{N}_n$ is the last step of Algorithm 1. We can formally define a partial order $<_x$ derived from the process $\mathcal{P}_x$ in the following way.

Definition 8. *Let* $\mathcal{P}_x = \mathcal{N}_n = (\mathcal{B}_n, \mathcal{E}_n, \mathcal{R}_n, \mathcal{A}_n)$ *be the process generated by* x. *We define a* **directed acyclic graph** $<_x^{init}$ *and a* **partial order** $<_x$, *both on* $\mathcal{E}_n$ *as follows:*

1. *For all* $\alpha, \beta \in \mathcal{E}_n$,
$$\alpha <_x^{init} \beta \iff \alpha(\mathcal{R}_n \circ \mathcal{R}_n)\beta \vee \alpha(\mathcal{R}_n \circ \mathcal{A}_n)\beta \vee \alpha(\mathcal{A}_n^{-1} \circ \mathcal{R}_n)\beta$$
2. *For all* $\alpha, \beta \in \mathcal{E}_n$, $\alpha <_x \beta \iff \alpha(<_x^{init})^+\beta$ □

The above construction is illustrated in Figure 5 (upper part illustrates (1) of Definition 8, and $\mathcal{P}_{cab}$ produces $<_{cab}$) and in Figure 6 ($\mathcal{P}_x$ produces $<_x^{init}$, and $<_x^{init}$ produces $<_x$). In most cases many different x's can generate the same process $\mathcal{P}_x$. The idea is that if $\mathcal{P}_x = \mathcal{P}_y$ then x and y are different observations of the same behaviour, so they are equivalent (w.r.t. concurrent behaviour) c.f. [17, 18]. Recall that for every sequence x, $\lhd_x$ denotes a total order defined by x (see Notation 1(3)).

Lemma 1. *For each interval firing sequence x,* $\mathsf{total}(<_x) = \{\lhd_y \mid \mathcal{P}_x = \mathcal{P}_y\}$.

Proof. (*sketch*) First we show $\lhd_x \in \mathsf{total}(<_x)$. Let $x = \alpha_1 \dots \alpha_n$. Let P_x^i denote a process defined by the prefix $\alpha_1 \dots \alpha_i$ of x, and let $(<_x^{init})^i$ denote a directed acyclic graph generated by P_x^i. By Algorithm 1, $(<_x^{init})^{i+1}$ is derived from $(<_x^{init})^i$ by adding α_{i+1}, but we always have $\neg(\alpha_{i+1}(<_x^{init})^{i+1}\alpha_k)$ for all $k \le i$. Hence $\lhd_x$ is an extension of $<_x$, so $\lhd_x \in \mathsf{total}(<_x)$. Since $\mathcal{P}_x = \mathcal{P}_y$ implies $<_x = <_y$, then $\{\lhd_y \mid \mathcal{P}_x = \mathcal{P}_y\} \subseteq \mathsf{total}(<_x)$.

Suppose $\lhd \in \mathsf{total}(<_x)$. Let $y \in (\mathcal{E}_n)^*$ such that $\lhd = \lhd_y$. Note that $y = \beta_1 \dots \beta_n$, where $\beta_1, \dots, \beta_n$ is a permutation of $\alpha_1, \dots, \alpha_n$. We can show by induction on the length of x that $\mathcal{P}_x = \mathcal{P}_y$. The proof is straightforward but lengthy and is omitted. Hence $\mathsf{total}(<_x) \subseteq \{\lhd_y \mid \mathcal{P}_x = \mathcal{P}_y\}$. □

Lemma 1 states that total orders defined by all sequences that can generate a process (occurrence activator net) $\mathcal{P}_x$ are just total extensions of a partial order $<_x$ that is defined by the process $\mathcal{P}_x$.

We will now define formally interval orders and interval order structures generated by interval firing sequences of $\mathcal{N}$.

Definition 9. *Let $x \in \mathsf{InSeq}(\mathcal{T}^*)$, $\mathcal{P}_x = \mathcal{N}_n = (\mathcal{B}_n, \mathcal{E}_n, \mathcal{R}_n, \mathcal{A}_n)$ be the process generated by x, and let $\widehat{E}_n = \{t^i \mid Bt^i \in \mathcal{E}_n \wedge Et^i \in \mathcal{E}_n\} \subseteq \widehat{T}$.*
We define the relations $\blacktriangleleft_x, \prec_x, \sqsubset_x$ on $\widehat{E}_n$, and the tuple S^x as follows:

1. *$a^i \blacktriangleleft_x b^j \overset{df}{\Longleftrightarrow} Ea^i \lhd_x Bb^j$,*
2. *$a^i \prec_x b^j \overset{df}{\Longleftrightarrow} Ea^i <_x Bb^j$,*
3. *$a^i \sqsubset_x b^j \overset{df}{\Longleftrightarrow} Ba^i <_x Eb^j$, and*
4. *$S^x = (\widehat{E}_n, \prec_x, \sqsubset_x)$.* □

Corollary 1. *1. The relation $\blacktriangleleft_x$ is an **interval order**.*
*2. The tuple S^x is an **interval order structure**.*

Proof. By Theorem 1 we have (1) and by Theorem 2 we have (2). □

The interval order structure S^x will be called **induced by process** $\mathcal{P}_x$.

Each $\mathcal{P}_x$ is generated from $\mathcal{N}$ by an interval sequence x and each interval sequence x defines an interval order $\blacktriangleleft_x$. The set of all interval orders that can be derived from $\mathcal{P}_x$ or $<_x$ is defined as follows.

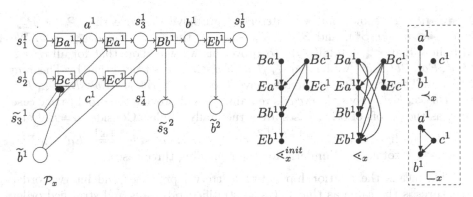

Fig. 6. An example of a process $\mathcal{P}_x$, the directed acyclic graph $\prec_x^{init}$, the partial order $\prec_x$, the relations $\prec_x$, $\sqsubset_x$ and the interval order structure $S^x = (\{a^1, b^1, c^1\}, \prec_x, \sqsubset_x)$. The (interval representation) net here is $\mathcal{N}$ from Figure 3, and $x = BaBcEaEcBbEb$.

Definition 10. *For each interval firing sequence x, we define,*

1. $\mathsf{interv}(\prec_x) = \{\blacktriangleleft_y \mid \lhd_y \in \mathsf{total}(\prec_x)\}$.
2. $interv(\mathcal{P}_x) = \{\blacktriangleleft_y \mid \mathcal{P}_x = \mathcal{P}_y\}$. □

The main result of this section states that for every interval firing sequence x, an interval process $\mathcal{P}_x$ and interval order structure S^x describe the same concurrent behaviour, so they can be seen as equivalent concepts.

Theorem 3. *For each interval firing sequence x,*

$$interv(S^x) = \mathsf{interv}(\prec_x) = interv(\mathcal{P}_x).$$

Proof. First we prove $\mathsf{interv}(\prec_x) = interv(\mathcal{P}_x)$. By Lemma 1, we have $\mathsf{total}(\prec_x) = \{\lhd_y \mid \mathcal{P}_x = \mathcal{P}_y\}$. Hence $\blacktriangleleft_y \in \mathsf{interv}(\prec_x) \iff \lhd_y \in \mathsf{total}(\prec_x) \iff \mathcal{P}_x = \mathcal{P}_y$
$\iff \blacktriangleleft_y \in interv(\mathcal{P}_x)$. Thus $\mathsf{interv}(\prec_x) = interv(\mathcal{P}_x)$.

We will now show $interv(S^x) = \mathsf{interv}(\prec_x)$. First we will prove $interv(S^x) \subseteq \mathsf{interv}(\prec_x)$. Let $\blacktriangleleft_y \in \mathsf{interv}(\prec_x)$, i.e. $\mathcal{P}_x = \mathcal{P}_y$. Consider the relation $\prec_x$. We have:
$$a^i \prec b^j \overset{\text{Def.9(2)}}{\iff} Ea^i <_x Bb^j \overset{\mathcal{P}_x = \mathcal{P}_y}{\iff} Ea^i <_y Bb^j \overset{\text{Lem.1}}{\implies} Ea^i \lhd_y Bb^j \overset{\text{Def.9(1)}}{\iff} a^i \blacktriangleleft_y b^i.$$
Hence $\blacktriangleleft_y$ is an extension of $\prec_x$. For the relation $\sqsubset_x$ we have: $a^i \sqsubset b^j \overset{\text{Def.9(3)}}{\iff}$
$Ba^i <_x Eb^j \overset{\mathcal{P}_x = \mathcal{P}_y}{\iff} Ba^i <_y Eb^j \overset{\text{Lem.1}}{\implies} Ba^i \lhd_y Eb^j \iff \neg(Eb^j \lhd_y Ba^i) \overset{\text{Def.9(1)}}{\iff}$
$\neg(b^j \blacktriangleleft_y a^i) \iff a^i \blacktriangleleft_y \frown b^j$, so $\blacktriangleleft_y$ extends $\sqsubset_x$ too. Hence $\blacktriangleleft_y \in interv(S^x)$.

Now we show $interv(\mathcal{P}_x) \subseteq \mathsf{interv}(\prec_x)$ *(sketch)*. Let $\blacktriangleleft \in interv(S^x)$ and let $\lhd_\blacktriangleleft$ be a total order representation of $\blacktriangleleft$ via Theorem 1, i.e. $a^i \blacktriangleleft b^j \iff Ea^i \lhd_\blacktriangleleft Bb^j$. Let $x_\blacktriangleleft \in \mathcal{E}_n$ be the sequence representation of the total order $\lhd_\blacktriangleleft$, i.e. $\lhd_\blacktriangleleft = \lhd_{x_\blacktriangleleft}$, where $\lhd_{x_\blacktriangleleft}$ is the total order generated by $x_\blacktriangleleft$. By Definition

9, $\blacktriangleleft = \blacktriangleleft_{x_\blacktriangleleft}$. To show that $\blacktriangleleft \in$ interv$(<_x)$, we have to prove that $\mathcal{P}_x = P_{x_\blacktriangleleft}$. Since $\blacktriangleleft \in interv(S^x)$, and $S^x = (\mathcal{E}_n, \prec_x, \sqsubset_x)$, then $\prec_x \subseteq \blacktriangleleft$ and $\sqsubset_x \subseteq \blacktriangleleft^\frown$. We will show that $\lhd_\blacktriangleleft \in$ total$(<_x)$. To prove this we will show that for all $\alpha, \beta \in \{Ba^i, Ea^i, Bb^j, Eb^j\}$ we have $\alpha <_x \beta \implies \alpha \lhd_\blacktriangleleft \beta$. First note that by Theorem 2(1) and Theorem 1(1) we already have $Ba^i <_x Ea^i$, $Bb^j <_x Eb^j$, $Ba^i \lhd_\blacktriangleleft Ea^i$ and $Bb^j \lhd_\blacktriangleleft Eb^j$, so only four cases remain. We will provide the proof to one case only, as the proofs of other cases are structurally similar. Consider $\alpha = Ea^i$ and $\beta = Bb^j$. We have $Ea^i <_x Bb^j \overset{\text{Def.9}(2)}{\Longleftrightarrow} a^i \prec_x b^j \implies a^i \blacktriangleleft b^j \overset{\text{Th.1}}{\Longleftrightarrow} Ea^i \lhd_\blacktriangleleft Bb^j$. Hence $\lhd_\blacktriangleleft \in$ total$(<_x)$. Similarly for the remaining three cases. $\square$

This means the relationship between interval processes and interval order structures is the same as that between stratified processes and stratified order structures described and analyzed in [11,17,18]. Figures 3 and 6 illustrate the results presented above. Figure 3 illustrates the entire procedure, but does not gives the details of the step from $\mathcal{P}_y$ to S^y for a given sequence $y = BaBcEaEcBbEb$. Figure 6 illustrates the relationships between $\mathcal{P}_x$, $<_x^{init}$, $<_x$ and $S^x = (\widehat{E}_n, \prec_x, \sqsubset_x)$, for a given $x = BaBcEaEcBbEb$ and the net $\mathcal{N}$ from Figure 3. Note that the relationship from Figure 6 is valid for any $x \in \{BaEaBbEbBcEc, BcEcBaEaBbEb, BaBcEcEaBbEb, BaBcEaEcBbEb, BcBaEcEaBbEb, BcBaEaEcBbEb, BaBcEaBbEbEc, BaBcEaBbEcEb, BcBaEaBbEbEc, BcBaEaBbEcEb\}$. Also for each x as above, interv$(\mathcal{P}_x) =$ interv$(S^x) = \{<_2^N, <_3^N, <_4^N\}$, where $<_2^N, <_3^N, <_4^N$ are these of Figure 2 (when a^1, b^1, c^1 are replaced by a, b, c).

The net N_{io} from Figure 4 can generate only interval behaviours. It generates neither sequences nor step sequences that start from the marking $\{s_1, s_2\}$ and end at $\{s_4, s_5\}$. This also means that the nets N_{io}, CN_{io}, and AN_{io} generate no appropriate process, if the process derivation is based on a firing sequence or firing step sequence, and this includes all techniques presented in [4,14,16,17,20,25,27] and all their modifications. On the other hand, the interval representation of N_{io}, the net $\mathcal{N}_{io}$ generates interval sequences, for example $z = BaBcEaBbEcEb$, that lead from $\{s_1, s_2\}$ to $\{s_4, s_5\}$. The interval sequence z generates the process $\mathcal{P}_z$, which in turn describes the interval order $<_z$ which equals $<_4^N$ (again with a^1, b^1, c^1 replaced by a, b, c). Since $<_4^N$ is the only observation generated by N_{io}, we have $S^z = (\{a^1, b^1, c^1\}, \prec_z, \sqsubset_z)$, where $\prec_z = <_4^N$ and $\sqsubset_z = (<_4^N)^\frown$, and interv$(\mathcal{P}_z) =$ interv$(S^z) = \{<_4^N\}$.

We will now show that the model based on the concept of step sequences and stratified processes can be defined in terms of interval processes with identical results, which could be seen as a *validation of our approach*.

Let $\mathsf{N} = (P, T, F, I, C_{init})$ be an ENI system, $\mathcal{N} = (\mathcal{P}, \mathcal{T}, \mathcal{F}, \mathcal{I}, C_{init})$ be its interval representation, $x = A_1 \ldots A_n$ be a *firing step sequence* of N, and let $ifs(x)$ be the *set of interval firing sequences* of $\mathcal{N}$ corresponding to x, i.e.
$$ifs(x) = \{z \mid z = x_1 \ldots x_n, x_i \in A_i^{BE}, \text{ for } i = 1 \ldots n\}.$$
Let $\overline{x} \in ifs(x)$ and assume that $length(\overline{x}) = k$. Let $P_x = N_n = (B_k, E_k, R_k, A_k)$ be a process derived from N by using Algorithm 2 and step

firing sequence x, and let $\mathcal{P}_{\overline{x}} = \mathcal{N}_n = (\mathcal{B}_k, \mathcal{E}_k, \mathcal{R}_k, \mathcal{A}_k)$ be a process derived from $\mathcal{N}$ by using Algorithm 1 and interval firing sequence $\overline{x}$. We also define $strat(P_x) = \{<_y|\ P_x = P_y\}$ (c.f. [17]), and for each set X, let $\mathtt{strat}(X)$ denote the set of all stratified orders on X. The followig result has been proved in [14].

Theorem 4 ([14,17]). *For every firing step sequence x,*

$$strat(P_x) = strat(S^x),$$

where S^x is a stratified order structure derived from P_x. □

The last two results of this paper show that for firing step sequences, i.e. when runs are represented by stratified orders, standard stratified order processes of [14,17] and our interval processes produce the same results.

Lemma 2. *For each firing step sequences x, y and each $\overline{x} \in ifs(x)$, $\overline{y} \in ifs(y)$, we have*

$$P_x = P_y \iff \mathcal{P}_{\overline{x}} = \mathcal{P}_{\overline{y}}.$$

Proof. (*Sketch*)   By induction on the number of steps of x, using the specific properties of Algorithms 1 and 2, and the reasoning similar to the one used in the proof of Proposition 2. □

Theorem 5. *For every firing step sequence x, we have*

$$strat(P_x) = interv(\mathcal{P}_{\overline{x}}) \cap \mathtt{strat}(\mathcal{E}_n).$$

Proof. (*Sketch*) Let $< \in strat(P_x)$. This means there is a step sequence $y = B_1 \ldots B_r$ such that $< = \lhd_y$, where $\lhd_y$ is a stratified order defined by y, and $P_x = P_y$. By Lemma 2, $\mathcal{P}_{\overline{x}} = \mathcal{P}_{\overline{y}}$, so $<_{\overline{x}} \in interv(\mathcal{P}_{\overline{x}})$, and by Proposition 2, $\blacktriangleleft_{\overline{x}} = \lhd_y$ (where $\blacktriangleleft_{\overline{x}}$ is an interval order defined by the sequence $\overline{x}$), and $\blacktriangleleft_{\overline{x}} \in \mathtt{strat}(\mathcal{E}_n)$, so $strat(P_x) \subseteq interv(\mathcal{P}_{\overline{x}}) \cap \mathtt{strat}(\mathcal{E}_n)$. Let $< \in interv(\mathcal{P}_{\overline{x}}) \cap \mathtt{strat}(\mathcal{E}_n)$. This means there is an interval sequence z such that $\lhd_z$ represents $<$ via Theorem 1 and $\mathcal{P}_z = \mathcal{P}_{\overline{x}}$. Since $<$ is a stratified order, by Proposition 2 there is a set of steps $B_1, \ldots, B_r$ such that $z = z_1 \ldots z_r$ and $z_i \in B_i^{BE}$, $i = 1, \ldots, r$. Define $z' = B_1 \ldots B_r$. By Proposition 2 again, $< = <_{z'}$, where $\lhd_{z'}$ is the stratified order defined by z'. Clearly $\overline{z'} = z$. By Lemma 2(2), $P_x = P_{z'}$, so $\lhd_{z'} \in strat(P_x)$. Hence $interv(\mathcal{P}_{\overline{x}}) \cap \mathtt{strat}(\mathcal{E}_n) \subseteq strat(P_x)$. □

The last two results are partially illustrated by the far right part of Figure 3. For $x = \{a, c\}\{b\}$, we have $ifs(x) = \{BaBcEaEcBaBb, BaBcEcEaBaBb, BcBaEaEcBaBb, BcBaEcEaBaBb\}$, so $y = BaBcEaEcBaBb \in ifs(x)$. We can show by inspection that $interv(\mathcal{P}_y) = \{<_2^N, <_3^N, <_4^N\}$ and $interv(\mathcal{P}_y) \cap \mathtt{strat}(\{a^1, b^1, c^1\}) = \{<_2^N, <_3^N\}$. Moreover, using the results of [14,17], we may show that $strat(P_x) = \{<_2^N, <_3^N\}$, as required by Theorem 5.

8   Final Comments

In this paper we have provided both an interval order operational semantics and an interval process semantics for Petri nets with inhibitor arcs. From this interval process semantics we then derived an interval 'true concurrency' semantics in terms of interval order structures.

We started with transforming a given net N with inhibitor arcs into another net $\mathcal{N}$ that is called the interval interpretation of N. We assume that all behavioural properties of N are defined by appropriate behavioural properties of $\mathcal{N}$. Then we define both operational and process semantics of $\mathcal{N}$, and show how an interval order structure that characterizes N is derived from a given interval process of $\mathcal{N}$, i.e. its interval representation. When operational semantics is restricted to step sequences, or stratified orders, our model produces the same results as that of [14,17]. It is possible to derive interval processes directly from N, without using $\mathcal{N}$ or explicit complementary places, but some intuition is then lost, so we do not explore this issue here. Last, but not least, we would like to point out that some nets with inhibitor arcs produce *only* pure interval behaviours, i.e. they generate neither firing sequences nor firing step sequences, only interval firing sequences. The net N_{io} from Figures 2 and 4 is one of such nets. If observations are only represented as step sequences, then N_{io} generates no behaviour at all. However, if runs are represented as interval orders, then it generates an observation (system run) that is exactly the interval order $<_4^N$. This cannot be modeled by standard semantics so behaviours of such nets can only be analyzed using our model. Concurrent systems are known for generating extremely complex behaviours, so there is a need for tools that can adequately model all of them, even if some do not occur often.

While adding activator arcs to our model is almost obvious (we are using them to represent processes anyway), an extension to general Place/Transition nets (as [16] did with the model of [14,17]) is a serious future research project.

Acknowledgments. We would like to thank the anonymous referees, Raymond Devillers and Adam Lenarčič for their comments and useful suggestions.

References

1. Abraham, U., Ben-David, S., Magidor, M.: On global-time and inter-process communication. In: Semantics for Concurrency, Workshops in Computing, pp. 311–323. Springer (1990)
2. Agerwala, T., Flynn, M.: Comments on capabilities, limitations and "correctness" of Petri nets. Computer Architecture News **4**(2), 81–86 (1973)
3. Baldan, P., Busi, N., Corradini, A., Pinna, G.M.: Domain and event structure semantics for Petri nets with read and inhibitor arcs. Theoretical Computer Science **323**, 129–189 (2004)
4. Busi, N., Pinna, G.M.: Process semantics for place/transition nets with inhibitor and read arcs. Fundamenta Informaticae **40**(2,3), 165–197 (1999)
5. Chiola, G., Donatelli, S., Francheschinis, G.: Priorities, inhibitor arcs and concurrency in P/T-nets. In: Proc. of ATPN 1991 (Applications and Theory of Petri Nets), Gjern, Denmark, pp. 182–205 (1991)

6. Fishburn, P.C.: Intransitive indifference with unequal indifference intervals. Journal of Mathematical Psychology **7**, 144–149 (1970)
7. Fishburn, P.C.: Interval Orders and Interval Graphs. John Wiley, New York (1985)
8. Gaifman, H., Pratt, V.: Partial order models of concurrency and the computation of function. In: Proc. of LICS 1987 (Logic in Computer Science), pp. 72–85
9. Goltz, U., Reisig, W.: The non-sequential behaviour of Petri nets. Information and Control **57**(2), 125–147 (1983)
10. Janicki, R.: Relational Structures Model of Concurrency. Acta Informatica **45**, 279–320 (2008)
11. Janicki, R., Kleijn, J., Koutny, M.: Quotient monoids and concurrent behaviours. In: Martin-Vide, C. (ed.) Scientific Applications of Language Methods, pp. 311–385. Imperial College Press, London (2010)
12. Janicki, R., Koutny, M.: Invariants and paradigms of concurrency theory. In: Aarts, E.H.L., van Leeuwen, J., Rem, M. (eds.) PARLE 1991. LNCS, vol. 506, pp. 59–74. Springer, Heidelberg (1991)
13. Janicki, R., Koutny, M.: Structure of Concurrency. Theoretical Computer Science **112**, 5–52 (1993)
14. Janicki, R., Koutny, M.: Semantics of Inhibitor Nets. Information and Computation **123**(1), 1–16 (1995)
15. Janicki, R., Koutny, M.: Fundamentals of Modelling Concurrency Using Discrete Relational Structures. Acta Informatica **34**, 367–388 (1997)
16. Juhás, G., Lorenz, R., Mauser, S.: Complete process semantics for inhibitor nets. In: Kleijn, J., Yakovlev, A. (eds.) ICATPN 2007. LNCS, vol. 4546, pp. 184–203. Springer, Heidelberg (2007)
17. Kleijn, H.C.M., Koutny, M.: Process Semantics of General Inhibitor Nets. Information and Computation **190**, 18–69 (2004)
18. Kleijn, J., Koutny, M.: Formal Languages and Concurrent Behaviour. Studies in Computational Intelligence **113**, 125–182 (2008)
19. Lamport, L.: The mutual exclusion problem. Journal of ACM **33**(2), 313–326 (1986)
20. Montanari, U., Rossi, F.: Contextual nets. Acta Informatica **32**(6), 545–596 (1995)
21. Murata, T.: Petri nets: Properties, analysis and applications. Proc. of IEEE **77**(4), 541–579 (1989)
22. Nielsen, M., Rozenberg, G., Thiagarajan, P.S.: Behavioural Notions for Elementary Net Systems. Distributed Computing **4**, 45–57 (1990)
23. Peterson, J.L.: Petri nets theory and the modelling of systems. Prentice-Hall (1981)
24. Rozenberg, G., Engelfriet, J.: Elementary net systems. In: Reisig, Wolfgang, Rozenberg, Grzegorz (eds.) APN 1998. LNCS, vol. 1492, pp. 12–121. Springer, Heidelberg (1998)
25. Vogler, W., Semenov, A., Yakovlev, A.: Unfolding and finite prefix for nets with read arcs. In: Sangiorgi, D., de Simone, R. (eds.) CONCUR 1998. LNCS, vol. 1466, pp. 501–516. Springer, Heidelberg (1998)
26. Wiener, N.: A contribution to the theory of relative position. Proc. of the Cambridge Philosophical Society **17**, 441–449 (1914)
27. Winkowski, J.: Process of Contextual Nets and Their Characteristics. Fundamenta Informaticae **33**, 1–31 (1998)
28. Zuberek, W. M.: Timed Petri nets and preliminary performance evaluation. In: Proc. of the 7-th Annual Symp. on Computer Architecture, La Baule, France, pp. 89–96 (1980)

An SRN-Based Resiliency Quantification Approach

Dario Bruneo[1]([⊠]), Francesco Longo[1], Marco Scarpa[1], Antonio Puliafito[1],
Rahul Ghosh[2], and Kishor S. Trivedi[3]

[1] Dipartimento DICIEAMA, Università degli Studi di Messina, Messina, Italy
{dbruneo,flongo,mscarpa,apuliafito}@unime.it
[2] Xerox Research Center, Bengaluru, India
rahul.ghosh@xerox.com
[3] Duke University, Durham, USA
kst@ee.duke.edu

Abstract. Resiliency is often considered as a synonym for fault-tolerance and reliability/availability. We start from a different definition of resiliency as the ability to deliver services when encountering unexpected changes. Semantics of change is of extreme importance in order to accurately capture the real behavior of a system. We propose a resiliency analysis technique based on stochastic reward nets that allows the modeler: (1) to reuse an already existing dependability or performance model for a specific system with minimal modifications, and (2) to adapt the given model for specific change semantics. To automate the model analysis an algorithm is designed and the modeler is provided with a formalism that corresponds to the semantics. Our algorithm and approach is implemented to demonstrate the proposed resiliency quantification approach. Finally, we discuss the differences between our approach and an alternative technique based on deterministic and stochastic Petri nets and highlight the advantages of the proposed approach in terms of semantics specification.

Keywords: Resiliency · Stochastic reward nets · Change semantics · Deterministic and stochastic petri nets

1 Introduction

In complex systems, a notion of built-in *resiliency* allows one to face the uncertainties that can happen beyond the normal behavior of the system originally envisioned during the design stage. Such uncertainties could be related to unexpected situations or sudden events that affect the way the system operates. Moreover, legacy systems could undergo redesign in order to adapt to new requirements and to include new functionalities.

Nevertheless, quantifying the resiliency can be a complex task. One of the main issues is the lack of systematic approach for quantifying resiliency metrics. The term resiliency is used in different fields and its definition is diverse

R. Devillers and A. Valmari (Eds.): PETRI NETS 2015, LNCS 9115, pp. 98–116, 2015.
DOI: 10.1007/978-3-319-19488-2_5

[1–3]. Many researchers consider resiliency as a synonym for fault-tolerance and reliability/availability. However, fault tolerance benefits can be captured by traditional dependability measures, i.e., reliability, availability, maintainability, safety. Sterbenz *et al.* [4] defined resiliency as the combination of trustworthiness (dependability, security, and performability) and tolerance (survivability, disruption tolerance, and traffic tolerance).

In our work, we start from such a definition considering resiliency as the ability of a system to carry out its work when facing sudden and unexpected *changes*. In particular, we propose an approach for the analytical modeling of resiliency considering changes in the operating conditions of systems. The changes we are referring to here are beyond the envelope of system configurations already considered during the design stage and thus beyond fault tolerance. Examples can be workload variations, (deliberate) changes in the number of available resources, system functionalities that can be enabled/disabled according to specific conditions or necessities, and so on.

This paper presents a formalism for quantifying the resiliency of a system via stochastic reward nets (SRNs) [5]. Our contributions are summarized below.

(1) We formally present a resiliency quantification technique based on the notion of change. A classification of changes is provided and the procedure to map the changes in the system behavior onto the changes in the corresponding SRN model is shown.

(2) We highlight the importance of introducing the correct semantics of the change that the system experiences on the SRN model. A novel approach is described showing how various semantics can be associated with a given change. This approach shows that even with the same output measure of interest (e.g., the average number of requests in the queue) different numerical results are obtained based on the change semantics.

(3) We introduce the modeling formalisms namely *changing functions* and *behavioral rules* allowing the modeler to force the correct change semantics on the SRN model.

(4) We present two algorithms that can be easily used by practitioners in order to model resiliency-related behaviors. In contrast to the traditional view of synonymizing resiliency with dependability, we show how resiliency can be quantified also with respect to performance measures.

(5) We implemented the algorithms in the Stochastic Petri Net Package (SPNP) [6] and show numerical results obtained by applying them to a simple running example based on a $M/M/1/r$ queue.

(6) We discuss the differences between our technique and a possible alternative based on the use of deterministic and stochastic Petri nets (DSPNs), showing the advantages of our technique from the modeler point of view.

The rest of the paper is organized as follows. In Section 2, we report the definition of change on which our notion of resiliency is grounded, formalize the problem, and propose a running example that will be used throughout the paper. In Section 3, we address the challenges mentioned in Section 2, and present our approach for resiliency quantification using SRNs. In Section 4, we formally describe the proposed algorithm while in Section 5 we discuss differences between our approach and a DSPN based approach. Related research is presented in Section 6. Finally, in Section 7, we provide concluding remarks and discuss future work.

2   Resiliency Quantification

This section presents our definition of change followed by the problem statement. We also present a running example that will be used subsequently to demonstrate the proposed approach.

2.1   Definition of Change

One of the key points of our proposed resiliency analysis strategy is the concept of change. In fact, different aspects have to be taken into account by the modeler when modeling the change a system is undergoing. First of all, it is possible to classify changes into two different sets: *unpredictable changes* and *programmed changes*. Unpredictable changes are the ones that are beyond the system administrator's control. They happen in an asynchronous manner and are consequences of external factors on the considered system. Programmed changes are voluntarily applied by the system administrator in order to adapt the system to new conditions. They are usually planned and thus synchronous. Consider a change which models the variation in the number of system resources. Then, an example of unpredictable change could be the failure of a set of system resources caused by an electrical outage. In contrast, an example of programmed change could be the planned power outage of a set of computing resources, e.g., for the newly emerged purpose of energy saving. Note that, from the system's perspective, programmed change is still an example of sudden change that is not considered within the design envelope. This is because the change plan can be made during the operational time and not during the design time.

In some cases the same change can exhibit *different semantics*. For example, if the change is related to the powering-off of a certain number of computing resources, two different behaviors can be considered, whether each resource can complete its work before shutdown or not. For this reason, the modeler has to clearly specify such semantics in order to quantify the resiliency correctly. In fact, in the powering-off example, if the resources have to wait for the work completion before shutdown, a certain time is elapsed before the change is completed (i.e., all the selected resources have been powered-off) while, in the other case, the change could be considered instantaneous. Thus, we can also classify changes considering their duration. The changes that can be applied instantaneously will be termed as *immediate changes* while we will refer to *gradual changes* when the change duration cannot be neglected. As clarified later in more details, associating a semantics to the considered changes is important so that the model is realistic and accurate.

2.2   Problem Formulation

Following the definitions in Section 2.1, we formalize the resiliency analysis approach. Let T_c denote the time at which the change is initiated and d denote the
duration of the change (in case of immediate changes $d = 0$). We are interested
in the analysis of the system behavior in the time interval $[0, \infty)$ starting from
the knowledge of:

- the system configuration before the change, i.e., in the interval $[0, T_c)$;
- the (dynamic) system configuration during the change, i.e., in the interval
  (T_c, T_d) (that is particularly meaningful only in the case of gradual changes);
- the new system configuration after the change, i.e., in the interval (T_d, ∞);

where $T_d = T_c + d$.

It is worth noting that, in the case of programmed changes, the time instant
T_c is a deterministic quantity. On the other hand, in the case of unpredictable
changes, given that we are interested in analyzing the system behavior at the
change occurrence, we can force the change to happen without introducing any
stochastic aspect, still considering T_c as a deterministic quantity. In fact, if the
system has already reached a steady state, its evolution in time after the change
does not depend on the actual time instant at which the change occurs. Thus,
the modeler can choose the value of T_c as it is more convenient for the analysis.
Note that this is not true in the case in which the change occurs when the system
has not yet reached a steady state. However, this case is out of the scope of this
paper.

On the contrary, the time instant T_d is intrinsically a stochastic quantity
because the completion of the change depends on the system internal behavior
which can not be deterministic. Since no other change is applied to the system
after time instant T_c, the analysis in the intervals (T_c, T_d) and (T_d, ∞) can be
performed as a single step (i.e., as a single analysis in the interval (T_c, ∞)). Yet,
it is important to remark that, during the analysis in the interval (T_c, T_d), the
change semantics have to be enforced in order to increase the accuracy of the
obtained results with respect to the real behavior of the system.

2.3   Running Example

In order to analyze all the different aspects related to resiliency quantification,
consider a simple system that will be used as a running example. The system
we wish to analyze is an $M/M/1/r$ queue with a finite buffer size of $r - 1$
(as shown in Fig. 1(a)). When the number of requests present in the system
reaches r ($r-1$ requests in the queue plus one being served), further requests are
dropped. We are interested in analyzing the system behavior when the buffer size
is reduced. Specifically, we consider the case in which, at a certain time instant,
the maximum number of requests in the system decreases from the value r to
r^*. Two possible change semantics can be easily identified:

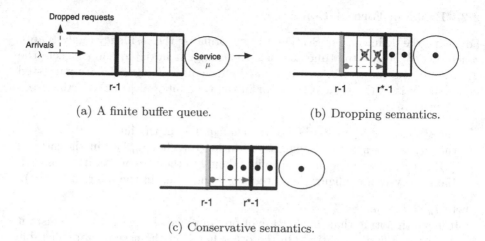

(a) A finite buffer queue.   (b) Dropping semantics.

(c) Conservative semantics.

Fig. 1. The running example

- *dropping* semantics - when the change is applied, if there are more than r^*-1 customers waiting in the queue, all the excess requests are immediately dropped (see Fig. 1(b));
- *conservative* semantics - when the change is applied, if there are more than r^*-1 customers waiting in the queue, the excess requests are still maintained in the queue waiting for the service. New requests will be enqueued only when the number of waiting customers becomes lower than $r^* - 1$ (see Fig. 1(c)).

Observe that the dropping semantics corresponds to an immediate change. In fact, at the time the change is applied, the queue length is immediately reduced and the system starts behaving as the new configuration (an $M/M/1/r^*$ queue). On the other hand, the conservative change corresponds to a gradual change leaving the system in an intermediate configuration until the number of customers in excess are served. At the time the change is applied, the queue length is preserved and the system cannot be represented neither as an $M/M/1/r$ queue (new requests are rejected when the queue length is less than $r - 1$ but greater than $r^* - 1$) nor as an $M/M/1/r^*$ (as the temporary queue length could be greater than $r^* - 1$).

3   Using SRN for Resiliency Quantification

The notion of resiliency discussed in the previous section can be analyzed using different formalisms that are able to opportunely represent the system as well as to model its behavior. Here, we focus on SRNs. In this section, we first informally discuss how SRNs can be used to perform a resiliency analysis. Then, we describe an SRN model for our running example trying to highlight how the change semantics can be enforced to the real behavior of the system. Finally, we present a formal description of how a resiliency analysis can be conducted through the use of SRNs.

3.1 Resiliency Analysis though SRNs

SRNs are an extension of generalized stochastic Petri nets (GSPNs), where every tangible marking of the net can be associated with a reward rate thus facilitating the computation of a variety of performance measures. Key features of SRNs are: (1) each transition may have an enabling function (also called a guard) so that a transition is enabled only if its marking-dependent enabling function is true; (2) marking dependent arc multiplicities are allowed; (3) marking dependent firing rates are allowed; (4) transitions can be assigned different priorities; (5) besides traditional output measures obtained from a GSPN, such as throughput of a transition and mean number of tokens in a place, more complex measures can be computed by using reward functions.

From a resiliency point of view, the notion of change in the system operating conditions has to be mapped onto the corresponding changes in the SRN model. One of the advantages of our approach is that the modeler is allowed to reuse an existing SRN model to adapt it to the resiliency analysis and to the specific change semantics with minimal modifications. The modeler is formally guided by providing such a semantics without having to extensively modify the SRN model. We identified the following changes that could be used by the modeler to represent resiliency-related behaviors:

- Variation in the rate of a transition (e.g., to model a change in the system workload or in the system service rate).
- Variation in the total number of tokens in a set of places (e.g., to model resource failure/repair or power-off/power-on).
- Variation in the guard function of a transition (e.g., to model the enforcement/disablement of specific system tasks or functionalities).
- General topological changes in the net (e.g., to model complex changes involving several system components).

From an SRN model point of view, such changes can be classified as *structural* and *non-structural* changes. Non-structural changes are those that keep the reachability graph of the SRN unaltered. For example, a variation in the rate of a transition does not affect either the number of states or the number of state transitions. Structural changes are those that cause the reachability graph of the SRN to be significantly modified, in terms of number of states and/or state transitions. In fact, dropping of states or creation of new states (either transient, recurrent, or both) can be caused by the enforcement of a change in the SRN model. For example, an increase in the total number of tokens in a set of places can definitely cause an increase in the number of states in the corresponding reachability graph.

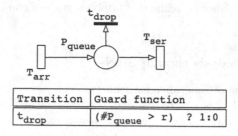

Transition	Guard function
t_{drop}	$(\#P_{queue} > r)$? 1:0

Fig. 2. An SRN model of the finite buffer queue running example

3.2   An SRN Model for the Running Example

For the running example, a corresponding SRN model is provided in Fig. 2 where: i) the exponentially distributed transition T_{arr} (with rate λ) represents the arrival process; ii) the exponentially distributed transition T_{ser} (with rate μ) models the service process; iii) place P_{queue} represents the system, each token in such a place modeling a request being served or waiting in the queue; iv) the immediate transition t_{drop}, along with its associated guard function, models the dropping of new incoming requests in the case the buffer is full.

Assume that the resiliency analysis needs to be conducted by reducing the maximum number of requests in the system from 4 to 2. In the SRN model, after setting the parameter r to 4 and 2, we obtain the two (reduced) reachability graphs[1] depicted in Fig. 3 where the label associated with each state represents the number of tokens in place P_{queue}. Such reachability graphs model the system evolution before and after the change. At the change occurrence, a mapping from one reachability graph to another has to be carried out. This can be done by computing the state probabilities after the change as a function of the state probabilities before the change. We call this operation *probability mapping* and we represent it in Fig. 3 with circle-headed arrows connecting the state of the reachability graph before the change with the state of the reachability graph after the change. In particular, in Fig. 3 the probability mapping related to the dropping semantics is reported. In this case, since the requests are immediately dropped, the probability to have two requests in the system immediately after the change is given by the sum of the probabilities to have two, three, or four requests immediately before the change. This is graphically depicted in Fig. 3 through a *many-to-one* mapping from states S_2, S_3, and S_4 in the reachability graph before the change and the state S_2' in the reachability graph after the change. With respect to the other states, not directly affected by the change, a *one-to-one* mapping has to be performed.

The probability mapping is not a straightforward operation as it needs to label, search, and recognize corresponding states in the two reachability graphs.

---

[1] In rest of the paper, we will use to the term reachability graph to refer to the reduced reachability graph including tangible markings only.

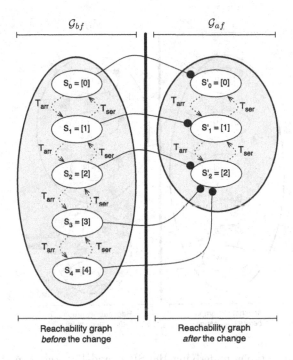

Fig. 3. Reachability graphs underlying the SRN model of Fig. 2 in the case of dropping semantics. Each state is labeled with the number of tokens in place P_{queue} ($[\#P_{queue}]$).

Hence, an automatic procedure able to perform this operation is of interest. Moreover, some specific change semantics can not be easily obtained only by considering the reachability graphs before and after the change and by mapping the corresponding probabilities. In fact, in order to force the conservative semantics in our running example, the reachability graphs depicted in Fig. 4 should be obtained, where a set of transient states is present. Such a set implements the gradual change behavior of the system dealing with the situations in which three or more requests are already present in the system when the change occurs. In such situations, according to the conservative semantics, new requests should not be accepted but the customers already present in the system should be served. This behavior is implemented in the reachability graphs of Fig. 4 by disabling event T_{arr} and enabling event T_{ser} in states S'_3 and S'_4. It is worth noting that this set of (transient) states would not be generated by simply analyzing the SRN model of Fig. 2 after the change but they require an ad-hoc procedure able to discover them. Moreover, such states could have a direct impact on the probability mapping. In fact, in this case only one-to-one mappings are required since the two reachability graphs have the same states.

Of course, based on the modeler's requirements, other ways to implement the same change semantics in the SRN model of Fig. 2 could be followed. Nev-

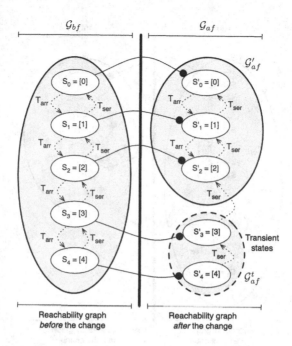

Fig. 4. Reachability graphs underlying the SRN model of Fig. 2 in the case of conservative semantics. Each state is labeled with the number of tokens in place P_{queue} ($[\#P_{queue}]$).

ertheless, the above discussion highlights the necessity for a formalization of a resiliency analysis approach based on SRNs.

3.3   A Formalization

We formally describe how the problem formulated in Section 2.2 can be addressed through the use of SRNs. Suppose that our system is modeled through an SRN $\mathcal{M}$ which can be parameterized by two different sets of parameters $\mathcal{P}_{bf}$ and $\mathcal{P}_{af}$ modeling the system behavior in the time intervals $[0, T_c)$ and (T_c, ∞), respectively. This gives rise to two different underlying reachability graphs, $\mathcal{G}_{bf}$ (before the change) and $\mathcal{G}_{af}$ (after the change). While the graph $\mathcal{G}_{bf}$ can be obtained by parameterizing $\mathcal{M}$ with the sets of parameters $\mathcal{P}_{bf}$ and by performing a reachability graph exploration, the graph $\mathcal{G}_{af}$ can be considered as composed by two sub-graphs, $\mathcal{G}'_{af}$ and $\mathcal{G}^t_{af}$. The graph $\mathcal{G}'_{af}$ can be obtained in a way similar to $\mathcal{G}_{bf}$ by using the set of parameters $\mathcal{P}_{af}$. The graph $\mathcal{G}^t_{af}$ is composed of transient states only, representing the (dynamic) system behavior during the change, i.e., in the interval (T_c, T_d), depending on the semantics associated with the change. In general, $\mathcal{G}^t_{af}$ can be composed of disjoint sub-graphs but they will eventually be connected to $\mathcal{G}'_{af}$.

The analysis of the system behavior in the interval $[0, \infty)$ with a change at time instant T_c can be conducted by performing a transient analysis of $\mathcal{G}_{bf}$ in the time interval $[0, T_c)$ followed by a transient analysis of $\mathcal{G}_{af}$ in the time interval (T_c, ∞). At the change occurrence (time instant T_c), the initial state probability vector associated with graph $\mathcal{G}_{af}$, $\boldsymbol{\pi}_{af}(T_c)$, has to be initialized using the state probabilities obtained at the end of the transient analysis in the previous time interval, i.e., as a function of the probability vector associated with $\mathcal{G}_{bf}$, $\boldsymbol{\pi}_{bf}(T_c)$:

$$\boldsymbol{\pi}_{af}(T_c) = f(\boldsymbol{\pi}_{bf}(T_c)). \tag{1}$$

In the analysis thus formalized, we can highlight the following challenges:

– Starting from the change semantics, how do we obtain the reachability graph $\mathcal{G}_{af}^t$? Also, how do we link it to $\mathcal{G}_{af}'$ in order to obtain $\mathcal{G}_{af}$?
– How do we perform the probability mapping represented by eq. (1)?

In the following section, we propose two algorithms that implement the resiliency quantification technique formalized above and address these challenges.

4   A Resiliency Quantification Technique

The proposed technique allows us to analyze structural and non-structural changes that can produce very different state spaces before and after the change (in terms of dropping of states or creation of new states). Moreover, it allows easy representation of different change semantics by discovering new transient states and automating the probability mapping. Our goal is to develop a new SRN-based formalism that gives modelers a high-level tool to represent resiliency-related behaviors in a user-friendly way. In rest of this section, we present such a formalism for the case where states are dropped in SRN model after the change. Nevertheless, the proposed approach and the algorithms can address the creation of new states after the change as well.

Our approach takes as input an SRN model $\mathcal{M}$ along with two distinct sets of parameters $\mathcal{P}_{bf}$ and $\mathcal{P}_{af}$ representing the behavior of the system before and after the change, respectively. The modeler is allowed to specify a set of *changing functions* $\mathcal{C}_f$ and a set of *behavioral rules* $\mathcal{B}_r$ in order to enforce a specific semantics during the change. Changing functions operate on the markings of the reachability graph before the change $\mathcal{G}_{bf}$ allowing the modeler to specify how each state is instantaneously transformed at the change occurrence. In their more general form, changing functions can be defined in a probabilistic way allowing the modeler to associate a set of changes with different probabilities. Thus, for each marking in $\mathcal{G}_{bf}$ more than one state could be obtained. Note that the modeler is allowed to express changing functions in terms of high-level components of the nets, e.g., places, transitions, tokens. For example, through a changing function the modeler can force an instantaneous modification in the number of tokens in a specific place. In fact, from a syntactic point of view, changing functions are similar to guard functions. Thus, the modeler does not need to exactly know the reachability graph of $\mathcal{M}$, neither before nor after the change.

Behavioral rules operate during the reachability graph exploration phase allowing the modeler to inhibit the visit of specific states during the change completion. Also in this case, such functions can be expressed in terms of high-level components of the net. Through behavioral rules the modeler can force the number of tokens in a place to remain constant, increase, or decrease. She can also enable or disable specific transitions during the change completion.

Algorithm 1 implements the proposed technique starting from the already generated reachability graphs parameterized by $\mathcal{P}_{bf}$ and $\mathcal{P}_{af}$ ($\mathcal{G}_{bf}$ and $\mathcal{G}'_{af}$, respectively). Algorithm 1 produces the reachability graph after the change $\mathcal{G}_{af}$ and the corresponding probability vector at the change occurrence π_{af}. If necessary, the reachability graph $\mathcal{G}'_{af}$ is integrated with the set of additional transient states $\mathcal{G}^t_{af}$ on-the-fly and its initial probability vector $\pi_{af}(T_c)$ is computed as a function of the probability vector $\pi_{bf}(T_c)$. The algorithm scans each state in $\mathcal{G}_{bf}$ (line 7). On line 9, each state s is modified according to the changing functions and thus obtaining a set $\mathcal{S}$ of modified states with their associated probabilities (we denote p_m as the probability that the state s is modified into the transformed state s_m). Such states are searched in $\mathcal{G}_{af}$ and if found their probabilities are mapped (line 12). Note that probabilities are summed up (presence of the $+$ $=$ operator) because more than one state $s \in \mathcal{G}_{bf}$ can be transformed into the same state $s_m \in \mathcal{G}_{af}$. If such states are not found, function $FirstTangibleReachedSet(\cdot)$ computes the probabilities of tangible set of states $\mathcal{T}$ that are reachable in a single hop. Function $FirstTangibleReachedSet(\cdot)$ loads the token configuration in $\mathcal{M}$ and starts a one-hop state space exploration considering the set of parameters $\mathcal{P}_{af}$ (line 15)[2] (we denote p_n as the probability that a tangible state s_n is reached from a state s_m in a single hop). Each such state is searched in $\mathcal{G}_{af}$ and if found its probability is set (lines 16-18). Note that, also in this case the $+$ $=$ operator is used because more than one state $s \in \mathcal{G}_{bf}$ can eventually be mapped to the same state $s_n \in \mathcal{G}_{af}$. Otherwise, for all the states an additional state space exploration is performed by function $Explore()$ that stops as soon as a state in $\mathcal{G}_{af}$ is found (line 20). Then, the newly generated reachability graph and its corresponding probability vector are merged with $\mathcal{G}_{af}$ and its probability vector π_{af} (lines 22-24). On line 13 and 18, the $FirstTangibleReachedSet(\cdot)$ and $Explore(\cdot)$ functions take the set of behavioral rules as additional parameter. These behavioral rules force the exploration avoiding the visit of specific states. If new states are found during the exploration and need to be modified, the set of changing functions can also be provided to the $Explore(\cdot)$ function as an additional parameter.

Considering the model in Fig. 2, changing functions and behavioral rules can be used to force the desired behavior. For example, if the behavior represented by the state space in Figure 3 needs to be forced, the modeler has to exploit the following changing function:

$$if(\#P_{queue} > 2) \ then \ \#P_{queue} = 2$$

---

[2] Loops of vanishing states are opportunely managed if present.

Algorithm 1. *apply_change(·)*

---

    input   : An SRN $\mathcal{M}$, two sets of **parameter** $\mathcal{P}_{bf}$ and $\mathcal{P}_{af}$, two **reachability**
                graph $\mathcal{G}_{bf}$ and $\mathcal{G}'_{af}$, a vector of **probability** at change occurrence $\boldsymbol{\pi}_{bf}$,
                a set of **changing function** C_f, a set of **behavioral rules** B_r.
    output: A **reachability** graph $\mathcal{G}_{af}$ and a corresponding vector of
                probability at change occurrence $\boldsymbol{\pi}_{af}$.

1 **begin**
2   **declare** $\boldsymbol{\pi}_{af}, \boldsymbol{\pi}_T$: **vector of probability**;
3   **declare** $\mathcal{G}_{af}, \mathcal{G}_T$: **reachability graph**;
4   **declare** S, T: **set of couples** <**state, probability**>;
5     $\boldsymbol{\pi}_{af} \longleftarrow 0$;
6     $\mathcal{G}_{af} \longleftarrow \mathcal{G}'_{af}$;
7   **foreach** $s \in \mathcal{G}_{bf}$ **do**
8         $S \longleftarrow \emptyset$;
9         $S \longleftarrow Modify(s, C_f)$;
10   **foreach** $< s_m, p_m > \in S$ **do**
11   **if** $s_m \in \mathcal{G}_{af}$ **then**
12             $\boldsymbol{\pi}_{af}[s_m] + = p_m \cdot \boldsymbol{\pi}_{bf}[s]$;
13   **else**
14             $T \longleftarrow \emptyset$;
15             $T \longleftarrow FirstTangibleReachedSet(s_m, \mathcal{M}, \mathcal{P}_{af}, B_r)$;
16   **foreach** $< s_n, p_n > \in T$ **do**
17   **if** $s_n \subset \mathcal{G}_{af}$ **then**
18                    $\boldsymbol{\pi}_{af}[s_n] + = p_n \cdot p_m \cdot \boldsymbol{\pi}_{bf}[s]$;
19   **else**
20                   $\mathcal{G}_T \longleftarrow Explore(s_n, \mathcal{M}, \mathcal{P}_{af}, \mathcal{G}_{af}, C_f, B_r)$;
21                   $\boldsymbol{\pi}_T \longleftarrow 0$;
22                   $\boldsymbol{\pi}_T[s_n] + = p_n \cdot p_m \cdot \boldsymbol{\pi}_{bf}[s]$;
23                   $\mathcal{G}_{af} \longleftarrow \mathcal{G}_{af} \cup \mathcal{G}_T$;
24                   $\boldsymbol{\pi}_{af} \longleftarrow \boldsymbol{\pi}_{af} \cup \boldsymbol{\pi}_T$;

25   **return** $\mathcal{G}_{af}, \boldsymbol{\pi}_{af}$;

---

where the notation $\#P$ indicates the number of tokens in place P. On the other hand, if the behavior represented by the state space in Fig. 4 needs to be forced, the modeler has to use the following behavioral rules that allow to specify that, during the change, new requests are not accepted until the exceeding requests are served:

– no immediate changes are allowed in number of tokens in place P_{queue};
– only decreasing variation in the number of tokens in place P_{queue} are allowed;

At a net level, such behavioral rules correspond to disabling transitions t_{drop} and T_{arr} and are taken into account by function $Explore(\cdot)$ during the reachability graph generation. The procedure also forces the algorithm to skip those events that are not compatible with the required behavior.

In order to demonstrate the working of the algorithm, we show how the state S_3 is processed in the running example with the changing and behavioral rules defined above. Consider the dropping semantics shown in Fig. 3. In this case, the token configuration of state S_3 is modified using the changing function. Thus, we obtain a new token configuration in which $\#P_{queue} = 2$. Such a new token configuration is searched and found in the reachability graph after the change (state S_2') and its corresponding probability is mapped into the new one. If the conservative semantics is adopted (Fig. 4) no changing functions are used. In that case, the state S_3 is not modified and its token configuration is searched in the reachability graph after the change. If the configuration is not found then the first tangible reachable set is obtained using the behavioral rules presented above. Transition t_{drop} being disabled, state S_3 becomes a tangible state even when the maximum number of requests in the system r is set to 2. At this point, a new state S_3' is generated in the reachability graph after the change and the probability mapping is performed. Subsequently, the new state S_3' is explored using the behavioral rules that allow only transition T_{ser} to be enabled. The firing of such a transition will force the graph to reach a state in which the token configuration is such that $\#P_{queue} = 2$. Once this token configuration is found in the reachability graph after the change (state S_2'), the exploration process is stopped.

The resiliency analysis described in Section 3.3 can then be conducted according to Algorithm 2. Algorithm 2 computes the value of a metric m in the time interval $[0, \infty)$ for a model $\mathcal{M}$ when a change is enforced at time instant T_c. Also in this case, the change is modeled by considering a set of SRN parameters $\mathcal{P}_{bf}$ before the change and a set of SRN parameters $\mathcal{P}_{af}$ after the change. Moreover, the change semantics is represented through a set of changing functions $\mathcal{C}_f$ and a set of behavioral rules $\mathcal{B}_r$. Algorithm 2 makes use of Algorithm 1 to enforce the change semantics. First of all, the reachability graph and the initial probability vector of the model at time instant 0 is obtained through function $generate\_state\_space(\cdot)$ (line 5). Then, the value of measure m in the time interval $[0, T_c)$ is computed through the function $solve(\cdot)$ (line 6). At line 7, function $generate\_state\_space(\cdot)$ is exploited again to obtain the reachability graph and the initial probability vector of the model after the change. Both the reachability graph and the initial probability vector are then modified in order to enforce the change semantics and to perform the probability mapping at line 8 (calling function $apply\_change(\cdot)$ described in Algorithm 1). Finally, the model is solved again to compute the value of metric m in the time interval (T_c, ∞) (line 9) and the complete vector containing the analysis results is returned (line 10).

Algorithms 1 and 2 have been implemented in the SPNP tool [6] and we applied them to the SRN of the running example computing the mean number of requests in the system, i.e., the mean number of tokens in place P_{queue}. Fig. 5 shows the value of such a metric when at time $T_c = 30s$ the maximum number of requests in the system is reduced from 4 to 2. System parameters have been set as follows: $\lambda = 10.2s^{-1}$, $\mu = 0.1s^{-1}$. Results show the importance of enforcing the correct change semantics by the modeler. In fact, while in the case of

---

Algorithm 2. *resiliency_analysis()*

---

    input   : An SRN $\mathcal{M}$, two sets of **parameter** $\mathcal{P}_{bf}$ and $\mathcal{P}_{af}$, a set of **changing**
           function $\mathcal{C}_f$, a set of **behavioral rules** $\mathcal{B}_r$, a **time instant** T_c when
           change is applied, a **measure** to be computed m.
    output: A vector of **float** containing the value of measure m in the interval
           $[0,\infty)$.

1 **begin**
2   **declare** $\boldsymbol{\pi}_{bf}(0)$, $\boldsymbol{\pi}_{af}(T_c)$: vector of **probability**;
3   **declare** $\mathcal{G}_{bf}$, $\mathcal{G}'_{af}$, $\mathcal{G}_{af}$: **reachability graph**;
4   **declare** $v_{[0,T_c)}$, $v_{(T_c,\infty)}$: vector of **float**;
5     $\mathcal{G}_{bf}, \boldsymbol{\pi}_{bf}(0) \longleftarrow$ *generate_state_space*$(\mathcal{M}, \mathcal{P}_{bf})$;
6     $v_{[0,T_c)}, \boldsymbol{\pi}_{bf}(T_c) \longleftarrow$ *solve*$(\mathcal{G}_{bf}, \boldsymbol{\pi}_{bf}(0), m, T_c)$;
7     $\mathcal{G}'_{af}, \boldsymbol{\pi}_{af}(T_c) \longleftarrow$ *generate_state_space*$(\mathcal{M}, \mathcal{P}_{af})$;
8     $\mathcal{G}_{af}, \boldsymbol{\pi}_{af}(T_c) \longleftarrow$ *apply_change*$(\mathcal{M}, \mathcal{P}_{bf}, \mathcal{P}_{af}, \mathcal{G}_{bf}, \mathcal{G}'_{af}, \boldsymbol{\pi}_{bf}(T_c), \mathcal{C}_f, \mathcal{B}_r)$;
9     $v_{(T_c,\infty)} \longleftarrow$ *solve*$(\mathcal{G}_{af}, \boldsymbol{\pi}_{af}(T_c), m, \infty)$;
10   **return** $v_{[0,T_c)} \cup v_{(T_c,\infty)}$;

---

dropping semantics an immediate fall in the metric value can be observed, in the case of conservative semantics the variation is smoother. Moreover, important resiliency-based performance indexes can be defined. For example, in the case of conservative semantics, we can compute the time needed to obtain a value of the expected number of requests in the system less or equal to the new value of r^*. This is given by the intersection of the curve representing the expected number of requests in the system with the straight line at $y = r^*$. This value can represent an estimation of the expected time (d) necessary for the change to complete. In the example shown in Fig. 5, such a value is equal to 19s.

5   An Analogy with the DSPN Approach

It is possible to approach the resiliency quantification problem using deterministic and stochastic Petri nets (DSPNs) similar to what has been done for phased mission systems (PMSs) [7]. From the modeler point of view, the DSPN approach consists of building a model characterized by two layers. The phase net (PHN) models the switching between different phases of the system through the use of deterministic transitions. The system net (SN) represents the behavior of the system during the different phases and this is performed by forcing a dependency between the parameters of the SN and the state of the PHN. As the state of the PHN changes, some of the parameters of the SN are changed in order to model the behavior in the newly reached phase.

    Assume that only two phases are present. In this case, from the solution point of view, the whole state space underlying the DSPN consists of two reachability sub-graphs compared to the reachability graphs before and after the change in our SRN approach. These sub-graphs are connected by the transitions derived from the firing of the deterministic transition of the PHN. Then, the first reachability graph is solved starting from the initial probability vector. Subsequently, a

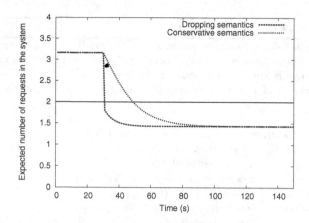

Fig. 5. Expected number of requests in the system when the change is applied at time $T_c = 30s$ under different change semantics

branching probability matrix is used in order to compute the initial probability vector of the second reachability graph that is eventually solved. Such branching probability matrix can be automatically generated by considering the transitions from the first subset of states to the second one.

Using the DSPN approach it is possible to analyze the resiliency of the finite buffer queue described in the running example. In Fig. 6, a corresponding DSPN model is presented. The SN is exactly the same of the SRN model of Fig. 2. The resiliency analysis can be performed using a PHN where transition T_{change} represents the change arrival modeled through its deterministic firing time (T_c). The behavior of the system before and after the change is represented through the parameter r that varies from 5 to 3. This variation influence the guard function associated with transition t_{drop}.

Fig. 6(b) represents the DSPN reachability graph in which each state is labeled with the corresponding token distribution through the 3-vector $[\#P_{queue}, \#Phase_1, \#Phase_2]$. Note that the semantics associated with the change is embedded in the model and it cannot be explicitly expressed. In fact, it is possible to observe that this model intrinsically implements the dropping semantics. Starting from states S_3 and S_4, once the change is applied, the system will reach state S_7. Thus it will instantaneously drop all the exceeding requests and start behaving as an M/M/1/2 queue.

To highlight such a phenomenon, let us consider a second DSPN model for the running example (see Fig. 7) in which the finite buffer size is modeled through the inhibitor arc from place P_{queue} to transition T_{arr} with multiplicity r. Even though the two DSPNs are identical in modeling the M/M/1/r queue and produce the same results with respect to all the measures of interest (e.g., mean number of requests in the system, dropping probability, dropping rate), they cannot be considered equivalent when performing a resiliency analysis. This is mainly due to the embedded changing semantics that gives rise to different

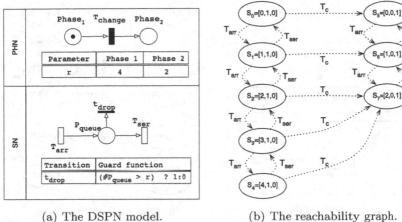

(a) The DSPN model.   (b) The reachability graph.

Fig. 6. A first DSPN model for the running example. Each state is labeled with the number of tokens in places $\#P_{queue}$, $\#Phase_1$, and $\#Phase_2$ ($[\#P_{queue}, \#Phase_1, \#Phase_2]$).

behaviors when the buffer size changes. In the model of Fig. 7(a), at the change occurrence, the exceeding requests are not dropped and are kept in the queue until they are served. This gives rise to the presence of the transient states intrinsically implementing the conservative semantics as shown in Fig. 7(b).

Motivated by this simple example, the following general considerations can be argued regarding the issues related to resiliency analysis using DSPNs.

(i) Usually, a specific change semantics is embedded in the model and the modeler would not be completely aware of it while enforcing the change during a resiliency analysis.

(ii) Equivalent models with the same semantics for a standard analysis could present different embedded change semantics. Also in this case, the modeler will not be aware of the differences between the two models during resiliency analysis. Thus, there could be a mismatch between the desired and the actual behavior of the system during the change.

(iii) The use of a specific model (with a specific embedded change semantics) could be mandatory; being part of a more complex system or being already available and difficult to modify. In this case, it would not be easy for the modeler to force the desired change behavior.

(iv) In the case of structural changes, significant modifications of the model could be necessary to implement the change via the addition/removal of transitions and/or places. This procedure could be time-consuming and error-prone.

Such issues are due to the fact that the DSPN approach is a purely high-level technique that completely hides the underlying state space model from the modeler. In our running example, the modeler could not be aware of the fact that,

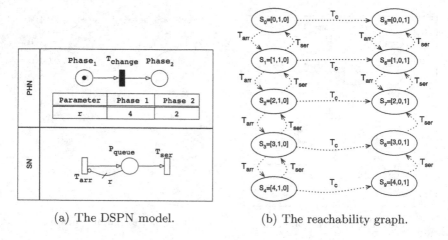

(a) The DSPN model.   (b) The reachability graph.

Fig. 7. A second DSPN model for the running example. Each state is labeled with the number of tokens in places $\#P_{queue}$, $\#Phase_1$, and $\#Phase_2$ ($[\#P_{queue}, \#Phase_1, \#Phase_2]$).

while in the model depicted in Fig. 6 the whole state space of the DSPN is obtained by simply juxtaposing the state spaces of the SN before the change and the SN after the change, in the model of Fig. 7 additional transient states are generated.

Considering all these aspects, we can summarize the advantages of our technique w.r.t. the DSPN approach:

(i) the modeler is made explicitly aware of the presence of a specific change semantics while performing a resiliency analysis of the modeled system;
(ii) the modeler is allowed to force a specific change semantics through the use of a set of changing functions and behavioral rules even if this semantics is different from the one embedded in the model;
(iii) when the structural changes are enforced, the use of changing functions allows to avoid significant modifications of the model making the procedure faster and less error-prone.

6   Related Research

In [8], Wang et al. describe resiliency analysis of supply chain networks using Petri nets. Authors describe the states of a supply chain network into three categories: loss-making, profitable and overloaded. Depending on the demand-supply of different firms in the supply chain network, the overall status of a company is determined using Petri nets based models. Authors claim that such approach can capture the resiliency of the overall network. However, sudden changes, e.g., failure of one or more firms, which could lead to structural changes of the Petri net has not been discussed in their work. In [9], Tavana et al. include repair time in resiliency quantification and provide a Petri net based model for resiliency analysis. We strongly disagree with such approach because both redundancy and repair are considered as fault-tolerance of the system. In [10] et al., Liu et al. use a Petri net based model to quantify the resiliency of the system as degraded performance during failure. Such approach is commonly known as performability modeling and we argue that notion of resiliency is much broader than the performability assessment of the system. In [11], Rodriguez et al. propose a UML model for resiliency quantification and subsequently translates it into a DSPN model. However, their notion of resiliency is synonymous with availability and do not capture sudden unexpected changes on the system. In summary, even though past research have used Petri-net based models for resiliency quantification, in all cases, the notion of resiliency was quantified by availability or fault-tolerance measures.

7 Conclusions and Future Work

The specification of the correct change semantics is an important challenge during resiliency analysis of systems. We provided an SRN based approach that is able to automate the resiliency analysis of a system. Specifically, our approach allows the modeler to describe the change semantics without relying on the semantics embedded in the original system model. The importance of this aspect and its impact on the accuracy of the results have been illustrated through the use of a simple running example based on a $M/M/1/r$ queue.

In future, more complex scenarios will also be investigated where our technique can be applied. A comparison of the accuracy will be done by validating the numerical results with respect to the measurements from a real system.

References

1. DeBardeleben, N., et al.: High-end computing resilience: Analysis of issues facing the hec community and path-forward for research and development, White paper, January 2010
2. Laprie, J.C.: From dependability to resilience. In: DSN (2008)
3. Simoncini, L.: Resilient computing: an engineering discipline. In: IPDPS (2009)
4. Sterbenz, J.P., et al.: Resilience and survivability in communication networks: Strategies, principles, and survey of disciplines. Elsevier Computer Networks, June 2010
5. Ciardo, G., et al.: Automated generation and analysis of markov reward models using stochastic reward nets. In: Linear Algebra, Markov Chains and Queuing Models. Springer (1993)
6. Hirel, C., Tuffin, B., Trivedi, K.S.: SPNP: stochastic petri nets. version 6.0. In: Haverkort, B.R., Bohnenkamp, H.C., Smith, C.U. (eds.) TOOLS 2000. LNCS, vol. 1786, pp. 354–357. Springer, Heidelberg (2000)
7. Mural, I., Bondavalli, A., Zang, X., Trivedi, K.: Dependability modeling and evaluation of phased mission systems: a dspn approach. In: Dependable Computing for Critical Applications 7, pp. 319–337, January 1999

8. Wang, J., Ip, W., Muddada, R., Huang, J., Zhang, W.: On petri net implementation of proactive resilient holistic supply chain networks. International Journal of Advanced Manufacturing Technology **69**(1–4), 427–437 (2013)
9. Tavana, M., Busch, T., Davis, E.: Modeling operational robustness and resiliency with high-level petri nets. International Journal of Knowledge-Based Organizations **1**(2), 17–38 (2011)
10. Liu, M., Hutchison, D.: Towards resilient networks using situation awareness. In: PGNET (2011)
11. Rodriguez, R., Merseguer, J., Bernardi, S.: Modelling and analysing resilience as a security issue within uml. In: SERENE (2010)

Non-atomic Transition Firing
in Contextual Nets

Thomas Chatain[1]($\boxtimes$), Stefan Haar[1], Maciej Koutny[2], and Stefan Schwoon[1]

[1] INRIA and LSV, CNRS and ENS Cachan, Cachan, France
chatain@lsv.ens-cachan.fr
[2] University of Newcastle-upon-Tyne, Newcastle upon Tyne, UK

Abstract. The firing rule for Petri nets assumes instantaneous and simultaneous consumption and creation of tokens. In the context of ordinary Petri nets, this poses no particular problem because of the system's asynchronicity, even if token creation occurs later than token consumption in the firing. With read arcs, the situation changes, and several different choices of semantics are possible. The step semantics introduced by Janicki and Koutny can be seen as imposing a two-phase firing scheme: first, the presence of the required tokens is checked, then consumption and production of tokens happens. Pursuing this approach further, we develop a more general framework based on explicitly splitting the phases of firing, allowing to synthesize coherent steps. This turns out to define a more general non-atomic semantics, which has important potential for safety as it allows to detect errors that were missed by the previous semantics. Then we study the characterization of partial-order processes feasible under one or the other semantics.

1 Introduction

There are some aspects of concurrent behaviour that cannot be modeled by sequences of actions nor by partial orders alone (c.f. [9,11]). An example is the 'earlier than or simultaneous' (that is, 'not later than') relationship [11], for which neither sequences nor partial orders are expressive enough. Consider, for example, a priority system with three actions: a, b, and c such that c has higher priority than both a and b. Initially, a and b can be executed simultaneously, while c is blocked. Moreover, completing a or b permanently enables action c. Using sequences of actions, we cannot capture the execution where a and b are executed in the same run of the system, as both (ab) and (ba) would violate the priority constraint. However, a sequence $(\{a, b\})$, representing a step in which actions a and b are executed simultaneously, faithfully reflects a possible scenario in which both a and b are executed. Consider now a modified system in which executing a no longer enables action c. In such a case, two executions involving the actions a and b are possible, namely $(\{a, b\})$ and (ab). Now, this behavior is *not* reflected by the partial order in which a and b are concurrent; for in that

---

This work is partially supported by the UK EPSRC project UNCOVER.

R. Devillers and A. Valmari (Eds.): PETRI NETS 2015, LNCS 9115, pp. 117–136, 2015.
DOI: 10.1007/978-3-319-19488-2_6

case, sequence (*ba*) would emerge as a valid system behaviour, which it is *not* according to the above specification. To cover such cases, [12] used structures richer than causal partial orders and, in this particular case, introduced the notion of a 'weak causality' between *a* and *b*, meaning that '*a* can be earlier than or simultaneous with *b*', but 'not later than *b*'. In the resulting model, causality (partial order) is augmented with weak causality leading to *stratified order structures* [8,10,12], which extend the standard causal partial orders if the underlying concurrent system does not exhibit features like priorities in the above example. Stratified order structures have been successfully applied to model, e.g., inhibitor and priority systems and asynchronous races (see, e.g. [12,14,16]). Extensions of the standard partial order model of concurrency to cover features such as priorities as well as inhibitor and read arcs in the elementary net systems are systematically discussed in [17].

Let us turn now to the more specific model class of Petri nets. Many distributed systems allow read-only access to some data. These non-destructive accesses can be done concurrently by several components of the system. In order to model these read-only accesses with Petri nets, a classical method is to design a loop in which some transition consumes and rewrites a token on the same place. Nevertheless this technique is not satisfactory when one is dealing with causal semantics because the consumption of the token artificially enforces an order on the events accessing the same data.

In order to solve this problem, read arcs were added to Petri nets [5,22]. This extension is now quite commonly used, and partial order semantics were proposed for this new model [3,4,28,31]. In the same vein, inhibitor arcs were also introduced [5,12]. Their expressive power is similar to the one of read arcs in the case of bounded nets. Finite complete prefixes of Petri nets with read arcs (also called contextual Petri nets) were first defined in the restricted case of *read-persistent nets* [29], and later in the general case [32]. Efficient procedures exist for the computation and analysis of finite complete prefixes for safe Petri nets with read arcs [2,25].

In the present paper, we push the analysis of contextual Petri nets further in the direction of collective, or non-atomic, firing of several transitions jointly, in one *step*, where a step is seen here as a set of transitions (or multi-set in the case of non safe nets). Giving a semantics that allows this is not problematic in ordinary Petri nets; a step is enabled iff the current marking is bigger than the sum of all presets of its transitions, both seen as vectors whose dimension is the number of places. With read arcs, the situation changes, and several different choices of step semantics are possible. The one introduced in [12] can be seen as imposing a two-phase firing scheme: first, the presence of the required tokens is checked, then consumption and production of tokens happens. Here, we develop a more general framework based on explicitly splitting the phases of firing, allowing to synthesize coherent steps. This turns out to define a more general non-atomic semantics. We will recall the fundamentals of Contextual Petri nets in Section 2, and develop the non-atomic sequential semantics in Section 3. In Section 4, we continue with the study of non-sequential, partial order semantics with non-atomic firing; finally, Section 5 concludes.

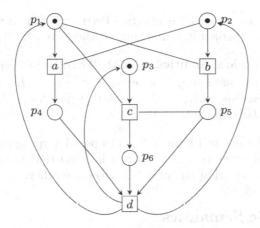

Fig. 1. A contextual Petri net

2   Contextual Petri Nets

2.1   Definition

We consider only *safe* contextual Petri nets (PNs), i.e. PNs where there is never more than one token in a place. We discuss the general case in Section 5.

Definition 1 (Contextual Petri Net (PN)). *A contextual Petri net is a tuple* $(P, T, pre, cont, post, M_0)$ *where* P *and* T *are finite sets of places and transitions respectively, pre and post map each transition* $t \in T$ *to its (nonempty) preset denoted* $^\bullet t \overset{\text{def}}{=} pre(t) \subseteq P$, *its (possibly empty) context denoted* $\underline{t} \overset{\text{def}}{=} cont(t) \subseteq P \setminus {}^\bullet t$ *and its (possibly empty) postset denoted* $t^\bullet \overset{\text{def}}{=} post(t) \subseteq P$; $M_0 \subseteq P$ *is the* initial marking.

We usually denote $^\bullet \underline{t} \overset{\text{def}}{=} {}^\bullet t \cup \underline{t}$. For simplicity, we assume that for any transition t, its context is disjoint from its preset and postset.

A contextual Petri net is represented as a graph with two types of nodes: places (circles) and transitions (rectangles). Presets are represented by arrows from places to transitions, postsets by arrows from transitions to places, and contexts by undirected edges between places and transitions. The initial marking is represented by tokens in places. Figure 1 shows an example of a contextual Petri net. The transition a, for instance, has p_1 in its preset, p_2 in its context and p_4 in its postset.

2.2   Atomic Semantics

A *marking* of a safe contextual Petri net is a set $M \subseteq P$ of marked places. A Petri net starts in its *initial marking* M_0. A transition $t \in T$ is *enabled* in a marking M if all the places of its preset and context are marked, i.e. $^\bullet t \cup \underline{t} \subseteq M$. Then t can *fire* from M, leading to the marking $M' \overset{\text{def}}{=} (M \setminus {}^\bullet t) \cup t^\bullet$.

Again, we consider only *safe* contextual Petri nets, that is we assume that if a transition $t \in T$ is enabled in a marking M, then $(M \setminus {}^{\bullet}t) \cap t^{\bullet} = \emptyset$.

Definition 2 (Atomic semantics, a-run). *We call* firing sequence of N under the atomic semantics, *or* a-run, *any sequence* $\sigma \stackrel{\text{def}}{=} (t_1 \ldots t_n)$ *of transitions for which there exist markings* $M_1, \ldots, M_n$ *such that for all* $i \in \{1, \ldots, n\}$, *firing* t_i *from* M_{i-1} *is possible and leads to* M_i.

For instance, the net in Figure 1 has two possible firing sequences: (a) and (bc). However, it is never possible to fire d because that would require to fire both a and b first, and firing one of a, b disables the other.

3   Non-atomic Semantics

In this section, we discuss two semantics for concurrent firing of multiple transitions. One is the well-known *step semantics* [11], in which multiple transitions can fire simultaneously. This is typically the case of a and b in the net of Figure 1, which are enabled simultaneously and have disjoint presets, but cannot fire together according to the atomic semantics. The step semantics can be interpreted as first checking whether all members of a set of transitions can fire, and then firing them either simultaneously or one by one, in any order. We then introduce a new, so-called *interval semantics*, which allows a more liberal choice of checking and firing transitions in a set.

We present the semantics under the assumption that the underlying net is safe even under these two semantics, which allow more possibilities than the atomic one.

3.1   Step Semantics

We first recall the step semantics [11].

Definition 3 (Step semantics, s-run). *Let* N *be a PN. We call* s-run *of* N *any sequence* $\sigma \stackrel{\text{def}}{=} (T_1 \ldots T_n)$ *of sets of transitions for which there exist markings* $M_1, \ldots, M_n$ *such that for all* $i \in \{1, \ldots, n\}$,

- *every* $t \in T_i$ *is enabled in* M_{i-1},
- *the presets of the transitions in* T_i *are disjoint, and*
- $M_i = (M_{i-1} \setminus \bigcup_{t \in T_i} {}^{\bullet}t) \cup \bigcup_{t \in T_i} t^{\bullet}$.

In the example of Figure 1, the step semantics allows one to fire a and b in one step since they are both enabled in the initial state and ${}^{\bullet}a \cap {}^{\bullet}b = \emptyset$. This gives the s-run $(\{a, b\})$ in addition to the others which were already possible under the atomic semantics; for instance the a-run involving b followed by c, (denoted (bc) for the atomic semantics), is simply rewritten as the s-run $(\{b\}\{c\})$ under the step semantics. However, transition d remains dead since none of these s-runs contains all of a, b, and c.

The intuitive model underlying the step semantics is that all the transitions in the step can first check, in any order, whether they are enabled and not in conflict with one another. Once the checks have been performed, they can all fire, again in any order. Put differently, if we denote the checking phase of a transition t by t^- and its firing phase by t^+, then every step consists of any permutation of the actions of type t^- (for all transitions t in the step), followed by any permutation of the actions t^+. The notion introduced in Definition 4 formalizes this intuition.

Definition 4 ($s^{\pm}$-run). *For every s-run $(T_1 \dots T_n)$ of a contextual Petri net N, every concatenation $u_1^-.u_1^+.\cdots.u_n^-.u_n^+$ of sequences u_i^- and u_i^+, is a $s^{\pm}$-run of N, where every u_i^- is a permutation of the set $\{t^- \mid t \in T_i\}$ and every u_i^+ is a permutation of the set $\{t^+ \mid t \in T_i\}$ (remember that T_i is a set of transitions of N).*

For example, the s-run $(\{b\}\{c\})$ yields the $s^{\pm}$-run $(b^-b^+c^-c^+)$ and the s-run $(\{a,b\})$ yields four $s^{\pm}$-runs: $(a^-b^-a^+b^+)$, $(a^-b^-b^+a^+)$, $(b^-a^-a^+b^+)$ and $(b^-a^-b^+a^+)$.

3.2   Splitting Transitions for Understanding Steps

Definition 4 formalizes a new semantics of PNs, in which the firing of a transition does not happen atomically, but in two steps, the checking of the pre-conditions and the actual execution. In this section, we generalize this idea.

The left-hand side of Figure 2 shows a part of the net in Figure 1, which consists of transition a with its preset $\{p_1\}$, context $\{p_2\}$, and postset $\{p_4\}$. The construction on the right-hand side of 2 illustrates the idea of splitting firing transitions into two phases:

- Every transition t is split into t^- and t^+.
- Every place p is duplicated to p^c (meaning token in p available for consumption) and p^r (meaning token in p available for reading).

Similar ideas about splitting transitions can be found in several works, for instance in [27].

Intuitively, if we apply this construction to all transitions from Figure 1, then the $s^{\pm}$-runs of that net correspond to a-runs of the newly constructed net. The following Definition 5 provides the precise details of the construction.

Definition 5 ($split(N)$). *For every contextual Petri net $N = (P, T, pre, cont, post, M_0)$, we define the contextual Petri net $split(N) \stackrel{\text{def}}{=} (P', T', pre', cont', post', M_0')$ where*

- T' *contains two copies, denoted t^- and t^+ of every transition $t \in T$.*
- P' *contains two copies, denoted p^c and p^r of every place $p \in P$, plus one place p_t per transition $t \in T$.*
- $^{\bullet}t^- \stackrel{\text{def}}{=} \{p^c \mid p \in {}^{\bullet}t\}$

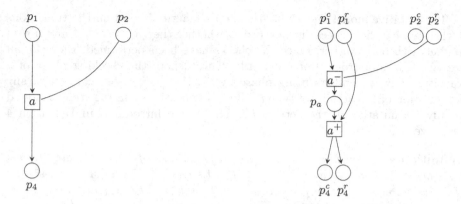

Fig. 2. The splitting of transition a (left) into a^- and a^+ (right)

- $t^- \stackrel{\text{def}}{=} \{p^r \mid p \in \underline{t}\}$
- $t^- {}^\bullet \stackrel{\text{def}}{=} \{p_t\}$
- ${}^\bullet t^+ \stackrel{\text{def}}{=} \{p^r \mid p \in {}^\bullet t\} \cup \{p_t\}$
- $\underline{t}^+ \stackrel{\text{def}}{=} \emptyset$
- $t^+ {}^\bullet \stackrel{\text{def}}{=} \{p^c \mid p \in t^\bullet\} \cup \{p^r \mid p \in t^\bullet\}\}$
- $M_0' \stackrel{\text{def}}{=} \{p^c \mid p \in M_0\} \cup \{p^r \mid p \in M_0\}$

We now formally prove the intuition mentioned above:

Lemma 1. *Every $s^\pm$-run $\sigma^\pm$ of N is a a-run of $split(N)$. Moreover $\sigma^\pm$ reaches the marking $\{p^c \mid p \in M\} \cup \{p^r \mid p \in M\}$, where M is the marking of N reached after the s-run σ from which $\sigma^\pm$ is obtained.*

Proof. We proceed by induction on the length of σ. The case $\sigma = ()$ is trivial. Now, let $\sigma^\pm = u_1^-.u_1^+. \cdots . u_n^-.u_n^+$ be a $s^\pm$-run obtained from a s-run $\sigma = (T_1 \dots T_n)$, assume the property true for $u_1^-.u_1^+. \cdots . u_{n-1}^-.u_{n-1}^+$ and denote M_{n-1} the marking reached after $(T_1 \dots T_{n-1})$. By induction hypothesis, $u_1^-.u_1^+. \cdots . u_{n-1}^-.u_{n-1}^+$ reaches the marking $\{p^c \mid p \in M_{n-1}\} \cup \{p^r \mid p \in M_{n-1}\}$ of $split(N)$. The fact that T_n is a valid step from M_{n-1} implies that $\bigcup_{t \in T_n} {}^\bullet \underline{t} \subseteq M_{n-1}$ and that the presets of the transitions in T_n are disjoint. This allows one to fire all the $t^-, t \in T_n$ in any order and reach the marking $\{p^c \mid p \in M_{n-1} \setminus \bigcup_{t \in T_n} {}^\bullet \underline{t}\} \cup \{p^r \mid p \in M_{n-1}\} \cup \{p_t \mid t \in T_n\}$ of $split(N)$. Now the $t^+, t \in T_n$, are all enabled and their presets are disjoint. They can in turn be fired in any order, reaching the desired marking of $split(N)$. $\qquad \square$

Note that the converse of Lemma 1 does not hold. For instance, for the net N from Figure 1, the net $split(N)$ admits the a-run $a^-b^-b^+c^-c^+a^+$, which is not an $s^\pm$-run of N.

3.3   Interval Semantics

We have seen that the construction $split(N)$ admits firing sequences that cannot be mapped back to executions under either the atomic or the step semantics. In this section, we shall introduce a new, so-called *interval semantics*, which is more general than the step semantics, and whose interpretation on a net N does correspond to the feasible executions in $split(N)$.

Definition 6 (Interval semantics, i-run). *Every a-run of $split(N)$ is called* i-run *of N, or* run *of N under the interval semantics.*

Coming back to the example of Figure 1, transition d can fire under the interval semantics, for instance after the i-run $a^-b^-b^+c^-c^+a^+d^-d^+$ where transitions b and c complete the firing during the period in which a fires. Under the atomic semantics, a and b are in conflict, which prevents d from firing. Under the step semantics, a and b can fire in the same step, but then c cannot fire. Under the interval semantics, d can also fire.

Recall that we introduced t^- and t^+ to represent different phases during the execution of transition t. An obvious question is whether the new semantics can lead to runs in which a transition 'gets stuck' during its execution. The following Lemma 2 affirms that this is not the case: once t^- is fired, nothing can hinder t^+ from firing, too.

Definition 7 (complete i-run). *An i-run is* complete *if every t^- is matched by a t^+.*

Lemma 2. *Every i-run can be completed: for every i-run σ, there exists a suffix μ which matches all the unmatched t^-, and such that $\sigma\mu$ is an i-run.*

Proof. As long as a t^- is unmatched, $^\bullet t^+$ remains included in the marking: no other transition consumes these tokens. Hence it suffices to fire all the t^+ corresponding to the unmatched t^-, in any order.   □

3.4   Comparison of Sequential Semantics

This section provides a brief summary and comparison of the previously discussed semantics. To simplify the comparison, we first need a technical definition that allows to represent atomic runs in a form comparable to i-runs. The following Definition 8 simply makes explicit the assumption that the firing of a transition is atomic: in terms of i-runs, every t^- is immediately followed by the corresponding t^+.

Definition 8 ($a^\pm$-run). *For every a-run $(t_1 \ldots t_n)$, the sequence $t_1^- t_1^+ \ldots t_n^- t_n^+$ is called an* $a^\pm$-run.

We can now turn to comparing the different sequential semantics based on (complete) i-runs. It is immediate that every $a^\pm$-run of a contextual Petri net N

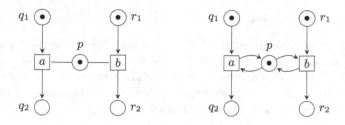

Fig. 3. Example illustrating the effect of read-arcs on partial-order semantics

is an $s^{\pm}$-run of N. Also, by Lemma 1, every $s^{\pm}$-run is an i-run, and by Lemma 2, every i-run can be made complete.

Let N be a PN, and denote by $Atomic_N$ the set of its $a^{\pm}$-runs, by $Step_N$ the set of its $s^{\pm}$-runs, and by $Interval_N$ the set of its i-runs. Then we have the following relation:

$$Atomic_N \subseteq Step_N \subseteq Interval_N$$

Note that, in general, the subset inclusions are strict, as we have seen in previous examples. The strictness holds even when N does not contain any read arcs. E.g., if N contains three enabled transitions a, b, c, whose presets are all disjoint, then $a^-b^-c^-a^+b^+c^+ \in Step_N \setminus Atomic_N$ and $a^-b^-a^+c^-b^+c^+ \in Interval_N \setminus Step_N$. However, the set of reachable markings remains the same under all three semantics when no read arcs are present.

4   Non-atomicity and Partial Order Semantics

Consider a PN N with read arcs such as in the left part of Figure 3. It is easy to see that if one replaces a read arc in a net by a pair of arrows forming a loop (see, e.g., the net N' in the right-hand side of Figure 3), then any a-run of N remains an a-run of N', and vice versa, and that both nets have the same reachable markings. However, one of the reasons why read arcs have attracted the attention of the Petri net community is that they change the step semantics of the net. E.g., both nets admit the s-runs ($\{a\}\{b\}$) and ($\{b\}\{a\}$), but N additionally admits the s-run ($\{a, b\}$). The splitting operation provided in the previous section preserves this difference: $split(N')$ admits the two s-runs ($a^-a^+b^-b^+$) and ($b^-b^+a^-a^+$), while $split(N)$ admits additional runs, e.g. ($a^-b^-a^+b^+$).

We first present processes as partial-order semantics for nets under atomic semantics. These definitions are standard [3,4,28,31]. Then, as well as for the sequential semantics, we define the partial-order semantics of a net N under the non-atomic semantics by applying partial-order atomic semantics to $split(N)$. This gives processes where every transition firing is split into two events e^- and e^+. These processes give sufficiently detailed information to understand how a scenario can or cannot be fired under non-atomic semantics.

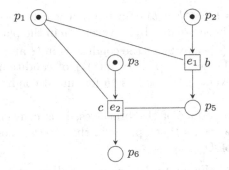

Fig. 4. A process representing the a-run (bc) of the contextual Petri net of Figure 1. Technically, the condition labeled p_1 is coded as $(\perp, p_1)$, the event e_1 (labeled b) is coded as $(\{(\perp, p_2)\}, \{(\perp, p_1)\}, b)$ and e_2 as $(\{(\perp, p_3)\}, \{(\perp, p_1), (e_1, p_5)\}, c)$

Anyway, in the end, we propose an abstract view of the processes where the e^- and e^+ are abstracted back to a single event e. These abstract processes strictly generalize the processes of the original net under atomic semantics. We characterize the conditions under which an abstract process is feasible under any of the atomic, step or interval semantics.

4.1 Processes Under Atomic Semantics

Processes are a way to represent an execution of a Petri net so that the actions (called events) are not totally ordered like in firing sequences, but only partially ordered by weak (or conditional) and strong (or unconditional) *causality* relations which indicate the dependencies between events due to creation, consumption and reading of tokens.

An execution of a Petri net N is represented as a labeled Petri net where every transition, called *event* and labeled by a transition t of N, stands for an occurrence of t, and every place, called *condition* and labeled by a place p of N, refers to a token produced by an event in place p or to a token of the initial marking. The arcs represent the creation and consumption of tokens.

Figure 4 shows a process representing the a-run (bc) of the contextual Petri net of Figure 1.

Because fresh conditions are created for the tokens created by each event, every condition has either no input arc (if it is an initial condition) or a single input arc, coming from the event that created the token. Symmetrically, each place has no more than one output arc since a token can be consumed by only one event in an execution.

We will define the mapping Π from the a-runs of a safe Petri net to their partial order representation as processes. We use a canonical coding like in [6]. This coding is illustrated in Figure 4.

Each process will be a set E of *events*. Every event e is itself a triple $({}^\bullet e, \underline{e}, \tau(e))$ that codes an occurrence of the transition $\tau(e)$ in the process. ${}^\bullet e$

and $\underline{e}$ are sets of pairs $b \stackrel{\text{def}}{=} (^\bullet b, \pi(b))$. Such a pair is called a *condition* and refers to the token that has been created by the event $^\bullet b$ in the place $\pi(b)$. We say that the event $e \stackrel{\text{def}}{=} (^\bullet e, \underline{e}, \tau(e))$ *consumes* the conditions in $^\bullet e$ and *reads* the conditions in $\underline{e}$. It also *creates* the set $\{(e, p) \mid p \in \tau(e)^\bullet\}$ of conditions, which we denote $e^\bullet$. A virtual initial event $\bot$ is used as $^\bullet b$ for initial conditions. By convention $\bot^\bullet \stackrel{\text{def}}{=} \{\bot\} \times M_0$.

To summarize the coding of the processes, it is convenient to define a set D_N, such that all the events that appear in the processes of a contextual Petri net N, are elements of D_N.

Definition 9 (D_N). *We define D_N as the smallest set satisfying:*

for all $B_1, B_2 \subseteq \bigcup_{e \in D_N \cup \{\bot\}} e^\bullet$ such that $\pi_{|B_1 \cup B_2}$ is injective,
*   for all $t \in T$,*
$$\pi(B_1) = {}^\bullet t \wedge \pi(B_2) = \underline{t} \implies (B_1, B_2, t) \in D_N.$$

Notice that this inductive definition is initialized by the fact that $\bot \in D_N \cup \{\bot\}$.

We need a last notion before defining the mapping Π from a-runs to processes: the set of conditions that remain at the end of a set E of events (meaning that they have been created by an event of E, and no event of E has consumed them) is $\uparrow(E) \stackrel{\text{def}}{=} \bigcup_{e \in E \cup \{\bot\}} e^\bullet \setminus \bigcup_{e \in E} {}^\bullet e$. Because N is safe, the restriction of π to $\uparrow(E)$ will be injective when E is a process and $\pi(\uparrow(E))$ will be the marking reached at the end of E.

Definition 10. *The function Π that maps each firing sequence $(t_1 \ldots t_n)$ to a process is defined as follows:*

- $\Pi(\epsilon) \stackrel{\text{def}}{=} \emptyset$
- $\Pi((t_1 \ldots t_{n+1})) \stackrel{\text{def}}{=} E \cup \{e\}$, *where*
    - $E \stackrel{\text{def}}{=} \Pi((t_1 \ldots t_n))$ *and*
    - *the event $e \stackrel{\text{def}}{=} (\pi_{|\uparrow(E)}^{-1}(^\bullet t_{n+1}), \pi_{|\uparrow(E)}^{-1}(\underline{t_{n+1}}), t_{n+1})$ represents the last firing of the sequence.*

Causality. We define the relation $\rightarrow$ on the events as: $e \rightarrow e' \stackrel{\text{def}}{\Longleftrightarrow} e^\bullet \cap {}^\bullet e' \neq \emptyset$. The reflexive transitive closure $\rightarrow^*$ of $\rightarrow$ is called the *unconditional* or *strong causality* relation.

If two events e and f are causally related ($e \rightarrow^* f$), then:

- e occurs in every process where f occurs, and
- if a process contains e and f, then e occurs before f.

Because of the read arcs, two events e and f may satisfy the second item without being in strong causal relation. This happens when e reads a condition that is consumed by f. This phenomenon is captured by the relation $\rightsquigarrow$ defined as $e \rightsquigarrow f \stackrel{\text{def}}{\Longleftrightarrow} \underline{e} \cap {}^\bullet f \neq \emptyset$. Combining $\rightarrow$ and $\rightsquigarrow$, we get the *conditional* or *weak causality*, denoted $\nearrow$, and defined as $e \nearrow f \stackrel{\text{def}}{\Longleftrightarrow} (e \rightarrow f) \vee (e \rightsquigarrow f)$.

For every event e, we denote $\lceil e \rceil \stackrel{\text{def}}{=} \{f \in E \mid f \rightarrow^* e\}$, and for all set E of events, $\lceil E \rceil \stackrel{\text{def}}{=} \bigcup_{e \in E} \lceil e \rceil$.

Branching processes, conflicts, unfoldings. Each process represents one execution of the net. One often uses the partial order representation to represent also *sets* of executions. This is done simply by superimposing several processes and merging their common prefixes; technically, this operation is nothing but the set union of the processes. The result is called a *branching process*. The most obvious difference between branching processes and processes is that branching processes may contain two distinct events e and e' which have a common pre-condition ($^\bullet e \cap {}^\bullet e' \neq \emptyset$). This is called a *conflict* and implies that e and e' never occur together in the same process, since, in a process each condition corresponds to a precise occurrence of a token in a place, created by an event and possibly consumed by another one.

For branching processes of contextual Petri nets, another source of incompatibilities between events needs to be considered: contrary to the strong causality relation $\rightarrow$, the weak causality relation $\nearrow$ may have some cycles. The events involved in such cycle are incompatible because, when an event is added to a process, it is never the predecessor by $\nearrow$ of an older event. This situation arises between the events representing an occurrence of a and an occurrence of b from the initial marking of the net of Figure 1, and corresponds to the fact that the firing of one disables the other in the atomic semantics.

The maximal branching process, obtained by superimposing all the processes of a net N, is called the *unfolding* of N.

4.2   Processes Under Non-atomic Semantics

In Section 3, we have defined non-atomic sequential semantics of a contextual Petri net N using the construction $split(N)$. every (complete) run σ of $split(N)$ under atomic semantics is interpreted as a run of N under non-atomic semantics.

We can now move very naturally to partial order non-atomic semantics.

Definition 11 ((Complete) split process). *For every (complete) i-run σ of a contextual Petri net N, $\Pi(\sigma)$ is called a (complete) split process of N.*

Figure 5 represents a split process of the contextual Petri net N of Figure 1. Weak and strong causality relations in the split process show precisely what are the interleavings of the a^-, a^+, b^-, b^+, c^-, c^+ which make possible a scenario where a, b and c occur.

This representation as split process has the interest of showing a very detailed view of the execution of a contextual Petri net under non-atomic semantics. We propose now a more abstract representation with only one event per transition firing. This representation generalizes the partial order semantics under atomic semantics, in the sense that every process under the atomic semantics is an abstraction of a split process.

The intuition behind the abstraction is the following. We remark that in a complete split process E of N, every event $e^- \in E$ representing an occurrence of a transition t^- of $split(N)$ creates a unique condition b corresponding to a

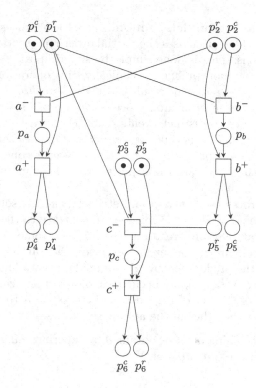

Fig. 5. A process of the splitting of the contextual Petri net N of Figure 1. Transitions a^- and b^- are concurrent, as well as a^+ and c^+. Hence the process represents the 4 i-runs $(a^-b^-b^+c^-c^+a^+)$, $(a^-b^-b^+c^-a^+c^+)$, $(b^-a^-b^+c^-c^+a^+)$ and $(b^-a^-b^+c^-a^+c^+)$. After this process, transition d (split to d^-d^+) becomes fireable.

token in p_t, and this condition is consumed by a unique event e^+ representing the occurrence of t^+.

The abstraction merges e^- and e^+ and deletes b. It also merges the two copies of the created tokens (occurrences of p^c and p^r).

Figure 6 shows the abstraction of the complete split process of Figure 5.

Definition 12 (Abstract processes, _abstr_, α). *We define the abstraction of a complete split process E as:*

$$abstr(E) \stackrel{\text{def}}{=} \{\alpha(e^+) \mid e^+ \in E^+\}$$

where E^+ is the set of events of E representing the occurrence of a transition t^+ of $split(N)$, and α is defined inductively by:

- $\alpha(\bot) \stackrel{\text{def}}{=} \bot$ *and*
- $\alpha(e^+) \stackrel{\text{def}}{=} (\{(\alpha(f^+), p) \mid (f^+, p^c) \in {}^\bullet e^-\},$
  $\{(\alpha(f^+), p) \mid (f^+, p^r) \in \underline{e^-}\},$
  $t)$

where t is the transition of N such that e^+ represents an occurrence of t^+.

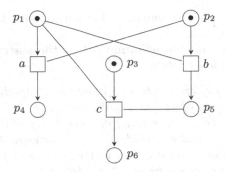

Fig. 6. The abstraction of the split process of Figure 5. This abstract process is feasible only under the interval semantics. With the atomic semantics, a and b cannot fire together. With the step semantics, they can fire 'simultaneously'. But this consumes the token in p_1 which is required to enable c.

We call $abstr(E)$ an abstract process *of N under interval semantics.*

Notice that the elements in $abstr(E)$ are members of the set D_N (Definition 9); this means they have the same shape as the events that occur in the processes of N under atomic semantics.

What is more: abstractions of processes of $a^\pm$ runs coincide with processes of a-runs.

Theorem 1. *For every a-run $(t_1 \ldots t_n)$, the process of $(t_1 \ldots t_n)$ is also the abstraction of the split process of the $a^\pm$-run $(t_1^- t_1^+ \ldots t_n^- t_n^+)$:*

$$abstr(\Pi((t_1^- t_1^+ \ldots t_n^- t_n^+))) = \Pi((t_1 \ldots t_n)) .$$

Proof. We first remark that the final conditions $\uparrow(abstr(E))$ of the abstraction of a complete split process E are the $(\alpha(f^+), p)$ with $(f^+, p^c) \in \uparrow(E)$ (or equivalently $(f^+, p^r) \in \uparrow(E)$): by definition of the abstraction, the conditions in $abstr(E)$ are the $(\alpha(f^+), p)$ with $p \in t^\bullet$ and $t^+ = \tau(f^+)$; and those that are final in $abstr(E)$ are those that are not consumed by any other $\alpha(e^+)$, which (by definition of $\alpha(e^+)$ and because E is complete) is equivalent to saying that (f^+, p^c) is not consumed by any e^- of E.

Then we prove the theorem by induction on the size of the a-run, using the inductive definitions of Π and α. The occurrences of t^- and t^+ at the end of the $a^\pm$-run are represented in $\Pi((t_1^- t_1^+ \ldots t_n^- t_n^+))$ by two events e^- and e^+, and α maps precisely e^+ to the event e of $\Pi((t_1 \ldots t_n))$ which represents the firing of t_n: the conditions in ${}^\bullet e^-$ being by definition final conditions of $\Pi((t_1^- t_1^+ \ldots t_{n-1}^- t_{n-1}^+))$, the $(\alpha(f^+), p)$ which occur in the definition of $\alpha(e^+)$ are the final conditions of $\Pi((t_1 \ldots t_{n-1}))$ which occur in the definition of the event e in $\Pi((t_1 \ldots t_n))$. $\qquad\square$

A direct consequence of this theorem is that every process of N under the atomic semantics, is also an abstract process of N.

We can also notice that the map α, and by consequence the abstraction *abstr* itself, are injective.

An important thing for the following is how the abstraction preserves the weak and strong causality relations.

Lemma 3. *We have explained when defining the abstraction that every event representing an occurrence of a t^- in a split process of N is followed in the process by a uniquely defined event representing the occurrence of the corresponding t^+. We use the notation e^- and e^+ to identify this correspondence. Moreover this pair of events appears in the abstraction as the event $\alpha(e^+)$, which we denote e. Similarly, for every pair of conditions $(e^+, p^c), (e^+, p^c)$, merged in the abstraction to the condition $(\alpha(e^+), p)$, we denote b^c and b^r and b.*

Using these notations, we have the following properties:

- *for every e, $e^- \to e^+$*
- *for every e and f, $e \to f \iff e^+ \to f^-$.*
- *$\rightsquigarrow$ occurs in a split process only between an e^- and an f^+. It is preserved by the abstraction: $e \rightsquigarrow f \iff e^- \rightsquigarrow f^+$.*

Proof.

- The causality $e^- \to e^+$ simply comes from the condition representing the token created by e^- in place p_t, and consumed by e^+.
- $e \to f$ implies that there exists a condition $b \in e^\bullet \cap {}^\bullet f$. If $b \in e^\bullet \cap {}^\bullet f$, then $b^c \in e^{+\bullet} \cap {}^\bullet f^-$; the other case is $b \in e^\bullet \cap \underline{f}$ and implies $b^r \in e^{+\bullet} \cap {}^\bullet f^-$. In both cases, we have $e^{+\bullet} \cap {}^\bullet f^- \neq \emptyset$, and then $e^+ \to f^-$.
- The only case where a condition is read by an event and consumed by another in a split process is when the condition (call it b^r) represents a token in a p^r, and $b^r \in \underline{e^-} \cap {}^\bullet f^+$ for some e and f. This appears in the abstraction as a place $b \in \underline{e} \cap {}^\bullet f$. $\square$

4.3   Characterization of Abstract Processes Feasible with the (Atomic, Step, Interval) Semantics

We propose a direct characterization of the abstract processes without using split processes. We have already remarked that abstract processes are subsets of D_N; now we give the conditions under which a subset of D_N is an abstract process for one or the other semantics.

Theorem 2 (Atomic semantics). *Every set $E \subseteq D_N$ of events is an abstract process of N under the atomic semantics iff*

- *$\lceil E \rceil \subseteq E$ (i.e. E is causally closed),*
- *for every $e, e' \in E$, $e \neq e' \implies {}^\bullet e \cap {}^\bullet e' = \emptyset$ (i.e. E contains no conflict), and*
- *the restriction $\nearrow_{|E}$ of $\nearrow$ to E is acyclic (i.e. its transitive closure $\nearrow_{|E}{}^+$ is irreflexive).*

Proof. Since abstract processes of N coincide with processes under the atomic semantics (see Theorem 1), this amounts to expressing the conditions under which a set $E \subseteq D_N$ of events is a process of N under the atomic semantics, which is a classical result of previous works about partial order semantics of contextual nets [3,4,28,31].

Briefly, the idea is that, by the inductive definition of the events of a process (see Definition 10), all the processes are causally closed and contain no conflicts. Also, when an event e is added to a process (again like in Definition 10), it has no successor by $\nearrow$ in the process. The consequence is that the processes contain no cycle of $\nearrow$.

Conversely, every set E of events that satisfies our three conditions is a process: it suffices to take the events of E in a sequence $(e_1 \ldots e_{|E|})$ compatible with the weak causality relation (i.e. such that $e_i \nearrow e_j$ implies $i < j$). This is possible because $\nearrow$ is acyclic. We get that the sequence $\sigma \overset{\text{def}}{=} (\pi(e_1) \ldots \pi(e_{|E|}))$ is a a-run of N and $\Pi(\sigma) = E$.   □

Theorem 3 (Step semantics). *Every set $E \subseteq D_N$ of events is an abstract process of N under the step semantics iff*

- *$\lceil E \rceil \subseteq E$,*
- *for every $e, e' \in E$, $e \neq e' \implies {}^\bullet e \cap {}^\bullet e' = \emptyset$, and*
- *the composition $\nearrow_{|E}^+ \to_{|E}$ of relations $\nearrow_{|E}^+$ and $\to_{|E}$ is irreflexive.*

Proof. Here the principle is the one developed for stratified order structures [8,10,12]. Consider a step to be executed after an $s^\pm$-run represented by a split process E'. The events corresponding to all the t^- are added first to the split process (first layer), and then the events corresponding to the t^+ (second layer). In the split process, the (weak and strong) causal dependencies involving the new events go only from the events of E' to the new events and from the first layer to the second layer. After abstraction, the two layers are merged into a single one, among which only weak causal dependencies may exist and may even have cycles (like the events labeled a and b in Figure 6). But no causal dependency exists from the new events to the old ones, which implies that $\nearrow_{|E}^+ \to_{|E}$ is irreflexive on the abstract process E.

Conversely, every set E of events that satisfies our three conditions is an abstract process of N under the step semantics: the fact that $\nearrow_{|E}^+ \to_{|E}$ be irreflexive allows one to partition the events of E into sets E_i such that only $\rightsquigarrow$ dependencies are possible between the events of an E_i, and the other causal dependencies go only from an E_i to an E_j with $i < j$. The sequence of E_i gives a sequence of steps whose split process is mapped to E by the abstraction.   □

Theorem 4 (Interval semantics). *Every set $E \subseteq D_N$ of events is an abstract process of N under the interval semantics iff*

- *$\lceil E \rceil \subseteq E$,*
- *for every $e, e' \in E$, $e \neq e' \implies {}^\bullet e \cap {}^\bullet e' = \emptyset$, and*
- *$\nearrow_{|E} \to_{|E}^+$ is acyclic (i.e. $(\nearrow_{|E} \to_{|E}^+)^+$ is irreflexive).*

Proof. E is an abstract process of N under the interval semantics iff it is the abstraction of a process E' of $split(N)$ under the atomic semantics. The abstraction mapping $abstr$ being injective, it defines a unique candidate for E'. One checks easily that $E' \subseteq D_{split(N)}$. We know that E' is a process of $split(N)$ iff it satisfies the conditions recalled in Theorem 2. It remains to show that they are equivalent to the conditions of the present theorem applied to $E = abstr(E')$. The equivalence of the conditions about the causal pasts ($\lceil E' \rceil \subseteq E'$ iff $\lceil E \rceil \subseteq E$) and about absence of conflicts are straightforward. The more interesting point is the correspondence between the acyclicity conditions: $\nearrow_{|E} \rightarrow_{|E}^+$ is acyclic iff $\nearrow_{|E'}$ is acyclic. This point derives from the properties of preservation of weak and strong causality by abstraction given in Lemma 3: they give immediately that every cycle for $\nearrow_{|E} \rightarrow_{|E}^+$ yields a cycle in $\nearrow_{|E'}$. The converse also holds because $\rightsquigarrow$ appears in E only between an e^- and an f^+, as $e^- \rightsquigarrow f^+$. Hence, if this weak causality dependency is concatenated with another one, giving $e^- \rightsquigarrow f^+ \nearrow g$, then the causal dependency $f^+ \nearrow g$ must be strong: $f^+ \rightarrow g$. In the end, this implies that every cycle of the $\nearrow_{|E'}$ relation provides a cycle of the $\nearrow_{|E'} \rightarrow_{|E'}^+$ relation. By Lemma 3, this cycle yields a cycle for $\nearrow_{|E} \rightarrow_{|E}^+$ in the abstracted process. $\qquad\square$

Summary. As a summary, we just want to confirm, at the level of abstract processes, our intuition that the interval semantics is more permissive than the step semantics, which is in turn more permissive than the atomic semantics. Namely, we compare the conditions about cycles of causality dependencies that appear in the three theorems above. It is true that if $\nearrow_{|E} \rightarrow_{|E}^+$ has a cycle, the cycle contains at least one strong causality dependency $e \rightarrow f$ and we have $f \nearrow_{|E}^+ \rightarrow_{|E} f$. It is also true that if $f \nearrow_{|E}^+ \rightarrow_{|E} f$, then $f \nearrow_{|E}^+ f$.

When there is no read arc, anyway, they all collapse (at the level of abstract or split processes).

Theorem 5. *For every Petri net N without read arcs (i.e. $\underline{t} = \emptyset$ for all t), the abstract processes under the three semantics coincide.*

Proof. In this case the weak and strong causality relations coincide, and, because the strong causality relation is acyclic by construction of the events, the conditions of acyclicity in the three previous theorems are all automatically verified. $\qquad\square$

4.4   The End

One could now wonder what happens if $split(N)$ be itself interpreted under step or interval semantics. The answer is: nothing; and this gives an end to our story! By its structure, $split(N)$ has the property that the three semantics generate the same abstract processes (and the same split processes too, since abstraction is injective).

Theorem 6. *For every contextual occurrence net N, every abstract process of $split(N)$ under the interval semantics is also an abstract process of $split(N)$ under the step and atomic semantics.*

Proof. We show that for every set of events $E \subseteq D_{split(N)}$, if $\nearrow_{|E}$ has a cycle, then $\nearrow_{|E} \rightarrow_{|E}^{+}$ has a cycle too. By Lemma 3, $\rightsquigarrow$ appears in E only between an e^- and an f^+, as $e^- \rightsquigarrow f^+$. Hence, if this weak causality dependency is concatenated with another one, giving $e^- \rightsquigarrow f^+ \nearrow g$, then the causal dependency $f^+ \nearrow g$ must be strong: $f^+ \rightarrow g$. In the end, this implies that every cycle of the $\nearrow_{|E}$ relation provides a cycle of the $\nearrow_{|E} \rightarrow_{|E}^{+}$ relation.   □

5 Discussion

We have shown, within a general framework obtained by an adequate splitting of transitions, how a novel non-atomic firing semantics emerges for contextual nets, and studied the resulting concurrent processes, which provide a deeper insight into complex dynamics of distributed systems.

A key motivation for the research presented in this paper comes from concurrent behaviours as exhibited by systems with a semantics that cannot be captured by sequences of actions (i.e., the atomic semantics). While the step semantics of, e.g., [8,10,15,26] provides an expressive operational semantics, it still does not represent the most general case. It was argued in [30], and analysed in detail in [11], that the most general observational semantics can be represented by the interval semantics. Invariant structures for such a semantics have been proposed in [10,19], and analysed in detail in [13]. A calculus for temporal reasoning about interval semantics was introduced in [1] where thirteen basic relations between time intervals that are qualitative rather than quantitative (no exact numeric spans are represented) were investigated. These relations and the operations on them form an interval algebra for which several distinct subalgebras of different expressiveness and tractability have since been investigated, e.g., in [21,23].

An example of recent application of concurrency semantics based on step sequences was the paper [7] which investigated the behaviour of GALS (Globally Asynchronous Locally Synchronous) systems in the context of VLSI circuits. The specification of a system was given in the form of a Petri net N, and the aim was to re-design the system to optimize signal management, by grouping together concurrent events. More precisely, by looking at the concurrent reachability graph of N (i.e., one based on the step semantics), one aims at discovering events that appear in 'bundles', so that they all can be executed in a single clock tick (in effect, pruning the concurrent reachability graph). The resulting bundling is envisaged to reduce signal management, reducing the cost of scheduling and control, and improving system performance. The paper proposes a method that derives a combination of bundles that represents the temporal activities the designer requires. Careful selection of bundles is essential so that the pruned behaviour of the fully asynchronous model still exhibits some characteristics of its parent and is persistent. *Step semantics* and *step persistence* are hence important features that will guarantee true persistent behaviour for mixed synchronous-asynchronous (GALS) models.

An interesting question from a practical point of view is how to construct abstract processes resp. the abstract unfolding automatically. One possibility requiring little work would be to translate a net N into $split(N)$, then unfold it with the tool CUNF, which efficiently generates the unfolding for the atomic semantics [24]. The resulting unfolding could then be transformed into an abstract unfolding by merging pairs of conditions labeled p^c, p^r and pairs of events labeled t^-, t^+, respectively; the pairs to merge are identified uniquely by definition of the abstraction. A more intriguing question is whether the abstract unfolding can also be generated directly from the net N. A starting point are the results presented in Section 4.3, which characterize the events that belong to the unfolding. However, checking those conditions directly would be inefficient. Existing unfolding tools compute, e.g., a *concurrency relation* that allows to identify possible events more quickly, see, e.g., [2]. Transferring these results does not seem straightforward, and moreover, the issue of how to compute a finite *marking-complete prefix* of the unfolding would require attention. These questions promise to be interesting future work.

We have restricted ourselves to safe nets for technical simplicity and hence readability. However, there are no major obstacles for extending our work to non safe contextual nets. Unfoldings can be defined easily for the very large class of *semi-weighted nets* [3,20]. Simply, we lose uniqueness of the process representing a firing sequence, which prevents us from using our function Π (Definition 10). More importantly, in split processes of safe nets, for every condition (f^+, p^r) consumed by an event e^+, the corresponding (f^+, p^c) is consumed by e^-. For non safe nets, an e^+ may consume another condition labeled p^r, created by another event, say f'. This would induce 'superfluous' causality between f' and e^+. Taking this into account would make Lemma 3 and the following more tedious.

Future work should also include more general non-atomic semantics, in particular for boolean nets [18].

References

1. Allen, J.F.: Maintaining knowledge about temporal intervals. Commun. ACM **26**(11), 832–843 (1983)
2. Baldan, P., Bruni, A., Corradini, A., König, B., Rodríguez, C., Schwoon, S.: Efficient unfolding of contextual Petri nets. Theor. Comput. Sci. **449**, 2–22 (2012)
3. Baldan, P., Corradini, A., Montanari, U.: Contextual Petri nets, asymmetric event structures, and processes. Information and Computation **171**(1), 1–49 (2001)
4. Busi, N., Pinna, G.M.: Non sequential semantics for contextual P/T nets. In: Billington, J., Reisig, W. (eds.) ICATPN 1996. LNCS, vol. 1091, pp. 113–132. Springer, Heidelberg (1996)
5. Christensen, S., Hansen, N.D.: Coloured Petri nets extended with place capacities, test arcs and inhibitor arcs. In: Ajmone Marsan, M. (ed.) ICATPN 1993. LNCS, vol. 691, pp. 186–205. Springer, Heidelberg (1993)

6. Engelfriet, J.: Branching processes of Petri nets. Acta Informatica **28**(6), 575–591 (1991)
7. Fernandes, J., Koutny, M., Pietkiewicz-Koutny, M., Sokolov, D., Yakovlev, A.: Step persistence in the design of GALS systems. In: Colom, J.-M., Desel, J. (eds.) PETRI NETS 2013. LNCS, vol. 7927, pp. 190–209. Springer, Heidelberg (2013)
8. Gaifman, H., Pratt, V.R.: Partial order models of concurrency and the computation of functions. In: Proceedings, Symposium on Logic in Computer Science, pp. 72–85. IEEE Computer Society (1987)
9. Janicki, R.: Relational structures model of concurrency. Acta Inf. **45**(4), 279–320 (2008)
10. Janicki, R., Koutny, M.: Invariants and paradigms of concurrency theory. In: Aarts, E.H.L., van Leeuwen, J., Rem, M. (eds.) PARLE 1991. LNCS, vol. 506, pp. 59–74. Springer, Heidelberg (1991)
11. Janicki, R., Koutny, M.: Structure of concurrency. Theoretical Computer Science **112**(1), 5–52 (1993)
12. Janicki, R., Koutny, M.: Semantics of inhibitor nets. Inf. Comput. **123**(1), 1–16 (1995)
13. Janicki, R., Koutny, M.: Fundamentals of modelling concurrency using discrete relational structures. Acta Inf. **34**, 367–388 (1997)
14. Juhás, G., Lorenz, R., Mauser, S.: Synchronous + concurrent + sequential = earlier than + not later than. In: Sixth International Conference on Application of Concurrency to System Design (ACSD 2006), pp. 261–272. IEEE Computer Society (2006)
15. Juhás, G., Lorenz, R., Mauser, S.: Causal semantics of algebraic Petri nets distinguishing concurrency and synchronicity. Fundam. Inform. **86**(3), 255–298 (2008)
16. Kleijn, H.C.M., Koutny, M.: Process semantics of general inhibitor nets. Inf. Comput. **190**(1), 18–69 (2004)
17. Kleijn, J., Koutny, M.: Causality in extensions of Petri nets. T. Petri Nets and Other Models of Concurrency **7**, 225–254 (2013)
18. Kleijn, J., Koutny, M., Pietkiewicz-Koutny, M., Rozenberg, G.: Step semantics of boolean nets. Acta Informatica **50**(1), 15–39 (2013)
19. Lamport, L.: The mutual exclusion problem: part I - a theory of interprocess communication. J. ACM **33**(2), 313–326 (1986)
20. Meseguer, J., Montanari, U., Sassone, V.: On the semantics of place/transition Petri nets. Mathematical Structures in Computer Science **7**(4), 359–397 (1997)
21. Monica, D.D., Goranko, V., Montanari, A., Sciavicco, G.: Expressiveness of the interval logics of allen's relations on the class of all linear orders: complete classification. In: Proceedings of the 22nd International Joint Conference on Artificial Intelligence, IJCAI/AAAI 2011, pp. 845–850 (2011)
22. Montanari, U., Rossi, F.: Contextual nets. Acta Inf. **32**(6), 545–596 (1995)
23. Nebel, B., Bürckert, H.: Reasoning about temporal relations: A maximal tractable subclass of allen's interval algebra. J. ACM **42**(1), 43–66 (1995)
24. Rodríguez, C.: Verification Based on Unfoldings of Petri Nets with Read Arcs. PhD thesis, Laboratoire Spécification et Vérification, ENS Cachan, France, December 2013
25. Rodríguez, C., Schwoon, S.: Verification of Petri nets with read arcs. In: Koutny, M., Ulidowski, I. (eds.) CONCUR 2012. LNCS, vol. 7454, pp. 471–485. Springer, Heidelberg (2012)
26. Vogler, W.: A generalization of trace theory. RAIRO Informatique théorique et Applications **25**(2), 147–156 (1991)

27. Vogler, W.: Fairness and partial order semantics. Inf. Process. Lett. **55**(1), 33–39 (1995)
28. Vogler, W.: Partial order semantics and read arcs. Theoretical Computer Science **286**(1), 33–63 (2002)
29. Vogler, W., Semenov, A., Yakovlev, A.: Unfolding and finite prefix for nets with read arcs. In: Sangiorgi, D., de Simone, R. (eds.) CONCUR 1998. LNCS, vol. 1466, pp. 501–516. Springer, Heidelberg (1998)
30. Wiener, N.: A contribution to the theory of relative position. Proc. of the Cambridge Philosophical Society **33**(2), 313–326 (1914)
31. Winkowski, J.: Processes of contextual nets and their characteristics. Fundamenta Informaticae **36**(1) (1998)
32. Winkowski, J.: Reachability in contextual nets. Fundamenta Informaticae **51**(1–2), 235–250 (2002)

Discrete Parameters in Petri Nets

Nicolas David[1]($^{\boxtimes}$), Claude Jard[1], Didier Lime[2], and Olivier H. Roux[2]

[1] University of Nantes, LINA, Nantes, France
{nicolas.david1,claude.jard}@univ-nantes.fr
[2] École Centrale de Nantes, IRCCyN, Nantes, France
didier.lime@ec-nantes.fr, olivier-h.roux@irccyn.ec-nantes.fr

Abstract. With the aim of significantly increasing the modeling capability of Petri nets, we suggest that models involve parameters to represent the weights of arcs, or the number of tokens in places. We consider the property of coverability of markings. Two general questions arise: "Is there a parameter value for which the property is satisfied?" and "Does the property hold for all possible values of the parameters?". We show that these issues are undecidable in the general case. Therefore, we also define subclasses of parameterised networks, depending on whether the parameters are used on places, input or output arcs of transitions. For some subclasses, we prove that certain problems become decidable, making these subclasses more usable in practice.

Keywords: Petri net · Parameters · Coverability

1 Introduction

The introduction of parameters in models aims to improve genericity. It also allows the designer to leave unspecified aspects, such as those related to the modeling of the environment. This increase in modeling power usually results in greater complexity in the analysis and verification of the model. Beyond verification of properties, the existence of parameters opens the way to very relevant issues in design, such as the computation of the parameters values ensuring satisfaction of the expected properties.

We chose to explore the subject on concurrent models whose archetype is that of Petri nets. We consider discrete parameterisation of markings (the number of tokens in the places of the net) or weight of arcs connecting the input or output places to transitions. We call these Petri nets parameterised nets or PPNs.

We consider the general properties of coverability and, to a lesser extent, reachability (that are often the basis for the verification of more specific properties).

First issues are:

Work partially supported by ANR project PACS (ANR-14-CE28-0002) and Pays de la Loire research project AFSEC.

R. Devillers and A. Valmari (Eds.): PETRI NETS 2015, LNCS 9115, pp. 137–156, 2015.
DOI: 10.1007/978-3-319-19488-2_7

– Is there a value of the parameters such that the property is satisfied?
– Is the property satisfied for all possible values of the parameters?

Given the modeling power offered by PPNs, we first study the decidability of these issues. Since in the general case, they are undecidable, we then examine decidable subclasses.

Related work. There is not much work on Petri nets with parameters. One example is regular model checking [3] for algorithmic verification of several classes of infinite-state systems whose configurations can be modeled as words over a finite alphabet. The main idea is to use regular languages as the representation of sets of configurations, and finite-state transducers to describe transition relations. This is only possible for particular examples including parameterised systems consisting of an arbitrary number of homogeneous finite-state processes connected in a regular topology, and systems that operate on linear data structures. Parameters are also introduced in models such as predicate Petri nets [8], in the aim to have more concise models, in particular to take into account symmetries in the model [4]. Domains of values are generally finite. Parameterised verification on timed systems has also been studied in several papers since its introduction by Alur et al. in [1]. Parameterisation of time uses continuous parameters. In this paper, we focus on discrete parameters on untimed Petri nets.

The remainder of the paper is structured as follows: Section 2 re-visits the semantics of Petri Nets and introduces discrete parameters in Petri Nets. Section 3 presents the undecidability results. Section 4 introduces subclasses of our parameterised models. Section 5 answers decidability results over those subclasses and underlines issues encountered with reachability. Section 6 concludes and points to future work.

2   Definitions

Notations

$\mathbb{N}$ is the set of natural numbers. $\mathbb{N}^*$ is the set of positive natural numbers and $\mathbb{N}_\omega$ is the classic union $\mathbb{N} \cup \{\omega\}$ where for each $n \in \mathbb{N}$, $n + \omega = \omega$, $\omega - n = \omega$, $n < \omega$ and $\omega \le \omega$. $\mathbb{Z}$ is the set of integers. Let X be a finite set. 2^X denotes the powerset of X and $|X|$ the size of X. Let $V \subseteq \mathbb{N}$, a V-valuation for X is a function from X to V. We therefore denote V^X the set of V-valuations on X. Given an alphabet Σ, we denote as Σ_ϵ the union $\Sigma \cup \{\epsilon\}$ where ϵ is the silent action. Given a set X, let $k \in \mathbb{Z}$ and $x \in X$, we define a linear expression on X by the following grammar: $\lambda ::= k \mid k * x \mid \lambda + \lambda$. Given a linear expression λ on X and a $\mathbb{N}$-valuation ν for X, $\nu(\lambda)$ is the integer obtained when replacing each element x in X from λ, by the corresponding value $\nu(x)$.

2.1   Petri Nets and Marked Petri Nets

Definition 1 (Petri Net). *A Petri Net is a 4-tuple $\mathcal{N} = (P, T, Pre, Post)$ where P is a finite set of places, T is a finite set of transitions, Pre and Post $\in$*

$\mathbb{N}^{|P| \times |T|}$ are the backward and forward incidence matrices, such that $Pre(p,t) = n$ with $n > 0$ when there is an arc from place p to transition t with weight n and $Post(p,t) = n$ with $n > 0$ when there is an arc from transition t to place p with weight n.

Given a Petri Net $\mathcal{N} = (P, T, Pre, Post)$, we denote $Pre(\bullet, t)$ (also written $\bullet t$) as the vector $(Pre(p_1,t), Pre(p_2,t), ..., Pre(p_{|P|},t))$ i.e. the tth column of the matrix Pre. The same notation is used for $Post(\bullet, t)$ (or $t^\bullet$).

Definition 2 (Marking). *A marking of a Petri Net* $\mathcal{N} = (P, T, Pre, Post)$ *is a vector* $m \in \mathbb{N}^{|P|}$.

If $m \in \mathbb{N}^{|P|}$ is a marking, $m(p_i)$ is the number of tokens in place p_i. We can define a partial order over markings.

Definition 3 (Partial Order). *Let* $\mathcal{N}$ *be a Petri Net such that* $\mathcal{N} = (P, T, Pre, Post)$, *let m and m' be two markings of* $\mathcal{N}$. *We define* $\leq$ *as a binary relation such that* $\leq$ *is a subset of* $\mathbb{N}^{|P|} \times \mathbb{N}^{|P|}$ *defined by:*

$$m \leq m' \Leftrightarrow \forall p \in P, m(p) \leq m'(p) \tag{1}$$

Definition 4 (Marked Petri Net). *A marked Petri Net (PN) is a couple* $\mathcal{S} = (\mathcal{N}, m_0)$ *where* $\mathcal{N}$ *is a Petri Net and m_0 is a marking of* $\mathcal{N}$ *called the initial marking of the system.*

An example of *marked Petri Net* is given in Figure 1.

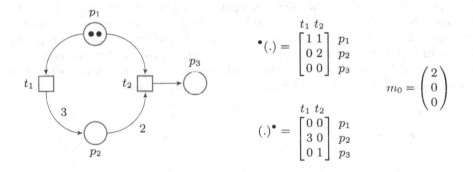

Fig. 1. A Marked Petri Net

2.2 Operational Semantics

Augmenting Petri Nets with markings leads to the notion of enabled-transitions and firing of transitions. Given a marked Petri Net $\mathcal{S}$, a transition $t \in T$ is said *enabled by a marking m* when $m \geq Pre(\bullet, t)$.

Definition 5 (PN Semantics). *The semantics of PN is a transition system* $\mathcal{S}_T = (Q, q_0, \rightarrow)$ *where,* $Q = \mathbb{N}^{|P|}$, $q_0 = m_0$, $\rightarrow \in Q \times T \times Q$ *such that,*

$$m \xrightarrow{t_i} m' \Leftrightarrow \begin{cases} m \geq {}^\bullet t_i \\ m' = m - {}^\bullet t_i + t_i^\bullet \end{cases} \tag{2}$$

This relation holds for sequences of transitions:

- $m \xrightarrow{w} m'$ if w is the empty word and $m = m'$
- $m \xrightarrow{wt} m'$ if $\exists m'', m \xrightarrow{w} m'' \wedge m'' \xrightarrow{t} m'$ where $w \in T^*$ and $t \in T$.

Definition 6 (Reachability set). *Given a PN,* $\mathcal{S} = (\mathcal{N}, m_0)$, *the reachability set of* $\mathcal{S}$, $RS(\mathcal{S})$ *is the set of all reachable markings of* $\mathcal{S}$ *i.e.* $RS(\mathcal{S}) = \{m \mid \exists w \in T^*, m_0 \xrightarrow{w} m\}$

2.3 Parametric Petri Nets

We would like to use less rigid modeling in order to model systems where some data are not known *a priori*. Therefore, in this subsection, we extend the previous definitions by adding a set of parameters *Par*. Working with Petri nets and discrete parameters leads to consider two main situations: the first one involves parameters on markings, by replacing the number of tokens in some places by parameters, the second one involves parameters as weights. The same parameter can be used in both situations. Using parameters on markings can be easily understood as modeling an unfixed amount of resources that one may want to optimise. Let us consider a concrete example to illustrate parameterised weights. In a production line, we consider two operations: first, to supply raw material, we need to unpack some boxes containing an amount λ_1 of resources, as depicted in Figure 2, and at the end, we need to pack end products in boxes of capacity λ_2, as in Figure 3. This is part of a whole packaging process that one may want to optimise. The level of abstraction induced by parameters permits to leave those values unspecified in order to perform an early analysis.

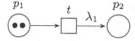
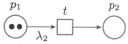

Fig. 2. Unpacking raw material   **Fig. 3.** Packing end products

Definition 7 (Parametric Petri Net). *A parametric Petri Net,* $\mathcal{NP}$ *is a 5-tuple* $\mathcal{NP} = (P, T, Pre, Post, Par)$ *such that* P *is a finite set of places of* $\mathcal{NP}$, T *is a finite set of transitions of* $\mathcal{NP}$, *Par is a finite set of parameters of* $\mathcal{NP}$, *Pre and Post* $\in (\mathbb{N} \cup Par)^{|P| \times |T|}$

Intuitively, a parametric Petri net is a Petri net where the number of tokens involved in a transition is parameterised as depicted in Figure 4.

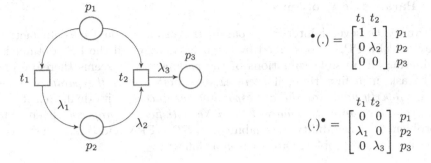

$$\bullet(.) = \begin{bmatrix} t_1 & t_2 \\ 1 & 1 \\ 0 & \lambda_2 \\ 0 & 0 \end{bmatrix} \begin{matrix} p_1 \\ p_2 \\ p_3 \end{matrix}$$

$$(.)^\bullet = \begin{bmatrix} t_1 & t_2 \\ 0 & 0 \\ \lambda_1 & 0 \\ 0 & \lambda_3 \end{bmatrix} \begin{matrix} p_1 \\ p_2 \\ p_3 \end{matrix}$$

Fig. 4. A Parametric Petri Net

Definition 8 (Parametric marking). *Given a parametric Petri Net* $\mathcal{NP} = (P, T, Pre, Post, Par)$, *a parametric marking is a* $|P|$-*dimensional vector* μ *of linear expressions on* $\mathbb{N} \cup Par$.

Modeling with parameters means using parameters over weights and markings rather than setting numeric values everywhere. Therefore we may also use a parametric initial marking.

Definition 9 (Parametric PN or PPN). *A parametric marked Petri Net (PPN) is a couple,* $\mathcal{SP} = (\mathcal{NP}, \mu_0)$ *where* $\mathcal{NP}$ *is a Parametric Petri Net and* μ_0 *is the parametric initial marking of* $\mathcal{NP}$.

PPNs can be used to design systems where some parts have not been analysed or where we need to keep flexibility. We now need to define a way to instantiate classic Petri nets from our parametric marked Petri Nets, in order to define a semantics.

Definition 10 (Parametric Semantics). *Let* $\mathcal{SP} = (P, T, Pre, Post, Par, \mu_0)$ *be a PPN, we consider the set of valuations* $\mathbb{N}^{Par}$. *Let* $\nu \in \mathbb{N}^{Par}$, *we define* $\nu(\mathcal{SP})$ *as the PN obtained from* $\mathcal{SP}$ *by replacing each parameter* $\lambda \in Par$ *by* $\nu(\lambda)$, *its valuation by* ν, *i.e.* $\nu(\mathcal{SP}) = (P, T, Pre', Post', m_0)$ *where* $\forall i \in [\![1, |P|]\!], \forall j \in [\![1, |T|]\!]$,

$$Pre'(i,j) = \begin{cases} Pre(i,j) & if \ Pre(i,j) \in \mathbb{N} \\ \nu(Pre(i,j)) & if \, Pre(i,j) \in Par \end{cases} \tag{3}$$

$$Post'(i,j) = \begin{cases} Post(i,j) & if \ Post(i,j) \in \mathbb{N} \\ \nu(Post(i,j)) & if \, Post(i,j) \in Par \end{cases} \tag{4}$$

$$m_0(i) = \begin{cases} \mu_0(i) & if \qquad\qquad \mu_0(i) \in \mathbb{N} \\ \nu(\mu_0(i)) & if \, \mu_0(i) \, is \, a \, linear \, expression \, on \, Par \end{cases} \tag{5}$$

A marked Petri Net is an *instance* of a parametric marked Petri net.

2.4   Parametric Problems

We can define several interesting parametric problems on PPNs. In fact, the behaviour of a PPN is described by the behaviours of all the PNs obtained by considering all possible valuations of the parameters. It seems therefore obvious to ask, in a first time, if *there exists valuations for the parameters such that a property holds for the corresponding instance* and its dual, *i.e.*, if *every instance of the parametric marked Petri Net satisfies the property*. Given a class of problem $\mathcal{P}$ (coverability, reachability,...), $\mathcal{SP}$ a PPN and ϕ is an instance of $\mathcal{P}$, parameterised problems are written as follows:

Definition 11 ($\mathcal{P}$-Existence problem). *($\mathcal{E}$-$\mathcal{P}$): Is there a valuation $\nu \in \mathbb{N}^{Par}$ s.t. $\nu(\mathcal{SP})$ satisfies the property ϕ ?*

Definition 12 ($\mathcal{P}$-Universality problem). *($\mathcal{U}$-$\mathcal{P}$): Does $\nu(\mathcal{SP})$ satisfies the property ϕ for each $\nu \in \mathbb{N}^{Par}$?*

This paper focuses on *reachability* and *coverability* issues.

Definition 13 (Reachability). *Let $\mathcal{S} = (\mathcal{N}, m_0) = (P, T, Pre, Post, m_0)$ and m a marking of $\mathcal{S}$, $\mathcal{S}$ reaches m iff $m \in RS(\mathcal{S})$.*

Definition 14 (Coverability). *Let $\mathcal{S} = (\mathcal{N}, m_0) = (P, T, Pre, Post, m_0)$ and m a marking of $\mathcal{S}$, $\mathcal{S}$ covers m if there exists a reachable marking m' of $\mathcal{S}$ such that m' is greater or equal to m i.e.*

$$\exists m' \in RS(\mathcal{S}) s.t. \ \forall p \in P, m'(p) \geq m(p) \tag{6}$$

We recall that reachability [9] and coverability [7] are decidable on classic Petri nets. In the context of parametric Petri nets, coverability leads to two main problems presented previously, that is to say: the *existence problem*, written ($\mathcal{E}$-cov) and the *universal problem*, written ($\mathcal{U}$-cov). For instance, ($\mathcal{U}$-cov) asks: *"Does each valuation of the parameters implies that the valuation of the parametric P/T net system covers m ?"* i.e.

$$m \text{ is } \mathcal{U}\text{-coverable in } \mathcal{SP} \Leftrightarrow \begin{cases} \forall \nu \in \mathbb{N}^{Par}, \ \exists m' \in RS(\nu(\mathcal{SP})) \\ \qquad\qquad \text{s.t. } m' \geq m \end{cases} \tag{7}$$

We can similarly define $\mathcal{E}$-reach and $\mathcal{U}$-reach for parameterised reachability.

3   Undecidability Results for the General Case

In their paper suming-up results of decidability for reset-nets and corresponding subclasses, Dufourd, Finkel and Schnoebelen noticed that *"Reachability is known to become undecidable as soon as the power of Petri nets is increased"* [5], for instance, adding *reset arcs* [2] or *inhibitor arcs* [6] makes reachability undecidable. In this section, we focus on showing that adding parameters to PN leads to undecidability. More specifically, ($\mathcal{U}$-cov) and ($\mathcal{E}$-cov) are undecidable on PPNs.

As we will proceed by reduction to the halting problem (and counter bound-edness problem) for counter machines to answer our problem, we first recall some definitions. A 2-Counters Machine has a pointer and a tape which contains finite number of instructions in three types: *increment, decrement* and *zero-test*. The pointer reads the tape to execute increment or decrement instructions sequentially. When the pointer reaches a *zero-test* instruction, then it will jump to a certain position on the tape and continue. Formally, it consists of two counters c_1, c_2, a set of states $P = \{p_0, ...p_m\}$, a terminal state labelled *halt* and a finite list of instructions $l_1, ..., l_s$ among the following list:

- increment: increase c_k by one and go to next state, where $k \in \{1, 2\}$
- decrement: decrease c_k by one and go to next state, where $k \in \{1, 2\}$
  zero-test: if $c_k = 0$ go to state p_j else go to state p_l, where $p_j, p_l \in P \cup \{halt\}$ and $k \in \{1, 2\}$

We can assume without restriction that the counters are non negative integers *i.e.* that the machine is well-formed in the sense that a *decrement instruction* is guarded by a *zero-test* and that the counters are initialised to zero. It is well known that the *halting problem* (whether state *halt* is reachable) and the *counters boundedness problem* (whether the counters values stay in a finite set) are both *undecidable* as proved by Minksy [10].

Theorem 1 (Undecidability of $\mathcal{E}$-cov on PPN). *The $\mathcal{E}$-coverability problem for PPN is undecidable*[1].

Proof. We proceed by *reduction from a 2-counters machine*. Given a Minksy 2-counters machine $\mathcal{M}$, we construct a PPN that simulates it, $\mathcal{SP}_{\mathcal{M}}$, as follows.

- Each counter c_i is modeled by two places C_i and $\neg C_i$. The value of the counter is encoded by the number of tokens in C_i.
- For each state p of $P \cup \{halt\}$ a 1-bounded place p is created in the net.
- The instructions of the previous definition are modeled by the transitions and arcs depicted in Figure 5.
- A unique additional place π with an additional transition θ serves to initialise the net. The initial marking is composed of one token in π and one token in the place p corresponding to the initial state p of $\mathcal{M}$.

Initially, only θ can be fired, which leads to the initial configuration of the machine (state p_0 and counters values null), with one token in p_0, no tokens in C_1 and C_2 and a parameterised number of tokens in $\neg C_i$. The value of this parameter will therefore represent the upper bound of the counter over the instructions sequence. We have to verify that each time $m(C_i) + m(\neg C_i) = \lambda$. First we show that $\mathcal{SP}_{\mathcal{M}}$ simulates $\mathcal{M}$ by verifying the behaviour of each instruction:

---

[1] We can be more accurate by specifying that we need at least 1 parameter used on 6 distinct arcs. The question remains opened for fewer parameterised arcs.

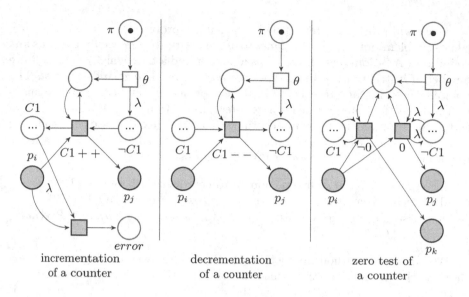

Fig. 5. Modeling a counter with PPN

- *Increment instruction:* As C_i models the counter, the transition $C_i + +$ adds one token in C_i, removes one token from $\neg C_i$ and changes the *current state* by removing the token from p_i and adding a token in p_j. The *error* states is marked iff the incrementation instruction is performed whereas we have already reached the upper bound over the execution. This state will be useful for the second proof.
- *Decrement instruction:* As C_i models the counter, the transition C_i - - removes one token from C_i, adds one token in $\neg C_i$ and changes the *current state* by removing the token from p_i and adding a token in p_j. We recall the machine is well-formed.
- *Zero Test:* As C_i models the counter, and as we know the sum of tokens available in C_i and $\neg C_i$, there is no token in C_i iff there are λ tokens in $\neg C_i$. According to this test the *current state* is updated by removing the token from p_i and adding a token in p_j or p_k. The value of the counter is left unchanged.

   & Coverability is undecidable :
We will show that given a 2-counters machine $\mathcal{M}$, *(a)* $\mathcal{M}$ halts (it reaches the *halt* state) iff *(b)* there exists a valuation ν such that $\nu(\mathcal{SP}_\mathcal{M})$ covers the corresponding p_{halt} place.

- *(a)* $\Rightarrow$ *(b)* First, let us assume that $\mathcal{M}$ halts. As $\mathcal{M}$ halts, the execution of the machine is finite. On this execution the two counters are bounded by c_{lim1} and c_{lim2}. Let c_{lim} be the maximum of those two values. Let ν be the valuation such that $\nu(\lambda) = c_{lim}$. By the previous explanation, $\mathcal{SP}_\mathcal{M}$ simulates $\mathcal{M}$. Moreover, the valuation ν ensures that $\mathcal{SP}_\mathcal{M}$ does not reach a deadlock state where p_{error} is marked. Therefore, when $\mathcal{M}$ reaches *halt*, $\mathcal{SP}_{\mathcal{M}}$ will add 1 token in p_{halt}. So, a marking where there is one token in p_{halt} is coverable.

- $(b) \Rightarrow (a)$ We proceed by contrapositive. Let us assume that $\mathcal{M}$ does not halt. We want to show that there is no valuation ν such that $\nu(\mathcal{SP}_{\mathcal{M}})$ adds a token in p_{halt}. Let us consider the two following distinct alternatives:
  - If the counters are bounded along the execution, either the value of λ is less than the maximum value of the counters and error will be reached during some increment resulting in a deadlock, or the value of λ is big enough so that error is never marked, but, in this case, then, as the machine does not halt, it means that it does not reach *halt*. So there is no instruction that leads to *halt* in $\mathcal{M}$. Therefore, according to the previous explanation, there is no transition that adds a token in p_{halt}.
  - If at least one counter is not bounded, then for any given valuation ν, we will reach an instruction $inc(c_i)$, where i is 1 or 2, and $c_i = \nu(\lambda)$. Therefore, a token will be added in p_{error} leading to a deadlock. So $\mathcal{SP}_{\mathcal{M}}$ will not cover a terminal state.

The undecidability of the halting problem on the 2-counters machine gives the undecidability of the $\mathcal{E}$-coverability problem.

Theorem 2 (Undecidability of $\mathcal{U}$-cov on PPN). *The $\mathcal{U}$-coverability problem for PPN is undecidable.*

Proof. $\mathcal{U}$ Coverability is undecidable:

We proceed by *reduction from a 2-counters machine*. We use the same construction as in the previous proof. We denote m_{error} the marking were $m_{error}(p) = 0$ for each $p \in P$ except $m_{error}(p_{error}) = 1$. We will show that given a 2-counter machine $\mathcal{M}$, *(a)* the counters are unbounded along the instructions sequence of $\mathcal{M}$ (counters boundedness problem) iff *(b)* for each valuation ν, $\nu(\mathcal{SP}_{\mathcal{M}})$ covers the m_{error}.

- $(a) \Rightarrow (b)$ First, let us assume that on a given instruction sequence, one counter of $\mathcal{M}$ is unbounded. By the second alternative considered in the proof for $\mathcal{E}$-cov we proved that for any valuation, a token will be added in p_{error}.
- $(b) \Rightarrow (a)$ Reciprocally, by contrapositive, we want to show that if the counters are bounded, there exists a valuation ν such that $\nu(\mathcal{SP}_{\mathcal{M}})$ does not cover m_{error}. This comes directly from the previous proof. As the counters are bounded along the instructions sequence, we consider a valuation ν such that $\nu(\lambda) = c_{lim}$ where c_{lim} is an upper bound of the values of the counters. By construction, there is no possibilities to add a token in p_{error}, otherwise, it means that $\mathcal{SP}_{\mathcal{M}}$ took an incrementation transition meaning that c_{lim} is not an upper bound.

The undecidability of the counters boundedness problem on the 2-counters machine gives the undecidability of the $\mathcal{U}$-coverability problem.

4   Subclasses of Parametric Petri Nets

4.1   Introducing Subclasses

On the one hand, our parametric model increases the modeling power of Petri nets but on the other hand, using parameters leads to complex models where properties become undecidable. In order to obtain parameterised models that are easier to analyse and therefore can be used in practice, we should reduce the power of modeling. We will therefore introduce some subclasses of the PPN in which we restrict the use of parameters to only markings, which could be used to model arbitrary number of identical processes, to only output arcs, which, we will see, is a bit more general or to only input arcs, which could model synchronizations among arbitrary numbers of identical process, and finally some combinations of those.

The following subclasses have therefore a dual interest. From a modeling point of view, restrict the use of parameters to tokens, output or input can be used to model concrete examples such as respectively processes or synchronisation of a given number of processes. From a theoretical point of view, it is interesting to introduce those subclasses of PPN in a concern of completeness of the study.

Definition 15 (P-parametric PN). *A P-parametric marked Petri Net (P-PPN), $\mathcal{SP} = (\mathcal{NP}, \mu_0)$ where $\mathcal{NP}$ is a Parametric Petri Net such that Pre and Post $\in \mathbb{N}^{|P| \times |T|}$ and μ_0 is a parametric marking of $\mathcal{NP}$.*

A P-PPN is a classic Petri net with a parametric initial marking.

Definition 16 (T-parametric PN). *A T-parametric Petri Net (T-PPN), $\mathcal{SP} = (\mathcal{NP}, m_0)$ where $\mathcal{NP}$ is a Parametric Petri Net and m_0 is a marking of $\mathcal{NP}$*

Intuitively, using parameters on outputs means we will create parametric markings. To complete this study, we can extract a subclass in which parameters involved in the Pre matrix and parameters involved in the Post matrix correspond to disjoints subsets of parameters. *i.e. $par(Pre) \cap par(Post) = \emptyset$* where *par* is the application that maps to the set of parameters involved in a matrix (or a vector). We call this subclass *distinctT-PPN*[2]. We can even refine the subclass of distinctT-PPN by considering the two distinct classes of *Pre-T-parametric PPN* (preT-PPN), where $Post \in \mathbb{N}^{|P|}$ and *Post-T-parametric PPN* (postT-PPN), where $Pre \in \mathbb{N}^{|P|}$.

As we introduced several subclasses, it is interesting to study whether one of this subclass is more expressive than the other. We will show that P-PPN and postT-PPN are related. Therefore, we introduce here some useful definitions. Our translations add *silent actions* that detail the beahviour of the Petri nets. Therefore, we introduce a labelling function Λ from the set of transitions T to

---

[2] Studying the undecidability proof, it is relevant to think that using different parameters for the input and the output would reduce the modeling power.

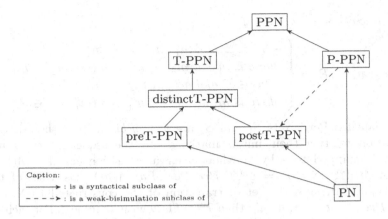

Fig. 6. Subclasses of PPN

$\Sigma_\epsilon, \Lambda : T \rightarrow \Sigma_\epsilon$, such that $\Sigma_\epsilon \subseteq T \cup \{\epsilon\}$ and $\Lambda(t_i)$ equals either t_i or ϵ. We extend the previous definitions by using $m \xrightarrow{t} m'$ or $m \xrightarrow{\Lambda(t)} m'$ depending on the context[3]. For instance, $m \xrightarrow{\epsilon^*} m'$ means that m leads to m' by using zero or more internal ϵ-transitions. Given two markings m and m' we write:

$$m \xrightarrow{\alpha}_\epsilon m' \leftrightarrow m \xrightarrow{\epsilon^*} \xrightarrow{\alpha} \xrightarrow{\epsilon^*} m' \text{ with } \alpha \neq \epsilon \qquad (8)$$

Definition 17 (Weak-Simulation). *Given two labelled marked Petri nets,* $\mathcal{S}_1 = (P_1, T_1, F_1, \Lambda_1, \Sigma_\epsilon, m_1^0)$ *and* $\mathcal{S}_2 = (P_2, T_2, F_2, \Lambda_2, \Sigma_\epsilon, m_2^0)$, *a binary relation* $\mathcal{R} \subseteq \mathbb{N}^{|P_1|} \times \mathbb{N}^{|P_2|}$ *is a simulation if*

$$\forall(m_1, m_2) \in \mathcal{R} \Leftrightarrow \begin{cases} \forall \alpha \in \Sigma \text{ and } m_1' \text{ s.t. } m_1 \xrightarrow{\alpha}_\epsilon m_1', \\ \exists m_2' \text{ s.t. } m_2 \xrightarrow{\alpha}_\epsilon m_2' \text{ and } (m_1', m_2') \in \mathcal{R} \end{cases} \qquad (9)$$

If we can find a weak-simulation $\mathcal{R} \subseteq \mathbb{N}^{|P_1|} \times \mathbb{N}^{|P_2|}$ such that $(m_1^0, m_2^0) \in \mathcal{R}$ we say that $\mathcal{S}_2$ weakly simulates $\mathcal{S}_1$, which means intuitively that $\mathcal{S}_2$ can match all the moves of $\mathcal{S}_1$. Moreover if we can find another weak-simulation $\mathcal{R}' \subseteq \mathbb{N}^{|P_1|} \times \mathbb{N}^{|P_2|}$ such that $\mathcal{S}_1$ weakly simulates $\mathcal{S}_2$, we say that $\mathcal{S}_1$ and $\mathcal{S}_2$ are *weakly co-similar.*

Definition 18 (Weak-Bisimulation). *Given two labelled PN,* $\mathcal{S}_1 = (P_1, T_1, F_1, \Lambda_1, \Sigma_\epsilon, m_1^0)$ *and* $\mathcal{S}_2 = (P_2, T_2, F_2, \Lambda_2, \Sigma_\epsilon, m_2^0)$, *a binary relation* $\mathcal{R} \subseteq \mathbb{N}^{|P_1|} \times$

---

[3] Indeed, if we consider the alphabet A equals to the set of the transition T of the Petri Net, and L as the identity function, the two definitions are equivalent. Using labelling is more general and allows to introduce non deterministic behaviours.

$\mathbb{N}^{|P_2|}$ *is a weak-bisimulation* [4] *if*

$$\forall (m_1, m_2) \in \mathcal{R} \Leftrightarrow \begin{cases} -\ \forall \alpha \in \Sigma \ and \ m_1' \ s.t. \ m_1 \xrightarrow{\alpha}_\epsilon m_1' \\ \quad there \ is \ m_2' s.t. \ m_2 \xrightarrow{\alpha}_\epsilon m_2' \ and \ (m_1', m_2') \in \mathcal{R} \\ -\ \forall \alpha \in \Sigma \ and \ m_2' \ s.t. \ m_2 \xrightarrow{\alpha}_\epsilon m_2' \\ \quad there \ is \ m_1' s.t. \ m_1 \xrightarrow{\alpha}_\epsilon m_1' \ and \ (m_1', m_2') \in \mathcal{R} \end{cases} \quad (10)$$

Two labelled Petri Nets $\mathcal{S}_1$ and $\mathcal{S}_2$ are *weakly bisimilar* if there is a weak bisimulation relating their initial markings. In the sequel, every transition called θ is mapped to ϵ by Λ whereas for a transition called t, $\Lambda(t) = t$. If the original PPN, $\mathcal{SP} = (P, T, Pre, Post, Par, \Lambda, \mu_0)$, has a set of transition T and T' denotes the set of transition of the constructed PPN, $\mathcal{SP}' = (P', T', Pre', Post', Par, \Lambda', \mu_0')$ then $T' = T \cup \Theta$ with $T \cap \Theta = \emptyset$. For each $t \in T$, $\Lambda(t) = t$ and for each θ in Θ, $\Lambda(\theta) = \epsilon$.

4.2   Translating P-PPN to postT-PPN

In order to simulate the behaviour of parameterised places, we translate those places in a parameterised initialisation process that needs to be fired before firing any other transitions in the net. The idea relies on using a new place π and a new transition θ enabled by this place, such that $\theta^\bullet$ initializes a P-PPN, as showed in Figure 7. We define the initial marking $m_0 = (0, ..., 0, 1)$ *i.e.* $\forall p \in P$, $m_0(p) = 0$ and $m_0(\pi) = 1$. We will show that $\mathcal{SP}'$ and $\mathcal{SP}$ are weakly-bisimilar by showing that each behaviour of $\mathcal{SP}$ can be done in $\mathcal{SP}'$ if we begin by firing θ and reciprocally.

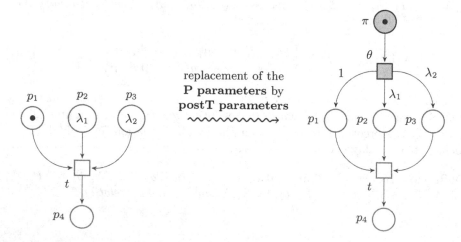

Fig. 7. From P-PPN to postT-PPN

---

[4] There exists several definitions of bisimulation, for instance preserving deadlocks or epsilon-branching, but the one we use is sufficient for our purpose.

Lemma 3. $\forall \nu \in \mathbb{N}^{Par}$, $\nu(\mathcal{SP})$ and $\nu(\mathcal{SP}')$ are weakly bisimilar.

Note that each path in $\mathcal{SP} = (P, T, Pre, Post, Par, \Lambda, \mu_0)$ can be done in $\mathcal{SP}' = (P', T', Pre', Post', Par, \Lambda', m'_0)$ by adding θ at the beginning. And reciprocally, each path in $\mathcal{SP}'$ begins by θ so is written $\theta.w$ where w is a path in $\mathcal{SP}$.

Proof. Let $\nu \in \mathbb{N}^{Par}$ a valuation of the parameters. We want to show that $\nu(\mathcal{SP})$ and $\nu(\mathcal{SP}')$ are weakly bisimilar. Let $\nu(\mu_0)$ be the parametric initial marking of $\nu(\mathcal{SP})$ and $\nu(m'_0) = m'_0$ the initial marking of $\nu(\mathcal{SP}')$. The only transition firable from m'_0 is θ and $m'_0 \xrightarrow{\theta} \nu(\mu_0)$ as shown in Figure 7. From $\nu(\mu_0)$, $\mathcal{SP}$ and $\mathcal{SP}'$ are isomorphic. So $\nu(\mathcal{SP}_1)$ and $\nu(\mathcal{SP}_2)$ are weakly-bisimilar.

Those results underline that using parameters on outputs is more powerfull than using parameters on markings. We can conclude that T-PPN are more expressive than PPN.

4.3 Translating postT-PPN to P-PPN

We will show that from a postT-PPN, $\mathcal{SP}_1 = (P_1, T_1, Pre_1, Post_1, Par_1, \Lambda_1, m_1^0)$ we can construct a P-PPN, $\mathcal{SP}_2 = (P_2, T_2, Pre_2, Post_2, Par_2, \Lambda_2, \mu_2^0)$ that weakly-simulates the behaviours of the postT-PPN. Reciprocally, the postT-PPN also weakly-simulates the behaviours of the P-PPN built.

For each transition t and place p such that the arc (t, p) is weighted by a parameter, we construct the net depicted in Figure 8 which replace this arc [5]. Therefore, $T_1 \subseteq T_2$. As previously, we introduce two labelling functions Λ_1 and Λ_2 from T_1 (resp. T_2) to T_ϵ such that, for each $t \in T_1$, $\Lambda_1(t) = \Lambda_2(t) = t$ and $\Lambda_2(t) = \epsilon$ otherwise (*i.e.* for each $t \in T_2 \backslash T_1$).

Lemma 4. $\forall \nu \in \mathbb{N}^{Par}$, $\nu(\mathcal{SP}_1)$ and $\nu(\mathcal{SP}_2)$ are weakly cosimilar.

Proof. We will prove the 2 weak-simulations.

- $\forall \nu \in \mathbb{N}^{Par}$, $\nu(\mathcal{SP}_2)$ simulates $\nu(\mathcal{SP}_1)$. Let us consider $\nu \in \mathbb{N}^{Par}$, $\nu(\mathcal{SP}_1)$ has the following behaviour: each time t is fired, $\nu(\lambda)$ tokens are created in p. In $\mathcal{SP}_2$, it is possible to generates $\nu(\lambda)$ tokens in p after firing the sequence $t\ \theta_{t,p,1}^{\nu(\lambda)}\ \theta_t\ \theta_{t,p,2}^{\nu(\lambda)}$, labeled $t\epsilon^*$. Moreover, this sequence resets the sub-net constructed for the weak-simulation. As the other transitions of the network are not affected, monotony gives directly the weak-simulation.
- $\forall \nu \in \mathbb{N}^{Par}$, $\nu(\mathcal{SP}_1)$ simulates $\nu(\mathcal{SP}_2)$. Reciprocally, a marking with $\nu(\lambda)$ tokens in p allows to simulate the behaviours of every marking such that $m(p) \leq \nu(\lambda)$ according to monotony therefore, the reachable markings induced by creating less than $\nu(\lambda)$ tokens in $\mathcal{SP}_2$ are simulated by the one with $\nu(\lambda)$ tokens, and therefore by $\mathcal{SP}_1$. As the other transitions of the network are not affected, monotony gives directly the weak-simulation.

---

[5] Notice that if several labeled arcs come from the same transition, some places and transitions of the Figure 8 should be duplicated according to indices.

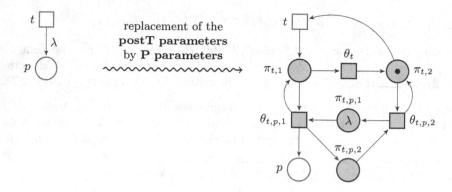

Fig. 8. From postT-PPN to P-PPN

Therefore, $\mathcal{SP}_1$ and $\mathcal{SP}_2$ are *weakly co-similar*.

Remark 1. This is not a weak bisimulation. Indeed, if $\mathcal{SP}_2$ adds 3 tokens in p (leading to a marking m_2) whereas $\mathcal{SP}_1$ adds $\nu(\lambda) = 4$ tokens in p (leading to a marking m_1). Then any transitions needing more than 3 tokens could only be fired from m_1 in $\mathcal{SP}_1$ only. Here the two simulations relations are not reciprocal: m_1 would simulates m_2 but m_2 would not.

5   Decidability Results

We will now consider the parameterised properties defined in Section 2 and the different subclasses of parameterised models of Section 4. Table 1 sums up the results that we present in this section.

Table 1. Decidability results for parametric coverability and reachability

	$\mathscr{U}$-problem		$\mathscr{E}$-problem	
	Reachability	Coverability	Reachability	Coverability
preT-PPN	?	?	?	D
postT-PPN	?	D	?	D
PPN	U	U	U	U
distinctT-PPN	?	?	?	D
P-PPN	?	D	D	D

5.1   Study of Parameterised Coverability

The easiest proofs rely on monotony. Indeed, some instances simulate other instances. We recall that the *zero valuation* (written 0) is the valuation that maps every parameter to zero.

Lemma 5. *Decidability of $\mathcal{U}$-coverability on postT-PPN (resp. P-PPN) can be reduced to a test with the zero valuation.*

Proof. For postT-PPN and P-PPN, the zero valuation is the one allowing the lowest amount of behaviours for coverability *i.e.* it is the most restrictive valuation for coverability. Indeed, considering a marking m that we try to cover, m is $\mathcal{U}$-coverable if and only if there is a firing sequence w such that $m_0 \xrightarrow{w} m1 \geq m$ in the 0-instanced postT-PPN (or P-PPN). Formally, given a postT-PPN or a P-PPN $\mathcal{SP}$ and a marking m, we have:

$$\exists \nu \text{ s.t. } m \text{ is not coverable in } \nu(\mathcal{SP}) \text{ iff } m \text{ is not coverable in } 0(\mathcal{SP})$$

Indeed, for any valuation ν we can fire w in the ν-instanced PPN, leading to a marking $m2 \geq m1$ by monotony. Moreover, on the instance of a PPN (*i.e.* on a PN), the coverability is known decidable, so we can answer to the problem on the zero instanced postT-PPN (or P-PPN). If the answer is *no*, then we have found a counter example. Else, monotony directly implies that using a greater valuation ν will provide at least behaviours covering the current ones. The *winning behaviour* that allowed to answer yes for the zero-instance will still works on this ν-instance. So every instance will satisfy the coverability.

Therefore we can claim that $\mathcal{U}$-cov is decidable on postT-PPN and P-PPN. Let us consider $\mathcal{E}$-cov for the same subclasses.

Theorem 6. *$\mathcal{E}$-cov is decidable on P-PPN.*

Proof. Decidability of $\mathcal{E}$-cov on P-PPN:
We consider a P-PPN, $\mathcal{SP}_1$. We will now build a PN $\mathcal{S}_2$ with *token-canons* that will supply the parameterised places of $\mathcal{SP}_1$ as depicted in Figure 9. Each *token-canon* consists in two places π_p, π'_p and two transitions θ_p, θ'_p. θ_p supplies p of $\mathcal{S}_2$. Moreover, each transition of $\mathcal{SP}_1$ is added as an input and an output of π'_p, meaning that the net is blocked as long as every θ'_p has not been fired. This is repeated for each place initially marked by a parameter. We initialize $\mathcal{S}_2$ with 1 token in each π_p. So for each valuation ν of $\mathcal{SP}_1$, firing the sequence $\theta_p^{\nu(\lambda_p)} \theta'_p$ for each parameterised place p leads to a marking m_2 equals to the valuation of the initial marking of $\mathcal{SP}_1$. Moreover, the θ-transitions added have been fired, so every π'_p is marked. The two nets have now the same behaviour. This shows that $\mathcal{S}_2$ simulates any valuation of $\mathcal{SP}_1$. Therefore, the existence of a valuation such that a given marking is covered can be reduced to the coverability of the same marking (completed with 0 for each π_p and 1 for each π'_p added) which is known decidable as a classic coverability problem on an unbounded Petri net.

Corollary 7. *$\mathcal{E}$-cov is decidable on postT-PPN.*

Proof. Decidability of $\mathcal{E}$-cov on postT-PPN:
We proved in previous section that postT-PPN and P-PPN are weakly-cosimilar. Therefore, given a postT-PPN we can built a P-PPN which is weakly-co-similar.

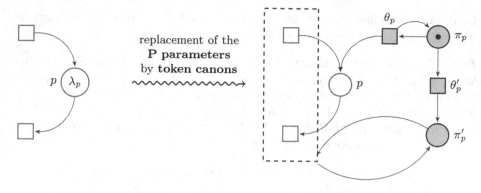

Fig. 9. From PPN to PN

Moreover, as coverability can be reduced to firing transition (by adding an observer transition), weak-simulation holds coverability. Theorem 6 gives us the decidability.

Theorem 8. $\mathscr{E}$-cov is decidable for preT-PPN.

Proof. $\mathscr{E}$-cov for the preT-PPN is decidable:
Let us consider a preT-PPN and a marking m that we try to cover. For an input transition with a weight of zero, we do not require the input place to be marked. Therefore, in terms of *input parameters*, by monotony, the zero valuation is the most permissive one for firing. Thus, there is at some valuation a firing sequence w such that $m_0 \overset{w}{\to} m_1 \geq m$ if and only if we can fire w in the *0-instanced* one, leading to a marking $m_2 \geq m_1$. Formally, given a preT-PPN $\mathcal{SP}$, we have:

$$m_0 \overset{w}{\to} m_1 \geq m \text{ in } \nu(\mathcal{SP}) \text{ iff } m_0 \overset{w}{\to} m_2 \geq m \text{ in } 0(\mathcal{SP}) \text{ with } m_2 \geq m_1$$

Informally, it means that the zero instance of the preT-PPN has the greatest amount of behaviours (in terms of coverability). Therefore it is the one which is necessary and sufficient to satisfy the $\mathscr{E}$-cov of m, meaning that if it does not satisfy the property, monotony implies that any instance of the preT-PPN will not satisfy either. If the *0-instanced* net covers m, we have a witness for the $\mathscr{E}$-cov.

Corollary 9. $\mathscr{E}$-cov is decidable for distinctT-PPN.

Proof. $\mathscr{E}$-cov for the distinctT-PPN is decidable:
As we can create a partition over Par between Par_{Pre} and Par_{Post}, respectively sets of parameters involved on inputs and outputs which are disjoint. We can consider the partial valuation $0_{|Par_{Pre}}$, which maps every parameter of Par_{Pre} to 0. We therefore get a postT-PPN on which the problem is decidable. Moreover, the post-PPN built is the one with the greatest amount of behaviours for coverability as explained previously. Considering that, if we cannot find any instance of this postT-PPN satisfying the property, we cannot find any instance of this distinctT-PPN satisfying it either.

5.2   Study of Parameterised Reachability

In classic Petri nets *decidability of reachability* certainly implies *decidability of coverability*. Indeed, given a marked Petri Net and a coverability problem, we can construct another marked Petri Net over which the previous coverability problem is equivalent to a reachability problem.

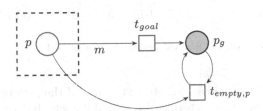

Fig. 10. Reducing Coverability to Reachability

Actually, with notations of Figure 10 covering a marking m is equivalent to reach the marking with only one token in place p_g in the net augmented with this new place p_g, a new transition t_{goal} such that ${}^\bullet t_{goal} = m$, with $Post(p_g, t_{goal}) = 1$ and, for each place p, a transition $t_{empty,p}$ such that: if p is not equal to p_g, $Pre(p, t_{empty,p}) = 1$, $Pre(p_g, t_{empty,p}) = 1$ and $Post(p_g, t_{empty,p}) = 1$. It is clear that the same can be done for PPN, which implies that *decidability of $\mathscr{E}$-reachability* implies *decidability of $\mathscr{E}$-coverability* and *decidability of $\mathscr{U}$-reachability* implies *decidability of $\mathscr{U}$-coverability*. Section 3 provides therefore the undecidability of ($\mathscr{E}$-reach) and ($\mathscr{U}$-reach) in the general case of PPN.

Theorem 10. *$\mathscr{E}$-reach is decidable on P-PPN.*

Proof. We can trivially adapt the conclusion of the proof of Theorem 6. We keep the same construction: the existence of a valuation such that a given marking is reached can be reduced to the reachability of the same marking (completed with 0 for each π_p and 1 for each π'_p added) which is known decidable as a classic reachability problem on an unbounded Petri net.

Nevertheless, for the other subclasses, the decidability of reachability is more complex. Intuitively, increasing the valuation used to instanciate a preT-PPN (resp. a postT-PPN) leads to disable (resp. enable) transitions, *i.e.* the coverability of a marking, but this is not sufifcient to deduce the exact number of tokens involved, *i.e.* reachability.

Figure 11 presents a preT-PPN. It is obvious that using the 0-valuation leads to enable the firing of t in any case, so it allows to cover any amount of tokens in p_2. In Figure 11(a), the coverability set is $CS_0 = \{m | m \leq (2,1,\omega)\}$. On the other hand, increasing the valuation leads to potentially disable t. We will therefore reduce the coverability set as we strengthen the pre-condition to fire t: in Figure 11(b), the coverability set is $CS_1 = \{m | m \leq (2,1,0) \vee m \leq (1,0,1)\} \subseteq CS_0$, and in Figure 11(c), we have $CS_2 = \{m | m \leq (2,1,0) \vee m \leq$

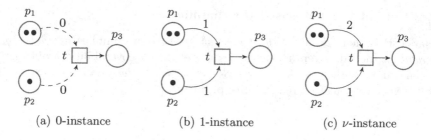

(a) 0-instance   (b) 1-instance   (c) ν-instance

Fig. 11. Several instances of a preT-PPN

$(0,0,1)\} \subseteq CS_1$. Nevertheless, this strengthening of the pre-condition, does not imply general consequences in terms of reachability sets. Indeed, in Figure 11(a), the reachability set is $\{(2,1,n)|n \in \mathbb{N}\}$, whereas in Figure 11(b) we can reach $\{(2,1,0),(1,0,1)\}$ and in Figure 11(c), we can reach $\{(2,1,0),(0,0,1)\}$.

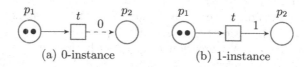

(a) 0-instance   (b) 1-instance

Fig. 12. Several instances of a postT-PPN

Equivalent observations rise from the study of Figure 12. When increasing the valuation, we may fire at least the same transitions, therefore, the coverability set is increasing: Figure 12(a) can cover any markings lower or equal to $(2,0)$ and can reach the set $\{(2,0),(1,0),(0,0)\}$ whereas Figure 12(b) can cover markings lower or equal to $(2,0),(1,1)$ or $(0,2)$ but can reach the set $\{(2,0)(1,1)(0,2)\}$.

6   Conclusion

6.1   Main Results

In this paper, we have introduced the use of discrete parameters and suggested parametric versions of the well known reachability and coverability problems. The study of the decidability of those problems leads to the results summed up in Figure 13 for coverability (Classes inside a dashed outline are decidable for the two corresponding parametric coverability problems).

We recall that the other results are presented in Tab 1.

6.2   Future Work

If we have strong intuitions for several empty cases such as decidability of $\mathscr{U}$-Coverability on preT-PPN and distinctT-PPN which would join the intuition

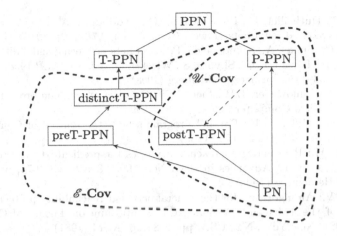

Fig. 13. What is decidable among the subclasses ? *(for coverability)*

that using the same parameters on inputs and outputs considerably increases the power of modeling of classic Petri nets, a deeper study should be carried to answer the decidability of Parametric-Reachability for instance. Being able to treat these parameterised models constitutes a scientific breakthrough in two ways:

- It significantly increases the level of abstraction in models. We will therefore be able to handle a much larger and therefore more *realistic class of models.*
- The existence of parameters can also address more relevant and *realistic verification issues.* Instead of just providing a binary response on the satisfaction or not of an expected property, we can aim to *synthetise* constraints on the parameters ensuring that if these constraints are satisfied, the property is satisfied. Such conditions for the proper functioning of the system are essential information for the designer.

Acknowledgments. We wish to thank the anonymous reviewers, who helped us to improve the paper by their suggestions.

References

1. Alur, R., Henzinger, T.A., Vardi, M.Y.: Parametric real-time reasoning. In: Proceedings of the Twenty-fifth Annual ACM Symposium on Theory of Computing, STOC 1993, New York, NY, USA, pp. 592–601. ACM (1993)
2. Araki, T., Kasami, T.: Some decision problems related to the reachability problem for Petri nets. Theoretical Computer Science **3**(1), 85–104 (1976)
3. Bouajjani, A., Jonsson, B., Nilsson, M., Touili, T.: Regular model checking. In: Emerson, E.A., Sistla, A.P. (eds.) CAV 2000. LNCS, vol. 1855, pp. 403–418. Springer, Heidelberg (2000)

4. Chiola, G., Dutheillet, C., Franceschinis, G., Haddad, S.: A symbolic reachability graph for coloured petri nets. Theor. Comput. Sci. **176**(1–2), 39–65 (1997)
5. Dufourd, C., Finkel, A., Schnoebelen, P.: Reset nets between decidability and undecidability. In: Larsen, K.G., Skyum, S., Winskel, G. (eds.) ICALP 1998. LNCS, vol. 1443, pp. 103–115. Springer, Heidelberg (1998)
6. Jones, N.D., Landweber, L.H., Lien, Y.E.: Complexity of some problems in Petri nets. Theoretical Computer Science **4**, 277–299 (1977)
7. Karp, R.M., Miller, R.E.: Parallel program schemata. Journal of Computer and System Sciences **3**(2), 147–195 (1969)
8. Lindqvist, M.: Parameterized reachability trees for predicate/transition nets. In: Rozenberg, G. (ed.) Advances in Petri Nets 1993. LNCS, vol. 674, pp. 301–324. Springer, Heidelberg (1993)
9. Mayr, E.W.: An algorithm for the general petri net reachability problem. In: Proceedings of the Thirteenth Annual ACM Symposium on Theory of Computing, STOC 1981, New York, NY, USA, pp. 238–246. ACM (1981)
10. Minsky, M.L.: Computation: Finite and Infinite Machines. Prentice-Hall Inc., Upper Saddle River (1967)

Negotiation Programs

Javier Esparza[1] and Jörg Desel[2]([envelope])

[1] Fakultät für Informatik, Technische Universität München, Munich, Germany
esparza@tum.de
[2] Fakultät für Mathematik und Informatik,
FernUniversität, Hagen, Germany
joerg.desel@fernuni-hagen.de

Abstract. We introduce a global specification language for distributed negotiations, a recently introduced concurrent computation model with atomic negotiations combining synchronization of participants and choice as primitive. A token game on distributed negotiations determines reachable markings which enable possible next atomic negotiations. In a *deterministic* distributed negotiation, each participant can always be engaged in at most one next atomic negotiation. In a *sound* distributed negotiation, every atomic negotiation is enabled at some reachable marking, and from every reachable marking the final marking of the distributed negotiation can be reached. We prove that our specification language has the same expressive power as sound and deterministic negotiations, i.e., every program can be implemented by an equivalent sound and deterministic negotiation and every sound and deterministic negotiation can be specified by an equivalent program, where a program and a negotiation are equivalent if they have the same Mazurkiewicz traces and thus the same concurrent runs. The translations between negotiations and programs require only linear time.

1 Introduction

Multi-party negotiation as a concurrent computation model has been recently introduced in [1,2] as a formalization of the negotiation paradigm given e.g. in [3,4]. In this model, distributed negotiations are described by combining atomic negotiations, called *atoms*. Each atom has a number of *parties* (the set of agents involved in it), and a set of possible *outcomes*. The parties of an atom agree on an outcome, which transforms the internal state of the parties, and determines the atoms each party is ready to engage in next. If each agent is always willing to engage in at most one atom, the negotiation is called *deterministic*.

For an example, consider the left part of Figure 1, which shows a deterministic negotiation with agents 1 to 4. Atoms are represented by black bars with white circles (*ports*) for the respective participating agents. Initially all agents are ready to engage in the *initial atom* n_0, where they decide whether to start discussing a proposal (outcome y(es)) or not (n(o)). If the agents agree on n, then the negotiation terminates with the *final atom* n_f. If they agree on y, then the agents build two teams to study and modify the proposal in parallel: agents

© Springer International Publishing Switzerland 2015
R. Devillers and A. Valmari (Eds.): PETRI NETS 2015, LNCS 9115, pp. 157–178, 2015.
DOI: 10.1007/978-3-319-19488-2_8

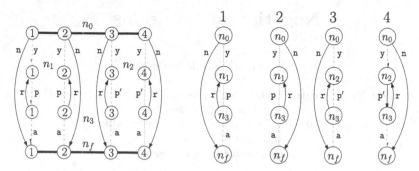

Fig. 1. Two negotiations between four agents

1 and 2 "move" to atom n_1, and agents 3 and 4 to n_2. After n_1 and n_2, the four agents decide in n_3 whether to accept (outcome a) or reject (r) the revised proposal; in case of rejection, the two teams work again on revisions.

Negotiations can deadlock. For instance, if, in our example, the r-arc from port 2 of atom n_3 would lead to n_f rather than to n_1, then the negotiation reaches a deadlock after the execution of $y p p' r p'$. Loosely speaking, a negotiation is *sound* if each atom can be executed in some reachable state and, whatever its current state, it can always finish, i.e., execute the final atom. In particular, soundness implies deadlock-freedom.

In this paper we investigate negotiations from a programming language point of view. Negotiations can be seen as concurrent compositions of flowcharts, one for each agent. For example, the negotiation on the left of Figure 1 is the composition of the four flowcharts shown on the right. So, just as flowcharts (or if-goto programs) model unstructured sequential programs, negotiations model unstructured concurrent programs. The Böhm-Jacopini theorem, often called the Structure Theorem [5][1], states that every flowchart has an equivalent structured program [5–7]. This raises the question we investigate in the paper: Is there a "Structure Theorem" for negotiations similar to the Böhm-Jacopini theorem for sequential computation? We give a positive answer for deterministic negotiations with a surprising twist: We exhibit a programming language with the same expressive power as *sound* deterministic negotiations. In other words, every syntactically correct program is guaranteed by construction to be sound, *and* for every sound deterministic negotiation there is an equivalent program exhibiting the same degree of concurrency. A similar question has frequently been studied for process models given as Petri nets or BPMN-diagrams, relating these models to programs in some execution language such as BPEL. In this setting, by now only partial solutions have been obtained. For example, [8] shows how to find so-called blocks in diagrams, each corresponding to a XOR-split/XOR-join-couple or to an AND-split/AND-join-couple. Process models with nested blocks are always sound and can easily be translated in a programming language, but not all sound process models have nested blocks.

---

[1] See [6], which convincingly argues that it should be considered a folk theorem.

agent a_1, a_2, a_3, a_4
outcome $y, n, a, r : \{a_1, \ldots, a_4\}; p : \{a_1, a_2\}; p' : \{a_3, a_4\}$

do [] y : $(p \parallel p') \circ$
      do [] a : **end** [] r : $(p \parallel p')$ **loop od**
      end
  [] n : **end**
od

Fig. 2. Program equivalent to the negotiation of Figure 1

An example program of our language is given in Figure 2. This program is equivalent to the negotiation of Figure 1. The first two lines of the program specify the agents of the system, and, for each outcome, the set of agents that have to agree to choose the outcome. The outer **do** $\cdots$ **od** block corresponds to the atom n_0. The block offers a choice between outcomes y and n; in the language, outcomes are prefixed by the [] operator. After outcome y, the two outcomes p and p' can be taken concurrently (actually, p is here an abbreviation of **do** p : **end od**, a block with only one possible outcome). The operator $\circ$ is the *layer composition* operator of Zwiers [9]. In every execution of $P_1 \circ P_2$, all actions of P_1 in which an agent a participates take place before all actions of P_2 in which a participates. If the sets of agents involved in P_1 and P_2 are disjoint, then P_1 and P_2 can be executed concurrently, and in this case we write $P_1 \parallel P_2$ (our language has only layer composition as primitive, and concurrent composition is just a special case). Finally, the block **do** [] a : **end** [] r : $(p \parallel p')$ **loop od** offers a choice between two alternatives, corresponding to the outcomes a and r. The alternatives are labeled with the keywords **end** and **loop** respectively, which indicate what happens after the chosen alternative has been executed: in the case of a **loop**, the block restarts, and for an **end** it terminates.

While we have presented both negotiations and negotiation programs as dataless computational models, data can easily be added to both. In fact, in [1, 2] each agent is assumed to have an internal state (which can be given by the valuation of a set of local variables), and an outcome of an atom with a set X of agents is assigned a state transformer relation which only applies to the internal states of the involved agents. For programs, we can assign to each agent a set of local variables, and to each outcome of an atom a guarded command over (a subset of) the local variables of the participating agents of the atom. For instance, assume that the purpose of the negotiation of Figure 1 is to fix a price. Agent a_i stores his current proposal for the price in a local variable x_i ($1 \leq i \leq 4$). The outcome n (no need to negotiate) is assigned the guard $x_1 = x_2 = x_3 = x_4$, while y is assigned its negation. The outcome p is assigned a command $x_1, x_2 := f(x_1, x_2)$, where f represents a (possibly nondeterministic) function that returns an agreed price between agents a_1 ad a_2. We proceed similarly with p' and a function g. If the two proposed prices agree, the program terminates. Otherwise, a new price is negotiated by means of a third function h, and sent to the four agents.

agent a_1 **var** x_1 **:int**

. . .

agent a_4 **var** x_4 **:int**

```
 1   do [] ¬(x₁ = x₂ = x₃ = x₄) :
 2          {x₁, x₂ := f(x₁, x₂) ‖ x₃, x₄ := g(x₃, x₄)} ∘
 3          do [] (x₂ = x₃) : end
 4             [] (x₂ ≠ x₃) :
 5                x₂, x₃ = h(x₂, x₃) ∘
 6                   {x₁, x₂ := f(x₁, x₂) ‖ x₃, x₄ := g(x₃, x₄)}
 7                end
 8          od  loop
 9       [] (x₁ = x₂ = x₃ = x₄) :  end
10   od
```

Fig. 3. A concrete program corresponding to the abstract program of Figure 2

Figure 3 shows a concrete negotiation program with data which corresponds to the abstract program of Figure 2. The i-th agent stores its current price in a variable x_i. If the prices are initially different, then agents 1 and 2 and agents 3 and 4 build two teams and come up with new suggestions for the price, a process encapsulated in the functions f and g. The new suggestions are stored in x_2 and x_3. If x_2 and x_3 are not equal, then agents 2 and 3 come up with a new suggestion (function h), which is then sent again to the two teams.

Notice that, according to the above recursive procedure, the set of agents executing the guards $(x_2 = x_3)$ and $(x_2 \neq x_3)$ must be equal, and this set must be a superset of the set of agents executing lines **5** and **6**. Since all variables appear in these lines, all agents must participate in the execution of the guards. If only agents a_2 and a_3 execute the guards, then the program may deadlock, because after line 2, process 1 does not know whether it has to execute line 6 or finish.

The paper is structured as follows. In the following section, we recall definitions and notations for negotiations. Section 3 introduces negotiation programs formally. In Section 4, we show how to derive a negotiation from a program. Section 5 is devoted to the converse direction, which is based on a technical result given in Section 6. Our result can be viewed as a solution to the *realizability problem*, as posed for other models, which will be discussed in Section 7.

2   Negotiations: Syntax and Semantics

We recall the main definitions of [1] for syntax and semantics of negotiations. However, here we do not consider states of agents and their transformations. Throughout the paper, we fix a finite set A of *agents* representing potential parties of negotiations.

Definition 1. *A negotiation atom, or just an* atom, *is a pair* $n = (P_n, R_n)$, *where* P_n *is a nonempty set of* parties *(participants) and* R_n *is a finite, nonempty set of* results. *For each result* r, *the pair* (n, r), *also denoted by* r_n, *is the* outcome *of* n.

A negotiation is a composition of atoms. We add a *transition function* $\mathfrak{X}$ that assigns to each triple (n, a, r) consisting of an atom n, a party a of n, and a result r of n a set $\mathfrak{X}(n, a, r)$ of atoms, the set of atomic negotiations agent a is ready to engage in after the atom n, if the result of n is r.

Definition 2. *Given a finite set of atoms* N, *let* $T(N)$ *denote the set of triples* (n, a, r) *such that* $n \in N$, $a \in P_n$, *and* $r \in R_n$.
A negotiation is a tuple $\mathcal{N} = (N, n_0, n_f, \mathfrak{X})$, *where* $n_0, n_f \subset N$ *are the initial and final atoms, and* $\mathfrak{X} : T(N) \to 2^N$ *is the transition function, such that*
   (1) every agent of A *participates in both* n_0 *and* n_f;
   (2) for every $(n, a, r) \in T(N)$: $\mathfrak{X}(n, a, r) = \emptyset$ *iff* $n = n_f$.
The negotiation $\mathcal{N}$ *is* deterministic *if* $|\mathfrak{X}(n, a, r)| = 1$ *for each* $(n, a, r) \in T(N)$ *satisfying* $n \neq n_f$. *We write* $\mathfrak{X}(n, a, r) = n'$ *instead of* $\mathfrak{X}(n, a, r) = \{n'\}$.

In this paper we consider only deterministic negotiations. In the graphical representation of a deterministic negotiation, an arc from the port of agent a in atom n, labeled by r, leads to the port of a in the unique atom of $\mathfrak{X}(n, a, r)$. In the negotiation of Figure 1, the atom n_0 has possible results y and n while n_1 only has the result p. By definition, the final atom n_f has results, too. Since after each outcome (n_f, e) no agent is ready to engage in any atom, these results are not represented in the figure. Whenever we choose disjoint names for results, as we did in this example, we do not have to distinguish results and outcomes.

A *marking* of a negotiation $\mathcal{N} = (N, n_0, n_f, \mathfrak{X})$ is a mapping $x \colon A \to 2^N$. Intuitively, $x(a)$ is the set of atoms that agent a is currently ready to engage in next. The *initial* and *final* markings, denoted by x_0 and x_f respectively, are given by $x_0(a) = \{n_0\}$ and $x_f(a) = \emptyset$ for every $a \in A$.

A marking x *enables* an atom n if $n \in x(a)$ for every $a \in P_n$. If x enables n, then n can take place and its parties agree on a result r; we say that the outcome (n, r) *occurs*. The occurrence of (n, r) produces a next marking x' given by $x'(a) = \mathfrak{X}(n, a, r)$ for every $a \in P_n$, and $x'(a) = x(a)$ for every $a \in A \setminus P_n$. We write $x \xrightarrow{(n,r)} x'$ to denote this, and call it a *small step*. By this definition, always either $x(a) = \{n_0\}$ or $x(a) = \mathfrak{X}(n, a, r)$ for some atom n and outcome r. Therefore, for deterministic negotiations, $x(a)$ always contains at most one atom. We write $x_1 \xrightarrow{\sigma}$ to denote that there is a sequence $\sigma = (n_1, r_1) \ldots (n_k, r_k) \ldots$ of small steps such that $x_1 \xrightarrow{(n_1,r_1)} x_2 \xrightarrow{(n_2,r_2)} \cdots \xrightarrow{(n_k,r_k)} x_{k+1} \cdots$ We call σ *occurrence sequence* from the marking x_1, or enabled by x_1. If σ is finite then we write $x_1 \xrightarrow{\sigma} x_{k+1}$ and call x_{k+1} *reachable* from x_1. If x_1 is the initial marking, then we call σ *initial occurrence sequence*. If moreover x_{k+1} is the final marking, then σ is a *large step*.

The marking x_f can only be reached by the occurrence of (n_f, e) (e being a possible result of n_f), and it does not enable any atom. Any other marking that does not enable any atom is considered a *deadlock*.

We represent a marking x of the negotiation of Figure 1 by the vector $(x(1), x(2), x(3), x(4))$. With this notation, one of the occurrence sequences is:

$$(n_0, n_0, n_0, n_0) \xrightarrow{y} (n_1, n_1, n_2, n_2) \xrightarrow{p} (n_3, n_3, n_2, n_2) \xrightarrow{p'}$$
$$(n_3, n_3, n_3, n_3) \xrightarrow{a} (n_f, n_f, n_f, n_f) \xrightarrow{e} (\emptyset, \emptyset, \emptyset, \emptyset)$$

Following [10,11], we introduce a notion of well-behavedness of negotiations:

Definition 3. *A negotiation is* sound *if* (a) *every atom is enabled at some reachable marking, and* (b) *every initial occurrence sequence is either a large step or can be extended to a large step.*

Sound negotiations are necessarily deadlock-free. A sound negotiation also has no livelocks, i.e., it cannot reach a behaviour from which it is impossible to reach the the final marking. However, sound negotiations may not terminate. In the rest of this paper, we often consider the set of all sound and deterministic negotiations. We introduce the abbreviation *SDN* for the elements of this set.

Two distinct atoms which are both enabled at a reachable marking are *concurrently enabled*. Hence two possible next outcomes (n_1, r_1) and (n_2, r_2) are concurrent if $n_1 \neq n_2$, and they are *alternative* if $n_1 = n_2$ and $r_1 \neq r_2$. In an occurrence sequence, concurrently occurring outcomes are ordered arbitrarily. Conversely, two subsequent outcomes in an occurrence sequence occur concurrently if and only if the sets of agents participating in the respective atoms are disjoint. This fact is utilized by the concurrent semantics of negotiations, the *Mazurkiewicz trace semantics*.

A Mazurkiewicz trace language [12] is based on a finite alphabet Σ (of events) and a *dependence relation* $D \subseteq \Sigma \times \Sigma$ which is reflexive and symmetric. The *independence relation* $I = (\Sigma \times \Sigma) \setminus D$ is symmetric and irreflexive. Two subsequent independent events of a sequential observation of a concurrent run can be interchanged, and the resulting sequence is an observation of the same run, whereas the order of two subsequent dependent events matters.

Given any finite sequence σ of events over Σ, $[\sigma]$ denotes the least set of sequences which contains σ and is closed under permutation of subsequent independent events (i.e., if $\sigma_1 \, a \, b \, \sigma_2 \in [\sigma]$ and $(a, b) \in I$ then $\sigma_1 \, b \, a \, \sigma_2 \in [\sigma]$). Each such $[\sigma]$ is called a *trace*, and each set of traces is a *trace language*. Formally, a trace language is defined on a *distributed alphabet* (Σ, I), where Σ is an alphabet and $I \subseteq \Sigma \times \Sigma$ is an independence relation.

Traces can be composed in a natural way: for $\sigma_1, \sigma_2 \in \Sigma^*$, $[\sigma_1] \cdot [\sigma_2] := [\sigma_1 \sigma_2]$ (it is easy to see that this is well-defined, i.e., for $[\sigma_1'] = [\sigma_1]$ and $[\sigma_2'] = [\sigma_2]$ we have $[\sigma_1 \sigma_2] = [\sigma_1' \, \sigma_2']$). Similarly, we define composition of trace languages: if A and B are sets of traces, then $A \cdot B := \{a \cdot b \mid a \in A, b \in B\}$.

The Kleene star applied to a trace, $[\sigma]^*$, denotes the languages of all $[\sigma]^i$, for $i = 0, 1, 2, \ldots$. Similarly, for a trace language A, A^* is the union of all A^i.

Definition 4. *Let* $\mathcal{N}$ *be a negotiation and let* Σ *be the set of all outcomes of* $\mathcal{N}$. *Define the independence relation* I *by* $((n_1, r_1), (n_2, r_2)) \in I$ *if* $P_{n_1} \cap P_{n_2} = \emptyset$ *(i.e.,* n_1 *and* n_2 *are independent if they have disjoint sets of agents). The set of*

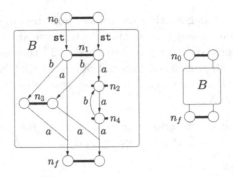

Fig. 4. Boxes

traces *of* $\mathcal{N}$, *denoted by* $T(\mathcal{N})$, *is the set of traces over* (Σ, I) *given by* $T(\mathcal{N}) = \{[\sigma] \mid \sigma \text{ is a large step of } \mathcal{N}\}$.

The outcomes $(n_1, \mathbf{p})$ and $(n_2, \mathbf{p}')$ of the negotiations of Figure 1 are independent. The set of traces is the set $\{[\sigma] \mid \sigma \in (\mathbf{n} + \mathbf{y}\,\mathbf{p}\,\mathbf{p}'\,(\mathbf{r}\,\mathbf{p}\,\mathbf{p}')^* \mathbf{a})\}$ (we abbreviate an outcome (n, r) to the result $\mathbf{r}$). For instance, we have $[\mathbf{y}\,\mathbf{p}\,\mathbf{p}'\,\mathbf{r}\,\mathbf{p}\,\mathbf{p}'\,\mathbf{a}] = \{\mathbf{y}\,\mathbf{p}\,\mathbf{p}'\,\mathbf{r}\,\mathbf{p}\,\mathbf{p}'\,\mathbf{a}, \mathbf{y}\,\mathbf{p}'\,\mathbf{p}\,\mathbf{r}\,\mathbf{p}\,\mathbf{p}'\,\mathbf{a}, \mathbf{y}\,\mathbf{p}\,\mathbf{p}'\,\mathbf{r}\,\mathbf{p}'\,\mathbf{p}\,\mathbf{a}, \mathbf{y}\,\mathbf{p}'\,\mathbf{p}\,\mathbf{r}\,\mathbf{p}'\,\mathbf{p}\,\mathbf{a}\}$.

It is convenient to assume that the initial and final atoms of a negotiation are distinct and have one single result each, for which we use the symbols $\mathbf{st}$ and $\mathbf{end}$, respectively. We will moreover require that no port of the initial atom has an ingoing arc. If the initial atom n_0 does not satisfy this, then we add a new initial atom n'_0 with a single result $\mathbf{st}$ and set $\mathcal{X}(n'_0, a, \mathbf{st}) = n_0$ for each agent a. For the final atom, we can easily replace all the results by a single result $\mathbf{end}$.

Definition 5. *A negotiation* $\mathcal{N} = (N, n_0, n_f, \mathcal{X})$ *is* normed *if* n_0 *and* n_f *are distinct and have one single result, called* $\mathbf{st}$ *for* n_0 *and* $\mathbf{end}$ *for* n_f*, and satisfies* $n_0 \notin \mathcal{X}(n, a, r)$ *for each atom* n*,* $a \in P_n$ *and* $r \in R_n$*. The* normed trace semantics *of* $\mathcal{N}$ *is the set of traces* $[\![\mathcal{N}]\!] = \{\sigma \mid \mathbf{st}\ \sigma\ \mathbf{end} \in T(\mathcal{N})\}$.

We use the abstract graphical representation of a normed negotiation shown in Figure 4; we draw a box around its *body* and give it a name, in this case B. Due to the convention above, for each agent there is exactly one arc connecting its port in the initial atom to the body. However, there may be several arcs from the body to the port of an agent in the final atom, although we represent them as one arc. Observe that a negotiation is completely determined by its body, the initial and final atoms just play the rôle of a wrapper.

3 Negotiation Programs

In this section, we provide a language for the specification of negotiations. As we have abstracted from states and state transformations of negotiations, we also abstract from data but concentrate on the communication between agents.

Agents can agree on negotiation outcomes. For the language, we therefore define a set of *outcome names* or *names* $\mathcal{R}$ (without stating anything about atomic negotiations yet). We fix a function $\ell\colon \mathcal{R} \to 2^A$ that assigns to each name a nonempty set of agents, intuitively the set of agents that have to agree on the outcome to be taken. For every set $X \subseteq A$, we denote by $\mathcal{R}_X$ the set of names $\mathbf{r} \in \mathcal{R}$ such that $\ell(\mathbf{r}) = X$.

Definition 6. *Let* $\mathcal{NP}$ *be the grammar consisting of the following productions for every* $X \subseteq A$, *every* $X' \subseteq X$, *and every* $Y, Z \subseteq X$ *such that* $Y \cup Z = X$:

$$prog[X] ::= \epsilon$$
$$\mathbf{do}\ \{[]\ endalt[X]\}^+\ \{[]\ loopalt[X]\}^*\ \mathbf{od}$$
$$prog[Y] \circ prog[Z]$$
$$endalt[X] ::= name[X]\colon prog[X']\ \mathbf{end}$$
$$loopalt[X] ::= name[X]\colon prog[X']\ \mathbf{loop}$$
$$name[X] ::= element\ of\ \mathcal{R}_X$$

where, as usual, ϵ *is the empty expression,* $\{\}^+$ *stands for "one or more instances of", and* $\{\}^*$ *for "zero or more instances of".*

For every $X \subseteq A$, *the* negotiation programs over X *are the expressions derivable in* $\mathcal{NP}$ *from the nonterminal* $prog[X]$.

In the rest of the paper we use P_X to denote a program over the set X of agents. With this syntax, if $P_{X'}$ is a subprogram of P_X, then necessarily $X' \subseteq X$.

Intuitively, the semantics of negotiation programs is as follows:

- ϵ stands for a terminated negotiation
- **do** body **od** describes a negotiation starting with an atomic negotiation among the agents of X, in which they agree on one of the alternatives in the body. If they agree on an end-alternative $\mathbf{a}\colon P_{X'}$ **end**, then the program continues with $P_{X'}$ and terminates when (and if) $P_{X'}$ terminates. If they agree on a loop-alternative $\mathbf{a}\colon P_{X'}$ **loop**, then, after $P_{X'}$ terminates (if it does), the program restarts.
- $P_Y \circ P'_Z$ combines sequential and concurrent composition. If $Y \cap Z = \emptyset$, then P_Y and P'_Z are executed concurrently, and we may write $P_Y \parallel P'_Z$ instead of $P_Y \circ P'_Z$.

Formally, the semantics of a negotiation program is a set of traces over a distributed alphabet. We define the alphabet first.

Definition 7. *Given a set of agents* A, *outcome names* $\mathcal{R}$ *and a labeling function* ℓ *as above, the* distributed alphabet over A *is the pair* (Σ, I), *where* $\Sigma = \mathcal{R}$ *and* $(\mathbf{a}, \mathbf{b}) \in I$ *iff* $\ell(\mathbf{a}) \cap \ell(\mathbf{b}) = \emptyset$. *That is, two outcome names are independent if their corresponding sets of agents are disjoint.*

The semantics *of a negotiation program* P_X *over a set of agents* $X \subseteq A$ *is the set of traces* $[\![P_X]\!]$ *over the distributed alphabet* (Σ, I) *inductively defined as follows, where* E_X^i *and* L_X^j *denote end- and loop-alternatives, respectively:*

$$[\![\epsilon]\!] = \{[\epsilon]\}$$

$$[\![\textbf{do} \ \overset{k}{\underset{i=0}{[\!]}} \ E_X^i \ \overset{m}{\underset{j=1}{[\!]}} \ L_X^j \ \textbf{od}]\!] = \left(\bigcup_{j=1}^{m} [\![L_X^j]\!] \right)^* \cdot \left(\bigcup_{i=0}^{k} [\![E_X^i]\!] \right)$$

$$[\![a\!:\!P_{X'}]\!] = \{[a]\} \cdot [\![P_{X'}]\!]$$

$$[\![P_Y \circ P_Z']\!] = [\![P_Y]\!] \cdot [\![P_Z']\!]$$

We use an abbreviation for **do**···**od** constructs with only one alternative (which must be an **end**-alternative): we shorten **do** $[\!]\,a\,:\,\epsilon$ **end od** to just a.

In our example, the body of the program shown in Figure 2 has the same semantics as the negotiation of Figure 1. Observe that we need to duplicate the subprogram (p $\|$ p$'$). This is, however, already necessary in sequential computations. Consider the degenerate negotiation with only one agent obtained by "projecting" the negotiation of Figure 1 onto the first agent (shown on the right of the figure). The language of the program is given by the regular expression yp(rp)*a, which also contains two occurrences of p. No regular expression for this language contains only one occurrence of p.

The main result of this paper, proved in the next sections, shows the equivalence between negotiation programs and sound deterministic negotiations, where a negotiation program and a SDN are equivalent if they have the same set of Mazurkiewicz traces. This equivalence not only preserves the occurrence sequences, but also concurrency. In particular, in the SDN for a program $P_1 \| P_2$, the negotiations for P_1 and P_2 are indeed executed concurrently. So the theorem shows that every specification is deadlock-free and can be implemented, and every sound implementation can be specified.

Theorem 1. *(a) For every negotiation program P there is a normed SDN $\mathcal{N}$ with the same set of agents such that $[\![P]\!] = [\![\mathcal{N}]\!]$. Moreover, the number of atoms and outcomes of $\mathcal{N}$ is equal to the number of do-blocks of P plus 2, and the total number of outcomes of $\mathcal{N}$ is equal to the total number of alternatives of P plus 1.*

(b) For every normed SDN $\mathcal{N}$ there is a negotiation program P with the same set of agents such that $\|P\| = \|\mathcal{N}\|$.

In (b), the size of P can be exponential in the size of $\mathcal{N}$. This is already the case for negotiations with one single agent, in which $\mathcal{N}$ is essentially a deterministic finite automaton, and P corresponds to a regular expression for this automaton, which can be exponentially larger than the automaton itself.

4   From Programs to Normed SDNs

We show that for every negotiation program P there is a normed SDN $\mathcal{N}$ such that $[\![P]\!] = [\![\mathcal{N}]\!]$, by induction over the structure of P. First we give a SDN for the empty program, and then we give deterministic negotiations for $P_1 \circ P_2$ and **do** $[\!]_{i=1}^{k} \, \mathsf{a}_i\!:\!P_i$ **end** $[\!]_{j=k+1}^{k+\ell} \, \mathsf{a}_j\!:\!P_j$ **loop**, assuming we have produced negotiations for all P_i. In all cases, the proof that the negotiation is sound and has the same traces as the program follows easily from the definitions, and is omitted.

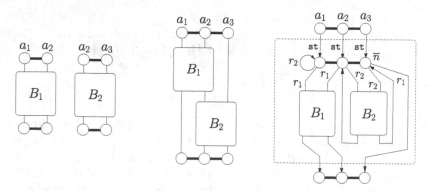

Fig. 5. The concatenation and the prefix operation

Definition 8. *The empty normed negotiation over a set X of agents is $\mathcal{N}_X^\epsilon = (\{n_0, n_f\}, n_0, n_f, \mathcal{X})$ with $\mathcal{X}(n_0, a, st) = n_f$, $\mathcal{X}(n_f, a, end) = \emptyset$ for each $a \in X$.*

Lemma 1. $\llbracket \epsilon \rrbracket = \{[\epsilon]\} = \llbracket \mathcal{N}_X^\epsilon \rrbracket$ *for every $\emptyset \neq X \subseteq A$.*

Figure 5 illustrates the concatenation (middle) of two negotiations (left) with bodies B_1, B_2 over two not disjoint sets of agents.

Definition 9. *Let $\mathcal{N}_1 = (N_1, n_{01}, n_{f1}, \mathcal{X}_1)$, $\mathcal{N}_2 = (N_2, n_{02}, n_{f2}, \mathcal{X}_2)$ be negotiations over (not necessarily disjoint) sets of agents A_1, A_2 satisfying $N_1 \cap N_2 = \emptyset$. The negotiation $\mathcal{N}_1 \circ \mathcal{N}_2 = (N, n_0, n_f, \mathcal{X})$ over agents $A_1 \cup A_2$ is defined by:*

- $N = (N_1 \setminus \{n_{01}, n_{f1}\}) \cup (N_2 \setminus \{n_{02}, n_{f2}\}) \cup \{n_0, n_f\}$

- $\mathcal{X}(n_0, a, st) = \begin{cases} \mathcal{X}_1(n_{01}, a, st) \text{ if } a \in A_1 \\ \mathcal{X}_2(n_{02}, a, st) \text{ if } a \in A_2 \setminus A_1 \end{cases}$

- *For every $n \in N_1$, for every $a \in P_n, r \in R_n$:*

$$\mathcal{X}(n, a, r) = \begin{cases} \mathcal{X}_1(n, a, r) \text{ if } \mathcal{X}_1(n, a, r) \neq n_{f1} \\ n_f \text{ if } \mathcal{X}_1(n, a, r) = n_{f1}, a \in A_1 \setminus A_2, \\ \mathcal{X}_1(n_{01}, a, r) \text{ if } \mathcal{X}_1(n, a, r) = n_{f1}, a \in A_1 \cap A_2, \end{cases}$$

- *For every $n \in N_2$, for every $a \in P_n, r \in R_n$:*

$$\mathcal{X}(n, a, r) = \begin{cases} \mathcal{X}_2(n, a, r) \text{ if } \mathcal{X}_2(n, a, r) \neq n_{f2} \\ n_f \text{ if } \mathcal{X}_1(n, a, r) = n_{f2} \end{cases}$$

Lemma 2. *If $\llbracket P_1 \rrbracket = \llbracket \mathcal{N}_1 \rrbracket$ and $\llbracket P_2 \rrbracket = \llbracket \mathcal{N}_2 \rrbracket$, then $\llbracket P_1 \circ P_2 \rrbracket = \llbracket \mathcal{N}_1 \circ \mathcal{N}_2 \rrbracket$.*

Prefixing negotiations by an atom that chooses which negotiation to execute next is illustrated in Figure 5 (right) for the special case of **do** [] $r_1 \colon P_1$ **end** [] $r_2 \colon P_2$ **loop od**, where P_1, P_2 are programs over agents $\{a_1, a_2\}$ and $\{a_2, a_3\}$, respectively. As for concatenation, the textual definition is a bit laborious.

Definition 10. *Let* $\mathcal{N}_1, \ldots \mathcal{N}_{k+\ell}$ *be negotiations over (not necessarily disjoint) sets of agents* $A_1, \ldots, A_{k+\ell}$. *Let* $\mathcal{N}_i = (N_i, n_{0i}, n_{fi}, \mathcal{X}_i)$ *for every* $1 \leq i \leq k + \ell$, *where the* N_i *are pairwise disjoint. The negotiation*

$$choice[\mathcal{N}_1, \ldots, \mathcal{N}_k; \mathcal{N}_{k+1}, \ldots, \mathcal{N}_{k+\ell}] = (N, n_0, n_f, \mathcal{X})$$

over agents $A = \bigcup_{i=1}^{k+\ell} A_i$ *is defined as follows:*

- $N = \{\bar{n}, n_0, n_f\} \cup \bigcup\limits_{i=1}^{k+\ell} N_i \setminus \{n_{0i}, n_{fi}\}$

- $\mathcal{X}(n_0, a, \mathbf{st}) = \bar{n}$ *for every* $a \in A$

- *For every* $1 \leq i \leq k$: $\mathcal{X}(\bar{n}, a, r_i) = \begin{cases} \mathcal{X}_i(n_{0i}, a, r_i) & \text{if } a \in A_i \\ n_f & \text{if } a \notin A_i \end{cases}$

- *For every* $k + 1 \leq i \leq k + \ell$: $\mathcal{X}(\bar{n}, a, r_i) = \begin{cases} \mathcal{X}_i(n_{0i}, a, r_i) & \text{if } a \in A_i \\ \bar{n} & \text{if } a \notin A_i \end{cases}$

- *For every* $1 \leq i \leq k$, $n \in N_i$, $a \in P_n$, $r \in R_n$:

$$\mathcal{X}(n, a, r) = \begin{cases} \mathcal{X}_i(n, a, r) & \text{if } \mathcal{X}_i(n, a, r) \neq n_{fi} \\ n_f & \text{if } \mathcal{X}_i(n, a, r) = n_{fi} \end{cases}$$

- *For every* $k + 1 \leq i \leq k + \ell$, $n \in N_i$, $a \in P_n$, $r \in R_n$:

$$\mathcal{X}(n, a, r) = \begin{cases} \mathcal{X}_i(n, a, r) & \text{if } \mathcal{X}_i(n, a, r) \neq n_{fi} \\ \bar{n} & \text{if } \mathcal{X}_i(n, a, r) = n_{fi} \end{cases}$$

Lemma 3. *Let* $P = \text{do } []_{i=1}^{k} a_i : P_i \text{ end } []_{j=k+1}^{k+\ell} a_j : P_j \text{ loop.}$ *If* $[\![P_i]\!] = [\![\mathcal{N}_i]\!]$ *for every* $1 \leq i \leq k + \ell$, *then* $[\![P]\!] = [\![choice[\mathcal{N}_1, \ldots \mathcal{N}_k; \mathcal{N}_{k+1}, \ldots, \mathcal{N}_{k+\ell}]]\!]$.

5   From Normed SDNs to Programs

We show that for every normed SDN N there is a negotiation program P with the same agents such that $[\![P]\!] = [\![N]\!]$. For this we use the results of [1,2] on *reduction rules*. Although we generally abstract from data aspects in this paper, states and state transformations are helpful to understand the reduction rules.

Each agent $a \in A$ has a (possibly infinite) nonempty set Q_a of *internal states*. We denote by Q_A the cartesian product $\prod_{a \in A} Q_a$. For each atom n and result $r \in R_n$, there is a *state transformer* $\delta_n(r)$ representing a non-deterministic state transforming function (this non-determinism is not related to the previously defined determinism of negotiations). Formally, $\delta_n(r)$ is a left-total relation $\delta_n(r) \subseteq Q_A \times Q_A$ satisfying: if $((q_{a_1}, \ldots, q_{a_{|A|}}), (q'_{a_1}, \ldots, q'_{a_{|A|}})) \in \delta_n(r)$ then $q_{a_i} = q'_{a_i}$ for all $a_i \notin P_n$ (only the internal states of parties of n can be transformed). We assign to each large step $\sigma = (n_0, r_0) \ldots (n_f, r_f)$ a transformer $\delta_\sigma = \delta(n_0, r_0) \cdots \delta(n_f, r_f)$ (concatenation is the usual concatenation of relations). The *summary transformer* of negotiation N and result r_f of the final atom n_f, $\delta_N(r_f)$, is the union of all δ_σ for large steps σ ending with (n_f, r_f).

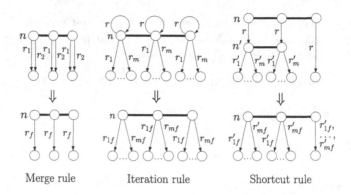

Merge rule   Iteration rule   Shortcut rule

Fig. 6. The reduction rules

Two negotiations $\mathcal{N}_1$ and $\mathcal{N}_2$ over A are *semantically equivalent*, denoted $\mathcal{N}_1 \equiv \mathcal{N}_2$, if either both are not sound or if both are sound, their final atoms have the same results and $\delta_{\mathcal{N}_1}(r_f) = \delta_{\mathcal{N}_2}(r_f)$ for every final result r_f.

A *reduction rule*, or just a rule, is a binary relation on the set of negotiations. Given a rule R, we write $\mathcal{N}_1 \xrightarrow{R} \mathcal{N}_2$ for $(\mathcal{N}_1, \mathcal{N}_2) \in R$. A rule R is *correct* if $\mathcal{N}_1 \xrightarrow{R} \mathcal{N}_2$ implies that $\mathcal{N}_1 \equiv \mathcal{N}_2$) and therefore in particular that $\mathcal{N}_1$ is sound iff $\mathcal{N}_2$ is sound.

Given a set of rules $\mathcal{R} = \{R_1, \ldots, R_k\}$, we denote by $\mathcal{R}^*$ the reflexive and transitive closure of $R_1 \cup \ldots \cup R_k$. We say that $\mathcal{R}$ is *complete with respect to a class of negotiations* if $\mathcal{N} \xrightarrow{\mathcal{R}^*} \mathcal{N}_{min}$ holds for every negotiation $\mathcal{N}$ in the class, where $\mathcal{N}_{min}$ is a minimal negotiation of that class. In the class of sound negotiations, each minimal negotiation has a single atom, which is both initial and final. In the class of normed sound negotiations, each minimal negotiation has two atoms, an initial and a final one, and the initial one has only one result, $\mathtt{st}$, which sends all agents to the final atom.

Given a reduction rule R, we say that R^{-1} is its associated *synthesis rule*. By the definition of completeness, for every normed SDN $\mathcal{N}$ over the set X of agents there is a chain $\mathcal{N}_X^\epsilon = \mathcal{N}_1 \equiv \mathcal{N}_2 \equiv \ldots \equiv \mathcal{N}_m = \mathcal{N}$ where each negotiation is obtained from the previous one through the application of a synthesis rule.

We will prove the existence of a sequence $\epsilon = P_1 \equiv P_2 \equiv \ldots \equiv P_m = P$ of programs such that $[\![P_i]\!] = [\![\mathcal{N}_i]\!]$ for every $1 \le i \le n$. We do so by proving the following statement for each synthesis rule R^{-1} in the following complete set of reduction rules: if $(\mathcal{N}, \mathcal{N}') \in R^{-1}$ and there is P such that $[\![P]\!] = [\![\mathcal{N}]\!]$, then there exists P' such that $[\![P']\!] = [\![\mathcal{N}']\!]$.

We repeat the correct and complete set of rules for normed SDNs from [2]. Rules are described by a *guard* and an *action*; $\mathcal{N}_1 \xrightarrow{R} \mathcal{N}_2$ holds if $\mathcal{N}_1$ satisfies the guard and $\mathcal{N}_2$ is a possible result of applying the action to $\mathcal{N}_1$. The rules introduced in [1,2] are summarized in Figure 6. The transformations of state transformers (δ_n) are actually not important in the present context but are provided for the sake of completeness.

Merge rule. Intuitively, this rule (Figure 6, left) merges two outcomes with identical next enabled atoms into one single outcome with a fresh label.

Guard: N contains an atom n with distinct outcomes $r_1, r_2 \in R_n$
  such that $\mathcal{X}(n, a, r_1) = \mathcal{X}(n, a, r_2)$ for every $a \in A_n$.
Action: (1) $R_n \leftarrow (R_n \setminus \{r_1, r_2\}) \cup \{r_f\}$, with r_f being a fresh label.
  (2) For all $a \in P_n$: $\mathcal{X}(n, a, r_f) \leftarrow \mathcal{X}(n, a, r_1)$.
  (3) $\delta(n, r_f) \leftarrow \delta(n, r_1) \cup \delta(n, r_2)$.
Iteration rule. The rule replaces the iteration of an outcome r followed by some other outcome by one outcome r_f with the same effect (Figure 6, middle).

Guard: N contains an atom n with an outcome r
  such that $\mathcal{X}(n, a, r) = n$ for every party a of n.
Action: (1) $R_n \leftarrow \{r'_f \mid r' \in R_n \setminus \{r\}\}$, with r'_f being a fresh label.
  (2) For all $a \in P_n$: $\mathcal{X}(n, a, r'_f) \leftarrow \mathcal{X}(n, a, r') \setminus \{n\}$.
  (3) For every $r'_f \in R_n$: $\delta_n(r'_f) \leftarrow \delta_n(r)^* \, \delta_n(r')$.

Shortcut rule. The shortcut rule merges the outcomes of two atoms that can occur subsequently into one single outcome with the same effect (Figure 6, right).

Given atoms n, n', we say that (n, r) *unconditionally enables* n' if $P_n \supseteq P_{n'}$ and $\mathcal{X}(n, a, r) = n'$ for every $a \in P_{n'}$. If (n, r) unconditionally enables n' then, for *every* marking x that enables n, the marking x' given by $x \xrightarrow{(n,r)} x'$ enables n'. Moreover, n' can only be disabled by its own occurrence.

Guard: N contains two distinct atoms $n, n' \neq n_0$
  such that (n, r) unconditionally enables n'.
Action:
(1) $R_n \leftarrow (R_n \setminus \{r\}) \cup \{r'_f \mid r' \in R_{n'}\}$, with r'_f being fresh labels.
(2) For all $a \in P_{n'}$, $r' \in R_{n'}$: $\mathcal{X}(n, a, r'_f) \leftarrow \mathcal{X}(n', a, r')$.
  For all $a \in P \setminus P_{n'}$, $r' \in R_{n'}$: $\mathcal{X}(n, a, r'_f) \leftarrow \mathcal{X}(n, a, r)$.
(3) For all $r' \in R_{n'}$: $\delta_n(r'_f) \leftarrow \delta_n(r) \delta_{n'}(r')$.
(4) If $\mathcal{X}^{-1}(n') = \emptyset$ after (1)-(3), then remove n' from N, where
  $\mathcal{X}^{-1}(n') = \{(\tilde{n}, \tilde{a}, \tilde{r}) \in T(N) \mid n' \in \mathcal{X}(\tilde{n}, \tilde{a}, \tilde{r})\}$.

Theorem 2. *[1,2] The merge, shortcut, and iteration rules are complete and correct for the class of deterministic negotiations (and thus preserve soundness as well as unsoundness). Moreover, every SDN with k atoms can be completely reduced by means of a polynomial number (in k) of applications of the rules.*

For defining according program rules, it is convenient to introduce *labeled programs*, in which each **do...od**-block carries a label. Two blocks carry the same label if and only if they are syntactically identical.

A labeled program P over a set of agents A *matches* a normed negotiation $\mathcal{N} = (N, n_0, n_f, \mathcal{X})$, denoted by $P \sim_A \mathcal{N}$, if each block P' of P is labeled with an atom $n' \in N \setminus \{n_0, n_f\}$ having the same agents and outcomes as P', and for each atom $n' \in N \setminus \{n_0, n_f\}$ some block of P is labeled by n.

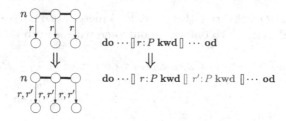

Fig. 7. Program rule for the (inverse of the) merge rule

For each of the rules above we prove the following statement: if $(\mathcal{N}, \mathcal{N}') \in R^{-1}$ and there is a negotiation program P such that $[\![P]\!] = [\![\mathcal{N}]\!]$ and $P \sim_A \mathcal{N}$, then there exists a negotiation program P' such that $[\![P']\!] = [\![\mathcal{N}']\!]$, and $P' \sim_A \mathcal{N}'$. For the merge and iteration rules this is very simple, but the shortcut rule is nontrivial.

In the rest of the section, **kwd** (for keyword) stands for either **end** or **loop**.

Merge rule.

Lemma 4. *Let* $(\mathcal{N}, \mathcal{N}') \in M^{-1}$, *where* M *is the binary relation of the merge rule. If there is* P *such that* $[\![P]\!] = [\![\mathcal{N}]\!]$ *and* $P \sim_A \mathcal{N}$, *then there exists* P' *such that* $[\![P']\!] = [\![\mathcal{N}']\!]$, *and* $P' \sim_A \mathcal{N}'$.

Proof. Let (n, r) be the outcome of $\mathcal{N}$ to which the synthesis rule is applied. Since $P \sim_A \mathcal{N}$, all blocks of P labeled by n are identical and have the form

$$n :: \mathbf{do} \cdots [] \, r : P_r \ \mathbf{kwd} \, [] \cdots \mathbf{od} \tag{1}$$

for some program P_r. If P' is the result of replacing all blocks labeled by n by

$$n :: \mathbf{do} \cdots [] \, r : P_r \ \mathbf{kwd} \, [] \, r' : P_r \ \mathbf{kwd} \, [] \cdots \ \mathbf{od}$$

then we clearly have $[\![P']\!] = [\![\mathcal{N}']\!]$, and $P' \sim_A \mathcal{N}'$.   □

Observe that, due to the duplication of P_r, the size of P' can be essentially twice the size of P.

Iteration rule.

Lemma 5. *Let* $(\mathcal{N}, \mathcal{N}') \in I^{-1}$, *where* I *is the binary relation of the iteration rule. If there is* P *such that* $[\![P]\!] = [\![\mathcal{N}]\!]$ *and* $P \sim_A \mathcal{N}$, *then there exists* P' *such that* $[\![P']\!] = [\![\mathcal{N}']\!]$, *and* $P' \sim_A \mathcal{N}'$.

Proof. Let n be the atom of $\mathcal{N}$ to which the synthesis rule adds one more outcome, and let X be the set of agents of n. Since $P \sim_A \mathcal{N}$, all blocks of P labeled by n are identical and have the form

$$n :: \mathbf{do} \ \overset{m}{\underset{i=1}{[]}} \ r_i : P_i \ \mathbf{kwd}_i \ \mathbf{od} \tag{2}$$

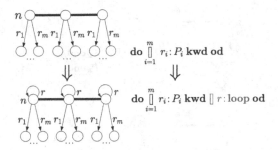

Fig. 8. Program rule for the (inverse of the) iteration rule

Let P' be the result of replacing all blocks labeled by n by

$$n :: \textbf{do} \ \underset{i=1}{\overset{m}{\big[\big]}} \ r_i : P_i \ \textbf{kwd}_i \ \big[\big] \ r : \textbf{loop} \ \textbf{od}$$

Then we clearly have $[\![P']\!] = [\![\mathcal{N}']\!]$, and $P' \sim_A \mathcal{N}'$.   □

Shortcut rule. The shortcut rule presents a problem, illustrated in Figure 9. The left part of the figure represents an application of the synthesis rule. Let $(\mathcal{N}, \mathcal{N}') \in S^{-1}$ be this application, where S is the binary relation of the shortcut rule. The program for $\mathcal{N}$ must contain a block labeled by n with set of agents $\{a_1, a_2, a_3\}$ and two outcomes r_1, r_2, as shown in the upper-right part of the figure. Assume, as shown in the figure, that P_1 and P_2 have $\{a_1, a_2\}$ and $\{a_1, a_2, a_3\}$ as sets of parties, respectively. Then the program for $\mathcal{N}'$ must still contain a **do**-block P for the atom n, but now with a single outcome r leading to a second **do**-block P' with two outcomes r'_1 and r'_2, leading to the programs P_1 and P_2. Since the outcome r only has a_1 and a_2 as parties, P' has to be a program derived from the nonterminal $\langle\text{prog}\rangle_{\{a_1, a_2\}}$. But then, since P_2 has $\{a_1, a_2, a_3\}$ as parties, it cannot be a subprogram of P'.

Fortunately, we can *sidestep* the problem by having a close look at the completeness proofs of [1, 2]. Those proofs imply the following result: completeness is retained if the shortcut rule is restricted to two special cases.

Definition 11. *The* one-outcome shortcut rule *is like the shortcut rule, but with the additional condition in its guard that the atom n' has only one outcome. The* same-parties shortcut rule *is like the shortcut rule, but with the additional condition in its guard that atoms n and n' have identical sets of parties.*

The proof of this completeness result is non-trivial, and we delay it to Section 6. Assuming the result holds, we show next that we find program transformations matching the inverses of the one-outcome and same-parties shortcut rules.

Lemma 6. *Let $(\mathcal{N}, \mathcal{N}') \in O^{-1}$, where O is the binary relation of the one-outcome shortcut rule. If there is P such that $[\![P]\!] = [\![\mathcal{N}]\!]$ and $P \sim_A \mathcal{N}$, then there exists P' such that $[\![P']\!] = [\![\mathcal{N}']\!]$, and $P' \sim_A \mathcal{N}'$.*

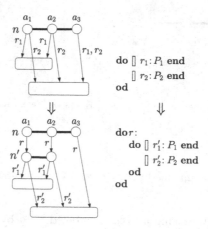

do [] $r_1 \colon P_1$ **end**
   [] $r_2 \colon P_2$ **end**
od

do $r \colon$
   do [] $r_1' \colon P_1$ **end**
      [] $r_2' \colon P_2$ **end**
   od
od

Fig. 9. The naïve program rule for the shortcut rule fails

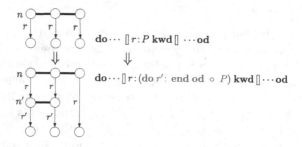

do $\cdots$ [] $r \colon P$ **kwd** [] $\cdots$ **od**

do $\cdots$ [] $r \colon (\textbf{do } r' \colon \textbf{ end od} \circ P)$ **kwd** [] $\cdots$ **od**

Fig. 10. Program rule mimicking the (inverse of the) one-outcome shortcut rule

Proof. Let n be the atom of N with an outcome r to which the inverse of the one-outcome rule is applied. Given a set T of traces, let $T[n, r, n', r']$ be the result of replacing in T each trace of the form $[\sigma_1 (n, r) \sigma_2]$ by the trace $[\sigma_1 (n, r) (n', r') \sigma_2]$. It follows easily from the definition of N and N' that $[\![N']\!] = [\![N]\!][r, r']$. The construction is illustrated in Figure 10.

Since $P \sim_A N$, all blocks of P labeled by n are identical and have the form

$$B = n :: \textbf{do} \cdots [] \; r \colon P_r \; \textbf{kwd} \; [] \; \ldots \textbf{od} \; .$$

Let $P[B/B']$ be the result of replacing all blocks labeled by n by

$$B' = n :: \textbf{do} \cdots [] \; r \colon (\textbf{do } r' \colon \textbf{end od} \circ P_r) \; \textbf{kwd} \; [] \; \ldots \textbf{od} \; .$$

By the definition of the program semantics we have $[\![B']\!] = [\![B]\!][n, r, n', r']$. We prove $[\![P[B/B']]\!] = [\![P]\!][n, r, n', r']$ by induction on the structure of P, which, taking $P' = P[B/B']$, concludes the proof.

– If $P = B$, then apply $P[B/B'] = B'$ and $[\![B']\!] = [\![B]\!][n, r, n', r']$.

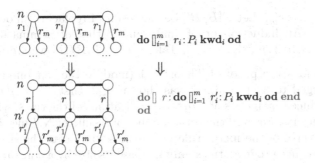

do $[]_{i=1}^{m}$ $r_i : P_i$ **kwd**$_i$ **od**

do $[]$ $r :$ **do** $[]_{i=1}^{m}$ $r'_i : P_i$ **kwd**$_i$ **od end**
od

Fig. 11. Program rule for the (inverse of the) same-parties shortcut rule

– If $P = $ **do** $[]_{i=1}^{m}$ $r_i : P_i$ **kwd**$_i$ **od**, where **kwd**$_i$ = **end** for $1 \leq i \leq m'$ and **kwd**$_i$ = **loop** for $m' < i \leq m$, then $P[B/B'] = $ **do** $[]_{i=1}^{m}$ $r_i : P_i[B/B']$ **kwd**$_i$ **od**. By induction hypothesis $[\![P_i[B/B']]\!] = [\![P_i]\!][n, r, n', r']$, and so we get

$$[\![P[B/B']]\!]$$
$$= (\bigcup_{i=m'+1}^{m} [\![P_i[B/B']]\!])^* \bigcup_{j=1}^{m'} [\![P_j[B/B']]\!]$$
$$= (\bigcup_{i=m'+1}^{m} [\![P_i]\!][n,r,n',r'])^* \bigcup_{j=1}^{m'} [\![P_j]\!][n,r,n',r'] \quad \text{(induction hypothesis)}$$
$$= \bigcup_{j=1}^{m'} \bigcup_{i=m'+1}^{m} ([\![P_i]\!][n,r,n',r'])^* [\![P_j]\!][n,r,n',r']$$
$$= \bigcup_{j=1}^{m'} \bigcup_{i=m'+1}^{m} ([\![P_i]\!]^* [\![P_j]\!]) [n,r,n',r']$$
$$= ((\bigcup_{i=m'+1}^{m} [\![P_i]\!])^* \bigcup_{j=1}^{m'} [\![P_j]\!]) [n,r,n',r']$$
$$= [\![P]\!][n,r,n',r']$$

– If $P = P_1 \circ P_2$, then

$$[\![P[B/B']]\!]$$
$$= [\![P_1[B/B']]\!] \cdot [\![P_2[B/B']]\!]$$
$$= [\![P_1]\!][n,r,n',r'] \cdot [\![P_2]\!][n,r,n',r'] \quad \text{(induction hypothesis)}$$
$$= ([\![P_1]\!] \cdot [\![P_2]\!])[n,r,n',r']$$
$$= [\![P_1 \circ P_2]\!][n,r,n',r']$$

$\square$

Lemma 7. *Let* $(\mathcal{N}, \mathcal{N}') \in O^{-1}$*, where O is the binary relation of the same parties shortcut rule. If there is P such that $[\![P]\!] = [\![\mathcal{N}]\!]$ and $P \sim_A \mathcal{N}$, then there exists P' such that $[\![P']\!] = [\![\mathcal{N}']\!]$, and $P' \sim_A \mathcal{N}'$.*

Proof. Let n be the atom of $\mathcal{N}$ with outcome r to which the inverse of the same-parties rule is applied. Given a set T of traces, let $T[n, r, n', r'_1, \ldots, r'_m]$ be the result of replacing in T each trace of the form $[\sigma_1(n, r_i)\sigma_2]$ by the trace $[\sigma_1(n, r)(n', r'_i)\sigma_2]$. It follows easily from the definition of $\mathcal{N}$ and $\mathcal{N}'$ that $[\![\mathcal{N}']\!] = [\![\mathcal{N}]\!][n, r, n', r'_1, \ldots, r'_m]$. Figure 11 illustrates this construction.

Since $P \sim_A \mathcal{N}$, all blocks of P labeled by n are identical. Let B be the syntactic expression of the block. Let $B' = $ **do** $r : B$ **end od**. Then $[\![B']\!] = $

$[\![B]\!][n, r, n', r'_1, \ldots, r'_m]$. Let $P[B/B']$ be the result of replacing all occurrences of B in P by B'. An induction proof analogous to that of Lemma 6 shows that $[\![P[B/B']]\!] = [\![B]\!][n, r, n', r'_1, \ldots, r'_m]$. Taking $P' = P[B/B']$ we are done. $\square$

This concludes the proof of Theorem 1 (modulo the remaining proof obligation discharged to Section 6). It was shown in [2] that every SDN $\mathcal{N}$ can be completely reduced by means of $O(a^4 \cdot r)$ applications of the rules, where a and r are the number of atoms and the total number of results of $\mathcal{N}$. Since the program rule for the inverse of the merge rule can at most duplicate the size of the program, and the other program rules only increase its size by a constant, we obtain an upper bound of $O(2^{a^4 \cdot n})$ for the size of the program P equivalent to $\mathcal{N}$. A program of linear size can be obtained by enriching the programming language with procedures. Instead of duplicating program P_r in the proof of Lemma 4, we call twice a procedure with body P_r.

6   Completeness of Rules for Normed SDNs

It remains to show that the merge, iteration, one-outcome shortcut and same-parties shortcut rules are complete for normed SDNs, i.e., that they reduce every normed SDN to a negotiation with just two atoms.

Definition 12. *A* cycle *of a negotiation* $\mathcal{N}$ *is a sequence of outcomes* (n_1, r_1), $\ldots, (n_k, r_k)$ *such that there are agents* $a_1, \ldots, a_k$ *and* $n_2 \in \mathcal{X}(n_1, a_1, r_1)$, $n_3 \in \mathcal{X}(n_2, a_2, r_2)$, $\ldots, n_1 \in \mathcal{X}(n_k, a_k, r_k)$. *The negotiation* $\mathcal{N}$ *is called* cyclic *if it contains a cycle, and* acyclic *otherwise.*

We consider the acyclic and cyclic cases separately.

The completeness of the rules (merge, iteration, one-outcome shortcut and same-parties shortcut) in the acyclic case was proven in [1]:

Lemma 8. *The merge rule, iteration rule, one-outcome shortcut rule and same-parties shortcut rule are complete for sound deterministic acyclic SDNs.*

Proof. This claim is an immediate consequence of Lemma 1 in [1] (our one-outcome shortcut rule is called d-shortcut rule there). Actually, Lemma 1 in [1] states that whenever the merge rule and the same-parties shortcut rule are not applicable to a sound deterministic acyclic negotiation then every agent participates in all atoms with more than one output. If the negotiation under consideration is not minimal yet, we can apply the shortcut rule to atoms n and n'. Since the same-parties shortcut rule is not applicable, n' has less parties than n, and hence not all agents participate in n'. Therefore n' can have only one outcome, and the conditions of the one-outcome shortcut rule are satisfied. $\square$

For the cyclic case, we have a closer look to the results of [2]:

Definition 13. *A* loop *is an occurrence sequence* σ *such that* $x \xrightarrow{\sigma} x$ *for some marking* x *reachable from the initial marking* x_0. *A* minimal loop *is a loop* σ *satisfying the property that there is no other loop* σ' *such that the set of atoms in* σ' *is a proper subset of the set of atoms in* σ.

Lemma 9 (Lemma 1 of [2]).

(1) Every cyclic SDN has a loop.
(2) The set of atoms of a minimal loop generates a strongly connected subgraph of the graph of the considered negotiation.

Usually, more than one atom is involved in a loop, and these atoms have different sets of parties. For sound deterministic negotiations, it was proven in [2] that at least one of these atoms involve all parties that participate in any of these atoms. These atoms are called *synchronizers* of the loop. In turn, a synchronizer of one loop can synchronize other loops as well. For a single atom n we consider the *fragment* of the negotiation which is constituted by all atoms and outcomes appearing in any loop synchronized by the atom n (which is nonempty only if n is a synchronizer of at least one loop). Each fragment is cyclic by construction. Now we are looking for a fragment with the property that all its cycles pass through its generating synchronizer n. It is not difficult to see that this property is satisfied by minimal fragments, which do not properly include any smaller ones: if a cycle of a fragment does not pass through the generating synchronizer n, then there is an according loop for this cycle, which again has a synchronizer n', and the fragment generated by n' is smaller than the one generated by n.

The procedure introduced in [2] shows that a minimal fragment generated by a synchronizer n can be viewed as an acyclic sound negotiation starting with n and ending with (a copy of) n, and can thus be reduced by the same rules as for the acyclic case. This procedure ends with a minimal cycle, which enables the iteration rule. After applying this rule, the cycle vanishes. The complete procedure deletes this way cycle by cycle, until the negotiation is acyclic and can be reduced to a minimal one as above.

Another important point made in [2] is that the atoms of a minimal fragment enjoy the following property: Each atom is either a synchronizer (and has hence the same parties as the generating atom) or has no *exits*, which means that all outcomes of the atom are also outcomes of the fragment. This implies that it suffices to apply the restricted same-parties and one-outcome shortcut rules instead of the general shortcut rule also for the acyclic case, as we will argue next. We have recalled above that the restricted rules suffice for sound and deterministic acyclic negotiations, and we reduce the fragment exactly like a corresponding acyclic negotiation. If a same-parties shortcut rule is applied in the fragment, then the same rule applies to the entire negotiation. The one-outcome shortcut rule, however, requires that the reduced negotiation (called n' in the definition) has only one output. Even if this is the case within the fragment, additional outputs might exist in the entire negotiation. However, in this case this atom must be a synchronizer, and thus all parties of the fragment participate in this atom. In particular, it cannot have less parties than the other atom of the rule (called n in the definition), which implies that the additional guard of the same-parties rule is also fulfilled. In other words: For each application of the one-outcome shortcut rule in the fragment, which is not at the same time an application of the same-parties shortcut rule, the reduced atom (n') has only one outcome in the negotiation, too, and hence, the same application of the shortcut rule in the negotiation is also a one-outcome shortcut reduction.

These considerations, all from [2], prove the following lemma:

Lemma 10. *The merge rule, iteration rule, one-outcome shortcut rule and same-parties shortcut rule are complete for sound deterministic cyclic SDNs.*

Finally, recall that completeness of a set of rules means that each negotiation can be reduced to a minimal one. Minimal negotiations have a single atom, whereas minimal normed negotiations have two. Since we apply the reduction rules to normed negotiations, we still have to show that we are always able to end the reduction procedure with a minimal normed negotiation.

Theorem 3. *The merge rule, iteration rule, one-outcome shortcut rule and same-parties shortcut rule are complete for normed SDNs.*

Proof. This proof is heavily based on Lemma 8 and Lemma 10. We only have to show that for every normed SDN N at least one rule can be applied that does not spoil the normedness property.

By definition of the rules, application of the merge rule or of the iteration rule transforms a normed SDN into a normed SDN. For the shortcut rule, the derived negotiation might be not normed, if the rule is applied to the initial atom n_0 and its unique successor. However, it suffices to consider the restricted variants of the one-outcome shortcut rule and the same-parties shortcut rule. We moreover rule out the case that the negotiation before transformation is already a minimal normed one, i.e., we assume that it has more than two atoms. For the one-outcome shortcut rule, in the resulting negotiation, the initial atom still has one outcome only, by definition of the shortcut rule. For the same-parties shortcut rule, however, this is not necessarily the case. So we consider this case in the sequel and assume that the same-parties shortcut rule can be applied to the initial atom n_0 and its successor n_1 of a normed negotiation.

By definition of a normed negotiation, none of the ports of the initial atom has an ingoing arc. Since the same-parties shortcut rule is applicable, n_1 contains the same parties as n_0, and since n_0 is the initial atom, all agents participate in both atoms. So it is obvious that the negotiation obtained after deletion of n_0, taking n_1 as initial atom, is also sound (but not normed in general). This smaller negotiation N' can be reduced to a minimal negotiation by the merge rule, the iteration rule and the two restricted variants of the shortcut rule. We consider two cases: If N' is already minimal, it consists of a single atom. Then the considered negotiation with n_0 is already a minimal normed SDN. If N' is not minimal, then one of the rules can be applied to N'. The same rule can be applied to N, referring to the same involved atoms. □

7   Conclusions

We have introduced a specification language for deterministic negotiations. The language has a very special feature: every program of the language is sound (the program can terminate from every reachable state, meaning in particular that the program is deadlock-free) *and* every sound negotiation can be specified in the language. So the language provides a syntactic characterization of soundness.

Design requirements for distributed systems are often captured with the help of scenarios, specifying the interactions that take place between sequential processes. There exist different formal notations for scenarios, depending on the underlying communication mechanism between processes. Formal notations also permit to specify multiple scenarios by means of operations like choice, concatenation, and repetition. A set of scenarios specified using such operations can be viewed as an early model of the system analyzable using formal techniques.

A key feature of scenario-based notations is that they present a global view of the system as a set of concurrent executions representing use cases. While this view is usually more intuitive for developers, implementations require a concurrent composition of sequential models, i.e., of state machines. A specification is realizable if there exists a set of state machines, one for each sequential component, whose set of concurrent behaviours coincides with the set globally specified. The *realizablity problem* consists of deciding if a given specification is realizable and, if so, computing a realization, i.e., a set of state machines. The problem has been studied for various formalisms.

For negotiations, the realizability problem reads as follows: given a syntactically correct negotiation program, is there a sound deterministic negotiation with the same behaviour? The results of this paper show that, for deterministic negotiations, the realizability problem is far more tractable than in other languages, because the answer to the above question is always positive. In turn, negotiation programs are expressively complete: every sound deterministic negotiation diagram has an equivalent negotiation program. Finally, negotiation programs can be distributed in linear time. We provided an algorithm to derive a deterministic negotiation from a program that generalizes classical constructions to derive an automaton from a regular expression. The negotiation is then projected onto its components.

References

1. Esparza, J., Desel, J.: On negotiation as concurrency primitive. In: D'Argenio, P.R., Melgratti, H. (eds.) CONCUR 2013. LNCS, vol. 8052, pp. 440–454. Springer, Heidelberg (2013)
2. Esparza, J., Desel, J.: On negotiation as concurrency primitive II: deterministic cyclic negotiations. In: Muscholl, A. (ed.) FOSSACS 2014. LNCS, vol. 8412, pp. 258–273. Springer, Heidelberg (2014)
3. Davis, R., Smith, R.G.: Negotiation as a metaphor for distributed problem solving. Artificial Intelligence **20**(1), 63–109 (1983)
4. Jennings, N.R., Faratin, P., Lomuscio, A.R., Parsons, S., Wooldridge, M.J., Sierra, C.: Automated negotiation: prospects, methods and challenges. Group Decision and Negotiation **10**(2), 199–215 (2001)
5. Böhm, C., Jacopini, G.: Flow diagrams, turing machines and languages with only two formation rules. Commun. ACM **9**(5), 366–371 (1966)

6. Harel, D.: On folk theorems. Commun. ACM **23**(7), 379–389 (1980)
7. Kozen, D., Tseng, W.-L.D.: The Böhm–Jacopini theorem is false, propositionally. In: Audebaud, P., Paulin-Mohring, C. (eds.) MPC 2008. LNCS, vol. 5133, pp. 177–192. Springer, Heidelberg (2008)
8. Vanhatalo, J., Völzer, H., Koehler, J.: The refined process structure tree. Data Knowl. Eng. **68**(9), 793–818 (2009)
9. Zwiers, J.: Compositionality, Concurrency and Partial Correctness-Proof Theories for Networks of Processes, and Their Relationship. LNCS, vol. 321. Springer, Heidelberg (1989)
10. van der Aalst, W.M.P.: The application of Petri nets to workflow management. J. Circuits, Syst. and Comput. **8**(1), 21–66 (1998)
11. van der Aalst, W.M.P., van Hee, K.M., ter Hofstede, A.H.M., Sidorova, N., Verbeek, H.M.W., Voorhoeve, M., Wynn, M.T.: Soundness of workflow nets: classification, decidability, and analysis. Formal Asp. Comput. **23**(3), 333–363 (2011)
12. Diekert, V., Rozenberg, G., Rozenburg, G.: The book of traces, vol. 15. World Scientific (1995)

Nested-Unit Petri Nets: A Structural Means to Increase Efficiency and Scalability of Verification on Elementary Nets

Hubert Garavel[1,2,3,4](✉)

[1] Inria, Montbonnot-Saint-Martin, France
[2] Université Grenoble Alpes, LIG, 38000 Grenoble, France
[3] CNRS, LIG, 38000 Grenoble, France
[4] Saarland University, Saarbr ücken, Germany
hubert.garavel@inria.fr
http://convecs.inria.fr

Abstract. Perti nets can express concurrency and nondeterminism but not hierarchy. This article presents an extension of Perti nets, in which places can be grouped into so-called "units" expressing sequential components. Units can be recursively nested to reflect the hierarchical nature of complex systems. This model called NUPN (Nested-Unit Perti nets) was originally developed for translating process calculi to Perti nets, but later found also useful beyond this setting. It allows significant savings in the memory representation of markings for both explicit-state and symbolic verification. Five tools already implement the NUPN model, which is also part of the next edition of the Model Checking Contest.

1 Introduction

Process calculi and Perti nets are two major branches of concurrency theory and have been extensively compared from many different viewpoints. Regarding the ways in which the hierarchical structure of complex systems can be formally described, process calculi have features that low-level Petri nets are lacking. This is precisely the issue adressed in the present article, which proposes to extend Perti nets with hierarchical structuring features inspired from process calculi.

Our proposal is rooted in a longstanding effort to develop the comprehensive CADP toolbox [22] for the design and verification of concurrent systems. The toolbox includes an efficient compiler [21,23,24] for LOTOS, a value-passing process calculus standardized by ISO [40]. This compiler translates LOTOS to labelled transition systems using, as an intermediate step, interpreted Perti nets that possess a hierarchical structure reflecting the concurrent structure of the source LOTOS specifications. Actually, the suggestion that the Perti nets generated by the compiler could retain structural information from the LOTOS source was formulated in 1988 by Eric Madelaine during a meeting; following this remark, the concept of "nested units" described in this article was progressively identified and refined as the most useful kind of information to be preserved.

© Springer International Publishing Switzerland 2015
R. Devillers and A. Valmari (Eds.): PETRI NETS 2015, LNCS 9115, pp. 179–199, 2015.
DOI: 10.1007/978-3-319-19488-2_9

For twenty-five years, this concept has been in use, but internally to the CADP toolbox only. Specifically, the LOTOS compiler uses two different types of hierarchically-structured nets: an interpreted Petri net (which comprises variables, expressions, assignments, guards, etc.) and an elementary net (which is a data-less abstraction of the former by removing all value-passing information). The present article is about this latter model, initially called BPN (*Basic Petri Net*) until we realized that this acronym was heavily overloaded[1]; for this reason, the acronym was changed to NUPN[2] (*Nested-Unit Petri Net*) in 2013.

Recently, this model found a new application field in the framework of the Model Checking Contest. For the 2014 edition of the contest, the software tools built around the NUPN model helped to correct and complete the descriptions (structural and behavioural properties) of the P/T nets proposed as challenges to the competitors; additionally, six new challenges were automatically derived from realistic process-calculus specifications using the NUPN tools. For the 2015 edition of the contest, NUPN will move from the back- to the front-office and become visible to competitors, as certain challenges will be provided as P/T nets enriched with NUPN information.

The present article is organised as follows. Sec. 2 defines the NUPN model and states its main properties. Sec. 3 does an extensive review of the state of the art to position the NUPN model with respect to related work. Sec. 4 indicates how the representation of markings can be optimized for NUPNs in both explicit-state and symbolic verification settings. Sec. 5 provides an overview of implementation efforts to equip the NUPN model with file formats, software tools, and collections of benchmarks. Finally, Sec. 6 gives concluding remarks and draws open perspectives for future work.

2   Nested-Unit Perti nets

2.1   Structure

This subsection defines the "structural" aspects of the NUPN model; these correspond to the description of syntax and static semantics for a computer language.

Definition 1. *A (marked) Nested-Unit Petri Net (acronym: NUPN) is a 8-tuple* $(P, T, F, M_0, U, u_0, \sqsubseteq, \text{unit})$ *where:*

1. *P is a finite, non-empty set; the elements of P are called* places.
2. *T is a finite set such that $P \cap T = \varnothing$; the elements of T are called* transitions.
3. *F is a subset of $(P \times T) \cup (T \times P)$; the elements of F are called* arcs.
4. *M_0 is a subset of P; M_0 is called the* initial marking.
5. *U is a finite, non-empty set such that $U \cap T = U \cap P = \varnothing$; the elements of U are called* units.

---

[1] BPN is used elsewhere as an acronym for *Backward Petri Net, Basic Petri Net* (as opposed to Colored Petri Net), *Batch Petri Net, Behavioural Petri Net, Biochemical Petri Net, Bounded Petri Net, Business Process Net,* B(PN)^2, etc.

[2] To be pronounced: "*new PN*".

6. u_0 is an element of U; u_0 is called the root unit.
7. $\sqsubseteq$ is a binary relation over U such that $(U, \sqsupseteq)$ is a tree with a single root u_0, where $(\forall u_1, u_2 \in U)\ u_1 \sqsupseteq u_2 \overset{\text{def}}{=} u_2 \sqsubseteq u_1$; thus, $\sqsubseteq$ is reflexive, antisymmetric, transitive, and u_0 is the greatest element of U for this relation; intuitively, $u_1 \sqsubseteq u_2$ espresses that unit u_1 is transitively nested in or equal to unit u_2.
8. unit is a function $P \rightarrow U$ such that $(\forall u \in U \setminus \{u_0\})\ (\exists p \in P)\ \text{unit}\,(p) = u$; intuitively, $\text{unit}\,(p) = u$ expresses that unit u directly contains place p.

We have chosen to base our definitions on elementary nets rather than P/T nets, the main difference being that elementary nets are ordinary (i.e., all arc weights are equal to one) and usually expected to be safe (i.e., each place can contain at most one token). We however use the terms "places" and "transitions" rather than their counterparts "conditions" and "events" in elementary nets. Notice that, despite the fact that NUPNs have been originally designed for process calculi, no particular assumption is made about place or transition labelling. The next definition provides useful notations derived from Def. 1.

Definition 2. Let $(P, T, F, M_0, U, u_0, \sqsubseteq, \text{unit})$ be a NUPN, and let u, u_1, and u_2 be any three units of U:

- $u_1 \sqsubset u_2 \overset{\text{def}}{=} (u_1 \sqsubseteq u_2) \wedge (u_1 \neq u_2)$ is the strict nesting partial order.
  disjoint $(u_1, u_2) \overset{\text{def}}{=} (u_1 \not\sqsubseteq u_2) \wedge (u_2 \not\sqsubseteq u_1)$ characterizes pairs of units neither equual nor nested one in the other.
- subunits*$(u) \overset{\text{def}}{=} \{u' \in U \mid (u' \sqsubset u)\}$ gives all units transitively nested in u.
- subunits$(u) \overset{\text{def}}{=} \{u' \in U \mid (u' \sqsubset u) \wedge (\nexists u'' \in U)\ (u' \sqsubset u'') \wedge (u'' \sqsubset u)\}$ gives all units directly nested in u.
- leaf$(u) \overset{\text{def}}{=} (\text{subunits}\,(u) = \varnothing)$ characterises the minimal elements of $(U, \sqsubseteq)$.
- places$(u) \overset{\text{def}}{=} \{p \in P \mid \text{unit}\,(p) = u\}$ gives all places directly contained in u; these are called the local places (or proper places) of u.
- places*$(u) \overset{\text{def}}{=} \{p \in P \mid (\exists u' \in U)\ (u' \sqsubseteq u) \wedge (\text{unit}\,(p) = u')\}$ gives all places transitively contained in u or its sub-units.
- $\widetilde{U} \overset{\text{def}}{=} \{u \in U \mid \text{places}\,(u) \neq \varnothing\}$ is the set of all units but u_0 if the root unit has no local place.

Proposition 1. Let $(P, T, F, M_0, U, u_0, \sqsubseteq, \text{unit})$ be a NUPN. The family of sets places(u), where $u \in \widetilde{U}$, is a partition of P.

Proof. It follows from item 8 of Def. 1 that all sets in the family are not empty. It follows from the definitions of places and unit that all sets in the family are pairwise disjoint. From these same definitions and the fact that unit is totally defined, it follows that the union of all sets in the family is equal to P.

2.2 Execution

This subsection defines the dynamic semantics of the NUPN model, namely the "token game" rules for computing markings and firing transitions. In a nutshell, the rules for a NUPN $(P, T, F, M_0, U, u_0, \sqsubseteq, \text{unit})$ are exactly the same as those for an elementary net (P, T, F, M_0); that is, the unit-related part $(U, u_0, \sqsubseteq, \text{unit})$ does not influence the execution of the NUPN.

Definition 3. *Let $(P, T, F, M_0, U, u_0, \sqsubseteq, \text{unit})$ be a NUPN. Let t be a transition:*

- *The* pre-set *of t is the set of places defined as $\bullet t \overset{\text{def}}{=} \{p \in P \mid (p, t) \in F\}$.*
- *The* post-set *of t is the set of places defined as $t^\bullet \overset{\text{def}}{=} \{p \in P \mid (t, p) \in F\}$.*
- *A* marking *M is defined as a set of places $(M \subseteq P)$.*
- *A transition t is* enabled *in some marking M iff it satisfies the predicate* enabled $(M, t) \overset{\text{def}}{=} (\bullet t \subseteq M)$.
- *A transition t can* safely fire *from some marking M iff it satisfies the predicate* safe-fire $(M, t) \overset{\text{def}}{=}$ enabled $(M, t) \wedge ((M \setminus \bullet t) \cap t^\bullet = \varnothing)$
- *A transition t can* weakly fire *from some marking M_1 to another marking M_2 iff* enabled $(M_1, t) \wedge (M_2 = (M_1 \setminus \bullet t) \cup t^\bullet)$, *which we note $M_1 \overset{t}{\longrightarrow} M_2$.*
- *A transition t can* strictly fire *from some marking M_1 to another marking M_2 iff* safe-fire $(M_1, t) \wedge (M_2 = (M_1 \setminus \bullet t) \cup t^\bullet)$.
- *A marking M is* reachable *from the initial marking M_0 iff $M = M_0$ or there exist $n \geq 1$ transitions $t_1, t_2, ..., t_n$ and n markings $M_1, M_2, ..., M_n$ such that $M_0 \overset{t_1}{\longrightarrow} M_1 \overset{t_2}{\longrightarrow} M_2 ... \overset{t_n}{\longrightarrow} M_n$.*
- *The NUPN is* safe *(or one-safe) iff for each reachable marking M and transition t,* enabled $(M, t) \Rightarrow$ safe-fire (M, t). *In such case, the weak-firing and strict-firing rules coincide.*

Definition 4. *Let $(P, T, F, M_0, U, u_0, \sqsubseteq, \text{unit})$ be a NUPN. Given a marking M and a unit u, let the* projection *of M on u be defined as $M \rhd u \overset{\text{def}}{=} M \cap \text{places}(u)$.*

Proposition 2. *Let $(P, T, F, M_0, U, u_0, \sqsubseteq, \text{unit})$ be a NUPN. Any marking M can be expressed as $M = (M \rhd u_1) \uplus ... \uplus (M \rhd u_n)$, where $u_1, ..., u_n$ are the units of $\widetilde{U}$, and where $\uplus$ denotes the disjoint set union.*

Proof. This directly follows from Prop. 1, given that the family places (u_1), ..., places (u_n) is a partition of P.

2.3 Unit Safeness

This subsection introduces the so-called *unit-safeness* property, which does not exist in "classical" Perti nets and plays a central role in the NUPN model.

Definition 5. *Let $(P, T, F, M_0, U, u_0, \sqsubseteq, \text{unit})$ be a NUPN. A marking $M \subseteq P$ is said to be* unit safe *iff it satisfies the predicate defined as follows:* unit-safe $(M) \overset{\text{def}}{=} (\forall p_1, p_2 \in M) (p_1 \neq p_2) \Rightarrow$ disjoint $(\text{unit}(p_1), \text{unit}(p_2))$; *that is, all places of a unit-safe marking are contained in disjoint units.*

Proposition 3. *Let $(P, T, F, M_0, U, u_0, \sqsubseteq, \text{unit})$ be a NUPN. For each marking M and unit u,* unit-safe $(M) \Rightarrow \text{card}(M \rhd u) \leq 1$; *that is, a unit-safe marking cannot contain two different local places of the same unit.*

Proof. By contradiction. If card $(M \triangleright u) > 1$, there exist at least two different places p_1 and p_2 in $M \cap$ places (u). Because p_1 and p_2 both belong to places (u), it follows that unit $(p_1) =$ unit (p_2), then $\neg$disjoint (unit (p_1), unit (p_2)), and finally $\neg$unit-safe (M).

Proposition 4. *Let* $(P, T, F, M_0, U, u_0, \sqsubseteq, \text{unit})$ *be a NUPN. For each marking M and units (u, u'), one has:* unit-safe $(M) \wedge (M \triangleright u \neq \varnothing) \wedge (u' \sqsubseteq u \vee u \sqsubseteq u') \Rightarrow (M \triangleright u' = \varnothing)$; *that is, if a unit-safe marking contains a local place of some unit u, it contains no local place of any ancestor or descendent unit u' of u.*

Proof. By contradiction. If $M \triangleright u' \neq \varnothing$ then M contains at least one place $p \in$ unit (u) and at least one place $p' \in$ unit (u'). If $u' \sqsubseteq u$ or $u \sqsubseteq u'$ then $\neg$disjoint (u, u'), hence $\neg$unit-safe (M). Notice, still assuming that unit-safe $(M) \wedge (u' \sqsubseteq u \vee u \sqsubseteq u')$, that the reverse implication $(M \triangleright u = \varnothing) \Rightarrow (M \triangleright u' \neq \varnothing)$ does not hold, as tokens can be absent from both u and u'.

Prop. 4 can be given an intuitive explanation in a process calculus setting. Consider a process term of the form $\boxed{B_1}$; ($\boxed{\boxed{B_2}}$ || $\boxed{B_3}$) ; $\boxed{B_4}$ where B_1, B_2, B_3, and B_4 are sequential process terms, and where square boxes denotes the units enclosing the places corresponding to these terms. The above proposition states that: (i) while B_1 or B_4 execute, neither B_2 nor B_3 can execute, because they are in descendent units of the unit containing B_1 and B_4; and (ii) while B_2 and/or B_3 execute, neither B_1 nor B_4 can execute, because they are in an ascendent unit of the units containing B_2 and B_3. Reasoning on "forks" and "joins" is another way to grasp the intuitive meaning of nested units.

Definition 6. *Let* $N = (P, T, F, M_0, U, u_0, \sqsubseteq, \text{unit})$ *be a NUPN. N is said to be unit safe iff it is safe and all its reachable markings are unit safe.*

Thus, a unit-safe NUPN is also safe. The converse implication does not hold; consider e.g., a safe NUPN with a single unit u_0 and two places p_1 and p_2 contained in u_0; let M_0 be $\{p_1, p_2\}$: this initial marking is safe but not unit safe.

Notice that, if NUPN definitions would be based on (ordinary) P/T nets rather than elementary nets, with markings defined as place multisets (i.e., functions $P \to \mathbb{N}$) rather than place subsets, unit safeness could be simply defined as the condition that all reachable markings are unit safe, which would imply safeness as a particular case of not having more than one token in the same unit.

An important issue is an efficient decision procedure to determine whether a "syntactically well-formed" NUPN (according to Def. 1) is unit safe or not. This issue will be further discussed in Sec. 6. The following conditions give preliminary, yet useful checks that can be easily performed.

Proposition 5. *Let* $N = (P, T, F, M_0, U, u_0, \sqsubseteq, \text{unit})$ *be a NUPN. Let t be a transition.*

1. *If $\neg$unit-safe (M_0) then N is not unit safe.*
2. *If $\neg$unit-safe $(\bullet t)$ then either N is not unit safe or t is not quasi-live.*
3. *If $\neg$unit-safe $(t\bullet)$ then either N is not unit safe or t is not quasi-live.*

Proof. Item 1 directly follows from Def. 6 given that M_0 is a reachable marking. Items 2 and 3: by contradiction. Assuming both that N is unit safe and t is quasi-live, it follows from the latter condition that there exist two reachable markings M_1 and M_2 such that $M_1 \xrightarrow{t} M_2$; consequently, ${}^{\bullet}t \subseteq M_1$ and $t^{\bullet} \subseteq M_2$. If either ¬unit-safe $({}^{\bullet}t)$ or ¬unit-safe $(t^{\bullet})$ then either ¬unit-safe (M_1) or ¬unit-safe (M_2); thus, N is not unit safe.

The unit-safeness property can be reformulated as a system of linear inequalities over the tokens present in reachable markings. Notice that such constraints differ from the traditional S-invariants, which are linear equations.

Proposition 6. *Let $(P, T, F, M_0, U, u_0, \sqsubseteq, \text{unit})$ be a safe NUPN. N is unit safe iff any reachable marking M satisfies the following system of inequalities:*

$$(\forall u \in \tilde{U}) \, (\forall u' \in \tilde{U} \mid u \sqsubseteq u') \, \sum_{p \in \text{places}\,(u) \cup \text{places}\,(u')} x_p \leq 1 \qquad (I_{u,u'})$$

where each variable x_p is equal to 1 if place p belongs to M, or 0 otherwise.

Proof. Direct implication: If N is unit safe, then unit-safe (M) is true. Prop. 3 ensures all inequalities $(I_{u,u'})$ with $u = u'$, since $\sum_{p \in \text{places}\,(u)} x_p = \text{card}\,(M \triangleright u)$. Prop. 4 ensures all inequalities $(I_{u,u'})$ with $u \sqsubset u'$, taking into account that $u \neq u' \Rightarrow \sum_{p \in \text{places}\,(u) \cup \text{places}\,(u')} x_p = \text{card}\,(M \triangleright u) + \text{card}\,(M \triangleright u')$ and that, from Prop. 4, $(M \triangleright u \neq \varnothing) \Rightarrow (M \triangleright u' = \varnothing)$ and $(M \triangleright u' \neq \varnothing) \Rightarrow (M \triangleright u = \varnothing)$, i.e., $(M \triangleright u = \varnothing) \vee (M \triangleright u' = \varnothing)$, which leads to $\text{card}\,(M \triangleright u) + \text{card}\,(M \triangleright u') \leq 1$ after applying Prop. 3 twice. Reverse implication: If N is not unit safe, but safe, there exists some reachable marking M such that ¬unit-safe (M). Thus, there exist two distinct places p_1 and p_2, and two units $u_1 = \text{unit}\,(p_1)$ and $u_2 = \text{unit}\,(p_2)$ such that ¬disjoint (u_1, u_2), i.e., $u_1 \sqsubseteq u_2$ or $u_2 \sqsubseteq u_1$. In both cases, $\sum_{p \in \text{places}\,(u_1) \cup \text{places}\,(u_2)} x_p \geq x_{p_1} + x_{p_2} = 2$, so that M violates inequality (I_{u_1,u_2}) if $u_1 \sqsubseteq u_2$, and/or violates inequality (I_{u_2,u_1}) if $u_2 \sqsubseteq u_1$.

We now study the preservation of NUPN properties under the abstraction (somehow related to the concept of "place fusion" in Coloured Perti nets [42]) given in [23] to determine which pairs of units can execute concurrently.

Definition 7. *Let $N = (P, T, F, M_0, U, u_0, \sqsubseteq, \text{unit})$ be a NUPN. Let N_α denote the 8-tuple $(P', T, F', M'_0, U, u_0, \sqsubseteq, \text{unit}')$ derived from N by merging, in each unit u, all the local places of u into a single place local to u. Formally:*

- *Let $P' \subseteq P$ denote the places of N_α after merging: $\text{card}\,(P') = \text{card}\,(\tilde{U})$.*
- *Let α be the abstraction function $P \to P'$ that maps each place of N to its corresponding place in N_α.*
- *Let $F' \subseteq (P' \times T) \cup (T \times P')$ be the finest arc relation that satisfies $(\forall p \in P) \, (\forall t \in T) \, (F(p,t) \Rightarrow F'(\alpha(p), t)) \wedge (F(t,p) \Rightarrow F'(t, \alpha(p)))$.*
- *Let $M'_0 \subseteq P'$ be equal to $\{\alpha(p) \mid p \in M_0\}$.*
- *Let unit' be the function $P' \to U$ defined by $(\forall p \in P) \, \text{unit}'(\alpha(p)) = \text{unit}\,(p)$.*

Proposition 7. *Let N be a NUPN and let N_α be defined as in Def. 7. Then:*
1. *N_α is also a NUPN.*
2. *If N is safe, N_α is not necessarily safe.*
3. *If N is unit safe, N_α is not necessarily unit safe.*

Proof. For item 1, it easily follows that, because N satisfies all the conditions of Def. 1, N_α also satisfies these conditions. For item 2, consider the following NUPN $N = (P, T, F, M_0, U, u_0, \sqsubseteq, \mathsf{unit})$ given by $P = \{p_0, p_1, p_2\}$, $T = \{t\}$, $F = \{(p_0, t), (t, p_1), (t, p_2)\}$, $M_0 = \{p_0\}$, $U = \{u_0, u\}$, $u \sqsubset u_0$, $\mathsf{unit}(p_0) = u_0$, $\mathsf{unit}(p_1) = u_0$, and $\mathsf{unit}(p_2) = u$; N is safe (but not unit-safe). In N_α, places p_0 and p_1 are merged together (e.g., into p_0), and $F' = \{(p_0, t), (t, p_0), (t, p_2)\}$, meaning that transition t is turned into a self-loop on p_0 and can accumulate infinitely many tokens in p_2; hence, N_α is not safe. For item 3, consider the same NUPN N as for item 2 but with a different initial marking $M_0 = \{p_1\}$; M_0 is the only reachable marking, so that N is unit safe; for the same reason as with item 2, N_α is not safe, and thus not unit safe (notice that t is not quasi-live, which suggests that preservation could hold under stronger assumptions).

2.4   Expressiveness

This subsection discusses the expressiveness of the NUPN model by showing its ability to encode mainstream forms of Perti nets.

As mentioned above, a unit-safe NUPN is safe, which implies that its underlying elementary net is also safe. The following proposition establishes the converse implication.

Proposition 8. *Let (P, T, F, M_0) be any ordinary, safe P/T net (i.e., a safe elementary net). There exists at least one 4-tuple $(U, u_0, \sqsubseteq, \mathsf{unit})$ such that $(P, T, F, M_0, U, u_0, \sqsubseteq, \mathsf{unit})$ is a unit-safe NUPN.*

Proof. Let $p_1, ..., p_n$ be the places of P, where $n = \mathrm{card}(P) \geq 1$. Let $u_0, u_1, ..., u_n$ be $(n+1)$ units and let $U = \{u_0, u_1, ..., u_n\}$. Let $\sqsubseteq$ be the relation defined by $(\forall u \in U)\, (u \sqsubseteq u) \wedge (u \sqsubseteq u_0)$; $(U, \sqsupseteq)$ is clearly a tree with a single root u_0. Let unit be the function $P \to U$ such that $(\forall i \in \{1, ..., n\})\ \mathsf{unit}(p_i) = u_i$, meaning that only the root unit u_0 has no local place. Therefore, the NUPN $(P, T, F, M_0, U, u_0, \sqsubseteq, \mathsf{unit})$ satisfies all the structural conditions of Def. 1. This NUPN is safe because (P, T, F, M_0) is safe. This NUPN is also unit safe, as any marking $M \subseteq P$ (reachable or not) satisfies $\mathsf{unit\text{-}safe}(M)$ because, for any two distinct places (p_i, p_j) in M, $\mathsf{disjoint}(\mathsf{unit}(p_i), \mathsf{unit}(p_j)) = \mathsf{disjoint}(u_i, u_j) = \mathit{false}$ since $i > 0$, $j > 0$, and $i \neq j$.

Notice that this simple encoding (each place in a distinct unit) is not necessarily the only one: there may exist better encodings with fewer units having more local places each; this issue will be discussed in Sec. 6. Also, this encoding justifies why Def. 1 allows the root unit to have no local place, whereas all other units must have at least one — this latter condition preventing the existence of useless "empty" units in a NUPN.

The next proposition establishes that NUPNs subsume *communicating automata*, i.e., sequential state machines that execute in parallel and possibly synchronize on (some of) their transitions. In the Petri net framework, communicating automata are easily expressed using so-called *state-machine components* (see, e.g., [52, p. 557], and [3] for a survey).

Proposition 9. *Let (P, T, F, M_0) be any ordinary P/T net possessing a state-machine decomposition. There exists at least one 4-tuple $(U, u_0, \sqsubseteq, \text{unit})$ such that $(P, T, F, M_0, U, u_0, \sqsubseteq, \text{unit})$ is a unit-safe NUPN.*

Proof. The existence of a state machine decomposition implies that: (i) there exists a collection of place sets $P_1, ..., P_n$ that is a partition[3] of P, and (ii) for each $i \in \{1, ..., n\}$, the subnet $N_i = (P_i, T_i, F_i, M_0 \cap P_i)$ restricted to P_i is a state machine, i.e., $\text{card}\,(M_0 \cap P_i) = 1$ and $(\forall t \in T_i)\ \text{card}\,({}^\bullet t) = \text{card}\,(t^\bullet) = 1$. Let $u_0, u_1, ..., u_n$ be $(n + 1)$ units and let $U = \{u_0, u_1, ..., u_n\}$. Let $\sqsubseteq$ be the relation defined by $(\forall u \in U)\ (u \sqsubseteq u) \land (u \sqsubseteq u_0)$; $(U, \sqsupseteq)$ is clearly a tree with a single root u_0. Let unit be the function $P \to U$ totally defined as follows: $(\forall i \in \{1, ..., n\})\ (\forall p \in P_i)\ \text{unit}\,(p) = u_i$, meaning that only the root unit u_0 has no local place. The NUPN $(P, T, F, M_0, U, u_0, \sqsubseteq, \text{unit})$ satisfies all the structural conditions of Def. 1. This NUPN is safe because (P, T, F, M_0) is state-machine decomposable, thus safe. Due to the state-machine decomposition, each reachable marking M has the form $\{p_1, ..., p_n\}$ where each p_i belongs to P_i; thus, for any two distinct places (p_i, p_j) in M, $\text{disjoint}\,(\text{unit}\,(p_i), \text{unit}\,(p_j)) = \text{disjoint}\,(u_i, u_j) = false$ since $i > 0$, $j > 0$, and $i \neq j$; the NUPN is therefore unit safe. $\square$

Nested units have the same theoretical expressiveness as communicating automata/state machines, but are more convenient for at least two reasons:

1. They add the notion of hierarchy to the concepts of concurrency and nondeterminism already present in elementary nets. This is similar to the escalation from communicating state machines to Statecharts [34] and hierarchical communicating state machines [1].

2. For each state machine P_i, these exists a S-invariant, which states that $\sum_{p \in \text{places}\,(P_i)} x_p = 1$, where M is any reachable marking and x_p the number of tokens M has in place p. This S-invariant is a consequence of the constraint that each transition of the subnet N_i must have exactly one input place and one output place in P_i. On the contrary, each unit u_i is not ruled by a S-invariant but a boundedness inequality of the form $\sum_{p \in \text{places}\,(u_i)} x_p \leq 1$ (cf. Prop. 6). The possibility of having no token in a unit has proven useful when encoding safe nets as NUPNs (cf. proof of Prop. 8); in practice, it also provides greater modelling flexibility:

   - It enables a unit not to have a token in the initial marking and to get a token later (e.g., when the unit is launched by a "fork" transition).
   - It enables a unit to lose its token (either when the unit normally completes with a "join" transition, or when it is abruptly terminated by a transition implementing, e.g., the LOTOS "disable" operator [40] or the raise of an exception [25]).
   - It allows a transition to have an input place in a given unit but no output place in this unit, or even no output place at all. The latter case is useful to model process terms ending with deadlock, such as "a; **stop**", for which the transition implementing action a needs no output place (the smaller the net, the more efficient the verification).

---

[3] Notice that some authors do not require $P_1, ..., P_n$ to be pairwise disjoint.

3   Comparison with Related Work

Although the concept of units for encapsulating Petri-net places belonging to the same sequential process was briefly mentioned, from a process-calculus point of view, in prior publications by the author [21,23,24], the present article is the first to specifically cover this topic and provide a broad synthesis from a Petri-net perspective.

One classically distinguishes between three different Petri-net classes ranked by increasing conciseness and expressiveness of the models they can describe: elementary nets (the most fundamental class), P/T nets, and high-level nets. In such a classification, NUPNs are above elementary nets because of the concept of hierarchy brought by units, and below high-level nets, the tokens of which may carry data. NUPNs are incomparable to P/T nets, as the latter allow multiple tokens per place but lack hierarchical structure; however, as mentioned above, one can easily convert P/T nets to NUPNs and vice versa.

The literature on Perti nets is so abundant, and so many extensions of Perti nets have already been proposed, that it would be no surprise if the ideas underlying the NUPN model had already been also published elsewhere. However, to the best of our knowledge, it is not the case. Specifically, the following comparisons can be drawn between NUPNs and the various approaches proposed in the literature:

1. *High-level Perti nets:* According to [37], there have been three generations of high-level extensions to Perti nets, successively introducing data, hierarchy, and object orientation. The generation that brought hierarchical extensions to Perti nets [18] [39,42] [19] [35,36] was developed independently from our concept of nested units [21,24], at the same time or slightly later; actually, the need for hierarchy in Perti nets had been recognized long before, together with early extension proposals, e.g., [54,55] [58] [63] [46,47] [59,60]. All these hierarchical extensions differ from nested units in several respects:
    - The motivation is not the same. The stated objectives of hierarchical extensions are: (i) to remedy a distinct weakness of traditional "flat" Perti nets, which provide no means to represent the structure of real-world systems and tend to become large, complex, and thus difficult to review and maintain, even for small-size systems; (ii) to equip nets with means for abstraction, encapsulation, and information hiding based on hierarchical structuring; (iii) to support top-down development methodologies ("divide and conquer"), which ease the modelling of involved systems by recursively decomposing them into modules of smaller, more manageable complexity; and (iv) to support bottom-up development methodologies ("reuse"), which enable systems to be designed by assembling components. Such hierarchical extensions are primarily intended to human specifiers who model systems using Perti nets, often with the help of diagram editors. On the contrary, NUPNs are not supposed to be produced or read by humans, but automatically generated and analyzed by computer tools, as NUPN was designed as a "machine-to-machine" formalism for increasing the efficiency of verification algorithms.

- The technical details are different. The common concept to all hierarchical Petri net extensions is the notion of *subnet* (also called *component*, *module*, *page*, *submodel*, or *subsystem*). A subnet usually aggregates *common* (also: *elementary*, *normal*, or *ordinary*) nodes, which are places or transitions, and *macro* (also: *abstract*, *substitution*, or *super*) nodes, which are special places or transitions, each of which represents a subnet. A hierarchical Petri net can be translated to a "flat" Petri net by substituting each macro node with its corresponding subnet, in the same way as macro-expansion is performed by text preprocessors. There is usually some notion of *interface*, often achieved by dedicated places or transitions. The NUPN model does not fit at all into this framework. Units are not subnets, as they only contain places (but neither transitions nor arcs), do not provide abstraction, and have no interfaces. Units are not macro-places either, because the sets of units and places are disjoint, and because no unit can be used where a place can (arcs and transitions are totally unrelated to units); moreover, replacing a unit by a single place does not always preserve the crucial unit-safeness property (cf. Prop. 7 above). Translating a NUPN to a "flat" Petri net does not require any kind of substitution (only the information about units has to be dropped). Finally, some hierarchical Petri net extensions allow certain places (especially, interface places) to be shared between several subnets, whereas such sharing is forbidden by the tree-like hierarchy of the NUPN model, in which each place (directly) belongs to a single unit.
- The intended behavioural semantics is also different. It is often stated that subnets are the Petri-net equivalent for subroutines (i.e., procedures and functions) and modules of programming languages; this is not the case with units, which focus on the concurrent structure of sequential processes running in parallel. In particular, when NUPNs are generated from process calculi, all of which have a built-in construct to define procedures (i.e., by associating an identifier to a given behavioural term so that it can be called multiple times), unit creation does not arise from the procedure calls themselves but from the occurrences of parallel composition operators; said differently, a call to a procedure that is fully sequential will create no unit of its own, unless it occurs as an operand of some parallel composition operator.
- Moreover, NUPN units have to satisfy the unit-safeness property, which has no counterpart in subnets. Even if certain properties are sometimes defined for subnets (e.g., uniformness, conservativeness, and state-machine property in [42, Sec. 4.1]), such properties are merely optional.

2. *Nested Perti nets* [49, 50] and *Object Perti nets* [48, 64, 65]: Such models describe Perti nets whose tokens are also Perti nets, thus inducing a multi-level hierarchy of "nets within nets"; in comparison, NUPNs are much simpler, as they only have data-less tokens.
3. *Translation from process calculi to nets*: The concept of nested units is a distinctive trait of the CÆSAR compiler for LOTOS [21, 24]. The same idea was implicitly present in a later LOTOS compiler, IBM's LOEWE software

[43,44] that translated LOTOS to Extended Finite State Machines, a formalism that inherently represents the concurrent structure that Perti nets without hierarchical extensions cannot express. Noticeably, for other process calculi than LOTOS, nested units have not been used by the translation approaches generating Perti nets from CCS [12] [26–28] [53] [13,20,51] [9,10] [30,31], CSP [29], CCS+CSP [56,57] [61,62], ACP [66], and OCCAM [32,38]. We believe, however, that many of these approaches could be easily adapted to produce NUPN-like structured models rather than "flat" nets.

4. *Petri Box Calculus* [4], *Box Algebra* [5,8], *Petri Net Algebra* [6,7], and *Asynchronous Box Calculus* [16,17]: These are process calculi specifically designed so that all process terms of these calculi can be compositionally translated to equivalent Petri-net fragments called *boxes*. At first sight, these boxes may bear some similarity to NUPN units, but there are enough radical differences between both models to sustain the claim that units are not boxes:

   – Units enclose places only, whereas boxes are nets and thus contain places as well as transitions.
   – Units are just based upon elementary nets, whereas boxes are based upon labelled Perti nets, meaning that additional information must be attached to box places (namely, a three-value attribute: entry, exit, or internal) and to box transitions (namely, actions or multisets of actions belonging to some communication alphabet).
   – Regarding structural properties, units only require a proper partitioning of places, whereas boxes lay totally different kinds of constraints, such as: each transition must have at least one input and one output place; a box must have at least one entry and one exit place; entry places have no incoming arcs and exit places have no outgoing arcs; etc.
   – Regarding behavioural properties, both units and boxes usually assume that each place has at most one token (with the notable exception of the Asynchronous Box Calculus [16,17], which extends the box approach to nets that are not one-safe, thus going beyond the capabilities of NUPNs). But units also require the aforementioned, stronger unit-safeness property (which is not mandatory for boxes), whereas boxes require a *cleanness* property, which expresses that tokens should progress from entry to exit places without staying in any of the nonexit places (this property is irrelevant for units, the places of which are not labelled and which can lose their tokens). Also, unit safeness leads to inequality relations (see Prop. 6), whereas box properties are naturally expressed in terms of equality relations (S-invariants) [4,14,15].
   – Any Petri net generated by the translation of a process term containing parallel composition has several units but only one box. Indeed, when translating a parallel composition $p_1 \| p_2$, the two units corresponding to p_1 and p_2 are kept side by side and enclosed into a third unit, whereas the two boxes corresponding to p_1 and p_2 are merged into one single box. Said differently, units remain *after* the translation is complete, whereas boxes only exist *during* the translation.

4 Efficient Marking Encodings for Unit-Safe NUPNs

It is well known that the safeness property of Perti nets allows to optimize the encoding of reachable markings by keeping, for each place, a single bit rather than an integer number. Therefore, each marking of a safe Petri net with N places is usually represented, in explicit-state verification, by a bit string with N bits, and in symbolic verification, by a BDD (*Binary Decision Diagram*) with N Boolean variables. In the sequel, this linear encoding will be called *scheme (a)* and used as a reference point in future comparisons.

The unit-safeness property of NUPNs allows to further optimize marking representation by taking into account all linear inequalities (cf. Prop. 6) that constrain the space of reachable markings. Let $(P, T, F, M_0, U, u_0, \sqsubseteq, \text{unit})$ be a unit-safe NUPN. Let $n \stackrel{\text{def}}{=} \text{card}(\widetilde{U})$ be the number of units having local places, and let $u_1, ..., u_n$ denote these units of $\widetilde{U}$. For each $u_i \in \widetilde{U}$, let $N_i \stackrel{\text{def}}{=} \text{card}(\text{places}(u_i))$ be the number of local places in u_i.

From Prop. 2, we know that any marking M can be represented by its projections $M \triangleright u_1, ..., M \triangleright u_n$. The result of Prop. 3 (at most one local place in each unit has a token) can be exploited to optimize the representation of these projections. Indeed, each $M \triangleright u_i$ is either empty or reduced to a singleton containing one of the N_i local places of u_i, leading to $(N_i + 1)$ different options. It is thus possible [21, Sec. 8.3.1] to store $M \triangleright u_i$ using only $\lceil \log_2(N_i + 1) \rceil$ bits (in explicit-state verification) or Boolean variables (in symbolic BDD-based verification), where $\lceil x \rceil$ denotes the smallest integer greater than or equal to x. This optimized representation will be called *scheme (b)*.

A slightly different encoding is proposed in [45, Sec. 4.1], which suggests to use one bit or Boolean variable to express whether u_i has a token or not[4], and $\lceil \log_2(N_i) \rceil$ more bits to store $M \triangleright u_i$ when u_i has a token. This encoding will be called *scheme (c)*. It is less compact than scheme (b), as it costs $(\lceil \log_2(N_i) \rceil + 1)$ bits or Boolean variables, but is claimed to favour global reduction of BDD size.

For nested units, further optimization is possible, based on the result of Prop. 4 (when a unit has a token, none of its ascendent or descendent units has a token). In particular, if a unit u has sub-units (i.e., subunits$(u) \neq \varnothing$), its local places and the local places of its sub-units can never have tokens simultaneously [45]; this suggests to use one bit or Boolean variable to encode whether there is or not a token in places(u), and to perform *overlapping* by using the same bits or Boolean variables to encode the presence of tokens either in places(u) or in places*$(u) \setminus$ places(u). Following this approach, the number $\nu(u_i)$ of bits or Boolean variables needed for a non-leaf unit u_i is given by the recursive definition $\nu(u_i) \stackrel{\text{def}}{=} 1 + \max\left(\lceil \log_2(N_i) \rceil, \sum_{u \in \text{subunits}(u_i)} \nu(u)\right)$. For a leaf unit u_j, one can opt either for $\nu(u_j) \stackrel{\text{def}}{=} \lceil \log_2(N_j + 1) \rceil$ if scheme (b) is chosen, or for $\nu(u_j) \stackrel{\text{def}}{=} (\lceil \log_2(N_j) \rceil + 1)$ if scheme (c) is preferred.

---

[4] [45] only introduces this bit when ¬leaf(u_i); however, this bit is required for both leaf and non-leaf units, as any unit can lose its token for the reasons given in Sec. 2.4, unless the unit satisfies stronger assumptions (i.e., is a state machine).

Scheme (b) without overlapping is the approach implemented in the CADP toolbox [22], in both explicit-state setting (CÆSAR tool for LOTOS, when invoked with option "-e7old") and symbolic setting (CÆSAR.BDD tool for NUPNs). We observed that BDD-based verification clearly outperforms the explicit-state approach on data-less models such as NUPNs. We assessed these five encoding/overlapping combinations on a collection of 3524 "non-trivial" NUPNs (i.e., such that $card\,(U) < card\,(P)$), with the following results:

scheme	overlapping	number of bits or Boolean variables	average size
(a)	no	$\sum_{i \in \{1,...,n\}} N_i$ (i.e., N)	100.00%
(b)	no	$\sum_{i \in \{1,...,n\}} \lceil \log_2(N_i + 1) \rceil$	40.52%
(c)	no	$\sum_{i \in \{1,...,n\}} (\lceil \log_2(N_i) \rceil + 1)$	46.44%
(b)	yes	$\nu(u_0) \mathsf{with leaf}\,(u_j) \Rightarrow \nu(u_j) = \lceil \log_2(N_j + 1) \rceil$	39.35%
(c)	yes	$\nu(u_0) \mathsf{with leaf}\,(u_j) \Rightarrow \nu(u_j) = \lceil \log_2(N_j) \rceil + 1$	44.94%

It appears that schemes (b) or (c) alone provide a marking-size reduction greater than 50%. Overlapping seems to have a much lower impact (less than 2%) but this may be an artefact on our current NUPN collection, in which communicating automata largely predominate over hierarchical models.

These experimental results could be expanded in at least three directions: (i) besides the number of Boolean variables, the number of BDD nodes allocated could be considered, (ii) overlapping is perhaps not the only reduction possible and better approaches could be investigated, e.g., by precomputing information about units that can execute concurrently [23]; and (iii) the potential impact of nested units for optimizing the transition relation (and not only marking representation) should also be studied.

Beyond the case of BDDs, it is likely that unit safeness could also permit savings when exploring the state space of NUPNs with other kinds of decision diagrams than BDDs. Of particular interest would be the investigation of MDDs (*Multi-valued Decision Diagrams*) and MTBDDs (*Multi-Terminal BDDs*), which are often deemed superior to BDDs for reachability analysis of Perti nets [2] [11]. Regarding SDDs (*Hierarchical Symbolic Set Diagrams*) [33], discussions with Alexandre Hamez led to the finding that unit safeness permits to keep only one SDD variable per unit, with satisfactory results (see Sec. 5.3).

5   Implementation of NUPN

The NUPN model is actually used for concrete applications. This section reviews the file formats and software tools that implement this model.

5.1   The ".nupn" File Format

The CADP toolbox [22] provides a textual format[5] for storing NUPNs in files that are assumed to have the ".nupn" extension. This format was designed to

---

[5] The definition is available from http://cadp.inria.fr/man/caesar.bdd.html

be concise, easy to produce and to parse by programs, and also readable by humans. Here is a small commented example:

```
!creator caesar        The NUPN was created by the CÆSAR tool.
!unit_safe             The creator tool warrants that unit-safeness holds.
places #5 0...4        There are 5 places numbered from 0 to 4.
initial place 0        The initial marking contains only place 0.
units #3 0...2         There are 3 units numbered from 0 to 2.
root unit 0            The root unit is unit 0.
U0 #1 0...0 #2 1 2     Unit 0 contains 1 place (0) and 2 sub-units (1, 2).
U1 #2 1...2 #0         Unit 1 contains 2 places (1, 2) and no sub-unit.
U2 #2 3...4 #0         Unit 2 contains 2 places (3, 4) and no sub-unit.
transitions #3 0...2   There are 3 transitions numbered from 0 to 2.
T0 #1 0 #2 1 3         Trans. 0 has 1 input place (0) and 2 output places (1, 3).
T1 #1 1 #1 2           Trans. 1 has 1 input place (1) and 1 output place (2).
T2 #1 3 #1 4           Trans. 2 has 1 input place (3) and 1 output place (4).
```

Non-ordinary and/or non-safe P/T nets can be encoded in this format by erasing information about arc multiplicity and token counts in the initial marking. To this aim, the ".nupn" format provides pragmas (namely, !multiple_arcs and !multiple_initial_tokens) to retain part of the erased information, so as to preserve a few behavioural properties — in addition to the structural ones.

5.2 The ".pnml" File Format

The NUPN model is not supported by the PNML standard [41] but there is a simple way to enrich a PNML file with NUPN-related information. This can be done without leaving the PNML framework, by inserting into a ".pnml" file, which describes an ordinary, safe P/T net (P, T, F, M_0), a "toolspecific" section that adds the description of $(U, u_0, \sqsubseteq, \text{unit})$. This is the approach followed for the Model Checking Contest, which has specified the format of such "toolspecific" section in natural language, XSD (XML Schema Definition), DTD (Document Type Definition), RNC (RELAX NG Compact Syntax), and RMG (RELAX NG XML Syntax)[6]. Here is the "toolspecific" section corresponding to the NUPN example of Sec. 5.1:

```
<toolspecific tool="nupn" version="1.1">
   <size places="5" transitions="3" arcs="7"/>
   <structure units="3" root="u0" safe="true">
      <unit id="u0">
         <places>p0</places>
         <subunits>u1 u2</subunits>
      </unit>
      <unit id="u1">
         <places>p1 p2</places>
         <subunits/>
      </unit>
      <unit id="u2">
         <places>p3 p4</places>
         <subunits/>
      </unit>
   </structure>
</toolspecific>
```

---

[6] These definitions are available from http://mcc.lip6.fr/nupn.php

5.3   Tools for NUPN

At present, the NUPN model is implemented in six tools developed at three different academic institutions:

1. CÆSAR[7] translates a (value-passing) LOTOS specification into a hierarchical interpreted Petri net. When invoked with option "-nupn", CÆSAR stores in a ".nupn" file the (unit-safe by construction) NUPN model corresponding to this interpreted Petri net. CÆSAR relies on options "-concurrent-units" and "-dead-transitions" of the CÆSAR.BDD tool (see below) to detect units that execute simultaneously (this information is useful to data-flow analysis [23]) and transitions that are not quasi-live in the NUPN (such transitions are neither quasi-live in the interpreted Petri net, and thus can be removed).

2. PNML2NUPN[8] is a tool developed by Lom-Messan Hillah. It translates a ".pnml" file containing an ordinary, safe P/T net into a ".nupn" file using the encoding scheme given for the proof of Prop. 8 (i.e., each place in a separate unit). If the P/T net is not ordinary or not safe, the ".nupn" file is still generated, but tagged with the special pragmas mentioned in Sec. 8.

3. EXP.OPEN[9] is a tool developed by Frédéric Lang. Its latest version can convert a set of finite-state automata that execute concurrently and synchronize as specified by process-calculi operators and/or synchronization vectors into a ".nupn" file using the encoding scheme given for the proof of Prop. 9.

4. CÆSAR.BDD[10] is a tool developed by Damien Bergamini in 2004 and progressively extended since then. It reads a ".nupn" file, checks that the NUPN is well-formed, and performs various actions depending on the command-line options. Option "-pnml" implements the inverse functionality of PNML2NUPN by translating the NUPN into a ".pnml" file, which embeds a "toolspecific" section (see Sec. 5.2). Option "-mcc" computes usual structural and behavioural properties and automatically generates a Petri net description form in LaTex according to the conventions of the Model Checking Contest; in 2014, the combined use of PNML2NUPN and CÆSAR.BDD enabled the author to detect and correct fourty erroneous properties in the contest's database of models. Options "-concurrent-units", "-dead-transitions", and "-exclusive-places" perform forward reachability analysis to obtain accurate information about places, transitions, and units. CÆSAR.BDD relies on BDDs, as implemented by Fabio Somenzi's CUDD software library[11].

5. CÆSAR.SDD is an emulation of CÆSAR.BDD written by Alexandre Hamez. Rather than BDDs, CÆSAR.SDD uses A. Hamez's library[12] for Hierarchical Set Decision Diagrams (SDDs) and takes advantage of unit safeness

---

[7] See http://cadp.inria.fr/man/caesar.html
[8] See http://pnml.lip6.fr/pnml2nupn
[9] See http://cadp.inria.fr/man/exp.open.html
[10] See http://cadp.inria.fr/man/caesar.bdd.html
[11] See http://vlsi.colorado.edu/~fabio/CUDD
[12] See https://github.com/ahamez/libsdd

to allocate only one SDD variable per unit (instead of one SDD variable per place with ordinary P/T nets). Preliminary experiments indicate that CÆSAR.SDD performs reachability analysis faster and can process large NUPNs that CÆSAR.BDD fails to handle.

6. PNMC[13] is a Petri Net model checker developed by Alexandre Hamez. PNMC is also built on the aforementioned SDD library, and is able to parse the "`toolspecific`" section of PNML files to exploit unit safeness. Although PNMC is a very recent tool, it ranked second in the "State Space" category at the 2014 edition of the Model Checking Contest.

5.4   NUPN Benchmarks

To obtain NUPN models, one can use PNML2NUPN, which translates any ordinary, safe P/T net into a NUPN, albeit with one place per unit. To better take advantage of NUPN-specific properties, one can write higher-level specifications in LOTOS (or in any language, such as LNT, that automatically translates to LOTOS) and generate a (structured) NUPN model using CÆSAR.

Such higher-level generated models are already available from the data base of models for the Model Checking Contest[14]. A present, six NUPNs are in the data base, and more will be added for the 2015 edition of the contest.

We will publish in 2015 the VLPN (*Very Large Perti nets*) benchmark suite[15], a collection of 350 large-size NUPN models, which will be given in both ".`nupn`" and ".`pnml`" formats, and will provide tool developers with realistic examples and challenging problems.

6   Conclusion

The NUPN (*Nested-Unit Petri Net*) model is an extension of Perti nets with additional information about concurrent structure, i.e., decomposition into hierarchically nested sequential processes. For twenty-five years, this model has remained hidden in the internals of the CÆSAR compiler for LOTOS [21,23,24]. With the advent of the Model Checking Contest, it became manifest that NUPN could be of interest to a broader community, as this model combines three major advantages:

– *It is easy to generate when Perti nets are produced from higher-level, structured descriptions.* This can be seen, e.g., on three main types of such descriptions. First, in the case of communicating automata, each automaton directly corresponds to a NUPN unit. Second, in the case of process calculi, the parallel composition operators determine NUPN units that are unit safe by construction; straightforward optimizations help to reduce the depth of unit nesting according to the associativity property of parallel composition; such

---

[13] See https://github.com/ahamez/pnmc
[14] See http://mcc.lip6.fr/models.php
[15] See http://cadp.inria.fr/resources/vlpn

an approach is implemented in the CÆSAR compiler. Third, in the case of high-level Perti nets, we believe that existing unfolding algorithms could be easily modified to retain in NUPN units all hierarchy-related information that is usually lost when generating "flat" unfolded Perti nets.

- *It allows significant improvements in state-space exploration and verification of behavioural properties.* As explained above, the unit-safeness property permits logarithmic savings in the encoding of markings, both in explicit-state and symbolic settings. Our longstanding observations with the CÆSAR compiler, conforted by recent experimental results obtained on certain benchmarks of the Model Checking Contest, confirm the real benefits of this approach in terms of performance and scalability.
- *It is not a disruptive extension that would require major overhaul in software tools.* Adding support for NUPN in an existing Petri-net tool only requires limited changes, namely: (i) being able to read NUPN information, which is easy if the tool already embedds a PNML parser, and (ii) take advantage of the NUPN information to optimize the representation of markings. The implementation of transition firings can remain unchanged, unless one wishes to use NUPN information to perform extra (e.g., partial-order) reductions.

As regards future research directions, we believe that the NUPN model raises a number of interesting issues:

1. *Is there an algorithm to determine if certain NUPNs are unit-safe without building their marking reachability graph?* Prop. 5 gives some necessary conditions for unit safeness concerning, e.g., the initial marking or the input/output places and quasi-liveness of particular transitions, but having a more general, efficient decision procedure would be desirable.

2. *What is the best algorithmic approach to compute behavioural properties of a NUPN, such as deadlock freeness, quasi-liveness, etc.?* At present, there are merely fragmentary answers to this question. For instance, we implemented and compared two state-space exploration approaches for NUPN, an explicit-state one and a symbolic one based on BDDs, both with the scheme (b) reduction made possible by the presence of units; clearly, the BDD-based implementation outperforms the explicit-state one. Also, recent results reported by Alexandre Hamez indicate that SDDs often scale better than BDDs when analyzing NUPN models. The application of other types of decision diagrams (ADDs, DDDs, MDDs, MTBDDs, etc.) to NUPN models remains to be investigated. It is also likely that information about the concurrent structure of NUPN models can be profitably exploited to perform state-space reductions based on partial orders and stubborn sets.

3. *How to optimally translate a given ordinary, safe P/T net to a NUPN?* As mentioned above, such a P/T net can be easily converted to a NUPN by putting each place in a distinct unit, but no algorithmic improvement can be expected from such a simple approach that makes no attempt at discovering the concurrent structure of the net. A better translation should target at reducing the number of units while maximizing the number of places per

unit. There have been many publications on how to decompose a Petri net into concurrent state machines; however, the NUPN hierarchy of nested units is likely to raise new challenges compared to prior approaches that merely target a flat composition of state machines.

4. *How does the concept of nested units extend to high-level nets?* The NUPN model defined in the present article is based on elementary nets; yet, nested units were originally introduced not for such "data-less" low-level nets, but for the interpreted Perti nets generated by the CÆSAR compiler as an intermediate model for the translation of LOTOS. It would therefore be interesting to study whether nested units can also be applied to other forms of high-level Perti nets, such as colored nets and predicate/transition nets.

5. *Can nested units support the unbounded creation/destruction of concurrent processes?* The NUPN model and the unit-safeness property have been designed to represent algebraic terms in which processes are launched and terminated dynamically, yet in a finite way, as in, e.g., "$B_1 ; (B_2 || B_3) ; B_4$" or "**process**$P = B_1 ; (B_2 || B_3) ; B_4 ; P$". However, for algebraic terms not having such a finite-control property, e.g., "**process**$P = B_1 ; (B_2 || P)$", the corresponding Petri nets can still be expressed as NUPNs, but the safeness and unit-safeness properties no longer hold and, ideally, should be replaced with other, more general flow relations.

Acknowledgments. This article was written under the aegis of the Alexander-von-Humboldt foundation. Frédéric Lang provided valuable comments about this article. Alexander Graf-Brill simplified the counterexample given for item 3 of Prop. 7. The author is grateful to Alexandre Hamez, Lom-Messan Hillah, and Fabrice Kordon for their support in making the NUPN model broadly available.

References

1. Alur, R., Yannakakis, M.: Model Checking of Hierarchical State Machines. In: Proc. ACM SIGSOFT Int. Symp. on Foundations of Software Engineering, pp. 175–188. ACM (1998)
2. Arora, N.: Comparison of Encoding Schemes for Symbolic Model Checking of Bounded Perti nets. Master thesis, paper 11511, Iowa State University, USA (2010)
3. Bernardinello, L., De Cindio, F.: A survey of basic net models and modular net classes. In: Rozenberg, G. (ed.) APN 1992. LNCS, vol. 609, pp. 304–351. Springer, Heidelberg (1992)
4. Best, E., Devillers, R., Hall, J.G.: The box calculus: a new causal algebra with multi-label communication. In: Rozenberg, G. (ed.) APN 1992. LNCS, vol. 609, pp. 21–69. Springer, Heidelberg (1992)
5. Best, E., Devillers, R.R., Koutny, M.: The box algebra - a model of nets and process expressions. In: Donatelli, S., Kleijn, H. (eds.) ICATPN 1999. LNCS, vol. 1639, pp. 344–363. Springer, Heidelberg (1999)
6. Best, E., Devillers, R.R., Koutny, M.: A Unified Model for Nets and Process Algebras. In: Handbook of Process Algebra, chap. 14. Elsevier (2001)
7. Best, E., Devillers, R.R., Koutny, M.: Petri Net Algebra. EATCS Monographs in Theoretical Computer Science. Springer (2001)

8. Best, E., Devillers, R.R., Koutny, M.: The Box Algebra = Perti nets + Process Expressions. Information and Computation 178(1) (2002)
9. Boudol, G., Castellani, I.: Three equivalent semantics for CCS. In: Guessarian, I. (ed.) Semantics of Systems of Concurrent Processes. LNCS, vol. 469, pp. 96–141. Springer, Heidelberg (1990)
10. Boudol, G., Castellani, I.: Flow Models of Distributed Computations: Three Equivalent Semantics for CCS. Information and Computation 114(2) (1994)
11. Ciardo, G., Zhao, Y., Jin, X.: Ten Years of Saturation: A Petri Net Perspective. Transactions on Perti nets and Other Models of Concurrency 6900 (2012)
12. de Cindio, F., de Michelis, G., Pomello, L., Simone, C.: Milner's Communicating Systems and Perti nets. In: APN 1982, Informatik-Fachberichte, vol. 66. Springer (1982)
13. Degano, P., De Nicola, R., Montanari, U.: A Distributed Operational Semantics for CCS Based on Condition/Event Systems. Acta Inf. 26(1/2) (1988)
14. Devillers, R.R.: Construction of S-invariants and s-components for refined petri boxes. In: Marsan, M.A. (ed.) APN 1993. LNCS, vol. 691, pp. 242–261. Springer, Heidelberg (1993)
15. Devillers, R.R.: S-Invariant Analysis of General Recursive Petri Boxes. Acta Informatica 32(4) (1995)
16. Devillers, R.R., Klaudel, H., Koutny, M., Pommereau, F.: An algebra of non-safe petri boxes. In: Kirchner, H., Ringeissen, C. (eds.) AMAST 2002. LNCS, vol. 2422, pp. 192–207. Springer, Heidelberg (2002)
17. Devillers, R.R., Klaudel, H., Koutny, M., Pommereau, F.: Asynchronous Box Calculus. Fundamenta Informaticae 54(4) (2003)
18. Dittrich, G.: Specification with Nets - Report on Activities in Connection with Requirements Capture with Nets. In: Pichler, F., Moreno-Díaz, R. (eds.) EUROCAST 1989. LNCS, vol. 410. Springer (1989)
19. Fehling, R.: A concept of hierarchical Perti nets with building blocks. In: Rozenberg, G. (ed.) APN 1991. LNCS, vol. 674, pp. 148–168. Springer, Heidelberg (1991)
20. Francesco, N.D., Montanari, U., Yankelevich, D.: Axiomatizing CCS, Nets and Processes. Science of Computer Programming 21(3) (1993)
21. Garavel, H.: Compilation et Vérification de Programmes LOTOS. Doctorate thesis, Université Joseph Fourier (Grenoble), November 1989
22. Garavel, H., Lang, F., Mateescu, R., Serwe, W.: CADP 2011: A Toolbox for the Construction and Analysis of Distributed Processes. Springer International Journal on Software Tools for Technology Transfer (STTT) 15(2), April 2013
23. Garavel, H., Serwe, W.: State Space Reduction for Process Algebra Specifications. Th. Comp. Sci. 351(2), February 2006
24. Garavel, H., Sifakis, J.: Compilation and verification of LOTOS specifications. In: Proc. 10th Int. Symp. on Protocol Specification, Testing and Verification (PSTV 1990), North-Holland, June 1990
25. Garavel, H., Sighireanu, M.: On the introduction of exceptions in LOTOS. In: Proc. Int. Joint Conf. on Formal Description Techniques and Protocol Specification, Testing, and Verification FORTE/PSTV 1996, IFIP. Chapman & Hall (1996)
26. Goltz, U.: On representing CCS programs by finite Perti nets. In: Chytil, M., Janiga, L., Koubek, V. (eds.) MFCS 1988. LNCS, vol. 324, pp. 339–350. Springer, Heidelberg (1988)
27. Goltz, U.: CCS and Perti nets. In: Guessarian, I. (ed.) Semantics of Systems of Concurrent Processes. LNCS, vol. 469, pp. 334–357. Springer, Heidelberg (1990)
28. Goltz, U., Mycroft, A.: On the relationship of CCS and Perti nets. In: Paredaens, J. (ed.) ICALP 1984. LNCS, vol. 172, pp. 196–208. Springer, Heidelberg (1984)

29. Goltz, U., Reisig, W.: CSP-programs with individual tokens. In: Rozenberg, G., Genrich, H.J., Roucairol, G. (eds.) APN 1984. LNCS, vol. 188, pp. 169–196. Springer, Heidelberg (1984)

30. Gorrieri, R., Montanari, U.: Distributed Implementation of CCS. In: Rozenberg, G. (ed.) APN 1991. LNCS, vol. 674, pp. 244–266. Springer, Heidelberg (1991)

31. Gorrieri, R., Montanari, U.: On the Implementation of Concurrent Calculi in Net Calculi: Two Case Studies. Theoretical Computer Science 141(1&2) (1995)

32. Hall, J.G., Hopkins, R.P., Botti, O., de Cindio, F.: A Petri Net Semantics of OCCAM2. Tech. report 329, Univ. of Newcastle upon Tyne, Computing Lab. (1991)

33. Hamez, A., Thierry-Mieg, Y., Kordon, F.: Building Efficient Model Checkers using Hierarchical Set Decision Diagrams and Automatic Saturation. Fundamenta Informaticae 94(3–4) (2009)

34. Harel, D.: Statecharts: A Visual Formalism for Complex Systems. Sci. Comput. Program. 8(3), 231–274 (1987)

35. He, X.: A formal definition of hierarchical predicate transition nets. In: Billington, J., Reisig, W. (eds.) APN 1996. LNCS, vol. 1091, pp. 212–229. Springer, Heidelberg (1996)

36. He, X., Lee, J.: A Methodology for Constructing Predicate Transition Net Specifications. Software, Practice & Experience 21(8) (1991)

37. He, X., Murata, T.: High-Level Perti nets - Extensions, Analysis, and Applications. In: Electrical Engineering Handbook. Elsevier Academic Press (2005)

38. Hopkins, R.P., Hall, J.G., Botti, O.: A basic-net algebra for program semantics and its application to OCCAM. In: Rozenberg, G. (ed.) Advances in Perti nets. LNCS, vol. 609, pp. 179–214. Springer, Heidelberg (1992)

39. Huber, P., Jensen, K., Shapiro, R.M.: Hierarchies in Coloured Perti nets. In: Rozenberg, G. (ed.) APN 1991. LNCS, vol. 483, pp. 313–341. Springer, Heidelberg (1989)

40. ISO/IEC: LOTOS - A Formal Description Technique Based on the Temporal Ordering of Observational Behaviour. International Standard ISO/IEC 8807 (1989)

41. ISO/IEC: High-level Perti nets - Part 2: Transfer Format. International Standard ISO/IEC 15909-2 (2011)

42. Jensen, K.: Coloured Perti nets - Basic Concepts, Analysis Methods and Practical Use - Vol. 1. EATCS Monographs on Th. Computer Science. Springer (1992)

43. Karjoth, G.: Implementing LOTOS specifications by communicating state machines. In: Cleaveland, R. (ed.) CONCUR 1992. LNCS, vol. 630, pp. 386–400. Springer, Heidelberg (1992)

44. Karjoth, G., Binding, C., Gustafsson, J.: LOEWE: A LOTOS Engineering Workbench. Computer Networks and ISDN Systems 25(7) (1993)

45. Kerbrat, A.: Méthodes Symboliques pour la Vérification de Processus Communicants: Etude et Mise en Œuvre. Doct. thesis, Univ. J. Fourier (Grenoble) (1994)

46. Kotov, V.E.: An algebra for parallelism based on Perti nets. In: Winkowski, J. (ed.) MFCS 1978. LNCS, vol. 64, pp. 39–55. Springer, Heidelberg (1978)

47. Kotov, V.E., Cherkasova, L.: On structural properties of generalized processes. In: Rozenberg, G., Genrich, H.J., Roucairol, G. (eds.) APN 1984. LNCS, vol. 188, pp. 288–306. Springer, Heidelberg (1984)

48. Kummer, O., Wienberg, F., Duvigneau, M., Schumacher, J., Köhler, M., Moldt, D., Rölke, H., Valk, R.: An extensible editor and simulation engine for Perti nets: renew. In: Cortadella, J., Reisig, W. (eds.) ICATPN 2004. LNCS, vol. 3099, pp. 484–493. Springer, Heidelberg (2004)

49. Lomazova, I.A.: Nested Perti nets - a Formalism for Specification and Verification of Multi-Agent Distributed Systems. Fundamenta Informaticae 43(1–4) (2000)

50. Lomazova, I.A.: Nested Perti nets: Multi-level and Recursive Systems. Fundamenta Informaticae 47(3–4) (2001)
51. Montanari, U., Yankelevich, D.: Combining CCS and Perti nets Via Structural Axioms. Fundamenta Informaticae 20(1/2/3) (1994)
52. Murata, T.: Perti nets: Analysis and Applications. Proc. of the IEEE 77(4) (1989)
53. Nielsen, M.: CCS and its relationship to net theory. In: Brauer, W., Reisig, W., Rozenberg, G. (eds.) APN 1986 (Part I). LNCS, vol. 255, pp. 393–415. Springer, Heidelberg (1986)
54. Noe, J.D.: Nets in Modeling and Simulation. In: Brauer, W. (ed.) Net Theory and Applications. LNCS, vol. 84, pp. 347–368. Springer, Heidelberg (1980)
55. Noe, J.D., Nutt, G.J.: Macro E-Nets for Representation of Parallel Systems. IEEE Transactions on Computers C-22(8), August 1973
56. Olderog, E.R.: Operational petri net semantics for CCSP. In: Rozenberg, G. (ed.) APN 1987. LNCS, vol. 266, pp. 196–223. Springer, Heidelberg (1986)
57. Olderog, E.R.: Nets, Terms, and Formulas: Three Views of Concurrent Processes and Their Relationship. Cambridge University Press (1991)
58. Peterson, J.L.: Perti nets. ACM Computing Surveys 9(3) (1977)
59. Suzuki, I., Murata, T.: Stepwise Refinements of Transitions and Places. In APN 1981, Informatik-Fachberichte, vol. 52. Springer (1981)
60. Suzuki, I., Murata, T.: A Method for Stepwise Refinement and Abstraction of Perti nets. Journal of Computer and System Sciences 27(1) (1983)
61. Taubner, D.: Finite Representations of CCS and TCSP Programs by Automata and Perti nets. LNCS, vol. 369. Springer (1989)
62. Taubner, D.: Representing CCS Programs by Finite Predicate/Transition Nets. Acta Informatica 27(6) (1989)
63. Valette, R.: Analysis of Perti nets by Stepwise Refinements. Journal of Computer and System Sciences 18(1) (1979)
64. Valk, R.: Perti nets as token objects: an introduction to elementary object nets. In: Desel, J., Silva, M. (eds.) ICATPN 1998. Lecture Notes in Computer Science, vol. 1420, pp. 1–25. Springer, Heidelberg (1998)
65. Valk, R.: Object Perti nets: using the nets-within-nets paradigm. In: Desel, J., Reisig, W., Rozenberg, G. (eds.) ACPN 2003. Lecture Notes in Ccomputer Science, vol. 3098, pp. 819–848. Springer, Heidelberg (2003)
66. van Glabbeek, R.J., Vaandrager, F.W.: Petri net models for algebraic theories of concurrency. In: de Bakker, J.W., Nijman, A.J., Treleaven, P.C. (eds.) PARLE 1987. LNCS, vol. 259, pp. 224–242. Springer, Heidelberg (1987)

Charlie – An Extensible Petri Net Analysis Tool

Monika Heiner[1]([✉]), Martin Schwarick[1], and Jan-Thierry Wegener[2]

[1] Brandenburg Technical University, Cottbus, Germany
{monika.heiner,martin.schwarick}@b-tu.de
[2] University Blaise Pascal, Clermont-Ferrand II, France
jan-thierry.wegener@isima.fr

Abstract. *Charlie* is an extensible thread-based Java tool for analysing Petri nets. Its built-in functionalities apply standard analysis techniques of Petri net theory (e.g. invariants, siphon/trap property) to determine structural and behavioural properties of place/transition Petri nets, complemented by explicit CTL and LTL model checking. *Charlie* comes with a plugin mechanism, which permits to easily extend its basic functionality as it has been demonstrated for, e.g., structural reduction and time-dependent Petri nets. *Charlie's* primary focus is teaching. For this purpose, it has a rule system comprising standard theorems of Petri net theory to possibly decide further properties based on the already determined ones. All applied rules are reported by default, so the user may keep track of all analysis steps. The tool is in use for model verification of technical systems, especially software-based systems, as well as for model validation of natural systems, i.e. biochemical networks, such as metabolic, signal transduction, and gene regulatory networks. It is publicly available at http://www-dssz.informatik.tu-cottbus.de/DSSZ/Software/Charlie.

Keywords: Analysis tool · Place/transition petri nets · Stochastic Petri nets · Time-dependent petri nets · Place/transition invariants · Siphon/-trap property · Explicit CTL/LTL model checking · Java · Threads · Plugin

1 Introduction

This paper gives an overview of the software tool *Charlie* which rounds off our Petri net toolset comprising (so far) *Snoopy* [21,33] for the construction and animation/simulation of hierarchically structured qualitative and quantitative (stochastic, continuous, hybrid) Petri nets, *Marcie* [23,24] for symbolic and simulative CTL/CSRL model checking of qualitative and stochastic Petri nets, *Patty* [35] for playing the token game within a standard web browser, and *S4* [27] - *Snoopy's* stand-alone steering server for the collaborative simulation of quantitative Petri nets.

Charlie set out as a Java tool to analyse standard place/transition nets, with primary focus on teaching Petri net theory. Its design builds on the experience gained over about 20 years while working with the Integrated Net Analyser (INA) previously developed at the Humboldt University Berlin by Peter H. Starke [40].

© Springer International Publishing Switzerland 2015
R. Devillers and A. Valmari (Eds.): PETRI NETS 2015, LNCS 9115, pp. 200–211, 2015.
DOI: 10.1007/978-3-319-19488-2_10

The development of *Charlie* began in 2006 by Martin Schwarick [37], later supported by various students. Among those are most notably Andreas Franzke [13] who reengineered the graphical user interface and the basic architecture of *Charlie*'s code, exploiting now also thread-based parallelism; and Ansgar Fischer [11], who extended the capabilities by the analysis of time-dependent Petri nets. The redesign made one of the more recent developments possible: the plugin system [41] contributed by Jan Wegener allows for flexibility and convenient configurability of the software package. Since then, the ongoing development takes advantage of *Charlie*'s regular use for teaching and the feedback from numerous users worldwide.

Charlie is first of all an analysis tool for standard place/transition Petri nets capable of performing various static and dynamic analyses of the standard body of Petri net theory, including methods building on the incidence matrix, siphons and traps, reachability and coverability graph, which are complemented by explicit CTL and LTL model checking. However, the analyses building on a finite reachability graph support also place/transition Petri nets enriched by special arcs, the so-called extended Petri nets. *Charlie*'s plugin mechanism has been used to enhance its basic functionality, including structural reduction and the dedicated support of time-dependent Petri nets by reachability graph analysis.

A distinguished feature of *Charlie* is its rule system, which is crucial for *Charlie*'s use in teaching the standard body of Petri net theory. The rule system comprises the most important standard theorems to possibly decide further properties based on the already determined ones. All applied rules are reported by default, so the user may keep track of all analysis steps.

Outline. The next section gives a summary of the main functionalities, including *Charlie*'s rule system and plugin mechanism. We continue with a sketch of selected aspects of *Charlie*'s architecture, some typical application scenarios, and a brief comparison with related tools. The paper concludes with hints how to install *Charlie*.

2 Functionalities

2.1 Basics

Input. *Charlie* reads standard *place/transition Petri nets* (defined by three finite sets: the set of initialised places, the set of transitions, and the set of weighted arcs), and *extended Petri nets* which additionally permit four special (weighted) arcs to conveniently express context conditions: read arcs (often also called test arcs), inhibitor arcs, reset arcs, and equal arcs, see [24] for definitions. This net class is strictly more powerful than the class of standard place/transition Petri nets. The use of special arcs may affect a model's analysability. However, *Charlie* does not check for any incompatibilities, but assumes that users know, what they are doing!

Charlie accepts Petri nets which have been created with Snoopy, preferably in the toolset's proprietary human-readable text file format ANDL (Abstract

Net Description Language) [21], but also the file formats APNN (Abstract Petri Net Notation) [7], and INA's PNT files (plain text file). *Charlie* understands all special arcs, but any additional information is ignored, e.g., stochastic/deterministic firing rates of stochastic/continuous transitions in quantitative Petri nets, or the colours of tokens, places, transitions, etc. in coloured Petri nets. With other words, only the net structure and the initial marking are considered.

The support of the Petri Net Markup Language (PNML), the XML-based standard exchange format of the Petri net community, is in preparation. Beyond that, it is rather straightforward to extend *Charlie* to read any further formats by help of *Charlie*'s plugin mechanism, see [41] for details.

Interface. *Charlie* comes with an intuitive and easy to use Graphical User Interface (GUI), written in Java. *Charlie*'s GUI has been inspired by the analysis tool INA, which is most obvious in the result vector, compare Figure 1, lower half, left hand side. An overview and explanation of all abbreviations can be

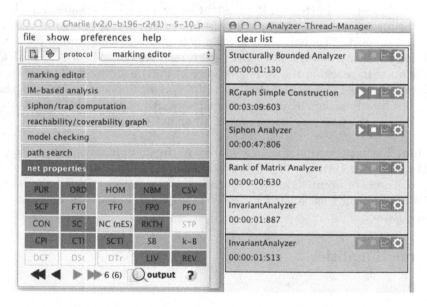

Fig. 1. Screenshot of *Charlie*'s GUI, here with two separate windows. The window on the left shows the standard features without any extensions. Starting from top: menu bar, followed by some buttons for quick access to often used functions, and the entry bars to the dialogue boxes for the different analysers. Next, the special dialogue "net properties" (which has been opened) shows all properties *Charlie* knows of. A property is marked green, if the Petri net under investigation fulfils this property; it is marked red, if the property is not fulfilled. Properties not decided yet are shown in grey, while a yellow colour indicates non-binary information (e.g., the net class, which is here beyond Extended Simple). The control buttons at the bottom switch through the results of the individual analysis steps, and trigger the "output" and "help" windows. The window on the right shows all started analyser threads: three have finished, one is still running, one was suspended, and one was aborted.

found in [4, 26]. The analysers, each performing one of *Charlie*'s analysis tasks, run in parallel by use of Java threads, compare Figure 1, right hand side. *Charlie* comes with a simple marking editor for the convenient exploration of different markings without having to repeatedly edit and re-read the entire Petri net.

Additionally, *Charlie* has been equipped with a textual user interface to support the embedding of individual analysis tasks into external tools, see [13] for details.

Manual. There is no *Charlie*-specific manual, besides Chapter 8 in [4], but there are three built-in options to learn more about *Charlie*'s technical notions and rules:

- *a tool tip window* pops up when the curser is above a property in the result vector;
- *the question mark* in the lower right corner goes to a help window with all rules, which are hierarchically structured, i.e., clicking on an underlined rule opens/closes a subset of rules;
- *help/F1* → *abbreviations* yields full text explanations of all technical notions.

2.2 Main Analysis Features

The ultimate analysis aim is to decide behavioural net properties; first of all the three orthogonal ones – boundedness, liveness, reversibility, going with more detailed properties, comprising boundedness degree, dynamic conflict freeness, number of dead states, and existence of dead transitions. *Charlie* offers the following analysers to possibly decide these properties.

Structural analysis. The determined structural properties include pure, ordinary, homogenous, non-blocking multiplicity, conservative, structural conflict free, existence of boundary nodes (input/output places/transitions), connected, strongly connected, and the net class (state machine, marked graph, (extended) free choice, extended simple); see [26] for definitions.

IM-based analysis. Analysis techniques building on the incidence matrix (IM) include the rank theorem [39], structural boundedness test, place/transition invariants, and (abstract) dependent transition sets (ADT sets) [19]. The incidence matrix can also be exported; supported formats: Matlab, CSV, text file.

Siphon/trap computation. Siphons and traps can be separately computed, or as far as required to determine the Siphon/Trap Property (STP). By default, the STP computation is aborted when a siphon without a sufficiently marked trap is found. The flag 'create all' triggers the computation of all minimal siphons. There is also a place set analyser which determines for an arbitrary place set, if it is a siphon, bad/sound siphon [22], or (maximal) trap.

Reachability/coverability graph. Options for reachability graph construction include: check boundedness, single/maximal step, and stubborn set reduction. By default, the coverability graph is constructed, if bounded-ness has not been decided yet. If the construction terminates, the number of nodes (states), edges (state transitions), and strongly connected components (SCCs) is shown. The graph can be visualised (by use of the JUNG library) with all SCCs coloured.

Model checking. There are explicit model checkers for Computational Tree Logic (CTL) and Linear Time Logic (LTL) formulae, which can either be read from a file or directly written within a *Charlie* analysis session. In the face of current standard computing techniques, we recommend the use of *Marcie* for state spaces beyond 500 000 states.

Path search. Search options cover shortest/longest paths between a source and sink specified either by a (sub-) marking, a state identifier from the reach-ability graph or a predicate (filter file). The path found can be exported as marking sequence, transition sequence, or Parikh vector.

Upon loading a Petri net, the first analyser (structural analysis) is automat-ically triggered due to the negligible computational costs. All other analysers have to be started explicitly. Analysers run in parallel, which permits to start a competition, e.g. between STP and reachability graph computation when one wants to decide liveness for extended simple nets.

Several (multi-) sets of nodes (places or transitions) computed with *Charlie* can be read by Snoopy for visualisation of the results, e.g., subnets induced by place/transition invariants, siphons, traps, or Parikh vectors (characterising a path search result).

2.3   The Rule System

Not every property to be decided has to be computed by an analyser. *Charlie* is aware of a number of well-known theorems from the standard body of Petri net theory, e.g. the fact that a Petri net which is covered by place invariants (CPI) is structurally bounded (SB). By applying theorems to already computed results one may save a great deal of computational time. The implementation of theorems is done with *Charlie*'s rule system.

A rule consists of a pair of result sets – the pre-conditions and the post-conditions. When an analyser has finished its analysis, the rule system checks if a rule can be applied to the results obtained so far, i.e., if there exists a rule with all pre-conditions fulfilled. If a rule can be applied, all results in the post-condition are set.

An example for an implemented rule is the well-known theorem from above: CPI involves SB. In *Charlie* this means that if the currently loaded Petri net is covered by place invariants and an analyser sets the property "covered by place invariants" to "true", then the rule in question is applied to the results and the property "structurally bounded" is set to "true" as well. This example demonstrates a strong point of *Charlie*'s rule system: especially for larger nets, the rule system may drastically decrease the analysis costs by avoiding tedious computations.

By default, every rule, which *Charlie* is about to apply needs to be confirmed by the user; compare Figure 2. This adds an educational value, and supports debugging as well. But *Charlie* can also be configured to silently accept all rules, making it more convenient for research purposes. More detailed information about *Charlie*'s rule system can be found in [13].

Fig. 2. *Charlie* asks the user for applying a rule. *Charlie* handles each property separately. Thus, there is a rule for "k-bounded", and there is a rule for "structurally bounded" as well, although the property "structurally bounded" implies the property "k-bounded".

2.4   The Plugin System

Previously, users had only a few possibilities of configuring *Charlie* according to their needs. By help of the more recently added plugin mechanism, a user can decide which analysers are required. This improves the flexibility and configurability of the tool and thus improves its general usability. For example, the analysis of time-dependent Petri nets is provided as plugin. Thus, only users who are interested in analysing time-dependent Petri nets will see a further dialogue box containing the options for analysing them.

Plugins for *Charlie* are easy to deploy, for the user and for the software developer as well. It is rather straightforward to implement new analysers for *Charlie* due to the standardisation and abstraction of the basic classes, which are required for writing new analysers; compare Section 3.

The plugin mechanism permits also to expand the set of supported rules. New rules can build on the predefined properties like CPI or SB, but developers have also the possibility to add their own properties which can then be used in the rule system. The expansion of the rule system is swiftly implemented and thus helps to save time spent for implementing new analysers which finally increases the overall productivity. Furthermore, users who want *Charlie* to be extended are able to write their own extensions, without having to interact with *Charlie*'s core development team.

The required background knowledge and a detailed explanation of the steps to be taken to develop new plugins for *Charlie* can be found in [41]. We also provide on Charlie's website the source code for one plugin, demonstrating the overall organisation of plugins as well the addition of new rules and properties.

2.5   Extended Functionalities

We provide five plugins on *Charlie*'s website to extend its basic functionality. These plugins are completely independent, any combination can be chosen.

GUI for command line tools. A flexible plugin for GUI-based communication with external command line tools. It can be easily configured by means of an XML description as it has been done for *Marcie* [36];

Structural reduction. A plugin helping to structurally reduce a Petri net. There are several reduction rules to choose from, see Chapter 5 in [40] for details.

Time-dependent Petri nets. A plugin for the analysis of time-dependent Petri nets under various options, e.g. [31]; see [11] for details.

Conflict graphs. A plugin that computes and displays transition conflict graphs, which are crucial for the mathematical approach presented in [29] to solve the problem of reconstructing biochemical networks from wet lab data.

ODEs analysis. A plugin for the structural analysis of continuous Petri nets [8,14] defining systems of Ordinary Differential Equations (ODEs). Properties supported include a continuous variation of the Siphon/Trap Property (the trap is replaced by an initially marked place invariant) [1] and the deficiency criterion of Feinberg graphs [38].

3   Architecture

We confine ourselves to a brief overview of those parts of the class hierarchy, a user might be most interested in – the hierarchy of the plugin system. All classes necessary for writing a basic plugin are located in sub-packages of `charlie.plugin`.

- The package `charlie.plugin.analyzer` contains the classes to write new analysers and their options. Here, also all classes are stored which are necessary to extend the rule system.
- The classes stored in the package `charlie.plugin.gui` have to be extended for amending the GUI.
- The class `PluginPlaceTransitionNetReader`, which can be found in the package `charlie.plugin.io`, is required for providing a reader.

Figure 3 gives the UML diagram with the class hierarchy of the most important classes of the package `charlie.plugin.analyzer` and their super classes, and Figure 4 the UML diagram with the class hierarchy of the packages `charlie.plugin.gui` and `charlie.plugin.io`. Classes that do not have a super class either extend `java.lang.Object` or, in the case of `JPanel`, another class of the standard Java library. In the diagrams, the abstract methods of the classes are given, as well as some important methods and constructors.

The plugins are loaded in a non-deterministic order, and so far only during the start-up phase. Currently there is no way of loading or unloading any of the plugins at runtime. The classes are loaded in the following order: first all analysers, then all rule extenders, followed by the computational dialogues, and finally all readers.

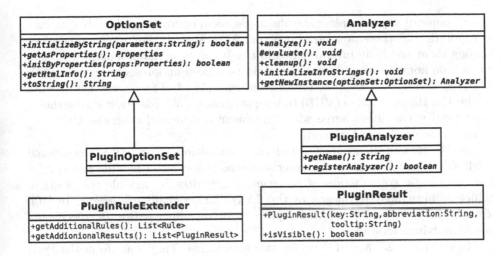

Fig. 3. Class hierarchy and abstract methods in the package `charlie.plugin.analyzer`. Coding conventions: "+" – public, "#" – protected, bold italic – abstract methods.

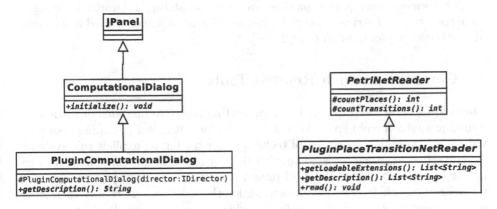

Fig. 4. Class hierarchy and abstract methods in the packages `charlie.plugin.gui` (left) and `charlie.plugin.io` (right); see Figure 3 for coding conventions.

4 Applications

Charlie is in worldwide use for teaching (see, e.g., [4,16,17]) and research (see, e.g., [10,12,18,30,32,34]). Since 2010, *Charlie* has been downloaded more than 2 000 times. We describe a couple of application scenarios in more details.

In 2007, a case study in model-driven Synthetic Biology was carried out by a multi-disciplinary team of undergraduate students from Glasgow University as part of the international Genetic Engineered Machine competition (iGEM) [15,17]; *Charlie* contributed to the design validation of a novel self-powering electrochemical biosensor.

A couple of papers explore specific biochemical networks, and apply *Charlie*'s computation of transition invariants and ADT sets [19] for model validation; among them are: hemojuvelin-hepcidin axis involved in maintaining the human body iron homeostasis [12], cephalostatin 1-induced apoptosis in leukemic cells [32], bioenergetics of Halobacterium Salinarum [34], and an interaction network of the Von Hippel-Lindau (VHL) tumour suppressor [30]. Ideally, it can be shown that Petri net analyses agree with experimental evidence, otherwise they may trigger new wet lab experiments.

In [3], structural properties and place/transition invariants are computed with *Charlie* and used to characterise a molecule-centred module concept for the systematic construction of biochemical networks by module composition, which is illustrated by means of the JAK/STAT signalling pathway. In [10], *Charlie* helps in exploring general patterns in signalling pathways, specifically for identifying crosstalks.

In contrast, [25] and [18] bridge two formalisms. They start from the Petri net representation of an ODE system (i.e., continuous Petri nets) and apply invariant analysis performed with *Charlie* to identify the main components of a signalling network.

A step-wise analysis of signalling and gene regulatory networks applying a wide spectrum of Petri net theory by help of *Charlie* is demonstrated in a couple of textbook chapters, see [5, 6, 20, 26, 28].

5   Comparison with Related Tools

There are several Petri net tools for supporting selective methods of static and dynamic analysis techniques. However, we are not aware of any other tool providing a comparable collection of techniques, or having an explicit rule system.

Nevertheless, some tools come with their own plugin system. There are two major approaches in the design of plugin systems. Some tools provide a ready-to-use framework for the developer, while others let the users call their own program and thus only work as a front-end for other analysers. Both approaches have their pros and cons. An advantage of the first approach is that the developer does not need to implement basic classes, e.g., a representation of the Petri net to be analysed, and thus saves a lot of time. On the other hand, the developer is – more or less – bound to the specific framework, and it may take some time to get used to the framework.

Charlie itself provides a framework for writing analysers. Another tool following this approach is the "Platform Independent Petri net Editor" (PIPE) [9], dedicated to performance evaluation of stochastic Petri nets. Thus, its analysis functionality is not comparable with *Charlie*.

The program "TIme petri Net Analyzer" (Tina) [2] allows users to include their own programs. These add-on programs can then be called by Tina, while Petri nets are drawn with Tina's built-in editor. The analysis functionality of Tina is not comparable with *Charlie* as its focus is on analysing various kinds of time-dependent Petri nets.

6   Installation

Charlie is a Java application; thus, it is available for Windows, Mac OS and Linux, and its execution requires a Java Runtime Environment (version 1.6 or higher). *Charlie* can be obtained free of charge for academic use from its website http://www-dssz.informatik.tu-cottbus.de/charlie.html. The installation package (jar file) contains all dependencies, no other libraries need to be manually installed; see *Charlie*'s website for more information, specifically for all deployed third party libraries.

Installing a plugin is a cakewalk: copy the zipped plugin file to the *plugin* folder of *Charlie*'s installation path. When downloading a plugin from *Charlie*'s website, please ensure that it is not automatically unpacked. To uninstall a plugin, simply remove the file from the *plugin* folder.

There is no such thing as error-free software. Please submit your bug reports or comments via *Charlie*'s bug tracker which you find on its website, or send an email to `charlie@informatik.tu-cottbus.de`.

References

1. Angeli, D., De Leenheer, P., Sontag, E.: A Petri net approach to the study of persistence in chemical reaction networks. Mathematical biosciences **210**(2), 598–618 (2007)
2. Berthomieu, B., Vernadat, F.: Time Petri nets analysis with Tina. In: Proc. QEST 2006, pp. 123–124. IEEE CS Press (2006)
3. Blätke, M., Dittrich, A., Rohr, C., Heiner, M., Schaper, F., Marwan, W.: JAK/-STAT signalling - an executable model assembled from molecule-centred modules demonstrating a module-oriented database concept for systems and synthetic biology. Molecular BioSystem **9**(6), 1290–1307 (2013)
4. Blätke, M., Heiner, M., Marwan, W.: Tutorial - Petri Nets in Systems Biology. Otto von Guericke University Magdeburg, Centre for Systems Biology, Tech. rep. (2011)
5. Blätke, M., Heiner, M., Marwan, W.: BioModel Engineering with Petri Nets, chap. 7, pp. 141–193. Elsevier Inc. (2015)
6. Blätke, M., Rohr, C., Heiner, M., Marwan, W.: A Petri Net based Framework for Biomodel Engineering, pp. 317–366. Modeling and Simulation in Science, Engineering and Technology. Springer, Birkhäuser Mathematics (2014)
7. Buchholz, P., Kemper, P.: A toolbox for the analysis of discrete event dynamic systems. In: Halbwachs, N., Peled, D.A. (eds.) CAV 1999. LNCS, vol. 1633, pp. 483–486. Springer, Heidelberg (1999)
8. David, R., Alla, H.: Discrete, Continuous, and Hybrid Petri Nets. Springer (2004)
9. Dingle, N.J., Knottenbelt, W.J., Suto, T.: PIPE2: a tool for the performance evaluation of generalised stochastic Petri Nets. ACM SIGMETRICS Performance Evaluation Review **36**(4), 34–39 (2009)
10. Donaldson, R.: Modelling and Analysis of Structure in Cellular Signalling Systems. Ph.D. thesis, University of Glasgow (2012)
11. Fischer, A.: State-space-based Analysis of time-dependent Petri nets (in German). Diploma thesis, BTU Cottbus, Dep. of CS (2009)

12. Formanowicz, D., Kozak, A., Głowacki, T., Radom, M., Formanowicz, P.: Hemojuvelin-hepcidin axis modeled and analyzed using Petri nets. Journal of biomedical Informatics **46**(6), 1030–1043 (2013)

13. Franzke, A.: Charlie 2.0 - a multi-threaded Petri net analyser. Diploma thesis, BTU Cottbus, Dep. of CS (2009)

14. Gilbert, D., Heiner, M.: From petri nets to differential equations - an integrative approach for biochemical network analysis. In: Donatelli, S., Thiagarajan, P.S. (eds.) ICATPN 2006. LNCS, vol. 4024, pp. 181–200. Springer, Heidelberg (2006)

15. Gilbert, D., Heiner, M., Rosser, S., Fulton, R., Gu, X., Trybiło, M.: A case study in model-driven synthetic biology. In: Hinchey, M., Pagnoni, A., Rammig, F.J., Schmeck, H. (eds.) 2nd IFIP Conference on Biologically Inspired Collaborative Computing (BICC 2008). IFIP, vol. 268, pp. 163–175. Springer, Boston (2008)

16. Gratie, D., Petre, I.: Quantitative Petri Nets Models for the Heat Shock Response. Tech. Rep. 1068, Turku Centre for Computer Science (2013)

17. Gu, X., Trybiło, M., Ramsay, S., Jensen, M., Fulton, R., Rosser, S., Gilbert, D.: Engineering a novel self-powering electrochemical biosensor. Systems and synthetic biology, pp. 1–12 (2010)

18. Hardy, S., Iyengar, R.: Analysis of Dynamical Models of Signaling Networks with Petri Nets and Dynamic Graphs, pp. 225–251. Springer (2011)

19. Heiner, M.: Understanding Network Behaviour by Structured Representations of Transition Invariants - A Petri Net Perspective on Systems and Synthetic Biology, pp. 367–389. Natural Computing Series. Springer (2009)

20. Heiner, M., Donaldson, R., Gilbert, D.: Petri Nets for Systems Biology, chap. 3, pp. 61–97. Jones & Bartlett Learning, LCC (2010)

21. Heiner, M., Herajy, M., Liu, F., Rohr, C., Schwarick, M.: Snoopy – a unifying petri net tool. In: Haddad, S., Pomello, L. (eds.) PETRI NETS 2012. LNCS, vol. 7347, pp. 398–407. Springer, Heidelberg (2012)

22. Heiner, M., Mahulea, C., Silva, M.: On the Importance of the Deadlock Trap Property for Monotonic Liveness. In: Int. Workshop on Biological Processes & Petri Nets (BioPPN), satellite event of Petri Nets 2010, pp. 39–54 (2010)

23. Heiner, M., Rohr, C., Schwarick, M.: MARCIE – model checking and reachability analysis done efficiently. In: Colom, J.-M., Desel, J. (eds.) PETRI NETS 2013. LNCS, vol. 7927, pp. 389–399. Springer, Heidelberg (2013)

24. Heiner, M., Schwarick, M., Tovchigrechko, A.: DSSZ-MC – a tool for symbolic analysis of extended petri nets. In: Franceschinis, G., Wolf, K. (eds.) PETRI NETS 2009. LNCS, vol. 5606, pp. 323–332. Springer, Heidelberg (2009)

25. Heiner, M., Sriram, K.: Structural analysis to determine the core of hypoxia response network. PLoS ONE **5**(1), e8600 (2010)

26. Heiner, M., Gilbert, D., Donaldson, R.: Petri nets for systems and synthetic biology. In: Bernardo, M., Degano, P., Zavattaro, G. (eds.) SFM 2008. LNCS, vol. 5016, pp. 215–264. Springer, Heidelberg (2008)

27. Herajy, M., Heiner, M.: A steering server for collaborative simulation of quantitative petri nets. In: Ciardo, G., Kindler, E. (eds.) PETRI NETS 2014. LNCS, vol. 8489, pp. 374–384. Springer, Heidelberg (2014)

28. Liu, F., Heiner, M.: Petri Nets for Modeling and Analyzing Biochemical Reaction Networks, chap. 9, pp. 245–272. Springer (2014)

29. Marwan, W., Wagler, A., Weismantel, R.: A mathematical approach to solve the network reconstruction problem. Mathematical Methods of Operations Research **67**(1), 117–132 (2008)

30. Minervini, G., Panizzoni, E., Giollo, M., Masiero, A., Ferrari, C., Tosatto, S.: Design and Analysis of a Petri Net Model of the Von Hippel-Lindau (VHL) Tumor Suppressor Interaction Network. PloS one **9**(6), e96986 (2014)

31. Popova-Zeugmann, L., Heiner, M.: Worst-case analysis of concurrent systems with Duration Interval Petri Nets. In: Schnieder, E.; Abel, D. (eds.) Proc. 5. EKA 1997, Braunschweig, May 1997, IfRA 1997), pp. 162–179 (1997)

32. Rodriguez, E.M.: A Mathematical Model For Cephalostatin 1-Induced Apoptosis In Leukemic Cells. Ph.D. thesis, University of the Philippines, College of Science, Institute of Mathematics (2008)

33. Rohr, C., Marwan, W., Heiner, M.: Snoopy - a unifying Petri net framework to investigate biomolecular networks. Bioinformatics **26**(7), 974–975 (2010)

34. del Rosario, R., Mendoza, E., Oesterhelt, D.: Modelling the Bioenergetics of Halobacterium Salinarum with Petri Nets. Journal of Computational and Theoretical Nanoscience **6**(8), 1965–1976 (2009)

35. Schulz, K.: An Extension of the Snoopy Software to Process and Manage Petri Net Animations (in German). Bachelor thesis, BTU Cottbus, Dep. of CS, November 2008

36. Schwarick, M., Rohr, C., Heiner, M.: Marcie - model checking and reachability analysis done efficiently. In: Proc. QEST 2011. pp. 91–100. IEEE CS Press (2011)

37. Schwarick, M.: A Petri net analysis tool (in German). Diploma thesis, BTU Cottbus, Dep. of CS (2006)

38. Shinar, G., Feinberg, M.: Structural Sources of Robustness in Biochemical Reaction Networks. Science **327**, 1389–1391 (2010)

39. Silva, M., Teruo, E., Colom, J.M.: Linear algebraic and linear programming techniques for the analysis of place/transition net systems. In: Reisig, W., Rozenberg, G. (eds.) APN 1998. LNCS, vol. 1491, pp. 309–373. Springer, Heidelberg (1998)

40. Starke, P.H., Roch, S.: INA, Integrated Net Analyzer, Version 2.2, Manual. Humboldt University Berlin, Dep. of CS (2003)

41. Wegener, J., Schwarick, M., Heiner, M.: A Plugin System for Charlie. In: Proc. International Workshop on Concurrency, Specification, and Programming (CS&P 2011), pp. 531–554. Białystok University of Technology (2011)

Petri Nets with Structured Data

Eric Badouel[1], Loïc Hélouët[1(✉)], and Christophe Morvan[1,2]

[1] INRIA Rennes Bretagne Atlantique, Rennes, France
{eric.badouel,loic.helouet}@inria.fr
[2] Université Paris-Est,Créteil, France
christophe.morvan@u-pem.fr

Abstract. This paper proposes Structured Data Nets (StDN), a Petri net extension that describes transactional systems with data. In StDNs, tokens are structured documents. Each transition is attached to a query, guarded by patterns, (logical assertions on the contents of its preset) and transforms tokens. We define StDNs and their semantics. We then consider their formal properties: coverability of a marking, termination and soundness of transactions. Unrestricted StDNs are Turing complete, so these properties are undecidable. We thus use an order on documents, and show that under reasonable restrictions on documents and on the expressiveness of patterns and queries, StDNs are well-structured transition systems, for which coverability, termination and soundness are decidable.

1 Introduction

Web services and business processes are now widely used applications. Many solutions exist to design such systems, but their formal verification remains difficult due to the tight connection of workflows with data [14,20,28]. For instance, in an online shop one faces situations where a workflow depends on data (*if the age of the client is greater than* 50, *then propose service S*), and conversely data depend on a flow (*return an offer with the minimal price proposed among the 5 first values returned by sub-contractors*). These systems have to be open: they must accept user inputs and manage multiple concurrent interactions. Openness also raises robustness issues: a system must avoid interferences among distinct transactions, and be robust for all inputs, including erroneous or obfuscated ones. Last, a transactional system usually manages its own data: catalog, clients database, stock,... which contents influences the execution of transactions.

Thus, exact descriptions of transaction systems lead naturally to infinite state models with infinite data and zero tests, that can be captured only by Turing powerful formalisms for which verification problems are undecidable. As a consequence, one has to work with abstractions of these systems to apply automated analysis techniques. Coarse grain approximations can rely on finite discretizations of data or on bounds on the number of transactions in a system. These straightforward techniques allow one to get back to the familiar models of finite state systems or (variants of) Petri nets for which verification techniques

© Springer International Publishing Switzerland 2015
R. Devillers and A. Valmari (Eds.): PETRI NETS 2015, LNCS 9115, pp. 212–233, 2015.
DOI: 10.1007/978-3-319-19488-2_11

are well-studied and decidable (model-checking for automata, coverability and reachability techniques for Petri nets). However, such bounded discretization that completely abstracts from data is usually too coarse.

This paper introduces *Structured Data nets* (StDN), a variant of Petri nets where tokens are structured documents, and transitions transform data. A token represents a piece of information that either belongs to a database associated with the system, or is attached to some ongoing transaction. Each transition of an StDN is attached a query, that is used to transform data, and is guarded by patterns expressing constraints on tokens in its input places. When firing a transition, the corresponding input documents are consumed and new documents computed as the result of queries applied to the input documents are produced in its output places. Fresh data are introduced in the system using an input transition that non-deterministically produces new documents corresponding to new transactions. Termination of a transaction is symbolized by the consumption of a document by an output transition. We define structured documents as trees whose nodes carry information given by lists of attributes/values (*à la* XML). We show that considering documents of bounded depth labeled by well-quasi ordered values, one can provide a well-quasi ordering on documents. We define StDNs and their semantics, and we consider formal properties of this model, such as coverability of a marking, termination and soundness of transactions. In their full generality, StDNs are Turing complete, so all these properties are undecidable. However, we prove that as soon as StDN manipulate well-quasi ordered documents, and meet some reasonable restrictions on the expressive power of patterns and queries (monotonous with respect to ordering), StDNs are well-structured transition systems. If in addition an StDN meets effectiveness requirements, well-structure yields that coverability of a marking is decidable. As a consequence, termination and soundness are also decidable. All these properties hold for a single initial marking of a net, but can be extended to handle symbolically unbounded sets of initial markings satisfying constraints defined by a pattern. Even if some information systems can not be represented by these well-structured StDNs, this decidable setting lays at a reasonable level of abstraction: it does not fix an *a priori* bound on the number of transactions, nor impose finiteness of data values.

Our model borrows elements from Petri nets, but also from data-centric models such as AXML [2] and business artifacts [25]. It is not the first extension of Petri nets which handles complex types attached to tokens: Petri nets with token carrying data have been proposed by [20]. For this extension, coverability of a configuration is decidable. However, data is not really transformed through the workflow, and is mainly used to adapt the structure of flows of an affine nets at runtime. Nested nets, which use low-level Petri nets as tokens have been proposed in [22]. In this model, nets can be moved from one place to another, interact with the higher level, or with their peers inside a place. We will show that our model is more expressive than nested nets. In particular, it models a notion of transaction, while nested nets leave their tokens anonymous. Our nets are close in spirit to PrT−Nets [15], that modify structured data via manipulations that are guarded by First Order predicates. However, StDNs use guarding mechanisms that can not be encoded in FO. Another variant that manipulates and transforms structured data is defined in [21] (XML nets). Places of an XML net carry data and are constrained by DTDs, and transitions perform data manipulations described in a query language. The model presented in this paper is close in spirit to XML nets, but keeps XML transfomations as abstract as possible, and emphasizes on semantics, decidability and formal properties of the model. Colored Petri nets [19] can also be considered as Petri nets with data. However, it is well-known that colors give a huge expressive power to nets, and can be used to encode arithmetic operations. It is hence hard to find a reasonable syntactic subclass of colored nets that is amenable to verification. Yet, our model could be simulated with complex coloring mechanisms.

Several formalisms handling data have also been designed outside the Petri net community. **Programming languages** such as BPEL [6] and ORC [23] have been proposed. BPEL is the de facto standard to design business processes. A BPEL specification describes a set of independent communicating agents. Coordination is achieved through message-passing. Interactions are grouped into sessions implicitly through *correlations*, which specify data values that uniquely identify a session—for instance, a purchase order number. ORC [23] is a programming language for the orchestration of services. It allows algorithmic manipulation of data, with an orchestration overlay to start services and synchronize their results. **Data-centric approaches** such as *Active XML* (AXML) [2] or *tree pattern rewriting systems* (TPRS) [14] define web services as a set of guarded rules that transform structured documents described, for instance, in XML. They do not make workflows explicit, and do not have a native notion of transaction either. To implement a workflow in an AXML specification, one has to integrate explicitly control states to AXML documents, guards and rules. Decidability of coverability has been proved for the subclass of "positive" AXML [3], in which rules can only append data to a document, and for TPRS manipulating documents of bounded depth. **Artifact-centric approaches** such as *business artifacts* [25] describe the logic of transactions for systems equipped with databases. The workflow of a transaction is defined using automata, or logical rules. A transaction carries variables, which are instantiated by values collected along the workflow or entered by the user. Verification of business artifacts has been proved feasible in a restricted setting [10]. In their original version, business artifacts only consider sequential processing of cases. They have inspired *Guard Stage Milestones* (GSM) [18], that allows parallelism among tasks. Recently we have introduced a grammar based artifact-centric case management system [7] which enables transparent distribution of tasks. One can also mention several initiatives to model web services in the π**-calculus** community. *Session types* [17] have been proposed as a formal model for web services. The expressive power of the whole π-calculus and session types do not allow for verification of reachability or coverability properties. [4] uses WSTS to show that a fragment of spatial logic that can express safety properties is decidable for well-typed π-calculus processes. An effective forward coverability algorithm for π-calculus with bounded depth has been proposed in [28]. Last, several formalisms such as μ-se [9], CASPIS [8], COWS [27], have been proposed to model web services.

This paper is organized as follows: Section 2 introduces the basic elements of our model, namely documents and tree patterns. Section 3 shows how documents can be ordered. Section 4 defines Structured Data Nets, and their semantics. We then consider formal properties of this model, and in particular coverability of a marking, termination, and soundness of transactions in Section 5. Section 6 concludes this work and gives future lines of research.

2   Documents and Tree Patterns

Our model of net is a variant of Petri nets manipulating structured data. These data are encoded as trees, and queried using tree patterns and queries.

A *tree* $T = (V, E, \text{root}_T)$ consists of a set V of vertices with a distinguished vertex, $\text{root}_T \in V$, called the *root* of the tree, together with a set of *edges* $E \subseteq V \times (V \setminus \{\text{root}_T\})$, such that for every vertex $v \in V \setminus \{\text{root}_T\}$ there exists a unique path from the root to v, i.e. a finite sequence $v_0, \ldots, v_n$ such that $v_0 = \text{root}_T$, $(v_{i-1}, v_i) \in E$ for $1 \leq i \leq n$ and $v_n = v$. In particular, *(i)* every vertex but the root $v \in V \setminus \{\text{root}_T\}$ has a unique predecessor, i.e. a vertex v' such that $(v', v) \in E$, and the root has no predecessor. A tree is *labelled* in A if it comes equipped with a labelling function $\lambda : V \to A$. The *depth* of a tree T is the maximal length of a sequence of consecutive edges in T.

Tokens of Structured Data Nets are *documents* represented by finite trees whose nodes are labelled with attribute/value pairs, i.e. by a finite set of equations of the form $a = v$ where tag a denotes a data field or an attribute and v its associated value. For that purpose we let a *tag system* $\tau = (\Sigma, \mathbb{D})$ consist of a set Σ of tags and a set $\mathbb{D}$ indexed by Σ such that for every $\sigma \in \Sigma$, the set $\mathbb{D}_\sigma$ of possible values for attribute σ is non-empty. A *valuation* $\nu \in \text{Val}_\tau$ associated with a tag system $\tau = (\Sigma, \mathbb{D})$ is a partial function $\nu : \Sigma \to \mathbb{D}$ whose domain of definition, denoted $\text{tag}(\nu)$, is finite and such that $\forall \sigma \in \text{tag}(\nu), \nu(\sigma) \in \mathbb{D}_\sigma$.

Definition 1 (Documents). *A document $D \in \text{Doc}_\tau$ associated with a tag system τ is a finite tree labelled by valuations in Val_τ.*

If v is the node of a document, we let $\text{tag}(v)$ be a shorthand for $\text{tag}(\lambda(v))$ and let $v \cdot \sigma$ denote $\lambda(v)(\sigma)$ when $\sigma \in \text{tag}(v)$. We use *tree patterns* to address boolean properties of trees. A tree pattern is also a labelled finite tree, whose edges are partitioned into ordinary edges and ancestor edges, and whose nodes are labelled by constraints. A *constraint*, denoted by $C \in \text{Cons}_\tau$, is defined by a partial function[1] $C : \Sigma \to \wp(\mathbb{D})$ whose domain, denoted $\text{tag}(C)$, is finite and such that $\forall \sigma \in \text{tag}(C), C(\sigma) \subseteq \mathbb{D}_\sigma$. For instance if $\mathbb{D}_\sigma$ is the set of integers then $5 \leq \sigma \leq 20$ constrains the value of σ to lay within the set of integers ranging between 5 and 20, and $\sigma =?$ allows σ to take value in the whole set of integers.

Definition 2 (Tree Pattern). *A tree pattern, $P \in \text{Pat}_\tau$, is a tuple $P = (V, Pred, Anc, \lambda)$, where $Pred, Anc \subseteq V \times V$ are disjoint set of edges and $(V, Pred \cup Anc, \text{root}_P, \lambda)$ is a finite tree labelled by constraints in Cons_τ.*

---

[1] $\wp(\mathbb{D})$ denotes the set of subsets of $\mathbb{D}$

As for documents, we let tag(v), for v a node of a tree pattern, be an abbreviation for tag($\lambda(v)$) and let $v \cdot \sigma$ denote $\lambda(v)(\sigma)$ when $\sigma \in$ tag(v). We further let $v \cdot \sigma =?$ as an shorthand for $v \cdot \sigma = \mathbb{D}_\sigma$ which means that v must carry the tag σ but the value of this tag is not constrained. This situation should not be confused with $\sigma \notin$ tag(v) which does not constrain node v to carry tag σ (see Figure 1 for an illustration). Pattern satisfaction is formally defined as follows:

Definition 3 (Pattern Satisfaction). *A document* $D = (V_D, E_D, \text{root}_D, \lambda)$ *satisfies a tree pattern* $P = (V_P, \text{Pred}, \text{Anc}, \lambda_P)$, *denoted* $D \models P$, *when there exists an injective map* $h : V_P \to V_D$ *such that:*

1. $h(\text{root}_P) = \text{root}_D$,
2. $\forall v \in V_P \quad$ tag(v) $\subseteq$ tag($h(v)$),
3. $\forall v \in V_P \; \forall \sigma \in$ tag(v) $\quad h(v) \cdot \sigma \in v \cdot \sigma$,
4. $\forall (v, v') \in \text{Pred}_P \quad (h(v), h(v')) \in E_D$, and
5. $\forall (v, v') \in \text{Anc}_P \quad (h(v), h(v')) \in E_D^*$ (where E_D^* denotes the reflexive and transitive closure of E_D).

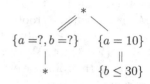

Fig. 1. A tree Pattern

Figure 1 is a tree pattern where the single and double edges denote respectively predecessor (Pred) and ancestor (Anc) relations. Furthermore, $* = \{\}$ denotes the empty constraint. It describes the set of trees which have five nodes v_0, v_1, v_2, v_3, and v_4 with the following properties. v_0 is the root of the tree v_1 is not a leaf node (i.e. it has at least one successor node v_2) and it carries tags a and b (tag(v_1) $\supseteq \{a, b\}$) with no particular constraints on their values: $\lambda(v_1)(a) = \mathbb{D}_a, \lambda(v_1)(b) = \mathbb{D}_b$. Node v_3 is an immediate successor to the root, it carries tag a (tag(v_2) $\supseteq \{a\}$) and the value attached to tag a is 10. Node v_4 is some successor node of v_3 tagged by b and the value attached to b is lower than 30. Requiring pattern matching to hold at the root of a document is not a limitation. Indeed, for a pattern P with root v, one can design a new pattrern P' that has an additional node v' such that $(v', v) \in$ Anc and $\lambda_{P'}(v') = \{\}$. Then, P' holds at the root of a document D iff P holds *at some node* of D. On the other hand, we use a child relation in patterns, and not only an ancestor relation. This implies that matching is not a simple embedding relation (in the usual sense used for graphs), but a strict embedding preserving edge types. Though defining patterns with child relation makes them less frequently monotonous, in allows to use a reasonnable subset of the XPATH standard [29] as patterns in StDNs.

3 Ordering Trees

We do not distinguish between isomorphic trees, i.e. when there exists a bijection $\varphi : V_T \to V_{T'}$ between their respective sets of vertices such that $(v, v') \in E_T \iff (\varphi(v), \varphi(v')) \in E_{T'}$ (and thus also $\varphi(\text{root}_T) = \text{root}_{T'}$), and $\lambda(v) = \lambda(\varphi(v))$.

If $(A, \leq)$ is an ordered set (resp. a quasi ordered set, i.e. $\leq$ is a reflexive and transitive relation) then the set of trees labelled in A can be ordered (resp.

quasi ordered) by setting $T_1 \leq T_2$ for any pair of trees $T_1 = (V_1, E_1, \text{root}_1, \lambda_1)$, $T_2 = (V_2, E_2, \text{root}_2, \lambda_2)$, when there exists an injective map $f : V_1 \to V_2$ such that:

1. $f(\text{root}_1) = \text{root}_2$,
2. $(v, v') \in E_1 \implies (f(v), f(v')) \in E_2$, and
3. $\forall v \in V_1, \lambda_1(v) \leq \lambda(f(v))$.

Hence $T_1 \leq T_2$ if T_2 can be obtained from T_1 by adding new edges and/or replacing existing labels by greater ones. For instance, given an order relation, $\leq_\sigma$, on $\mathbb{D}_\sigma$ and a subset of tags, $\Sigma' \subseteq \Sigma$, one obtains a quasi order on Doc_τ associated with the quasi order on valuations Val_τ given by:

$$\nu \leq_{\Sigma'} \nu' \iff \text{tag}(\nu) \cap \Sigma' \subseteq \text{tag}(\nu') \ \wedge \ \forall \sigma \in \text{tag}(\nu) \cap \Sigma' \quad \nu(\sigma) \leq_\sigma \nu'(\sigma)$$

Thus, restricted to tags in Σ', valuation ν' has a larger domain and associates greater values to tags for which both ν and ν' are defined (see Figure 2 for an illustration). Note that $\Sigma' \subseteq \Sigma'' \implies \leq_{\Sigma''} \subseteq \leq_{\Sigma'}$.

Definition 4 (Monotony). *A pattern P is* monotonous *if, for any pair of documents (D_1, D_2), $D_1 \leq_{\Sigma'} D_2$ and $D_1 \models P$ implies $D_2 \models P$ where Σ' is the set of tags occurring in P.*

$D_1 \cdot \{u = 2, y - 9\}$ $D_2 \cdot \{a \quad 4\}$ $P_1 \cdot \{a = ?\}$ $P_2 \cdot \{a = ?\}$
| | || ||
$\{b = 5\}$ $\{b = 3\}$ $\{5 \leq c \leq 11\}$ $\{10 < d\}$
/   \   /   \
$\{c = 10\}$ $\{d = 20\}$ $\{c = 15\}$ $\{d = 30\}$
                                         | |
                                    $\{e = 12\}$ $\{f = 4\}$

Fig. 2. Documents and patterns: Assume all the domains $\mathbb{D}_\sigma$ are given by the set $\mathbb{N}$ of natural numbers with their usual ordering, then $D_1 \leq_{\{a,c,d\}} D_2$. Pattern P_1 is not monotonous since $D_1 \leq_{\{a,c\}} D_2$, $D_1 \models P_1$ and $D_2 \not\models P_1$. Pattern P_2 is monotonous.

As illustrated in Figure 2, a pattern that imposes upper bounds on attribute values is not monotonous. Let us recall that a *well quasi order* (wqo) is a quasi order that is *well-founded*: any infinite sequence $x_1, \ldots, x_n, \ldots$ contains two elements x_i and x_j such that $i < j$ and $x_i < x_j$. Equivalently, a quasi order is a wqo if it contains no infinite strictly decreasing sequences nor infinite antichains (sets of pairwise incomparable elements). Let $\uparrow x = \{y \mid x \leq y\}$ denote the *upward closure* of an element x. A set X is *upward closed* if $\uparrow X = X$. Any upward closed set in a wqo has a *finite* basis (a set $B(X) \subseteq X$ such that $\bigcup_{x \in B(X)} \uparrow x = X$). This property ensures the existence of a finite representation for infinite upward closed sets of elements. Finding a wqo on structured data can serve to finitely represent collections of data of arbitrary sizes, or to allow symbolic manipulations on families of trees. However, in contrast with Kruskal's theorem, which states that tree *embedding* is a well quasi order on the set of finite trees, the set $(\mathrm{Doc}_\tau, \leq_{\Sigma'})$ is in general not a wqo even if the set of tags is finite and their domains are finite or well quasi ordered. In fact, $(\mathrm{Doc}_\tau, \leq_{\Sigma'})$ is a *strict rooted inclusion*. It is needed to models faithfully differences in databases contents and documents growth, but allows construction of sets of pairwise incomparable elements of arbitrary sizes (as shown in Figure 3).

$$\{a = 0\}$$
$$|$$
$$\{b = 0\}$$
$$\vdots$$
$$\{b = 0\}$$
$$|$$
$$\{a = 0\}$$

Fig. 3. Let us consider tag system $\tau = (\{a, b\}, \mathbb{D})$, with $\mathbb{D}_a = \mathbb{D}_b = \{0\}$ and the tree shown next, denoted $a.b^k.a$, whose root v_0, tagged a with $\lambda(v_0)(a) = 0$, is followed by a sequence $v_1, \ldots, v_k$ of nodes tagged b with value $\lambda(v_i)(b) = 0$, and ends with a node v_{k+1} tagged a, with $\lambda(v_{k+1})(a) = 0$. The set of trees $\{a.b^k.a \mid k \in \mathbb{N}\}$ consists of pairwise incomparable elements for $\leq_{\{a,b\}}$, hence they form an infinite antichain, whereas they form a chain for tree embedding.

This problem (existence of sets of pairwise incomparable elements of arbitrary sizes) can be avoided by restricting to trees of bounded depth. Let us denote $\mathrm{Doc}_{\tau, \leq n}$ the set of documents whose depth is less or equal to n. In order for $(\mathrm{Doc}_{\tau, \leq n}, \leq_\Sigma)$ to be a wqo one must also assume that the set of tags, Σ, is finite. If it is not the case, the family of trees reduced to their root and all labelled with distinct tag would constitute an infinite antichain.

Proposition 1. *Let* $\tau = (\Sigma, \mathbb{D})$ *a tag system where* Σ *is a finite set,* $\Sigma' \subseteq \Sigma$, *and* $n \in \mathbb{N}$. *If, for all* $\sigma \in \Sigma'$, $(\mathbb{D}_\sigma, \leq_\sigma)$ *is a wqo then* $(\mathrm{Doc}_{\tau, \leq n}, \leq_{\Sigma'})$ *is a wqo.*

Proof. First, note that since two documents that only differ on tags that do not belong to Σ' are equivalent for the equivalence relation induced by the quasi order $\leq_{\Sigma'}$, one can assume without loss of generality that $\Sigma' = \Sigma$. We know by [11] that the set of graphs $\mathcal{G}_\Sigma^n$, of bounded depth labelled by well quasi ordered tags, and ordered by strict subgraph inclusion $\leq$ is a well quasi order. Therefore the same result holds for trees of bounded depth labelled by wqo, ordered by rooted strict subgraph inclusion $\leq^r$. Indeed one has $T \leq^r T' \iff \overline{T} \leq \overline{T'}$ where $\overline{T}$ is obtained from T by adding a node labelled with a new symbol and by adding an edge from this node to the root of T. This additional node is the root of $\overline{T}$ and any strict labelled-graph embedding from $\overline{T}$ to $\overline{T'}$ necessarily relates their roots (because of their common label which does not appear elsewhere) and therefore also their unique successor nodes, i.e. the roots of T and T'. So it remains to prove that the order relation $\nu \leq_\Sigma \nu' \iff \mathrm{tag}(\nu) \subseteq \mathrm{tag}(\nu') \ \wedge \ \forall \sigma \in \mathrm{tag}(\nu) \ \nu(\sigma) \leq_\sigma \nu'(\sigma)$ on valuations Val_τ is a wqo. This order relation can be expressed as: $\nu \leq_\Sigma \nu' \iff \forall \sigma \in \Sigma' \ \nu(\sigma) \leq_\sigma^\perp \nu'(\sigma)$ where a valuation is viewed as a function $\nu : \Sigma \to \mathbb{D} \cup \{\perp\}$ where $\perp$ is a new element added to each of the sets $\mathbb{D}_\sigma$ as a least element ($x \leq_\sigma^\perp y \iff x = \perp \vee x \leq_\sigma y$) and by letting $\nu(\sigma) = \perp \iff \sigma \notin \mathrm{tag}(\nu)$. Then $(\mathbb{D}_\sigma \cup \{\perp\}, \leq_\sigma^\perp)$ is a wqo for every $\sigma \in \Sigma'$. As, the Cartesian product of a *finite* family of wqos is a wqo, we have that $(\mathrm{Val}_\tau, \leq_\Sigma)$ is a wqo. $\qquad\square$

4   Structured Data Nets

StDns are designed to model complex workflows with data, such as transactions. In StDNs, interactions are handled as follows: a new case (a structured document) is created and attached a unique identifier. It then follows a workflow, collecting data in the system. When the transaction is completed, the computed values are returned to the caller. During the workflow, several parallel threads may have been created, and a part of the data of the case (client's name, ...) can be stored in the system for later use.

For convenience, we distinguish two particular transitions that are used to initiate and terminate cases. A transition t_{in}, with no incoming place, which delivers to the input place p_{in} a token representing a new transaction. A transition t_{out}, with no outgoing place, which unconditionally consumes any token from the output place p_{out}.

In addition to case management, transactional systems are often required to meet properties such as isolation of transactions. Isolation means that two transactions do not influence one another. This is achieved on one hand by allowing concurrency, which is a native feature of all Petri nets variants, but also by forbidding undesired side effects of a transaction. In a web store, for instance, paying a command should not trigger delivery of someone else's items in another transaction. Isolation is often implemented by attaching a session number to a case. Formalisms such as BPEL [26] allow for more elaborated mechanisms called *correlations* to filter and group messages sharing commonalities. In general, it is not useful to remember exactly the identity of a session, nor to order session identities. A mechanism allowing to differentiate distinct sessions suffices. In [5], we have proposed session systems whose configurations are represented as graphs, and sessions as components of these graphs. In *structured data nets* isolation of transactions is handled by assigning an identifier to each individual token, thus inducing a partition on the set of tokens. More precisely, a token is a pair $T = (D, id)$ where D is a document, the value of the token, and $id \in \mathbb{N}$ indicates when $id = 0$ that the data D is part of the local database of the system. Otherwise, $id \neq 0$ provides the identifier of the transaction that D belongs to. Thus identifiers of transactions are positive integers.

Roughly speaking, each input arc (p, t) for $p \in {}^\bullet t$ in a structured data net is attached a guard given by a tree pattern $\langle p, t \rangle$. Transition t is enabled in a marking M if in every of its input place $p \in {}^\bullet t$ one can find a token $T_p = (D_p, id_P) \in M(p)$ such that $D_p \models \langle p, t \rangle$ and all non-null identifiers id_P coincide. The latter condition ensures that all the pieces of information, but those belonging to the local database, are concerned with the same transaction. These tokens are then removed from the current marking and some new tokens should be added to each of its output places $p \in t^\bullet$. For that purpose, each output arc (t, p) for $p \in t^\bullet$ is attached a query $\langle t, p \rangle$ that describes how to compute the value of the token(s) to add in place $p \in t^\bullet$ from the vector of input documents $(D_p)_{p \in {}^\bullet t}$ which enabled the firing of the transition. Queries can produce multisets of tokens. We denote by $\mathcal{M}(A)$ the multisets with elements in set A. Every $X \in \mathcal{M}(A)$ is a map $X : A \to \mathbb{N}$, where $X(a)$ gives the multiplicity of element $a \in A$ in X. We further let $\mathcal{M}_f(A)$ define the set of finite multisets, i.e., the subset of $\mathcal{M}(A)$ which contains the multisets X such that $X(a) \neq 0$ for a finite number of elements $a \in A$.

Definition 5 (Query). *An n-ary query $Q : (Doc_\tau)^n \rightarrow \wp(\mathcal{M}_f(Doc_\tau))$ is a function that non-deterministically produces a finite multiset of documents from a vector of documents given as input.*

A query is *simple* when it non-deterministically returns an ordinary set: $\mathrm{Im}(Q) \subseteq \wp(Doc_\tau)$. A query is *deterministic* if it returns a singleton: $\mathrm{Im}(Q) \subseteq \mathcal{M}_f(Doc_\tau)$. As illustrated in Figure 4, non-deterministic queries can be used to specify non-deterministic choices of the environment. Non-simple queries can be used to produce several documents, and design creation of concurrent threads.

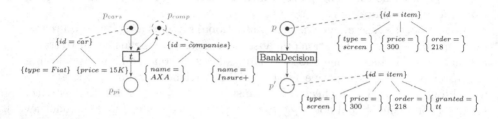

Fig. 4. The leftmost example depicts a part of broking system for a car insurance system. Place p_{cars} contains structured documents depicting cars and their price. A token in p_{comp} lists several insurance companies. The place p_{pi} is the starting point to ask pro-forma invoices to companies. The transition t creates one structured document per insurance company that appears in the database, by application of query $\langle t, p_{pi} \rangle$ attached to flow arc from t to place p_{pi}. The net on the right models a part of an online shop in which a payment of some bought item needs to be granted by a bank. Transition BankDecision models this decision. The query $\langle BankDecision, p' \rangle$ attaches a new child to the document's root indicating bank's decision with a boolean. Hence, it non-deterministically returns the input document augmented with either a true or a false boolean tag.

We leave voluntarily the queries underspecified, as our aim is to define generic properties of nets depending on properties of their documents, query language, and flow structure, but abstracting away as much as possible the query language. Several mechanisms have been proposed to query structured data. Standard query languages such as XQuery [30] and Xpath [29] use patterns to extract information from trees, and are usually described formally as tree pattern queries. The definition of structured data nets is as follows:

Definition 6 (Structured Data Net). *Let τ be a tag system. A structured data net, or StDN, is a structure $\mathcal{N} = (P, P_{DB}, T, F, \langle \cdot, \cdot \rangle)$ where P is a set of places, $P_{DB} \subseteq P$ is a subset of places corresponding to the local database of the net, T is a set of transitions, $F \subseteq P \times T \cup T \times P$ is a set of flow arcs, and map $\langle \cdot, \cdot \rangle : F \rightarrow Pat_\tau \cup \mathcal{Q}_\tau$ associates each input arc $(p, t) \in F$ to a pattern $\langle p, t \rangle \in Pat_\tau$ and each output arc $(t, p) \in F$ to a query $\langle t, p \rangle \in \mathcal{Q}_\tau$.*

The respective sets of input and output elements of $x \in P \cup T$, *preset* and *postset* are denoted $^\bullet x = \{y \mid (y,x) \in F\}$ and $x^\bullet = \{y \mid (x,y) \in F\}$. The map $\langle \cdot, \cdot \rangle$ associates each input arc $(p,t) \in F$ to a pattern $\langle p,t \rangle \in \mathrm{Pat}_\tau$ and each output arc $(t,p) \in F$ to an n-ary query $\langle t,p \rangle \in \mathcal{Q}_\tau$ where $n = |^\bullet t|$ is the number of input places of t with a given enumeration of this set of places. We furthermore require that StDNs possess two places p_{in} and p_{out}, and two transitions t_{in} and t_{out} such that $^\bullet t_{in} = \emptyset$, $t_{in}^\bullet = \{p_{in}\}$, $^\bullet t_{out} = \{p_{out}\}$, $t_{out}^\bullet = \emptyset$, $p_{out}^\bullet = \{t_{out}\}$, and $\langle p_{out}, t_{out} \rangle = tt$ is the trivial pattern reduced to its root labeled with the empty constraint $* = \{\}$, i.e. tt is the pattern matched by any document. Any transition such that $^\bullet t \cap P_{DB} \neq \emptyset$ has also input places in $P \setminus P_{DB}$ ensuring that a transition acts on the database only in the context of the processing of a particular transaction. Finally t_{in} is the unique transition with an empty preset, t_{out} is the unique transition with an empty postset, and any place in $P \setminus P_{DB}$ has non-empty preset and postset.

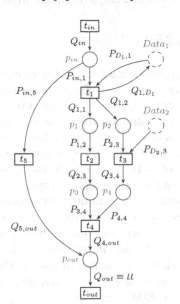

Fig. 5. We assume in this example that all queries are simple and all but Q_{in} are deterministic. Then input transition t_{in} creates non deterministically a new transaction by putting a token in place p_{in} containing a document (e.g. a form) together with a new identifier. According to the shape of the token but also to the data contained in place $Data_1$ transitions t_5 and t_1 may be enabled. For instance t_1 may correspond to the nominal behaviour while t_5 is used when the document is incomplete or ill-formed. In the latter case the document is immediately transferred to the output place p_{out}. In the former case the treatment is split by t_1 into two threads (concurrent actions t_2 and t_3) and the respective results are aggregated by transition t_4. Then the output transition t_{out} can withdraw the terminated transaction from the system.

Definition 7 (Behaviour of StDNs). *A token $T = (D, id) \in \mathrm{Tok}_\tau$ is made of a document $D \in \mathrm{Doc}_\tau$ and a non-negative integer $id \in \mathbb{N}$. A marking $M : P \to \mathcal{M}_f(\mathrm{Tok}_\tau)$ assigns a finite multiset of tokens to each place such that for all $(D, id) \in M(p)$ one has $id = 0$ if and only if $p \in P_{DB}$. Transition $t \neq t_{in}$ is enabled in marking M and firing transition t in marking M leads to marking M', denoted as $M[t\rangle M'$, when*

1. *$\exists id, \forall p \in {}^\bullet t, \ \exists T_p = (D_p, id_p) \in M(p) \quad s.t. \quad D_p \models \langle p, t \rangle, \ and \ p \notin P_{DB} \Rightarrow id_p = id$,*

2. *$\forall p \in t^\bullet, \ \exists X_p \in \langle t, p \rangle \left((D_p)_{p \in {}^\bullet t} \right)$,*

3. *Let id and X_p be respectively defined from 1. and 2. $\forall p \in t^\bullet \ M'(p) = M''(p) \cup \{(D, id_p) \mid D \in X_p\}$ where $id_p = id$ if $p \notin P_{DB}$ and $id_p = 0$ if*

$p \in P_{DB}$, and $\forall p \notin t^\bullet$ $M'(p) = M''(p)$; where M'' is the marking given by:

$$M''(p) = \begin{cases} M(p) \ if \ p \notin {}^\bullet t \\ M(p) \setminus \{(D_p, id_p)\} \ if \ p \in {}^\bullet t \end{cases}$$

The behaviour of transition t_{in} is similar except that since it has no input place it is always enabled and no identifier results from the enabling condition. It creates a new identifier associated with the tokens created in input place p_{in}.

When conditions 1 and 2 in Definition 6 are met we say that transition t is *enabled* in marking M, denoted $M[t\rangle$. Note that the firing relation $M[t\rangle M'$ is non-deterministic due to the fact that first, one may find several token sets that satisfy the patterns associated with the input places of t, and second, the queries associated with the output places may also be non-deterministic. Marking M' is *reachable* from marking M when there exists a sequence of transition firings leading from M to M'. We denote $\mathcal{R}(M)$ the set of markings reachable from M.

5   Properties of Structured Data Nets

The main motivation for using formal notations and semantics is to derive automated tools to reason on the corresponding systems. For transactional systems, one may want to check that a request with correct type is always processed in a finite amount of time, regardless of current data. Another issue can be to guarantee that a payment on an online store is always followed by the sending of the purchased item to the buyer. Last, one may want to check some simple business rules on transactions, confidentiality of some data, etc. In most cases, the properties to check do not deal with global states of the modeled system, but rather on the status of one particular transaction plus a limited environment. Hence the properties of interest for StDNs are closer to coverability properties than to reachability properties. In this section we formalize and address decidability of reachability, coverability, termination (whether all transactions terminate), and soundness (the question of whether all transactions terminate without leaving pending threads in the system). We can formalize reachability, coverability, termination and soundness as follows for an StDN with respect to a given initial marking M_0. We will assume w.l.o.g. that M_0 contains no transaction: $\forall p \in P \setminus P_{DB}, M_0(p) = \emptyset$. Indeed, one can always add to an existing net without transactions in its initial marking another net that initializes some places with a chosen contents, to obtain a given marking M_0 (up to identifiers attached to documents). Then, all problems can be brought back to similar problems with transaction-free initial markings.

Reachability: Is a given marking M reachable from the initial marking: $M \in \mathcal{R}(M_0)$?

Coverability: Is a given marking M smaller than some reachable marking: $\exists M' \in \mathcal{R}(M_0)$ *s.t.* $M \leq M'$? (For a given order relation $\leq$ on markings)

Termination of a transaction: Given a marking M such that a new transaction has just been created ($M(p_{in})$ contains a token (D, id) which is the only token with identifier id in M), can one reach a marking M' such that $M(p_{out})$ contains a token (D', id) ? Does one always reach such a marking from M ? Is termination possible or granted for any initial case given by a marking M or respectively for all initial cases in which the considered document satisfies a given pattern P ?

Soundness: Given a marking M such that a new transaction has just been created, $(M(p_{in})$ contains a token (D, id) in $M(p_{in})$ which is the only token with identity id in M), can one always reach a marking M' such that $M(p_{out})$ contains a token (D', id) and at the same time avoid markings in which p_{out} contains a token (D', id) and another place contains a token of the form (D'', id) (the case is not completely terminated)?

All questions above are undecidable if no restriction is imposed on the nature of documents or queries. In the rest of the section, we consider a class of StDN which is proved to be effective well-structured transition systems, a property that guarantee the decision of coverability.

Theorem 1 (Undecidability). *Reachability, coverability, termination and soundness are undecidable problems for StDNs.*

Proof. We encode a Turing machine into an StDN. We recall that a Turing machine is made of an infinite bi-directional tape divided in both directions into an infinite number of consecutive cells and a finite state device that can read and write the cell being examined by a read/write head and that can also move that head along the tape in both direction. A cell contains a 0 or a 1, initially every cell has the default value 0. More precisely a Turing machine consists of a finite set of states Q with some initial state q_0 and a finite set of instructions of the form $[q, x, \omega, q']$ where q and q' are states, $x \in \{0, 1\}$ is the possible value of the cell, and $\omega \in \{0, 1, L, R\}$ is an operation that corresponds respectively to writing 0 or 1 in the current cell or moving the r/w-head to the left or to the right. A configuration is a triple $(q, u, v) \in Q \times \{0, 1\}^\omega \times \{0, 1\}^\omega$ made of a state $q \in Q$ and two infinite words coding respectively the content of the left part of the tape, read from right-to-left, and the right part of the tape, read from left-to-right. The r/w-head is positioned on the first cell of the right-part of the tape. The transitions of the Turing machine are given as follows:

1. Writing a value $y \in \{0, 1\}$ on the current cell: $(q, u, x \cdot v) \xrightarrow{[q,x,y,q']} (q', u, y \cdot v)$.

2. Right move: $(q, u, x \cdot v) \xrightarrow{[q,x,R,q']} (q', x \cdot u, v)$.

3. Left move: $(q, y \cdot u, x \cdot v) \xrightarrow{[q,x,L,q']} (q', u, y \cdot x \cdot v)$.

$$\{state = q\}$$

$$\{l = u_1\} \qquad\qquad \{r = v_1\}$$
$$\vdots \qquad\qquad\qquad \vdots$$
$$\{l = u_n\} \qquad\qquad \{r = v_m\}$$
$$\mid \qquad\qquad\qquad \mid$$
$$\{l = \natural\} \qquad\qquad \{r = \natural\}$$

A reachable configuration (q, u, v) contains only a finite number of non-null elements therefore one can encode a configuration with a tree as shown next where $\forall i > n, u_i = 0$ and $\forall i > m, v_i = 0$. We let $[q, u, v]$ denote this tree (even though the representation is not unique). In terms of this representation the moves of the Turing machine can be simulated with the rules:

1. Writing a value $y \in \{0,1\}$ on the current cell: $[q, u, x \cdot v] \xrightarrow{[q,x,y,q']} [q', u, y \cdot v]$.

2. $[q, u, x \cdot v] \xrightarrow{[q,x,R,q']} [q', x \cdot u, v]$ and $[q, u, \sharp] \xrightarrow{[q,0,R,q']} [q', 0 \cdot u, \sharp]$.

3. $[q, y \cdot u, x \cdot v] \xrightarrow{[q,x,L,q']} [q', u, y \cdot x \cdot v]$ and $(q, \sharp, x \cdot v) \xrightarrow{q,x,L,q'} (q', \sharp, 0 \cdot x \cdot v)$.

Each of these rules can straightforwardly be represented by a transition r with ${}^\bullet r = r^\bullet = \{p_{in}\}$ where pattern $\langle p_{in}, r \rangle$ describes those configurations that enable rule r and query $\langle r, p_{in} \rangle$ describes the effect of r on such a configuration. Pattern $\langle t_{in}, p_{in} \rangle = \{[\sharp, q_0, \sharp]\}$ produces the initial configuration. We complete the description of the StDN by adding one transition $halt_{q,x}$ from p_{in} to place p_{out} for each pair of state q and symbol x for which there is no move of the machine of the form $(q, x, -, -)$ where pattern $\langle p_{in}, halt_{q,x} \rangle$ tests that the state is q and the symbol read is x and query $\langle halt_{q,x}, p_{out} \rangle$ witnesses the halting of the Turing machine by creating a specific token, e.g. the empty configuration $[\sharp, q_0, \sharp]$, in the output place. For this StDN reachability or coverability of the final marking with one token in p_{out} are equivalent to termination or soundness thus all these properties are undecidable.   □

This result is not surprising, as reachability or coverability are usually undecidable for Petri nets with extended tokens like colored Petri nets. However, one may note several important issues from the encoding of a Turing machine. First, deterministic queries are sufficient for this encoding. Second, three distinct tags and finite domains of values are sufficient to encode a configuration of a Turing machine. An immediate question is whether one can rely on the structure of the data and on simple restrictions to obtain decidability results. A first obvious useful restriction is to bound the depth of documents manipulated by the system. By Proposition 1 the set of documents manipulated by the StDN is a wqo when the domains of the data fields, attached to tree nodes, are wqos. This restriction is reasonable, as it is unlikely that documents grow arbitrarily during their lifetime in a system. Similarly, databases of arbitrary sizes can be represented as unbounded sets of bounded depth documents in places of P_{DB}.

Definition 8. *An StDN is well quasi ordered (is a wqo StDN for short), when*

 i) the domains of values used by document data fields are well quasi ordered (finite sets, integers, vectors of integers,...), with effective comparison (one can can effectively decide if $x \leq_\sigma y$), and

 ii) there exists a bound on the depth of all documents appearing in $\mathcal{R}(M_0)$.

Let us comment on the restrictions in Definition 8. Assuming wqo values in documents still allows to work with infinite domains like integers. However, this restriction forbids to attach structured data such as queues of unbounded sizes to nodes. Within the context of transactional systems, this is not a severe limitation. Note also that checking whether $\mathcal{R}(M_0)$ contains only bounded depth documents is obviously undecidable. However, this property is frequently met, and is not a severe limitation either: Most of transactional systems can be seen as protocols working with a finite number of data fields or using finite forms, in which a finite number of entries needs to be filled. Hence, applying a query usually does not increase too much the size of a document. One shall also note that the depth of standard structured documents is usually very low: the structure helps decomposing an entry into data fields, i.e. decomposing a concept into sub-concepts (a person is described as someone with a first name and last name) and it is recognized [24] that 99% of XML documents have depth smaller than 8, and that the average depth of XML documents is 4. Note also that the depth restriction does not mean finiteness of manipulated data: trees of arbitrary width still comply with this restriction, and data values attached to nodes need not be chosen from finite domains. This allows for instance for the manipulation of XML documents containing arbitrary numbers of records. Still, as shown at the end of this section, considering well quasi ordered StDNs is not enough to obtain decidability.

Let us define the ordering relation on the set of markings induced by the ordering of documents, and thus ultimately by the ordering of the data values appearing in these documents. The powerset of an ordered or quasi ordered set $(A, \leq)$ is equipped with the quasi order $\leq$ where $X \leq Y$ when an injective map $h : X \to Y$ exists such that $\forall x \in X\ x \leq h(x)$. For multisets $X, Y \in \mathcal{M}(A)$ we similarly let $X \leq Y \iff [\![X]\!] \leq [\![Y]\!]$ where $[\![X]\!] = \{(x,i) \mid x \in X \wedge 1 \leq i \leq X(x)\}$ denotes the set of occurrences of X. Markings are compared component-wise up to an injective renaming of their transactions. More precisely, we let $M_1 \leq M_2$ when there exists an injective map $h : \mathbb{N} \to \mathbb{N}$ such that $h(0) = 0$, and for every place p and every $i \in \mathbb{N}$ one has $\pi_i(M_1(p)) \leq \pi_{h(i)}(M_2(p))$ where $\pi_i(M(p)) = \{D \mid (D, i) \in M(p)\}$ denotes the multiset of documents in $M(p)$ with identifier i. As the comparison between two markings is performed up to a renaming of transactions, the exact identifier of a token does not matter. The only concern is whether two tokens with the same (respectively with different) identifier(s) are mapped to tokens with the same (resp. with different) identifier(s). Hence, we can equivalently consider markings as partitions of a multiset [2] of pairs from $P \times \mathrm{Doc}_{\tau, \leq n}$. As a partition of a set X is a set of subsets of X, any quasi order on X extends (using twice the powerset extension) to a quasi order on the set of partitions of X. With this representation $M_1 \leq M_2$ when the two partitions are comparable for the extension to partitions of the ordering $\leq$ on $P \times \mathrm{Doc}_{\tau, \leq n}$ given by $(p, D) \leq (p', D')$ when $p = p'$ and $D \leq D'$.

Proposition 2. *The set of markings over bounded depth documents whose data have well quasi ordered domains is a wqo.*

Proof. From proposition 1, we know that $(\mathrm{Doc}_{\tau, \leq n}, \leq)$ is a wqo. Since the set of places is finite, the ordering relation on $P \times \mathrm{Doc}_{\tau, \leq n}$ is also a wqo. Last, the product of two wqos forms a wqo [16], and we have seen that extending the ordering to multisets and then to partitions also yields a wqo. Hence, the ordering on markings over documents of bounded depth is a wqo.   □

---

[2] by partition of a multiset X we mean a partition of the set $[\![X]\!]$ of occurrences of X.

An immediate followup to well quasi orderedness is to set restrictions to obtain well-structured transition systems (WSTS) and reuse existing results to check coverability. An n-ary query Q is said to be *monotonous* when

$$(\forall i \in \{1, \ldots, n\} \quad D_i \leq D_i') \implies Q(D_1, \ldots, D_n) \leq Q(D_1', \ldots, D_n')$$

Proposition 3. *A wqo StDN with monotonous patterns and queries is a WSTS, more precisely* $(M_1[t\rangle M_1' \wedge M_1 \leq M_2) \implies (\exists M_2', M_2[t\rangle M_2' \wedge M_2 \leq M_2')$

Proof. According to Definition 7 we distinguish the initial transition t_{in}, which is responsible for the creation of new identifiers, from the other transitions.
If $t = t_{in}$**:** The transition t_{in} is not guarded, and results in a non-deterministic creation of new documents $D_1, \ldots, D_k$ with a fresh identity id in place p_{in}, namely $M_1' = M_1 \uplus \{(p, (D_1, id)) \cup \cdots \cup (p, (D_k, id))\}$. Then, one can find a fresh integer id' that is not used in M_2 so that $M_2[t_{in}\rangle M_2'$ where $M_2' = M_2 \uplus \{(p, (D_1, id')) \cup \cdots \cup (p, (D_k, id'))\}$. As $M_1 \leq M_2$, there exists an injective map h such that for every place p and every $x \in Dom(h)$, $\pi_x(M_1(p)) \leq \pi_{h(x)}(M_2(p))$. We extend this map by letting $h(id) = id'$ to get $\pi_{id}(M_1'(p)) \leq \pi_{id'}(M_2'(p))$ and thus $M_1' \leq M_2'$.

General case $(t \in T \setminus \{t_{in}\})$**:** This transition is enabled when all the patterns $P_1 = \langle p_1, t \rangle, \ldots, P_k = \langle p_1, t \rangle$ attached to flows from places $p_1, \ldots, p_k$ in ${}^\bullet t$ to t are satisfied by some documents $D_1, \ldots, D_k$, with the same identifier id for documents located in places ${}^\bullet t \setminus P_{DB}$, and with identifier 0 for documents from ${}^\bullet t \cap P_{DB}$. Upon firing, t consumes $D_1, \ldots D_k$ from ${}^\bullet t$, and outputs a set of newly created documents $D_1', \ldots D_{k'}'$ with identifier id in places of $t^\bullet \setminus P_{DB}$, and with identifier 0 in places of $t^\bullet \cap P_{DB}$ where $\{D_1', \ldots D_{k'}'\} = \cup_{p \in t^\bullet} X_p$ for some $X_p \in \langle t, p \rangle(D_1, \ldots, D_k)$. As $M_1 \leq M_2$, there exists an injective mapping h such that for every identifier x and every place p, $\pi_x(M_1(p)) \leq \pi_{h(x)}(M_2(p))$. This also yields, for each identifier x and each place p a map $\varphi_{p,x} : \pi_x(M_1(p)) \to \pi_{h(x)}(M_2(p))$, such that $D_i \leq \varphi_{p,x}(D_i)$. Let us denote by $\varphi = \bigcup \varphi_{p,x}$ the union of all these maps for $p \in P$, and x an identifier used in M_1

Since guards are monotonous and $D_i \leq \varphi(D_i)$, one has $\varphi(D_i) \models P_i$. From the monotony of queries we deduce that for every place $p \in {}^\bullet t$, there exists $X_p' \in \langle t, p \rangle(\varphi(D_1), \ldots, \varphi(D_k))$ with $X_p \leq X_p'$. Thus transition t is enabled in marking M_2 and $M_2[t\rangle M_2'$ with $M_2'(p) = (M_2 \setminus (\{\varphi(D_1), \ldots, \varphi(D_k)\} \cap M_2(p))) \cup X_p'$.

Let us now prove that $M_1' \leq M_2'$. We can design a set of injective maps $\varphi_{p,x}' : \pi_x(M_1'(p)) \to \pi_{h(x)}(M_2'(p))$ witnessing $M_1' \leq M_2'$. For every $D_i \in M_1(p) \cap M_1'(p)$, we define $\varphi_{p,x}'(D_i) = \varphi_{p,x}(D_i)$, as the documents that were not consumed remain unchanged and hence comparable in both markings. Then, for each newly created document D_i' in X_p, as $X_p \leq X_p'$, we necessarily have a document D_j' in X_p' such that $D_i' \leq D_j'$. Hence we can set $\varphi_{p,x}'(D_i') = D_j'$, and obtain $D \leq \varphi_{p,x}'(D)$ for every $D \in M_1'(p)$. Hence, the map $\varphi' = \bigcup \varphi_{p,x}'$ witnesses $M_1' \leq M_2'$. □

Coverability can be decided using a standard backward algorithm. For a set of markings X, we let $pre(X) = \{M \mid \exists t \in T, M' \in X, M[t\rangle M'\}$. We also let $basis(X)$ be a basis for an upward closed set X. Let M be the marking that one tries to cover. The algorithm iteratively computes basis for the sets of markings from which a marking in $\uparrow M$ can be reached in a finite number of steps. The algorithm starts from the set $X_0 = \{M\}$, that is a basis for all markings greater than M. Then it builds iteratively $X_{i+1} = X_i \cup basis(pre(\uparrow X_i))$, and stops when a fixed-point is reached, or as soon as there exists $M' \in X_i$ such that $M' \leq M_0$, indicating that there exists a sequence of transitions from M_0 to a marking greater than M. It was proved in [1,13] that this algorithms is correct and terminates for *effective* WSTS where effectiveness means that *i)* the comparison relation $\leq$ is effective and *ii)* (backward-effectiveness) one can effectively build a finite basis for $pre(\uparrow M)$.

Corollary 1 (Coverability). *Coverability is decidable for backward-effective wqo-StDN with monotonous patterns and queries.*

Proof. It remains to show that the comparison among markings is effective. For any pair of documents $D_1, D_2 \in Doc_\tau$, one can effectively check for the existence of a mapping from D_1 to D_2, and compare the values of paired data fields, as we have assumed that the domains of these data-fields are effective wqos. Then finding an identity preserving mapping among contents of places (finite multisets) is also effective. □

Backward effectiveness means that from an upward closed set of markings one can effectively build a finite representation of the data input to a transition that might have generated these contents. This property is easily met if the effect of a transition on a place is to aggregate finite amount of data collected from its input places (for instance the sum of positive integers collected in forms), or to append a new branch to a document (in this case, the input data can be obtained by considering subtrees of the documents appearing in the original marking).

Let us now show that this result on coverability allows to prove more properties. For a pattern P, we define $Sym(P)$ the *symbolic set of initial cases* induced by P as the set of documents satisfying P. We are now ready to address the termination, soundness, and coverability for symbolic sets of initial cases. The latter coverability question makes sense if one assumes that the query $\langle t_{in}, p_{in} \rangle$ generates $Sym(P)$. This is not always the case, and the set of documents generated by $\langle t_{in}, p_{in} \rangle$ needs not satisfy a single pattern P. It may even be the case that this set of initial cases is not upward closed (for instance, a query can generate documents which nodes carry only odd integer values). The coverability problem for the set of initial cases induced by P can be rephrased as follows: assuming $IMG(\langle t_{in}, p_{in} \rangle) = Sym(P)$, and given a marking M to cover, can one find an initial marking M_0 such that $M_0(p_{in}) \in Sym(P)$ and there exists M' greater than M in $\mathcal{R}(M_0)$?

Theorem 2. *Termination, soundness, and coverability for symbolic set of initial cases defined by a monotonous pattern are decidable properties on the class of backward-effective wqo-StDN with monotonous patterns and queries.*

Proof. The **termination** of a case associated with an identifier id is equivalent to the coverability of the marking with one token $(D_\perp, id)$ in place p_{out} (and all other places empty) by the marking resulting from the initialization of this case (using transition t_{in}) where $D_\perp$ is the least document (reduced to an untagged root). Decidability of **soundness** also stems from decidability of coverability. An StDN is sound if it terminates and whenever place p_{out} contains a token, one cannot find another place containing a token with the same identifier, i.e. for each place $p \in P \setminus \{p_{out}\}$ the marking M_p with token $(D_\perp, id)$ in both place p_{out} and p and with no other tokens is not coverable from the initial marking.

Coverability, termination and soundness have solutions for a single given initial marking, i.e. for a particular chosen case. We would like to consider whether transactions terminate or cover a given marking M for all or for some possible inputs to the system. We suppose that the set of results output by query $\langle t_{in}, p_{in} \rangle$ is the **symbolic set of documents** from $\mathrm{Doc}_{\tau, \leq n}$ that satisfy a particular monotonous pattern P. Then, one can compute the set $BSat(P)$ of documents obtained by replacing ancestor edges of P by sequences of edges with untagged nodes in such a way that the depth of the obtained document remains smaller than n, and replacing each constraint γ on values attached to a node of P by a value selected from a basis for the upward closed set of values satisfying γ. This basis exists as P is monotonous, and the domains are wqos. This set $BSat(P)$ forms a basis for all documents conforming to pattern P. Noticing that $\mathcal{R}(M) \leq \mathcal{R}(M')$ when $M \leq M'$ for wqo and backward effective StDNs with monotonous queries and patterns, coverability and termination can be verified for all cases initiated by $\langle t_{in}, p_{in} \rangle$ if it can be proved for all elements in $BSat(P)$. Note that it is sufficient to compute the fixed-point returned by the backward coverability algorithm and then compare this set with all minimal elements in $BSat(P)$.   □

The above decidability results do not extend to reachability:

Theorem 3 (Undecidability of reachability). *Reachability is undecidable, even for backward effective wqo-StDN with monotonous patterns and queries.*

Proof. An StDN can easily simulate reset Petri nets for which reachability is undecidable [12]. We need only to deal with place p_{in} (in order to conform with Definition 6 we can assume a transition t from p_{in} to p_{out} such that pattern $\langle p_{in}, t \rangle$ is never satisfied). The content of place p_{in} encodes a particular marking of the reset net: A document D with a root node and a child labeled p with n children indicates that place p of the reset net contains n tokens. This set of tokens can be manipulated as a whole, incremented or decremented by monotonous queries. Enabledness of a transition can be encoded by a pattern that tests the existence of a token in some place p, i.e. they are trees with a root, a child node tagged p and one children. Monotonous queries can be used to increment or decrement the number of children of a particular node tagged by p, encoding consumption or creation of tokens. Last, a query can remove all children of a document, simulating a reset arc. Such queries are monotonous, and transitions using this kind of queries are also backward effective. It is also obvious that one can design a transition that will fire only once, produce a set of documents encoding the initial marking of a reset net, and will then ignore all transactions produced by $\langle t_{in}, p_{in} \rangle$. Undecidability of the reachability problem for reset nets [12] concludes the proof. $\square$

This negative result should not be seen as a severe limitation: reachability is usually undecidable outside the class of Petri nets, and when considering transactional systems, properties of interest are usually not expressed in terms of global states. Let us remark from the above proof that encoding a reset Petri net with an StDN is straightforward. StDN can also simulate nested nets [22]. Nested nets are high-level nets, which tokens are markings of low-level nets (which can be easily modeled by structured documents of bounded depth, with a single id). They can evolve individually inside a place as standard Petri nets, or interact with the higher-level net (which can be simulated by a transition of an StDN). Synchronizations inside places of nested nets (involving two token-nets in a place) can also occur. In StDN, transitions use only one document from each place; however, synchronization inside a place p can be simulated by first moving one document from p, to another place p' and then firing a transition that uses this document and another document from p.

Proposition 4. *Well quasi orderedness of an StDN is undecidable. Coverability, reachability and termination problems are undecidable for wqo StDNs.*

Proof. We design a wqo StDN that encodes a two counters machine. A two counters machine is given as a pair of counters C_1, C_2 holding non-negative integers and a finite list of instructions $l_1, \ldots l_n$ each of which, except the last one, is of one of the following forms: *i)* $l_i : inc(C_\ell)$ meaning that we increment counter C_ℓ and then go to the following instruction, *ii)* $l_j :$ **if** $(C_\ell = 0)$, l_k **else** $dec(C_j)$, $l_{k'}$ indicating that if counter C_ℓ is null we must proceed to instruction l_k otherwise we decrement this counter and go to instruction $l_{k'}$. The machine halts when it reaches the last instruction $l_n : Halt$. A configuration of a counter machine is given by the value of its counters, and the current instruction line. The machine usually starts at instruction 0, with counters set to 0. It is well-known that one cannot decide if a counter machine halts. For any counter machine, we can define an StDN (represented in Figure 6) that encodes the moves of the machine.

First, we can encode a counter machine configuration as a document with three nodes: a root, and its left and right children. The root is tagged by an instruction number from $l_1, \ldots, l_n$, the left and right children are tagged by c_1 and c_2 respectively with values given by non-negative integers. The corresponding documents are of bounded depth with values from wqo domains. For each instruction of the form $l_i : inc(C_\ell)$, we design a transition t_i with ${}^\bullet t_i = t_i^\bullet = p_{in}$ such that $P_i = \langle p, t_i \rangle$ is the pattern reduced to a root whose tag has value l_i and $Q_i = \langle t_i, p \rangle$ is the query that transforms a document into a document with root l_{i+1}, and such that the value attached to the node with tag c_ℓ is incremented by one, and the other one is left unmodified. For each instruction of the form $l_j :$ **if** $(C_\ell = 0)$, l_k **else** $dec(C_j)$, $l_{k'}$ we design two transitions $t_{j,Z}$ and $t_{j,NZ}$ such that $P_{j,Z} = \langle p_{in}, t_{j,Z} \rangle$ is a pattern testing if the root of a document is labeled by l_j, and the value of node with tag c_ℓ is zero, $Q_{j,Z} = \langle t_{j,Z}, p_{in} \rangle$ is the query that transforms a document into a document with root l_k, and such that the values

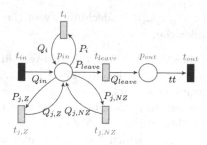

Fig. 6. Encoding a counter Machine with wqo Structured Data Nets

attached to child nodes remain unchanged, $P_{j,NZ} = \langle p_{in}, t_{j,NZ} \rangle$ is the pattern testing if the root of a document is labeled by l_j, and the value of node with tag c_ℓ is greater than zero, $Q_{j,NZ} = \langle t_{j,NZ}, p_{in} \rangle$ is the query that transforms a document into a document with root $l_{k'}$, and such that the value attached to node with tag c_ℓ is decremented by one and the value attached to the other child node remains unchanged. The initial configuration of the counter machine is created by query $Q_{in} = \langle t_{in}, p_{in} \rangle$ that produces a document with root labeled l_0 and two children nodes tagged respectively by c_1, c_2 with values 0. We set M_0 as an initial marking in which all places are empty. Transition t_{leave} moves the token from place p to p_{out} if the root tag has value l_n, i.e. the machine halted. Clearly, the counter machine terminates iff one can reach a configuration in which p_{out} is not empty. Thus one cannot decide termination, and similarly the reachability or coverability (of the marking with just one token in p_{out}).

Let us now prove that one can not decide whether a net is wqo. One can add a transition t_{nobnd} to the above net such that $^\bullet t_{nobnd} = t_{nobnd}^\bullet = p_{out}$, $\langle p_{out}, t_{nobnd} \rangle = tt$, and $\langle t_{nobnd}, p_{out} \rangle$ is a query that increases the depth of a document by 1, by inserting a children with some tag a between the root and its first child (hence creating successive incomparable documents). Then the counter machine terminates iff the corresponding StDN is not wqo.   □

Even though well quasi orderedness of a net is undecidable, acceptable restrictions ensure this property. In many systems, queries are used to extract data from a data-set (a list of records). The result is also a list of records that can be again assembled as a bounded depth document. Other queries compute new values from data-sets (sums, means, etc.) and insert the results is a new document (a "form") of bounded depth and size. So, one can restrict to queries that produce only documents of bounded depth, which values domains are finite sets or wqo sets such as integers without harming too much the expressiveness of the model. Form filling queries that manipulate integers, rationals or strings are also very often backward effective, provided the mechanisms used to select the nodes carrying the values of interest to fill a form are monotonous.

6   Conclusion

This paper has addressed an extension of Petri Nets whose transitions manipulate structured data via patterns and queries. Without limitations, this model is Turing Powerful. However, under some restrictions on the nature of queries and on the shape of documents some interesting properties, such as coverability, are decidable. We believe that limiting data to structured documents of bounded depth with wqo labels is a sensible approach: many information systems use strings, booleans, etc, but do not need real values with arbitrary precision.

Several improvements might be investigated. An important issue is to identify classes of data operations that allow StDNs to fall into decidable subclasses. Our coverability proof relies on backward effectiveness of transitions to guarantee effectiveness of the WSTS associated to a wqo StDN with monotonous queries and patterns. This does not identify a particular class of queries. To be practical, we would like to identify classes of non-trivial monotonous queries that ensure effectiveness. Decidability results for positive active XML [3], for instance, use another form of monotonicity: they assume that a document can only grow, which can be an adequate assumption in case management systems. Considering positive StDN could be a way to ensure effectiveness. Another improvement lies in pattern expressiveness: currently, only individual constraints on data values are attached to nodes. One could, however, consider patterns with constraints of the form $v.\sigma \leq v'.\sigma'$, involving values of several nodes, sets of patterns requiring matching on several documents from a place, boolean combinations of patterns,... and see how these extensions affect positive results. Another line of research concerns symbolic manipulation of upward closed sets of documents. So far, we have considered coverability for symbolic set of initial cases, but we can imagine to define symbolic sets of initial markings, database contents, or target markings to cover. We also want to consider extensions of the model with some essential features for web services and transactional systems, for example allowing for transaction cancellation. Such feature is currently not handled by our model: one can even remark that an StDN might not be sound, even when it is wqo and backward effective.

References

1. Abdulla, P.A., Cerans, K., Jonsson, B., Tsay, Y-K.: General decidability theorems for infinite-state systems. In: Proc. of LICS 1996, pp. 313–321. IEEE (1996)
2. Abiteboul, S., Benjelloun, O., Manolescu, I., Milo, T., Weber, R.: Active XML: A Data-Centric Perspective on Web Services. In: BDA02 (2002)
3. Abiteboul, S., Benjelloun, O., Milo, T.: Positive active XML. In: Proc. of PODS 2004, pp. 35–45. ACM (2004)
4. Acciai, L., Boreale, M.: Deciding safety properties in infinite-state pi-calculus via behavioural types. In: Albers, S., Marchetti-Spaccamela, A., Matias, Y., Nikoletseas, S., Thomas, W. (eds.) ICALP 2009, Part II. LNCS, vol. 5556, pp. 31–42. Springer, Heidelberg (2009)
5. Akshay, S., Hélouet, L., Mukund, M.: Sessions with an unbounded number of agents. In: ACSD 2014, vol. 4281, pp. 166–175. IEEE (2014)

6. Andrews, T., Curbera, F., Dholakia, H., Goland, Y., Klein, J., Leymann, F., Liu, K., Roller, D., Smith, D., Thatte, S., Trickovic, I., Weerawarana, S.: Business process execution language for Web services (BPEL4WS). version 1.1 (2003)
7. Badouel, E., Hélouët, L., Kouamou, G.-E., Morvan, C.: A grammatical approach to data-centric case management in a distributed collaborative environment. In: SAC 2015. ACM (2015)
8. Boreale, M., Bruni, R., De Nicola, R., Loreti, M.: Sessions and pipelines for structured service programming. In: Barthe, G., de Boer, F.S. (eds.) FMOODS 2008. LNCS, vol. 5051, pp. 19–38. Springer, Heidelberg (2008)
9. Bruni, R., Lanese, I., Melgratti, H., Tuosto, E.: Multiparty Sessions in SOC. In: Lea, D., Zavattaro, G. (eds.) COORDINATION 2008. LNCS, vol. 5052, pp. 67–82. Springer, Heidelberg (2008)
10. Damaggio, E., Deutsch, A., Vianu, V.: Artifact systems with data dependencies and arithmetic. ACM Trans. Database Syst. **37**(3), 22 (2012)
11. Ding, G.: Subgraphs and well-quasi-ordering. Journal of Graph Theory **16**(5), 489–502 (1992)
12. Dufourd, C., Finkel, A., Schnoebelen, P.: Reset nets between decidability and undecidability. In: Larsen, K.G., Skyum, S., Winskel, G. (eds.) ICALP 1998. LNCS, vol. 1443, p. 103. Springer, Heidelberg (1998)
13. Finkel, A., Schnoebelen, P.: Well-structured transition systems everywhere!. Theor. Comput. Sci. **256**(1–2), 63–92 (2001)
14. Genest, B., Muscholl, A., Wu, Z .: Verifying recursive active documents with positive data tree rewriting. In Proc. of FSTTCS 2010, volume 8 of LIPIcs, pp. 469–480. Schloss Dagstuhl - Leibniz-Zentrum fuer Informatik (2010)
15. Genrich, H.J.: Predicate/transition nets. In: Brauer, W., Reisig, W., Rozenberg, G. (eds.) Petri Nets: Central Models and Their Properties, Advances in Petri Nets 1986. LNCS, vol. 254, pp. 207–247. Springer, Heidelberg (1986)
16. Higman, G.: Ordering by divisibility in abstract algebras. Proc. London Math. Soc. **3**(2), 326–336 (1952)
17. Honda, K., Yoshida, N., Carbone, M.: Multiparty asynchronous session types. In: POPL, pp. 273–284. ACM (2008)
18. Hull, R., Damaggio, E., Fournier, F., Gupta, M., Heath III, F.T., Hobson, S., Linehan, M., Maradugu, S., Nigam, A., Sukaviriya, P., Vaculin, R.: Introducing the guard-stage-milestone approach for specifying business entity lifecycles (invited talk). In: Bravetti, M. (ed.) WS-FM 2010. LNCS, vol. 6551, pp. 1–24. Springer, Heidelberg (2011)
19. Jensen, K.: Coloured Petri Nets - Basic Concepts, Analysis Methods and Practical Use, vol. 1, 2nd edn. Monographs in Theoretical Computer Science, An EATCS Series (1996)
20. Lazic, R., Newcomb, T., Ouaknine, J., Roscoe, A.W., Worrell, J.: Nets with tokens which carry data. Fundam. Inform. **88**(3), 251–274 (2008)
21. Lenz, K., Oberweis, A.: Modeling interorganizational workflows with XML nets. In: 34th Annual Hawaii International Conference on System Sciences (HICSS-34) (2001)
22. Irina, A.: Lomazova and Ph. Schnoebelen. Some decidability results for nested Petri nets. In: Perspectives of System Informatics, pp. 208–220 (1999)
23. Misra, J., Cook, W.: Computation orchestration. Software and Systems Modeling **6**(1), 83–110 (2007)
24. Mlynkova, I., Toman, K., Pokorný, J.: Statistical analysis of real XML data collections. In: Proc. of International Conference on Management of Data 2006, pp. 15–26. Tata McGraw-Hill (2006)

25. Nigam, A., Caswell, N.S.: Business artifacts: An approach to operational specification. IBM Syst. J. **42**, 428–445 (2003)
26. OASIS. Web Services Business Process Execution Language. Technical report, OASIS (2007). http://docs.oasis-open.org/wsbpel/2.0/OS/wsbpel-v2.0-OS.pdf
27. Pugliese, R., Tiezzi, F.: A calculus for orchestration of Web services. J. Applied Logic **10**(1), 2–31 (2012)
28. Wies, T., Zufferey, D., Henzinger, T.A.: Forward analysis of depth-bounded processes. In: Ong, L. (ed.) FOSSACS 2010. LNCS, vol. 6014, pp. 94–108. Springer, Heidelberg (2010)
29. World Wide Web Consortium. XML path language (xpath). Technical report, W3C. W3C Recommendation (1999). http://www.w3.org/TR/xpath
30. World Wide Web Consortium. XQuery 1.0: An XML Query Language. Technical report, W3C. W3C Recommendation (1999). http://www.w3.org/TR/xquery

On the Reversibility of Live Equal-Conflict Petri Nets

Thomas Hujsa[1]([⊠]), Jean-Marc Delosme[2], and Alix Munier-Kordon[3]

[1] LIAFA, Université Paris Diderot - Paris 7 and CNRS UMR 7089, Paris, France
Thomas.Hujsa@liafa.univ-paris-diderot.fr
[2] Université d'Evry-Val-D'Essonne, IBISC, 91025 Evry, France
Jean-Marc.Delosme@ibisc.univ-evry.fr
[3] Sorbonne Universités, UPMC Paris 06, UMR 7606, LIP6, 75005 Paris, France
Alix.Munier@lip6.fr

Abstract. A Petri net is reversible if its initial marking is a home marking, a marking reachable from any reachable marking. This property is fundamental in man-made systems as it lets a system return to its initial state using only internal operations.

Necessary and sufficient conditions are already known for the reversibility of well-formed Choice-Free and ordinary Free-Choice nets. Like the homogeneous Join-Free nets, these nets constitute subclasses of Equal-Conflict nets. In this larger class, the reversibility property is not well understood.

This paper provides the first characterization of reversibility for all the live Equal-Conflict systems by extending, in a weaker form, a known condition that applies to the Choice-Free and Free-Choice subclasses. We also show that this condition is tightly related to the Equal-Conflict class and does not apply to several other classes.

Keywords: Reversibility · Home markings · Liveness · Weighted petri nets · Characterization · Equal-conflict · Join-free · Choice-free · Free-choice

1 Introduction

Liveness and reversibility are behavioral properties of Petri nets that are fundamental for many real world applications. These systems (such as embedded or flexible manufacturing systems) have to keep all their functions (transitions) active over time, a condition modeled by the liveness property. These systems often also require a steady, regular, behavior and the possibility of returning to some particular states (markings) using only internal operations, a condition modeled by the reversibility property.

A system is *live* if any transition can be fired after a finite number of steps from any reachable marking. The markings that are reachable from every

T. Hujsa — The work of this author is supported by Digiteo / Project Tatami.

R. Devillers and A. Valmari (Eds.): PETRI NETS 2015, LNCS 9115, pp. 234–253, 2015.
DOI: 10.1007/978-3-319-19488-2_12

reachable marking–when they exist–are called *home markings*. A Petri net is *reversible*, or *cyclic*, if its initial marking is a home marking, in which case all reachable markings are home markings. Reversibility avoids a costly transient phase and favors a steady behavior from the start. Besides, it often simplifies substantially the study of the reachability graph.

Importance of Weights. In this study, we focus on weighted Petri nets, which are well suited to the modeling of real-life systems. In the domain of embedded systems, Synchronous Data Flow graphs [8], equivalent to particular weighted Petri nets, have been introduced to model the communications between a finite set of periodic processes. In the domain of flexible manufacturing systems (FMS), the weights make possible the modeling of bulk consumption or production of resources [15]. In these cases, weights allow a compact representation of the volumes of data or resources exchanged.

Important Weighted Subclasses. We focus on subclasses of weighted Petri nets that are defined by structural restrictions. A net is *homogeneous* if each place has all its outputs weights equal. The Equal-Conflict systems form a homogeneous subclass where transitions that have a common input place share the same set of input places.

This class generalizes several important subclasses of Petri nets. It contains the Choice-Free systems, also known as output non-branching systems [3], in which every place has at most one output transition. Weighted T-systems—equivalent to Synchronous Data Flow graphs—are Choice-Free systems where each place has at most one input transition. The homogeneous Join-Free Petri nets form a subclass of Equal-Conflict nets in which each transition has at most one input place. The homogeneous S-systems are homogeneous Join-Free systems in which each transition has at most one output place.

Previous Results. The problem of checking the reversibility property is decidable [1,4], although its complexity is unknown. If the system is supposed to be bounded, a naive exponential algorithm would check the strong connectedness of its reachability graph. Moreover, neither one of the properties of liveness and reversibility implies the other [11].

The relation between liveness and reversibility has been studied in several weighted subclasses. The systems considered are often bounded, that is, with a bounded number of tokens in every place for all the reachable markings. Well-formedness is also commonly assumed for the net, ensuring the boundedness of the system for any initial marking and the existence of at least one live marking. Liveness and reversibility are equivalent for any well-formed T-system [14]. For well-formed Choice-Free systems, a characterization of reversibility was expressed in terms of the reversibility of particular subsystems under the liveness assumption in [7]. For the same class, a necessary and sufficient condition for the conjunction of liveness and reversibility was given in [15], which also applies to well-formed ordinary Free-Choice nets [5]. To our knowledge, no result of similar strength exists for homogeneous S-systems, hence for larger classes.

Nevertheless, for Equal-Conflict systems, some characterizations of liveness have been uncovered. Under the well-formedness assumption, there exist a structural necessary and sufficient condition of liveness [17] and a checking method [16]. Also, the existence of reachable home markings is a necessary condition for the combined liveness and boundedness of an Equal-Conflict system [17].

Liveness and reversibility have been studied in many other classes, notably liveness in [2] and reversibility in [6].

Contributions. Our main contribution is a necessary and sufficient condition of reversibility for live, not necessarily bounded, Equal-Conflict systems. It is based on the existence of a *feasible T-sequence*, which is a sequence returning to the initial marking and where each transition is fired at least once.

The existence of a T-sequence is a necessary and sufficient condition for a well-formed Choice-Free system to be both live and reversible [15]. We exhibit a simple counter-example for the homogeneous S-system class. Consequently, the condition does not extend to the Equal-Conflict class.

We show easily that the existence of a feasible T-sequence is a necessary condition for a system to be both live and reversible. The major result is the proof that, for live Equal-Conflict systems, the existence of a T-sequence is also a sufficient condition of reversibility. We also provide various counter-examples showing that this characterization does not extend to several larger classes.

Organization of the Paper. In Section 2, we give general definitions, detail notations and properties of Petri nets, and define the subclasses that we study in the paper. In Section 3, we investigate the relationship between liveness and reversibility in weighted Petri nets and several bounded subclasses. We also introduce the notion of T-sequence and highlight its importance for the reversibility property. In Section 4, we explore a particular definition of fairness in Equal-Conflict nets and exploit it to prove the characterization of reversibility for all the live Equal-Conflict systems. In Section 5, we show by means of counter-examples that this characterization of reversibility does not extend to several classes of Petri nets. Finally, Section 6 is our conclusion.

2   Definitions, Notations and Properties

We first recall definitions and notations for weighted nets, markings, systems and firing sequences. Classical notions, such as liveness and boundedness, are formalized. Lastly, special classes of nets, including Choice-Free, Join-Free and Equal-Conflict nets, are recalled.

2.1   Weighted and Ordinary Nets

A *(weighted) net* is a triple $N = (P, T, W)$ where:

- the sets P and T are finite and disjoint, T contains transitions and P places,

- $W : (P \times T) \cup (T \times P) \mapsto \mathbb{N}$ is a weight function.

$P \cup T$ is the set of the nodes of the net.

An arc leads from a place p to a transition t (respectively a transition t to a place p) if $W(p, t) > 0$ (respectively $W(t, p) > 0$). An *ordinary* net is a net whose weight function W has values in $\{0, 1\}$.

The *incidence matrix* of a net $N = (P, T, W)$ is a place-transition matrix C defined as

$$\forall p \in P \ \forall t \in T, \quad C[p, t] = W(t, p) - W(p, t)$$

where the weight of each non-existing arc is 0. The weight function W can be represented by two place-transition matrices *Pre* and *Post* defined as follows: $\forall p \in P, \forall t \in T, Pre[p, t] = W(p, t)$ and $Post[p, t] = W(t, p)$. Consequently, the incidence matrix can be defined as $C = Post - Pre$.

The *pre-set* of the element x of $P \cup T$ is the set $\{w | W(w, x) > 0\}$, denoted by ${}^\bullet x$. By extension, for any subset E of P or T, ${}^\bullet E = \bigcup_{x \in E} {}^\bullet x$. The *post-set* of the element x of $P \cup T$ is the set $\{y | W(x, y) > 0\}$, denoted by $x^\bullet$. Similarly, $E^\bullet = \bigcup_{x \in E} x^\bullet$.

We denote by max_p^N the maximum output weight of p in the net N. The simpler notation max_p is used when no confusion is possible.

A *join-transition* is a transition having at least two input places.

2.2 Markings, Systems and Firing Sequences

A *marking* M of a net N is a mapping $M : P \to \mathbb{N}$. A *system* is a couple (N, M_0) where N is a net and M_0 its initial marking.

A marking M of a net N *enables* a transition $t \in T$ if $\forall p \in {}^\bullet t, M(p) \geq W(p, t)$. Generalizing to sets, a set T of transitions is enabled by M if every transition of T is enabled by M. A marking M *enables* a place $p \in P$ if $M(p) \geq max_p$. Generalizing to sets, a set P of places is enabled by M if every place of P is enabled by M.

The marking M' obtained from M by firing an enabled transition t, denoted by $M \xrightarrow{t} M'$, is defined by $\forall p \in P, M'(p) = M(p) - W(p, t) + W(t, p)$.

A *firing sequence* σ on the set of transitions T is a mapping $\{1, \ldots, n\} \to T$ with $n \geq 1$, or $\mathbb{N} \to T$; it is finite of length n in the first case and infinite otherwise. A firing sequence $\sigma = t_1 t_2 \cdots t_n$ is *feasible* if the successive markings obtained, $M_0 \xrightarrow{t_1} M_1 \xrightarrow{t_2} M_2 \cdots \xrightarrow{t_n} M_n$, are such that M_{i-1} enables the transition t_i for any $i \in \{1, \cdots, n\}$. We note $M_0 \xrightarrow{\sigma} M_n$.

The *Parikh vector* $\vec{\sigma} : T \to \mathbb{N}$ associated with a finite sequence of transitions σ maps every transition t of T to the number of occurrences of t in σ.

A marking M' is said to be *reachable* from the marking M if there exists a feasible firing sequence σ such that $M \xrightarrow{\sigma} M'$. The set of markings reachable from M is denoted by $[M\rangle$.

A *home marking* is a marking that can be reached from any reachable marking. Formally, M is a home marking in the system (N, M_0) if $\forall M' \in [M_0\rangle, M \in [M'\rangle$. A system is *reversible* if its initial marking is a home marking.

2.3   Liveness and Boundedness

Liveness and boundedness are two basic properties ensuring that all transitions of a system $S = (N, M_0)$ can always be fired and that the overall number of tokens remains bounded. More formally,

- A system S is *live* if for every marking M in $[M_0\rangle$ and for every transition t, there exists a marking M' in $[M\rangle$ enabling t.
- S is *bounded* if there exists an integer k such that the number of tokens in each place never exceeds k. Formally, $\exists k \in \mathbb{N}\ \forall M \in [M_0\rangle\ \forall p \in P,\ M(p) \leq k$. S is k-*bounded* if, for any place $p \in P$, $k \geq \max\{M(p)|M \in [M_0\rangle\}$.
- A system S is *well-behaved* if it is live and bounded.

A marking M is live (respectively bounded) for a net N if the system (N, M) is live (respectively bounded). The structure of a net N may be studied to ensure the existence of an initial marking M_0 such that (N, M_0) is live and bounded:

- N is *structurally live* if a marking M_0 exists such that (N, M_0) is live.
- N is *structurally bounded* if the system (N, M_0) is bounded for each M_0.
- N is *well-formed* if it is structurally live and structurally bounded.

The algebraic properties of consistency and conservativeness are necessary conditions for well-formedness for all weighted Petri nets [10,13]. They are defined next in terms of the existence of particular annulers of the incidence matrix.

2.4   Semiflows, Consistency and Conservativeness

Semiflows are particular left or right annulers of an incidence matrix C that is supposed to be non-empty:

- A P-semiflow is a non-null vector $X \in \mathbb{N}^{|P|}$ such that $X^T \cdot C = 0$.
- A T-semiflow is a non-null vector $Y \in \mathbb{N}^{|T|}$ such that $C \cdot Y = 0$.

We denote by $\mathcal{I}(V)$ the set of the indices of the vector V. The *support* of a vector V, denoted by $|V|$, is defined as the largest subset of $\mathcal{I}(V)$ being associated to non-zero components of V, meaning that $\forall i \in |V|, V[i] \neq 0$ and $\forall i \in \mathcal{I}(V) \setminus |V|$, $V[i] = 0$. A P-semiflow is *minimal* if the greatest common divisor of its components is equal to 1 and its support is not a proper superset of the support of any other P-semiflow. Minimal T-semiflows are defined similarly.

We denote by $\mathbb{1}^n$ the column vector of size n whose components are all equal to 1. The conservativeness and consistency properties are defined as follows using the incidence matrix C of a net N:

- N is *conservative* if a P-semiflow $X \in \mathbb{N}^{|P|}$ exists for C such that $X \geq \mathbb{1}^{|P|}$.
- N is *consistent* if a T-semiflow $Y \in \mathbb{N}^{|T|}$ exists for C such that $Y \geq \mathbb{1}^{|T|}$.

The net on Figure 1 is conservative and consistent.

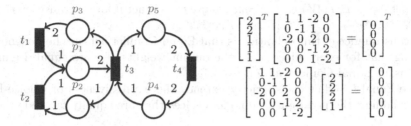

Fig. 1. This weighted net is conservative (the left vector $[2, 2, 1, 1, 1]$ is a P-semiflow and its components are ≥ 1) and consistent (the right vector $[2, 2, 2, 1]^T$ is a T-semiflow and its components are ≥ 1).

2.5 Choice-Free Nets, Join-Free Nets and Subclasses

The following basic subclasses of weighted Petri nets are defined by structural restrictions on the number of inputs or outputs of nodes. By studying these particular structures, the understanding of the behavior has been improved in several larger classes [12, 17].

In Choice-Free nets, each place has at most one output transition, meaning that choices are not allowed. More formally, $N = (P, T, W)$ is a *Choice-Free net* if $\forall p \in P$, $|p^\bullet| \leq 1$.

In Join-Free nets, each transition has at most one input place, meaning that synchronizations are not allowed. More formally, $N = (P, T, W)$ is a *Join-Free net* if $\forall t \in T$, $|{}^\bullet t| \leq 1$.

The net of Figure 1 is Choice-Free but not Join-Free: t_3 is a join-transition.

A net N is a *Fork-Attribution net* (or FA net) if it is a Choice-Free net and a Join-Free net. A net is an *S-net* if every transition has at most one input and one output. A net is a *T-net* if every place has at most one input and one output.

2.6 Equal-Conflict Relation, Sets, Nets and Larger Classes

In order to consider nets that are more expressive than the basic Choice-Free or Join-Free classes, some choices or synchronizations must be allowed.

However, in presence of structural choices, the behavior depends on the resolution of conflicts, which is limited by the preconditions of the conflicting transitions and by the current marking. When these preconditions are identical, all the alternatives are equivalent and the study of the behavior is simplified.

This notion of equal preconditions is captured by the next relation on the transitions of any weighted net, which was defined in [17].

Let $N = (P, T, W)$ be a net. Two transitions t, t' of T are in *equal conflict relation* if $Pre[P, t] = Pre[P, t'] \neq \mathbb{0}^{|P|}$, where $Pre[P, t]$ denotes the t-th column of the matrix Pre. It is an equivalence relation on the set of transitions, and each equivalence class is an *equal conflict set*.

We deduce that an equal conflict set is enabled by a marking M if and only if at least one transition of this set is enabled by M.

A net $N = (P, T, W)$ is an *Equal-Conflict* (EC) net if for all transitions t and t' of N, ${}^\bullet t \cap {}^\bullet t' \neq \varnothing \Rightarrow Pre[P, t] = Pre[P, t']$.

A consequence of this definition is that Equal-Conflict nets are homogeneous, meaning that for every place p, all the output weights of p are equal. Figure 2 contains an Equal-Conflict net on the left.

The Equal-Conflict class strictly extends the expressiveness of Choice-Free nets by adding the possibility to model choices that are equally favored.

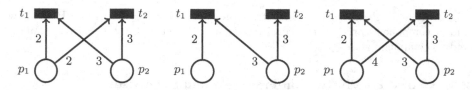

Fig. 2. The net on the left is an Equal-Conflict net. In the middle, ${}^\bullet t_1 = \{p_1, p_2\} \neq \{p_2\} = {}^\bullet t_2$, hence the net is not Equal-Conflict. On the right, the pre-sets of both transitions are equal, however it is not Equal-Conflict since it is not homogeneous: the output weights of p_1 are not all equal.

Finally, we recall the following well-known classes, whose weighted versions generalize the Equal-Conflict class.

Free-Choice nets are ordinary (unit-weighted) Equal-Conflict nets. The weighted generalization of this class encompasses the Equal-Conflict nets and is depicted on the right in Figure 2.

A net $N = (P, T, W)$, either ordinary or weighted, is *Asymmetric-Choice* if $\forall p_1, p_2 \in P$, $p_1^\bullet \cap p_2^\bullet \neq \varnothing \Rightarrow p_1^\bullet \subseteq p_2^\bullet$ or $p_2^\bullet \subseteq p_1^\bullet$. A weighted homogeneous Asymmetric-Choice net is shown in the middle of Figure 2.

Figure 3 represents the inclusion relations between the special subclasses of weighted Petri nets considered in this paper.

3   Liveness, Reversibility and T-sequences

We recall known results and provide examples that explain some interactions between liveness and reversibility in weighted subclasses. We then introduce the notion of T-sequence and study its importance in relation with these properties.

3.1   Previous Results on the Reversibility of Live Systems

Since we are interested in systems that are both live and reversible, we first illustrate some relations between these properties. While, under the well-formedness assumption, liveness is equivalent to reversibility in weighted T-systems [14], it does not imply reversibility in weighted Fork-Attribution systems and homogeneous S-systems, as illustrated in Figure 4.

Thus, since a live system may not be reversible, other notions, such as T-sequences, must be introduced to study the reversibility property.

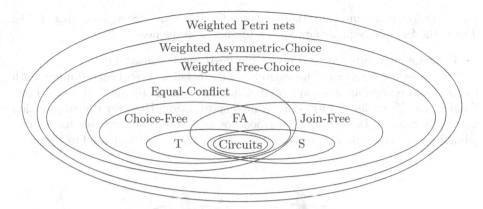

Fig. 3. Some classes and subclasses of weighted systems.

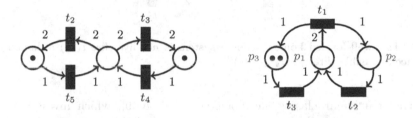

Fig. 4. On the left, a live S-system. On the right, a live Fork-Attribution system. None of them is reversible.

3.2 T-sequences

We introduce next the notion of *T-sequence* and show that the existence of such a sequence is necessary to have both liveness and reversibility.

Definition 1 (T-sequences, partial T-sequences). *Consider a Petri net with set of transitions T. A T-sequence is a sequence whose Parikh vector is equal to a T-semiflow whose support is T. A partial T-sequence is a sequence whose Parikh vector is equal to a T-semiflow whose support is different from T.*

The alternative expressions *feasible* or *realizable T-semiflow* may be found in the literature when there exists a feasible (partial or not) T-sequence. Such a sequence, when feasible at the initial marking, defines *weak reversibility* in [14].

The next lemma provides a necessary condition to obtain both liveness and reversibility.

Lemma 1. *If a system $S = (N, M_0)$ is live and reversible, then it enables a T-sequence.*

Proof. Suppose that the system is live and reversible. By the liveness assumption, there exists a feasible sequence σ_0 whose support is the set of all transitions. By the reversibility assumption, there exists a feasible sequence σ_1 returning to M_0. Thus, the feasible sequence $\sigma_0 \sigma_1$ is a feasible T-sequence.   □

Consequently, any live and reversible Petri net is consistent.

In the other direction, the existence of a feasible T-sequence implies both liveness and reversibility in (weighted) Choice-Free nets [15] and (ordinary) Free-Choice nets [5] under the well-formedness assumption. However this implication is false in general. Indeed, a well-formed homogeneous S-system may have a feasible T-sequence while it is neither live nor reversible, as illustrated in Figure 5.

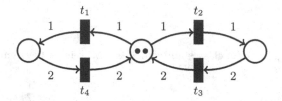

Fig. 5. This well-formed homogeneous S-system is not live (fire $t_1 t_2$) although a T-sequence is feasible (fire $t_1 t_1 t_4 t_2 t_2 t_3$).

Other particular classes have been studied in [9], which investigates the relationship between the reversibility property and the existence of reachable markings that enable a partial T-sequence associated to a minimal T-semiflow.

This fact justifies the study of reversibility under liveness hypothesis in the next section. We also show in that section that the existence of a feasible T-sequence is sufficient for reversibility in the Equal-Conflict class when liveness is assumed.

4   Reversibility of Live Equal-Conflict Systems

Under the liveness hypothesis, we investigate the reversibility property in Equal-Conflict systems, which may be unbounded. First, we define a notion of fairness and develop an associated property for sequences. Then, we use the fairness to facilitate the proof of the characterization of reversibility for all live Equal-Conflict systems.

4.1   Fairness in Equal-Conflict Systems

Taking inspiration from [17], we define a *fairness* property adapted to the Equal-Conflict class. Then, we present a result about fairness that will prove useful for the study of the reversibility property.

Definition 2 (Fairness in Equal-Conflict systems). *An infinite firing sequence is* globally fair *if it fires every transition of the system an infinite number of times. An infinite firing sequence is* locally fair *if*

- *when an equal conflict set contains a transition that is fired an infinite number of times, all of its transitions are fired an infinite number of times, and*
- *when an equal conflict set is enabled, one of its transitions is fired after a finite number of firings.*

The following theorem is similar to a result of [17] which uses a slightly different definition of fairness. Comparing with [17], we replace the boundedness and strong connectedness assumptions by the liveness assumption.

Theorem 1 (Fairness in live Equal-Conflict systems). *Let S be a live Equal-Conflict system. An infinite sequence σ that is feasible in S is globally fair if and only if it is locally fair.*

Proof. If σ is globally fair, it is easy to see that σ is locally fair. Let us prove the converse. Suppose that σ is locally fair.

Denote by Q the set of the equal conflict sets containing a transition that occurs infinitely often in σ and by $\overline{Q}$ the set of the other equal conflict sets. The set Q is non-empty since there is only a finite number of equal conflict sets and σ is infinite. If $\overline{Q}$ is empty, then we are done. Now suppose that $\overline{Q}$ is non-empty.

By definition of Q and by the local fairness assumption, all the transitions of the sets in Q are fired an infinite number of times in σ, while all the transitions of the sets in $\overline{Q}$ are fired a finite number of times and become forever non-enabled after the firing of a finite prefix sequence σ_0 of σ. Denote by M the marking reached by firing σ_0 in S and by σ' the infinite suffix sequence of σ satisfying $\sigma = \sigma_0 \sigma'$.

By the liveness assumption, there exists a transition t in $\overline{Q}$ and a finite sequence σ_1 feasible at M such that σ_1 contains only transitions of Q and enables t. The sequence σ_1 may not be a prefix of σ', however all the transitions of Q are fired an infinite number of times in σ'. We deduce that a finite prefix sequence σ_2 of σ' exists such that $\vec{\sigma}_2 \geq \vec{\sigma}_1$. Moreover, since only transitions of $\overline{Q}$ are structurally allowed to remove tokens from the inputs of t, the transition t becomes enabled after the firing of the finite sequence $\sigma_0 \sigma_2$, contradicting the fact that every transition of $\overline{Q}$ stays forever non-enabled after the firing of σ_0. Thus, $\overline{Q}$ is empty and σ is globally fair. □

In the following, we will use fair sequences to study the reversibility of live Equal-Conflict systems.

4.2 A Characterization of Reversibility under the Liveness Assumption

By Lemma 1, in every live Petri net, the existence of a feasible T-sequence is necessary for reversibility. We show that it is also sufficient for the class of live Equal-Conflict nets.

To obtain the sufficiency, we show that after the firing of any feasible sequence, we can use the T-sequence to construct another sequence that leads to the initial marking.

Starting from an initial marking, any firing sequence that is a prefix of a feasible T-sequence can be trivially completed to reach the initial marking again. More generally, any firing sequence that solves conflicts by following the local ordering induced by the adequate multiple of the T-sequence can be completed to reach the initial marking. However, if a transition is fired that solves a conflict by following a different ordering, the possibility to reach the initial marking is not ensured anymore. The occurrences of other transitions in the same conflicting set that should have been fired earlier are called *delayed occurrences*.

The proof of the characterization is constructive and makes use of two algorithms that compute this sequence. The first algorithm (Algorithm 1) fires at least all the delayed occurrences and returns the corresponding sequence σ_t. The second algorithm (Algorithm 2) starts after the end of the first algorithm and builds a sequence σ_t' returning to the initial marking. These two sequences are illustrated in Figure 6.

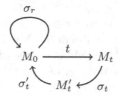

Fig. 6. If the T-sequence σ_r is feasible and t is fired, then Algorithm 1 builds the sequence σ_t and Algorithm 2 computes the sequence σ_t', which returns to the initial marking.

Notations. For every transition t, we denote by E^t the equal conflict set containing t. We introduce σ^n, n being a positive integer, to denote the concatenation of the sequence σ taken n times, and represent its infinite concatenation by σ^∞.

The notation $K_{t_i}^n(\sigma)$, $n \geq 1$, or more simply $K_i^n(\sigma)$, denotes the largest prefix sequence of σ preceding the n-th occurrence of t_i in σ, thus containing $n-1$ occurrences of t_i. For example, considering the sequence $\sigma = t_1\, t_2\, t_1\, t_3\, t_1\, t_2\, t_3$, $K_{t_1}^3(\sigma) = t_1\, t_2\, t_1\, t_3$ and $K_{t_3}^1(\sigma) = t_1\, t_2\, t_1$.

Consider an equal-conflict set E and sequences τ and κ such that $\vec{\tau} < \vec{\kappa}$. Assume there exists a transition t in E for which $\vec{\tau}(t) < \vec{\kappa}(t)$. Consider for each transition t' in E such that $\vec{\tau}(t') < \vec{\kappa}(t')$, its next occurrence in κ after its $\vec{\tau}(t')$-th occurrence. The transition t' in E whose next occurrence is the first to appear in κ is returned by a function, called the next transition function and denoted by $tnext(E, \tau, \kappa)$. Figure 7 illustrates these notations.

Algorithm 1 determines a way of firing the delayed occurrences while following the local ordering induced by the T-sequence in every other equal conflict set. Lemma 2 shows the termination of this algorithm. Then, Lemma 3 provides an equality indicating a match between occurrence counts.

The next technical lemma proves the termination of Algorithm 1, which computes a particular sequence σ_t and is illustrated in Figure 8.

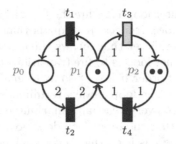

Fig. 7. The equal conflict sets are $E^{t_1} = \{t_1, t_3\}$, $E^{t_2} = \{t_2\}$ and $E^{t_4} = \{t_4\}$. Consider the feasible sequence $\sigma = t_4\,t_4\,t_1\,t_3\,t_1\,t_2\,t_3$. The subsequences of σ obtained by projection on each set, $\sigma_1 = t_1\,t_3\,t_1\,t_3$, $\sigma_2 = t_2$ and $\sigma_4 = t_4\,t_4$, define local orderings. Define $\tau = t_3\,t_4\,t_1$. Then $\vec{\sigma} > \vec{\tau}$, and the next transition to be fired in E^{t_1} is the one whose next occurrence appears first in σ_1. Since $\vec{\tau}(t_1) = 1$ and $\vec{\tau}(t_3) = 1$, we deduce that $tnext(E^{t_1}, \tau, \sigma) = t_1$.

Algorithm 1. Construction of a sequence σ_t that fires the delayed transitions of E^t by following the ordering of the T-sequence σ_r

---

Data: The system (N, M_t) obtained by firing t in S, the feasible T-sequence σ_r.
Result: The sequence σ_t that is feasible in (N, M_t) and fires the delayed occurrences of $\kappa_0 = K_t^1(\sigma_r)$.

1   $\tau := t$;

2   **while** $\exists\, t' \in E^t \setminus \{t\},\ \vec{\kappa}_0(t') > \vec{\tau}(t')$ **do**

3   **while** *the equal conflict set E^t is not enabled* **do**

4   Among the transitions that belong to enabled equal conflict sets, fire the transition t_i whose next occurrence after the $\vec{\tau}(t_i)$-th appears first in $(\sigma_r)^\infty$;

5          $\tau := \tau\, t_i$;

6   **end**

7   Fire the transition $t_j = tnext(E^t, \tau, \kappa_0)$;

8      $\tau := \tau\, t_j$;

9   **end**

10   τ is of the form $t\,\sigma_t$;
11   **return** σ_t

Lemma 2. *Let (N, M_0) be a live Equal-Conflict system in which a T-sequence σ_r is feasible. Then, for every transition t enabled by M_0, with $M_0 \xrightarrow{t} M_t$, Algorithm 1 terminates and computes the sequence σ_t that is feasible at M_t.*

Proof. Consider the marking M_t reached by firing a transition t from M_0. We prove that Algorithm 1 computes such a sequence σ_t that is feasible at M_t.

The objective of the outer loop is to fire the transitions different from t in E^t until the number of their occurrences in τ equals that in κ_0. Every time E^t is enabled, a firing occurs in this set that follows the order of κ_0 until completion.

The objective of the inner loop is to fire transitions that do not belong to E^t by following the associated order in $(\sigma_r)^\infty$ so as to enable E^t.

Let us show that the inner loop always terminates and enables E^t. First, by the liveness assumption, every reachable marking enables at least one equal conflict set. Now suppose that the inner loop does not terminate. Consequently, an infinite feasible sequence τ is fired that never enables E^t. Since the firings in the loop follow the order of $(\sigma_r)^\infty$ and the support of σ_r is T, the sequence τ is locally fair, thus globally fair by Theorem 1, contradicting the fact that E^t never becomes enabled. We deduce that E^t becomes enabled and the inner loop terminates.

We now prove the termination of the algorithm. Since the inner loop always terminates, a transition t_j is fired at the end of every iteration of the outer loop such that $\vec{\kappa}_0(t_j) > \vec{\tau}(t_j)$ and t_j is concatenated to the current τ, decreasing the number of remaining steps to attain $\vec{\kappa}_0(t_j)$. Hence the outer loop terminates. $\square$

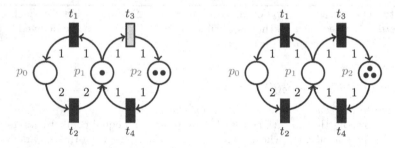

Fig. 8. Consider the T-sequence $\sigma_r = t_1 t_4 t_1 t_2 t_3$, which is feasible for the system (N, M_0) on the left. Setting $t = t_3$, (N, M_t) is pictured on the right. Since the first output transition of p_1 to be fired in σ_r is $t_1 \neq t_3$, two occurrences of t_1 are delayed. Starting from the system on the right, Algorithm 1 constructs the sequence σ_t that fires the delayed occurrences while following the local ordering in every other place. Before the loop, $\tau = t_3$ and $\kappa_0 = K^1_{t_3}(\sigma_r) = t_1 t_4 t_1 t_2$. The sequence computed is $\sigma_t = t_4 t_1 t_4 t_1$.

In Algorithm 1, the firings that did not belong to E^t followed the order of σ_r^∞. At the end, there is no delayed occurrence of any transition in E^t. We deduce the next property on the number of occurrences in τ.

Lemma 3 (Property of $\tau = t\,\sigma_t$). *Let $S = (N, M_0)$ be a live Equal-Conflict system in which a T-sequence σ_r is feasible. Consider the sequence σ_t constructed by Algorithm 1 after the firing of any transition t in S. Consider the sequences $\tau = t\,\sigma_t$ and $\kappa = \sigma_r^\alpha$ where $\alpha \geq 1$ is the smallest integer such that $\vec{\tau} \leq \alpha \cdot \vec{\sigma}_r$. Then, for each equal-conflict set E such that $t_u = tnext(E, \tau, \kappa)$ is defined, with $m = \vec{\tau}(t_u) + 1$ and $K_u = K^m_u(\kappa)$, and for every transition $t' \in E$, $\vec{\tau}(t') = \vec{K}_u(t')$. For every other equal-conflict set E, for each transition t' in E, $\vec{\tau}(t') = \vec{\kappa}(t')$.*

Proof. Algorithm 1 terminates by Lemma 2. At the end of the outer loop, for every equal-conflict set E such that $t_u = tnext(E, \tau, \kappa)$ with $\vec{\tau}(t_u) < \vec{\kappa}(t_u)$, two cases have to be considered.

If t_u does not belong to E^t, then all firings of E appeared in the same order and are as many in τ as in K_u in the inner loop. We deduce that every transition t' of E satisfies $\vec{\tau}(t') = \vec{K}_u(t')$. Otherwise, t_u belongs to E^t and the first loop fired precisely all the occurrences of E^t that belong to κ_0, in addition to the first unique firing of t. Thus, every transition t' of E^t satisfies $\vec{\tau}(t') = \vec{K}_u(t')$.

Finally, in every other equal-conflict set, there is no transition t_u such that $\vec{\tau}(t_u) < \vec{\kappa}(t_u)$. Since $\vec{\tau} \le \vec{\kappa}$, we deduce the second equality. $\qquad\square$

At the end of Algorithm 1, take the example of Figure 8, with $E^{t_1} = \{t_1, t_3\}$, $E^{t_2} = \{t_2\}$, $E^{t_4} = \{t_4\}$, $\tau = t_3 \sigma_t = t_3 t_4 t_1 t_4 t_1$ and $\kappa = (\sigma_r)^2$.

For E^{t_1}, $tnext(E^{t_1}, \tau, \kappa) = t_1$, $K_1 = t_1 t_4 t_1 t_2 t_3$, $\vec{\tau}(t_1) = 2 = \vec{K}_1(t_1)$ and $\vec{\tau}(t_3) = 1 = \vec{K}_1(t_3)$.

For E^{t_2}, $tnext(E^{t_2}, \tau, \kappa) = t_2$, $K_2 = t_1 t_4 t_1$ and $\vec{\tau}(t_2) = 0 = \vec{K}_2(t_2)$.

For E^{t_4}, the second equality of the lemma is satisfied: $\vec{\tau}(t_4) = 2 = \vec{\kappa}(t_4)$.

Using Lemma 3, the next theorem shows that Algorithm 2 builds a sequence σ'_t that is feasible after the firing of $\tau = t \sigma_t$ and reaches the initial marking. The sequence is illustrated in Figure 6 and an application of this second algorithm is presented in Figure 9.

Algorithm 2. Computation of the feasible sequence σ'_t

Data: The sequences $\tau = t \sigma_t$ and $\kappa = (\sigma_r)^\alpha$, the marking M'_t such that
$$M_0 \xrightarrow{\tau} M'_t$$
Result: The completion sequence σ'_t that is feasible in (N, M'_t) such that
$$M'_t \xrightarrow{\sigma'_t} M_0$$

1 **while** $\vec{\tau} \ne \vec{\kappa}$ **do**
2 $\quad$ Fire the transition t_i whose next occurrence after its $\vec{\tau}(t_i)$-th appears first in $\quad \kappa$;
3 $\quad$ $\tau := \tau t_i$;
4 **end**
5 τ is of the form $t \sigma_t \sigma'_t$;
6 **return** σ'_t

Theorem 2. *Let $S = (N, M_0)$ be a live Equal-Conflict system, with $N = (P, T, W)$. Suppose there exists a feasible T-sequence σ_r in S. For every transition t enabled by M_0 such that $M_0 \xrightarrow{t} M_t$, there exists a sequence σ^* that is feasible at M_t such that $\sigma = t \sigma^*$ is a T-sequence satisfying $\vec{\sigma} = k \cdot \vec{\sigma}_r$ for some integer $k \ge 1$.*

Proof. In the rest of the proof, we note $\kappa_0 = K_t^1(\sigma_r)$ the largest prefix sequence of σ_r preceding the first occurrence of t, meaning that σ_r is of the form $\kappa_0 \, t \, \sigma_2$, while the sequence κ_0 does not contain any occurrence of t. This sequence is well-defined since the support of $\vec{\sigma}_r$ is T.

If t is the first transition of E^t to be fired following the order of σ_r, meaning that κ_0 does not contain any occurrence of transitions in E^t, then the sequence κ_0 does not use any token from the input places of t, thus one can execute κ_0 after the firing of the first occurrence of t and the sequence $t \, \kappa_0 \, \sigma_2$ is feasible at M_0. Hence, $\sigma^* = \kappa_0 \, \sigma_2$.

Otherwise, t is not the first transition in E^t to be fired following the order of σ_r, meaning that κ_0 contains at least one occurrence of another transition of E^t. We show next that Algorithm 2, whose inputs are the sequences computed by Algorithm 1, completes τ up to κ by following the order of the remaining unfired occurrences in κ. We deduce that the sequence σ^* obtained at the end reaches the initial marking.

To achieve this objective, we prove that the following loop invariant $I(k)$ is true for $k \geq 0$:

$I(k)$: "at the end of iteration k, for every transition t_u such that $\vec{\tau}(t_u) < \vec{\kappa}(t_u)$ and $t_u = tnext(E^{t_u}, \tau, \kappa)$, then for every transition t_j of E^{t_u}, $\vec{\tau}(t_j) = \vec{K}(t_j)$, where K denotes the sequence $K_u^m(\kappa)$ and m is the value $\vec{\tau}(t_u) + 1$".

Before starting the loop, $k = 0$ and Lemma 3 applies.

Now assume that k iterations of the loop occurred and $I(k)$ is true. During iteration $k + 1$, a new transition t_i is fired following the order of κ. At the end of iteration $k + 1$, for every transition t_u such that $\vec{\tau}(t_u) < \vec{\kappa}(t_u)$ and $t_u = tnext(E^{t_u}, \tau, \kappa)$, we denote by K' the sequence $K_u^{m'}(\kappa)$ where $m' = \vec{\tau}(t_u) + 1$ and consider two cases. First, if t_u does not belong to E^{t_i}, then K' is the same sequence as in the previous iteration and for every transition t_j of E^{t_u}, $\vec{\tau}(t_j)$ has not changed either, thus $\vec{\tau}(t_j) = \vec{K}'(t_j)$. Otherwise, if t_u belongs to E^{t_i}, implying $E^{t_i} = E^{t_u}$, then K' contains the same number of occurrences of every transition t_j of E^{t_i} as in the sequence K associated to t_i in the previous iteration, except for t_i, whose number has been incremented by one. Besides, the only transition whose number of occurrences in τ has been incremented by one is t_i. Consequently, for every transition t_j of E^{t_u}, we have $\vec{\tau}(t_j) = \vec{K}'(t_j)$. We deduce finally that all the equalities that are supposed to be true at the end of iteration k remain true at the end of iteration $k + 1$.

Hence, the invariant is true at every iteration of the loop. Furthermore, by definition of the t_i chosen at every step, for which we define the current value $m = \vec{\tau}(t_i) + 1$ and the sequence $K = K_i^m(\kappa)$, all the occurrences in K are already present in the sequence τ of the current iteration. Thus, at the beginning of every iteration, for every transition $t_j \in T$, $\vec{\tau}(t_j) \geq \vec{K}(t_j)$.

Moreover, the sequence K is feasible at M_0 and leads to a marking that enables t_i, by definition of the feasible sequence κ. Thus, τ fired the input transitions of the input places of t_i at least as many times as in K. Then, the invariant implies that the transitions of E^{t_i} fired exactly as many times in K as in τ. Thus, the input places of t_i received at least the number of tokens they would receive by firing K from M_0, implying that t_i is enabled.

We deduce that the loop completes $\vec{\tau}$ up to $\vec{\kappa}$ and terminates.

Finally, since κ is of the form $(\sigma_r)^\alpha$ for some integer $\alpha > 0$, the feasible sequence $t\,\sigma^*$ is a T-sequence.   □

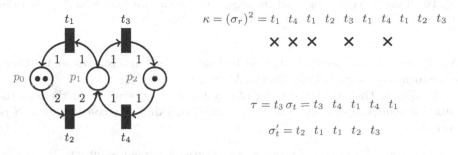

$$\kappa = (\sigma_r)^2 = t_1\ \ t_4\ \ t_1\ \ t_2\ \ t_3\ \ t_1\ \ t_4\ \ t_1\ \ t_2\ \ t_3$$

$$\times\ \times\ \times\ \quad\times\quad\ \ \times$$

$$\tau = t_3\,\sigma_t = t_3\ \ t_4\ \ t_1\ \ t_4\ \ t_1$$

$$\sigma'_t = t_2\ \ t_1\ \ t_1\ \ t_2\ \ t_3$$

Fig. 9. On the left, the system obtained at the end of Algorithm 1 and the corresponding value of τ on the right. The crosses indicate the occurrences of transitions in κ that have been fired in $\tau = t\,\sigma_t$, setting $t = t_3$. In Algorithm 2, $\alpha = 2$ and $\kappa = (\sigma_r)^2$. Following the ordering of κ, the sequence $\sigma'_t = t_2\,t_1\,t_1\,t_2\,t_3$ is fired, leading to the initial marking. Finally, after the initial firing of t_3, the sequence $\sigma_t\,\sigma'_t = t_4\,t_1\,t_4\,t_1\,t_2\,t_1\,t_1\,t_2\,t_3$ returns to the initial marking.

The next corollary provides the characterization of reversibility for all live Equal-Conflict systems and is illustrated in Figure 10.

Corollary 1. *Consider a live Equal-Conflict system $S = (N, M_0)$ such that $N = (P, T, W)$. The system S is reversible if and only if it enables a T-sequence.*

Proof. For the necessity, Lemma 1 applies.

We prove the sufficiency next. Suppose there exists a feasible T-sequence σ_r in the live system S. We show that after the firing of any feasible sequence σ, with $M_0 \xrightarrow{\sigma} M'$, there exists a feasible sequence σ^* that leads to the initial marking. For that purpose, we show by induction on the length n of σ the property $P(n)$:

"If a sequence σ of length n is feasible in a live Equal-Conflict system $S = (N, M_0)$ and a feasible T-sequence, denoted by σ_r, exists in S, then there exists a feasible sequence σ^* such that $M_0 \xrightarrow{\sigma\,\sigma^*} M_0$."

If $n = 0$, σ and σ^* are empty sequences and the initial marking is reached.

Otherwise, suppose $n > 0$, with $\sigma = t\,\sigma'$, note $M_0 \xrightarrow{t} M \xrightarrow{\sigma'} M'$, and assume that the property $P(n-1)$ is true. Applying Theorem 2, there exists a sequence σ'_t that is feasible at M such that $M \xrightarrow{\sigma'_t} M_0$ and the sequence $t\,\sigma'_t$ is a T-sequence. Thus, the T-sequence $\sigma'_t\,t$ is feasible at M. Applying the induction hypothesis on the sequence σ' of size $n-1$, which is feasible in the live system

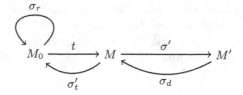

Fig. 10. If the T-sequence σ_r and the sequence $\sigma = t\,\sigma'$ are feasible at M_0, then the sequence $\sigma^* = \sigma_d\,\sigma'_t$ is feasible at M' and leads to M_0.

(N, M), we obtain a sequence σ_d that is feasible at M' and returns to M. Thus, the sequence $\sigma^* = \sigma_d\,\sigma'_t$ is feasible at M' and leads to M_0.

We deduce that after the firing of any feasible sequence in S, there exists a feasible sequence that returns to the initial marking. We conclude that S is reversible. □

Some examples of the previous sections provide some insight into the conditions of this characterization. Indeed, Figure 4 pictures non-reversible systems that are Equal-Conflict, live and do not enable any T-sequence. Figure 5 depicts a non-reversible system that is Equal-Conflict, non-live and enables a T-sequence.

5   T-sequences in Larger Classes

In the previous section, we showed that the existence of a feasible T-sequence is necessary and sufficient for reversibility in live Equal-Conflict systems, which are not necessarily bounded.

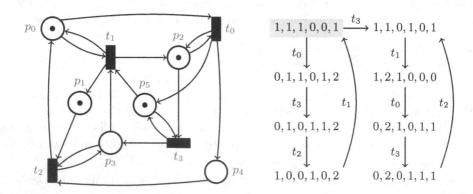

Fig. 11. The system allows the T-sequence $t_0\,t_3\,t_2\,t_1$. Liveness, boundedness and non-reversibility of the system can be deduced from its reachability graph on the right. Multiplying the input and output weights of p_0 by 2 yields a system in which any transition firing preserves the overall number of tokens. We deduce that $(2, 1, 1, 1, 1, 1)^T$ is a conservativeness vector, hence the net is structurally bounded. Since it is also structurally live, it is well-formed.

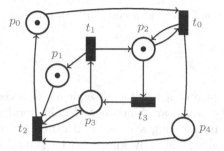

Place p	Output set $p^{\bullet}$
p_0	t_0
p_1	t_2
p_2	t_0, t_3
p_3	t_1, t_2
p_4	t_2

Fig. 12. This ordinary Asymmetric-Choice system is unbounded since the place p_1 is unbounded (fire $(t_3\, t_1)^{\alpha}$ for any positive integer α). It is live since t_1 and t_3 can always be fired after a finite number of firings, thus allowing new firings of t_0 and t_2. It is not reversible since there is always an occurrence of t_1 between two occurrences of t_2. The system allows the T-sequence $t_0\, t_3\, t_2\, t_1$.

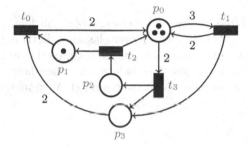

Fig. 13. In this weighted Free-Choice system, the T-sequence $t_1\, t_3\, t_2\, t_0$ is initially enabled. The place p_1 is unbounded (fire the sequence $(t_3\, t_2\, t_3\, t_2\, t_0)^{\alpha}$ for any positive integer α), thus the system is unbounded. Two consecutive firings of t_1 are not possible, and t_0 is either enabled by a firing of t_1 followed by a firing of t_3, or by two firings of t_3 with a firing of t_2 in between. Firing only occurrences of t_2 and t_3 generates tokens in p_1 that cannot be destroyed. Hence the system is not reversible. After any firing sequence, it is possible to send three tokens back to p_0 while p_1 contains one or more tokens. Such a marking enables the T-sequence and we deduce the liveness.

Now we provide some counter-examples for this condition in other subclasses of Petri nets. They are all strongly connected, live, and not reversible systems allowing a T-sequence.

First, the characterization does not carry over to systems that are just well-formed, even if the net is ordinary, as shown in Figure 11, which is inspired from a system of [5].

Second, it does not apply either to the class of ordinary Asymmetric-Choice systems, as shown by the unbounded system of Figure 12.

Last, it does not extend to weighted Free-Choice systems, even when they are very close to Join-Free, as illustrated in Figure 13 where the system has only one synchronization—a join-transition with just two inputs—that distinguishes it from the Join-Free class. We have not found yet a counter-example belonging to the Join-Free class.

6   Conclusion

In any weighted Petri net, the existence of a feasible T-sequence is necessary to have both liveness and reversibility, which are fundamental behavioral properties for embedded and flexible manufacturing systems and other real-world applications. This necessary condition was already known to be sufficient for well-formed, strongly connected, weighted Choice-Free and ordinary Free-Choice systems. It is no longer sufficient for the well-formed homogeneous S-systems, a class with both choices and weights included in the Equal-Conflict class.

By taking the liveness property as an assumption, we relaxed this condition and proved that it is sufficient for reversibility in all the live Equal-Conflict systems. Petri nets of this expressive class may not be strongly connected nor be bounded.

Finally, we exhibited several counter-examples, all live, non-reversible and allowing a T-sequence, belonging to larger classes of Petri nets.

As a consequence, extensions of our new characterization of reversibility would require more constraints. We believe that non-homogeneous Join-Free nets, bounded or not, or homogeneous bounded Asymmetric-Choice nets are worth investigating.

References

1. Araki, T., Kasami, T.: Decidable Problems on the Strong Connectivity of Petri Net Reachability Sets. Theoretical Computer Science **4**(1), 99–119 (1977)
2. Barkaoui, K., Couvreur, J.-M., Klai, K.: On the equivalence between liveness and deadlock-freeness in petri nets. In: Ciardo, G., Darondeau, P. (eds.) ICATPN 2005. LNCS, vol. 3536, pp. 90–107. Springer, Heidelberg (2005)
3. Best, E., Darondeau, P.: Petri net distributability. In: Clarke, E., Virbitskaite, I., Voronkov, A. (eds.) PSI 2011. LNCS, vol. 7162, pp. 1–18. Springer, Heidelberg (2012)
4. de Frutos Escrig, D., Johnen, C.: Decidability of Home Space Property. Tech. Rep. LRI-503, Univ. de Paris-Sud, Centre d'Orsay, LRI (1989)
5. Desel, J., Esparza, J.: Free Choice Petri Nets, Cambridge Tracts in Theoretical Computer Science, vol. 40. Cambridge University Press, New York (1995)
6. Haddad, S., Mairesse, J., Nguyen, H.T.: Synthesis and Analysis of Product-form Petri Nets. Fundamenta Informaticae **122**(1–2), 147–172 (2013)
7. Hujsa, T., Delosme, J.-M., Munier-Kordon, A.: On the reversibility of well-behaved weighted choice-free systems. In: Ciardo, G., Kindler, E. (eds.) PETRI NETS 2014. LNCS, vol. 8489, pp. 334–353. Springer, Heidelberg (2014)
8. Lee, E.A., Messerschmitt, D.G.: Synchronous Data Flow. Proceedings of the IEEE **75**(9), 1235–1245 (1987)
9. López-Grao, J.-P., Colom, J.-M.: Structural Methods for the Control of Discrete Event Dynamic Systems – The Case of the Resource Allocation Problem. In: Seatzu, C., Silva Suárez, M., van Schuppen, J.H. (eds.) Control of Discrete-event Systems. LNCIS, vol. 433, pp. 257–278. Springer, Heidelberg (2013)

10. Memmi, G., Roucairol, G.: Linear Algebra in Net Theory. In: Brauer, W. (ed.) Net Theory and Applications. LNCS, vol. 84, pp. 213–223. Springer, Heidelberg (1980)
11. Murata, T.: Petri Nets: Properties, Analysis and Applications. Proceedings of the IEEE **77**(4), 541–580 (1989)
12. Recalde, L., Teruel, E., Silva, M.: SC*ECS: a class of modular and hierarchical cooperating systems. In: Billington, J., Reisig, W. (eds.) Application and Theory of Petri Nets 1996. LNCS, vol. 1091, pp. 440–459. Springer, Heidelberg (1996)
13. Sifakis, J.: Structural properties of petri nets. In: Winkowski, J. (ed.) Mathematical Foundations of Computer Science. LNCS, vol. 64, pp. 474–483. Springer, Heidelberg (1978)
14. Teruel, E., Chrzastowski-Wachtel, P., Colom, J.M., Silva, M.: On Weighted T-systems. In: Jensen, K. (ed.) Application and Theory of Petri Nets 1992. LNCS, vol. 616, pp. 348–367. Springer, Heidelberg (1992)
15. Teruel, E., Colom, J.M., Silva, M.: Choice-Free Petri Nets: A Model for Deterministic Concurrent Systems with Bulk Services and Arrivals. IEEE Transactions on Systems, Man and Cybernetics, Part A **27**(1), 73–83 (1997)
16. Teruel, E., Silva, M.: Liveness and home states in equal-conflict systems. In: Marsan, M.A. (ed.) Application and Theory of Petri Nets 1993. LNCS, vol. 691, pp. 415–432. Springer, Heidelberg (1993)
17. Teruel, E., Silva, M.: Structure Theory of Equal Conflict Systems. Theoretical Computer Science **153**(1&2), 271–300 (1996)

SNAKES: A Flexible High-Level Petri Nets Library
(Tool Paper)

Franck Pommereau[(✉)]

IBISC, University of Évry/Paris-Saclay, 23 bd de France,
91037 Évry Cedex, France
franck.pommereau@ibisc.univ-evry.fr

Abstract. SNAKES (SNAKES is the Net Algebra Kit for Editors and Simulators) is a general purpose Petri nets library, primarily for the Python programming language but portable to other ones. It defines a very general variant of Python-coloured Petri nets that can be created and manipulated through the library, as well as executed to explore state spaces. Thanks to a variety of plugins, SNAKES can handle extensions of Petri nets, in particular algebras of Petri nets [4,26]. SNAKES ships with a compiler for the ABCD language that is precisely such an algebra. Finally, one can use the companion tool Neco [14] that compiles a Petri net into an optimised library allowing to compute efficiently its state space or perform LTL model-checking thanks to library SPOT [8,13]. This paper describes SNAKES' structure and features.

Keywords: Petri nets library · Prototyping · Simulation · Model-checking

1 SNAKES in a Nutshell

SNAKES is a general purpose Petri net library for the Python programming language (but we show in Section 4 that it can be ported to other languages). Using SNAKES, one can create Petri nets, transform them (add/remove/... nodes, add/remove/... arcs, etc.), manipulate their markings, and also fire transitions (sequentially). SNAKES is not designed to perform analysis but because it can execute modelled nets, it may be used to explore traces or state spaces. However, a companion tool called Neco is preferred for this purpose and provides fast reachability and LTL explicit analysis.

SNAKES uses a very general variant of Python-coloured Petri nets (see Section 1.3): tokens can carry arbitrary Python objects, transitions guards are arbitrary Python expressions and arcs may be annotated with arbitrary Python variables or expressions. Moreover, SNAKES provides support for various Petri nets extensions: read arcs, whole-place arcs and inhibitor arcs. Because we use the same language for the library and the Petri nets annotations, users are provided

R. Devillers and A. Valmari (Eds.): PETRI NETS 2015, LNCS 9115, pp. 254–265, 2015.
DOI: 10.1007/978-3-319-19488-2_13

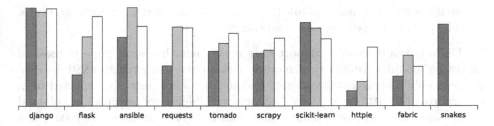

Fig. 1. SNAKES compared with the most popular Python projects on GitHub (on March 20th, 2015). From left to right, bars represent: ■ size of the project measured in number of source lines of code, ranging from 184.6k for Django to 3.7k for HTTPie; ▨ number of contributors, ranging from 1.0k for Ansible to 2 for SNAKES; □ popularity measured as the number of stars (GitHub's bookmarks) times the number of forks, ranging from 13.3k stars and 5.2k forks for Django to 2 stars and 1 fork for SNAKES (however, it is worth noting that SNAKES has moved to GitHub only since March 15th, 2015).

with great flexibility. In addition to this flexibility, a general plugin mechanism is provided to allow for redefining every aspect of SNAKES, like the firing rule in particular. For instance, in [23, 24] we show how SNAKES can be extended to support time Petri nets (which requires less than 100 lines of code); or in [25], we show how nets-within-nets, with transition firing synchronised between the nested levels of nets, can be implemented using less than 30 lines of code.

SNAKES has been developed since 2002, progressively growing to about 81.5k lines of portable Python, which represents quite a big effort as shown in Figure 1. One reason that increases the size of SNAKES is that it does not rely on external or system-dependant libraries and includes features that are not directly related to Petri nets, for instance: a LL(1) parser generator; tools for Python code parsing, refactoring and generation; tools for API documentation extraction and generation. On the other hand, this allows SNAKES to work out-of-the-box on any system with Python starting from version 2.5, including the 3.x series as well as alternative implementations like PyPy, Jython, IronPython, or stackless Python [27]. SNAKES is free software released under the GNU LGPL [10]. Because it is freely available, it is hard to say how many users it has, but we measured that the online documentation receives more than 300 unique visitors per month. SNAKES is available at https://github.com/fpom/snakes.

1.1 Modules and Plugins

The whole library comes as a Python package organised as a hierarchy of modules among which the main ones are:

- snakes is the top-level module that defines commonly used exceptions;
- snakes.data defines data structures like multisets, substitutions, etc.;
- snakes.typing defines a type system used to restrict the tokens in places;
- snakes.plugins gathers all the plugins provided with SNAKES (see below);
- snakes.pnml defines import/export functions to/from PNML (see below);

- snakes.nets is the main module that defines all the Petri net related structures like places, transitions, arcs, marking graph, etc.

Users typically need to import only snakes.nets that itself imports most of the other modules. At the time module snakes.pnml was written, PNML used to support only places/transitions nets and such nets are correctly imported from or exported to PNML by SNAKES. But nets with high-level features like coloured tokens are exported into a dialect that does not conform nowadays PNML, and reciprocally, high-level PNML cannot be loaded into SNAKES. Adding this support represents a huge work regarding the complexity of the latest standard.

The most useful plugins shipped with SNAKES are:

- gv allows to draw Petri nets using GraphViz [5] (see Figure 3 for pictures);
- ops provides nets compositions from algebras of Petri nets (sequence, choice, iteration and parallel composition);
- pids offers dynamic process identifiers creation and destruction [20];
- labels allows to annotate nets and their nodes with arbitrary values;
- let allows to assign variables within expressions, which is useful to avoid computing several times the same expression (more at the end of Section 1.3).

Generally, plugins are based on a set of hooks in the tools, allowing the plugin to perform a specific action when the hook is activated. SNAKES takes a more general approach: a plugin is basically a set of classes that extends the classes of a module (snakes.nets in general). This is thus much more general since anything can be extended or redefined. Moreover, it is also more flexible than standard classes inheritance because it is made dynamically, depending on which plugins are actually loaded. In order to avoid incompatible extensions and to simplify the use, plugins declare which other plugins they conflict with as well as which other they depend on.

1.2   Hello World

Figure 2 shows a simple example of SNAKES usage: this code loads snakes.nets extended with plugin gv (lines 1-3); creates a Petri net (line 4); adds three places (lines 5–7) and a transition (line 8); adds arcs (lines 9-11); draws the net once (line 12); gets the modes for the transition (line 13, the returned modes are given in the comment lines 14–17); fires the transition with one of these modes (line 18); and finally draws the net once more (line 19). The resulting pictures are displayed in Figure 3. One can note that places are here marked with string objects and that the output arc from transition "concat" to place "sentence" is labelled with a Python expression that concatenates three strings, two of which being obtained by consuming tokens in the other places.

1.3   Transition Firing

As said previously, every Petri net in SNAKES can be executed, *i.e.*, its transitions can be fired. To achieve this, we need to make a compromise between the

```
1   import snakes.plugins
2   snakes.plugins.load("gv", "snakes.nets", "snk")
3   from snk import *
4   pn = PetriNet("hello␣world␣in␣SNAKES")
5   pn.add_place(Place("hello", ["hello", "salut"]))
6   pn.add_place(Place("world", ["world", "le␣monde"]))
7   pn.add_place(Place("sentence"))
8   pn.add_transition(Transition("concat"))
9   pn.add_input("hello", "concat", Variable("h"))
10  pn.add_input("world", "concat", Variable("w"))
11  pn.add_output("sentence", "concat", Expression("h␣+␣'␣'␣+␣w"))
12  pn.draw("hello-1.eps")
13  modes = pn.transition("concat").modes()
14  # modes = [Substitution(h='salut', w='world'),
15  #     Substitution(h='salut', w='le monde'),
16  #     Substitution(h='hello', w='world'),
17  #     Substitution(h='hello', w='le monde')]
18  pn.transition("concat").fire(modes[2])
19  pn.draw("hello-2.eps")
```

Fig. 2. Python code for the "hello world" example

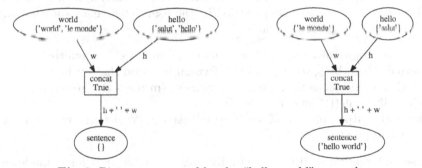

Fig. 3. Pictures generated by the "hello world" example

generality of nets definitions and some implementation restrictions. Informally, our definition is as follows: a Petri net is a tuple (S, T, ℓ, M) where,

- S is a finite set of places;
- T is a finite set of transitions, disjoint from S;
- ℓ is a labelling function such that
  - for all $s \in S$, $\ell(s)$ is the type of s, *i.e.*, a restriction on the tokens it may hold. This is implemented in snakes.typing as Boolean functions used to check whether tokens can be accepted or not,
  - for all $t \in T$, $\ell(t)$ is the guard of t, implemented as a Python expression,
  - for all $(x, y) \in (S \times T) \cup (T \times S)$, $\ell(x, y)$ is the annotation of the arc from x to y and is a multiset of expressions to specify the tokens produced or consumed through the arc;

– M is the marking, *i.e.*, a mapping from places to multisets of Python values.

In general, such a Petri net cannot be implemented, in particular in Python. For instance, imagine an arc from a place s to a transition t and labelled with a call to a function $f(x)$. To fire t, we would need, for each token value v in s to solve $v = f(x)$ in order to discover the possible bindings for variable x. This is clearly not feasible when f is an arbitrary Python function. So, SNAKES adopted the following restrictions:

– input arcs (in $S \times T$) cannot be labelled with expressions, but only with values, variables or combinations of them within structures that allow for pattern matching (currently, only tuples are implemented);
– all the variables used in a transition, its guard and surrounding arcs should appear on at least on one input arc so it can be bound.

Given this setting, the firing rule is quite straightforward and can be decomposed into two methods of a transition object t. First, t.modes() computes all the possible bindings of the transition's variables by matching input arcs annotations with respect to all the tokens available in input places. The second limitation above is not enforced but the modes of a transition that does not respect are simply not computed by SNAKES (see below about relaxing a bit this limitation); however, they could be provided by the user. Then, each such binding m is checked to be a mode as follows:

– for each input place s, check if "eval(ℓ(s,t), m)" yields a multiset of tokens actually held by s, where eval is a Python function that evaluates arbitrary Python expressions in a given environment (m plays this role here);
– check if "eval(ℓ(t), m)" returns True;
– for each output place s, check if every token in "eval(ℓ(t,s), m)" is accepted by the type of s.

The second method, t.fire(m), actually fires the transition for a mode m by consuming and producing the tokens as computed above.

To overcome a bit the limitation that every variable is bound from the input arcs, plugin let provides a function also called let that allows to bind new variables during the evaluation of an expression. In practice, this is useful only during the evaluation of the guard, for instance "x > 10 **and** let(y="f(x)", z="g(x)")" allows to introduce two new variables y and z whose values can be computed arbitrarily (here by calling functions f and g), and that can be used in the output arcs avoiding potential redundant calls to f and g. Note that let returns True if it can successfully bind the variables, and False otherwise (*e.g.*, if an expression yields an exception), which is adequate for its use in guards.

2   ABCD for Friendly Modelling

SNAKES being a library, it is mainly targeted towards developers and researchers who need to program with Petri nets. However, for the modeller, defining nets

```
1    buffer hello : str = "hello", "salut"
2    buffer world : str = "world", "le␣monde"
3    buffer sentence : str = ()
4    [ hello−(h), world−(w), sentence+(h + '␣' + w)]
```

Fig. 4. "Hello world" example revisited in ABCD

using SNAKES directly may be tedious. A user friendly syntax is thus desirable for users that mainly want to build models and explore them. For this purpose, SNAKES comes with a compiler for the ABCD modelling language (Asynchronous Box Calculus with Data) which is a process algebra with friendly Python-like syntax, that embeds full Python, and with a Petri nets semantics (see [26, sec. 3.3] for more details). The compiler translates ABCD code into Petri nets, called from the command line, it can draw the computed net or save it into a file (in SNAKES' PNML dialect) for a later use. It may also be called from a Python program to obtain a net object directly.

The example from Figure 2 could be expressed as shown in Figure 4. We can see that places are expressed as typed buffers (str is Python's type for strings) with an initial content (empty in the case of "sentence"), and transitions are expressed as atomic actions enclosed into square brackets within which the tokens consumed from or produced into buffers are specified. However, ABCD is not designed as a textual syntax for Petri nets and it cannot express any Petri net. Instead, it provides the modeller with a notion of control flow and parametrised processes with local data. This is illustrated in Figure 5 where two producers and two consumers share a buffer bag (defined line 1). Lines 2–4 define a net (which can be considered as a process factory) parametrised by a value mod, two instances of which being created in line 7 with distinct values for mod. Net prod declares a local buffer count, this means that every instance of prod has its own private copy of count. Line 4, the process itself consists of two atomic actions connected by an iteration operator "*". The left action increments the value in buffer count and produces in bag the current value of count modulo mod. The right action [False] is a special one that can never be executed; because it is used here as the exit of the iteration, process prod is forced to iterate forever producing values in bag. Net cons shows two more features: guards for atomic actions, given after keyword **if**, and sequential composition ";". We can also see the parallel composition "|" in the main process line 7. A fourth composition that is not shown here is the choice "+".

The ABCD compiler also features an interactive simulator that allows step-by-step execution of an ABCD model, directly on the source code, like when using a debugger for a programming language.

3   Efficient Model-Checking

SNAKES is first designed to be flexible and general, not to be efficient: instrumenting Python code from a Python program is definitely not the fastest way

```
1   buffer bag : int = ()
2   net prod (mod) :
3       buffer count : int = 0
4       [count−(x), count+(x+1), bag+(x % mod)] * [False]
5   net cons (div) :
6       ( [bag−(x) if x % div == 0] ; [bag−(x) if x % div != 0] ) * [False]
7   prod(5) | prod(7) | cons(2) | cons(3)
```

Fig. 5. A producer-consumer example in ABCD

to explore the state space of a Petri net. In order to do this efficiently, one can use tool Neco [14] that is available separately [11]. This tool compiles SNAKES Petri nets into fast native code with an optimised marking structure and per-transition optimised firing. Using the declared place types, it can type the variables on input arcs and generate Cython code [2], a dialect of Python extended with C types. Then, Cython code is compiled into C source code that is finally compiled into native code (all this process is automated). However, note that Neco compiles and optimises Petri nets, not the embedded Python code. So, if a Petri net embeds slow Python code and provides too few types (*e.g.*, in Figure 2 we did not provide any typing for the places, so they are constrained to the universal type object) Cython is forced to rely on the Python interpreter instead of generating fast C code. Neco can also compile ABCD models. In such a case, it exploits many properties of the resulting Petri net that are known by construction (for instance, control flow places are low-level 1-safe places and form 1-invariants on the sequential parts) and performs further optimisation during the compilation.

Apart from its compiler, Neco also features a tool to build the state space of a compiled net, and a tool to perform LTL model-checking on-the-fly. For the latter purpose, it relies on library SPOT [8] that is exactly the complement to Neco: on the one hand, Neco is able to construct a Kripke structure by firing the transitions of the compiled Petri net; on the other hand, SPOT can turn a LTL formula into a Bchi automaton and check on-the-fly the emptiness of its product with the Kripke structure.

Neco was awarded at the Model-Checking Contest 2013 (satellite event of the PETRI NETS conference) as the most efficient explicit LTL model-checker. Moreover, in many cases, it was the only tool to actually provide a result, which assesses its robustness. A tutorial for using Neco is available online [11].

4   SNAKES Out of Python

Using Cython [2] again, it is easy to create a C binding for SNAKES (*i.e.*, export its API to a C library) so it can be called from another programming language. This is not provided by default because there is not one unique binding of SNAKES, but instead one possible binding for every combination of plugins. Fortunately, writing such a binding is easy when we know where the technical difficulties are.

```
1   # here we write regular Python code to import SNAKES or other
2   # modules, load plugins, define functions, ...
3   cdef public int newnet (char *name) :
4       # here we just write regular Python code that uses SNAKES
5   cdef public int addplace (char *net, char *name, int tokens) :
6       # and so on...
```

Fig. 6. Cython source code of the binding (file `libsnk.pyx`)

Moreover, one advantage of writing the binding for each such use case is that we are able to produce an API that is exactly suited to our particular need.

The main difficulty is that, when calling SNAKES from another programming language, we shall send references to Python objects outside of the Python runtime. If it happens that an object is no more referenced from the Python runtime, it is garbage collected and the outer reference becomes dangling, which is likely to crash the program with a segmentation fault. To avoid this, we have to provide a storage for the objects with our own references. For instance, we may store net objects and provide access to them through their names.

So, basically, our binding consists of a Cython file `libsnk.pyx` as sketched in Figure 6 (see [22] for the full details). The Cython tool allows to compile this source into a dynamic library (`libsnk.so` under Linux) along with a C header file `libsnk.h` that can be used from a C program. The only constraint is to take care to initialise the Python runtime and the library before to call its functions.

To use SNAKES from another programming language than C, a simple possibility is to rely on SWIG that allows to automatically generate bindings of C libraries for almost 20 programming languages [1].

5   Use Cases

As explained already, it is very hard to have a clear picture of who is using SNAKES because it is freely available and very few users actually ask for support. Fortunately, there are works we known well about [6,7,12,14,15,21,29,30] and that illustrate typical use cases for SNAKES as listed below.

Prototyping tools. A prototype implementation of a massively parallel CTL* model-checking algorithm for ABCD models of security protocols allowed to assess scalability [15]. A new approach to process-symmetry reductions initially defined in [20] has been prototyped in Neco by generating Python code, showing a dramatic performance boost [12], and can be now ported to Cython.

Compilation from/to Petri nets. Neco compiler is entirely implemented in Python using SNAKES to handle the Petri nets and ABCD as an input language [14]. Apart from ABCD, the Petri net semantics of various other formalisms has been implemented using SNAKES, recently: a graphical variant of the π-calculus [30] and a modelling language dedicated to toxic risk assessment in biological and bio-synthetic systems [7].

Modelling. SNAKES is also used to create Petri net models, like in [21] where models of cloud services are represented as token-nets instrumented by a system-net that models the elasticity mechanism. For this task, SNAKES is presumably the only tool available because it allowed to create token-nets whose structures and markings are determined during the firing of the transitions in system-net. More often, an input language is used, like in [7,30], or ABCD is used like in [15]. ABCD has also been used to model peer-to-peer protocols for an industrial case of distributed storage system [6,29].

Analysis. Many modelling works are made with model-checking in perspective, but very often, only reachability analysis is performed to check safety properties and this is surprisingly often made directly using SNAKES [6,21,29]. Neco is also used to speedup state space computation [6] or to perform LTL model-checking [30]. Another kind of analysis is to collect data along a collection of randomly generated traces and to perform statistical analysis, either to assess performances [21] or to evaluate other quantitative information, like in [6] where the number of file loss of a peer-to-peer storage system is evaluated with respect to the percentage of malicious peers present in the system.

6   Conclusion

We have presented SNAKES that enables to develop Petri net tools with great flexibility regarding the variant of Petri nets, and allowing their execution for simulation purpose or for limited reachability analysis. Efficient LTL model-checking can be performed using Neco. SNAKES also ships with a compiler for the ABCD algebra of Petri nets allowing user-friendly modelling of high-level systems.

Ongoing and Future Work. Despite its age and reported stability, SNAKES is still considered as a beta software because it lacks a real development team to meet the standard expectations from a stable software. In particular, it is very hard to provide a roadmap of planned features because they are added in a demand-driven fashion and depend a lot on the time the author can spend. So, current version is 0.9.17 and is slowly converging towards 1.0, which will be reached when at least the following features will be covered:

- replace current PNML support that does not conform to the standards with simpler file formats and rely on third-party tools [17] to handle PNML;
- integrate Neco through a plugin to allow its use transparently and bring LTL model-checking directly to the users;
- fill a few holes in the documentation and perform minor code cleanup and simplification.

This does not mean that no other features will be introduced in the meantime, some in particular are very much desired:

- interactive simulation of any Petri net (in addition to ABCD processes), and fast automatic simulation coupled with statistical analysis of the traces;

- integration with other tools (user interfaces, analysers, etc.), in particular with CosyVerif [17], notably by supporting more inputs/outputs languages;
- genericity with respect to the annotation language by generalising the compilation approach;
- automated API generation to other languages by extending the API documentation extraction tool to generate Cython bindings as presented above;
- extend ABCD with a syntax for raw Petri nets, and with support for thread-like processes as defined in [20] and [26, sec. 4.3].

Interface with other tools and integration with other programming languages are two crucial features to open SNAKES to more researches out of the Python ecosystem. It looks very useful not to limit its use to one particular programming language so it can be helpful for a broader community.

Related Works. To the best of our knowledge, SNAKES is quite a unique tool in that there is no other such general purpose Petri net library aimed at tools developers, that is still actively developed and maintained. The Petri Net Kernel [19] used to have similar goals for Java or Python, depending on the version, but it received no update since October 2003.

Taking apart its purpose and considering only the Petri net variant proposed in SNAKES, we may find similarities with other high-level Petri nets tools. In particular, the coloured Petri nets [18] implemented in CPN tools [16] are also Petri nets annotated with a programming language which is a variant of ML in this case. A variant of coloured Petri nets coloured with the Haskell programming language was proposed in [28] but the project appears stopped since 2004. The TINA toolbox [3] supports interfacing with C code, allowing to implement guards for the transitions of a time Petri net, and to perform computation on transition firing. But this is quite far from providing C-coloured Petri nets because the net and C parts remain separated and the data is attached to the state instead of to the tokens, which is a serious limitation from a modelling perspective.

When considering Neco together with SNAKES, it becomes relevant to compare with explicit model-checkers for high-level Petri nets. CPN tools cited above can perform CTL-like model-checking on a fully computed state space, while Neco uses SPOT to perform LTL model-checking on-the-fly. This is similar to Helena [9] that also works with Petri nets annotated with an ad-hoc language; moreover, like Neco, Helena compiles the Petri net into C code in order to speedup transitions firing. However, this compilation is limited to the annotations and the marking, but not generalised to the whole Petri net structure like in Neco.

References

1. Beazley, D.M., Fulton, W.: SWIG – Simplified Wrapper and Interface Generator. http://www.swig.org
2. Behnel, S., Bradshaw, R., Dalcín, L., Florisson, M., Makarov, V., Seljebotn, D.S.: Cython – C-extensions for Python. http://cython.org

3. Berthomieu, B., Vernadat, F.: Time Petri nets analysis with TINA. In: Proc. of QEST 2006. IEEE Computer Society (2006)
4. Best, E., Devillers, R., Koutny, M.: Petri net algebra. Springer (2001)
5. Bilgin, A., Ellson, J., Gansner, E., Hu, Y., North, S.: Graphviz – Graph Visualization Software. http://graphviz.org
6. Chaou, S., Utard, G., Pommereau, F.: Evaluating a peer-to-peer storage system in presence of malicious peers. In: Proceedings of HPCS 2011. IEEE Computer Society (2011)
7. Di Guisto, C., Klaudel, H., Delaplace, F.: Systemic approach for toxicity analysis. In: Proc. of BioPPN 2014. Workshop Proceedings, vol. 1159. CEUR (2014)
8. Duret-Lutz, A.: LTL translation improvements in Spot. In: Proc. of VECoS 2011. Electronic Workshops in Computing, British Computer Society (2011)
9. Evangeliste, S.: HELENA, a high level net analyzer. http://lipn.univ-paris13.fr/evangelista/helena
10. Free Software Foundation: GNU Lesser General Public License. http://www.gnu.org/licenses/lgpl.html
11. Fronc, Ł.: Neco net compiler. http://code.google.com/p/neco-net-compiler
12. Fronc, Ł.: Effective marking equivalence checking in systems with dynamic process creation. In: Proc. of Infinity 2012. Electronic Proceedings in Theoretical Computer Science (2012)
13. Fronc, Ł., Duret-Lutz, A.: LTL model checking with neco. In: Van Hung, D., Ogawa, M. (eds.) ATVA 2013. LNCS, vol. 8172, pp. 451–454. Springer, Heidelberg (2013)
14. Fronc, Ł., Pommereau, F.: Building Petri nets tools around Neco compiler. In: Proc. of PNSE 2013 (2013)
15. Gava, F., Pommereau, F., Guedj, M.: A BSP algorithm for on-the-fly checking CTL* formulas on security protocols. The Journal of Supercomputing (2014)
16. Group, T.C.: CPN tools. http://cpntools.org
17. Haddad, S., Kordon, F., Petruci, L.: CosyVerif. http://cosyverif.org
18. Jensen, K., Kristensen, L.M.: Coloured Petri Nets, Monographs in Theoretical Computer Science, vol. 2. Springer (1997)
19. Kindler, E., Weber, M.: The Petri Net Kernel: An infrastructure for building Petri net tools. Software Tools for Technology Transfer 3 (1999)
20. Klaudel, H., Koutny, M., Pelz, E., Pommereau, F.: State space reduction for dynamic process creation. Scientific Annals of Computer Science 20 (2010)
21. Mohamed, M., Amziani, M., Belaïd, D., Tata, S., Melliti, T.: An autonomic approach to manage elasticity of business processes in the Cloud. Future Generation Computer Systems (2014) (To appear)
22. Pommereau, F.: SNAKES out of Python. http://www.ibisc.univ-evry.fr/fpommereau/SNAKES/snakes-out-of-python.html
23. Pommereau, F.: Quickly prototyping Petri nets tools with SNAKES. Petri net newsletter 10 (2008)
24. Pommereau, F.: Quickly prototyping Petri nets tools with SNAKES. In: Proc. of PNTAP 2008. ACM Digital Library. ACM (2008)
25. Pommereau, F.: Nets in nets with SNAKES. In: Proc. of MOCA 2009. Universität Hamburg, Dept. Informatik, Hamburg (2009)
26. Pommereau, F.: Algebras of coloured Petri nets. Lambert Academic Publishing (2010)
27. Python Software Foundation: Alternative Python implementations. http://www.python.org/download/alternatives

28. Reinke, C.: Haskell-coloured petri nets. In: Koopman, P., Clack, C. (eds.) IFL 1999. LNCS, vol. 1868, pp. 165–180. Springer, Heidelberg (2000)
29. Sanjabi, S., Pommereau, F.: Modelling, verification, and formal analysis of security properties in a P2P system. In: Proceedings of COLSEC 2010. IEEE Digital Library. IEEE Computer Society (2010)
30. Van Pham, V.: Modelling and analysing open reconfigurable systems. Ph.D. thesis, Univ. Évry / Paris-Saclay (2014)

Characterizing Stable Inequalities of Petri Nets

Marvin Triebel[(✉)] and Jan Sürmeli

Institut für Informatik, Humboldt-Universität zu Berlin, Berlin, Germany
{triebel,suermeli}@informatik.hu-berlin.de

Abstract. One way to express correctness of a Petri net N is to specify a linear inequality U, requiring each reachable marking of N to satisfy U. A linear inequality U is *stable* if it is preserved along steps. If U is stable, then verifying correctness reduces to checking U in the initial marking of N. In this paper, we characterize classes of stable linear inequalities of a given Petri net by means of structural properties. Thereby, we generalize classical results on traps, co-traps, and invariants. We show how to decide stability of a given inequality. For a certain class of inequalities, we present a polynomial time decision procedure.

Keywords: Petri net analysis · Inductive invariants · Linear inequalities · Stable properties · Traps · Co-traps · Invariants

1 Introduction

Distributed systems are inherently complex due to their native concurrency, local states and steps of each part of the system, and message exchange between the parts. Thus, precisely specifying and automatically verifying the correctness of a given distributed system is difficult or impossible. *Petri nets* are a well-known formalism to model the behavior of distributed systems. The combination of an intuitive graphical syntax and clear mathematical semantics enables formal specification and automatic verification of correctness of a model.

There are several approaches to specify the correctness of a Petri net N. Thereby, the usual trade-off is between a more expressive formalism, and the feasibility of deciding correctness. A simple formalism is to specify a *linear inequality* U over the *places* of N, requiring each reachable *marking* of N to satisfy U. Thereby, a place of N models a local condition, storage or buffer. A marking of N aggregates all local states to a global state by assigning a number of tokens to each place of N. Each place p in a linear inequality represents the number of tokens on p. For instance, $p \leq 1$ requires that every reachable marking assigns at most one token to p, $p_1 + p_2 \leq 1$ requires that p_1 and p_2 are never simultaneously marked, and $p_1 - p_2 \geq 0$ requires that the number of tokens on p_2 never exceeds the number of tokens on p_1. As a more involved example, consider a system that handles *requests* with *processors*, where each request requires the availability of two processors. Assume R and P to be the places containing the pending requests and the available processors, respectively. Then, the inequality

© Springer International Publishing Switzerland 2015
R. Devillers and A. Valmari (Eds.): PETRI NETS 2015, LNCS 9115, pp. 266–286, 2015.
DOI: 10.1007/978-3-319-19488-2_14

$Q - 2R \geq 0$ expresses a sufficient condition for the availablity of sufficiently many processors to handle all pending requests. This notion of correctness is a special class of safety properties, and has the following advantages: First, there exists rich theory on linear inequalities, namely linear algebra. Second, there exist well-known links between linear inequalities and structural properties of Petri nets, namely *invariants*, *traps*, and *co-traps*. Unfortunately, 2EXP is a lower bound for the complexity: We reduce *coverability* to validity of a single linear inequality, and 2EXP is a lower bound for the complexity of coverability [2]. Hence, checking correctness is not necessarily feasible in practice for all nets and linear inequalities. To the best of our knowledge, decidability of correctness described by such linear inequalities has neither been proven nor disproven yet.

However, for some linear inequalities, correctness of N can be easily verified: If a given linear inequality U is *stable* in the structure of N, that is, preserved along each (not necessarily reachable) step of N, then correctness of N reduces to checking U in the initial marking of N. Thus efficiently deciding stability can be very valuable for deciding correctness. There exist characterizations of stable inequalities by means of invariants, traps, and co-traps. However, these existing characterizations are incomplete: There exist stable linear inequalities that are neither linked to invariants, traps, nor co-traps.

In this paper, we tackle the two problems of

- characterizing sets of stable linear inequalities of a given net structure by means of structural properties, and
- providing decision procedures to check whether a given linear inequality is stable in a given net structure.

To this end, we introduce *generalized traps* and *generalized co-traps* as new structural properties based on traps and co-traps. We then characterize stable linear inequalities by means of sur-invariants [5], [23], generalized traps, and generalized co-traps, generalizing existing results. We show that stability of a given linear inequality is decidable, and provide a decision procedure for a subclass of linear inequalities running in polynomial time.

We structure our paper as follows: After introducing basic notions in Sect. 2, we discuss stable linear inequalities in Sect. 3. We characterize classes of stable linear inequalities in Sect. 4 to 6: We present a complete characterization by means of linear programming in Sect. 4, introduce inherently stable structural properties in Sect. 5, and study the opposite direction, that is, structural properties implied by stability, in Sect. 6. From these characterizations, we derive decision procedures in Sect. 7. In Sect. 8 we discuss related work, and conclude our paper in Sect. 9. We sketch a reduction from coverability to validity in the appendix of this paper.

2   Preliminaries

We write B^A for the set of all functions $A \to B$ from some set A into some set B. We write $\mathbb{Z}$ and $\mathbb{N}$ for the sets of integers and natural numbers (including 0), respectively. As usual, $x+y$ and xy denote the sum and product of two integers x and y, respectively. We write $|x|$ for the absolute value of an integer x. As usual, $\leq$ and $<$ denote the natural weak and strict order on integers, respectively. If needed, we extend these notions to the set $\mathbb{Z} \cup \{\infty\}$, with $x < \infty$ for all $x \in \mathbb{Z}$. We call $x \in \mathbb{Z} \cup \{\infty\}$ a *lower bound* of $X \subseteq \mathbb{Z}$ if $x \leq x'$ for all $x' \in X$. If it exists, we denote the *infimum*, that is, the greatest lower bound of X, as $\inf X$. As usual, $\inf \emptyset = \infty$.

We recall required notions on *vectors over integers*: Let $A = \{a_1, \ldots, a_n\}$ be an ordered set and $v \in \mathbb{Z}^A$. Then, we call v an *A-vector*, where $v[i]$ denotes $v(a_i)$ for all $1 \leq i \leq n$. For some $x \in \mathbb{Z}$, $xv \in \mathbb{Z}^A$ is defined by $(xv)[i] := xv[i]$ for $1 \leq i \leq n$. Let v and v' be A-vectors. As usual, $v + v'$ and $v \cdot v'$ denote their *sum* and *dot product*, respectively, defined by $(v + v')[i] := v[i] + v'[i]$ and $v \cdot v' := \sum_{i=1}^n v[i]v'[i]$. We write $\leq$ for the natural partial order on A-vectors with $v \leq v'$ iff for all $1 \leq i \leq n$: $v[i] \leq v'[i]$. If for all $1 \leq i \leq n$, $v[i] \geq 0$, we call v semi-positive. If for all $1 \leq i \leq n$, $v[i] \leq 0$, then we call v semi-negative. Let $B \subseteq A$. Then, the *characteristic A-vector* of B is the A-vector $\mathrm{char}_A(B) \in \{0,1\}^A$ with $\mathrm{char}_A(B)[i] := 1$ iff $a_i \in B$. If clear from the context, we dismiss the index, and simply write $\mathrm{char}(B)$ instead of $\mathrm{char}_A(B)$.

In the remainder of this section, we recall notions of Petri nets as they can be found in [21]. A *net structure* $S = \langle P, T, F \rangle$ consists of finite disjoint sets P and T of *places* and *transitions*, respectively, and a *flow relation* $F \subseteq (P \times T) \cup (T \times P)$. Let $x \in P \cup T$. Then, x is a *node* of S with *preset* ${}^\bullet x := \{y \mid yFx\}$ and *postset* $x^\bullet := \{y \mid xFy\}$. We always assume the set of places to be ordered: Then, each $t \in T$ induces the following three P-vectors: $t^- := \mathrm{char}({}^\bullet t)$, $t^+ := \mathrm{char}(t^\bullet)$, and $t^\Delta := t^+ - t^-$.

Each semi-positive P-vector m is a *marking* of S. The natural number $m[i]$ denotes the *number of tokens* on p_i in m. We say that p_i is *marked* in m, if $m[i] > 0$. Let $t \in T$. If $m \geq t^-$, then t is *enabled* in m in S, written $t \xrightarrow{m}_S$. Let $m' = m + t^\Delta$. If t is enabled in m in S, then m, t, and m' form a *step* of S resulting in marking m', written $m \xrightarrow{t}_S m'$. For $i = 1, 2$, let $m_i \xrightarrow{t_i}_S m'_i$ with $m'_1 = m_2$. Then, $m_1 \xrightarrow{t_1}_S m'_1$ and $m_2 \xrightarrow{t_2}_S m'_2$ are *subsequent*. As usual, we extend the notation of steps to subsequent steps such as $m_1 \xrightarrow{t_1}_S \ldots \xrightarrow{t_n}_S m'_n$, or $m_1 \xrightarrow{t_1 \ldots t_n}_S m'_n$. A marking m_2 is reachable from a marking m_1 in S, iff $m_1 = m_2$ or $m_1 \xrightarrow{\sigma} m_2$ for some transition sequence σ. We write $\mathrm{Reach}_S(m)$ for the set of all markings reachable from m.

3   Stable Linear Inequalities of Petri Nets

In this section, we discuss *stable linear inequalities*, and their connections to the well-known structural properties of *traps* and *co-traps*. Let for this section $S = \langle P, T, F \rangle$ with $P = \{p_1, \ldots, p_n\}$ be a net structure. A *P-inequality* is a linear inequality where each variable is a place from P. A P-inequality can be semi-positive, semi-negative or mixed, based on the weights of each variable.

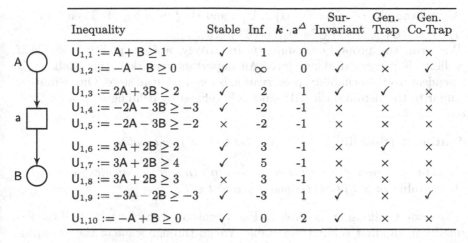

Inequality	Stable	Inf.	$k \cdot a^\Delta$	Sur-Invariant	Gen. Trap	Gen. Co-Trap
$U_{1,1} := A + B \geq 1$	✓	1	0	✓	✓	✗
$U_{1,2} := -A - B \geq 0$	✓	∞	0	✓	✗	✓
$U_{1,3} := 2A + 3B \geq 2$	✓	2	1	✓	✓	✗
$U_{1,4} := -2A - 3B \geq -3$	✓	-2	-1	✗	✗	✗
$U_{1,5} := -2A - 3B \geq -2$	✗	-2	-1	✗	✗	✗
$U_{1,6} := 3A + 2B \geq 2$	✓	3	-1	✗	✓	✗
$U_{1,7} := 3A + 2B \geq 4$	✓	5	-1	✗	✗	✗
$U_{1,8} := 3A + 2B \geq 3$	✗	3	-1	✗	✗	✗
$U_{1,9} := -3A - 2B \geq -3$	✓	-3	1	✓	✗	✓
$U_{1,10} := -A + B \geq 0$	✓	0	2	✓	✗	✗

Fig. 1. A net structure S_1 with inequalities $U_{1,1}, \ldots, U_{1,10}$. Definitions for the *infimum* of U w.r.t. t, sur-invariants, generalized traps and generalized co-traps can be found in Sect. 4, Sect. 5.1, Sect. 5.2, and Sect. 5.3, respectively.

Definition 1 (P-inequality, semi-positive, semi-negative, mixed). *Let k be a P-vector, and $c \in \mathbb{Z}$. Then, k and c induce the P-inequality $U = k \cdot P \geq c$ with weights k and constant c. If k is semi-positive (semi-negative), then U is semi-positive (semi-negative). If U is neither semi-negative nor semi-positive, then U is* mixed.

Thereby, P is merely a symbol representing the variables in the P-inequality. We can conceive P as a vector containing each place. Then, the written-out scalar product yields the common syntax as used in Fig. 1. The classes of semi-positive and semi-negative P-inequalities overlap in the cases where all weights are zero; the class of mixed P-inequalities is disjoint from the other classes. Our definition also covers inequalities of the form $k \cdot P \leq c$ which can be written as $-k \cdot P \geq -c$. As we only consider integer c, we can also express strict inequalities: For each integer x, we have $x > c$ iff $x \geq c + 1$.

Figure 1 shows a very simple net structure S_1 consisting of places A and B, and a transition a. Each entry in the first column of the accompanying table is an example for a P_1-inequality for $P_1 = \{A, B\}$.

We can *evaluate* a marking m in a P-inequality U by assigning $m[i]$ to each place p_i. Based thereon, we define *validity* of U in m in the obvious way:

Definition 2 (Value, satisfaction, validity). *Let $U = k \cdot P \geq c$ be a P-inequality. Let m be marking of S.*

- *$k \cdot m$ is the* value *of m in U.*
- *Marking m* satisfies *U, or synonymously, U is* valid *in m, iff $k \cdot m \geq c$. We write $\mathbb{M}(U)$ for the set of all U-satisfying markings of S.*
- *Petri net $\langle S, m \rangle$* satisfies *U, or synonymously, U is* valid *in $\langle S, m \rangle$, iff U is valid in each $m' \in \mathrm{Reach}_S(m)$.*

As an example, consider S_1, $U_{1,1}$, $U_{1,2}$ and $U_{1,8}$ from Fig. 1. Then, $(1\ 0) \in \mathbb{M}(U_{1,1}) \cap \mathbb{M}(U_{1,8})$, $(0\ 1) \in \mathbb{M}(U_{1,1})$, $(0\ 0) \in \mathbb{M}(U_{1,2})$.

We recall the property of *stability*. Intuitively, a P-inequality is stable if its validity is preserved along steps. An important remark is that stability is independent from reachability, preservation is required in all steps. Our definition is similar to the definition in [21], and only refined by defining t-stability for a given transition t.

Definition 3 (Stability). *Let* $t \in T$. *Let* U *be a* P-*inequality.*

- *U is t-stable in S iff for all steps $m \xrightarrow{t}_S m'$: $m \in \mathbb{M}(U)$ implies $m' \in \mathbb{M}(U)$.*
- *U is stable in S iff U is t-stable for each $t \in T$.*

The second column in the table in Fig. 1 contains a checkmark ($\checkmark$) if the P_1-inequality in the first column is a-stable. We go through some of the examples: Intuitively, $U_{1,1}$ is a-stable because the places A and B are equally weighted and a just "shifts" a token from A to B. Similarly, $U_{1,4}$ is stable: In each $U_{1,4}$-satisfying marking m, there is at most one token on A and B, and A and B are never marked at once: Thus, a is either disabled, or firing a leads to the marking $(0\ 1)$. In contrast to that, $U_{1,5}$ is not stable due to the satisfying marking $(1\ 0)$ which enables a, but firing a leads to the non-satisfying marking $(0\ 1)$. At first glance it may be counter-intuitive that $U_{1,8}$ is not a-stable, because $U_{1,6}$ and $U_{1,7}$ are both a-stable. This can be explained with the marking $m = (1\ 0)$ which enables a: Both $U_{1,6}$ and $U_{1,8}$ are valid in m. However, firing a from each of them has different consequences: $U_{1,6}$ stays valid because one token on B is sufficient to satisfy $U_{1,6}$. In contrast to that, $U_{1,8}$ becomes invalid, because one token on B is not sufficient to satisfy $U_{1,8}$. Marking m does not satisfy $U_{1,7}$, another token on either place is required; once there are at least two tokens in the net, $U_{1,7}$ is valid and stays valid, because the number of tokens does not change. The P_1-inequality $U_{1,10}$ requires at least as many tokens on B as on A, and is stable because a consumes tokens from A and produces tokens on B.

As mentioned in the introduction, stability of U reduces validity of U in some Petri net $\langle S, m \rangle$ to validity of U in m: If U is stable in S and valid in m, then U is valid in every marking $m' \in \text{Reach}_S(m)$.

Traps and *co-traps* (also known as siphons or structural deadlocks) are well-known structural properties inducing stable P-inequalities. Thereby, traps and co-traps are usually defined as sets of places with certain properties. Intuitively, a trap is a set Q of places with the following property: Once Q is marked, Q cannot become unmarked again – hence, tokens are trapped in Q. In contrast to that, a co-trap is a set of places Q that – once unmarked – can never be marked again. For technical reasons, we conceive a trap or co-trap as its induced P-inequality instead of a set of places:

Definition 4 (Trap, co-trap). *Let* $Q \subseteq P$ *be a set of places and* $t \in T$ *a transition. If* $t^- \cdot \text{char}(Q) \geq 1$ *implies* $t^+ \cdot \text{char}(Q) \geq 1$, *then* $\text{char}(Q) \cdot P \geq 1$ *is a t-trap. If* $t^+ \cdot \text{char}(Q) \geq 1$ *implies* $t^- \cdot \text{char}(Q) \geq 1$, *then* $-\text{char}(Q) \cdot P \geq 0$ *is* a t-co-trap. If U is a t-trap for each transition $t \in T$, then U is a trap. Likewise, if U is a t-co-trap for each $t \in T$, then U is a co-trap.

As mentioned before, all traps and co-traps are stable. The table in Fig. 1 contains the trap $U_{1,1}$ and the co-trap $U_{1,2}$. The table also contains examples of P_1-inequalities that are stable, but neither traps nor co-traps. Some of them are *generalized traps* or *generalized co-traps* as we will show in Sect. 5.2 and 5.3. Finally, there is the set of *canonical P-inequalities* which are trivially stable because they are valid in every marking: Let $Q \subseteq P$. Then, $U = \mathrm{char}(Q) \cdot \boldsymbol{P} \geq 0$ is a *canonical inequality*. Obviously, U is valid in each $\boldsymbol{m}$ of S, and thus also stable in S.

4   A Complete Characterization Based on Linear Programming

In this section, we provide a complete characterization of all stable P-inequalities of a given net structure $S = \langle P, T, F \rangle$ with $P = \{p_1, \ldots, p_n\}$. To this end, we define the *infimum* of a P-inequality U w.r.t. a given transition t in S. Intuitively, the infimum of U w.r.t. t is the least value of all markings $\boldsymbol{m}$ in U enabling t, or ∞ if t is disabled in every U-satisfying marking.

Definition 5 (Infimum of a P-inequality w.r.t. a transition). *Let $\boldsymbol{k}$ be a P-vector and $c \in \mathbb{Z}$. Let $t \in T$ be a transition. Let M_t be the set of all markings of S enabling t. Then,*

$$\inf{}_{t,S}(\boldsymbol{k} \cdot \boldsymbol{P} \geq c) := \inf\{\boldsymbol{k} \cdot \boldsymbol{m} \mid \boldsymbol{m} \in M_t \cap \mathbb{M}(\boldsymbol{k} \cdot \boldsymbol{P} \geq c)\}$$

is the infimum of $\boldsymbol{k} \cdot \boldsymbol{P} \geq c$ w.r.t. t in S.

Thereby, the infimum is well-defined, because the constant c is a lower bound for the set of all markings satisfying U. Figure 1 shows examples of infimums for different inequalities: E.g. $U_{1,1}$ has an infimum of 1, as the marking $(1\ 0)$ enables a and satisfies $U_{1,1}$. In contrast to that, no marking both satisfies $U_{1,2}$ *and* enables a, thus, the infimum $U_{1,2}$ is ∞. Regarding $U_{1,7}$, we see that the infimum is 5: We need at least one token on A to enable a; in order to satisfy $U_{1,7}$, we need to add another token; B has the lower weight, and putting a token on B leads to a value of 5.

Now we can use the infimum of a P-inequality w.r.t. a transition t for a characterization of all t-stable P-inequalities: Let U be the inequality $\boldsymbol{k} \cdot \boldsymbol{P} \geq c$. Then, U is t-stable iff the sum of the $\boldsymbol{k}$-weighted effect of t and the infimum of U w.r.t. t is greater than or equal to c.

Theorem 1. *Let $t \in T$ be a transition. Let $\boldsymbol{k}$ be a P-vector and $c \in \mathbb{Z}$. Then, the following are equivalent:*

1. $\boldsymbol{k} \cdot \boldsymbol{P} \geq c$ is a t-stable inequality.
2. $\inf_{t,S}(\boldsymbol{k} \cdot \boldsymbol{P} \geq c) + \boldsymbol{k} \cdot t^\Delta \ \geq \ c$.

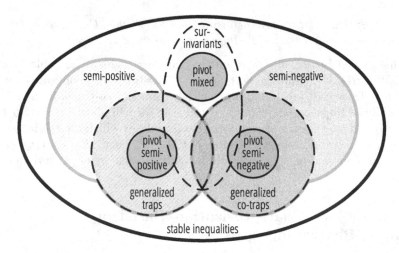

Fig. 2. Overview: Characterizations of stable P-inequalities. Thereby, pivot mixed, pivot semi-negative, pivot semi-positive denote the sets of stable pivot mixed, stable pivot semi-positive, and stable pivot semi-negative P-inequalities, respectively.

Proof. Let $U = \boldsymbol{k} \cdot \boldsymbol{P} \geq c$.

"1.⇒2." Let U be t-stable. If t is disabled in each $\boldsymbol{m} \in \mathbb{M}(U)$, then $\inf_{t,S}(U) = \infty$, and 2. trivially holds. Let t be enabled in at least one U-satisfying marking. Then, by Definition 5, $\inf_{t,S}(U) \geq c$, and there exists a marking $\boldsymbol{m}$ with $\boldsymbol{k} \cdot \boldsymbol{m} = \inf_{t,S}(U)$ and $\boldsymbol{m}$ enables t. Let $\boldsymbol{m} \xrightarrow{t}_S \boldsymbol{m}'$. By the firing rule, $\boldsymbol{k} \cdot \boldsymbol{m}' = \boldsymbol{k} \cdot (\boldsymbol{m} + \boldsymbol{t}^\Delta) = \boldsymbol{k} \cdot \boldsymbol{m} + \boldsymbol{k} \cdot \boldsymbol{t}^\Delta = \inf_{t,S}(U) + \boldsymbol{k} \cdot \boldsymbol{t}^\Delta$. Because U is t-stable, $\boldsymbol{k} \cdot \boldsymbol{m}' \geq c$. Therefore, $\inf_{t,S}(U) + \boldsymbol{k} \cdot \boldsymbol{t}^\Delta \geq c$.

"2.⇒1." Let $\inf_{t,S}(U) + \boldsymbol{k} \cdot \boldsymbol{t}^\Delta \geq c$. If $\inf_{t,S}(U) = \infty$, then t is disabled in each $\boldsymbol{m} \in \mathbb{M}(U)$, and U is trivially t-stable. Let $\boldsymbol{m} \in \mathbb{M}(U)$ and t be enabled in $\boldsymbol{m}$. Let $\boldsymbol{m} \xrightarrow{t}_S \boldsymbol{m}'$. Then, $\boldsymbol{k} \cdot \boldsymbol{m}' = \boldsymbol{k} \cdot (\boldsymbol{m} + \boldsymbol{t}^\Delta) = \boldsymbol{k} \cdot \boldsymbol{m} + \boldsymbol{k} \cdot \boldsymbol{t}^\Delta$. By Definition 5, $\boldsymbol{k} \cdot \boldsymbol{m} \geq \inf_{t,S}(U)$. Therefore, $\boldsymbol{k} \cdot \boldsymbol{m}' = \boldsymbol{k} \cdot \boldsymbol{m} + \boldsymbol{k} \cdot \boldsymbol{t}^\Delta \geq \inf_{t,S}(U) + \boldsymbol{k} \cdot \boldsymbol{t}^\Delta \geq c$. Hence, $\boldsymbol{m}' \in \mathbb{M}(U)$ and U is t-stable. $\square$

As an example, in Fig. 1 one can see that all inequalities are stable iff the sum of the infimum and $\boldsymbol{k} \cdot \boldsymbol{a}^\Delta$ is greater than or equal to the constant of the inequality.

5   From Structure to Stability

In this section, we extend the work on *sur-invariants* [5], [23] in Sect. 5.1, and generalize the existing structural properties of traps and co-traps to *generalized traps* and *generalized co-traps* in Sect. 5.2 and 5.3, respectively. We show that each of these structural properties implies stability. We discuss the converse of these statements in Sect. 6. Figure 2 summarizes the findings of Sect. 5 and 6. Let for this section $S = \langle P, T, F \rangle$ with $P = \{p_1, \ldots, p_n\}$ be a net structure.

5.1   Sur-Invariants

Let t be a transition. A P-inequality is a t-*sur-invariant* iff t has a semi-positive weighted effect.

Definition 6 (Sur-Invariant). *Let $t \in T$ be a transition. Let $U = \mathbf{k} \cdot \mathbf{P} \geq c$ be a P-inequality. Then, U is a t-sur-invariant iff $\mathbf{k} \cdot \mathbf{t}^\Delta \geq 0$.*

Figure 3 shows examples: Every transition of S_{3a} puts at least as many tokens on A as on B. In S_{3b}, each transition consuming from a 2-weighted place produces two tokens. In S_{3c}, we have an inverse effect.

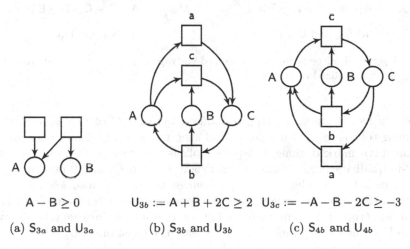

$$A - B \geq 0 \qquad U_{3b} := A + B + 2C \geq 2 \quad U_{3c} := -A - B - 2C \geq -3$$

(a) S_{3a} and U_{3a} (b) S_{3b} and U_{3b} (c) S_{4b} and U_{4b}

Fig. 3. Three sur-invariants U_{3a}, U_{3b} and U_{3c} of S_{3a}, S_{3b} and S_{3c}, respectively

Lemma 1. *Let $t \in T$ be a transition. Let U be a P-inequality. If U is a t-sur-invariant of S, then U is t-stable in S.*

Proof. If $\mathbb{M}(U) = \emptyset$ or $m \not\geq t^-$ for all $m \in \mathbb{M}(U)$, U is trivially stable. Otherwise, let $m \in \mathbb{M}(U)$ and $m \xrightarrow{t}_S m'$ be a step of S. Then, $\mathbf{k} \cdot \mathbf{m}' = \mathbf{k} \cdot (\mathbf{m} + \mathbf{t}^\Delta) = \mathbf{k} \cdot \mathbf{m} + \mathbf{k} \cdot \mathbf{t}^\Delta$. Because $m \in \mathbb{M}(U)$, we have $\mathbf{k} \cdot \mathbf{m} \geq c$. Because U is a sur-invariant, $\mathbf{k} \cdot \mathbf{t}^\Delta \geq 0$. Therefore, $\mathbf{k} \cdot \mathbf{m} + \mathbf{k} \cdot \mathbf{t}^\Delta \geq c$, and thus $\mathbf{k} \cdot \mathbf{m}' \geq c$ and $m' \in \mathbb{M}(U)$. $\square$

The converse does not hold, as $U_{1,4}$ and $U_{1,7}$ in Fig. 1 illustrate. Both P_1-inequalities are stable, but $\mathbf{k}a^\Delta = -1$ in both cases. Thus, $U_{1,4}$ and $U_{1,7}$ are not sur-invariants.

5.2   Generalized Traps

Here, we consider a P-inequality U of the form $\mathbf{k} \cdot \mathbf{P} \geq c$, where $\mathbf{k}$ and c are semi-positive. We derive conditions for U to be a *generalized t-trap* by generalizing

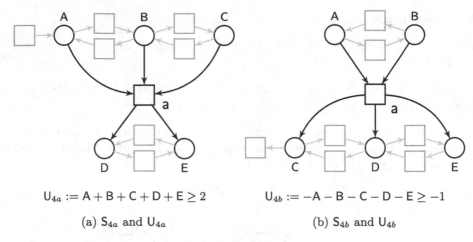

$$U_{4a} := A + B + C + D + E \geq 2 \qquad U_{4b} := -A - B - C - D - E \geq -1$$

(a) S_{4a} and U_{4a} (b) S_{4b} and U_{4b}

Fig. 4. A generalized trap and a generalized co-trap: U_{4a} is a generalized trap of S_{4a}, and U_{4b} is a generalized co-trap of S_{4b}

t-traps: By Definition 4, a t-trap is induced by a set Q of places, such that t consuming tokens from Q implies t producing tokens on Q. Thus, once marked, a t-trap stays marked along t-steps — tokens are "trapped". Hence, a t-trap is a P-inequality where a place p has weight 1 if $p \in Q$, and 0 otherwise. The constant of a trap is always 1. A *generalized t-trap* U is also a semi-positive inequality. However, the weights and the constant may differ from 0 and 1. We weaken the structural requirement as follows: U is a t-sur-invariant, or the value of t^+ in U is sufficiently high, that is, at least the constant of U.

Definition 7 (Generalized trap). *Let $t \in T$ be a transition. Let $U = \mathbf{k} \cdot \mathbf{P} \geq c$ be a semi-positive P-inequality. Then, U is a generalized t-trap if U is a t-sur-invariant or $\mathbf{k} \cdot \mathbf{t}^+ \geq c$.*

Figure 2 depicts the relationship between t-sur-invariants and generalized t-traps: The intersection between the two sets is the set of semi-positive t-sur-invariants. Therefore, U_{3b} from Fig. 3b is a generalized trap, as it is a semi-positive sur-invariant. Figure 4a shows another example for a generalized trap U_{4a}: First, S_{4b} is t-sur-invariant for every gray transition $t \neq \mathsf{a}$. Second, U_{4a} is a generalized a-trap but not an a-sur-invariant, as the weighted effect is negative.

We show that each generalized t-trap U is t-stable. If U is a t-sur-invariant, we can apply Lemma 1. Otherwise, we inspect a t-step from an arbitrary U-satisfying marking and apply semi-positivity of U:

Lemma 2. *Let $t \in T$ be a transition. Let U be a semi-positive P-inequality. If U is a generalized t-trap of S, then U is t-stable in S.*

Proof. If U is a t-sur-invariant, we can apply Lemma 1. Otherwise, we have $\mathbf{k} \cdot \mathbf{t}^+ \geq c$. If $\mathbb{M}(U) = \emptyset$ or $\mathbf{m} \not\geq \mathbf{t}^-$ for all $\mathbf{m} \in \mathbb{M}(U)$, then U is trivially stable. Otherwise, let $\mathbf{m} \in \mathbb{M}(U)$ and $\mathbf{m} \xrightarrow{t}_S \mathbf{m}'$ be a step. Then, $\mathbf{k} \cdot \mathbf{m}' = \mathbf{k} \cdot (\mathbf{m} + \mathbf{t}^{\Delta}) =$

$k \cdot m - k \cdot t^- + k \cdot t^+$. Because t is enabled in m, $m \geq t^-$. By assumption, k is semi-positive. Thus $k \cdot (m - t^-)$ is semi-positive. From $k \cdot t^+ \geq c$, we can thus conclude $k \cdot m' \geq c$, and $m' \in \mathrm{M}(U)$. $\qquad\square$

The converse does not hold, as $U_{1,7}$ in Fig. 1 illustrates. The P_1-inequality is semi-positive and stable, but it is neither a sur-invariant nor a generalized trap, as the weighted effect is -1 and $k \cdot a^+ = 2 < 4$.

Finally, we show that the classical trap theorem (every t-trap is t-stable) is an actual special case of Lemma 2. To this end, we first show that every t-trap is a generalized t-trap:

Lemma 3. *Let $t \in T$ be a transition. Let U be a t-trap of S. Then, U is a generalized t-trap of S.*

Proof. Let $U = k \cdot P \geq 1$. We show that $k \cdot t^\Delta < 0$ implies $k \cdot t^+ \geq 1$. If $k \cdot t^\Delta < 0$, there exists some place $p \in {}^\bullet t$ and $k[i] = 1$. Because U is a t-trap, there exists some j with $1 \leq j \leq n$ and $t^+[j] = 1$. Because k is semi-positive, we have $k \cdot t^+ \geq 1$. $\qquad\square$

It remains to be shown that there exists a generalized t-trap which is not a classical t-trap. This can be easily seen, as classical t-traps cannot have coefficients other than 0 or 1.

Likewise, we can show that each canonical P-inequality $\mathrm{char}(Q) \cdot P \geq 0$ for $Q \subseteq P$ is a generalized t-trap: The condition $\mathrm{char}(Q) \cdot t^+ \geq 0$ is trivially satisfied.

5.3 Generalized Co-traps

In this section we consider again a P-inequality U of the form $k \cdot P \geq c$, but in contrast to the previous section, now k and c are semi-negative. In the following, we introduce the notion of *generalized t-co-traps*. As a preparation, we show a sufficient condition for t-stability of semi-negative P-inequalities:

Lemma 4. *Let $t \in T$ be a transition. Let $U = k \cdot P \geq c$ a semi-negative P-inequality. If $k \cdot t^- < c$, then U is t-stable.*

Proof. If $\mathrm{M}(U) = \emptyset$, U is trivially stable. Otherwise, let $m \in \mathrm{M}(U)$. Then, $k \cdot m \geq c$. By assumption, $k \cdot t^- < c$. Thus $k \cdot t^- < c \leq k \cdot m$. Because k is semi-negative, $t^- \not\leq m$. Therefore, t is disabled in each marking $m \in \mathrm{M}(U)$ and U is trivially t-stable. $\qquad\square$

Now we are ready to introduce *generalized t-co-traps*, generalizing classical co-traps. By Definition 4, a t-co-trap is induced by a set of places Q, such that t producing tokens on Q implies t consuming tokens from Q. Thus, once Q is unmarked, it cannot be marked again by t-steps. For this reason, every t-co-trap is a semi-negative inequality where each place Q has weight -1, each place outside Q has weight 0, and the constant is 0. A *generalized t-co-trap* generalizes a t-co-trap in two ways: First, we allow arbitrary semi-negative weights instead of only -1 and 0. Second, the constant may be an arbitrary semi-negative number instead of only 0. Structurally, we require U is either a t-sur-invariant, or t-stable by the condition in Lemma 4.

Definition 8 (Generalized co-trap). *Let $t \in T$ be a transition. Let $U = \boldsymbol{k} \cdot \boldsymbol{P} \geq c$ be a semi-negative P-inequality. Then U is a generalized t-co-trap of S iff U is a t-sur-invariant, or $\boldsymbol{k} \cdot \boldsymbol{t}^- < c$.*

Figure 2 depicts the relationship between t-sur-invariants, generalized t-traps, and generalized t-co-traps: The intersection between the set of t-sur-invariants and the set of generalized t-co-traps is the set of semi-negative t-sur-invariants. The intersection of the set of generalized t-traps and generalized t-co-traps is non-empty — the weights of a P-inequality that is both a generalized t-trap and generalized t-co-trap are all 0.

Figure 3c depicts the generalized co-trap U_{3c}, because U_{3c} is a semi-negative sur-invariant. Figure 4b shows another, more interesting example of a generalized co-trap: U_{4b} is a t-sur-invariant for every gray transition $t \neq \mathsf{a}$. However, U_{4b} is a generalized a-co-trap but not an a-sur-invariant.

We show that each generalized t-co-trap U is t-stable. For the case that U is not a t-sur-invariant, we apply Lemma 4.

Lemma 5. *Let $t \in T$ be a transition. Let U be a semi-negative P-inequality. If U is a generalized t-co-trap of S, then U is t-stable in S.*

Proof. If U is a t-sur-invariant, we can apply Lemma 1. Otherwise, $\boldsymbol{k} \cdot \boldsymbol{t}^- < c$. Then, by Lemma 4, t is disabled in each $\boldsymbol{m} \in \mathbb{M}(U)$, and thus U is t-stable. □

The converse does not hold in general, as shown by $\mathsf{U}_{1,4}$ in Fig. 1. The semi-negative P_1-inequality is stable, but is not a generalized co-trap, as the weighted effect is negative and $\boldsymbol{k} \cdot \boldsymbol{a}^- = -1 \geq -3$.

Finally, we show that the classical co-trap theorem (every t-co-trap is t-stable) is an actual special case of the generalized co-trap theorem. To this end, we first show that every t-co-trap is a generalized t-co-trap:

Lemma 6. *Let $t \in T$ be a transition. Let U be a t-co-trap of S. Then, U is a generalized t-co-trap of S.*

Proof. Let $U = \boldsymbol{k} \cdot \boldsymbol{P} \geq 0$ be a classical t-co-trap with coefficients -1 and 0. We show that $\boldsymbol{k} \cdot \boldsymbol{t}^\Delta < 0$ implies $\boldsymbol{k} \cdot \boldsymbol{t}^- < 0$. If $\boldsymbol{k} \cdot \boldsymbol{t}^\Delta < 0$, there is some place $p_i \in t^\bullet$ and $\boldsymbol{k}[i] = -1$. Because U is a t-co-trap, there exists some j with $1 \leq j \leq n$ and $\boldsymbol{t}^-[j] = -1$. Because $\boldsymbol{k}$ is semi-negative, $\boldsymbol{k} \cdot \boldsymbol{t}^- < 0$. □

It remains to be shown that there exists a generalized t-co-trap which is not a classical t-trap. As every classical t-co-trap has only weights in $\{0, 1\}$, this can be easily seen.

6   From Stability to Structure

In this section, we discover structural properties of stable inequalities. As a first subclass with distinct structural properties, we introduce t-*sharp P-inequalities*. A P-inequality U is t-sharp if there exists a U-satisfying marking that enables t. Let for this section $S = \langle P, T, F \rangle$ with $P = \{p_1, \ldots, p_n\}$ be a net structure.

Definition 9 (*t*-sharp). *Let $U = k \cdot P \geq c$ be a P-inequality. Let $t \in T$ be a transition. Let M_t be the set of all markings enabling t. Then, U is t-sharp iff there exists a marking $m \in M_t$ with $k \cdot m = c$.*

We observe that a *P*-inequality U is *t*-sharp iff the infimum of U w.r.t. t coincides with the constant of U. Applying this argument and Theorem 1, we show that *t*-stability and *t*-sharpness together imply that U is a *t*-sur-invariant:

Lemma 7. *Let $t \in T$ be a transition. Let $U = k \cdot P \geq c$ be a P-inequality. If U is t-stable and t-sharp, then U is a t-sur-invariant.*

Proof. If U is *t*-sharp, then there exists a marking m, such that $k \cdot m = c$ and m enables t. Hence, m is in the set $M_t \cap \mathrm{M}(U)$ from Definition 5. Because $k \cdot m = c$, $k \cdot m$ is also an infimum of the set $\{k \cdot m' \mid m' \in \mathrm{M}(U)\}$. Therefore, $\inf_{t,S}(U) = c$. From Theorem 1 and *t*-stability of U, we get $\inf_{t,S}(U) + k \cdot t^\Delta \geq c$. Applying the assumption $\inf_{t,S}(U) = c$, we have $c + k \cdot t^\Delta \geq c$ which is equivalent to $k \cdot t^\Delta \geq 0$. Therefore, by Definition 6, U is a *t*-sur-invariant.   □

In the following, we investigate conditions for the *t*-sharpness of a *P*-inequality U. To this end, we introduce the class of *pivot P-incqualities*, and derive sufficient conditions for *t*-sharpness in Sect. 6.1. In Sect. 6.2 to 6.4 we apply these conditions to show that *t*-stable mixed pivot *P*-inequalities are *t*-sur-invariants, *t*-stable semi-positive pivot *P*-inequalities are generalized *t*-traps, and *t*-stable semi-negative pivot *P*-inequalities are generalized *t*-co-traps.

6.1   Pivot Inequalities

We identified *pivot P*-inequalities as a class of *P*-inequalities that can be easily syntactically characterized, and yield simple sufficient conditions for *t*-sharpness. A *P*-inequality is *pivot*, if there exists at least one place with absolute weight 1.

Definition 10 (Pivot P-vector, pivot P-inequality). *Let $U = k \cdot P \geq c$ be a P-inequality.*

1. *k is pivot iff there exists i with $1 \leq i \leq n$ and $|k[i]| = 1$.*
2. *U is pivot iff k is pivot.*

For an inequality it is easy to check whether it is a pivot inequality. Furthermore, we observe that every *t*-trap or *t*-co-trap is a pivot inequality, because all of its coefficients are 0 or 1.

In the following, we show sufficient conditions for *t*-sharpness for classes of pivot inequalities.

Lemma 8. *Let $t \in T$ be a transition. Let k be a pivot P-vector and $k[i] = 1$. Let $c \in \mathbb{Z}$. Let $k \cdot t^- \leq c$. Then, $U = k \cdot P \geq c$ is t-sharp.*

Fig. 5. A net structure S_5 with marking m_5 and an a-sharp inequality U_5

Proof. Let $P = \{p_1, \ldots, p_n\}$. We construct a marking m as follows: Let v be the P-vector defined by

$$v[j] := \begin{cases} c - k \cdot t^- & \text{if } i = j \\ 0 & \text{otherwise .} \end{cases}$$

Let $m = t^- + v$. We first show $k \cdot m = c$: $k \cdot m = k \cdot (t^- + v) = k \cdot t^- + k \cdot v = k \cdot t^- + k[i]v[i] = k \cdot t^- + c - k \cdot t^- = c$. From this, we can conclude $m \in \mathbb{M}(U)$. It remains to be shown that m enables t. Let $1 \le j \le n$. If $i \ne j$, then $m[j] = t^-[j]$. If $i = j$, then $m[j] = t^-[j] + c - k \cdot t^-$. By assumption, $k \cdot t^- \le c$, and also $c - k \cdot t^- \ge 0$. Therefore, $m[j] \ge t^-[j]$ and finally $m \ge t^-$ and t is enabled in m. Therefore, U is t-sharp. $\qquad\square$

We can use this to show the existence of such a marking if the pivot is negative and $k \cdot t^- \ge c$:

Lemma 9. *Let $t \in T$ be transition. Let k be a pivot P-vector and $k[i] = -1$. Let $c \in \mathbb{Z}$. Let $k \cdot t^- \ge c$. Then, $U = k \cdot P \ge c$ is t-sharp.*

Proof. We observe that $-k[i] = 1$ and $-k \cdot t^- \le -c$. Applying Lemma 8, there exists a marking m that enables t and $-k \cdot m = -c$. Then, $k \cdot m = c$. $\qquad\square$

Finally, we show a stronger existence lemma for mixed pivot P-inequalities:

Lemma 10. *Let $t \in T$ be a transition. Let k be a mixed pivot P-vector. Let $c \in \mathbb{Z}$. Then, $U = k \cdot P \ge c$ is t-sharp.*

Proof. We distinguish the cases $k[i] = 1$ vs. $k[i] = -1$ and $k \cdot t^- \le c$ vs. $k \cdot t^- > c$.

- Let $k[i] = 1$ and $k \cdot t^- \le c$. Then we can apply Lemma 8.
- Let $k[i] = -1$ and $k \cdot t^- \ge c$. Then we can apply Lemma 9.
- Let $k[i] = 1$ and $k \cdot t^- > c$. Because k is mixed, there exists $1 \le j \le n$ with $k[j] < 0$. Let $d = \frac{c - k \cdot t^-}{k[j]}$. Then, d is a rational number. Let κ be the least integer with $\kappa \ge d$.
  Let v be the P-vector defined by

$$v[\ell] := \begin{cases} \kappa & \text{if } \ell = j \\ c - k \cdot t^- - k[j]\kappa & \text{if } \ell = i \\ 0 & \text{otherwise.} \end{cases}$$

Let $m = t^- + v$. We show $k \cdot m = c$ as follows: $k \cdot m = k \cdot (t^- + v) = k \cdot t^- + k \cdot v = k \cdot t^- + k[j]\kappa + k[i](c - k \cdot t^- - k[j]\kappa) = k \cdot t^- + k[j]\kappa + c - k \cdot t^- - k[j]\kappa = c$. It remains to be shown that m is a marking enabling t. To this end, we show $v[\ell] \geq 0$ for all $1 \leq \ell \leq n$. First, we show $\kappa \geq 0$ by showing $d \geq 0$. We have $d = \frac{c - k \cdot t^-}{k[j]}$. By assumption $k \cdot t^- > c$ and $k[j] < 0$. Hence, $c - k \cdot t^- < 0$ and also $d \geq 0$. Now, we show $c - k \cdot t^- - k[j]\kappa \geq 0$. To this end, we use $0 \leq d \leq \kappa$ and $k[j] < 0$, and instead show $c - k \cdot t^- - k[j]d \geq 0$. $c - k \cdot t^- - k[j]d = c - k \cdot t^- - k[j]\frac{c - k \cdot t^-}{k[j]} = c - k \cdot t^- - c + k \cdot t^- = 0$. Hence, $m \geq t^-$ and t is enabled in m.

- Let $k[i] = -1$ and $k \cdot t^- < c$. Then, $-k[i] = 1$ and $-k \cdot t^- > c$. Thus by the previous part of the proof, there exists a marking m with $-k \cdot m = -c$ and m enables t. From this, we conclude $k \cdot m = c$.

Therefore, U is t-sharp. □

An example of $m = t^- + v$ as constructed in the proof can be seen in Fig. 5. At least one token is in every pre-place of a and $k \cdot m = 3$.

Combining Lemma 8 to 10 with Lemma 7, we show the following theorem:

Theorem 2. *Let $t \in T$ be a transition. Let $U = k \cdot P \geq c$ be a stable pivot P-inequality. Then each of the following conditions implies that U is a t-sur-invariant:*

1. *There exists $k[i] = 1$ and $k \cdot t^- \leq c$.*
2. *There exists $k[i] = -1$ and $k \cdot t^- \geq c$.*
3. *k is mixed.*

Proof. 1. Applying Lemma 8 yields t-sharpness, applying Lemma 7 and the assumption that U proves $k \cdot t^\Delta \geq 0$. Analogously, 2. and 3. are shown by replacing Lemma 8 by Lemma 9 and Lemma 10, respectively. □

6.2 Stable Mixed Pivot Inequalities Are Sur-Invariants

From Theorem 2, we can directly derive that all t-stable mixed pivot P-inequalities are t-sur-invariants. This yields the following characterization:

Theorem 3 (Sur-invariant theorem). *Let $t \in T$ be a transition. Let U be a mixed pivot P-inequality of S. Then, the following are equivalent:*

1. *U is t-stable in S.*
2. *U is a t-sur-invariant of S.*

Proof. "1.⇒2." Follows directly from Theorem 2.
"2.⇒1." Follows directly from Lemma 1. □

Figure 2 visualizes this relationship. As written in the caption of Fig. 2, mixed pivot stands for the set of all *stable* mixed pivot P-inequalities.

6.3   Stable Semi-positive Pivot Inequalities Are Generalized Traps

Applying Theorem 2, we show that each t-stable semi-positive pivot inequality is a generalized t-trap. There, the only remaining proof objective is to show that $k \cdot t^- > c$ implies $k \cdot t^+ \geq c$. Here, the main argument is that t is enabled in the U-satisfying marking t^-, and firing t yields the marking t^+. From t-stability, we can conclude that t^+ satisfies U. The combination of this result with Lemma 2 yields the following characterization:

Theorem 4 (Generalized trap theorem). *Let $t \in T$ be a transition. Let U be a semi-positive pivot P-inequality of S. Then, the following are equivalent:*

1. *U is t-stable in S.*
2. *U is a generalized t-trap of S.*

Proof. Let $U = k \cdot P \geq c$.

"**1.⇒2.**" We show that U is a generalized t-trap. We show that U is a t-sur-invariant or $k \cdot t^+ \geq c$.
    1. Let $k \cdot t^- \leq c$. Then, by Theorem 2, U is a t-sur-invariant.
    2. Let $k \cdot t^- > c$. Then, $t^- \in \mathbb{M}(U)$, t is enabled in l^-, and $t^- \xrightarrow{t}_S t^+$. Then, $t^+ \in \mathbb{M}(U)$, because U is stable. Thus, $k \cdot t^+ \geq c$.
"**2.⇒1.**" Follows directly from Lemma 2.   □

Figure 2 visualizes this relationship. As written in the caption of Fig. 2, semispspositive pivot stands for the set of all *stable* semi-positive P-inequalities. The sets mixed pivot and semi-positive pivot are disjoint because mixed means being neither semi-positive nor semi-negative.

6.4   Stable Semi-negative Pivot Inequalities Are Generalized Co-traps

Applying Theorem 2, we show that each t-stable semi-negative pivot inequality is a generalized t-co-trap. Here, the proof is very short: By Definition 8, $U = k \cdot P \geq c$ is a t-co-trap iff (1) U is a t-sur-invariant or (2) $k \cdot t^- < c$. By Theorem 2, the complement of case (2) implies case (1). The combination of this result with Lemma 2 yields the following characterization:

Theorem 5 (Generalized co-trap theorem). *Let $t \in T$ be a transition. Let U be a semi-negative pivot P-inequality of S. Then, the following are equivalent:*

1. *U is t-stable in S.*
2. *U is a generalized t-co-trap of S.*

Proof. Let $U = k \cdot P \geq c$.

"**1.⇒2.**" Let t be a transition of S. We show that U is a generalized co-trap by showing that U is a t-sur-invariant or $k \cdot t^- < c$. It is sufficient to that $k \cdot t^- \geq c$ implies that U is a t-sur-invariant, which we have shown in Theorem 2.

"2.⇒1." Follows directly from Lemma 5.   □

Figure 2 shows this relationship. As written in the caption of Fig. 2, semisp-snegative pivot is the set of *stable* semi-negative pivot inequalities. The intersection of the sets semi-negative pivot and semi-positive pivot is empty, because a P-inequality with semi-positive and semi-negative weights has zero weights, and thus is not pivot.

7   Deciding Stability of Linear Inequalities

As shown in the appendix, 2EXP is a lower bound for the complexity of deciding validity of an inequality. Thus, the computational effort is high and deciding validity may become infeasible for practical purposes. As validity of a stable inequality reduces to validity in the initial marking, deciding stability efficiently is of particular interest.

In this section, we show decidability of stability for arbitrary P-inequalities. We discuss the complexity of deciding stability, and distinguish between arbitrary and pivot P-inequalities. Let $S = \langle P, T, F \rangle$ be a net structure with $P = \{p_1, \ldots, p_n\}$. We assume the following input:

- A transition t given as two P-vectors t^+ and t^-.
- A P-inequality $U = k \cdot P \geq c$ given as the P-vector k and the integer c.

Theorem 1 directly provides the basis for deciding t stability: The condition on the infimum of U w.r.t. t is necessary and sufficient. From linear programming, we know that there exists some procedure solve that gets two P-vectors v, v' and an integer c as input, and solves the linear program $\inf\{v \cdot m \mid m \geq v', k \cdot m \geq c\}$ [17]. Now we can use solve to decide t-stability:

Theorem 6 (Decidability of stability). *Let $S = \langle P, T, F \rangle$ and $t \in T$. Let U be a P-inequality. Then, t-stability and stability of U are decidable problems.*

Proof. Let $U = k \cdot P \geq c$. Clearly, given input k, t^- and c, solve computes $\inf_{t,S}(U)$. Then, applying Theorem 1, compute $\inf_{t,S}(U) + k \cdot t^\triangle$, and compare it to c. Thus, t-stability is decidable. We can simply apply this procedure for each $t \in T$ to decide stability of U.   □

Regarding complexity, we argue that deciding t-stability is in NP, because the condition on $\inf_{t,S}(U)$ in Theorem 1 can be reduced to the decision variant of the linear optimization problem, which in turn is known to be in NP [19]. In particular, it is not necessary to actually solve the optimization problem by calling solve: It is sufficient to solve the decision variant. As we can decide stability by deciding t-stability for each $t \in T$, deciding stability is also in NP. We leave (dis-)proving NP-hardness of deciding stability to future work. However, NP as upper bound for the complexity bound is signifantly better than the lower bound 2EXP for deciding validity.

We apply Theorem 3 to 5 to show that deciding t-stability and stability is in P for the class of pivot inequalities. Thereby, we assume integer arithmetics and comparisons, and accessing a vector at a given index to have constant complexity.

Theorem 7 (Complexity of deciding stability for pivot inequalities). *Let* $S = \langle P, T, F \rangle$ *be a net structure and* $t \in T$. *Let* U *be a pivot* P-*inequality. Then, deciding* t-*stability and deciding stability of* U *are problems in* P. *In particular,* t-*stability and stability can be decided in* $\mathcal{O}(|P|)$ *and* $\mathcal{O}((|P| + |T|)^2)$, *respectively.*

Proof. Obviously, the class of U (mixed, semi-positive, semi-negative) can be determined in $\mathcal{O}(|P|)$. Given the class, one can decide t-stability by checking whether U is a t-sur-invariant (Theorem 3), generalized t-trap (Theorem 4), or generalized $t$spsco-trap (Theorem 5). Inspecting the respective definitions, we conclude that there are at most two dot-products to compute and compared with some constant. The dot-product of two P-vectors can be computed in $\mathcal{O}(|P|)$. Hence, deciding t-stability is in $\mathcal{O}(|P|)$. Hence, deciding t-stability of U is in P. Stability (in contrast to t-stability) can be decided by deciding t-stability for each transition t. Therefore, deciding stability is in $\mathcal{O}(|P||T|) \subseteq \mathcal{O}((|P| + |T|)^2)$. Hence, deciding stability of U is in P.   □

8   Related Work

Our notions of validity and stability of P-inequalities are the same as in [21]. However, we refine the definition of stability, as t-stability, where the parameter t is some transition. The relation between stability and t-stability is natural, and it is not a big step to switch between the two notions: The refined notion of t-stability removes universal quantification in favor of introducing a parameter.

The term stability is known and used in literature, as deciding validity for a stable property reduces to deciding validity in the initial marking. Thereby, a stable, valid property is often called an *inductive invariant*. In the following, we discuss works that study combinations of inductive invariants, structural properties and linear algebra. The usage of integer linear programming [10] is common in structural Petri net analysis [14], [20], [22]. In [14], the author computes valid linear equations by means of linear algebra. Under the additional assumption that every transition is quasi-live, every valid equation is also stable [21]. This does not hold for inequalities, as a simple argument one may take boundedness of a given place. Traps and co-traps are known at least since the early seventies [12]. Since then, they are a fundamental part in the theory of Petri nets [5], [8], [13], [18], [21], [23]. In practice, traps and co-traps are used as analysis techniques in the fields of flexible manufacturing systems [1], [7], and synthetic biology [13]. In this paper, we generalized the notions of traps and co-traps in order to characterize sets of stable inequalities. The concept of traps has also been generalized for *colored Petri nets* [8]. We restricted ourselves to elementary Petri nets, also known as P/T nets, and have not yet studied the influence of extensions such as token colors or hot vs. cold transitions. Different procedures for deciding and computing traps and co-traps are surveyed in [3]. Here, the focus is often on enumerating *minimal* traps and co-traps, that is, minimal w.r.t. set inclusion. We have not yet discovered such a notion as a *minimal generalized* trap or co-trap. Our procedures are only decision procedures for a given inequality. However, our characterizations cover strictly larger classes of stable inequalities. The idea of sur-invariants has already been introduced in [5], [23] where they appear as generalizations of transition invariants. The property of sur-invariants is implicitly mentioned in [22]. In this work, we continued the work on this topic.

In [15], the author provides a decision procedure for the stability of Presburger formulas by reducing stability to satisfiability. A P-inequality can be expressed as a Presburger formula [11]. On the one hand, Presburger formulas are more general than P-inequalities, therefore decidability of stability follows as a corollary from decidability of stability of Presburger formulas. On the other hand, our characterization by means of linear programming leads to a proof that deciding stability of P-inequalities is in NP. In contrast to that, deciding satisfiability of Presburger formulas has double exponential complexity [9]. In particular, our characterizations lead to a polynomial algorithm for the subclass of pivot inequalities.

In [16], the author studies inductive invariants in the context of reachability. They show the following: If a marking is not reachable, then there exists an inductive Presburger invariant proving this. This does not imply the existence of a stable P-inequality, as Presburger formulas are a strict super class of P-inequalities. The related class of stable *modulo-invariants* is discussed in [4] in the context of reachability.

The correctness notion in this paper only copes with very specific safety properties, namely, a given P-inequality is required to hold in every reachable marking. In order to cope with more involved safety properties or even liveness properties, one could consider P-inequalities as the atomic propositions of some temporal logics. If one chooses the temporal logics of CTL* [6], then the formula AG $k \cdot P \geq c$ mirrors the correctness notion in this paper. In contrast to that, the more involved formula AGEF $k \cdot P \geq c$ requires that from every reachable marking, there is a marking reachable that satisfies $k \cdot P \geq c$.

9 Conclusion and Future Work

In this paper, we studied stable P-inequalities of net structures. Thereby, a stable P-inequality is a linear inequality where each variable is a place, and validity is preserved along all steps. In Sect. 4, we provided a complete characterization of all stable P-inequalities by means of linear programming. Then, we tackled the problem of characterizing the set of stable P-inequalities by means of structural properties. To this end, we followed two directions: In Sect. 5, we studied stability-inducing structural properties, namely sur-invariants, and the newly introduced generalized traps and co-traps. In Sect. 6, we inspected cases where stability implies structural properties. To this end, we introduced *pivot P-inequalities*, that is, P-inequalities with at least one weight with absolute value 1. This class is syntactically characterized, and – to the best of our knowledge – did not gain attention before in the context of Petri nets. We showed that stability implies structural properties for all pivot P-inequalities. Together, Sect. 5 and 6 provide a complete characterization of all stable pivot P-inequalities by means of sur-invariants, generalized traps, and generalized co-traps. We applied the results of Sect. 4 to 6 in Sect. 7 to show that deciding stability is in NP for arbitrary P-inequalities, and in P for pivot P-inequalities. In contrast to that, we show in the appendix of this paper that deciding the validity of a given P-inequality in a Petri net is a remarkably more complex problem: In particular, we show that 2EXP is a lower bound for the complexity of deciding validity. As deciding validity of stable P-inequalities is trivial, we propose to decide stability before deciding validity. Verifying this proposal in a case study with Petri net models from practice would be an interesting endeavor which we leave for future work.

In the remainder of this section, we discuss some further ideas for future work. As a start, we have only shown that deciding stability is in NP. An interesting point would be to see whether this problem is also NP-hard. As already discussed in Sect. 8, we only provided decision procedures for stability. It would be desirable to have a procedure to enumerate a canonical, finite set of stable P-inequalities. Similarly, one can consider a case where some P-inequality U is not stable, but can be composed from finitely many stable P-inequalities $U_1, \ldots, U_n$. Here, the challenge is to find a stability-preserving composition operator. At first glance, addition and conjunction would be obvious choices; however, addition does not preserve stability (but validity), and the conjunction of two inequalities is generally not expressible as an inequality. As the conjunction of two P-inequalities is a Presburger formula [11], one could lift our results to Presburger formulas, or apply a mixed approach. The *trap/co-trap theorem* relates traps and co-traps with liveness of a Petri net. It would be interesting to find a similar theorem for generalized traps and generalized co-traps. In this context, it would be interesting to define a duality relation on generalized traps and co-traps, similar to "a set of places that is both a trap and a co-trap". From a practical point of view, it would be interesting to implement our decision procedures. Then, one could make a case study to compare the pure reachability-based approach to deciding validity, with the mixed approach of first checking stability.

If a P-inequality U is stable, every P-inequality that is equivalent to U is also stable. Therefore, an efficient procedure to construct an equivalent pivot P-inequality U' from U, if such U' exists, would be useful: Stability of U then reduces to stability of U'. A first approach could be to decide whether U is a multiple of some pivot P-inequality U' by finding the greatest common divisor of the coefficients.

Appendix: Reducing coverability to validity

We suspect validity of P-inequalities to be decidable, as a proof one would try to reduce validity to reachability by adding arcs to each transition such that one distinct place stores the value of the current marking. In this section, we reduce the problem of *coverability* to the problem of validity. Let $N = \langle S, m \rangle$ be a Petri net with $S = \langle P, T, F \rangle$. We inspect the complexity of deciding validity of a P-inequality $U = k \cdot P \geq c$ in N. To this end, we reduce *coverability* to validity, which has 2EXP as a lower bound for the complexity [2]. A marking m' is *coverable* in N iff there is a reachable marking m'' with $m' \leq m''$.

In order to facilitate our construction, we introduce arc weights. It is well known that arc weights can be considered "syntactic sugar" with respect to reachability, and do not add to expressive power. We can formally consider arc weights by changing the flow relation F to a flow *function*, mapping each pair $\langle x, y \rangle \in (P \times T) \cup (T \times P)$ to a natural number.

Let $\hat{p} \notin P$ and $\hat{t} \notin T$. For a given marking m', we define the net $N' := \langle S', m \rangle$ as follows: $S' := \langle P', T \cup \{\hat{t}\}, F' \rangle$, $P' := P \cup \{\hat{p}\}$, $F'(x, y) := F(x, y)$ for all $\langle x, y \rangle \in (P \times T) \cup (T \times P)$, $F'(p, \hat{t}) := m'(p)$ for all $p \in P$, $F'(\hat{t}, p) := m'(p)$ for all $p \in P$, $F'(\hat{t}, \hat{p}) := 1$, $F'(\hat{p}, \hat{t}) := 0$.

Let $U = k \cdot P' \geq 0$ be the P'-inequality with zero weights for all $p \in P$, and weight -1 for $\hat{p}$. We show that N' satisfies U iff m' is *not* coverable in N. To this end, we first observe that every step of S is also a step of S'. Let v be some P'-vector assigning 0 to all $p \in P$. If m'' is a marking of S with $m' \leq m''$, then we have

$$m'' + v \xrightarrow{\hat{t}}_{S'} m'' + v + v',$$

where v' is the P'-vector assigning 1 to $\hat{p}$ and 0 to all $p \in P$. Hence, if some marking m'' covering m' is reachable in N, then $\hat{p}$ can be marked in N'. Now, we observe that $\hat{p}$ cannot be marked in N' if m' is not coverable in N. Finally, N satisfies U iff $\hat{p}$ cannot be marked. Thus, m' is *not* coverable iff N' satisfies U.

References

1. Abdallah, I., ElMaraghy, H.: Deadlock prevention and avoidance in fms: A petri net based approach. The International Journal of Advanced Manufacturing Technology 14(10), 704–715 (1998)
2. Cardoza, E., Lipton, R., Meyer, A.R.: Exponential space complete problems for petri nets and commutative semigroups. In: Proceedings of the 8th Annual ACM Symposium on Theory of Computing, pp. 50–54 (1976)
3. Colom, J.M., Silva, M.: Convex geometry and semiflows in P/T nets. A comparative study of algorithms for computation of minimal p-semiflows. In: Proceedings of 10th International Conference on Applications and Theory of Petri Nets, Bonn, Germany, June 1989. Advances in Petri Nets 1990, pp. 79–112 (1989)
4. Desel, J., Neuendorf, K.P., Radola, M.D.: Proving nonreachability by modulo-invariants. Theoretical Computer Science 153(1–2), 49–64 (1996)
5. Desel, J.: Struktur und Analyse von Free-Choice-Petrinetzen. Deutscher Universitätsverlag, DUV Informatik (1992)
6. Emerson, E.A., Halpern, J.Y.: "sometimes" and "not never" revisited: On branching versus linear time temporal logic. J. ACM 33(1), 151–178 (1986)
7. Ezpeleta, J., Colom, J., Martinez, J.: A petri net based deadlock prevention policy for flexible manufacturing systems. IEEE Transactions on Robotics and Automation 11(2), 173–184 (1995)
8. Ezpeleta, J., Couvreur, J., Silva, M.: A new technique for finding a generating family of siphons, traps and st-components. application to colored petri nets. In: Advances in Petri Nets 1993, Papers from the 12th International Conference on Applications and Theory of Petri Nets, Gjern, Denmark, pp. 126–147 (1991)
9. Fischer, M.J., Rabin, M.O.: Super-exponential complexity of presburger arithmetic, pp. 27–41 (1974)

10. Garey, M.R., Johnson, D.S.: Computers and Intractability; A Guide to the Theory of NP-Completeness. W.H. Freeman & Co., New York, NY, USA (1990)
11. Ginsburg, S., Spanier, E.H.: Semigroups, presburger formulas, and languages. Pacific Journal of Mathematics 16(2), 285–296 (1966)
12. Hack, M.: Analysis production schemata by Petri nets. Master's thesis, Massachusetts Institute of Technology, Cambridge, Mass (1972)
13. Heiner, M., Gilbert, D., Donaldson, R.: Petri nets for systems and synthetic biology. In: Bernardo, M., Degano, P., Zavattaro, G. (eds.) SFM 2008. LNCS, vol. 5016, pp. 215–264. Springer, Heidelberg (2008)
14. Lautenbach, K.: Linear algebraic techniques for place/transition nets. In: Brauer, W., Reisig, W., Rozenberg, G. (eds.) Petri Nets: Central Models and Their Properties. Lecture Notes in Computer Science, vol. 254, pp. 142–167. Springer, Berlin Heidelberg (1987)
15. Leroux, J.: The general vector addition system reachability problem by presburger inductive invariants. Logical Methods in Computer Science 6(3) (2010)
16. Leroux, J.: Vector addition systems reachability problem (a simpler solution). In: Voronkov, A. (ed.) The Alan Turing Centenary Conference, Turing-100, Manchester UK June 22–25, 2012, Proceedings. EPiC Series, vol. 10, pp. 214–228 (2012)
17. Mitchell, J.E.: Branch-and-cut algorithms for combinatorial optimization problems. Handbook of applied optimization, pp. 65–77 (2002)
18. Murata, T.: Petri nets: properties, analysis and applications. In: Proceedings of the IEEE, pp. 541–580 (Apr 1989)
19. Papadimitriou, C.H.: On the complexity of integer programming. J. ACM 28(4), 765–768 (1981)
20. Pascoletti, K.H.: Diophantische Systeme und Lösungsmethoden zur Bestimmung aller Invarianten in Petri-Netzen. GMD-Bericht Nr. 160, R. Oldenbourg Verlag (1986)
21. Reisig, W.: Understanding Petri Nets: Modeling Techniques, Analysis Methods. Springer, Case Studies (2013)
22. Silva, M., Teruel, E., Colom, J.M.: Linear algebraic and linear programming techniques for the analysis of place or transition net systems. In: Lectures on Petri Nets I: Basic Models, Advances in Petri Nets, pp. 309–373 (1996)
23. Starke, P.H.: Analyse von Petri-Netz-Modellen, pp. 1–253 (1990)

Process Discovery Using Localized Events

Wil M.P. van der Aalst[1,2]([✉]), Anna Kalenkova[2], Vladimir Rubin[2],
and Eric Verbeek[1]

[1] Eindhoven University of Technology, P.O. Box 513,
5600 MB Eindhoven, The Netherlands
{w.m.p.v.d.aalst,h.m.w.verbeek}@tue.nl
[2] National Research University Higher School of Economics,
Moscow 101000, Russia
akalenkova@hse.ru

Abstract. Process mining techniques aim to analyze and improve conformance and performance of processes using event data. Process discovery is the most prominent process-mining task: A process model is derived based on an event log. The process model should be able to capture causalities, choices, concurrency, and loops. Process discovery is very challenging because of trade-offs between fitness, simplicity, precision, and generalization. Note that event logs typically only hold example behavior and cannot be assumed to be complete (to avoid overfitting). Dozens of process discovery techniques have been proposed. These use a wide range of approaches, e.g., language- or state-based regions, genetic mining, heuristics, expectation maximization, iterative log-splitting, etc. When models or logs become too large for analysis, the event log may be automatically decomposed or traces may be clustered before discovery. Clustering and decomposition are done automatically, i.e., no additional information is used. This paper proposes a different approach where a *localized event log* is assumed. Events are localized by assigning a non-empty set of *regions* to each event. It is assumed that regions can only interact through shared events. Consider for example the mining of software systems. The events recorded typically explicitly refer to parts of the system (components, services, etc.). Currently, such information is ignored during discovery. However, references to system parts may be used to localize events. Also in other application domains, it is possible to localize events, e.g., communication events in an organization may refer to multiple departments (that may be seen as regions). This paper proposes a generic process discovery approach based on localized event logs. The approach has been implemented in *ProM* and experimental results show that location information indeed helps to improve the quality of the discovered models.

1 Introduction

Today's systems record all kinds of events, e.g., social interaction, financial transactions, user-interface activities, and the use of (mobile) devices. As more

This work is supported by the Basic Research Program of the National Research University Higher School of Economics.

© Springer International Publishing Switzerland 2015
R. Devillers and A. Valmari (Eds.): PETRI NETS 2015, LNCS 9115, pp. 287–308, 2015.
DOI: 10.1007/978-3-319-19488-2_15

and more *event data* become available, the practical relevance of *process mining* further increases. Process mining techniques aim to discover, monitor and improve real processes by extracting knowledge from event logs [1]. The three most prominent process-mining tasks are: (i) *process discovery*: learning a process model from example behavior recorded in an event log, (ii) *conformance checking*: diagnosing and quantifying discrepancies between observed behavior and modeled behavior, and (iii) *performance analysis*: identifying bottlenecks, delays, and inefficiencies using the timestamps of events. Starting point for analysis is often an automatically discovered process model. In this paper, we focus on this first step, i.e., *learning a process model from event data.*

Input for process discovery is an *event log*. Each *event* in such a log refers to an *activity* (i.e., a well-defined step in some process) and is related to a particular *case* (i.e., a *process instance*). The events are partially ordered. Events related to a case describe one "run" of the process. Such a run is often referred to as a *trace*. It is important to note that an event log contains only example behavior.

Process discovery is challenging for a variety of reasons. Typically, only a fraction of the behavior possible can be observed and there is no explicit information on behaviors that are impossible, i.e., a sequence of activities that never occurred, may still happen in the future, but may also be impossible. Moreover, mixtures of choice, concurrency, and iteration may be difficult to uncover using merely an event log.

In this paper we propose to use "location information" present in most data sources. We assume that each event belongs to one or more *regions*. A region may be a software/hardware component, a service, a department, a team, or a geographic location. Regions can only interact through shared events just like communication involves multiple parties. We assume that events with non-overlapping sets of regions *cannot* influence each other directly. *This is comparable to the independence assumption often used in statistical analysis.*

Localized event logs combined with the independence assumption allow for a new decomposition approach. A *sublog* of the overall event log is created for every region. Then a *submodel* is created for each sublog. These submodels are merged into an *overall model.* Whereas traces at the global level are often unique showing only a fraction of the possible behavior, traces in the sublogs may have more repetitive behavior and easily cover all possible local behaviors. Therefore, location information may provide valuable information guiding decomposed discovery. This speeds up analysis and, most likely results in models better describing reality.

The idea to partition event logs is not new, see for example decomposition approaches [3,4] and trace clustering approaches [9,16,27]. However, unlike existing approaches we do not try to partition cases or activities through mining. Instead, we propose to exploit location information explicitly attached to events. Such information is often available or derivable.

The approach has been implemented in *ProM* and experiments using synthetic and real-life event logs demonstrate the value of location information.

The remainder of the paper is organized as follows. Section 2 discusses related work. Section 3 introduces preliminaries, including process models. Process mining, in particular control-flow discovery, is introduced in Section 4. Localized event logs, i.e., logs where events have one or more associated regions, are presented in Section 5. Such logs may be used for decomposed process discovery, as shown in Section 6. The experiments presented in Section 7 (using synthetic data and data from two real-life software systems) show that localized event logs allow for significantly better models. Section 8 concludes the paper.

2   Related Work

For an introduction to process mining, we refer to [1].

Process discovery, i.e., discovering a process model from a multiset of example traces, is a very challenging problem and various discovery techniques have been proposed [5–8,10,11,13,15,18,19,21,25,28,29]. Many of these techniques use Petri nets during the discovery process. It is impossible to provide a complete overview of all techniques here. Very different approaches are used, e.g., heuristics [13,28], inductive logic programming [15], state-based regions [5,11,25], language-based regions [8,29], and genetic algorithms [21]. Classical synthesis techniques based on regions [14] cannot be applied directly because the event log contains only example behavior. For state-based regions one first needs to create an automaton as described in [5]. Moreover, when constructing the regions, one should avoid overfitting. Language-based regions seem good candidates for discovering transition-bordered Petri nets for subnets [8,29]. Recently, a family of inductive mining approaches has been proposed by Leemans et al. [18,19]. These techniques can deal with incompleteness and infrequent behavior, but still provide formal guarantees (e.g., perfect fitness and rediscoverability for specific parameter settings). The approach presented in this paper can be used in conjunction with all existing process discovery approaches.

Also related is the work on decomposed process mining. In [2] two types of log decomposition are identified: *vertical decomposition* and *horizontal decomposition*. In a vertical partitioning complete cases are assigned to a group and end-to-end process models are discovered or checked. Traditional trace clustering techniques may be viewed as vertical decomposition techniques (not for scalability but for obtaining simpler models). Several authors have proposed such trace clustering techniques [9,16,27]. Here traces are grouped and simplified models are created per group. The approach in this paper is based on a horizontal decomposition (traces are split into subtraces) rather than a vertical decomposition. In a horizontal partitioning activities are assigned to (possibly overlapping) groups [2–4]. Cases are projected on subsets of activities, thus resulting in a sublog per group. A process fragment is discovered or checked per subgroup. The principles presented in [3,4] are used to prove the correctness of the approach proposed in this paper.

Different divide and conquer approaches are possible [3,4,12]. For example, one may decompose event logs and process models based on the refined process structure tree identifying Single-Entry Single-Exit (SESE) fragments [22,24]. This can only be done for conformance checking. Here, explicit location information is exploited to decompose *discovery* into relatively independent parts.

3   Process Models

The results presented in this paper do not depend on a particular representation. However, we use *labeled Petri nets* with designated *initial* and *final* markings to illustrate the approach. This section introduces the preliminaries needed in the remainder.

$\mathcal{B}(A)$ is the set of all multisets over some set A. For some multiset $b \in \mathcal{B}(A)$, $b(a)$ denotes the number of times element $a \in A$ appears in b. $b = [x^3, y^2, z]$ is a multiset having 6 elements: three x elements (i.e., $b(x) = 3$), two y elements (i.e., $b(y) = 2$), and one z element (i.e., $b(z) = 1$). Operators are defined as usual, e.g. $[x^2, y] \uplus [x, y, z] = [x^3, y^2, z]$ is the union of two multisets.

$\sigma = \langle a_1, a_2, \ldots, a_n \rangle \in X^*$ denotes a sequence over X of length n. $\langle \, \rangle$ is the empty sequence and $\sigma_1 \cdot \sigma_2$ is the concatenation of two sequences. $\sigma \restriction_Q$ is the projection of σ on Q, e.g., $\langle a, b, c, a, b, c \rangle \restriction_{\{a,c\}} = \langle a, c, a, c \rangle$.

Definition 1 (Sequence Projection). *Let X be a set and $Q \subseteq X$ one of its subsets. $\restriction_Q \in X^* \to Q^*$ is a projection function and is defined recursively: (1) $\langle \, \rangle \restriction_Q = \langle \, \rangle$ and (2) for $\sigma \in X^*$ and $x \in X$: $(\langle x \rangle \cdot \sigma) \restriction_Q = \sigma \restriction_Q$ if $x \notin Q$, and $(\langle x \rangle \cdot \sigma) \restriction_Q = \langle x \rangle \cdot \sigma \restriction_Q$ if $x \in Q$.*

Definition 2 (Applying Functions to Sequences). *Let $f \in X \nrightarrow Y$ be a partial function.[1] f may be applied to sequences of X using the following recursive definition (1) $f(\langle \, \rangle) = \langle \, \rangle$ and (2) for $\sigma \in X^*$ and $x \in X$:*

$$f(\langle x \rangle \cdot \sigma) = \begin{cases} f(\sigma) & \text{if } x \notin dom(f) \\ \langle f(x) \rangle \cdot f(\sigma) & \text{if } x \in dom(f) \end{cases}$$

Figure 1 shows a labeled Petri net composed of places $P = \{p1, p2, \ldots, p21\}$ and transitions $T = \{t1, t2, \ldots, t18\}$. The flow relation $F = \{(p1, t1), (t1, p2), (t1, p8), \ldots\}$ specifies the connections between places and transitions. A transition may have a label, e.g., transition $t1$ has label a. The label refers to the activity associated with the transition. Two transitions may have the same label, e.g., $t13$ and $t15$ correspond to the same activity. Note that transition $t4$ has no label, i.e., it does not correspond to a transition and is sometimes called "invisible".

Definition 3 (Labeled Petri Net). *A labeled Petri net is a tuple $N = (P, T, F, l)$ defining a finite set of places P, a finite set of transitions T (such that $P \cap T = \emptyset$), a flow relation $F \subseteq (P \times T) \cup (T \times P)$, and a labeling function $l \in T \nrightarrow \mathcal{U}_A$ where $\mathcal{U}_A$ is some universe of activity names. A marking of N is a multiset of places M, i.e., $M \in \mathcal{B}(P)$.*

A labeled Petri net $N = (P, T, F, l)$ defines a directed graph with nodes $P \cup T$ and edges F. A transition $t \in dom(l)$ has a label $l(t)$ that refers to some activity.

---

[1] A partial function $f \in X \nrightarrow Y$ has a domain $dom(f) \subseteq X$ and a range $rng(f) = \{f(x) \mid x \in dom(f)\} \subseteq Y$.

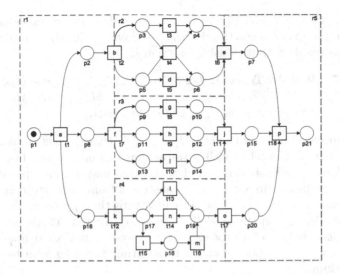

Fig. 1. Labeled Petri net with initial marking [p1] and final marking [p21]. The dashed lines refer to regions and will be explained later.

An invisible transition $t \in T \setminus dom(l)$ has no label and does not correspond to some observable activity. The state of a Petri net, called *marking*, is a multiset of places indicating how many *tokens* each place contains. The initial marking shown in Figure 1 is [p1]. Another marking of this Petri net is [p3, p5, p15, p19].

A transition $t \in T$ is *enabled* in marking M of net N, denoted as $(N, M)[t\rangle$, if each of its input places •t contains at least one token. An enabled transition t may *fire*, i.e., one token is removed from each of the input places •t and one token is produced for each of the output places t•. Transition $t1$ in Figure 1 is enabled in the initial marking. Firing $t1$ results in [p2, p8, p16]. In marking [p3, p5, p15, p19] five transitions are enabled: $t3, t4, t5, t14, t17$. Firing $t4$ results in marking [p4, p6, p15, p19].

$(N, M)[t\rangle(N, M')$ denotes that t is enabled in M and firing t results in marking M'. Let $\sigma = \langle t_1, t_2, \ldots, t_n \rangle \in T^*$ be a sequence of transitions. $(N, M)[\sigma\rangle$ (N, M') denotes that there is a set of markings $M_0, M_1, \ldots, M_n$ such that $M_0 = M$, $M_n = M'$, and $(N, M_i)[t_{i+1}\rangle(N, M_{i+1})$ for $0 \le i < n$. A marking M' is *reachable* from M if there exists a sequence σ such that $(N, M)[\sigma\rangle(N, M')$.

In this paper we consider Petri nets with a designated initial and final markings. The behavior considered are all *complete* firing sequences from the initial marking M_{init} to the final marking M_{final}.

Definition 4 (System Net). *A system net is a triplet $SN = (N, M_{init}, M_{final})$ where $N = (P, T, F, l)$ is a labeled Petri net, $M_{init} \in \mathcal{B}(P)$ is the initial marking, and $M_{final} \in \mathcal{B}(P)$ is the final marking. $\mathcal{U}_{SN}$ is the* universe of system nets.

Given a system net SN, $\phi(SN)$ is the set of all possible *visible* traces, i.e., complete firing sequences starting in M_{init} and ending in M_{final} projected onto the set of observable activities using function l.

Definition 5 (Visible Traces). *Let* $SN = (N, M_{init}, M_{final}) \in \mathcal{U}_{SN}$ *be a system net with* $N = (P, T, F, l)$. $\phi(SN) = \{l(\sigma) \mid (N, M_{init})[\sigma\rangle(N, M_{final})\}$ *is the set of* visible *traces starting in* M_{init} *and ending in* M_{final}.[2]

Given a universe of activities $\mathcal{U}_A$, $\mathcal{U}_T = \mathcal{U}_A{}^*$ is the universe of visible traces. $\phi(SN) \subseteq \mathcal{U}_T$ defines the set of visible traces that can be generated by SN. Note that transitions may be invisible and that there may be multiple transitions having the same label. However, $\phi(SN)$ abstracts from such internals.

In this paper, we use Petri nets to illustrate the approach. However, the results do not depend on the modeling language selected. Therefore, we define the more neutral notion of a process model. A system net SN defines a process model $PM = \phi(SN)$ if there is at least one firing sequence from the initial to the final marking.[3]

Definition 6 (Process Model). *A process model* PM *is a non-empty set of visible traces, i.e.,* $PM \subseteq \mathcal{U}_T$ *and* $PM \neq \emptyset$. $\mathcal{U}_{PM}$ *is the universe of process models.*

In the remainder we use the following shorthand to refer to the activities appearing in a model: $\alpha(PM) = \{a \mid \exists_{\sigma \in PM}\, a \in \sigma\}$.

4   Process Mining

Starting point for any process mining technique is an event log with partially ordered events referring to cases and activities. To introduce events logs formally, we need to introduce some notations. Next to the universe of activities $\mathcal{U}_A$, the universe of visible traces $\mathcal{U}_T$, and the universe of process models $\mathcal{U}_{PM}$, we assume four additional universes:

- $\mathcal{U}_E$ is the set of all possible event identifiers,
- $\mathcal{U}_C$ is the set of all possible case identifiers,
- $\mathcal{U}_{Attr}$ is the set of all possible attribute names, and
- $\mathcal{U}_{Val}$ is the set of all possible attribute values.

Definition 7 (Event Log). $L = (E, C, act, case, attr, \prec)$ *is an event log if:*
- $E \subseteq \mathcal{U}_E$ *is a set of events,*
- $C \subseteq \mathcal{U}_C$ *is a set of cases,*
- $act \in E \to \mathcal{U}_A$ *maps events onto activities,*

---

[2] Note that $l(\sigma)$ maps a firing sequence onto a trace of visible activities (see Definition 2).

[3] Note that the labeled Petri net may deadlock or livelock before reaching M_{final}. Such traces are not considered because they cannot be related to cases in the event log. It is up to the discovery approach to ensure some notion of soundness.

- $case \in E \rightarrow C$ maps events onto a set of cases,
- $attr \in E \rightarrow (\mathcal{U}_{Attr} \not\rightarrow \mathcal{U}_{Val})$ maps each event onto a partial function assigning values to some attributes, and
- $\prec \subseteq E \times E$ defines a partial order on events.[4]

$\mathcal{U}_L$ is the set of all possible event logs.

Any $e \in E$ uniquely identifies an event. $act(e)$ is the activity executed for case $case(e)$. There may be cases without events, but every event refers to precisely one case. Event may have any number of attributes, e.g., $attr(e)(timestamp) = $ 2015-01-19T22:51:30.700+01:00 denotes the time event e occurred. Definition 7 assumes a partial order on events. In literature often a total order is assumed within a case, i.e., a case corresponds to a sequence of events. However, sometimes one is not sure about the ordering of events, e.g., multiple events have happened on the same day without an explicit order. Moreover, we may know the actual causal dependencies based on analyzing dataflow dependencies. In both cases, a partial order is more appropriate.

In the remainder we use the following shorthand to refer to the activities appearing in an event log: $\alpha(L) = \{act(e) \mid e \in E\}$.

Definition 8 (Process Discovery Technique). *A process discovery technique* $disc \in \mathcal{U}_L \rightarrow \mathcal{U}_{PM}$ *maps event logs onto process models such that for any* $L \in \mathcal{U}_L$: $\alpha(L) = \alpha(disc(L))$.

A process discovery technique produces a process model for an event log. Here we only require that the set of activities in the event log $\alpha(L)$ matches the set of activities in the model $\alpha(disc(L))$. As discussed in Section 2, many discovery techniques have been proposed in literature. These may be viewed as specific instances of $disc$.

Process discovery is challenging because event logs are often far from complete and there are at least four competing quality dimensions: (1) *fitness*, (2) *simplicity*, (3) *precision*, and (4) *generalization* [1]. A model with good *fitness* allows for most of the behavior seen in the event log. A model has a perfect fitness if all traces in the log can be replayed by the model from beginning to end. The *simplest* model that may explain the behavior seen in the log is the best model. This principle is known as Occam's Razor. Fitness and simplicity alone are not sufficient to judge the quality of a discovered process model. For example, it is very easy to construct an extremely simple Petri net that is able to replay all traces in an event log (but also any other event log referring to the same set of activities).[5] Similarly, it is undesirable to have a model that only allows for the exact behavior seen in the event log. Remember that the log contains only example behavior and that many traces that are possible may not

---

[4] A partial order is a binary relation that is (1) irreflexive, i.e. $x \not\prec x$, (2) antisymmetric, i.e. $x \prec y$ implies $y \not\prec x$, and (3) transitive, i.e. if $x \prec y$ and $y \prec z$, then $x \prec z$.

[5] System net $SN = ((P, T, F, l), M_{init}, M_{final})$ with $P = \emptyset$, $T = \alpha(L)$, $F = \emptyset$, l the identity function, $M_{init} = [\,]$, and $M_{final} = [\,]$ can replay any case in L.

have been observed yet. A model is *precise* if it does not allow for "too much" behavior. A model that is not precise is "underfitting", i.e., the model allows for behaviors very different from what was seen in the log. At the same time, the model should generalize and not restrict behavior to just the examples seen in the log. A model that does not *generalize* is "overfitting". Overfitting means that an overly specific model is generated whereas it is obvious that the log only holds example behavior (i.e., the model explains the particular sample log, but there is a high probability that the model is unable to explain the next batch of cases).

Here we do not quantify the four quality dimensions and restrict ourselves to simple fitness notions such as perfect fitness and the fraction of perfectly fitting cases.

Definition 9 (Fitness). *Let $L = (E, C, act, case, attr, \prec) \in \mathcal{U}_L$ be an event log and $PM \in \mathcal{U}_{PM}$ a process model.*

- *A case $c \in C$ is perfectly fitting PM (notation $PM \rightsquigarrow c$) if and only if there exists a trace $\sigma = \langle a_1, a_2, \ldots, a_n \rangle \in PM$ and a bijection $f \in \{1, 2, \ldots n\} \to \{e \in E \mid case(e) = c\}$ such that $a_i = act(f(i))$ for $1 \le i \le n$ and $f(j) \not\prec f(i)$ for any $1 \le i \le j \le n$.[6]*
- *$fit(L, PM) = \{c \in C \mid PM \rightsquigarrow c\}$ is the set of perfectly fitting cases.*
- *$nofit(L, PM) = C \setminus fit(L, PM)$ is the set of non-fitting cases,*
- *$fitness(L, PM) = \frac{|fit(L,PM)|}{|C|}$ is the fraction of traces in the event log perfectly fitting the model, and*
- *L is perfectly fitting PM if $nofit(L, PM) = \emptyset$.*

Note that we use interleaving semantics for process models while events are partially ordered (to capture uncertainty or causalities). Event log L is perfectly fitting model PM if for any observed case c there is model trace that could explain the set of events observed for c. When making a *trade-off* between fitness, simplicity, precision, and generalization, we may end up with a model not ensuring perfect fitness (e.g., deliberately leaving out exceptional behavior).

5   Localized Event Logs

As mentioned in the introduction, we assume *localized* event logs, i.e., each event e has a non-empty set of regions $loc(e)$. If event e occurs exclusively inside region r (i.e., no interaction between regions), then $loc(e) = \{r\}$. If event e describes some form of interaction between two regions $r1$ and $r2$, then $loc(e) = \{r1, r2\}$. Any form of interaction (from communicating humans to function calls and service invocations) involves multiple entities (e.g., components, services, or departments), here called *regions*.

---

[6] A function $f \in X \to Y$ is bijective if there is a one-to-one correspondence between the elements of X and Y, i.e., function f is total, surjective and injective.

Definition 10 (Localized Event Log). *A localized event log $L_L = (L, R, loc)$ is composed of an event log $L = (E, C, act, case, attr, \prec) \in \mathcal{U}_L$, a set of locations (called regions) R, and a location function $loc \in E \rightarrow \mathcal{P}_{NE}(R)$.*[7]

Given an event e, $loc(e)$ defines the set of regions involved. As mentioned before, regions can only interact through shared events.

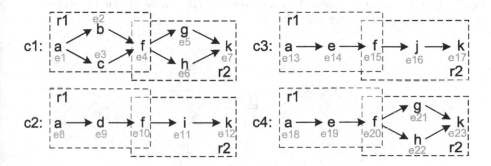

Fig. 2. Localized event log with 4 cases and 23 events

Figure 2 visualizes a small event log with $E = \{e1, e2, \ldots, e23\}$ (23 events), $C = \{c1, c2, c3, c4\}$ (4 cases), and $R = \{r1, r2\}$ (2 regions). Functions act and $case$ are also depicted in Figure 2: $act(e1) = a$, $case(e1) = c1$, $act(e2) = b$, $case(e2) = c1$, $act(e8) = a$, $case(e8) = c2$, etc. $\prec$ is only partially shown in Figure 2. Ordering relations of events in different cases are not depicted and only the transitive reduction of the ordering relations within a case is shown. Consider for example case $c1$. First activity a is executed (event $e1$) followed by both b (event $e2$) and c (event $e3$), then f (event $e4$) is executed followed by both g (event $e5$) and h (event $e6$). Case $c1$ concludes with the execution of activity k (event $e7$). We abstract from attributes here (i.e., $attr$ is not shown), e.g., each event e may have an associated timestamp $attr(e)(timestamp)$ and resource $attr(e)(resource)$. The location function loc is depicted using the shaded rectangles: $loc(e1) = \{r1\}$, $loc(e2) = \{r1\}$, $loc(e4) = \{r1, r2\}$, $loc(e5) = \{r2\}$, $loc(e20) = \{r1, r2\}$, $loc(e23) = \{r2\}$, etc. Note that all f events belong to both regions.

Classical discovery approaches consider all events to be potentially related. *However, based on the regions involved we may conclude that events are unrelated thus significantly simplifying process discovery.* Consider again the localized event log of Figure 2. Based on the four cases, one could conclude that d is always followed by i and that j is always preceded by e. However, we have seen only four cases and the next case may reveal new behavior. Process discovery should be able to deal with incompleteness. For non-trivial processes, typically most traces are globally unique, i.e., there is no other case following exactly the same path from start to finish. If there are many unique traces, one cannot assume global completeness. However, we may assume events to be *unrelated* unless they are

---

[7] $\mathcal{P}_{NE}(X) = \{Y \subseteq X \mid Y \neq \emptyset\}$, i.e., all non-empty subsets of X.

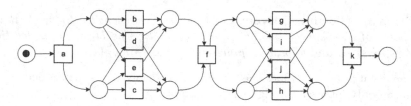

Fig. 3. Process model represented by a system net (the initial marking is shown; the final marking only marks the sink place)

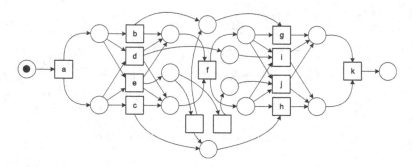

Fig. 4. Overfitting process model not taking into account the regions. Due to incompleteness, dependencies between $\{b, c, d, e\}$ and $\{g, h, i, j\}$ are derived that do not exist.

in the same region. Interaction between regions is possible only through shared events. Using this assumption, we could discover the process shown in Figure 3 using only the four cases of Figure 2. Without using such an assumption, we may end up with the process model shown in Figure 4. This model allows for the behavior exhibited by the four cases in Figure 2 and nothing more. In this overfitting model, e may be followed by g and h, or e may be followed by j, but e may not be followed by i. However, using the notion of regions in the localized event log, we know that the choice made in region $r1$ is unrelated to the choice made in region $r2$.

To illustrate the value of localized events consider the system net shown in Figure 5 (the final marking just marks place end). There are n concurrent parts each composed of k parallel activities. The model allows for:

$$pst_{all} = \frac{(n(k+2))!}{((k+2)!)^n}(k!)^n$$

possible (sequential) traces.[8] Note that we only consider sequential traces here. We may also consider the number of "directly follows" relations:

---

[8] Each of the n concurrent parts allows for $k! = k \times (k-1) \times \ldots \times 1$ sequential traces of length $k+2$ (abstracting from the fixed first activity as and the last activity ae which are invariable, but including ais and aie)). These n traces of length $k+2$ can be interleaved in $\frac{(n(k+2))!}{((k+2)!)^n}$ ways and there are $(k!)^n$ unique collections of such n traces.

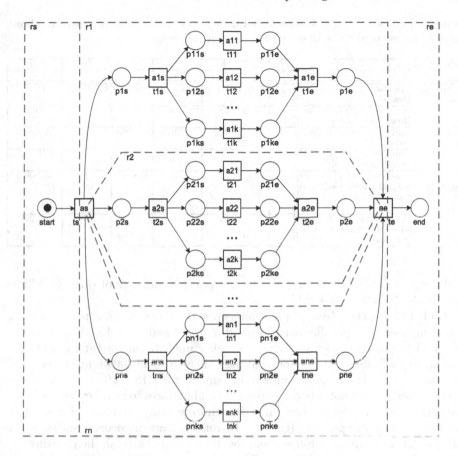

Fig. 5. A process composed of $n + 2$ subprocesses marked $rs, r1, r2, \ldots, rn, re$. Each of the n subprocesses in the middle has k parallel activities. For larger values of n and k this process is difficult to discover due to the many possible interleavings.

$$df_{all} = n + n(k + 1)(k + (n - 1)(k + 2)) + n(1 + (n - 1)(k + 2))$$

where a directly follows relation is a pair of activities such that one activity is directly followed in a sequential trace.[9] The directly follows relation is interesting because it is used by many process discovery algorithms to uncover causal relationships.

Let us now consider one of the concurrent parts (say ri with $i \in \{1, \ldots, n\}$). The submodel allows for $pst_i = k!$ possible (sequential) traces of length $k + 4$

---

[9] Activity as can be directly followed by n activities ($a1s \ldots ans$). Each ais activity (with $i \in \{1, \ldots, n\}$) can be directly followed by $k + (n - 1)(k + 2)$ activities. Each aij activity (with $i \in \{1, \ldots, n\}$ and $j \in \{1, \ldots, k\}$) can also be directly followed by $k + (n - 1)(k + 2)$ activities. Each aie activity (with $i \in \{1, \ldots, n\}$) can be directly followed by $1 + (n - 1)(k + 2)$ activities. Activity ae is never followed by another activity.

Table 1. Effects of n and k values in Figure 5 on the number of traces or direct successions that need to be observed for complete coverage

parameters	n	1	1	5	5	1	10	10
	k	1	5	1	5	10	1	10
overall process	number of unique traces	1	120	1.68E+8	7.91E+31	3628800	4.39E+24	4.17E+177
	number of directly follows relationships	4	32	200	1140	112	850	14080
single fragment	number of unique traces	1	120	1	120	3628800	1	3628800
	number of directly follows relationships	4	32	4	32	112	4	112
combined fragments	minimal number of global traces needed to cover all locally unique traces	1	120	1	120	3628800	1	3628800
	total number of local directly follows relationships	4	32	20	160	112	40	1120

(including as, ais, aie and ae). The corresponding number of directly follows relations is $df_i = k^2 + k + 2$.[10]

Table 1 shows the effects of parameters n and k (there are n concurrent parts each composed of k parallel activities). If $n = 10$ and $k = 10$, then there are 4.17×10^{177} unique traces. Clearly, it is highly unlikely (understatement) to see all of these possibilities. Per concurrent part, there are 3628800 unique traces, still a lot but nevertheless a spectacular reduction (factor 1.15×10^{171}). Process discovery algorithms do not rely on seeing all possible traces to avoid overfitting. For example, if there are loops there may be infinitely many possible behaviors (see for example the lower part of Figure 1). Therefore, many discovery algorithms use notions such as the directly follows relation. If $n = 10$ and $k = 10$, then the directly follows relation has 14080 elements. This reduces to 1120 if it suffices to see only the local directly follows relationships, i.e., *less than 8 percent of the overall direct successions need to be observed to discover the "correct" model!*

Figure 5 is a rather extreme example. However, it nicely shows that the same model can be discovered using smaller, less complete event logs by exploiting localization information in event logs. Compare this to statistics where assumptions about independence are used in predictions or when computing confidence intervals.

Definition 10 allows for two events that refer to the same activity but different regions. For process discovery, we would like to relate activities to a fixed number of regions. Hence, we aim at event logs that are *stable*.

Definition 11 (Stable). *A localized event log* $L_L = (L, R, loc)$ *with* $L = (E, C, act, case, attr, \prec)$ *is stable if for all* $e_1, e_2 \in E$ *with* $act(e_1) = act(e_2)$: $loc(e_1) = loc(e_2)$.

---

[10] Activity as can only be directly followed by ais in the submodel corresponding to ri. Activity ais can be directly followed by k activities. Each aij activity (with $j \in \{1, \ldots, k\}$) can be followed by k activities (aie and aij' with $j' \neq j$). Activity aie can only be directly followed by ae.

The localized event log of Figure 2 is stable, e.g., f events always refer to $r1$ and $r2$. A localized event log that is not stable can be "stabilized" by refining function $act \in E \to \mathcal{U}_A$. For example, function act can be replaced by act' where $act'(e) = (act(e), loc(e))$ for $e \in E$. The new function distinguishes activities having distinct sets of regions involved.

6 Decomposed Process Discovery

A localized event log can be transformed into a collection of sublogs, i.e., one event log per region. The sublogs are used to discover submodels. Finally, the submodels can be merged into a single overall process model. To create sublogs, we define a projection operator.

Definition 12 (Projection). *Let* $L = (E, C, act, case, attr, \prec)$ *be an event log and* $X \subseteq E$ *a subset of events.* $L \upharpoonright_X = (X, C, act \upharpoonright_X, case \upharpoonright_X, attr \upharpoonright_X, \prec')$ *with* $\prec' = (\prec \cap (X \times X))$.[11]

Definition 13 (Decomposed Discovery). *Let* $L_L = (L, R, loc)$ *be a localized event log with* $L = (E, C, act, case, attr, \prec)$ *and* $A = \alpha(L)$, *and let* $disc \in \mathcal{U}_L \to \mathcal{U}_{PM}$ *be a process discovery technique. For any region* $r \in R$, *we define the following shorthands:*
- $E_r = \{e \in E \mid r \in loc(e)\}$ *are the events of region* r,
- $L_r = L \upharpoonright_{E_r}$ *is the sublog of region* r,
- $A_r = \{act(e) \mid e \in E_r\}$ *are the activities of region* r, *and*
- $PM_r = disc(L_r)$ *is the process model discovered for region* r.

$PM_R = \{\sigma \in A^* \mid \forall_{r \in R}\ \sigma \upharpoonright_{A_r} \in PM_r\}$ *is the overall process model constructed by merging the individual models.*

Note that the smaller process models are merged by weaving the region-based subsequences.

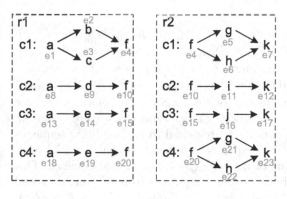

Figure 6 illustrates how event logs can be projected onto the different regions. Now a model can be discovered for each region and the models can be merged as defined next.

PM_R merges the subprocesses discovered for the $|R|$ sublogs. Activity sequence σ is a visible trace of PM_R if and only if $\sigma \upharpoonright_{A_r} \in PM_r$ (i.e., the projected sequence is a visible trace of the corresponding submodel) for each

Fig. 6. Two projected event logs based on the overall event log of Figure 2: one sublog for each region

---

[11] $f \upharpoonright_X$ is function f with the domain restricted to X, i.e., $dom(f \upharpoonright_X) = X \cap dom(f)$.

region $r \in R$. Like the rest of the paper, Definition 13 is not Petri net specific. However, the merging of the submodels into one overall model corresponds to the following union operator for system nets.

Definition 14 (Union of Nets). *Let $SN^1 = (N^1, M_{init}^1, M_{final}^1) \in \mathcal{U}_{SN}$ with $N^1 = (P^1, T^1, F^1, l^1)$ and $SN^2 = (N^2, M_{init}^2, M_{final}^2) \in \mathcal{U}_{SN}$ with $N^2 = (P^2, T^2, F^2, l^2)$ be two system nets with $P^1 \cap P^2 = \emptyset$.*

- $P^3 = P^1 \cup P^2$ *is the resulting set of places,*
- $A_S = rng(l^1) \cap rng(l^2)$ *is the set of shared activities (appearing in both regions),*
- $T_S^1 = \{t \in dom(l^1) \mid l^1(t) \in A_S\}$ *and* $T_S^2 = \{t \in dom(l^2) \mid l^2(t) \in A_S\}$ *are the transitions corresponding to shared activities,*
- $T^3 = \{(t_1, t_2) \in T_S^1 \times T_S^2 \mid l^1(t_1) = l^2(t_2)\} \cup \{(t_1, \gg) \mid t_1 \in T^1 \setminus T_S^1\} \cup \{(\gg, t_2) \mid t_2 \in T^2 \setminus T_S^2\}$ *is the resulting set of transitions,*[12]
- $dom(l^3) = \{(t_1, t_2) \in T^3 \mid t_1 \in dom(l^1) \vee t_2 \in dom(l^2)\}$, $l^3((t_1, t_2)) = l^1(t_1)$ *if* $t_1 \in dom(l^1)$ *and* $l^3((t_1, t_2)) = l^2(t_2)$ *if* $t_2 \in dom(l^2)$,
- $F^3 = \{(p, (t_1, x)) \in P^1 \times T^3 \mid (p, t_1) \in F^1\} \cup \{((t_1, x), p) \in T^3 \times P^1 \mid (t_1, p) \in F^1\} \cup \{(p, (x, t_2)) \in P^2 \times T^3 \mid (p, t_2) \in F^2\} \cup \{((x, t_2), p) \in T^3 \times P^2 \mid (t_2, p) \in F^2\}$,
- $N^1 \cup N^2 = (P^3, T^3, F^3, l^3)$ *is the union of N^1 and N^2, and*
- $SN^1 \cup SN^2 = (N^1 \cup N^2, M_{init}^1 \uplus M_{init}^2, M_{final}^1 \uplus M_{final}^2)$ *is the union of system nets SN^1 and SN^2.*

The above definition takes the union of two system nets, but this can be extended to any number of system nets. The following lemma shows that such union based on merging transitions indeed implements the composition used in Definition 13.

Lemma 1. *Let $SN^1, SN^2, \ldots, SN^n$ be n system nets with non-overlapping sets of places. $\phi(\bigcup_{1 \leq i \leq n} SN^i) = \{\sigma \in A^* \mid \forall_{1 \leq i \leq n} \ \sigma \restriction_{rng(l^i)} \in \phi(SN^i)\}$ with $A = \bigcup_{1 \leq i \leq n} rng(l^i)$ as the set of activities.*

Proof. Assume $n = 2$, $SN^1 \cup SN^2 = (N^1 \cup N^2, M_{init}^1 \uplus M_{init}^2, M_{final}^1 \uplus M_{final}^2)$, $N^1 = (P^1, T^1, F^1, l^1)$, $N^2 = (P^2, T^2, F^2, l^2)$, and $N^1 \cup N^2 = (P^3, T^3, F^3, l^3)$. The proof can be generalized for any number of system nets $n \geq 1$.

Let $\sigma \in \phi(SN^1 \cup SN^2)$, we need to show that $\sigma \restriction_{rng(l^1)} \in \phi(SN^1)$ and $\sigma \restriction_{rng(l^2)} \in \phi(SN^2)$. SN^1 can be seen as a projection of $SN^1 \cup SN^2$, i.e., places in P^2 are removed, places in P^1 are kept, transitions of the type $(\gg, t_2)$ are removed, and transitions of the type (t_1, t_2) or $(t_1, \gg)$ renamed to t_1. The firing sequence corresponding to σ in $SN^1 \cup SN^2$ corresponds to a firing sequence in SN^1 after renaming and removing transitions of the type $(\gg, t_2)$ from the sequence. This firing sequence is indeed possible because removing places from P^2 can never lead to blocking transitions. Hence, $\sigma \restriction_{rng(l^1)} \in \phi(SN^1)$. Similarly: $\sigma \restriction_{rng(l^2)} \in \phi(SN^2)$.

---

[12] Next to synchronizing transitions of the form (t_1, t_2), there are transitions of the form $(t_1, \gg)$ or $(\gg, t_2)$ that do no synchronize as these are local to one of the nets.

Let $\sigma \in A^*$ be such that $\sigma\lceil_{rng(l^1)} \in \phi(SN^1)$ and $\sigma\lceil_{rng(l^2)} \in \phi(SN^2)$, we need to show that $\sigma \in \phi(SN^1 \cup SN^2)$. $\sigma\lceil_{rng(l^1)} \in \phi(SN^1)$ defines a full firing sequence $\sigma_1 \in (T^1)^*$ with $l^1(\sigma_1) = \sigma\lceil_{rng(l^1)}$, i.e., a sequence of transitions starting in M_{init}^1 and ending in M_{final}^1. Similarly, $\sigma\lceil_{rng(l^2)} \in \phi(SN^2)$ defines a full firing sequence $\sigma_2 \in (T^2)^*$ with $l^2(\sigma_2) = \sigma\lceil_{rng(l^2)}$. Note that $l^1(\sigma_1)\lceil_{A_S} = l^2(\sigma_2)\lceil_{A_S} = \sigma\lceil_{A_S}$.

There exists a $\sigma_3 \in (T^3)^*$ such that $l^3(\sigma_3) = \sigma$, $f_1(\sigma_3) = \sigma_1$ and $f_2(\sigma_3) = \sigma_2$ with $dom(f_1) = \{(t_1, t_2) \in T^3 \mid t_1 \neq \gg\}$, $f_1(t_1, t_2) = t_1$, and $dom(f_2) = \{(t_1, t_2) \in T^3 \mid t_2 \neq \gg\}$, $f_2(t_1, t_2) = t_2$. Such a sequence exists because in σ both system nets agree on shared activities A_S and for any t_1 and t_2 with $l^1(t_1) = l^2(t_2) \in A_S$: $(t_1, t_2) \in T^3$ (i.e., all combinations have been included). Now, it is easy to see that σ_3 is indeed a firing sequence possible in $SN^1 \cup SN^2$: it starts in $M_{init}^1 \uplus M_{init}^2$ and ends in $M_{final}^1 \uplus M_{final}^2$. Since $l^3(\sigma_3) = \sigma$, $\sigma \in \phi(SN^1 \cup SN^2)$. □

The lemma is related to classical results on net composition [20]. Also see [3,4] for other properties preserved by the union of two system nets in relation to an event log.

Theorem 1 (Decomposed Discovery). *Let $L_L = (L, R, loc)$ be a stable localized event log and let $disc \in \mathcal{U}_L \rightarrow \mathcal{U}_{PM}$ be a process discovery technique. Let PM_R, PM_r, and L_r be as defined in Definition 13.*

- *$fit(L, PM_R) \subseteq \bigcap_{r \in R} fit(L_r, PM_r)$,*
- *$fitness(L, PM_R) \leq \frac{|\bigcap_{r \in R} fit(L_r, PM_r)|}{|C|}$,*
- *$fit(L, PM_R) = \bigcap_{r \in R} fit(L_r, PM_r)$ if $\prec$ defines a strict total order,[13]*
- *$fitness(L, PM_R) = \frac{|\bigcap_{r \in R} fit(L_r, PM_r)|}{|C|}$ if $\prec$ defines a strict total order.*

Proof. The second and fourth statement follow directly from the first and third statement respectively. To prove the first statement we need to show that for any $c \in fit(L, PM_R)$ and $r \in R$: $c \in fit(L_r, PM_r)$. Because $PM \rightsquigarrow c$ there is a trace $\sigma_R = \langle a_1, a_2, \ldots, a_n \rangle \in PM_R$ and a bijection $f \in \{1, 2, \ldots n\} \rightarrow \{e \in E \mid case(e) = c\}$ such that $a_i = act(f(i))$ for $1 \leq i \leq n$ and $f(j) \not\prec f(i)$ for any $1 \leq i \leq j \leq n$. Let $\sigma_r = \sigma_R\lceil_{A_r}$. Clearly, $\sigma_r \in PM_r$ due to the construction of PM_R (see Definition 13). c is not just an case in L but also a case in L_r (see Definition 12). Due to stability, the set of c events projected away matches the elements projected away in $\sigma_r = \sigma_R\lceil_{A_r}$. Hence, a smaller bijection can be created relating σ_r to the A_r events in c. Therefore, $c \in fit(L_r, PM_r)$.

The reverse does not necessarily hold if $\prec$ is just a partial order and not a total order. The partial order could be linearized differently in the region-based submodels. To prove the third statement we additionally need to show that for any $c \in L$ such that $c \in fit(L_r, PM_r)$ for all $r \in R$: $c \in fit(L, PM_R)$. Since $\prec$ is now a strict total order, there is one $\sigma = \langle a_1, a_2, \ldots, a_n \rangle$ describing the sequence of activities (not events) in case c. Let $\sigma_r = \sigma\lceil_{A_r}$. For all $r \in R$: $\sigma_r \in PM_r$ because $c \in fit(L_r, PM_r)$ and L_L is stable. Since $PM_R = \{\sigma \in A^* \mid \forall_{r \in R} \sigma\lceil_{A_r} \in PM_r\}$, we conclude that $\sigma \in PM_R$ and $c \in fit(L, PM_R)$. □

---

[13] A strict order is a partial order that is also trichotomous (exactly one of $x \prec y$, $y \prec x$ or $x = y$ holds).

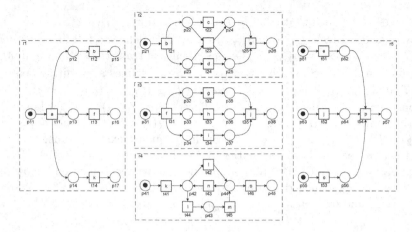

Fig. 7. Five discovered system nets: one for each region. The initial markings are indicated. The final markings are the states with all sink places marked with one token (not indicated explicitly).

Figure 7 shows the basic idea. Suppose that we take an event log created by simulating Figure 1 such that the event log is *locally* complete with respect to the directly follows relation. Now project the overall event log onto the five regions and discover a process model per region. In this case, discovery techniques may discover the five system nets shown in Figure 7. It is easy to see that these submodels indeed describe the corresponding sublogs well. The five system nets in Figure 7 may be merged using Definition 14. In this case we do not get Figure 7 immediately. However, after removing some of the redundant places (i.e., hanging places whose removal does not change the behavior), we get the original system net (modulo renaming of places).

The composition of an overall model from submodels used in Definition 13 (and the specific Petri-net realization in Definition 14), assumes *synchronous* communication. *Asynchronous* communication can be supported by introducing special "channel regions", these are regions with a *send* and *receive* activity. This corresponds to the system net $SN_a = ((\{p_{buffer}\}, \{t_{send}, t_{receive}\}, \{(t_{send}, p_{buffer}), (p_{buffer}, t_{receive})\}, l), [\ ], [\ ])$ with $l(t_{send}) = a_{send}$ and $l(t_{receive}) = a_{receive}$. The corresponding process $PM_a = \phi(SN_a)$ is a simple buffer and may be viewed as a region. Hence, results like the property expressed in Theorem 1 can also be applied in the asynchronous setting.

7   Experimental Results

The decomposition discovery approach was implemented as a plugin for *ProM* (www.processmining.org) – an open source framework aimed to develop and test process mining algorithms. The plugin takes a localized event log as input (in localized event logs regions are specified as additional event attributes) and produces a system net as a result. This plugin was added to the package called *LocalizedLogs* available in the *Nightly Build* of *ProM*. The *DivideAndConquer* package [26] is used to handle the sublogs and to merge the resulting models.

7.1 Synthetic Event Data

Consider the reference model of a booking process depicted in Figure 8. Figure 9 shows an event log, generated by this model. This event log is not complete with respect to the directly follows relation, e.g., in the small event log the *select hotel* activity never directly followed the *register* activity.

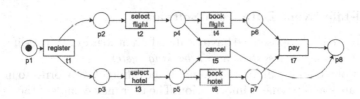

Fig. 8. A system net of a booking process with the initial and final markings [p_1] and [p_8] respectively

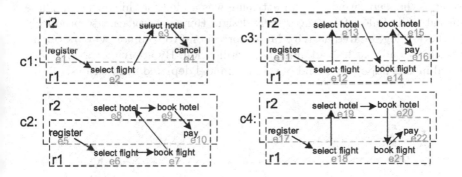

Fig. 9. A localized event log generated by the system net presented in Figure 8. There are two regions: one concerned with flights (*r1*) and one concerned with hotels (*r2*).

All the known discovery methods, including those that deal with incomplete logs, will not rediscover the initial model, because they cannot exploit localization information and demand some form of global completeness. The inductive mining approach [19], which is able to mine models from incomplete event logs, will discover the process model presented in Figure 10. The model is overfitting the event log with respect to the accidental ordering of two selection activities. Moreover, two loops are created. However, if we apply the approach proposed in this paper, we discover the initial system net (Figure 8) using the same discovery technique (after removing redundant hanging places, as described). This is possible because the event log in Figure 9 is complete per region.

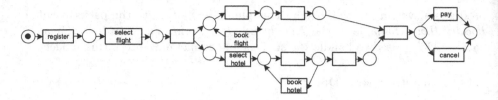

Fig. 10. The process model discovered by the inductive miner *without* exploiting localization information. Note that causalities between unrelated parts are inferred due to the incomplete event log.

7.2   Real-Life Event Data from Software

Using the approach proposed we have analyzed event logs of two real-life software systems: a *booking flight system* and a *banking system*.

The user of a booking flight system fills three different web forms to insert personal, insurance and payment information. The user may complete the web forms in any order. Thus, due to the event log complexity and incompleteness the direct application of the well-known discovery algorithms quickly results incomprehensible process models that contain misleading cycles and non-existing dependencies between activities. The overall event log was enriched with three regions corresponding to the web forms, i.e., an attribute was added for this purpose. These regions naturally follow from the system design. Hence, it was easy to produce a localized event log. Shared activity labels correspond to common window operations, such as load and unload, and data verification. By applying the approach presented in this paper, we could obtain the model depicted in Figure 11.

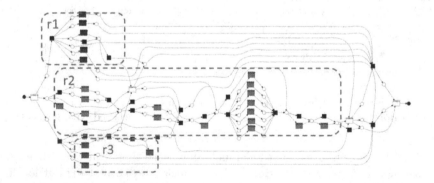

Fig. 11. A model of a booking flight system. Shared activities are highlighted in white, although it is not explicitly shown, they belong to all the regions.

The inductive mining approach was utilized as an underlying algorithm. The model obtained by directly applying the inductive miner contains 1809 connections between transitions, because of a global cycle, connecting almost all the transitions with each other, while the model constructed using regions contains only

177 connections.[14] Relations derived between different regions other than through overlapping activities are artifacts of the incompleteness of the event log.

The other software system under consideration is a banking system. This banking system handles requests and provides the user with the information about customer services. The banking system has a hierarchical structure and is represented by different program layers. Namely, it includes facade, services, data and common data access layers. Each request is received on the facade layer and then redirected to the next layer of the hierarchy. To treat layers as regions the event log was enriched with additional events, denoting request/response communications between layers and belonging to both communicating regions. The localized event log can be used to create the model. Again, the resulting model is simpler and our approach succeeds in handling incompleteness better than traditional approaches: the model contains 1986 connections between transitions instead of 19115, presented in the model obtained by applying the inductive miner directly on the event log. This multilayer model was represented as a model of interacting processes (or layers). A plugin for *ProM*, which constructs a BPMN [23] model of interacting processes from a set of system nets and a corresponding event log, was developed as well. This plugin is based on the BPMN-supporting plugins, described in [17]. It converts each system net to a BPMN process within a pool, each request or response activity is converted to a message event, and each pair of corresponding message events is connected by a message flow. Note that for this plugin each shared event should have an additional attribute to determine its type (send or receive event). The automatically generated BPMN model of the multilayer banking system is presented in Figure 12.

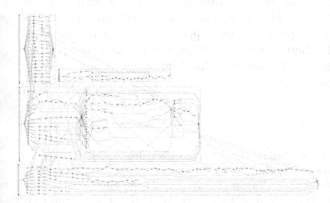

Fig. 12. A BPMN model discovered for a multilayer banking system

Thus, the decomposition discovery approach allows not only to improve the quality of the models discovered, but also assists in creating hierarchical models exploiting higher-level process notations like BPMN.

For models constructed from the real-life event logs using various discovery approaches: heuristic [13,28], inductive [18, 19], and ILP (language-based regions) [8,29] miners, quality metrics, such as *fitness*, *precision* and

---

[14] A pair (t_1, t_2) is a "connection" between visible transitions t_1 and t_2 (i.e., $t_1, t_2 \in dom(l)$) if and only if there exists a non-trivial path from t_1 to t_2, which does not go through other visible transitions.

generalization were obtained. Table 2 contains quality characteristics[15] of process models constructed directly from the event log, using the discovery approach specified, and the characteristics of corresponding process models constructed using localization information. Table 2 shows that the models constructed from the localized logs allow for more traces to fit and are more general, while the models constructed directly from the event logs tend to be more precise, but less fitting.

Table 2. Quality of process models discovered from the real-life event logs

Event logs	Discovery algorithms	Fitness	Trace fitness	Precision	Generalization
Booking system	Heuristic miner	0.00 / 0.13	0.64 / 0.75	0.55 / 0.32	0.89 / 0.90
	Inductive miner	0.23 / 1.00	0.85 / 1.00	0.22 / 0.16	0.98 / 1.00
	ILP miner	1.00 / 1.00	1.00 / 1.00	0.36 / 0.25	1.00 / 1.00
Banking system[16]	Inductive miner	0.25 / 1.00	0.84 / 1.00	0.14 / 0.06	0.97 / 1.00
	ILP miner	0.54 / 1.00	0.64 / 1.00	0.44 / 0.16	0.68 / 1.00

8 Conclusion

In this paper we presented a novel process discovery approach exploiting localization information, i.e., events refer to one or more regions. Such information is available in most application domains. In this paper, we illustrated this using event data from software systems. Such systems have an explicit architecture and events may be related to this architecture. Hence, it is easy to create localized event logs. Experiments show that such reasonably chosen information can be used to produce much better process models. Whereas conventional approaches require some global form of completeness, our approach only needs local completeness (within a region). Therefore, the resulting models are simpler, more general and allow more cases to fit. Moreover, localization information may be exploited to create hierarchical models.

References

1. van der Aalst, W.M.P.: Process Mining: Discovery. Conformance and Enhancement of Business Processes. Springer, Berlin (2011)
2. van der Aalst, W.M.P.: Distributed Process Discovery and Conformance Checking. In: de Lara, J., Zisman, A., (eds.) FASE 2012. LNCS, vol. 7212, pp. 1–25. Springer, Heidelberg (2012)

---

[15] *Fitness* is the fraction of perfectly fitting cases. *Trace fitness* is the measure of discrepancy between a log and a model. *Precision* is the fraction of additional cases, obtained during replay, which are not represented in the log. *Generalization* is the fraction of states visited during replay, which are covered by the model.

[16] Characteristics for the models constructed by the heuristic miner cannot be obtained in a reasonable amount of time.

3. van der Aalst, W.M.P.: A General Divide and Conquer Approach for Process Mining. In: Federated Conference on Computer Science and Information Systems (FedCSIS 2013), pp. 1–10. IEEE Computer Society (2013)
4. van der Aalst, W.M.P.: Decomposing Petri Nets for Process Mining: A Generic Approach. Distributed and Parallel Databases 31(4), 471–507 (2013)
5. van der Aalst, W.M.P., Rubin, V., Verbeek, H.M.W., van Dongen, B.F., Kindler, E., Günther, C.W.: Process Mining: A Two-Step Approach to Balance Between Underfitting and Overfitting. Software and Systems Modeling 9(1), 87–111 (2010)
6. van der Aalst, W.M.P., Weijters, A.J.M.M., Maruster, L.: Workflow Mining: Discovering Process Models from Event Logs. IEEE Transactions on Knowledge and Data Engineering 16(9), 1128–1142 (2004)
7. Agrawal, R., Gunopulos, D., Leymann, F.: Mining Process Models from Workflow Logs. In: Schek, H.-J., Alonso, G., Saltor, F., Ramos, I. (eds.) EDBT 1998. LNCS, vol. 1377, pp. 469–483. Springer, Berlin (1998)
8. Bergenthum, R., Desel, J., Lorenz, R., Mauser, S.: Process Mining Based on Regions of Languages. In: Alonso, G., Dadam, P., Rosemann, M. (eds.) International Conference on Business Process Management (BPM 2007). Lecture Notes in Computer Science, vol. 4714, pp. 375–383. Springer-Verlag, Berlin (2007)
9. Bose, R.P.J.C., van der Aalst, W.M.P.: Trace Clustering Based on Conserved Patterns: Towards Achieving Better Process Models. In: Rinderle-Ma, S., Sadiq, S., Leymann, F. (eds.) PM 2009 Workshops. LNBIP, vol. 43, pp. 170–181. Springer, Heidelberg (2010)
10. Carmona, J., Cortadella, J.: Process Mining Meets Abstract Interpretation. In: Balcazar, J.L. (ed.) ECML/PKDD 210. Lecture Notes in Artificial Intelligence, vol. 6321, pp. 184–199. Springer-Verlag, Berlin (2010)
11. Carmona, J., Cortadella, J., Kishinevsky, M.: A Region-Based Algorithm for Discovering Petri Nets from Event Logs. Business Process Management 2008, 358–373 (2008)
12. Carmona, J., Cortadella, J., Kishinevsky, M.: Divide-and-Conquer Strategies for Process Mining. In: Dayal, U., Eder, J., Koehler, J., Reijers, H.A. et al. (eds.) BPM 2009. LNCS, vol. 5701, pp. 327–343. Springer, Heidelberg (2009)
13. Cook, J.E., Wolf, A.L.: Discovering Models of Software Processes from Event-Based Data. ACM Transactions on Software Engineering and Methodology 7(3), 215–249 (1998)
14. Darondeau, P.: Unbounded Petri Net Synthesis. In: Desel, J., Reisig, W., Rozenberg, G. (eds.) ACPN 2003. LNCS, vol. 3098, pp. 413–438. Springer, Heidelberg (2004)
15. Goedertier, S., Martens, D., Vanthienen, J., Baesens, B.: Robust Process Discovery with Artificial Negative Events. Journal of Machine Learning Research 10, 1305–1340 (2009)
16. Greco, G., Guzzo, A., Pontieri, L., Saccà, D.: Discovering Expressive Process Models by Clustering Log Traces. IEEE Transaction on Knowledge and Data Engineering 18(8), 1010–1027 (2006)
17. Kalenkova, A., de Leoni, M., van der Aalst, W.M.P.: Discovering, Analyzing and Enhancing BPMN Models Using ProM. In: Business Process Management Demo Sessions (BPMD 2014), vol. 1295. CEUR Workshop Proceedings, pp. 36–40 (2014)
18. Leemans, S.J.J., Fahland, D., van der Aalst, W.M.P.: Discovering Block-Structured Process Models from Event Logs Containing Infrequent Behaviour. In: Song, M., Wohed, P. et al. (eds.): BPM 2013 Workshops. LNBIP, vol. 171, pp. 66–78, 2014. Springer, Heidelberg (2014)

19. Leemans, S.J.J., Fahland, D., van der Aalst, W.M.P.: Discovering Block-structured Process Models from Incomplete Event Logs. In: Ciardo, G., Kindler, E. (eds.) PETRI NETS 2014. LNCS, vol. 8489, pp. 91–110. Springer-Verlag, Berlin (2014)

20. Mazurkiewicz, A.: Semantics of Concurrent Systems: A Modular Fixed-Point Trace Approach. In: Rozenberg, G. (ed.) Advances in Petri Nets 1984. Lecture Notes in Computer Science, vol. 188, pp. 353–375. Springer-Verlag, Berlin (1984)

21. Alves de Medeiros, A.K., Weijters, A.J.M.M., van der Aalst, W.M.P.: Genetic Process Mining: An Experimental Evaluation. Data Mining and Knowledge Discovery 14(2), 245–304 (2007)

22. Munoz-Gama, J., Carmona, J., van der Aalst, W.M.P.: Single-Entry Single-Exit Decomposed Conformance Checking. Information Systems 46, 102–122 (2014)

23. OMG. Business Process Model and Notation (BPMN). Object Management Group, formal/2011-01-03 (2011)

24. Polyvyanyy, A., Vanhatalo, J., Völzer, H.: Simplified Computation and Generalization of the Refined Process Structure Tree. In: Bravetti, M., Bultan, T. (eds.) WS-FM 2010. LNCS, vol. 6551, pp. 25–41. Springr, Heidelberg (2011)

25. Sole, M., Carmona, J.: Process Mining from a Basis of Regions. In: Lilius, J., Penczek, W. (eds.) PETRI NETS 2010. LNCS, vol. 6128, pp. 226–245. Springer, Heidelberg (2010)

26. Verbeek, E.: Decomposed process mining with DivideAndConquer. Proceedings of the BPM Demo Sessions 2014, 1–5 (2014)

27. J. De Weerdt, M. De Backer, J. Vanthienen, and B. Baesens. Leveraging Process Discovery With Trace Clustering and Text Mining for Intelligent Analysis of Incident Management Processes. In: IEEE Congress on Evolutionary Computation (CEC 2012), pp. 1–8 (2012)

28. Weijters, A.J.M.M., van der Aalst, W.M.P.: Rediscovering Workflow Models from Event-Based Data using Little Thumb. Integrated Computer-Aided Engineering 10(2), 151–162 (2003)

29. van der Werf, J.M.E.M., van Dongen, B.F., Hurkens, C.A.J., Serebrenik, A.: Process Discovery using Integer Linear Programming. Fundamenta Informaticae 94, 387–412 (2010)

New Search Strategies for the Petri Net CEGAR Approach

Ákos Hajdu[1], András Vörös[1]($\boxtimes$), and Tamás Bartha[2]

[1] Department of Measurement and Information Systems,
Budapest University of Technology and Economics, Budapest, Hungary
vori@mit.bme.hu
[2] Institute for Computer Science and Control,
MTA SZTAKI, Budapest, Hungary

Abstract. Petri nets are a successful formal method for the modeling and verification of asynchronous, concurrent and distributed systems. Reachability analysis can provide important information about the behavior of the model. However, reachability analysis is a computationally hard problem, especially when the state space is infinite. Abstraction-based techniques are often applied to overcome complexity. In this paper we analyze an algorithm, which uses counterexample guided abstraction refinement. This algorithm proved its efficiency on the model checking contest. We examine the algorithm from a theoretical and practical point of view. On the theoretical side, we show that the algorithm cannot decide reachability for relatively simple instances. We propose a new iteration strategy to explore the invariant space, which extends the set of decidable problems. We also give proofs on the theoretical limits of our approach. On the practical side, we examine different search strategies and we present our new, complex strategy with superior performance compared to traditional strategies. Measurements show that our new contributions perform well for traditional benchmark models as well.

Keywords: Petri nets · Reachability analysis · Abstraction · CEGAR · ILP

1 Introduction

The development of complex, distributed and safety-critical systems requires mathematically precise proofs in order to ensure the suitability and correctness of the design. Formal modeling and verification methods provide such tools. However, a major drawback of using formal techniques is their computation and memory-intensive nature. Even for relatively small asynchronous and concurrent models, the state space and the set of possible behaviors can be unmanageably large, or even infinite. This is usually referred to as the "state space explosion" problem in the literature.

This problem also holds for one of the most popular modeling formalisms, Petri nets. The behavior of a Petri net model is determined by the set of reachable states and fireable transitions. Therefore, reachability analysis is an important

© Springer International Publishing Switzerland 2015
R. Devillers and A. Valmari (Eds.): PETRI NETS 2015, LNCS 9115, pp. 309–328, 2015.
DOI: 10.1007/978-3-319-19488-2_16

formal verification technique for Petri nets. The reachability problem answers the question whether a given state is reachable from the initial state of the modeled system. However, solving reachability is a computationally hard problem. Therefore, abstraction-based techniques are often involved to overcome complexity.

Wimmel and Wolf published an algorithm [18], which applies counterexample guided abstraction refinement to the reachability problem of Petri nets. Their algorithm proved its efficiency at the model checking contest in 2013 [10]. After its publication, we analyzed the algorithm regarding correctness and completeness, and published our results in [8]. Although the algorithm can solve many problems efficiently, we proved that it fails to decide reachability for relatively simple instances. In worse cases it may even give a wrong answer. We suggested improvements and we also extended the algorithm to be able to handle inhibitor arcs and submarking coverability problems. Furthermore, we proved that even the improved algorithm is incomplete due to its iteration strategy.

In this paper we continue our work with further theoretical and practical investigations. In Section 2 we introduce the theoretical background of our work. We present the algorithm of Wimmel and Wolf [18] and a brief overview of our previous findings [8] in Section 3. Then, we introduce our current results. On the theoretical side, we propose a new iteration strategy to be used during the phase that explores the invariant space (Section 4). We show that our new approach extends the set of decidable problems and we also give theoretical results on its limits. On the practical side, we examine the behavior of well-known search strategies (depth- and breadth-first search) for the solution space traversal and we also present our new, complex strategy combining the advantages of BFS and DFS (Section 5). We prove the efficiency of our new approaches with measurements on traditional benchmark models and on our special nets as well (Section 6). Finally, we conclude our work in Section 7.

2   Background

In this section we introduce the theoretical background of our work. First, we present Petri nets (Section 2.1), then we introduce reachability analysis (Section 2.2).

2.1   Petri Nets

Petri nets [13] are graphical models for concurrent and asynchronous systems, providing both structural and dynamical analysis. A discrete Petri net is a tuple $PN = (P, T, E, W)$, where P is the set of *places*, T is the set of *transitions*, with $P \neq \emptyset \neq T$ and $P \cap T = \emptyset$, $E \subseteq (P \times T) \cup (T \times P)$ is the set of *arcs* and $W: E \mapsto \mathbb{Z}^+$ is the weight function assigning weights $w^-(p_j, t_i)$ to the edge $(p_j, t_i) \in E$ and $w^+(p_j, t_i)$ to the edge $(t_i, p_j) \in E$. Places and transitions are numbered from zero in our work.

A *marking* of a Petri net is a mapping $m: P \mapsto \mathbb{N}$. If a place p contains k *tokens* in a marking m then $m(p) = k$. The initial marking is denoted by m_0.

Dynamic Behavior. A transition $t \in T$ is *enabled* in a marking m, if $m(p_j) \geq w^-(p_j, t)$ holds for each $p_j \in P$ with $(p_j, t) \in E$. An enabled transition t can *fire*, consuming $w^-(p_j, t)$ tokens from places $p_j \in P$ with $(p_j, t) \in E$ and producing $w^+(p_j, t)$ tokens on places $p_j \in P$ with $(t, p_j) \in E$. The firing of a transition t in a marking m is denoted by $m[t\rangle m'$ where m' is the marking after firing t.

A word $\sigma = t_1 t_2 \ldots t_n \in T^*$ is a *firing sequence*. A firing sequence is *realizable* in a marking m and leads to m' (denoted by $m[\sigma\rangle m'$), if $m[t_1\rangle \ldots [t_n\rangle m'$. The *Parikh image* of a firing sequence σ is a vector $\wp(\sigma) \colon T \mapsto \mathbb{N}$, where $\wp(\sigma)(t_i)$ is the number of the occurrences of t_i in σ. The empty firing sequence is denoted by ε.

2.2 Reachability Problem

A marking m' is *reachable* from m if a realizable firing sequence $\sigma \in T^*$ exists for which $m[\sigma\rangle m'$ holds. The set of all reachable markings from the initial marking m_0 of a Petri net PN is denoted by $R(PN, m_0)$. The reachability problem is to decide if $m' \in R(PN, m_0)$ holds for a given marking m'. The aim of reachability analysis is to solve the reachability problem by finding a realizable firing sequence $m_0[\sigma\rangle m'$. The reachability problem is decidable [12], but it is at least EXPSPACE-hard [11] and no upper bound is known yet.

State Equation. The *incidence matrix* of a Petri net is a matrix $C_{|P| \times |T|}$, where $C(i, j) = w^+(p_i, t_j) - w^-(p_i, t_j)$. The element $C(i, j)$ represents the change in the number of tokens in p_i after firing t_j. Let m and m' be markings of the Petri net, then the *state equation* takes the form $m + Cx = m'$. Any vector $x \in \mathbb{N}^{|T|}$ fulfilling the state equation is called a *solution*. Note, that for any realizable firing sequence σ leading from m to m', the Parikh image of the firing sequence fulfills the equation $m + C\wp(\sigma) = m'$. On the other hand, not all solutions of the state equation are Parikh images of a realizable firing sequence. Therefore, the existence of a solution for the state equation is a necessary but not sufficient criterion for reachability. A solution x is called *realizable* if a realizable firing sequence σ exists with $\wp(\sigma) = x$.

T-invariants. A vector $y \in \mathbb{N}^{|T|}$ is called a *T-invariant* if $Cy = 0$ holds. A realizable T-invariant represents the possibility of a cyclic behavior in the modeled system, since its complete occurrence does not change the marking. However, during firing the transitions of the T-invariant, some intermediate markings can be of interest. If each component of the T-invariant y is either zero or one we also denote y by enumerating the components with value one, e.g., $y = (1, 0, 1, 0)$ can be denoted by $y = \{t_0, t_2\}$.

Solution Space. The solution space of the state equation $m + Cx = m'$ is semi-linear. Each solution x can be written as the sum of a *base solution* and the linear combination of T-invariants [18], which can formally be written as

$x = b + \sum_i n_i y_i$, where $b \in \mathbb{N}^{|T|}$ is the base solution and $n_i \in \mathbb{N}$ is the coefficient of the T-invariant $y_i \in \mathbb{N}^{|T|}$.

3   CEGAR Approach on Petri Nets

In this section we introduce the CEGAR approach generally (Section 3.1) and we present an algorithm published by Wimmel and Wolf [18], which applies the CEGAR approach to the reachability problem of Petri nets (Section 3.2). After its publication, we examined the correctness and completeness of their algorithm [8]. These findings form a basis for our current work, so we introduce them briefly in Section 3.3.

3.1   CEGAR Approach

Abstraction is a general mathematical approach for solving hard problems. It hides the irrelevant details, so the abstract model can be handled easier. One such technique is existential abstraction [5], which means that the abstract model over-approximates the original one. Therefore, if an invariant holds in the abstract model, it also holds in the original model. However, if there is a counterexample for which the invariant does not hold, it might be caused by the over-approximation. Thus, every counterexample must be examined whether it has a corresponding concrete counterexample in the original model. If a concrete counterexample exists, the invariant does not hold in the original model. Otherwise, the abstract counterexample is spurious and the abstraction has to be refined using the information from the examination. This technique is called the "counterexample guided abstraction refinement" (CEGAR) and it is widely used in model checking [1], [4], [9].

3.2   Reachability Analysis of Petri Nets Using CEGAR

Wimmel and Wolf published an algorithm [18], which applies the CEGAR approach to the reachability analysis of Petri nets, using the state equation. Figure 1 shows an overview of their algorithm, while each step is detailed in this section.

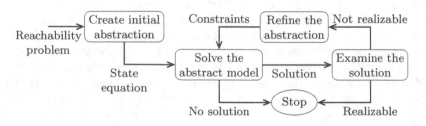

Fig. 1. Petri net CEGAR algorithm flowchart

Initial Abstraction. The input of the algorithm is a reachability problem $m' \in R(PN, m_0)$, which is transformed into the initial abstraction, namely the state equation of the form $m_0 + Cx = m'$.

Solving the Abstract Model. Solving the abstract model (i.e., the state equation) is an integer linear programming problem [6]. The ILP solver yields a minimal solution with respect to the cost function. In the algorithm of Wimmel and Wolf [18], the sum of the firing count of transitions is minimized in order to obtain trajectories with the shortest length.

The state equation is an over-approximation of the set of reachable markings, since its feasibility is a necessary, but not sufficient condition for reachability. Therefore, if no abstract solution exists, the target marking cannot be reached in the Petri net either. However, a solution of the abstract model may or may not be realizable by a firing sequence. Thus, further examinations are needed.

Examining the Solution. The solution of the state equation is a vector $x \in \mathbb{N}^{|T|}$, where $x(t)$ denotes the number of times a transition $t \in T$ has to fire in order to reach m' from m_0. However, x does not include any information about the order of the transition firings and whether they are enabled. Thus, the algorithm has to explore the state space of the Petri net with the limitation that each transition t can fire at most $x(t)$ times. If the target marking m' can be reached with this limit (i.e., x is realizable), it is a sufficient proof for reachability. Otherwise, x is a counterexample and the abstraction has to be refined.

Abstraction Refinement. If a solution x is not realizable, the ILP solver has to be forced to generate a different solution. This can be done by adding additional *constraints* (i.e., linear inequalities over transitions) to the state equation. The following two types of constraints were defined by Wimmel and Wolf [18].

– *Jump constraints* have the form $|t_i| < n$, where $n \in \mathbb{N}$, $t_i \in T$ and $|t_i|$ represents the firing count of the transition t_i. Jump constraints can be used to obtain different base solutions, exploiting their pairwise incomparability.
– *Increment constraints* have the form $\sum_{i=1}^{k} n_i |t_i| \geq n$, where $n_i \subset \mathbb{Z}$, $n \in \mathbb{N}$, and $t_i \in T$. Increment constraints can be used to reach non-base solutions, i.e., T-invariants are added in some linear combination.

After adding the new constraint, the state equation may become infeasible, or a new solution is obtained. Figure 2 presents the solution space. The bottom dots represent base solutions, while the cones represent the linear space formed by the T-invariants. The upper dots correspond to non-base solutions. Jumps are denoted by dashed arrows and increments by continuous arrows. The precise method for generating constraints and traversing the solution space is presented later in this section, but first, *partial solutions* are introduced.

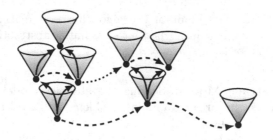

Fig. 2. Solution space of the state equation [18]

Partial Solutions. Given a Petri net $PN = (P, T, E, W)$ and a reachability problem $m' \in R(PN, m_0)$, a *partial solution* is a tuple $ps = (C, x, \sigma, r)$, where:

- C is the set of (jump and increment) constraints, together with the state equation they define the ILP problem,
- x is the minimal solution satisfying the state equation and the constraints belonging to the set C,
- $\sigma \in T^*$ is a maximal realizable firing sequence, with $\wp(\sigma) \le x$, i.e., each transition $t \in T$ can fire at most $x(t)$ times and enabled transitions must fire in some order,
- $r = x - \wp(\sigma)$ is the remainder vector.

Partial solutions are generated during the examination of the solution x by exploring the state space of the Petri net. For this purpose, Wimmel and Wolf use a "brute force" method with some optimization. The algorithm builds a tree with markings as nodes and occurrences of transitions as edges. The root of the tree is the initial marking m_0, and there is an edge labeled by t between nodes m_1 and m_2 if $m_1[t\rangle m_2$ holds. On each path leading from the root of the tree to a leaf, each transition t_i can occur at most $x(t_i)$ times. Each path to a leaf represents a maximal firing sequence, thus a new partial solution. The marking reached is referred to as the *final marking* of the partial solution.

A partial solution is called a *full solution* if $r = 0$ holds, thus $\wp(\sigma) = x$, which means that σ realizes the solution vector x. Wimmel and Wolf proved that for each realizable solution of the state equation a full solution exists. This full solution can be reached by continuously expanding the minimal solution of the state equation with constraints [18].

Consider now a partial solution $ps = (C, x, \sigma, r)$, which is not a full solution, i.e., $r \ne 0$. This means that some transitions could not fire enough times. There are three possible situations in this case:

1. x may be realizable by another firing sequence σ', thus a full solution $ps' = (C, x, \sigma', 0)$ can be found in the tree.
2. By adding jump constraints, greater, but pairwise incomparable solutions can be obtained.

3. For transitions $t \in T$ with $r(t) > 0$ increment constraints can be added to increase the token count in the input places of t, while the final marking m' must be unchanged. This can be achieved by adding new T-invariants to the solution. These T-invariants can "borrow" tokens for transitions in the remainder vector.

Generating Constraints. When a partial solution is not a full solution, both jump and increment constraints can be added, but they are applied on a different level:

- Jump constraints are generated from solution vectors of the state equation.
- Increment constraints are generated from partial solutions (which are obtained from solution vectors).

Jump Constraints. Given a solution vector x, for each transition $t_i \in T$ with $x(t_i) > 0$ a jump constraint c_i of the form $|t_i| < x(t_i)$ can be added to the state equation. If a new solution vector y_i is obtained after adding one of the constraints c_i, this process can be recursively repeated for y_i. Wimmel and Wolf proved that every base solution can be obtained using jump constraints [18].

Increment Constraints. Let $ps = (\mathcal{C}, x, \sigma, r)$ be a partial solution with $r > 0$. This means that some transitions could not fire enough times. Wimmel and Wolf use a heuristic to find the places and number of tokens needed to enable these transitions. If a set of places actually needs n $(n > 0)$ tokens, the heuristic estimates a number from 1 to n. If the estimate is too low, this method can be applied again, converging to the actual number of required tokens. The heuristic consists of the following three steps:

1. First, it builds a dependency graph to collect the transitions and places that are of interest. These are transitions that could not fire, and places that disable these transitions under the final marking of ps. An edge from a place p to a transition t means that p disables t, while an edge in the opposite direction means that firing t would increase the token count in p. Each source SCC[1] of the dependency graph has to be investigated, because it cannot get tokens from other components. Therefore, an increment constraint is needed.
2. The second step is to calculate the minimal number of missing tokens for each source SCC. There are two sets of transitions, $T_i \subseteq T$ and $X_i \subseteq T$. If one transition in T_i becomes fireable, it may enable all the other transitions of the SCC, while transitions in X_i cannot activate each other, therefore their token shortage must be fulfilled at once.
3. The third step is to construct an increment constraint c for each source SCC from the information about the places and their token requirements. These constraints will force transitions (with $r(t) = 0$) to produce tokens in the given places. Since the final marking is left unchanged, a T-invariant is added to the solution vector.

---

[1] Source strongly connected component, i.e., one without incoming edges from other components.

When applying the new constraint c, three situations are possible depending on the T-invariants in the Petri net:

- If the state equation and the set of constraints become infeasible, this partial solution cannot be extended to a full solution, therefore it is no longer of interest.
- If the ILP solver can produce a solution $x + y$ (with y being a T-invariant), new partial solutions can be found for y. If none of them helps getting closer to a full solution, the algorithm can get into an infinite loop, but no full solution is lost. A method to avoid this non-termination phenomenon will be discussed later in this section.
- If there is a new partial solution ps' where some transitions in the remainder vector could fire, this method can be repeated.

The following theorem of Wimmel and Wolf [18] states that if the reachability problem has a solution, it can be reached by the CEGAR approach:

Theorem 1. *If the reachability problem has a solution, a realizable solution of the state equation can be reached by continuously expanding the minimal solution with jump and increment constraints.*

Optimizations. Wimmel and Wolf also presented some methods for optimization [18]. In our current work, only the following T-invariant filtering optimization is important. After adding a T-invariant y to the partial solution $ps = (\mathcal{C}, x, \sigma, r)$, all the transitions of y may fire without enabling any transition in r, yielding a partial solution $ps' = (\mathcal{C}', x + y, \sigma', r)$ with $\wp(\sigma') = \wp(\sigma) + y$. The final marking and remainder vector of ps' is the same as in ps, therefore the same T-invariant y is added to the solution by the heuristic again, which can prevent termination. Thus, the algorithm cuts the search space at ps'. However, during firing the transitions of y, the algorithm could get closer to enabling a transition in r (without reaching the limit where it becomes enabled). These "better" intermediate markings should be detected, and be used as new partial solutions. Wimmel and Wolf gave a definition for better intermediate markings, which we generalized it in our former work [8]. Our definition is as follows.

Definition 1 (Better intermediate marking). *An intermediate marking m_i is considered better than the final marking m' of the firing sequence σ if there exists a transition t with $r(t) > 0$ and a place p with $(p, t) \in E$ for which $m'(p) < w^-(p, t) \land m_i(p) > m'(p)$ holds.*

This means that t is disabled by p and p had more tokens in the intermediate marking m_i than in the final marking m'.

3.3 Correctness and Completeness of the Algorithm

After Wimmel and Wolf published their algorithm, we examined the correctness and completeness properties and we published our findings in [8]. This section summarizes these results.

Correctness. We proved by a counterexample that the algorithm is incorrect due to an over-estimation in the increment constraint generating heuristic. In this case, incorrectness resulted in an answer "not reachable" for a reachable marking. We suggested a method to detect such situations giving the answer "not decidable". We also presented a new algorithm that tries to find the solution in such cases.

Completeness. We presented several subclasses of Petri nets for which the algorithm could not decide reachability and we suggested solutions to most of them. However, we proved that the improved algorithm is still incomplete due to its iteration strategy. In our current work we present a similar, but simpler proof (Section 4.1) and we propose a new iteration strategy to extend the set of decidable problems (Section 4.2).

4 New Iteration Strategy to Explore the Invariant Space

In this section we show that the algorithm of Wimmel and Wolf cannot decide reachability for relatively simple examples, because not every necessary invariant is explored (Section 4.1). We propose a new iteration strategy to traverse the invariant space by involving so-called "distant" invariants (Section 4.2). We show that this new approach extends the set of decidable problems and we also give theoretical results on its limitations. We also present a new filtering criterion (Section 4.3), which can avoid non-termination of the algorithm.

4.1 Proof of the Incompleteness

We prove the incompleteness of the algorithm published by Wimmel and Wolf [18] with the following example. Consider the Petri net PN in Figure 3 with the reachability problem $(1, 1, 0) \in R(PN, (0, 1, 0))$, i.e., producing a token in p_0. The vector $x_s = (1, 1, 1, 1, 1)$ is a solution, realized by the firing sequence $\sigma_s = t_3 t_1 t_0 t_2 t_4$.

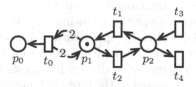

Fig. 3. A counterexample of completeness

The algorithm does the following steps. The minimal solution vector is $x_0 = (1, 0, 0, 0, 0)$, i.e., firing t_0. Since t_0 is not enabled, the only partial solution is $ps_0 = (\emptyset, x_0, \sigma_0 = \varepsilon, r_0 = (1, 0, 0, 0, 0))$. The algorithm finds that an additional token is required in p_1 and only t_1 can satisfy this need. With an increment constraint c_1: $|t_1| \geq 1$, the T-invariant $\{t_1, t_2\}$ is added to the new solution vector $x_1 = (1, 1, 1, 0, 0)$. Only t_2 and t_1 can fire (in this order), thus the only partial solution for x_1 is $ps_1 = (\{c_1\}, x_1, \sigma_1 = t_2 t_1, r_1 = r_0)$. This partial solution is skipped by the T-invariant filtering optimization, since the only difference from ps_0 is that all transitions of a T-invariant were fired. Furthermore, there are no better intermediate markings, since no additional token was "borrowed" from the T-invariant $\{t_1, t_2\}$. The algorithm terminates at this point, leaving the problem undecided. Without the filtering optimization, the algorithm would add the T-invariant $\{t_1, t_2\}$ again and again, preventing termination.

The problem is that the original algorithm does not recognize that although $\{t_1, t_2\}$ can fire, it only circulates the same token, instead of "lending" a new one. An extra token could be produced in p_2 (and then moved in p_1) using the T-invariant $\{t_3, t_4\}$. However, $\{t_3, t_4\}$ is not connected directly to p_1 (where the tokens are missing), so the iteration strategy of the algorithm does not try to involve it. We propose an extension to the iteration strategy in Section 4.2 in order to involve such "distant" invariants into the solution vector.

4.2 Involving Distant Invariants

Let y and z be T-invariants. We say that z is a distant invariant for y if z can produce tokens in a place connected to y. This can be written formally as follows.

Definition 2 (Distant invariant). *The T-invariant z is a distant invariant for the T-invariant y if a place p and transitions t_1, t_2 exist with $y(t_1) > 0$, $z(t_2) > 0$, $((t_1, p) \in E \vee (p, t_1) \in E)$, $w^+(p, t_2) - w^-(p, t_2) > 0$ and $y(t_2) = 0$.*

The definition states that y includes t_1, z includes t_2 and t_1 is connected to p, where the firing of t_2 increases the number of tokens. This way z can "borrow" tokens for y. The extra criterion $y(t_2) = 0$ is needed to ensure that we do not produce tokens for y by itself. In the example in Figure 3, $\{t_3, t_4\}$ is a distant invariant for $\{t_1, t_2\}$ because t_3 can produce tokens in p_2, which is connected to t_1 (and t_2).

When a transition in the remainder could not fire, the original algorithm tried to increase the token count on its input places. Our definition of distant invariants generalizes this concept the following way. When a partial solution is skipped by the T-invariant filtering optimization, it means that a T-invariant was fired, but could not "lend" enough tokens to enable a transition in the remainder. The basic idea of involving distant invariants is to try to increase the token count in any place connected to the filtered T-invariant. If some tokens can be produced, the filtered invariant will then be able to transfer them indirectly to the place that lacks tokens. There are two problems to be solved:

- How many tokens should be produced for the invariant that caused filtering?
- Termination criterion: if the distant invariant cannot help, adding it again can lead to non-termination.

Number of Tokens Produced in the Invariant. Estimating the required number of tokens is a hard problem, since the sum of the tokens in the places of a T-invariant may change during firing. Over-estimation can also be a problem: the final marking of the invariant may not be the "best" state regarding the number of tokens. Therefore, we produce only one token at a time and repeat this process if it was not enough.

Termination Criterion. When a distant invariant does not help, there are two possible cases. The distant invariant z could either not lend any tokens to the filtered invariant y or it could lend some, but not enough to enable a transition in the remainder.

The first case means that not only y lacks tokens, but z as well. Thus, we can now apply our strategy again, i.e., involving a distant invariant for $y + z$. This way we form a "chain" of distant invariants, which is defined formally as follows.

Definition 3 (Chain of distant invariants). *Let* $y_1, y_2, \ldots, y_n$ $(n \in \mathbb{N})$ *be T-invariants. We say that* $y_1 + y_2 + \ldots + y_n$, $n \in \mathbb{N}$ *is a chain of distant invariants if* y_{i+1} *is a distant invariant for* y_i *(for* $1 \leq i < n$). *A subchain of a chain* $y_1 + y_2 + \ldots + y_n$ *is a chain* $y_1 + y_2 + \ldots + y_k$, *with* $k \leq n$.

The definition of distant invariants ensures termination for such chains, since the newly involved distant invariant must have at least one transition that is not included in the previous ones and the number of transitions in a Petri net is finite.

The second case indicates that z could lend some tokens, but not enough. Therefore, we can involve distant invariants again for y. If z is the only distant invariant for y, this simply results in adding z again, but in general any distant invariant can be involved. However, if $y = y_1 + y_2 + \ldots + y_n$ is a chain, this would only produce tokens in places connected to y_n. Thus, we have to involve a distant invariant for every subchain in order to transfer the tokens to the originally filtered invariant (y_1).

Our new ideas above are formulated in Algorithm 1. The input of the algorithm is a partial solution ps' that was skipped due to ps and the number of better intermediate markings during the firing sequence of ps'. Partial solutions are extended to store a chain of distant invariants, which is initially 0.

At first we calculate the difference between the solution vectors of ps and ps' and we initialize the list of constraints with the constraints of ps'. The following two cases are possible.

- If the chain of $ps \neq 0$, some distant invariants were already involved. If there are better intermediate markings ($n_b > 0$), then these invariants helped (but not enough) to enable a transition in the remainder. In this case we can involve them again, so the chain of ps' is the same as in ps and we involve a distant invariant for every subchain.

Algorithm 1. Distant invariant algorithm

    Input   : ps': Partial solution skipped
                ps: Partial solution that caused skipping ps'
                n_b: Number of better intermediate markings for ps'
    Output : x: New solution vector found by involving distant invariants
1 $z \leftarrow$ difference invariant between ps and ps' ;
2 $C^* \leftarrow$ constraints of ps';
3 **if** *the chain of ps* $\neq 0$ $\wedge n_b > 0$ **then**
4   Chain of $ps' \leftarrow$ Chain of ps;
5   **for** *each subchain of ps'* **do**
6 | $C^* \leftarrow C^* \cup$ {constraint to involve a distant invariant for the subchain};
7   **end**
8 **end**
9 **else if** z *is a distant invariant for the chain of ps* **then**
10   Chain of $ps' \leftarrow$ Chain of $ps + z$;
11     $C^* \leftarrow C^* \cup$ {constraint to involve a distant invariant for the chain of ps'};
12 **end**
13 $x \leftarrow$ solve the state equation with C^*;
14 **return** x;

- Otherwise we extend the chain of ps with z and involve distant invariants only for the whole chain. However, we have to first check if z is really an extension to the chain of ps, since ps' can be a solution obtained by the original increment constraints.

Finding a constraint to involve a distant invariant for a chain (or subchain) y is quite straightforward. We get the places connected to the transitions of y and we create a constraint using the third step of the increment constraint generating heuristic to produce a token in these places. If no constraint can be found, the algorithm returns no new solution. If there are multiple distant invariants for y, all of them can be found using jump constraints from the original algorithm. Finally, we solve the state equation extended with C^* and return the solution (if found).

This new strategy can solve the example in Figure 3 trivially. As a complex example, consider the Petri net PN in Figure 4 with the reachability problem $(1,1,0,0,2) \in R(PN,(0,1,0,0,2))$, i.e., producing a token in p_0.

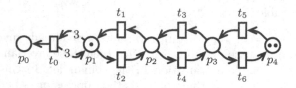

Fig. 4. Distant invariant example

The minimal solution of the abstract model is firing t_0, which is not enabled. Thus, the T-invariant $\{t_1, t_2\}$ is added twice in order to get two additional tokens in p_1. This invariant can fire but it does not help getting closer to enabling t_0 so the partial solution is skipped. At this point, our new algorithm tries to produce a token in any of the places connected to $\{t_1, t_2\}$, i.e., p_1 and p_2 by distant invariants. Therefore, the T-invariant $\{t_3, t_4\}$ is added once to the new solution. This invariant can also fire but does not help enabling t_0. The partial solution is skipped, and since $\{t_3, t_4\}$ is a distant invariant for $\{t_1, t_2\}$, the algorithm now tries to produce a token in places connected to the chain $\{t_1, t_2\} \cup \{t_3, t_4\}$, i.e., in p_1, p_2, and p_3. This implies that the invariant $\{t_5, t_6\}$ is added once. Firing this invariant does not enable t_0, but yields an extra token in p_1, which is a better intermediate marking. Thus, the partial solution is skipped but the algorithm now tries to involve distant invariants for every subchain, namely for $\{t_1, t_2\}$ and $\{t_1, t_2, t_3, t_4\}$, resulting in the addition of $\{t_3, t_4\}$ and $\{t_5, t_6\}$. The solution vector is now $(1, 2, 2, 2, 2, 2, 2)$, which can be realized by the firing sequence $t_5 t_5 t_3 t_3 t_1 t_1 t_0 t_2 t_2 t_4 t_4 t_6 t_6$.

Limitations. Although our new approach can solve a new range of problems, it also has some limitations. As an example consider the Petri net PN in Figure 5(a) with the reachability problem $(1, 1, 0) \in R(PN, (0, 1, 0))$, i.e., producing a token in p_0.

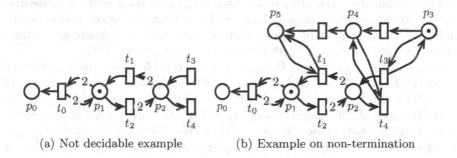

(a) Not decidable example   (b) Example on non-termination

Fig. 5. Example nets for the limitation of distant invariants

The minimal solution is firing t_0, which is not enabled. Thus, the T-invariant $\{t_1, t_2\}$ is added once in order to get an additional token in p_1. This invariant can fire, but it does not help getting closer to enabling t_0 so the partial solution is filtered. At this point the algorithm tries to produce tokens for $\{t_1, t_2\}$ using distant invariants, which implies adding $\{t_3, t_4\}$ once. This invariant can fire, lending a token in p_2. However, t_1 requires two tokens to fire and produce one in p_1. This partial solution is also filtered and there are no better intermediate markings, since we only count the tokens in places connected to the disabled transition t_0, which is p_1. The algorithm terminates at this point leaving the problem undecided.

A trivial idea for this example would be to extend the definition of better intermediate markings (Definition 1) to count tokens not only in places connected to the transition that cannot fire, but in places connected to the filtered T-invariant as well. This can be formalized as follows. Let $ps = (\mathcal{C}, x + y, \sigma, r)$ be a partial solution that was skipped due to the invariant y. Suppose that we obtained $ps' = (\mathcal{C}', x + y + z, \sigma', r)$ by involving the distant invariant z for y, which could not enable any transition in the remainder, thus ps' is skipped as well. Furthermore, suppose that no better intermediate marking was found using Definition 1 (as in the example in Figure 5(a)). Given a partial solution ps and a place p let $\max(ps, p)$ be $\max(m(p))$ during firing σ of ps from the initial marking m_0. Then the definition of better intermediate markings can be generalized in the following way.

Definition 4. *Given the partial solutions ps and ps' as described above, an intermediate marking m_i of σ' is considered better than the final marking m' if Definition 1 holds or a transition t with $y(t) > 0$ and a place p with $(p, t) \in E \vee (t, p) \in E$ exists for which $m_i(p) > \max(ps, p)$ holds.*

The generalized definition states that the intermediate marking is also considered better if there is a place connected to the filtered T-invariant, which contains more tokens than in any marking in the firing sequence of the previous partial solution. If a better intermediate marking exists for ps' using this definition, then we can involve z again. However, this definition would often lead to non-termination since the filtered T-invariant (y) is already enabled (otherwise it would not have been filtered). Thus, we cannot give an upper bound on the number of tokens in p, as opposed to our original definition, where we produce tokens in p until the transition that is disabled by p gets enabled.

As an example consider the Petri net PN in Figure 5(b) with the reachability problem $(1, 1, 0, 0, 0, 1) \in R(PN, (0, 1, 0, 1, 0, 0))$, i.e., producing a token in p_0 and moving the token from p_3 to p_5. This net works similarly to the net in Figure 5(a), but occurrences of the transitions t_3, t_4, and t_1 can only appear in this order, due to the upper part (places p_3, p_4, p_5) of the net. As in the previous example, $\{t_1, t_2\}$ is added first, then $\{t_3, t_4\}$. Suppose now, that we consider it a better intermediate marking when t_3 produced a token in p_2. This implies that $\{t_3, t_4\}$ is added again. Now t_4 can fire two times, producing two tokens in p_2. There are two possible sequels. If t_1 fires, it produces an extra token in p_1 and enables t_0. However, the extra tokens must be consumed in order to reach the final marking, but t_4 cannot fire after t_1. The search terminates on this path, since no more solutions can be found. The second case is that t_4 fires, which consumes the tokens from p_2 so t_1 cannot transfer them to p_1. Thus, t_0 is still not enabled, but we had a better intermediate state, since we had two tokens in p_2. Therefore, $\{t_3, t_4\}$ is added again and this process repeats avoiding termination.

The examples in Figure 5 show that the generalized definition (Definition 4) may help to decide reachability for some instances, but it may also yield non-termination.

4.3   New Filtering Criterion

Although a partial solution is skipped using the T-invariant filtering optimization, we may obtain new solutions from it through intermediate markings or distant invariants. This yields a new branch in the search space, which can also lead to non-termination.

There are special cases where T-invariants can either fire or not, both being a maximal firing sequence. As an example, consider the Petri net in Figure 4 and suppose that t_1, t_2, t_3, and t_4 each has to fire once. A possible maximal firing sequence is $t_2t_4t_3t_1$, but t_2t_1 is also maximal, since neither t_4 nor t_3 is enabled afterwards. When such invariants exist, it is possible that the following two partial solutions are obtained from $ps = (\mathcal{C}, x, \sigma, r)$ after adding the invariant y:

- $ps' = (\mathcal{C}', x + y, \sigma', r)$, with $\wp(\sigma') = \wp(\sigma) + y$, and
- $ps'' = (\mathcal{C}', x + y, \sigma, r + y)$.

In the first case, the invariant was fired (i.e., added to the firing sequence), while in the second case it was not fired (i.e., added to the remainder). The first case can be detected by the T-invariant filtering optimization. However, we found that the second case can also lead to non-termination if there are at least two T-invariants with this property.

To overcome this problem, we detect when a T-invariant is added to the remainder, i.e., we get $ps'' = (\mathcal{C}', x + y, \sigma, r + y)$ from $ps - (\mathcal{C}, x, \sigma, r)$. However, ps'' cannot be filtered immediately because the remainder is different so the abstraction refinement may add new invariants that can help. We only skip ps'' if ps was skipped by the original T-invariant filtering optimization, which also means that ps'' was obtained through intermediate markings or distant invariants.

5   Search Strategies

As already mentioned in Section 3.2, the algorithm of Wimmel and Wolf traverses the semi-linear solution space of the state equation. At each non-realizable solution, multiple (jump and/or increment) constraints can be applied, each yielding a new path in the solution space. However, the authors did not publish the strategy for the solution space traversal in [18]. An overview pseudo-code was published later in [19]. In this section we present three different search strategies: depth-first search (Section 5.1), breadth-first search (Section 5.2) and our new approach, a complex strategy (Section 5.3), which combines the advantages of DFS and BFS. Measurement results supporting our statements in this section can be found in Section 6.2.

5.1   Depth-First Search

Depth-first search (DFS) can be very effective regarding memory usage and computation time as well. It only stores one path of the solution space in memory at a time for backtracking purposes and it has a fast convergence if several invariants have to be added to reach a realizable solution. However, DFS has some disadvantages as well:

- It may not find the minimal solution by choosing a path, which contains a solution but not the minimal one.
- It may fail to terminate in an infinite solution space by choosing a path, where T-invariants can be added infinitely many times without finding a realizable solution.

The T-invariant filtering optimization (Section 3.2) and our new filtering criterion (Section 4.3) cuts the search space, but does not always detect infinite loops. We tried to give stronger criteria for cutting, but then realizable solutions were lost, reducing the set of decidable problems.

5.2 Breadth-First Search

Due to the problems of DFS, we implemented a breadth-first search (BFS) version of the algorithm as well. The number of base solutions can grow exponentially, but it is always finite so we still use DFS between the base solutions and only use BFS in the linear space of invariants. As opposed to DFS, it is less efficient, but always finds the minimal solution if the target marking is reachable. When the target marking is not reachable, BFS may fail to terminate in an infinite solution space. The T-invariant filtering optimization can prevent this in some cases and can also make the computational time shorter.

5.3 Complex Search

We also developed a new, complex search strategy, which combines the advantages of DFS and BFS. We traverse the base solutions using DFS as previously. When exploring the invariant space over a base solution our main strategy is DFS, but with a little BFS extension: at each solution x, we generate all partial solutions belonging to x, instead of continuing the search with the first one and filter them based on a partial order.

Ordering of Partial Solutions. We define an ordering over vectors and partial solutions as follows.

Definition 5 (Ordering of vectors). *A vector x is less than a vector y (denoted by $x < y$), if and only if $x(i) \leq y(i)$ for each index i and $x \neq y$.*

Definition 6 (Ordering of partial solutions). *A partial solution $ps_1 = (\mathcal{C}, x, \sigma_1, r_1)$ is less than a partial solution $ps_2 = (\mathcal{C}, x, \sigma_2, r_2)$ (denoted by $ps_1 < ps_2$), if and only if $r_2 < r_1$.*

A partial solution ps_1 is less than a partial solution ps_2 if the remainder r_2 is less than r_1. This means that ps_2 is closer to realization, since every transition fired in the sequence of ps_1 was also fired in ps_2, but ps_2 may have more fired transitions. Note that this is a partial order, since partial solutions ps_1, ps_2 may exist with $ps_1 \not< ps_2$ and $ps_2 \not< ps_1$, e.g., if $r_1 = (1, 0)$ and $r_2 = (0, 1)$.

Filtering Partial Solutions. For our filtering criterion we define maximal and minimal partial solutions.

Definition 7 (Maximal partial solution). *A partial solution ps of a solution x is maximal, if and only if no other partial solution ps' exists for x with ps < ps'.*

Definition 8 (Minimal partial solution). *A partial solution ps of a solution x is minimal, if and only if no other partial solution ps' exists for x with ps' < ps.*

The filtering criterion is quite simple, we only keep minimal and maximal partial solutions. Since the ordering is partial, there can be more than one minimal and maximal partial solutions.

We keep the maximal partial solution because it has a minimal remainder, i.e., it is the closest to realizing the solution vector. Also, the T-invariant filtering optimization works well for maximal partial solutions, since every T-invariant that can fire, must also fire (i.e., it is added to the firing sequence). A minimal partial solution has maximal remainder, i.e., not every enabled T-invariant was fired. This yields a slower convergence to a realizable solution. However, since the remainder is different from the remainder of the maximal partial solution, the abstraction refinement may involve different invariants.

6   Evaluation

We implemented our algorithm as a plug-in for the *PetriDotNet* [15] framework to evaluate its performance. We compared our approach to other tools and algorithms (Section 6.1) and we also measured the performance of the different search strategies (Section 6.2).

6.1   Comparison to Other Tools and Algorithms

We compared our algorithm to the implementation of Wimmel and Wolf, which is called the *SARA* tool [17]. We also compared our approach to the well-known saturation-based model checking algorithm [2], [14]. The results can be seen in Table 1, where *TO* refers to an unacceptable run-time (> 600 seconds), *ERR* means a run-time exception and *NS* implies that the algorithm terminated, but could not solve the problem.

The FMS model [3] represents a flexible manufacturing system. The parameter of the model determines the size of the state space, while the structure of the net is fixed. The results show that our algorithm outperforms both saturation and the SARA tool. The Kanban model [3] illustrates a production scheduling method. The parameter determines the size of the state space. We experienced that our algorithm can find a realizable solution quickly, but it examines many partial solutions before finding the full solution. The Dining philosophers model [7] is often used to show the problems of parallel programming and mutual exclusion. As the parameter grows, both the structure of the net and the state space becomes larger. Saturation and SARA performs better for these models.

Table 1. Comparison of our algorithm to SARA and saturation

Model	Our algorithm	SARA	Saturation
FMS-10	0,041 s	0,001 s	0,06 s
FMS-50	0,048 s	0,018 s	1,09 s
FMS-100	0,056 s	0,059 s	8,03 s
FMS-200	0,071 s	0,278 s	69,7 s
FMS-400	0,105 s	0,868 s	TO
FMS-800	0,226 s	3,537 s	TO
FMS-1600	0,317 s	ERR	TO
FMS-3200	0,65 s	ERR	TO
FMS-6400	1,274 s	ERR	TO
FMS-12800	2,54 s	ERR	TO
Kanban-10	0,032 s	0,03 s	0,002 s
Kanban-13	1,074 s	0,05 s	0,003 s
Kanban-16	3,055 s	0,09 s	0,01 s
Kanban-19	7,128 s	0,134 s	0,03 s
Kanban-22	16,039 s	0,2 s	0,03 s
Kanban-25	31,181 s	0,268 s	0,05 s
Dphil-10	0,078 s	0,005 s	0,01 s
Dphil-20	0,204 s	0,012 s	0,02 s
Dphil-30	0,399 s	0,021 s	0,03 s
Dphil-50	1,156 s	0,037 s	0,03 s
Dphil-100	6,989 s	0,094 s	0,04 s
Dphil-200	67,603 s	0,33 s	0,05 s
Distant1	0,027 s	0,001 s	-
Distant2	0,068 s	NS	-
Distant3	0,083 s	NS	-
Distant4	0,116 s	NS	-
Distant5	0,078 s	NS	-
Distant6	0,063 s	NS	-
Distant7	0,137 s	NS	-

The Distant models are built by us [16] to test our new iteration strategy, which involves distant invariants. The Distant1 and Distant3 models can also be seen in Fig. 3 and Fig. 4. After publishing our former proof of incompleteness [8], we contacted Wimmel and Wolf and they extended their implementation to be able to solve Distant1. However, the original algorithm cannot solve complex examples on distant invariants. As the state space of these models are infinite, saturation cannot handle these problems.

Due to the complexity of the models, further examination is required to determine how the structure and behavior of the models affect the performance of the algorithms and which algorithm is the most effective for a given type of models. This is an interesting future research direction.

6.2   Comparison of Search Strategies

The solution space (i.e., the abstract model) is usually small for the examples presented in Table 1, so every search strategy has a similar performance. We created models with many T-invariants (i.e., a large solution space) to evaluate the different search strategies. The results can be seen in Table 2, where the cost corresponds to the size of the solution, i.e., $\sum_{t \in T} x(t)$. The two parameters in the model name determine the number of invariants. The asterisk indicates a different ordering of places and transitions.

Table 2. Measurement results for different search strategies

	DFS		BFS		Complex	
Model	Time	Cost	Time	Cost	Time	Cost
Chain 1+2	0,04 s	7	0,055 s	7	0,039 s	7
Chain 1+3	0,095 s	13	0,828 s	13	0,1 s	13
Chain 1+4	0,291 s	21	85,24 s	21	0,288 s	21
Chain 1+4*	24,2 s	35	55,28 s	21	1,498 s	29
Chain 1+5	54,59 s	39	TO	31	56,36 s	39
Chain 2+2	0,076 s	11	0,277 s	11	0,074 s	11
Chain 2+3	0,197 s	19	12,768 s	19	0,288 s	23
Chain 2+3*	2,28 s	29	5,288 s	19	1,387 s	23

It is clear that DFS is more efficient than BFS regarding computational time. However, it often fails to find the minimal solution. Our combined strategy often outperforms DFS, while also being closer to the minimal solution.

7   Conclusions

In our paper we examined an abstraction-based algorithm for the reachability problem of Petri nets. From the theoretical point of view, we showed that the original algorithm cannot decide reachability for relatively simple nets. We presented a new iteration strategy based on distant invariants in order to overcome this deficiency. We also gave theoretical results on the limits of our new approach. From the practical point of view, we examined the behavior of the solution space traversal with DFS and BFS strategies and we also proposed a new, complex strategy based on a partial order between solutions. We demonstrated the efficiency of our new approaches with measurements.

Acknowledgments. This work was partially supported by the ARTEMIS JU and the Hungarian National Research, Development and Innovation Fund in the frame of the R5-COP (Reconfigurable ROS-based Resilient Reasoning Robotic Cooperating Systems) project.

References

1. Beyer, D., Henzinger, T., Jhala, R., Majumdar, R.: The software model checker Blast. International Journal on Software Tools for Technology Transfer **9**(5–6), 505–525 (2007)
2. Ciardo, G., Lüttgen, G., Siminiceanu, R.: Saturation: an efficient iteration strategy for symbolic state-space generation. In: Margaria, T., Yi, W. (eds.) TACAS 2001. LNCS, vol. 2031, pp. 328–342. Springer, Heidelberg (2001)
3. Ciardo, G., Zhao, Y., Jin, X.: Ten years of saturation: a Petri net perspective. In: Jensen, K., Donatelli, S., Kleijn, J. (eds.) ToPNoC V. LNCS, vol. 6900, pp. 51–95. Springer, Heidelberg (2012)
4. Clarke, E., Grumberg, O., Jha, S., Lu, Y., Veith, H.: Counterexample-guided abstraction refinement for symbolic model checking. J. ACM **50**(5), 752–794 (2003)
5. Clarke, E.M., Grumberg, O., Long, D.E.: Model checking and abstraction. ACM Trans. Program. Lang. Syst. **16**(5), 1512–1542 (1994)
6. Dantzig, G.B., Thapa, M.N.: Linear programming 1: introduction. Springer-Verlag New York Inc., Secaucus (1997)
7. Dijkstra, E.: Hierarchical ordering of sequential processes. Acta Informatica **1**(2), 115–138 (1971)
8. Hajdu, Á., Vörös, A., Tamás, B., Mártonka, Z.: Extensions to the CEGAR approach on Petri nets. Acta Cybernetica **21**(3), 401–417 (2014)
9. John, A., Konnov, I., Schmid, U., Veith, H., Widder, J.: Parameterized model checking of fault-tolerant distributed algorithms by abstraction. In: Formal Methods in Computer-Aided Design (FMCAD), pp. 201–209, October 2013
10. Kordon, F., Linard, A., Becutti, M., Buchs, D., Fronc, L., Hulin-Hubard, F., Legond-Aubry, F., Lohmann, N., Marechal, A., Paviot-Adet, E., Pommereau, F., Rodrígues, C., Rohr, C., Thierry-Mieg, Y., Wimmel, H., Wolf, K.: Web report on the model checking contest @ Petri net 2013, June 2013. http://mcc.lip6.fr
11. Lipton, R.: The Reachability Problem Requires Exponential Space. Research report, Yale University, Dept. of Computer Science (1976)
12. Mayr, E.W.: An algorithm for the general Petri net reachability problem. In: Proceedings of the Thirteenth Annual ACM Symposium on Theory of Computing, pp. 238–246. STOC 1981. ACM, New York (1981)
13. Murata, T.: Petri nets: Properties, analysis and applications. Proceedings of the IEEE **77**(4), 541–580 (1989)
14. Vörös, A., Darvas, D., Bartha, T.: Bounded saturation based CTL model checking. In: Proceedings of the 12th Symposium on Programming Languages and Software Tools, SPLST 2011 (2011)
15. Website of PetriDotNet. http://inf.mit.bme.hu/en/research/tools/petridotnet (online accessed March 22, 2015)
16. Website of the models used in the measurements. http://inf.mit.bme.hu/en/pn2015 (online accessed March 22, 2015)
17. Website of the SARA tool. http://www.service-technology.org/sara/index.html (online accessed March 22, 2015)
18. Wimmel, H., Wolf, K.: Applying CEGAR to the Petri net state equation. In: Abdulla, P.A., Leino, K.R.M. (eds.) TACAS 2011. LNCS, vol. 6605, pp. 224–238. Springer, Heidelberg (2011)
19. Wimmel, H., Wolf, K.: Applying CEGAR to the Petri net state equation. Logical Methods in Computer Science **8**(3) (2012)

Workflow Management Principles for Interactions Between Petri Net-Based Agents

Thomas Wagner^(✉) and Daniel Moldt

Department of Informatics, Informatics and Natural Sciences,
Faculty of Mathematics, Informatics and Natural Sciences,
University of Hamburg, Hamburg, Germany
http://www.informatik.uni-hamburg.de/TGI/

Abstract. Software agents can be considered as similar to humans interacting with one another to complete a complex activity or, in an organisational setting, a workflow. More so, agents can view their own behaviour as workflows, which can require other resources in order to be executed. This paper examines and describes an approach to consider agent behaviour as workflows and agents as both workflow engines and workflow resources. This approach can achieve a flexible and more uniform type of agent interaction. The paper describes the approach as a design pattern and blueprint. It also presents a first technical proof-of-concept. The general approach, concepts and prototype are based on and realised with reference Petri nets. This enables a clear transition between the conceptual approach and the practical realisation.

Keywords: Workflows · Agents · Integration · Interaction · Communication · Petri nets

1 Introduction

In an agent-oriented software system each agent provides its own part of the overall functionality. In order to achieve the overall system goal different agents need to interact. These interactions are predefined. This means that agents and their functionality are known in the execution environment (e.g. a directory service). When functionality is needed by other agents, it is looked up using preexisting (i.e. predefined at modelling time) knowledge. The agent requiring the functionality then directly communicates with the agent providing it.

This sort of interaction works well for agent systems in general. However, there are aspects which could be improved. These aspects include, but are not limited to, questions of availability and workload-balancing (e.g. fully utilising the available capacity), encapsulation (e.g. protecting critical system parts), or flexibility (e.g. dynamically changing service providers). These kinds of aspects can be handled by introducing helper constructs such as proxy agents. Yet, these kinds of constructs only tackle specific technical issues. This paper proposes a different way of handling the interaction between agents on a conceptual level.

A distributed agent system is, in its function, similar to a group of human individuals working together to achieve a common goal. The interactions between

© Springer International Publishing Switzerland 2015
R. Devillers and A. Valmari (Eds.): PETRI NETS 2015, LNCS 9115, pp. 329–349, 2015.
DOI: 10.1007/978-3-319-19488-2_17

such a group can be supported by a workflow system. A workflow consists of a set of tasks, which are executed individually to achieve an overall purpose.

Workflow principles, like task atomicity, control flow encapsulation and the separation between execution and resources, can be applied to agent interaction. Considering an agent's behaviour as workflows, agents become workflow engines and tasks represent sets of related actions. These tasks may require the functionality of other agents. At this point these other agents are considered in the same way as human users or workflow resources[1]. They complete tasks and send back the results to the task creator, which can continue in its behaviour.

The paper presents the overall approach in three incremental but distinct contributions. First, the similarities between agent and workflow systems are emphasised, resulting in a general perspective of agent systems as workflow systems. Building on this perspective the core details of agents as workflow engines and resources are described as a design pattern and blueprint. Finally, in order to validate the technical aspects of the pattern the WORKBROKER-prototype is introduced as a proof-of-concept. To illustrate the approach the paper uses simple examples. More complex scenarios and comparative case-studies are currently being developed, but are outside of the scope of this paper.

Additionally the approach contributes to our ongoing research of utilising and applying Petri nets in software engineering. On an abstract level, Petri nets are used to motivate and illustrate concepts, perspectives and ideas. But reference Petri nets [16] are also and more importantly used as the principal part of our executable code in the systems we create. We strive to realise any software artefact and concept as reference nets that are effortlessly embedded into and executed by the Java-based event formalism at the core of our runtime environment RENEW. This includes agents, workflows, objects, use-cases, etc. This paper presents a proof-of-concept that reference nets can be used to realise a combination of agent behaviour and workflows in the same way.

The paper contains eight sections. After this introduction Section 2 describes the technical background. Sections 3 to 5 present the three incremental contributions of the approach characterised above. Section 6 contains an overall discussion, Section 7 examines related work. The paper is concluded in Section 8.

2 Background

Reference nets [16] are a Petri net formalism following the nets-within-nets principles introduced in [21]. Tokens in reference nets are references to other reference nets or Java objects. This is used to build complex systems by nesting and interconnecting components. Communication between reference net instances is handled through synchronous channels [7]. The **Reference Net Workshop** (RENEW[2] [16,17]) serves as the modelling and execution environment for reference net systems. To support reference nets and Petri nets features RENEW utilises a Java-based event formalism at its core.

---

[1] To distinguish between human users and agents, we use the term *resource* for agents.
[2] RENEW is available at www.renew.de.

Reference nets have been used for the agent architecture and agent implementation adopted in this paper. Our reference architecture for multi-agent systems is called MULAN (**Mul**ti **A**gent **N**ets [20]). Agent systems in MULAN are defined on four layers. Each layer serves as the direct execution environment for the next one. The layers are: System, agent platform, agent, agent protocol (behaviour). CAPA (**C**oncurrent **A**gent **P**latform **A**rchitecture [9]) is an implementation of MULAN. CAPA utilises reference nets as the majority of the executable code to realise fully functioning agent systems following the FIPA (Foundation for Intelligent Physical Agents) standards for agents [10]. Decision making in CAPA is realised through nets which represent purely agent internal behaviour and can function proactively. Agent knowledge is stored in an internal knowledge base net which can be accessed by agent behaviours.

As described and compared in e.g. [6,20] there are several alternative agent architectures that could be used for similar purposes. However, MULAN offers the advantages of Java-based execution and reference nets (e.g. natural concurrency, mutual exclusion, expressiveness, nesting of nets, graphical representation). Through these advantages MULAN has proven itself over the years in many research and teaching projects.

For workflow aspects we use workflow nets [1], which model (business) processes as Petri nets. The reference net realisation of workflow nets uses a special transition called the task transition [13]. This transition is used to model workflow tasks with multiple operations (request, confirm, cancel) as a single transition for modelling. For execution the task transition is automatically translated into a complex net structure which realises the desired complex behaviour. Please note that aspects such as workflow soundness and correctness are outside of the scope of this paper. These aspects are currently being researched on top of the context described in this paper and will be presented at a later time.

3   General Perspective

Considering an agent system as a workflow system is a natural perspective. There are a number of similarities between the two types of systems. Both feature independent entities performing certain actions in a certain order with a high amount of collaboration and interaction.

In workflow systems human users perform tasks defined in workflows. Different users with different qualifications are needed to complete all tasks in the workflow. In agent systems software agents perform their functions as defined in their behaviour. Different agents providing different functionality are needed to complete the overall purpose of the system.

The key difference, in this context, is that a workflow system uses a workflow management system (WFMS) to distribute, manage and handle all things related to workflows and tasks. In an agent system the agents need to handle this management of their interactions on their own. There are helper constructs, such as directory services, but in general a software agent is responsible for deciding and handling what data is transmitted to which agent. This happens without

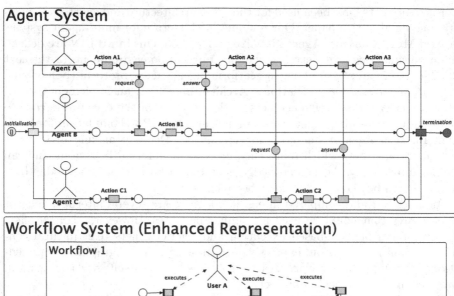

Fig. 1. Conceptual view of agent and workflow systems

any higher authority or guarantee that the work the agent wishes another agent to perform is actually done.

Figure 1 illustrates this perspective[3]. The upper part shows a Petri net representation of a regular agent system. Three agents perform actions and interact with one another. Basically, agent A alternates between performing an action and sending a request for an action to agents B and C respectively. Additionally agent C performs an independent action before it receives the request from agent A. Note that the initialisation and termination are part of the (implicit) system behaviour and are not assigned to one particular agent.

The lower part of Figure 1 shows a workflow system containing one workflow net. The representation has been enhanced with information about users and

---

[3] To keep the nets simple we limit ourselves to a basic example that uses mostly sequences and only one set of connected behaviour. More complex behaviour, including multiple, concurrent behaviours/workflows, is also supported and handled equally.

arranged to indicate the tasks they execute. The sequence of tasks A1, B1 and A2 is executed concurrently to the task C1. Once these tasks are finished the tasks C2 and A3 can be performed in sequence.

It is evident from Figure 1 that the two systems are very closely related. Except for the communication each agent action has a corresponding workflow task. Agents and users also correspond and the order of execution for actions and tasks is identical. There are two key differences between the workflow and agent views. The workflow considers the behaviour globally (i.e. for all users) and the assignment of tasks is not directly clear. In the agent view the behaviour is partitioned onto the three agents, which localises the behaviour and directly defines the assignment of actions. The global view explains the missing representation of communication in the workflow system. The unclear assignment of users is consolidated with the agent view if we assume unique user roles.

This means that the workflow view *can* be applied to the agent system if the communication and resource assignment are addressed. This application opens up a number of possibilities on how the behaviour of agents can be improved with established mechanisms used in workflow systems.

A complete application of the workflow view and all its aspects to agent systems is, however, not desirable. Some of the key qualities of agents are their autonomy, the encapsulation of data and functionality, and their ability to make certain decisions independently. These (and more) key qualities make agents as versatile as they are, especially in distributed environments. A complete application with a central master workflow that controls the behaviour of the agents globally would greatly diminish or even completely eliminate these qualities. Also, the approach should only be applied on the application level of agent systems and not on the meta and middleware level. The involved aspects can't adequately utilise the concepts and principles introduced by workflow management. This will be further discussed in Section 6.

To maintain the key qualities of agents a moderate approach is required. In Figure 1 each agent has its own behaviour "lane" which consists of the actions that it actually executes. These lanes are connected by the communication between agents but are, in general, independent. Still, the connection also states that actions B1 and C2 can only be performed once agent A has sent requests for them. Considering this, we can assume that these actions are like assignments agents B and C execute for agent A. This means that agent A's behaviour can be considered as a workflow in which actions B1 and C2 are tasks for other agents. The other actions (A1,A2,A3) are consequently tasks that are both controlled and executed directly by agent A.

Agent B is, under this consideration, only a resource for the workflow of agent A. Agent C, however, also executes action C1, which is independent from the other agents, but is a precondition to action C2. This means that Agent C controls a workflow and task of its own, but also acts as a resource for task C2 in agent A's workflow.

In other words, agents are considered in a dual capacity as both workflow engines and workflow resources. As engines they control their own behaviour defined and executed as a set of workflows. As resources they perform tasks

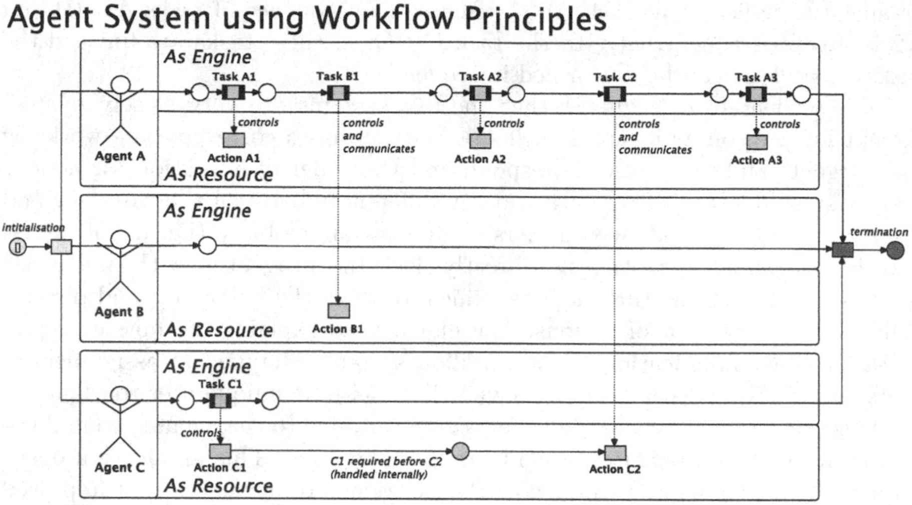

Agent System using Workflow Principles

Fig. 2. Conceptual view of an agent system using workflow principles

within their own or other agents' workflows and thus provide the actual functionality required for those tasks.

Figure 2 shows a net representation[4] of this view for the system from Figure 1. Agent behaviour now distinguishes between engine and resource aspects. On the engine side tasks control the actions or sets of actions of the resource side, which correspond to the actual functionality. Communication aspects, especially message exchange, are incorporated into the tasks as well. Figure 2 also takes into account that agent A controls tasks B1 and C2. Agent B exclusively acts as a resource for task B1. Agent C, however, controls the task C1 itself and acts as a resource for (the subsequent) task C2. Agents B and C retain their autonomy, as they can decide to deny requests from agent A.

The remaining key difference between agent and workflow systems is the infrastructure provided by a WFMS. A WFMS handles the communication and interaction between workflow users and engines. An agent system does not possess such a mechanism, therefor agents manage their own interactions. An intermediary system handling these aspects is the final part of the approach that needs to be provided. As a kind of middleware, it realises a process-infrastructure for agent systems by bridging the gap between agent workflow engines and agent workflow resources. It is responsible for workflow management aspects like task assignment and the mapping between tasks and actions. It also provides communication and synchronisation mechanisms. The components of the approach, especially the intermediary system and workflow engines, are aligned to the

---

[4] The dotted connections between tasks and actions are *not* Petri net arcs. They represent conceptual connections that need to be implemented by complex net structures like the task transition. This also applies to Figure 8.

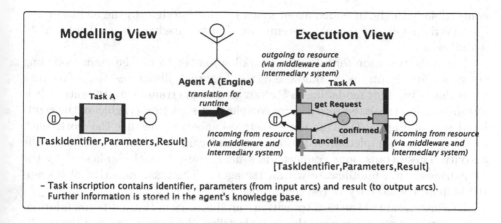

Fig. 3. Conceptual view of an agent workflow engine

components of the WfMC reference model for WFMS [12], though this is not further discussed in this paper.

4   Agents as Workflow Engines and Resources

This section presents the core details of how the perspective presented in the previous section can be realised as a design pattern. There are three major components in this perspective. Agents as workflow engines are described in Section 4.1. Agents as workflow resources are described in Section 4.2. Finally, the intermediary system is described in Section 4.3.

4.1   Agents as Workflow Engines

In order to control agent behaviour with workflows the task concept needs to be introduced into agent behaviour. Each set of related actions of the agent needs to be mapped into tasks. This is the main modelling challenge on the control/engine side of the agent behaviour.

Tasks are either performed by an agent itself or involve other agents. For modelling purposes they are handled exactly the same, they may however be handled differently at execution time. This will be discussed in Section 6.

The dependencies and order between the tasks need to be defined as well. Any additional information about the execution of the tasks (e.g. execution rules defining which agents are allowed to perform which tasks, parameters that are transmitted, results that are expected) needs to be made available to the executing agent as well. The result is a workflow representation of one behaviour of one particular agent. This needs to be applied to all behaviours of an agent.

Workflow nets [1] are well suited for the required representation and modelling aspects. Other workflow representations are also possible, if they are compatible with the intended agent system. With foresight to the inclusion into our Petri net-based agent systems we limit ourselves from here on to workflow nets.

The task transition for reference (workflow) nets ([13]) is the main modelling construct for agents as workflow engines. Figure 3 illustrates this. The task transition is used for modelling in RENEW as a single transition. At runtime it is automatically translated into a more complex net structure (visible on the right-hand side of Figure 3). This net structure enables requesting the workitem[5], confirming the completion of the activity and cancelling the execution of the activity. These transitions connect via synchronous channels (indicated by the grey arrows) to a middleware within the agent. The task transition also keeps the state of the activity in the central place.

The inscription of the task transition contains some of the additional information mentioned above, namely the task-identifier, the parameters and the result. The task-identifier can be used by the agent to query the remaining additional information stored in its knowledge base. Parameters and the result apply to variables on the incoming and outgoing arcs of the task transition.

When the agent executes such a workflow it controls the execution of the net through the middleware. The middleware communicates with the intermediary system and reports available workitems. These workitems are made available to eligible resources, which can then request them. The middleware receives information about the state of the task from the intermediary system. Any change of the state of the task is implemented by firing the corresponding transition within the task transition net structure. Another important function of the workflow engine is to ensure the isolation of case data for each instance of a workflow. Some of that data may be relevant only to the current case. This data may be stored directly in the workflow net instance for that case. Other data (e.g. obtained results) may be required in other workflows and should be extracted to the knowledge base of an agent beforehand.

Atomicity of tasks is another important aspect. The design of the task transition ensures atomicity within the workflow engine. Data or results can only be made available in the workflow outside of the task *after* its internal confirm transition has been fired. If the activity is cancelled the original input parameters are put back onto the precondition places by the internal cancel transition.

Workflows are started by an engine proactively (e.g. directly after initialisation) or reactively (e.g. after another workflow has been finished). Once all tasks of a workflow have been completed by resources, the engine has successfully finished the behaviour it controlled.

4.2   Agents as Workflow Resources

Agent workflow resources perform the tasks that are contained in the control workflows executed by the agent workflow engines. This means that these agents take on the same role as human users in a regular workflow system.

---

[5] An available task in an active workflow is called a *workitem*. An *activity* is a workitem assigned to a resource. This distinction clearly identifies the context.

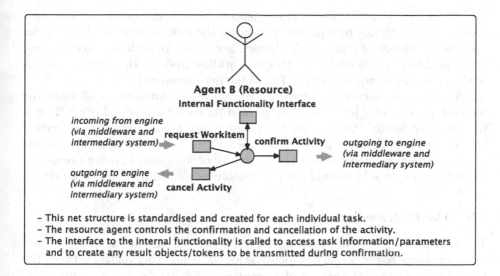

Fig. 4. Conceptual view of an agent workflow resource

When a task is activated in an agent workflow engine the intermediary system is informed. It polls the workitems from all active agent workflow engines. Depending on the technical implementation, the workitems may either be offered to the resources to be requested or they may be assigned automatically. If they are offered, a middleware within the resource agent receives lists of workitems (worklists) and decides which of these are requested. If workitems are assigned automatically, the middleware simply receives the information about the workitem.

When a requested or assigned workitem is received by the middleware it initiates the execution of the resulting activity. This is done by instantiating a standardised net structure. This net structure is shown in Figure 4, which illustrates the realisation of the agent workflow resource. It closely resembles the net structure contained within the task transition of the control workflow in the workflow engine. The operations performed in the net structure (request workitem, confirm/cancel activity) correspond to those in the control workflow. These operations are matched by the intermediary system. When an activity is cancelled the middleware handles any rollback aspects related to the resource.

The main difference between the net structure of the resource and that of the task transition is the interface to the internal functionality. When the activity is started, the central place is filled with data about the activity. This enables the interface to the internal functionality to fire, which in turn initiates the actions required to accomplish the activity. Note that, similar to the engine agent, all of these transitions are controlled by the middleware of the resource agent. Once the internal functionality has finished all the necessary actions the interface becomes active again and creates the result objects so the activity can be completed correctly by the middleware and intermediary system.

A task may require more complex behaviour and further interactions with other agents. This can be handled by allowing the internal functionality to initiate a new workflow to control this complex behaviour. In such cases the resource agent would act as an engine for this subworkflow in order to complete its task in the original engine's workflow. This is further discussed in Section 6.

While the net structure shown in Figure 4 is standardised for all tasks the internal functionality has to be implemented for each task individually[6]. This is the main modelling challenge on the resource side of the behaviour of agents. In combination with the partition of tasks on the control/engine side of the behaviour it completely realises the behaviour of its agent. In other words, the modelling challenge in regular agent behaviour is split into these two aspects.

4.3   The Intermediary System

The intermediary system bridges the gap between agent workflow engines and agent workflow resources. It is responsible for the connecting control between the task of an engine and the actions of a resource. It also handles the communication aspects between the different agents. This section will discuss the basics and concepts of an intermediary system. Section 5 will present a current technical prototype of such a system.

Both agent workflow engines and agent workflow resources connect to the intermediary system through their internal middleware. In general, the intermediary system itself consists of one or more specialised agents. These agents are the direct communication partners of the middlewares of engines and resources. The idea behind the intermediary system is illustrated in Figure 5.

An engine's middleware sends information about requestable workitems to the intermediary system and receives information about the state of workitems and activities in order to control the corresponding task transition. For engines the intermediary system is basically the central contact point of a system. It receives information about the state of all workflows in the workflow engines and provides status updates back to them.

Resource middleware receives information about requestable workitems or already automatically assigned activities from the intermediary system. Since this is a proactive behaviour the intermediary system needs to know about the available resources beforehand. Hence, resources need to register with the intermediary system before they can receive any information. The intermediary system also receives (manual) requests for available workitems and confirmations/cancellations of activities from the resources. These are the status updates sent to the engines.

An important function of the intermediary system is to match the requests, confirmations and cancellations between engines and resources. When a task becomes activated in an engine the middleware of the engine is notified of that. It creates a workitem and sends it to the intermediary system.

---

[6] Carefully modelled functionality can be reused in the context of multiple tasks.

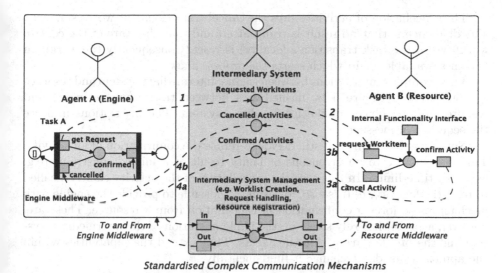

Fig. 5. Conceptual view of the role of the intermediary system

The information about requestable workitems is gathered by the intermediary system into worklists. These worklists are used regardless of whether the tasks are to be assigned to resources automatically or are manually requestable by the resources. For automatic assignment the worklist are processed for each available resource and decisions about the assignment made by the intermediary system. This, for example, can be based on availability or current workload of resources. The intermediary system can also isolate resources in critical or mutually exclusive (sections of) workflows through the worklists. Worklists for a resource only contain those workitems, which the resource is permitted to request. This is realised by comparing the role and type of a registered resource to the execution rule for that task (provided by the engine). For manual assignment the worklists are sent to each resource individually. The middleware of the resource then decides which workitems to request.

When such a request arrives at the intermediary system it forwards it to the engine. The engine has the ultimate control over whether or not the request is accepted. It either denies the request and the workitem remains available or it accepts the request and creates a new activity by firing the internal transition of the task. The resource receives this activity from the intermediary system. The middleware of the resource fires its own request transition and transmits the activity object via synchronous channel during firing. The resource can then perform the actions required for the activity.

When an activity is completed the resource agent's middleware fires the confirm transition. Activity and result are transmitted through the intermediary system to the engine agent. It receives the result and fires the confirm transition of the task transition. The execution of the workflow can then continue.

The cancellation of activities fires the cancel transitions but works similarly. The difference is that no result is transmitted and that the state of the control workflow (in the task transition's locality) is reset. Consequently the workitem becomes available again which starts the process anew.

These complex interactions between engine, intermediary system and resource are indicated in Figure 5 by dashed arcs between transitions in engine and resource and by places in the intermediary system. The inscriptions indicate the sequence of messages.

Note that the engine can still decide to refuse the confirmation of an activity. This may be due to an erroneous or faulty result or a missed constraint (e.g. exceeded time-limit). In this case the cancellation of the activity could be called to reset the local state. It is also, for example, feasible to provide the engine with mechanisms to force a confirmation or cancellation from a resource. These are, however, aspects that rely solely on the implementation of the intermediary system and the middleware within the agents. They extend the capabilities within the approach but don't change it fundamentally.

5   The WorkBroker Prototype

The current WORKBROKER-system is a prototype implementing and serving as a proof-of-concept for the design pattern described in the previous section. It focuses on the implementation of the intermediary system (see Section 4.3) as a CAPA agent system and utilises reference workflow nets. It is being developed in the context of two PhD theses and also as part of our annual teaching project. The project aims to create a process support environment for the PAOSE (PETRI NET-BASED, AGENT- AND ORGANIZATION-ORIENTED SOFTWARE ENGINEERING [5]) development approach.

The WORKBROKER is a subsystem of that environment. It is responsible for bridging the gap between engine agents executing workflows for PAOSE processes and resource agents directly supporting the developers. The subsystem's role in the overall system is specialised, but it is independently extended to be used on its own as a full-fledged intermediary system. The independence of system components is a typical perspective on agent-oriented systems. Consequently, each individual component (subsystem, agent etc.) requires more effort to be built. Nonetheless, the compositionality, resilience and robustness of systems built this way are improved.

Figure 6 shows part of the coarse design diagram[7] for the WORKBROKER-prototype. This represents the core functionality. Secondary aspects, like database access or monitoring, have been omitted.

Engine and resource roles provide the middleware for engines and resources. These roles can be assumed by multiple agents in the system (in addition to their other functional roles). The roles provide internal behaviour nets to these agents

---

[7] In PAOSE, the coarse design diagram provides an overview of system from which the architecture is derived.

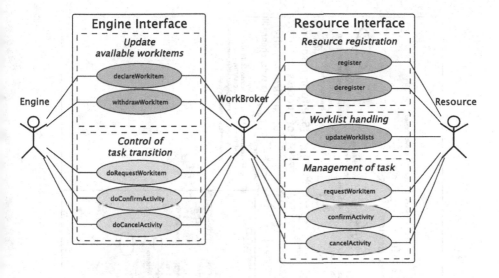

Fig. 6. Part of the Coarse Design Diagram of the WORKBROKER-prototype

which implement the functionality of the middleware. The WORKBROKER role implements the intermediary system.

The interactions between the roles can be classified into two interfaces with multiple grouped interactions (as illustrated in Figure 6). The interactions in *Control of task transition* of the engine interface and *Management of task* in the resource interface correspond to the core function of an intermediary system to match task operations (request/confirm/cancel) between engines and resources. They are always called in pairs (e.g. *confirmActivity* and *doConfirmActivity*) and are connected by functionality implemented within the WORKBROKER role. The remaining groups of interactions realise updating available workitems within the WORKBROKER, resource registration and worklist distribution.

To illustrate the implementation, part of the internal functionality of the WORKBROKER role is shown as an example in Figure 7. This is only part of the net that implements matching a confirmed activity between engine and resource. The overall net is too large to discuss in the scope of this paper. All interactions between this net and other nets (e.g. interactions) are realised through synchronous channels (indicated by *net:channelname(parameter)*). Additional details can be found in the emphasised, bracketed comments within the Figure.

The partial net in Figure 7 receives a request to confirm an activity from a *confirmActivity* interaction (**1.**). This initiates the *doConfirmActivity* interaction (not shown in the figure). That interaction communicates with the lower part of the net (**2.**) to determine the executing (owner) engine of the activity. Once the interaction is completed the result is handed back to the net (**3.**). If the engine agreed to the confirmation, the activity is removed from the internal list of the WORKBROKER (**4a.**). If the engine disagreed, the activity remains in the internal list (**4b.**). Finally, the resource is informed about the result (**5.**).

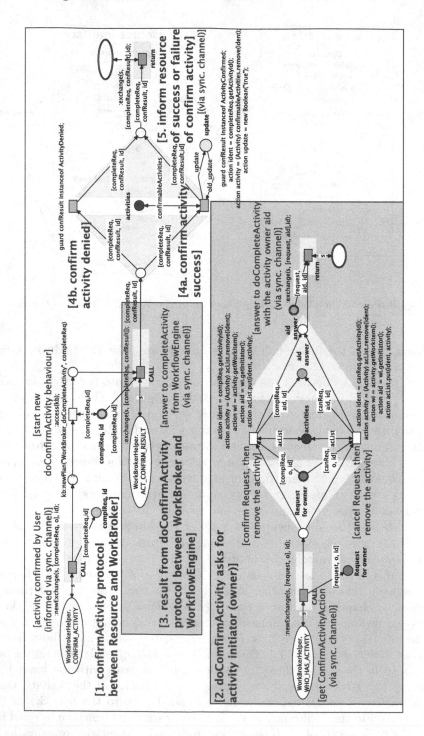

Fig. 7. Part of the WORKBROKER functionality for confirming activities

Even as a prototype of an intermediary system the WORKBROKER-prototype already realises key parts of the required core functionality. The involved middlewares allow the declaration of tasks by engines and the subsequent workitem requests and activity confirmations/cancellations by resources. The WORKBROKER role manages available workitems and administers between engines and resources. The prototype is, however, still limited in some points. The interface to declare tasks is currently limited to certain types of tasks in the context of the overall process support environment. Similarly, only certain resource functionality of the environment can be called. Standardised calls for resource functionality and the extension of the task interface for engines are currently under development.

6 Discussion

The approach described in the previous sections applies workflow management principles to the behaviour of and between software agents. Principles, like the separation between workflow engine (control flow) and workflow resource (functionality) and the introduction of tasks and task atomicity, have different effects on agent systems. This section discusses these effects, advantages and disadvantages, as well as some open questions to the approach.

As stated above, one major workflow principle introduced by the approach is the separation between engines and resources which leads to a decoupling between interacting agents. Agents no longer need to know their interaction partners beforehand. The matching between engines and resources is handled by the intermediary system. This allows for a more flexible choice of interaction partners. Different alternative resources may be considered by an engine as it has the ability to deny a request for a workitem. Furthermore the intermediary system can have a positive influence on the efficiency, as it can monitor workloads and take appropriate actions. It can also enforce security and encapsulation aspects by filtering worklists and preventing resources from requesting tasks they are not qualified or authorised for.

The central role of the intermediary system has some disadvantages though. There is an increased communicative overhead for the messages. But the individual messages are more standardised, as most of the exchanges deal with requesting workitems and confirming or cancelling activities. These exchanges would follow uniform patterns with differing parameters. This simplifies both modelling and implementing communication aspects.

Another disadvantage of the intermediary system is that, if it fails, the connection between engines and resources can be lost. A distributed implementation of the intermediary system could compensate for a partial failure. Such an implementation could utilise multiple agents on multiple platforms. If one of these agents failed the communication could be handled by the remaining agents.

A further major principle is the introduction of the task concept into agent behaviour. The task concept enhances the abstraction for the modeller. Multiple related actions can be combined into one task. This simplifies agent protocols, though the readability of these protocols becomes a major focus for an implementation. It needs to ensure that task descriptions contain all relevant information. Modellers also need to make sure to combine actions reasonably.

The task concept also introduces a kind of atomicity into agent behaviour. The ability to cancel tasks and reset the local state of the workflow is beneficial in multiple ways. Agents can reason about the quality of a result, decide to discard it and start the task over. They can also cancel an execution that violates expected completion time or other constraints.

The introduction of the task concept also affects the resource side. Functionality for a task can be modelled in small, reusable fragments, instead of large and interdependent protocols. This way it can be more easily exchanged or modified, since the control flow is encapsulated by the workflow in the workflow engine. As long as the interface to the workflow remains unchanged, the details of the implementation of the task functionality do not affect the workflows. Flexibility can also be supported by offering different variants of a task implementation instantiated depending on the system state at runtime.

An open question is how internal tasks should be handled. Internal tasks contain only actions the engine will perform as a resource itself. This means that the communication with the intermediary system is unnecessary. However, in some cases (e.g. high workload) it may be beneficial to delegate even internal tasks. One solution is to provide an optional shortcut for internal tasks in the engine middleware and let the engine decide at runtime.

As far as methodology is concerned the approach can be incorporated into the established PAOSE development approach ([5], see Section 5). PAOSE models a system along two main dimensions: Behaviour and structure. The behaviour, modelled as agent interactions, corresponds directly to the scope of workflows in the approach. The structure, defined through agent roles, can provide the basis for task execution rules and consequent assignment of tasks. From a technical perspective, an implementation of the intermediary system would have to be made available for PAOSE systems. As stated before, the WORKBROKER from Section 5 is currently being extended to that purpose. Exchanging other artefacts (e.g. agent protocol nets with workflow (fragments)) within PAOSE is unproblematic, as they are already realised as reference nets.

Another aspect related to tasks concerns subworkflows. The approach doesn't limit the complexity of the behaviour involved in a task. In fact, it is possible for a task to require interactions between the resource agent and other agents. This means that in order to accomplish a task a resource may need to initiate a new control workflow and execute it. The agent would be active as a resource for the task and as an engine for the workflow at the same time. This introduces a distinction into the workflows as proactive behaviour and reactive subworkflows.

This aspect is illustrated in Figure 8, which extends the previous example of Figure 2. Task B1 of agent A now causes agent B to start the reactive subworkflow B1. That subworkflow contains tasks that are performed by agents B and C. The result of that subworkflow is reported back to the resource functionality of agent B. Agent B then reports the termination and result back to task B1 in agent A, which is then confirmed.

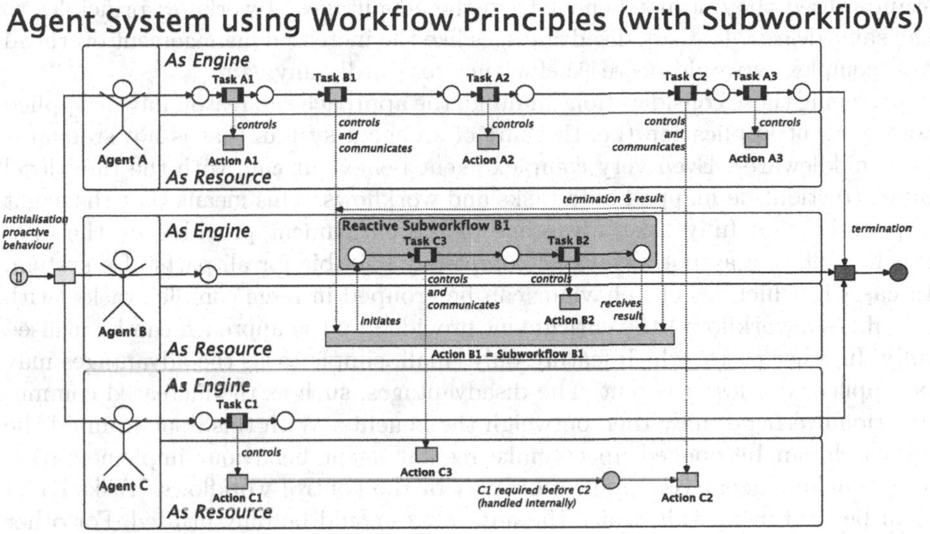

Agent System using Workflow Principles (with Subworkflows)

Fig. 8. Conceptual view of the handling of subworkflows

With this type of nesting of processes the approach can support very complex and interconnected behaviour. It also enables more complex interactions between agents to be combined into a single task (for the initiator). For example, subworkflow B1 in Figure 8 may also call resource functionality in agent A. In that case agent A would be a resource in the workflow of one of its own resources. These and more complex kinds of interdependencies can be handled through the use of subworkflows. The example in Figure 8 also emphasises the resource perspective on agents. Agent C acts as a resource for tasks C1 and C3. These are independent from one another and may be available concurrently. This means that agent C, like a human workflow user, can autonomously decide which task to complete first.

There are some apparent differences between agents and workflows that concern the applicability of the approach. Agents may run continuously, while workflows should always terminate. However, agents as artefacts of a software system should also always terminate at some point. Therefore, their individual behaviours, which this approach maps to workflows, should also terminate.

Another issue relates to the different levels of complexity agent and workflow systems can represent. In practice, some parts of an agent system cannot be reasonably realised as workflows. This applies to the standardised functions and mechanisms of the agent middleware (i.e. core functionality like initialisation, message handling, knowledge) and the meta-level of organisation, agent and behaviour management. Nonetheless, even these aspects can still be *regarded* as workflows. These aspects constitute a form of behaviour and the actions involved in it follow some kind of order. They can consequently be combined into tasks and workflows. However, as these aspects are mostly agent-internal or highly standardised they do not benefit from the advantages of workflow principles to the same degree. Instead, disadvantages like the increased management overhead and complexity would decrease efficiency for hardly any gain.

Keeping these considerations in mind, the approach can reasonably be applied to any agent application (i.e. the part of an agent system that is not standardised middleware). Even very complex agent behaviour can, with the right level of abstraction, be mapped onto tasks and workflows. This means that the agent application can fully take advantage of the enrichment provided by the approach. Still, it may not always be completely suitable for all parts of a system. In cases in which agent behaviour can be grouped in large complex tasks (with possible subworkflows) the enrichment provided by the approach can be utilised fully. In other cases, which feature only small, simple tasks the advantages may be applied to a lesser extent. The disadvantages, such as the increased communication overhead, may then outweigh the benefits. With this issue in mind the approach can be opened up to make regular agent behaviour implementation and standard agent communication part of the control workflows. Tasks could then be used in cases in which the advantages could be fully utilised. For other cases standard agent behaviour would be employed.

7 Related Work

Our approach combines agents and workflows. There are many such research efforts in several different contexts. But mostly, agents are used to realise and improve WFMS. Many examples for such agent-based WFMS can be found. [4] provides intelligent agents with a certain awareness of current workflows. The agent reasons about the most likely path a user might take in order to provide more efficient support. [19] uses agents to monitor workflows and coordinate resources in order to avoid delays in task execution. There are many more functions in workflow management for which agents can be used. [8] identifies twenty-four such functions and classifies over 100 publications into this scheme.

Our approach, on the other hand, falls into the rarer category, in which workflows are used to improve agent management. Another such approach is described in [14]. They propose to control the state of an agent with an internal workflow engine. One engine combines workflows from different engines into a master workflow. This way a certain degree of flexibility is achieved but the approach fails to explain how and by which agent the master workflow is executed. Such a master workflow for all aspects of an interaction impairs the autonomy of the agents and limits their capabilities. The paper also fails to address how the implementation of the task functionality is implemented and accessed.

A further approach to utilise workflow nets for agent interaction is described in [15]. In it, a predetermined plan is transformed into a workflow net for the cooperation between the currently active agents. It features less flexibility then our approach as the plan and workflow net need to be reevaluated and reformed if the agents change. In our approach resource allocation is dynamic and agents can easily be exchanged. The approach in [15] does, however, feature a strong formal basis dealing with workflow soundness and critical sections. These aspects are outside of the scope of this paper, but are being currently researched.

Our approach also shares some connections to service-oriented computing. [2,18] deal with partner synthesis in this context. This means that the configuration of a service requires a partner service to be considered controllable. Controllability is a correctness criterion for services. Applying these notions to the relation between engine and resource in our context can be used to improve areas like optimal resource assignment.

Interorganisational workflows are also a related topic. Their high degree of autonomy enables agents to be considered as independent organisations. Related concepts, like the ones presented in [3], may be used to improve the approach.

A topic directly related to our approach is presented in [11]. It enables modelling CAPA agent interactions in a subset of BPMN[8]. The ability to define agent behaviour directly in an established workflow notation will be used to improve our approach in the future. BPMN could enhance or possibly even replace the currently used workflow nets.

8 Summary and Outlook

This paper presents an approach on how to apply workflow management principles to agent interaction. The first stage in this research is an overall perspective on agent systems as workflow systems, with agents serving as workflow engines and resources. This unusual consideration serves as the basis for a design pattern, the second stage of the research. Lastly, the design pattern is realised in a technical proof-of concept, the WORKBROKER-prototype.

Examining the contributions of perspective, pattern and prototype, we have found several advantages that can improve interactions between agents: Enabling task atomicity in agent behaviour, dividing functionality into reusable and flexible fragments, decoupling the control flow from the functionality and standardising communication between agents are some of the effects that have been discussed. We are confident that, by continuing with our research efforts in this context, even more beneficial effects can be achieved.

The approach was developed in the context of a larger ongoing effort to combine and integrate agents and workflows. This integration effort aims to enable system modellers to use agents and workflows as modelling constructs on the same abstraction level. This provides an entity abstraction that can dynamically act as an agent, a workflow or both. This enables a modeller to utilise and combine properties of agents and workflows in an extensive yet structured way. A general description of the ideas can be found in [22].

By applying workflows to agent behaviour, this paper's approach represents one key part of that desired complete integration. In the future the approach will be extended on a conceptual level to support the integration efforts to an even greater effect. An extended technical implementation of the WORKBROKER-prototype will also be used to provide technical aspects of the integration.

---

[8] Business Process Model and Notation, http://www.omg.org/spec/BPMN/2.0/.

Work on the conceptual approach and technical implementation will also continue independently from the overall integration effort. This will focus on extending the WORKBROKER-prototype and incorporating it into the CAPA agent toolset. Another major focus will be the realisation of more, comparative case-studies and complex examples. This will enable us to validate and more concretely qualify the effects of the approach.

As a concluding observation, the approach, as a proof-of-concept, affirms the use of Petri nets in our own research and software engineering in general. We designed and implemented a net-based combination of agent behaviour and workflows. This combined software concept can now, thanks to the common basis of reference Petri nets, be easily embedded with existing, net-realised concepts, like the agents and components featured in MULAN and CAPA. Properties of nets, such as concurrency, expressiveness, nesting, etc., contributed greatly in creating models and systems in several projects. We will continue to design and implement diverse software engineering concepts with Petri nets to add them to our expanding toolset. We are confident this research will continue to validate our position that Petri nets are an appropriate and useful technique for practical software engineering.

References

1. van der Aalst, W.M.P.: Verification of work. In: Azéma, P., Balbo, G. (eds.) ICATPN 1997. LNCS, vol. 1248, pp. 407–426. Springer, Heidelberg (1997)
2. van der Aalst, W.M.P., Lohmann, N., La Rosa, M.: Ensuring correctness during process configuration via partner synthesis. Information Systems 37(6), 574–592 (2012)
3. van der Aalst, W.M.P., Lohmann, N., Massuthe, P., Stahl, C., Wolf, K.: Multiparty contracts: Agreeing and implementing interorganizational processes. Computer Journal 53(1), 90–106 (2010)
4. Both, F., Hoogendoorn, M., van der Mee, A., Treur, J., de Vos, M.: An intelligent agent model with awareness of workflow progress. Applied Intelligence 36(2), 498–510 (2012)
5. Cabac, L.: Multi-agent system: a guiding metaphor for the organization of software development projects. In: Petta, P., Müller, J.P., Klusch, M., Georgeff, M. (eds.) MATES 2007. LNCS (LNAI), vol. 4687, pp. 1–12. Springer, Heidelberg (2007)
6. Cabac, L.: Modeling Petri Net-Based Multi-Agent Applications. Agent Technology - Theory and Applications, vol. 5. Logos Verlag, Berlin (2010)
7. Christensen, S., Damgaard Hansen, N.: Coloured petri nets extended with channels for synchronous communication. In: Valette, R. (ed.) ICATPN 1994. LNCS, vol. 815, pp. 159–178. Springer, Heidelberg (1994)
8. Delias, P., Doulamis, A., Matsatsinis, N.: What agents can do in workflow management systems. Artificial Intelligence Review 35(2), 155–189 (2011)
9. Duvigneau, M., Moldt, D., Rölke, H.: Concurrent architecture for a multi-agent platform. In: Giunchiglia, F., Odell, J.J., Weiss, G. (eds.) AOSE 2002. LNCS, vol. 2585, pp. 59–72. Springer, Heidelberg (2003)
10. Foundation for Intelligent Physical Agents. FIPA Agent Management Specification (2003). http://www.fipa.org/specs/fipa00023/index.html

11. Haustermann, M.: BPMN-Modelle für petrinetzbasierte agentenorientierte Softwaresysteme auf Basis von Mulan/Capa. Master thesis, University of Hamburg, Department of Informatics, September 2014
12. Hollingsworth, D.: The workflow reference model. Technical report, WfMC (1995). Available at http://www.wfmc.org
13. Jacob, T.: Implementierung einer sicheren und rollenbasierten Workflowmanagement-Komponente für ein Petrinetzwerkzeug. Diploma thesis, University of Hamburg, Department of Computer Science (2002)
14. Korhonen, J., Pajunen, L., Puustjärvi, J.: Using transactional workflow ontology in agent cooperation. In: AIM Workshop, First EurAsian Conference on Advances in ICT. Tehran (2002)
15. Kotb Y.T.: Workflow-Net Based Cooperative Multi-Agent Systems. PhD thesis, The University of Western Ontario, Electronic Thesis and Dissertation Repository, August 2011. p. 228
16. Kummer, O.: Referenznetze. Logos Verlag, Berlin (2002)
17. Kummer, O., Wienberg, F., Duvigneau, M., Köhler, M., Moldt, D., Rölke, H.: Renew - the Reference Net Workshop. In: Veerbeek, E. (ed.) Tool Demonstrations. 24th International Conference on Application and Theory of Petri Nets (ATPN 2003). International Conference on Business Process Management (BPM 2003)., pp. 99–102, June 2003
18. Lohmann, N., Weinberg, D.: Wendy: A tool to synthesize partners for services. Fundamenta Informaticae **113**, 295–311 (2011)
19. Pla, A., Gay, P., Meléndez, J., López, B.: Petri net based agents for coordinating resources in a workflow management system. In: ICAART 2011 - Proceedings of the 3rd International Conference on Agents and Artificial Intelligence, Rome, Italy, January 28–30, pp. 514–523 (2011)
20. Rölke, H.: Modellierung von Agenten und Multiagentensystemen - Grundlagen und Anwendungen. Agent Technology-Theory and Applications, vol. 2. Logos Verlag, Berlin (2004)
21. Valk, R.: Petri nets as token objects: an introduction to elementary object nets. In: Desel, J., Silva, M. (eds.) ICATPN 1998. LNCS, vol. 1420, pp. 1–25. Springer, Heidelberg (1998)
22. Wagner, T., Quenum, J., Moldt, D., Reese, C.: Providing an agent flavored integration for workflow management. In: Jensen, K., Donatelli, S., Kleijn, J. (eds.) ToPNoC V. LNCS, vol. 6900, pp. 243–264. Springer, Heidelberg (2012)

Author Index

Alqarni, Mohammed 77

Badouel, Eric 212
Barbot, Benoît 1
Bartha, Tamás 309
Bruneo, Dario 98

Chatain, Thomas 117

David, Nicolas 137
Delosme, Jean-Marc 234
Desel, Jörg 157
Dumas, Marlon 33

Esparza, Javier 157

Garavel, Hubert 179
García-Bañuelos, Luciano 33
Ghosh, Rahul 98

Haar, Stefan 117
Hajdu, Ákos 309
Heiner, Monika 200
Hélouët, Loïc 212
Hujsa, Thomas 234

Janicki, Ryszard 77
Jard, Claude 137

Kalenkova, Anna 287
Koutny, Maciej 117
Kwiatkowska, Marta 1

Lime, Didier 137
Longo, Francesco 98
Lorenz, Robert 49

Moldt, Daniel 329
Morvan, Christophe 212
Munier-Kordon, Alix 234

Pommereau, Franck 254
Puliafito, Antonio 98

Roux, Olivier H. 137
Rubin, Vladimir 287

Scarpa, Marco 98
Schwarick, Martin 200
Schwoon, Stefan 117
Sürmeli, Jan 266

Triebel, Marvin 266
Trivedi, Kishor S. 98

van der Aalst, Wil M.P. 287
Verbeek, Eric 287
Vörös, András 309

Wagner, Thomas 329
Wegener, Jan-Thierry 200

Printed in the United States
By Bookmasters